DEPARTMENT OF ECONOMIC AND SOCIAL AFFAIRS

# Industrial Development for the 21ˢᵗ Century:

## Sustainable Development Perspectives

UNITED NATIONS
New York, 2007

# DESA

The Department of Economic and Social Affairs of the United Nations Secretariat is a vital interface between global policies in the economic, social and environmental spheres and national action. The Department works in three main interlinked areas: (i) it compiles, generates and analyses a wide range of economic, social and environmental data and information on which States Members of the United Nations draw to review common problems and to take stock of policy options; (ii) it facilitates the negotiations of Member States in many intergovernmental bodies on joint course of action to address ongoing or merging global challenges; and (iii) it advises interested Governments on the ways and means of translating policy frameworks developed in United Nations conferences and summits into programmes at the country level and, through technical assistance, helps build national capacities.

## Note

# Foreword

Since the United Nations Conference on Environment and Development in 1992 and the subsequent World Summit on Sustainable Development in 2002, significant efforts have been made in pursuit of sustainable development. At the September 2005 World Summit, the UN General Assembly reiterated that "sustainable development is a key element of the overarching framework for United Nations activities, in particular for achieving the internationally agreed development goals", including those contained in the Millennium Declaration and the Johannesburg Plan of Implementation (A/RES/59/227).

The United Nations Commission on Sustainable Development (CSD) will be holding its 15th session in the spring of 2007, focusing on policy options and practical measures to address challenges in the areas of energy for sustainable development, industrial development, air pollution/atmosphere, and climate change. This is clearly a very ambitious agenda and the issues are rather closely interlinked. Yet, the Commission will also need to consider each of these topics on its own terms. In order to inform the discussions on Industrial Development, the Division for Sustainable Development, which acts as Secretariat to the Commission, is publishing this book, which highlights key challenges for developing countries, across different regions and sectors, and how effectively and with what sorts of policies different countries have responded to them. At the same time, the topics addressed in the volume are directly relevant to the preparations for the next two-year cycle, more specifically to the themes "agriculture", "rural development", and "Africa".

The volume begins by examining industrial development as central to the process of structural transformation which characterises economic development. It points to the new challenges and opportunities facing today's industrialisers as a result of globalization, technological change and new international trade rules. The emergence of Southern multinationals and South-South investment is one new phenomenon explored. The next set of chapters focuses on key sectors with potential for developing countries. Two key themes emerge. First, traditional points of entry for late industrialisers – like textiles and clothing – have become even more intensely competitive than before, calling for innovative adaptive strategies. Second, countries may wish to broaden their development perspective, recognizing that "industry" narrowly defined does not exhaust the opportunities for producing high value added goods and services for international markets. Knowledge intensity is increasing across all spheres of economic activity, including agriculture and services which can offer promising development paths for some developing countries. The final section addresses social and environmental aspects of industrial development. Much evidence is presented that labour-intensive – but not necessarily other – patterns of industrial development can be highly effective in poverty reduction. A range of policies can promote industrial energy and materials efficiency, often with positive impacts on firms' financial performance as well as the environment. Promoting materials recycling and reuse is found to be an effective if indirect means of conserving energy. Finally, the growth of multinational interest in corporate social responsibility is traced, with consideration given to both the barriers and the opportunities this can pose for developing country enterprises linked to global supply chains.

We hope that this collective effort of staff members and external authors contributes to a successful outcome of CSD-15.

JoAnne DiSano
Director, Division for Sustainable Development

# Acknowledgements

This book benefited from critical feedback received at an Expert Group Meeting in September 2006 where draft chapters were reviewed and discussed. A number of specialists in different aspects of industrial development participated in the brainstorming on 'policy lessons', and many of those insights are incorporated in the concluding chapter. Special thanks are due to those who participated in the aforementioned meeting as paper discussants, including Jomo K. Sundaram, Rob Vos, Manuel Montes, Ralph Wahnschafft and David Le Blanc of UNDESA, and Dilek Aykut of The World Bank. The contribution of Under-Secretary General José Antonio Ocampo, who kindly agreed to have a summary of his comprehensive opening remarks included as an introduction to the volume, is gratefully acknowledged.

# Contents

**Foreword,** *JoAnne DiSano* ........................................................................ i i i

**Acknowledgements**........................................................................... v

**Introduction,** *José Antonio Ocampo*........................................................1

**Part 1 New Frontiers and Challenges**

**1.1**    Industrial development: Some stylized facts and policy directions,
        *Dani Rodrik* ...........................................................................7

**1.2**    Technology, globalization, and international competitiveness:
        Challenges for developing countries,
        *Carl Dahlman*........................................................................29

**1.3**    Developing country multinationals: South-South investment comes
        of age, *Dilek Aykut* and *Andrea Goldstein*...................................85

**Part 2 Sector Studies**

**2.1**    Natural resource-based industries: Prospects for Africa's agriculture,
        *Mónica Kjöllerström* and *Kledia Dallto*....................................119

**2.2**    The textiles and clothing industry: Adjusting to a post quota world,
        *Ratnakar Adhikari* and *Yumiko Yamamoto*..............................183

**2.3**    Services-led industrialization in India: prospects and challenges,
        *Nirvikar Singh*.......................................................................235

**Part 3 Social and Environmental Dimensions of Industrial Development**

**3.1**    Industrial development and economic growth:
        Implications for poverty reduction and income inequality,
        *Matleena Kniivilä*.................................................................295

**3.2**    Industrial energy and materials efficiency: What role for policies?,
        *Mohan Peck* and *Ralph Chipman*............................................333

**3.3**    From supply chains to value chains: A spotlight on CSR,
        *Malika Bhandarkar* and *Tarcisio Alvarez-Rivero*........................387

**The Way Forward**

        Policy lessons for 21st century industrializers
        *David O'Connor*....................................................................415

# Introduction

José Antonio Ocampo*

Economic development is fundamentally a process of structural transformation[1]. This involves the reallocation of productive factors from traditional agriculture to modern agriculture, industry and services, and the reallocation of those factors among industrial and service sector activities. If successful in accelerating economic growth, this process involves shifting resources from low- to high-productivity sectors. More broadly, sustained economic growth is associated with the capacity to diversify domestic production structure: that is, to generate new activities, to strengthen economic linkages within the country and to create domestic technological capabilities.

The industrial and modern service sectors typically contribute dynamically to this diversification process. Indeed, the evidence of the past quarter century – or, indeed, of the post-war era in the developing world – clearly indicates that rapid growth in the developing world has been invariably associated with diversification of production into manufacturing and modern services, while slow growth has been usually associated with swelling low-productivity services.

Reflection on industrial policies in developing countries should be concerned with three important dimensions: *innovations* (in a Schumpeterian sense), *linkages* (Hirschman), and *surplus labour* (Lewis). Those three dimensions are examined in turn.

*Innovation* should be considered in a broad sense, as the development of new economic activities or new ways of doing existing activities. It is important in this regard to recognize the role, not only of technological but also of non-technological innovations. For instance, developing new marketing networks and innovations in marketing, as well as the development of new organisational practices or structures are often more important than the adoption of new production technologies. Indeed, the ability to reap the benefits from new technologies often depends on innovations in distribution and organisation occurring simultaneously. The microeconomics literature has tended to focus too much on production, and too little on sales, marketing and distribution. Schumpeter's concept of "new combinations" captures much better this broad concept of innovation than the usual association of this concept with technological change in production.

Innovations, in turn, tend to be different in developing countries and in developed countries. For the former, technological change often consists in entering activities and sectors, or the adoption of technologies or marketing and organisational strategies, which are already well established in developed

* Under-Secretary General, Department of Economic and Social Affairs, United Nations, New York.

countries. For industrial countries, moving the technological frontier, or developing new non-technological practices are the major forms of innovation. Entrepreneurs are the ones who organize and lead such forays into unexplored territory. Their appetite for risk may, however, be dulled if the prospect of profiting from a successful discovery is small. Non-technological innovation, such as conquering a new market or developing a new marketing strategy, may be more important in the early stages of development but it can be easily imitated and is also difficult to protect through conventional forms of intellectual property rights.

It is also necessary to go beyond the neo-classical view, in which technological progress is exogenous and technology is often embodied in industrial equipment. On the contrary, the process of absorption of technology by firms is an active and costly process. Furthermore, the development of new activities may be fraught with coordination failures and entry costs vary across sectors. Most developing countries enter international markets with commodities or basic manufactures and assembly operations, because the production of high-tech products requires a pre-existing industrial and technological base. One of the main challenges of industrial policy is thus to understand better how to support the development, in a coordinated fashion, of production and technological capabilities in new economic activities. It is in this context that "clusters" of interlinked firms, trading goods and services as well as ideas and personnel, are seen as valuable features of the industrial landscape.

*Linkages* then are crucial to "systemic competitiveness" – i.e., with competitiveness that goes beyond the individual firm to become a feature of certain sectors in specific regions or of whole regions and countries. The development of linkages has both supply and demand side effects. The latter determine the magnitude of macroeconomic multipliers; the former are associated with the positive externalities that different economic agents generate among themselves through cost reductions induced by economies of scale and scope in production, lower transport and transaction costs (economies of agglomeration), the induced provision of more specialized inputs or services (economies of specialization), and the sharing of knowledge between firms and the development of human capital that can move between firms (knowledge spillovers). This implies that developing domestic linkages is more important than integration into world markets per se, and that not all patterns of integration into international markets have the same effect on economic growth. Thus, the countries that profit most from FDI are those whose domestic firms and institutions build domestic technological capability, both through investment in own R&D and workforce education and training, and through linkages created between domestic firms and foreign affiliates. At the same time, a successful export strategy is highly dependent on how the export sectors are integrated with other domestic economic activities, not least in terms of employment generation.

In developing countries, a sizeable part of the workforce is underemployed in low-productivity activities. As Lewis argued, this surplus labour is available in virtually unlimited supply to the modern sector, where it could be employed more productively. The absorption of this *surplus labour* or, in the opposite case, the incapacity to do so, is generally a more important determinant of overall factor productivity growth in developing countries than technological change per se. Thus far, globalization has had only a limited impact on surplus labour absorption. In fact, in some parts of the world, informal employment in low productivity sectors has grown with the liberalization of trade and the implementation of efficiency-increasing domestic economic reforms. In these cases, aggregate productivity may show a poor performance even if the modern sectors are immersed in a dynamic process of technological change. Industrial policies should thus aim at reducing surplus labour in the economy.

Taking into account surplus labour in the design of industrial policies can lead to very different prescriptions from those emerging from a neo-classical paradigm, which assumes full employment. Thus, industrial policies and the process of production sector restructuring generated by structural reforms should be measured against their potential effects on surplus labour in the economy. In this regard, linkages are once again crucial, since what matters from an employment perspective is the overall impact of industrial restructuring and development on job creation, even if many of the new jobs are in a growing service sector stimulated by and supporting industrial activity or, for that matter, in producing food crops and other agricultural products to satisfy changing consumer preferences.

\*\*\*

Let me mention, finally, two elements that must be taken into account in understanding the links between industrial policies and growth. The first is that domestic factors are not the sole determinant of domestic policies. The regional and global economic environments are also essential determinants of growth, an issue usually overlooked in the massive literature on economic growth in recent decades. During the so-called golden age of 1950-1973, most developing regions experienced rapid economic growth. In contrast, the final two decades of the twentieth century brought a large number of "growth collapses", with only a small number of developing economies able to sustain fast rates of growth. Furthermore, widening international inequality diminishes the growth prospects of the less advantaged countries. This is so because markets may exacerbate inequality, as successful countries accumulate richer endowments and as capital follows success, while those left behind remain more vulnerable to shocks in international financial and commodity markets.

Second, development is path-dependent, i.e., long-run growth prospects depend on an economy's trajectory. The importance of dynamic learning economies to economic development implies that the opportunities open to economic agents are largely determined by their production experience. Loss of experience may thus have cumulative effects on growth, as illustrated in the 1980s by the diverging experience of Latin America (which suffered major adverse macroeconomic shocks) and Asia (which did not). This is not, however, a recipe for fatalism à la the "history (or geography) is destiny" school of development. Several countries have been able to emerge from extended periods of relative stagnation or high economic volatility to embark on new development paths characterised by consistently high growth. Those experiences do, however, suggest the importance of government policy in helping create an environment which provides sufficient rewards to entrepreneurship and innovation, and also in addressing the coordination failures and informational externalities which can inhibit a sustainable process of industrial development.

***

The essays in this volume develop a number of the themes touched upon here – the importance of *patterns* of industrial diversification and the opportunities they provide for linkage and knowledge spillover (Rodrik); the need for a broader view of innovation, encompassing not only technology but also marketing, logistics, management and organization (Dahlman); the realization that FDI, including South-South investments, do not per se have a positive impact on the economic development of recipient countries (Aykut and Goldstein); the scope beyond industry – in certain areas of agriculture and services – for innovation, linkage and high-value-added production (Kjöllerström and Dallto; Singh); the employment-creating and poverty-reducing effects of different patterns of industrial development (Kniivilä); and the importance of the external environment to shaping industrial development prospects (Adhikari and Yamamoto; Dahlman). While not mentioned explicitly here, some of the essays which follow deal with the ways by which governments and corporations have been addressing the social and environmental impacts of industrial development (Peck and Chipman; Bhandarkar and Alvarez-Rivero).

## Notes

1 For further elaboration of the arguments here, see Ocampo (2005), "The Quest for Dynamic Efficiency: Structural Dynamics and Economic Growth in Developing Countries", in José Antonio Ocampo (editor), Beyond Reforms: Structural Dynamics and Macroeconomic Vulnerability, Stanford University Press, ECLAC and World Bank, Palo Alto, CA. See also United Nations (2006), World Economic and Social Survey 2006: Diverging Growth and Development, New York (Department of Economic and Social Affairs; E/2006/50/Rev.1/ST/ESA/306).

# Part 1

# New Frontiers and Challenges

# Industrial development: Some stylized facts and policy directions

Dani Rodrik*

## 1. Introduction

Structural issues were once at the core of thinking on economic development policies. Development economists of the "old school" understood well the fundamental role that structural transformation played in the course of development. In their thinking, the movement of labour from traditional activities in agriculture and other primary sectors to "modern" industry was the key to raising the economy's saving and investment rates and to fostering economic growth.[1] The faster the rate at which labour would move from traditional agriculture and low-productivity informal activities to the modern sector, the more rapid the rate of economic growth.

Of course not all modern activities need to take place within manufacturing industries. The expansion of non-traditional agriculture can play an important role in development (as it has notably in Chile). And the modernization of traditional agriculture can be a significant source of productivity gains (as with the green revolution). But historically rapid growth is associated first and foremost with the expansion of industrial activities.

Economic globalization has greatly increased the premium on manufacturing, particularly of the exportable kind. In recent decades rapidly growing developing countries have been able to grow much faster than earlier antecedents (Britain during the industrial revolution, the United States during its catch-up with Britain in the late 19th century, or European recovery in the post-war period). The reason for this is that world markets provide near-limitless demand for manufactured exports from developing countries. An expansion of non-tradables is self-limiting, as the domestic terms of trade eventually turns against non-tradables, choking off further investment and growth. And there are natural limits to export-led growth based on primary products, as country after country has discovered. Developing countries exporting manufactured products do not face such limits as long as they can latch on to new activities which face dynamic demand in rich countries' markets.

* John F. Kennedy School of Government, Harvard University.

Of course, it is not only manufactures that possess these characteristics, and there is always the danger that we associate "new products" and diversification too closely with manufactures and with a narrow view of industrialization. There are many service activities that are tradable, and many non-traditional natural-resource based products which provide potential for high growth. India has benefited tremendously from exports of Information Technology (IT) and Business Processing Outsourcing (BPO) services, and Chile has successfully diversified from copper into advanced fisheries and fruit products. In practice, what may prove key is the development of a sufficiently broad base of non-traditional tradables rather than of manufactures per se.

Despite all this, recent economic thinking on policy reforms pays scant attention to structural transformation and industrial development. The implicit view is that once the "economic fundamentals"—macroeconomic stability and well-functioning markets—are in place, structural transformation is an automatic process. As long as an economy is open to international trade, comparative advantage directs resources to where their contribution to national product is maximized. And even though there is a long tradition of studies on the natural-resource curse, contemporary thinking on policy has been very reluctant to favour some economic activities over others. Economic policies promoting manufacturing, or some manufacturing subsectors over others, are still frowned upon.

In reality, the expansion of manufacturing activities in low-income environments is fraught with externalities and spillovers of all kind. Entrepreneurs who make investments in non-traditional economic activities provide valuable demonstration effects for prospective entrants, they train workers and managers who can be employed in other firms, they generate technological learning which they cannot fully appropriate, and they provide inputs (and demand) for other activities which may not have started up otherwise. The social value of such investments greatly exceeds their private value.

The perspective adopted in this paper is therefore different. It takes as its starting point recent empirical evidence that places industrial development, and non-traditional manufactures in particular, in the driving seat of economic growth and development. This empirical work has generated some new stylized facts and has greatly increased our understanding of how manufacturing contributes to economic growth. The first half of the paper is devoted to discussing these stylized facts.

The second half of the paper presents a policy discussion around a bare-bones general-equilibrium model. The model is informed by the empirical evidence discussed in the first half of the paper and is built on a general learning spillover generated in the modern sector. It highlights the respective roles played in industrialization of three kinds of economic policies: trade liberalization, promotion of non-traditional exports, and current-account policies (including, critically, the exchange rate). The objective here is to move beyond specific industrial policies of the type discussed in Rodrik (2004) to a consideration of how the challenge of industrialization affects the stance of external policies more broadly.

## 2. Some important stylized facts of development

I begin by presenting some important empirical regularities, that recent research on patterns of economic growth has highlighted. These regularities underscore the importance of industrial development as an engine of economic growth. None of them will come as a big surprise to close observers of developing countries. What is significant is the growing body of systematic empirical evidence that now backs up the maintained hypotheses in the classical literature on development.

*1. Economic development requires diversification, not specialization*

Productive diversification is a key correlate of economic development. Poor countries produce a relatively narrow range of goods, while richer countries are engaged in a broad range of economic activities. This may sound obvious, but runs counter to one of the fundamental insights of trade theory. The principle of comparative advantage states that the gains from trade arise from specialization. According to the theory, it is by specializing in those activities that they are relatively good at—or relatively less bad at—that poor nations reap the benefits from engaging with the world economy. There is a large literature, typified by the Little-Scitovsky-Scott/Bhagwati-Krueger/Balassa studies of the 1970s,[2] that ascribes the underperformance of developing nations to their failure to let domestic resource flows be guided by the forces of comparative advantage.

But whatever role closure to international trade may have played in delaying economic growth, it is unlikely that failure to specialize has ever been the key obstacle to development. This is the clear message that emerges from a neat study by Imbs and Wacziarg (2003). These authors examined the patterns of sectoral concentration in a large cross-section of countries, as well as within countries over time. They discovered that as incomes increase, economies become less concentrated and more diversified. This process goes on until countries reach roughly the income level of Ireland. It is only at relatively high levels of income that further growth is associated with increased specialization. If sectoral concentration is graphed against income per capita, therefore, one obtains a U-shaped curve. A detailed analysis of export data by Klinger and Lederman (2004) arrives at a similar finding in trade: the number of new export products also follows an inverted U-curve in income.

Imbs and Wacziarg (2003) undertook a whole battery of robustness tests, and found that the regularity they had identified was a very strong one. In particular, the U-shaped pattern is present even when one focuses on the manufacturing sector alone, suggesting that what is going on here is not just a structural transformation from agriculture to industry, but also a process of diversification and expansion of the range of activities within manufacturing. The pattern is also not just a cross-section phenomenon (like Kuznets's famous inverted U-shape relationship between inequality and levels of development): it also holds within countries through time. The turnaround typically happens at a relatively late stage in development. Thus, in the words of Imbs and Wacziarg (2003, 64), "countries diversify over most of their development path." If economy-wide productivity growth were driven by specialization (driven in turn by openness to trade), we would observe a positive relationship between specialization and income levels, not the negative one that Imbs and Wacziarg have identified.

What does this imply for industrialization? It suggests that enhancing an economy's productive capabilities over an increasing range of manufactured goods is an integral part of economic development. The first order of business in development is to learn how to do new things, not to focus on what one already does well.

*2. Rapidly growing countries are those with large manufacturing sectors*
Figure 1 shows the trends in the share of manufacturing in GDP in five different regions of the world: East Asia and the Pacific, South Asia, Latin America and the Caribbean, Middle East and North Africa, and Sub-Saharan Africa. Compare first East Asia with Latin America. In 1965, the manufacturing industries of the two regions were of roughly similar size, accounting for around 25 per cent of GDP. By 1980, manufacturing's share had risen to almost 35 per cent of GDP in East Asia, while it remained still slightly above 25 per cent in Latin America—a difference of 10 per cent of GDP. And since the late 1980s, manufacturing has experienced a precipitous decline in Latin America, falling to a low of 15 per cent by 2004. The broader manufacturing base that East Asian countries were able to build—and maintain—is an important structural difference between these two regions.

None of the three remaining regions have managed to build large manufacturing bases either. As of 2004 the share of manufacturing in GDP hovered around the 15 per cent mark in Sub-Saharan Africa, South Asia, and Middle East and North Africa. The degree to which this performance can be ascribed to underlying factor endowments, rather than to a poor policy regime, is an interesting and important question to which I shall turn later.

*3. Growth accelerations are associated with structural changes in the direction of manufacturing*
The evidence on the importance of manufacturing discussed above relates to cross-country comparisons. But we can go beyond this evidence and ask a more specific question: are growth take-offs linked to the performance of manufacturing somehow?

While long-term growth has been rare among the universe of developing nations, growth accelerations that last a decade or so have been quite frequent. Two recent studies have taken advantage of the abundance of these growth accelerations to identify some stylized facts associated with such accelerations. In Hausmann, Pritchett, and Rodrik (2005) we looked at instances of growth acceleration (of 2 per cent or more) that were sustained for at least eight years and found more than 80 such episodes since the 1950s. Jones and Olken (2005) similarly focused on cases of what they called "start-stop" growth, identifying instances of both "up-breaks" (accelerations) and "down-breaks" (decelerations).

These sharp turning points in growth performance allow us to ask whether manufacturing plays a role in shaping growth performance. Johnson, Ostry, and Subramanian (2006) examined the cases of sustained growth accelerations identified by Hausmann, Pritchett, and Rodrik (2005) and found that nearly all these cases took place in the midst a rapid increase in the share of manufactures in total exports (see also Prasad, Rajan, and Subramanian 2006). Jones and Olken (2005) found that up-breaks were associated with increased manufacturing employment (as a share of economy-wide employment), while down-breaks witnessed declines in manufacturing employment. In Jones and Olken's (2005, p.17) words, "regime shifts [in economic growth] therefore see broad moves into and out of manufacturing rather than intra-manufacturing reallocation." All of these studies also document a rise in the share of trade (imports and exports) in GDP during growth accelerations.

*4. Specialization patterns are not pinned down by factor endowments*
This is all fine and well, a sceptic might say, but perhaps manufacturing capabilities and success are determined primarily by geography and factor endowments. East Asia had an abundance of labour and poor natural resources, so specializing in manufactures was a natural choice. Latin America is rich in natural resources, Sub-Saharan Africa in land, and the Middle East in oil. Maybe bad policy can ruin a nascent manufacturing sector, but can good policy play more than a limited role if factor endowments condemn an economy to specialize in primary products rather than industry?

The evidence suggests that factor endowments and policy both play a role in shaping production structure. In particular, successful countries have always pushed the limits of their static comparative advantage and diversified into new activities that are the domain of countries considerably richer than they are. If countries like China and India (and South Korea, Taiwan, Singapore, and Malaysia before them) have done so well, it is not primarily because their labour-endowment advantage gave them the ability to compete in labour-intensive manufactures. It is because they were able to quickly diversify into more sophisticated, technically-demanding activities that supported higher rates of economic growth.

It is possible to make this point more rigorously using a quantitative index developed in Hausmann, Hwang, and Rodrik (2006) which we called EXPY. The index measures the productivity level associated with a country's export specialization pattern. *EXPY* is calculated in two steps. First, using the 6-digit HS commodity classification (which yields more than 5,000 different commodities), we compute the weighted average of the incomes of the countries exporting each traded commodity, where the weights are the revealed comparative advantage of each country in that commodity (normalized so that the weights sum up to 1). This gives us the income level of that commodity, which we call *PRODY*. Next we calculate *EXPY* as the weighted average of the *PRODY* for each country, where the weights are the share of each commodity in that country's total exports.

As would be expected from the manner of its construction, *EXPY* is highly correlated with per-capita income: rich countries export goods that other rich countries export. A scatter plot of EXPY against per-capita GDP for 1992 is shown in Figure 2. But what is important from our perspective is that countries do not all lie on the regression line. Some countries are way below the regression line, while others are way above it. It is striking that China and India both stand out in the latter group. Both high-performing economies have export profiles that are especially skewed towards high productivity goods. In 1992, China's exports were associated with an income level that is three times higher than China's per-capita GDP at the time. While this gap has diminished over time, it still remains high.

It turns out that *EXPY* is not well explained by factor endowments and other economic fundamentals. The partial correlations between *EXPY* and human capital and institutional quality, controlling for per-capita GDP, are shown in Figures 3 and 4, respectively. These scatter plots use more recent trade data from 2002 to maximize the number of countries included. We find only a weakly positive partial correlation between *EXPY* and the stock of human capital (Figure 3), and virtually no partial correlation with our index of institutional quality, the "rule of law" (Figure 4).

While specialization patterns are not uniquely pinned down by a country's factor endowments, that does not mean that comparative advantage patterns are entirely idiosyncratic and up for grabs. African countries are unlikely to be able to make the jump to aerospace and semiconductors with their existing skill and capital endowments. But while the sophistication of a country's exports is determined in part by its overall productive capacity and its human capital endowment, policy also matters. Bangladesh's relative factor endowments are similar to China's—abundant in labour, and scarce in human and physical capital—yet the country has an *EXPY* that is roughly 50 per cent lower than China's. It is difficult to avoid the conclusion that China's determined efforts to acquire technology from abroad and diversify its exports are at the root of this difference (see Rodrik, 2006). I will return to the policy implications of this later in the paper.

*5. Countries that promote exports of more "sophisticated" goods grow faster*
Of course it could be that by pushing investments into sophisticated activities for which the economy has no innate comparative advantage China and other countries with similar policies have ended up penalizing their economies. That would be the natural reaction of a trade economist with strong faith in comparative advantage as a driver of economic performance. But the evidence speaks quite loudly on this score, and suggests otherwise. There is in fact a robust and positive relationship between the initial level of a country's *EXPY* and the subsequent rate of economic growth experienced by that country. Figure 5 is the relevant scatter plot: it shows the relationship between *EXPY* in 1992 and growth over the 1992-2003 period, holding initial levels of income constant. This is a positive and statistically significant relationship. We have obtained very similar results in panel settings (employing fixed effects for countries) with data going back to the 1960s: countries that experience a rise in *EXPY* subsequently grow more rapidly (see Hausmann, Hwang, and Rodrik, 2006). The evidence strongly suggests that industrial upgrading is a leading indicator of economic performance.[3]

*6. There is "unconditional" convergence at the level of individual products*
One reason that latching on to more sophisticated manufactured products promotes growth is that such products have productivity frontiers that are further away and therefore present greater room for technological catch-up. By starting to produce goods that countries much richer than them are currently producing, poor countries enlarge the scope of productivity improvements. Convergence in productivity levels with rich countries becomes an important force for economic growth.

This claim needs some explanation. Begin first with the neoclassical model of economic growth, which posits that countries have access to the same technologies. In this model, poorer countries converge to the income levels of rich countries through a process of human and physical capital accumulation. This theoretical prediction has found little support in the data, however. When one looks at the cross-national evidence on growth, there is no indication that poorer countries grow systematically more rapidly than richer countries.

This kind of convergence exercise is usually performed on aggregate data, typically GDP per capita. When Hwang (forthcoming) recently carried out a similar exercise using detailed, product-level data, he made a surprising and important discovery: economic convergence at the level of individual products is *unconditional*. In other words, when a country starts to produce a particular good, the productivity with which that good is produced—measured by either labour productivity or unit prices (an indicator of product quality)—converges to the frontier for that good unconditionally, regardless of any of the characteristics of the country in question. Moreover, the rate of convergence is quite rapid.

Note how different this finding is from the conditional convergence results that dominate the work on economic growth. The message of the conditional convergence literature is as follows: "what you need to do to converge to the income levels of rich countries is to get your policies and institutions in order." Hwang's (forthcoming) results say: "what you need to do to converge is to get a foothold in the goods that rich countries produce." The absence of unconditional convergence at the aggregate level must be due, in turn, to structural features of low-income economies. Poor countries remain poor because they are not producing the kind of goods that will carry them towards riches.

The presence of unconditional convergence at the product level is also important in that it sheds light to a related puzzle regarding *EXPY*. Remember that *EXPY* is calculated by looking at the type of goods that each country exports. Even at the 6-digit level of disaggregation, these goods can be quite dissimilar in terms of product quality and technological sophistication. Look for example at Table 1 where I compare the unit values of some of China's main electronics exports with those of three other comparators considerably richer than China (South Korea, Malaysia, and Singapore). For the most part, China's unit values are at the low end of the scale, and are sometimes a fraction of those of other countries. Looking at these numbers, one may have guessed that *EXPY* levels are likely to be quite misleading because they lump together countries producing albeit similar goods at very different levels of sophistication.

But Hwang's (forthcoming) results turn this inference on its head. If there is unconditional convergence at the 6-digit level, it means that countries starting to produce low unit-value goods within a product category will eventually experience significant increases in their unit values. In fact, the lower the unit value you start out with, the greater is the growth you will experience. And this will happen more or less automatically, without any special supportive policies in place.

But what is far from automatic is getting these new industries off the ground in the first place. Unconditional convergence kicks off only after entrepreneurs (and sometimes the state) decide to undertake the investments needed to get an industry going. And as we know, the process of economic diversification is rife with market failures. Coordination and learning externalities of many kinds block investment and entrepreneurship in new activities. These market failures and the kind of policy response they call for are reviewed in Rodrik (2004) and I will not dwell on them in this paper. Instead, in the next section I will place the discussion of the policy issues raised by industrial development in the broader context of economy-wide reform strategies.

*7. Some specialization patterns are more conducive than others to promoting industrial upgrading*

Another reason manufacturing promotes growth is that a specialization pattern based on manufactured goods presents a better platform for jumping on to new economic activities with unexploited productivity potential. A country with a broad-based manufacturing sector is more likely to take advantage of new opportunities than one which has specialized in a few primary-based products.

This idea is made more precise in the recent work of Hausmann and Klinger (2006). These authors start with the observation that the inputs and public goods that different industries need can vary quite a lot. A first-rate sanitary and phyto-sanitary regime for animal husbandry will enable a country to easily expand the range of animal products that it can produce and sell abroad, but will not help much in other parts of the product space (e.g., electronics) where the regulatory or human capital requirements may be quite different. Pulp and paper products require property rights to be well established in forestry and an adequate taxation regime for long-lived assets—institutional features that are largely irrelevant for, say, the auto parts industry. Transitions from old to new activities become harder when they involve novel institutional prerequisites. Everything else being the same, then, a country is better off producing goods that require institutional assets that can be used in a wide range of goods other than those already in production. This facilitates structural transformation and diversification.

The next observation, and one that they document at length, is that the product space is quite uneven in this sense of asset-specificity. Some economic activities require highly specific assets that do not allow jumps to other activities, while others require assets that permit such jumps. A major contribution of Hausmann and Klinger (2006) is that they actually provide a mapping of the product space along this particular dimension. Their metric for identifying the "distance" between any pair of goods, $A$ and $B$, is based on the likelihood that a country producing $A$ also produces $B$, and vice versa. Unsurprisingly, the part of the "forest" that contains manufactures is much denser than the part with natural resources or primary products.

The speed of structural transformation then depends on how dense the product space is—i.e., how many products there are close by—in the neighbourhood of the country's present product mix. Hausmann and Klinger (2006) show that the value of the "open forest" near the country's existing product mix–the *PRODY* of products that are nearby but which have not yet been exploited—determines how rapidly the country's *EXPY* rises. Putting all this differently, making the transition to manufactures helps not just because it pulls resources into higher productivity activities, but also because it makes future structural change easier.

### 3. A model of growth through industrial development

In this section I present a model that illustrates the key features discussed earlier and elucidates some of the policy issues that arise in this context. The central idea behind the model is that growth is driven through learning and enhanced capabilities accumulating in the industrial sector. I take this as a given and, in light of the preceding discussion, do not attempt to provide further microfoundations or evidence for it. While traditional exportables or non-tradables can also be a source of productivity gains for the economy, I follow the arguments in the preceding section by positing that it is non-traditional tradables which are the source of productive externalities. This allows me to use the model to clarify some policy issues.

#### 1. Production and technology

In a typical developing economy, much of the industrial sector is import competing and inward-looking. I call this the importables sector, producing output $q$. At the same time, there exist nascent industrial activities that are potentially competitive in world markets and which the country can eventually acquire comparative advantage in. I call this sector the non-traditional exportables, with output $x$. There is also a traditional exportable sector producing output $z$, and a non-tradable sector producing output $n$. Labour is the main factor of production. All tradable sectors operate with diminishing returns to scale while non-tradables operate under constant returns to scale.

The production functions for each activity can be written as follows:

$$q = Af(l_q) = Al_q^{\beta_q} \qquad \text{.... importables}$$

$$x = Ag(l_x) = Al_x^{\beta_x} \qquad \text{.... non-traditional exportables}$$

$$z = h(l_z) = \theta l_z^{\beta_z} \qquad \text{... traditional exportables}$$

$$n = l_n \qquad \text{... non-tradables}$$

Employment in each sector is denoted by $l$ with an appropriate sectoral subscript. The economy's total labour force is given exogenously by $\bar{l}$ with the following full employment constraint:

(1)      $\bar{l} = l_q + l_x + l_z + l_n \qquad$ ... full employment constraint

The parameters $\beta$ lie between 0 and 1 and calibrate the strength of diminishing returns in each sector, with $\beta \to 1$ representing the constant-returns to scale limit.

The parameter $A$ represents the level of productivity in the modern part of the economy (importables and non-traditional exportables). Its evolution over time is the main driver of economic growth. We posit that the rate at which $A$ rises over time is increasing with the level of economic activity in the modern sector at any point in time. This is meant to capture in general fashion the productivity promoting benefits of manufacturing, as discussed previously. The larger the modern sector, the more rapid the rate at which productivity increases.

(2)    $\dfrac{dA}{dt} = \pi(q + x),$    $\pi'>0,\ \pi''<0$    ... productivity growth

(We shall take $A$ to be fixed at any point in time for purposes of comparative statics.) The way this is formulated, what matters for productivity growth is the aggregate of output in the modern sector, regardless of whether resources are employed in importables or (non-traditional) exportables. This recognizes that domestic market oriented industry generates learning spillovers for exportables, just as exportable production may improve productivity elsewhere in the economy. In fact, the treatment here is symmetric with respect to the learning generated in the two types of economic activites.

### 2. Pricing and market equilibrium

I assume that all three tradable sectors are price takers in world markets, where prices are fixed to unity for convenience. Domestic prices depend on the nature of trade policies. I will consider two types of trade polices, import tariffs on importables (at ad-valorem rate $t$) and export subsidies on non-traditional exportables (at ad-valorem rate $s$). With these policies in place, domestic prices become $(1+t)$, $(1+s)$, and 1 respectively for importables, non-traditional exportables, and traditional exportables. The price of non-tradables is given by $p$.

Labour is assumed to be mobile across all four sectors. Therefore, there is a common wage rate in the economy, $w$, which is equal to the value of the marginal labour productivity in each sector. The conditions for labour-market equilibrium can be written as follows.

(3)       $w = (1+t)Af'(l_q) = (1+t)Al_q^{\beta_q}$

(4)       $w = (1+s)Ag'(l_x) = (1+s)Al_x^{\beta_x}$

(5)       $w = \theta h'(l_z) = \theta l_z^{\beta_z}$

(6)       $w = p$

Note that the wage rate has to equal the price of non-tradables goods as long as that technology is linear and as specified above.

### 3. External balance

The difference between domestic expenditures and domestic income has to be covered by net resource transfers from abroad, $B$. We express both national income and expenditures at world prices. National income is simply the sum of value added in the economy, $q+x+z+pn$. On the expenditure side, we assume for simplicity that neither of the exportables (traditional and non-traditional) is consumed at home. Therefore, total expenditure is the sum of consumption of importables and non-tradables. Assuming further that preferences are Cobb-Douglas, with $\alpha$ denoting the share of importables in expenditures ($0 < \alpha < 1$), and imposing the requirement that domestic demand and output of non-tradables have to equal each other, the external balance equation can be written as follows.

(7)     $\alpha pl_n - (1 - \alpha)(q + x + z) = B$          ... external balance

The interpretation of this equation is as follows. Note that $pl_n$ is the income generated in the non-tradables sector, of which $\alpha$ "leaks" into import demand. And $q+x+z$ is the income generated (at world prices) in the tradable sector, of which $(1- \alpha)$ is spent on non-tradables rather than importables. The balance between these two forces gives us the current account deficit, $B$. In the analysis of the system we can treat $B$ either as zero (imposing balance on the current account as an equilibrium condition) or as determined by exchange-rate and other macroeconomic policies from outside the system.

### 4. Equilibrium

The model has seven endogenous variables, $l_q$, $l_x$, $l_z$, $l_n$, $w$, $p$, $dA/dt$. There are seven independent equations (1)-(7) that can be used to provide implicit solutions for these, and to undertake comparative statics analysis. I will provide an informal discussion of the workings of the model below.

### 5. Discussion

The market failure around which the normative implications of this model work is the learning externality in the modern part of the economy. In the absence of policy intervention, the output of the modern sector, $q+x$, will be too low. This has severe dynamic implications here because the cost of the failure to internalize the externality is not just a static one, but also a dynamic one. When $q+x$ is too low, the economy's (productivity) growth rate is also too low. The first-best policy in this context consists of subsidizing both importables and non-traditional exportable production. But we are mainly concerned here with how this structural feature of the economy interacts with other standard reform policies.

Consider first import liberalization. In principle, one of the main advantages of import liberalization is that it ends up stimulating the production of exportables. By the Lerner symmetry theorem, removing import restrictions is tantamount to removing restrictions on exports. That is good news in the kind of framework modelled above, where exportables are a source of learning and productivity spillovers. But the model also identifies two important sources of bad news for import liberalization. First, to the extent that production of import-competing goods is also a source of productivity spillovers, import liberalization works at cross purposes with the need to generate new learning. Second, and more subtly, when only non-traditional exportables generate learning spillovers, import liberalization is also a very blunt instrument for producing the desirable export response.

The second point is an important one that is often overlooked in policy discussions, so it is worth spending some time on it. The fundamental rationale of the Lerner symmetry theorem is a general equilibrium one. When import tariffs are removed, the resources released by import competing activities have to be deployed elsewhere in the economy. When aggregate demand is managed appropriately so that neither unemployment nor trade deficits are allowed to become problems, exportables constitute those activities "elsewhere." But the theorem says nothing about the composition of the export supply response, which will depend on the supply elasticities of different export activities in general equilibrium. In the context of our model, we have two types of exportables, with the one that matters for growth being the non-traditional type. If import liberalization stimulates mainly traditional exports (say garments or agricultural products with minimal processing) rather than non-traditional products, the end result is bound to be disappointing. We end up with export growth but with little economic growth overall.

To see how this is possible in the context of our specific model, let us make the supply of traditional exportables highly elastic. To make the point as starkly as possible, assume that the output of traditional exportables can be expanded at near constant returns to scale (i.e., we let $\beta_z \to 1$). We ask what the consequences of a reduction in the import tariff are. In this case, it can be checked that the comparative statics of the model become very simple:

$$\frac{dl_q / l_q}{dt} = \frac{1}{(1+t)(1-\beta_q)} > 0 \qquad\qquad \frac{dl_x / l_x}{dt} = 0$$

Import liberalization reduces employment and output in the import-competing sector without stimulating any growth in non-traditional exports whatsoever. In this economy, productivity growth and economic growth will slow down since $q+x$ goes down unambiguously. What has happened is that traditional exports, being in much more elastic supply than non-traditional exports, have swallowed up all the resources released by the import competing activities.

A similarly negative outcome can arise also for a different reason. Now suppose that traditional and non-traditional exports do not differ in their supply elasticities, but that the import liberalization is accompanied by macroeconomic policies that allow the trade deficit to get larger (or equivalently, that enable capital inflows to rise). In our model this can be analyzed by letting $B$ rise as $t$ falls. This time, the export response will be sluggish across the board. Since $q$ goes down for sure following the import liberalization and the rise in $x$ is limited by the growing trade deficit, in all likelihood $q+x$ will decline once again. The effects on economic growth will be adverse.

We are now in a better position to understand why across-the-board import liberalization, of the type that countries in Latin America and elsewhere adopted in the late 1980s and thereafter have produced such disappointing results. While not intended that way, these reforms weakened the industrial base of their economies, and reduced productive dynamism overall. They squeezed the import-competing sectors without sufficiently stimulating new non-traditional exportables. We see the results in poor figures for growth and economy-wide Total Factor Productivity (TFP).

Contrast now the Latin American reform strategy with the archetypal Asian one. Asian countries reformed their economies in a different way, by focusing initially on providing non-traditional export activities direct inducements and subsidies. The specific policies employed varied, from export subsidies (in South Korea and Taiwan in the 1960s) to export processing zones (in Singapore and Malaysia in the 1970s) to Special Economic Zones (in China in the 1980s and 1990s). But in each case the focus was on targeted new exportables, rather than on import liberalization. In fact, in all of these countries, significant import liberalization was undertaken only after growth had reached a significant momentum.

In the context of our model, we can think of the Asian strategy as taking the form of an export subsidy, $s$. How does this work? Clearly, an increase in $s$ has a direct positive effect on the supply of non-traditional exportables, $x$. To the extent that this expansion crowds out import-competing activities, $q$ may well fall—which is the Lerner symmetry theorem working now in reverse. But since the export subsidy is targeted on non-traditional exportables only, this need not happen. The expansion of the non-traditional exportable sector may well come at the expense of the traditional exportable sector. In fact, when the supply of traditional exportables is highly elastic (the same assumption we made above in the context of the Latin American policy experiment), that is exactly what happens. So letting $\beta_z \to 1$ as before, the comparative statics with respect to $s$ yield:

$$\frac{dl_q/l_q}{ds} = 0 \qquad\qquad \frac{dl_x/l_x}{ds} = \frac{1}{(1+s)(1-\beta_x)} > 0$$

The export subsidy has no effect on production and employment in the import-competing sector, while it directly stimulates non-traditional exportables. In this case we have unambiguously growth promoting trade creation. Since $x$ increases while $q$ remains unchanged, the economy's rate of productivity growth is permanently higher.

This framework identifies therefore an important asymmetry between policies targeted at across-the-board trade liberalization and those that are targeted at improving production incentives for non-traditional exportables. The usual policy discourse frequently treats these two types of policies as if they were substitutes for each other. Appealing to the Lerner symmetry theorem, East Asia's export policies are often lumped together with import liberalization. Yet, once we allow for differences between traditional and non-traditional exports, we can begin to see how misleading these arguments are. The robust industrial base which generates economic growth requires strategic policies directed specifically to new economic activities. The trickle-down effects of import liberalization cannot be relied on to produce the intended effects. That is a key lesson from the comparative experience with policy reform.

Another important lesson has to do with macroeconomic management and exchange rate policy in particular. As can be seen from equation (7), the current account balance has a direct effect on the level of tradables production in the economy. Everything else being the same, larger capital inflows from abroad are associated with a bigger current account deficit, a higher $p$ and $w$, a more appreciated (lower) real exchange rate, and smaller output of tradables ($q+x+z$). (As usual, the real exchange rate is the relative price of tradables to non-tradables, which in our model is inversely related to $p$.) Countries that have opened themselves to capital inflows and have let their currencies float have typically experienced exactly these consequences. An appreciated currency and a volatile real exchange rate implied by turbulence in financial markets are hardly conducive to the expansion of new exportable activities. And conversely, an "undervalued" currency can be more potent than industrial policy in promoting industrialization.

What matters for incentives is the real exchange rate, while governments can control at best the nominal exchange rate. Many analysts dismiss the arguments above on the grounds that the real exchange rate is an endogenous variable over which the government may not have much control. But this flies in the face of both theory and evidence. On the theoretical front, the endogenous level of the real exchange rate is shaped by many policy decisions that the government has control over. Everything else being the same, restrictions on capital inflows, encouragement of capital outflows (for example, allowing domestic social security funds to invest abroad), sterilized intervention, tighter fiscal policies, and nominal devaluations (in the context of supportive demand-management policies) will all result in more competitive real exchange rates. And empirically, governments that have placed large weight on competitiveness in their conduct of monetary and exchange rate policies have indeed managed to maintain the real exchange rate at reasonably competitive levels (using a variety of instruments of the type listed above). China and India are a key exhibit in this respect. In both countries, competitive real exchange rates have been an explicit policy objective, and have played a fundamental role in fostering a large and diversified industrial base. There is also broader cross-national evidence which indicates that intervention and other monetary policies do affect the level of the real exchange rate over the medium term, with important consequences for economic growth (Sturzenegger and Yeyati, 2006).

One direct implication of these considerations is that a strict inflation targeting regime of the type that many countries have adopted (e.g., Chile, Brazil, Peru, South Africa, Turkey) is not particularly suited to the needs of industrial development and growth. In such monetary regimes, the central bank does not have a competitiveness target, and the level of the exchange rate becomes an issue only to the extent that it affects inflation. A typical consequence is long bouts of overvaluation (from the perspective of the health of tradables) along with substantial currency volatility over the medium term (driven largely by external developments and fluctuations in the appetite for emerging market assets). Evaluations of inflation targeting to date have focused almost exclusively on consequences for inflation and output volatility, rather than longer-term growth (see for example IMF, 2006). The framework put forth here suggests that there is an important cost to be paid—in terms of foregone growth over the longer term—for placing financial and monetary considerations in the driving seat of exchange rate policy.

## 4. Concluding remarks

The preceding discussion points to a two-pronged strategy in support of industrial development. What is needed is both a robust industrial policy targeted at new exportables, and a supportive exchange-rate policy that promotes production of tradables across the board. Without a relatively stable and competitive exchange rate, it is practically impossible to induce investment and entrepreneurship in tradables of any kind. But without more directly targeted industrial policies, exchange rate policies alone cannot be a very powerful tool for promoting diversification. A cheap domestic currency helps both traditional exporters and non-traditional ones. The secret of the success of high-growth economies lies in a combination of these two types of policies.

Let me add a few words on industrial policy, since there is much opposition to (and confusion on) this kind of policy intervention. What I understand by "industrial policy" is not an effort by the government to select particular sectors and subsidize them through a range of instruments (directed credit, subsidies, tax incentives, and so on). The critics of industrial policy are correct when they argue that governments do not have adequate knowledge to pick "winners." As discussed in Rodrik (2004) and Hausmann and

Rodrik (2006), industrial policy is more appropriately conceived as a *process* whereby the state and the private sector jointly arrive at diagnoses about the sources of blockage in new economic activities and propose solutions to them. Industrial policy requires the government to take an ex-ante stand neither on the activities to be promoted nor on the instruments to be deployed. It simply requires it to build the public-private institutional arrangements whereby information on profitable activities and useful instruments of intervention can be elicited.

Finally, while I have downplayed the role of "fundamentals" (e.g., human and physical capital endowments and institutional quality), that is not because I think they are unimportant, but because I wanted to emphasize that they are not the sole driving force behind specialization patterns. The problem with focusing exclusively on these fundamentals—at the expense of the type of policies just considered—is that it overlooks the diversification opportunities that can be pursued even with relatively poor institutions and at low levels of skills and capital. Had China and India simply focused on getting the fundamentals right, the former would not be an exporter of sophisticated electronics products today and the latter would not have become a world power in IT services. It is a reasonable guess that neither country would be growing as rapidly.

Figure 1. Manufacturing value added as % of GDP

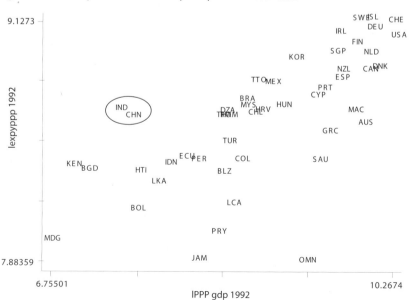

Source: Data are from the World Development Indicators database.
Obs.: The share of MVA in GDP has increased slightly in East Asia and the Pacific from the early
nineties to 2003 (2005 World Development Indicators).

Figure 2. Relationship between EXPY and per-capita incomes in 1992

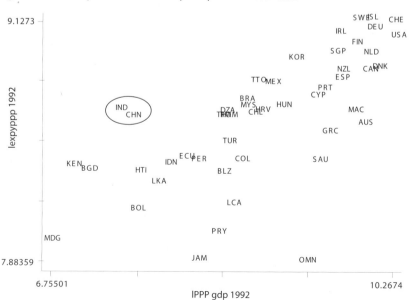

Figure 3. Partial scatter plot between EXPY and human capital

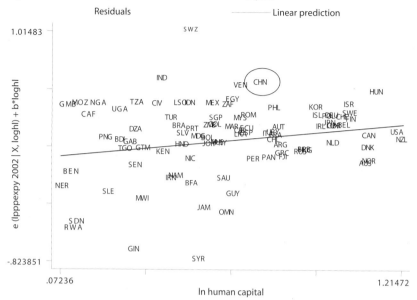

Figure 4. Partial scatter plot between EXPY and institutional quality

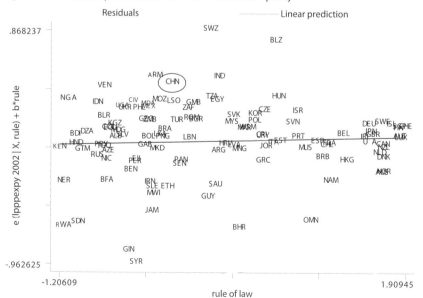

Figure 5. Relationship between initial level of EXPY and growth, controlling for initial income

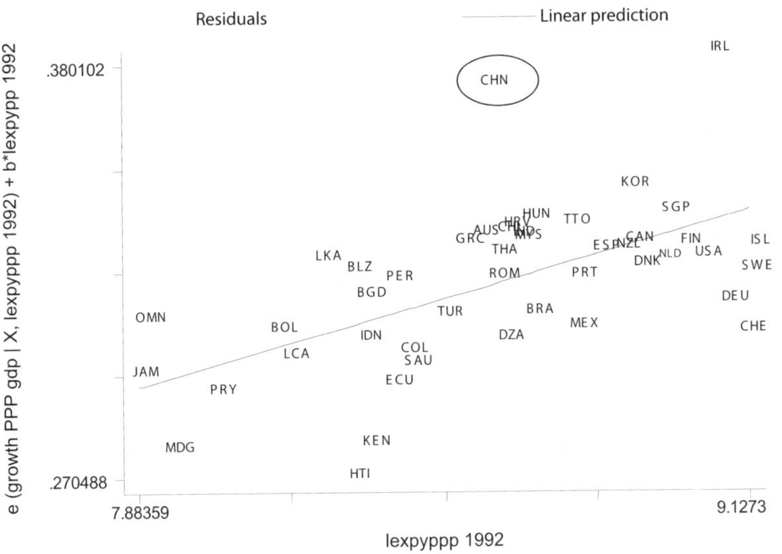

Residuals                               ——— Linear prediction

Table 1.
Unit value comparisons:
electrical goods and equipment exports
(US$ per unit, 2003)

| Product name | China | S. Korea | Malaysia | Singapore |
|---|---|---|---|---|
| Electric transformers, static converters and rectifier | 0.855 | 5.713 | 0.884 | 0.229 |
| Electric accumulators | 1.317 | 2.519 | 17.295 | 1.248 |
| Electric apparatus for line telephony, telegraphy | 14.488 | 66.581 | 46.995 | 36.496 |
| Electronic sound reproducing equipment, non-recording | 13.520 | 50.003 | 52.966 | 68.260 |
| Video recording and reproducing apparatus | 48.733 | 39.356 | 90.926 | 112.492 |
| Parts, accessories of audio, video recording equipment | 9.875 | 26.222 | 14.299 | n/a |
| Radio and TV transmitters, television cameras | 62.040 | 259.014 | 117.773 | 92.389 |
| Radio, radio-telephony receivers | 7.370 | 38.552 | 83.770 | 68.803 |
| Television receivers, video monitors, projectors | 72.903 | 17.987 | 144.185 | 195.939 |
| Parts for radio, tv transmission, receive equipment | 31.982 | 47.988 | 15.007 | n/a |
| Electronic printed circuits | 1.774 | 65.973 | 2.281 | 49.581 |
| Electronic integrated circuits and microassemblies | 1.101 | 960.988 | 1.478 | 2.337 |

Source: UN Comtrade Database and Rodrik (2005).

## Notes

1 Lewis (1954) provides the classic statement of this view.

2 The first of these was undertaken for the OECD, the second for the NBER, and the third for the World Bank.

3 There is the possibility of reverse causality of course, but in Hausmann, Hwang, and Rodrik (2006), we tried different instrumentation strategies, which yielded very similar results.

# Bibliography

Hausmann, R. and B. Klinger (2006), Structural transformation and patterns of comparative advantage in the product space, mimeo, Harvard University.

Hausmann, R., L. Pritchett and D. Rodrik (2005), Growth Accelerations, Journal of Economic Growth, 10, 2005, 303–29.

Hausmann, R., J. Hwang and D. Rodrik (2006), What You Export Matters, Harvard University, April.

Hausmann, R., and D. Rodrik, (2006), Doomed to Choose: Industrial Policy as Predicament, Harvard University, September.

Hwang, J. (forthcoming), Introduction of New Goods, Convergence, and Growth, Department of Economics, Harvard University.

Imbs, J. and R. Wacziarg (2003), Stages of Diversification, American Economic Review, 93(1), 63-86.

International Monetary Fund (2006), Inflation Targeting and the IMF, Prepared by Monetary and Financial Systems Department, Policy and Development Review Department, and Research Department, Washington, DC, March 16.

Johnson, S., J. Ostry and A. Subramanian (2006), Africa's Growth Prospects: Benchmarking the Constraints, IMF Working Paper, Washington D.C., International Monetary Fund.

Jones, B. F. and B. A. Olken (2005), The Anatomy of Start-Stop Growth, NBER Working Paper No. 11528, Cambridge, MA, National Bureau of Economic Research.

Klinger, B. and D. Lederman (2004), Discovery and Development: An Empirical Exploration of 'New' Products, World Bank, August.

Lewis, W. A. (1954), Economic Development with Unlimited Supplies of Labor, Manchester School of Economic and Social Studies, 22, 139-91.

Prasad, E., R. Rajan and A. Subramanian (2006), Foreign Capital and Economic Growth, Research Department, IMF, August.

Rodrik, D. (2004), Industrial Policy for the Twenty-First Century, Harvard University.

Rodrik, D. (2006), What's So Special About China's Exports, China & World Economy, 14(5), 1-19.

Sturzenegger, F. and E.L. Yeyati (2006), Fear of Floating or Fear of Sinking? Exchange Rate regimes in the 2000s, unpublished paper.

# Technology, globalization, and international competitiveness: Challenges for developing countries

Carl Dahlman*

## 1. Introduction

This paper traces the role of technology in economic growth and competitiveness, summarizes the strategies of the fastest growing economies over the last 50 years from the perspective of their technology strategy, summarizes some of the key global trends which are making it more difficult for developing countries to replicate the fast growth experience of the countries mentioned, and traces the impact of the rise of China on developing countries. The main argument of this paper is that technology is an increasingly important element of globalisation and of competitiveness and that the acceleration in the rate of technological change and the pre-requisites necessary to participate effectively in globalisation are making it more difficult for many developing countries to compete.

Section 2 gives a long-term perspective on technology and economic growth. Section 3 presents a global overview of changes in regional competitiveness as revealed by economic growth. Section 4 identifies some of the high performers in the last 50 years and reviews the strategies of the high performing East Asian economies comprising the well known "gang of four", plus three South East Asian countries. Section 5 reviews the strategies of the BRICM countries, the largest developing country economies (Brazil, Russia, India, China and Mexico). It also argues that it is harder for developing countries to replicate the success of the high performing East Asian countries for two main reasons. One relates to new elements in the global competitive environment. These are summarized in section 6. The other is the rapid rise of China (and to a lesser extent India). This is covered in Section 7, which also includes a preliminary analysis of the effects of the rapid rise of China on the rest of the world. Finally, Section 8 draws some conclusions. Developing countries must develop more technological capability and greater flexibility to succeed in the more demanding and asymmetric global environment. It is likely that the pressures of globalisation and greater international competition generate strong protectionist retrenchment in both developed and developing countries. These should be resisted. The world as a whole will be better off if developed countries focus on increasing their flexibility to adjust to changing comparative advantage resulting from rapid technical change, and developing countries focus on increasing their education, infrastructure, and technological capability. There remain however large asymmetries in the global system and greater efforts need to be made to provide some global balancing and transfer mechanisms.

* Georgetown University, Edmund A. Walsh School of Foreign Service.

## 2. Knowledge, technology, and growth in long-term perspective

### 2.1 Long-term trends

One of the best ways to see the role of knowledge in development, which is both sobering and enlightening, is to take a long historical perspective on both the growth of population and the increase in average per capita income (figure 1).[1] For the first 1,400 years of the past two millennia, the global population grew very slowly.[2] Although there were privileged elites with much higher income during this period, average per capita incomes hovered around $400 (in 1990 international US dollars). This figure is sobering in that it is roughly the same as that for today's poorest countries. Yet something remarkable began to happen around 1500. Both the global population and per capita income began to increase simultaneously. This shift was due to the convergence of many factors, in particular: better hygiene; the development of ingenious ways to harness wind and water power to augment human and animal energy; and advances in agricultural techniques such as irrigation, improved seeds, and multiple cropping. What is even more remarkable, when viewed from a long-term perspective, is how suddenly, even seemingly exponentially, both population and per capita incomes began to rise from the 1800s onward. This tremendous growth was in large part led by the development of the steam engine, whereby mankind was first able to harness fossil fuel energy for productive tasks. This augmentation of power enabled the industrial revolution with the corresponding proliferation of productive activity and expansion in the range of products and services brought to market.

As a compounding factor, further improvements in agriculture released a stream of labour into the recently arisen and relatively more productive industrial sectors. Simultaneous with these demographic changes and enhanced production technology, railroads and steamships supported scale economies and provided new opportunities for specialization and exchange. In the early nineteenth century, this broad social and economic transformation set the course toward the advanced standard of living which is today the hallmark of developed countries.

These first basic transformations were followed by successive radical inventions and corresponding institutional restructurings. Consider, for example, the advent of electricity. More or less suddenly, power could be distributed in discrete units including into the home for powering numerous labour saving devices. This technological change gradually released women into the workforce and increased output. Other examples include the following: gas and then electric lighting increased the length of the working day; the development of the gasoline engine untethered power from grids and led to more flexible transportation; the telegraph, and then the telephone reduced distance by making it possible to communicate and coordinate activities across space, enlarging markets and furthering opportunities for specialization and exchange. Eventually, the development of the semiconductor spawned the current information technology revolution which ought to be viewed as one more epochal innovation wave that transforms the organization of economic and social activity.[3] As such, development strategy today must be based upon the evolving productive and developmental logic of information technology and knowledge economics.

Regrettably, the benefits of all these many historical advances have not been equally spread. From the 1700s onward, per capita incomes diverged across countries and regions (figure 2). The benefits of increased per capita income concentrated first in England which spawned the industrial revolution, then spread to Western Europe, and soon thereafter to the United States (US). By the end of the 1800s, the US began to overtake Europe in many areas of industrial production.

Looking at figure 2, it is natural to ask: what accounts for the dazzling performance of the US? To a great extent, US growth was supported by a large internal market that allowed broader exploitation of transportation and communications advances starting with the railroad. Embracing these technologies brought large cost reductions from extensive economies of scale and scope. The US was also a land rich in natural resources including navigable rivers, arable land, timber, and minerals. Yet, more important than these contributing factors, the foundation of American economic growth was a fabric of institutions and an economic incentive regime which supported entrepreneurship, experimentation, and risk-taking. A core expression of this orientation, the US may be said to have invented the process of invention itself— when Thomas Alva Edison created the first industrial research and development (R&D) laboratory. After Edison, the industrial R&D lab was quickly imitated by many large US companies. By 1900 there were more industrial research laboratories in the US than in Europe.

Citing R&D as the core element in US economic growth may lead some to think that the solution to unequal economic growth is to create more research capability in the developing world. While this orientation may help, the innovation needs of developing countries are both simpler and more complex: simpler because to a large extent developing countries can attain increases in productivity by making effective use of existing knowledge; more complex, because the key requirements of technology-driven development are not just new knowledge.[4] In addition, development requires education, packages of technical skills, and a whole series of institutions, networks and capabilities which enable the effective use of existing knowledge and must be part of, or even precede, any serious effort to create new knowledge. Because addressing these constraints is critical for developing countries, the following sections offer greater detail on different aspects of innovation in order to lay the groundwork for explaining the strategies of different countries over time.

## 2.2 Innovation in the context of developing countries

Innovation in the context of developing countries is not so much a matter of pushing back the frontier of global knowledge, but more the challenge of facilitating the first use of new technology in the domestic context. Innovations should be considered broadly as improved products, processes, and business or organizational models. Development strategists ought to think not only of R&D and the creation of knowledge, but also attend to the details of its acquisition, adaptation, dissemination, and use in diversified local settings. It is useful to review what is involved in each of these five activities as this taxonomy will help structure the analysis of the most appropriate policies, institutions and capabilities necessary to increase innovation in the broad sense suggested here.

## 2.3 The creation, acquisition, adaptation, dissemination, and use of knowledge in developing countries

The *creation* of knowledge is the process of inventive activity. It is usually the result of explicit research and development effort normally carried out by scientists and engineers. The key institutions involved in the creation of knowledge are public R&D laboratories, universities, and private R&D centres. However, not all creation of knowledge is the result of formal R&D effort. Sometimes inventions come from the experience of production, or through informal trial and error; sometimes they come from serendipitous insight. Notably, the multiple origination of knowledge raises a measurement problem because not all R&D activity results in an invention, and not all inventions come from formal R&D activity. Nonetheless, various proxies are available to track knowledge, R&D effort, and their interconnections. Accordingly, the most standard proxies will be applied as needed in the following discussion.

For countries behind the technological frontier, *acquisition* of existing knowledge may be expected to yield higher increases in productivity than would flow from a similar scale investment in R&D or other efforts to push back the technological frontier. There are many means of technology transfer for private goods. Direct foreign investment, licensing, technical assistance, importation of technology as embodied in capital goods, components or products, copying and reverse engineering, and foreign study are the key channels. Also, more generally, easy communication allows access to technical information in printed or electronic form, especially including what can be accessed through the internet. Proprietary technology is usually sold or transferred on a contractual basis. But even proprietary technology may leak out depending on the strength of the Intellectual Property Rights (IPR) regime and its enforcement, and the reverse engineering capacity of users. However, despite significant proprietary constraints, much of the most useful technology is in the public domain or is owned by governments who could potentially put it in the public domain. As such, the key challenges for development strategy are less about the creation and acquisition process and more often related to the challenges of delivering technology and knowledge to those who need it.

Technologies often must undergo *adaptation* to be applicable in specific local conditions. This need is particularly clear in agriculture, where new technologies such as hybrid seeds are very sensitive to specific local conditions. To meet local needs, further research and experimentation is often required to adapt general agriculture solutions to specific temperature, soil, and water conditions as well as local pests. To a lesser extent, even industrial technologies have to be adapted to local conditions: access to raw materials, sources of power, labour traditions, various standards, and climate are just some of the local idiosyncrasies that leave their mark on industry. And yet, often the skills necessary to adapt technologies to local conditions are not too dissimilar from those necessary to create new technology. Similar to knowledge creation, adaptation also requires research and experimentation.

In the private sector, the *dissemination* of knowledge happens when enterprises expand, sell, or transfer their knowledge, or when other firms or organizations imitate or replicate the knowledge others have created. The efficient dissemination of knowledge requires appropriate mechanisms to educate potential users in the benefits of the related technology, often a process inclusive of broad educational advance, not just the provision of technical information.[5] Much dissemination also occurs through the sale of new machinery or other inputs that embody a new technology. There are also specialized institutions, such as agricultural research and extension systems, productivity organizations, and consulting firms that specialize in helping disseminate technologies. These efforts usually involve explicit training, demonstration projects, or technical assistance on how to use the technology.

To *use* new technologies usually requires literacy as well as specialized training. Also, beyond education, using new technology often requires access to complementary inputs and supporting industries, and access to finance for new equipment, inputs or purchase of the technology license. When it involves starting a new business, it is important to have a supportive regulatory environment, namely one without excessive red tape, but which at the same time has a strong rule of law, respects private property, and facilitates the enforcement of contracts. At the broadest level, knowledge use also requires macroeconomic stability and good governance. In short, it requires a well developed economic and institutional regime.

Countries have followed different strategies in how they created, acquired, adapted, disseminated or used knowledge for their development. Most countries that are behind the global technological frontier can take advantage of acquiring knowledge that already exists elsewhere in the world and adapting it for use in their local settings. This is most often done through trade and through formal technology transfer agreements. Foreign technology owners are not always willing to license their cutting edge technology.

Some countries explicitly try to attract foreign investors to bring their advanced foreign technology to their countries, while others do not. In addition, not all countries that have put in place foreign investment promotion policies have met with success. Countries have sometimes preferred to develop their own technology, rather than to rely (primarily) on foreign technology. Sections 4 and 5 of the paper will trace the strategies of the high performing countries and the largest developing countries. I will attempt to draw some conclusions on what works under what circumstances before considering some of the new elements of global competition (sections 6 and 7) which are affecting what may be feasible in the new, more demanding context.

## 3. Global overview of changing competitiveness

Before focusing on the strategies of the developing countries that have had the highest rates of growth in the last 50 years, it is useful to have a somewhat broader perspective of the relative performance of different regions. Figure 3 presents the shares of global GDP accounted for by the two largest single economies as well as the European Union (EU), plus the developing world divided into the six regions used by the World Bank.[6] This is done using two different sets of data. In Figure 3a, nominal exchange rates are used. In Figure 3b purchasing power parity (PPP) exchange rates are used.

As can be seen in Figure 3a, the share of the US in global value added declined during the seventies and eighties as Japan increased its share. The Japanese economy experienced very fast growth in the first half of the twentieth century based on copying and reverse engineering of technology developed in the West. This rapid growth was truncated during the World War II and its direct aftermath, but resumed soon thereafter, again, based on copying and reverse engineering of foreign technology. By the second half of the twentieth century, Japan innovated many elements of what came to be known as the Japanese production system, eventually becoming the fastest growing economy in the world. Japan has, however, not managed to recover fully from recession in the early 1990s.

The US, on the other hand, had faster growth in the second half of the nineties than the rest of the world and recovered most of its lost global GDP share by 2000. The rapid growth of the US in the last five years of the twentieth century, at an average annual rate of 5 per cent, was remarkable. Until then, it had been thought that countries at the frontier could not grow so fast. Its rapid growth was attributed to investments in information technology and organizational change which began to be made in the late 1980s and early 1990s when the country was trying to keep ahead of Japan. It is noteworthy that the EU also lost global GDP share, whether measured by the original EU 15 countries, or the expanded EU-25.[7]

In the developing world, the only region that continuously increased its share of global GDP was East Asia. All other regions lost global GDP share or at best barely maintained it. The remarkable growth of the East

Asian developing countries can be appreciated better when GDP is converted using PPP exchange rates as in Figure 3b. In that figure it can be seen that the share of the East Asian developing countries surpasses that of Japan and begins to approximate that of the US.

## 4. Countries with successful long-term growth

Only a handful of countries have made the transition from "developing" to "developed". Japan did it in the first half of the last century. The "gang of four" (Hong Kong, China; Republic of Korea, Singapore, and Taiwan, Province of China) did it in the second half of last century.

It is instructive to identify which countries have achieved high growth performance over the last 50 years and to compare their strategies and performance with that of the five largest developing countries (the BRICMs).[8] Table 1 presents the average annual rates of GDP growth for all countries that have grown at an average annual rate of 5 per cent or more between 1965 and 2004. It also includes the rates of growth for the last 14 years as well as the last 4 years to see how they have done in the more recent period.

On the high performer side, there are a couple of surprises. Pakistan has averaged annual growth above 5 per cent for both parts of the period, although its average growth rate has slowed over the last 14 years. It is now also a special case given the geopolitical developments since 9/11, and will not be covered here. Botswana is a special case due to its diamond trade and also will not be considered here. The other high performers are the familiar ones from East Asia. The original Asian "gang of four" (see above) make it to the group of high performers, in spite of the 1997 Asian crisis, which hit all of them hard. Hong Kong, Singapore, and Taiwan, however, experienced a somewhat slower average rate of growth for the last four years – a fact that may be related to the rapid rise of China. Three of what are sometimes called the next-tier Asian newly industrialized countries (NICs) – Indonesia, Malaysia and Thailand – also make it.[9] China, which did not receive much attention as a high performing country even at the beginning of the 1990s in spite of its track record, has been the best long-term performer of all and will be the central focus of section 6 of this paper.[10]

Among the other BRICMs, the two Latin American countries (Brazil and Mexico) grew at over 5 per cent annually in the first half of the period. In contrast, they grew at less than 3 per cent in the second half, slower than the global average, and have lost share in the global economy.[11] India, on the other hand, which grew at an average of only 3.3 per cent in the 1965-1980 period, grew at 5.8 per cent in the 1980-2004 period. Its growth has actually been accelerating, and for 2003-2005 it grew at 8 per cent annually. Russia went through a crisis and fragmentation with severe contraction of GDP during the transition, and even a significant drop of life expectancy. Since 1998, it has started to grow thanks to massive oil and gas exports, with an average growth of 6.8 per cent for 2000-2004.[12]

The high performing East Asian economies plus the BRICMs accounted in 2004 for 50 per cent of the world's population, 15 per cent of its gross
national income (33 per cent in PPP terms), and 25 per cent of its merchandise exports (see table 7). Given that these 12 economies account for 60 per
cent of the developing world's population, about 75 per cent of its GDP,
and 93 per cent of its merchandise exports, it is quite instructive and relevant to examine in more detail the strategies of the Asians compared to the
non-Asian BRICM countries that have not been performing as well.[13]

Table 2 maps their strategies in terms of the extent to which they have
relied on foreign direct investment or their own R&D and the extent to
which they are inward or outward oriented. All the successful Asian countries
have been outward oriented in their trade strategy while the non-East Asian
countries have been more inward oriented. An inward orientation means
that they have tended to protect the domestic market from outside competition and have also generally tried to develop their own technology. An outward orientation does not necessarily mean low tariff and non-tariff barriers.
It means that the countries have generally been open to outside ideas and
have used exports as a way to put pressure on domestic firms to improve their
capabilities even while there may have been some degree of protection. It is
also useful to distinguish between countries that have been relatively passive
in their openness to foreign direct investment (FDI) and those that have
been more strategic in using industrial policy extensively to induce FDI to
develop backward linkages and increase its contribution to the economy.[14]

This is just a rough characterization of the broad strategies of these
countries. As will be seen in the summaries below, there have been some
changes over time. Those changes are in themselves significant and will be
picked up again after this section, for they have implications for what other
countries will or will not be able to do. Tables 3, 4 and 5 provide some key
indicators for the "gang of four", the other high performing Asian
economies, and the BRICM countries respectively.[15]

## 4.1 The first wave of high performing East Asian economies[16]

*Republic of Korea: Autonomous technological development*
Korea's strategy is close to that of Japan. Like Japan, it relied very little on
FDI. Instead, initially it acquired a lot of its technology through trade, copying, reverse engineering and technology licensing.[17] When it became a competitive threat to the countries that were licensing technology, its companies
had to begin to invest in R&D to develop their own technology.[18] The government had a strong role in industrial policy. It used success in the export
market as the yardstick by which to measure performance. This also led to
the creation of large industrial conglomerates known as chaebols. These have
been part of the Korean success story because they have had deep pockets to
cross-subsidize risky ventures in new areas out of the profits of their more
competitive "cash cows". In 1965 Korea spent only 0.5 per cent of its GDP

on R&D and 80 per cent of the effort was undertaken by the government. By the mid 1990s it was spending over 2 per cent of GDP, more than 70 per cent of which was accounted for by the private sector, primarily the chaebols, who were having trouble obtaining licenses from foreign competitors. It was only after the 1997 financial crisis that Korea opened up to foreign investment to get foreign exchange into the economy from the sale of failed companies, but also to get access to more advanced foreign technology and to put pressure on domestic firms to perform better.[19] Even so, as can be seen from Table 3, among the "gang of four" Korea has relied the least on FDI. On the other hand, Korea invests the most in R&D and in higher education. It has one of the highest tertiary enrolment rates in the world.

*Hong Kong: Laissez-faire development*
Hong Kong, at the other extreme, is a laissez-faire economy with complete integration into the global trading system. Along with Singapore, it is one of the countries most dependent on trade and FDI for access to knowledge. The share of trade to GDP is over 300 per cent in both, and the average share of FDI to GDP has been over 20 per cent also in both. One of the special aspects of Hong Kong is that it has served as the gateway for business with China. Besides being a critical entrepot for China trade, Hong Kong was quick to outsource labour-intensive manufacturing activity to mainland China. It also developed extensive links with foreign buyers and became a transportation and logistics centre for trade in the region.[20] Being the gateway to China also gave it a special and privileged position in becoming a financial and service centre. Among the "gang of four", Hong Kong also used to be the one with the weakest education base. Hong Kong had the additional constraint of some uncertainty when it reverted back to China in 1999. In addition, it has been facing competition from Shanghai as part of China's explicit strategy to support Shanghai after 1990. As a result, in the 1990s the local government began to engage in more pro-active policy-making, beginning to invest more in R&D, higher education and infrastructure (e.g. information and communications technology – ICT – infrastructure and the new airport). Nevertheless, Hong Kong still lags on these counts vis-à-vis the other three economies.

*Singapore: Strategic use of foreign investment*
Singapore also had an open trade regime and depended very much on FDI for its technology. It had however a much stronger and activist government role than Hong Kong. While generally working with market principles, the government was heavily involved in attracting the kind of foreign investment which it thought would contribute the most to economic development. The development story of Singapore is one of moving quickly from cheap unskilled labour to becoming a knowledge-based economy. In the mid 1960s, after independence from the UK, it briefly entered a federation with

Malaysia. When that failed, Prime Minister Lee Kwan Yew opted for attracting outward oriented foreign investment based on cheap and disciplined labour. Singapore attracted foreign investment when most other countries (like India) were shunning it. Wage rates rose rapidly as the foreign firms came in. The government therefore invested heavily in secondary and technical tertiary education and in upgrading the skills of Singaporean workers in order to remain competitive.

Furthermore, it invested very heavily in developing a port and airport in order to become an efficient transhipment point for trade between South East Asia, Europe and the US. In the 1990s, it invested heavily in ICT to improve trade logistics and further reduce transactions costs.[21] By the end of the 1990s, the government also began to invest more in R&D and to position Singapore as a major educational hub for Asia. It has now become an important regional hub for finance, education, and regional corporate headquarters for multinational corporations (MNCs), and for medicine – all knowledge-based services.[22]

*Taiwan (Province of China): State-directed technological development*
Taiwan was somewhat in between the strong industrial policy approach of Korea and the more open trade but still government-directed approach of Singapore. Three special characteristics of Taiwan that are important to understanding its success are the role of the state, the Chinese diaspora, and the structure of industry. First, the government has had a strong role in its economic development. In the 1950s the key development strategy was import substitution under high tariff walls. The 1960s saw a switch to export orientation. In the period up to 1990, the government had a very active role in the economy. It made extensive use of tariff and non-tariff barriers and selective credit to favour specific sectors and to develop new industries.[23] In addition, the government was very strategic toward the use of FDI and actively encouraged the development of backward linkages and technology transfer.[24] Furthermore, the government set up special industrial parks, including the Hsinchu Science Based Industrial Park in the vicinity of universities and a large public research institute to stimulate technology development and the creation of new high technology enterprises.

Second, Taiwan has drawn very successfully on the large Chinese diaspora working in the high-tech industry around the world. The government developed various mechanisms such as wise men councils and periodic meetings to draw on the advice of this diaspora. It has also actively sought to attract back some of its nationals with high tech experience. A good example of its strong industrial policy as well as the link to the diaspora was the development of the science based industrial park of Hsinchu and the Industrial Technology Research Institute. This involved a strong role of government in developing the electronics industry and in attracting nationals back to Taiwan.[25] This was very successful in moving its electronics industry from simple assembly of electronic products, often for foreign companies, to developing its own chip making capability, and becoming an important own brand player in the global industry.

A third special characteristic of Taiwan is that, unlike Korea, its industrial sector has been made up primarily of small and medium-sized firms, rather than large chaebols with deep pockets to cross-subsidize risky ventures. The government has thus developed a strong supportive technological infrastructure such as technical information services and specialized public research institutes. It also developed special programs to create technological linkages between foreign firms and small domestic suppliers. As Taiwan's own wages rose, it offshored labour-intensive assembly industry to China, especially in Shenzhen and Guangdong. It kept its high-tech industry home. However, as China deepened its trade reforms and maintained rapid growth, and clearly became a dominant economy, Taiwanese investors started to transfer their high-tech manufacturing to the Chinese mainland. There are now "little Taipeis" all along the Chinese coast.

## 4.2 Strategies of the second wave of high performing East Asian economies

The second group of high performing East Asian economies (Indonesia, Malaysia, and Thailand) has been more similar in their industrial and technological strategy. Vietnam has been added to this group, although it only achieved annual growth rates above 5 per cent in the 1980-2004 period, because it is following in the footsteps of these other countries, albeit from a lower human capital and institutional base as a transition country to a market economy (see table 4). They have all been export oriented, although Malaysia, Thailand and Vietnam more so than Indonesia (the share of trade to GDP has been over 100 per cent for all but Indonesia). The first three also have had higher investment to GDP rates than Indonesia. In all of them FDI played a critical role in export growth, in Malaysia and Thailand more so than in the others. Malaysia and Thailand are also more advanced than Indonesia and Vietnam in investments in R&D and in education, particularly tertiary education. Malaysia is the most industrialized of the four and has the highest share of manufactured exports as well as the most technology-intensive manufactured exports. They were all negatively affected by the Asian financial crisis in 1997 (Vietnam least of all), but have recovered. Indonesia averaged growth of 4.8 per cent per annum from 1980 to 2004, and Malaysia and Thailand have grown above 6 per cent per annum. Vietnam, meanwhile, has been steadily increasing its average growth rate since the Asian financial crisis.

## 5. Strategies of the BRICM countries

Before summarizing the strategies of India and China, both of which merit more in-depth treatment, it is instructive to contrast the strategy or the East Asian NICs with those of the three BRICM countries that have not performed well—Brazil, Mexico, and Russia. On the face of it, these three countries should have been expected to perform better. All three are large economies, have a critical mass of trained professionals, and significant investments in R&D – though more so in Russia, and to some extent Brazil, than in Mexico. All have also achieved islands of technological excellence such as nuclear, space and aeronautics and deep oil exploration in Brazil; petroleum, glass, steel and cement in Mexico; and military and space technology in Russia. However, these islands of excellence have not permeated the economies but remain enclaves rather than the precursors of more general innovation capability.

## 5.1 Brazil: Still mostly a primary commodities exporter in spite of decades of government R&D effort

The Brazilian government has been focusing on science and technology for more than four decades. The military government of the 1960s saw technological capability as a strategic element and promoted investment in R&D and higher education institutions. Like India, it developed a large nuclear program. In addition, it has developed a strong space and aeronautics program. One island of excellence has been Embraer, now the world's third largest producer of aircraft, which was born as a spin-off of the aeronautics research institute. Brazil has also attracted FDI and has been second only to China in attracting the most volume among developing countries. However, Brazilian industry has not been very competitive in general. There are three key factors for this. One is that, along with India, Brazil is one of the most inward oriented of the large developing countries. It has thought of itself as a continental economy that could be nearly self-sufficient in almost everything. The share of trade in GDP is only 30 per cent and it also has high tariff and non-tariff barriers (Table 5).

Thus its domestic industry has not been subjected to pressures from international competition as much as the East Asian economies covered above. This has also meant that a lot of the foreign investment that came to Brazil has been oriented towards the protected internal market rather than towards using Brazil as an export platform as was the case for the Asian economies. As a result, together with India, Brazil has among the lowest ratios of manufactured exports to GDP and the lowest shares of high technology exports in manufactured exports. Second, Brazil has had much more macroeconomic instability. For firms, financial engineering has thus been more important than focusing on industrial engineering and developing a strong technological capability to export. Third, Brazil has very high costs of capital, high direct and indirect taxes, and high indirect labour costs as a result of high taxes on labour and rigidities in the labour market. As a result, Brazil has a very large informal economy (estimated by some at 40 per cent) and is not very competitive in manufactured exports.

A bright spot for Brazil, however, has been agricultural and mineral exports. In cereal production Brazil has high productivity because of good land and climatic conditions as well as successful agricultural research and extension programs by the Federal and some of the state governments. Brazil is also rich in many mineral resources with strong Brazilian companies such as CVRD (minerals), Petrobras (petroleum), and Gerdau (steel).[26] Agricultural and mineral exports have been growing very rapidly, mainly to feed China's increased demand. These natural resource driven exports have been important in raising Brazil's overall rate of growth in spite of continued competitive problems in its industrial sector.

## 5.2 Mexico: Falling behind in spite of being next to the United States

Mexico's experience is similar to Brazil's in many respects. However, it has been much more integrated into the global market through trade. The share of trade in GDP is nearly double that of Brazil. Part of this used to be petroleum exports, but Mexico also diversified into manufactured exports. This occurred initially through foreign investment in the "maquila" border assembly industry. Special provisions in the US tariff code – which imposed import duty only on foreign value-added when certain types of good were exported for assembly and re-imported – stimulated the growth of electronics assembly plants in Mexico. When Mexico joined NAFTA (North American Free Trade Agreement) in 1994, however, much of the advantage of this special import regime disappeared. At the same time, many firms found it more attractive to move their labour-intensive industries to China. NAFTA did, however, bring in more FDI focused on the US market and manufactured exports have increased. The share of manufactured exports in merchandise exports increased from 43 per cent to 80 per cent between 1990 and 2004. Nevertheless, Mexico was overtaken by China two years ago as the second largest exporter to the US.

Mexico has been losing competitiveness because of high transportation costs, electricity and other infrastructure costs, as well as the relatively low level of education of its labour force. Unlike the Asian high performers, it was not able to develop strong backward linkages from most of the foreign firms, particularly those in the maquila sector.[27] Mexico has spawned some large competitive domestic companies such as América Móvil (cellular telephone service provider), CEMEX (cement), FEMSA and GRUMA (food and beverages), Modelo (beer), and Nemak (auto engine cylinder heads), but most of them are expanding more abroad than in Mexico because of the difficult domestic conditions.

Mexico has invested much less than Brazil in R&D, as can be seen by the very low expenditures on R&D as a share of GDP (just 0.4 per cent of GDP vs. 1.0 per cent in Brazil).

## 5.3 Russia: Becoming a petro-economy with poor industrial competitiveness

As is well known, Russia was a scientific and technological super-power. With the economic crisis that followed the collapse of the Soviet Union in 1991, however, the scientific and technological support infrastructure suffered significant contraction. Many of the former mechanisms for transferring research output to production collapsed. In addition, as Russian industry was very outmoded, if not obsolete, and not geared up for competitive industrial production, there was also a significant contraction of the industrial base. Furthermore, most firms turned to import of technology, capital goods, and components rather than to the domestic scientific community or research labs for technology. As a result, Russia produces much basic science but few commercial applications. Russia has not been able to attract much FDI except to its oil and gas sector. Part of the reason it has not been successful is foreign investors' frustrations with bureaucracy and corruption as well as with a perceived lack of security of property rights in light of recent experience, e.g., with the re-nationalization of Yukos.

Until recently Russia was also not very well integrated into global trade. With the high international prices for oil and gas, Russia is now growing by exploiting its large natural gas and petroleum reserves. This is a very unbalanced growth, however, and Russia is in effect de-industrializing as the large foreign exchange inflows are generating Dutch disease effects. Virtually everything other than natural resources (and armaments) is losing competitiveness. In 2004, only 23 per cent of its exports were manufactured products and the share of manufacturing in total output has been falling too.

The Russian economy is a cautionary tale of the importance of an effective economic and institutional regime. Having a highly educated population and a strong scientific and technological capability without an effective economic and institutional regime has meant that Russia's strong knowledge assets have not been well deployed to increase economic growth and competitiveness.

## 5.4 India: Cautiously beginning to integrate into the global trade system

After independence from Britain in 1947, India embarked on its own development strategy. As a reaction to what was considered an exploitative colonial experience, the government developed a very autarkic, inward oriented strategy. The main elements of that strategy were import substitution, a large public sector with central planning, strong intervention in labour and capital markets, and over-regulation of business, including the reservation of 1,500 items for production by small-scale industry.

There were also very strong restrictions on FDI and on the licensing of foreign technology. During this period, technology policy focused very much on self reliance.[28] The Indian economy grew very slowly between 1950 and 1980 at what became known derisively as the "Hindu rate of growth" of 2 per cent to 3 per cent  per annum in contrast to rates of growth of 5 per cent to 10 per cent for many other Asian economies. However, one of the great successes of this period was the green revolution. The public agricultural research efforts of Indian institutions working with other public research institutions worldwide led to significant improvement in wheat varieties with higher productivity. The dissemination and use of these new improved varieties turned India from a grain importing country with periodic famines into a net agricultural exporter.

The 1980s saw the introduction of pro-business reforms initiated by Indira Gandhi and later carried out by Rajiv Gandhi. These included easing restrictions on capacity expansion by large firms, removal of many price controls, and the reduction of corporate taxes. These were followed in 1991 by a more significant liberalization of the economy as a result of severe balance of payments crisis. These reforms included liberalizing imports, reducing investment licensing, privatizing some state-owned enterprises, allowing automatic approval of FDI in some sectors, and reducing the number of products reserved for small-scale industry.[29]

The impact of this liberalization on the economy and on science and technology policy was significant. The average rate of growth for the economy jumped to 6.0 per cent for 1990-2000. Firms which had not had to worry much about efficiency in a protected and over-regulated domestic market suddenly woke up to the need to improve their products and services and to reduce their costs. Some parts of the public research infrastructure responded to the change in the overall incentive regime.[30] The impact of growing competitive pressure was also reflected in an increase in the number of private firms doing R&D and in the increase in their R&D relative to sales.

As part of the conditions for joining the WTO in 1995, India agreed to bring its intellectual property legislation into conformity with developed country standards. This was done through a series of amendments in 1999 and 2005. The opening up of foreign investment also brought stronger competitors into the domestic market.

Since 2000, India is showing greater participation in the global arena. Between 2000 and 2004 the Indian economy achieved an average annual growth rate of 6.2 per cent, and since 2003 it has actually been growing at 8 per cent. India's engineering talent began to be recognized globally thanks to the reputation its software engineers acquired in fixing the "Y2K bug". This launched its expansion into software services and business process outsourcing (BPO) globally. In addition, in the last five years an increasing number of MNCs are not only producing in India, but setting up their own R&D centres in the country, attracted largely by the relatively low cost and high level of human capital available locally, as well as the possibility of working round the clock with their other research centres thanks to digital networks. The result of this increased R&D investment by MNCs in India as well as some increased R&D investment by domestic firms has led to an estimated increase in R&D from an average of about 0.8 per cent of GDP for the 20 years up to 2003 to as much as 1.1 per cent of GDP in 2005.[31]

## 5.5 China: Embracing globalisation

There have been many building blocks to China's innovation strategy.[32] The first was massive importation of turnkey plants, mostly in heavy industry, from the Soviet Union in the 1950s as part of its initial industrialization drive. This ended with the Great Leap forward in 1958 when China went on a more autarkic technological development strategy ("a furnace in every back yard") and the Cultural Revolution of the 1960s. This was a period of turmoil and relative stagnation. In the early 1970s, Zhou Enlai proposed the "four modernizations" (agriculture, industry, science and the military). This led again to massive importation of technology, primarily from the West and Japan. Deng Xiaoping's decision to give farmers more autonomy over their production – the rural household responsibility system – was another milestone in China's reforms. This led to a strong increase in agricultural productivity. These reforms were eventually applied to the industrial sector, freeing enterprises to make more of their own decisions and to enjoy the rewards of good ones. The effect of these changes was to create a strong incentive for finding better and more efficient ways to produce. A third initiative, very important for the rural sectors, was the Spark program which aimed to speed the dissemination of agricultural technology. This was subsequently reinforced with the Torch Program aimed at disseminating more advanced technologies throughout the economy. A fourth measure was to create enclaves open to FDI with a near free trade regime in special economic zones (SEZs). Initially only a few were set up as pilot experiments. These performed very well, so the government expanded them gradually. When China decided to join the WTO in 1997, these were effectively expanded to the whole economy. Besides the SEZs, explicit measures were undertaken during the 1980s and 1990s to liberalize FDI rules.

Thus, China has been very effective at both disseminating knowledge domestically and tapping into global knowledge through trade and FDI. Among the large economies, China is the most integrated through trade. The share of merchandise and services trade in GDP in 2004 was 67 per cent. In addition, China has become the second largest host to FDI. The share of FDI inflows to GDP increased to 7 per cent at its peak and has averaged 5.1 per cent for the last 10 years.

China is now engaged in a major strategy to strengthen its own innovation. In 1998 it was investing just 0.7 per cent of GDP in R&D. Around 2002-2003, however, it decided to put more emphasis on own innovation. Between 2003 and 2004, China increased its investments in R&D by 50 per cent and by 2005 it was investing 1.4 per cent of GDP. For the new five-year plan China announced in December 2005 that it would be increasing its R&D expenditures to 2.0 per cent of GDP by 2010 and to 2.5 per cent (the average for developed countries) by 2025.[33] To put this in a global context, figure 4 presents R&D expenditures of the largest spending countries in PPP terms. The circles correspond to the absolute value being spent, the horizontal axis gives its share of GDP, and the vertical axis shows the number of scientists and engineers in R&D per million people. According to the OECD's latest Science, Technology and Industry Outlook, in 2004 China was the third largest national spender on R&D, but given it rapidly increasing expenditures, it probably overtook Japan by the end of 2006. However, it is still not as efficient in R&D as developed countries.

Thus, China has followed a five pronged strategy. One prong was to import a massive number of turnkey plants, first from the Soviet Union, then turnkey plants and capital goods from the West. A second has been to copy, reverse engineer and otherwise borrow as much foreign technology as possible. Like Japan, and Korea earlier, this has been facilitated by investments in human capital. A third has been to disseminate knowledge internally. The fourth was to tap foreign knowledge through trade and through FDI. Now that it is catching up in many sectors and that it is being seen as a major competitor, the fifth prong consists in beginning to innovate on its own account by increasing investments in R&D.

## 5.6 Conclusion

This section has traced the strategies of the successful high performing economies and contrasted them with those of Brazil, Mexico, and Russia which have not been performing as well. From the comparisons it may be inferred that the key elements of the successful strategies of the Asian economies have been a strong outward orientation, heavy use of foreign knowledge (including copying and reverse engineering and otherwise appropriating foreign knowledge), macroeconomic stability, high investment rates, and an economic incentive and institutional regime that demands improved performance. All of them except Korea and India made extensive use of FDI as a way to acquire foreign knowledge and to penetrate export markets. Korea opted not to rely on FDI, but to acquire knowledge through trade, and reverse engineering, and to invest substantially in its own R&D. It also invested massively in secondary and then tertiary education. These high levels of education facilitated its assimilation of foreign technology and the development of its own technological capability, including its large investments in R&D. India, which also opted to limit FDI until the last 15 years, followed a more autarkic strategy than Korea, as it did not rely much on acquiring foreign knowledge through trade. Unlike Korea, however it did not expand significantly its own R&D investments, nor did it invest much in expanding secondary and tertiary education. That is one of the reasons why its performance until the opening up in the 1990s was so poor. After 1991, as it drew more on foreign knowledge, its economic growth improved and eventually accelerated to over 8 per cent for the last three years.

Brazil and Mexico did get FDI, but much of it came for the protected domestic markets. Also, these countries did not make as massive investments in R&D and education as Korea. Russia did invest a lot in R&D, but most of it was focused on military objectives. Its commercial industrial technology was generally quite poor. Engagement with the global system through trade was limited, and this in turn limited knowledge acquisition and spillovers. It also had a poor economic and institutional regime which did not allocate resources to the most productive uses, leading to poor competitive performance. Its recent growth performance is based on natural resource rents rather than on technological capability.

Thus it appears that a common strategy for most of the high performers was to start with labour intensive exports and to gradually move up to more sophisticated products.

However, the simpler labour-intensive outward oriented strategies that worked in the past are no longer as easy to replicate for two reasons. One is that the global context has changed significantly. Some of these new trends and their implications for developing countries are developed in Section 6. The second is the speed, scale and scope of China's entry onto the global stage. It is pre-empting the simple labour-intensive growth strategy because its advantages are not only low cost but also very productive labour, as well as economies of scale in transportation and logistics. It is also moving up the technology ladder very quickly, and is fully plugged into international value chains and distribution systems. The implications of China's rise for other countries will be covered in Section 7.

## 6. Key global trends

The key global trends that are changing the global competitive context and therefore the possibilities for developing countries include: increasing speed in the creation and dissemination of knowledge; trade liberalization, globalisation, and physical disintegration of production; increased importance of integrated value chains; increased role of MNCs in production and distribution; and changing elements of competition.[34]

### 6.1 Increasing speed in creation and dissemination of knowledge

Advances in science, combined with the information revolution (itself a product of these advances), are driving an acceleration in the creation and dissemination of knowledge. It is now possible to codify and digitize much of our understanding of science. This permits modelling and simulation, which in turn further speeds up the understanding of science and the creation of new goods and services. The time between basic scientific discovery and commercial application is decreasing. This is particularly evident in biotechnology. The product life cycle of most manufactured products is also shrinking. This is evident in the electronic products industry, ranging from computers and mobile phones to consumer electronics.[35]

The increased importance of new technology can be seen in the increasing variety of goods and services produced. This can be appreciated in the increasing importance of manufactured products and services in trade. For the world as whole, the share of manufactured products in trade has increased from 58 per cent in 1965 to 65 per cent in 1980, 73 per cent in 1990 and 77 per cent in 2004. This is partly because the demand for manufactured products is more income-elastic than for primary commodities. Developing countries that do not have the capability to move into production of manufactured products therefore lose out on the possibility of benefiting from the most dynamic part of merchandise trade. In addition, the technological intensity of trade in manufactured goods is increasing. This can be seen in trade among OECD countries, which accounts for approximately two-thirds of world trade. For their trade in manufactures, which accounts for the bulk of their exports, over the last ten years the share of medium and high technology manufactured exports has increased from 59.8 per cent in 1994 to 64 per cent in 2003 (figure 5).

The implication of the speed-up in the creation and dissemination of knowledge is that developing countries need to find effective ways of tapping into the very rapidly growing stock of global knowledge. Those that are more advanced also have to invest more in their own R&D in order to compete with new frontier technological advances.

## 6.2 Trade liberalization

Since the GATT there has been a trend towards increasing liberalization in trade policy among most countries. In developing countries, average tariff levels have fallen from 34.4 per cent in 1980-83 to 12.6 per cent in 2000-2001; in developed countries they have fallen from 8.2 per cent in 1989-92 to 4.0 per cent in 2000.[36] In addition, non-tariff barriers have fallen. There is also a movement towards greater openness in trade in services, including not only financial and business services, but also education.[37] We are moving closer to free trade in manufactured products, but the same does not apply to agriculture. While movement of capital is increasingly free, this is not generally the case for labour, where international mobility has been concentrated among the highly skilled, for which some advanced countries have created special temporary immigration visas, particularly for information technology specialists.

Many services areas that were once considered non-tradable have now become tradable to the extent that they can be digitized and provided remotely, across national boundaries, through the internet. Thus we are moving to a system of freer trade which is bringing increasing competitive pressure to domestic markets the world over.

At the same time, there has been a strengthening in the rules and regulations of the international trading system. Some protectionist trade and industrial policies used effectively by some of the current developed countries as well as some of the Asian high performers to promote their industries and services are now not allowed under WTO rules.[38] Moreover, stronger enforceable sanctions against piracy of intellectual property through the TRIPS mechanism of the WTO now exist. As a result, it is now much harder for developing countries to use some of the policies that helped some countries acquire more advanced technology as part of their development strategy.

The challenge for developing countries is therefore to determine how best to be open to international competition while at the same time nurturing the development of their own production capabilities. If they liberalize too early, they run the risk of having their domestic industries wiped out by well established and stronger foreign competitors.

## 6.3 Globalisation

The two trends just discussed have led to a dramatic expansion of globalisation – the greater integration of economic and social activity around the world. The reduction in communication and transportation costs combined with trade liberalization has led to a dramatic expansion of trade. Imports and exports as a share of global GDP have increased from 40 per cent in 1990 to 55 per cent in 2004. In addition, the reduction of communications cost and the spread of the mass media have virtually created a "real time world", where events that happen in one place are instantly known worldwide.

Moreover, as the formerly inward oriented economies of China, India, and the former Soviet Union have increased their participation in the international trading system, the net effect is that the global labour force has effectively doubled (Freeman, 2006). This has strong implications for developed as well as developing countries. Developed countries are now facing competition from much lower cost workers, which is putting pressure on labour-intensive industries. Freeman goes on to argue that the doubling of the global labour force has increased the marginal productivity of capital. As a result, that share of value added that is going to capital has increased, while that which is going to labour has decreased. The principal beneficiaries of this globalisation and rebalancing of relative wages are the multinational corporations which are the most effective agents at intermediating and taking advantage of differences in global factor prices.

The implication of this increased globalisation for developing countries is that they are more exposed to everything that is happening worldwide. It also means that everything happens faster, so in addition to facing more competition, they have to develop greater capability than before in order to respond rapidly and adequately to new threats and opportunities.

## 6.4 Physical disintegration of production and increased importance of integrated supply chains

The reduction in transportation and communication costs combined with the digitalization of information has led to the physical *disintegration* of production. Because of lower transactions costs, different components of a final product are now manufactured in several different countries.[39] The product may then be assembled in yet another country and then distributed worldwide. The same applies to some services. This means that, to get products or services to the market, it is now more important than in the past to tap into global supply chains. Even R&D is being commoditized to some extent as it is being outsourced to specialized centres in different countries, including India and China.[40]

This is what is being called the two great "unbundlings".[41] It is useful to distinguish them because they have different trajectories and implications. The first unbundling is the end of the necessity to produce goods close to consumers. This has been going on for centuries but has been accelerated by the rapid decline in transportation costs in the last four decades, particularly since the widespread use of containers and bulk carriers. The impact of this has been that much manufacturing production, especially of the more standard and labour-intensive goods, is being transferred to developing countries with lower labour costs.

The second unbundling is the end of the need to perform most manufacturing stages near each other. This has been made possible by the rapidly falling costs of telecommunications and the possibility of codifying and digitizing tasks. The impact of this has been that many service tasks supporting manufacturing as well as other services have been offshored to countries with lower labour costs.[42]

The implication of these developments is that there are increased opportunities for those countries that can position themselves to take advantage of the two unbundlings. The major developing country beneficiary of the first unbundling has been China, which is becoming the manufacturing workshop of the world. The major beneficiary of the second unbundling has been India, thanks to its critical mass of higher educated English speaking technicians, engineers, and scientists. Other economies such as the Philippines, Vietnam, former Soviet republics with critical mass of highly skilled manpower, and some Caribbean English speaking island economies are also benefiting from digital trade made possible by this second unbundling. Most other developing countries without critical mass in the skills base, English language or the advanced telecommunications and other physical infrastructure have not benefited as much and are having trouble competing on both fronts.

Developed countries are also being impacted by increased globalisation and the two unbundlings. The first is more in keeping with the expectations of traditional trade and product cycle theory, which postulated that labour-intensive manufacturing would move to labour abundant countries. Under this theory it was expected that developed countries would stay ahead by moving into more skill- and technology-intensive sectors. However, the second unbundling is a newer phenomenon not foreseen by traditional trade theory. It was not anticipated that services could be traded virtually thanks to advances in information technology.

Various economists, including Alan Blinder (2006) and Gene Grossman et al. (2006) are beginning to focus on this phenomenon. Blinder has even gone as far as to call offshoring the third industrial revolution. Its most significant idiosyncrasy is that the dividing line between jobs that can be outsourced versus those that cannot is not related to skills. Many highly skilled and knowledge-intensive jobs can now be outsourced. Blinder (2006) estimates that the total number of jobs susceptible to offshoring may be two to three times the total number of current manufacturing jobs in the US.[43] This is an important new element not anticipated by economic policy in developed economies. It is no longer sufficient for developed countries to invest in higher education to stay ahead. They will need to focus on exploiting advantages in non-tradable services, transform their educational systems to prepare workers for those jobs, strengthen innovation and creativity, and put in place adequate trade adjustment mechanisms (Blinder, 2006).

## 6.5 Increased role of MNCs in production and distribution

One of the key drivers of globalisation with significant implications for developing country strategies is the increased role of MNCs. They are the key producers and disseminators of applied knowledge. They are estimated to account for at least half of total global R&D and more than two-thirds of business R&D.[44] MNCs disseminate knowledge directly through their operations in foreign countries and through licensing agreements. In addition, they often are the first to introduce new products, processes, or business and management methods in many foreign countries, providing examples and ideas for imitation by domestic companies. They also train workers, managers and researchers who may disseminate some of the knowledge and experience acquired while working for the multinational when they leave to work for another company or set up their own.

It is estimated that the value added by MNCs in their home countries plus that in foreign affiliates represents 27 per cent of global GDP.[45] On the trade side, it is estimated that affiliates of foreign firms account for one-third of world exports.[46] However, the influence of MNCs is greater than this. They affect a much larger share of GDP if one takes into account backward and forward linkages, as well as their role in demonstrating new technologies and putting pressure on domestic firms to upgrade production processes. Although there is no accurate estimate, probably more than half of the remaining trade is done through supply chains controlled by multinationals as part of vertical chains or through distribution chains.

In addition, MNCs are now operating much more as independent global agents.[47] Rather than responding to the needs of any country, even their original home country, their objective is to operate globally in the best way to increase returns to their investors, whoever they are and wherever they may be. This will increasingly put them at odds with the interests of their home countries (as they shift even high value, high skill jobs and functions, including research, out of their home base) as well as host countries (as one location is pit against another and resources are redeployed to wherever it is more profitable).

One of the implications of the increased role of MNCs in the generation of knowledge and in production and distribution of goods is that developing countries now need to pay more attention to how to attract and make the most effective use of foreign investment. Even Korea and Japan, which were the countries that made least use of FDI, have had to open up in the 1990s in order to get access to some cutting-edge technology that foreign firms are not willing to license. However, FDI to developing countries is very heavily concentrated in just a few of them. The top ten developing countries account for 65 per cent of the total FDI going to developing countries.[48] FDI goes to where it finds the most attractive profit opportunities, either to supply local markets, or to use those locations as export platforms for other markets. Most evidence shows that offering special tax and other incentives is usually not sufficient to offset major economic disadvantages perceived by foreign investors. Therefore, countries that cannot offer intrinsic advantages to attract FDI are going to have to find alternative ways of getting access to relevant foreign knowledge. These can include buying some of the technologies through arm's-length transactions, technical assistance, copying and reverse engineering, and own technological development, but these pose their own sets of challenges (as discussed above).

Another implication of this for developing countries is that they have to become integrated into global supply chains normally controlled by multinational producers or distributors (like Wal-Mart or other large retailers). Entry into supply chains is usually at the simpler levels such as making simple manufactured goods, producing simple components, or assembling subcomponents. Both getting into and moving to higher value added activities in vertical supply chains can be difficult. For the first, the supplier must demonstrate capability to produce to high standards of quality and timeliness in delivery; for the second, strengthened technological capabilities are required.[49]

Entering supply chains controlled by distributors such as Wal-Mart is also difficult. Usually production runs have to be large. Suppliers must also be able to maintain quality and timeliness. All three of these requirements make it difficult for smaller countries with smaller firms to enter these supply chains.[50] Their producers generally do not have the scale to produce the volumes required (Wal-Mart is sourcing over 25 billion dollars worth of goods from China, cuts out middlemen, and goes directly to the producers). In addition, a buyer like Wal-Mart exerts continued pressure on the suppliers to reduce costs and improve quality and speed of delivery.

It should be noted that there are only a few companies from developing countries which have managed to create and sell globally under their own brand names.[51] This indicates how difficult and expensive it is to develop own brand and distribution systems.

## 6.6    Changing elements of competition

Competitiveness used to be based (to a greater degree) on static comparative advantage. Today, competitiveness does not just depend on the cost of factors of production, or on a specific technological advantage. Rather, it depends on continuous innovation, high level skills and learning, an efficient communications and transport infrastructure, and a supportive enabling environment.[52] Each of these aspects is discussed below in greater detail.

*Innovation becoming a critical component*
In this context of rapid development and dissemination of new knowledge, innovation is becoming a more critical element of competitiveness. Firms have to be constantly innovating to avoid falling behind. This does not necessarily mean that they have to be moving the technological frontier forward. Only the most advanced firms do that. However, all firms need to be at least fast imitators and adopt, use and improve new technology in order not to fall behind. This puts a great deal of pressure on firms' technological capabilities. Moreover, innovation is not just a matter of new products or new processes and ways to produce them, but also better organization and management techniques, and better business models which facilitate doing business.[53] An example of what is essentially a very simple innovation is containerized cargo, which has greatly facilitated shipping manufactured products and dramatically cut down freight costs. An example of business innovation is the development of consumer product companies such as Dell, which subcontract production according to their design and specifications to third parties, eliminate distributors, and sell directly to the final consumer. Another example of a business innovation is Wal-Mart's monitoring of consumer demand from points of sale through electronic cash registers, linking that information to central ordering directly to producers all around the world, thereby eliminating intermediaries in production and distribution.

The implication of this for companies is that they have to make greater efforts to keep up with new technologies and new forms of business organization and production and distribution networks. This requires more investment in their technological capability to search for, acquire and adapt technology to their needs and in managing production and distribution systems. For those that are closer to the frontier, it means that they need to put more effort into real cutting edge innovations in technology and business.

*Education and skills as fundamental enablers*
Technological advance is very complementary with higher skills and more education.[54] As a result, education and skills are becoming more important in international competitiveness. MNCs make their location decisions partly based on the education and skills of the local workforces. This means that countries need to make more investments on increasing education and skills. Globally, there has been an increase in average educational attainment. There has been a strong increase in the number of persons with higher education. Because of the knowledge revolution, there is a need for people to learn a diverse range of new skills. This has given rise to what Peter Drucker termed the "knowledge worker" (Drucker, 1994). The knowledge worker is not just the PhD with very narrow and advanced education. S/he is the technician and the graduate of the junior college. In the United States, 35 per cent of students in tertiary education are older than the typical college age cohort of 18-24. Many are workers who are coming back to get their college degrees, or workers who already have college degrees but are coming back to obtain specialized training certificates or more advanced degrees. Thus there is a need to think in terms of systems of life-long learning.

This implies that developing countries need not only to expand primary education, but that they also need to expand the access and quality of secondary and tertiary education. This may be difficult given tight budgetary constraints, so many developing countries will have to rely more on tuitions and private provision of higher education. Increasing higher education may bring the risk of losing people to the brain drain if graduates cannot find good jobs locally. Thus developing country governments have to think through their higher education strategies more carefully. In addition, governments need to think of education and training as integrated systems for life-long learning and to start designing systems that will have multiple providers and multiple pathways to different levels of certification and qualification. They also have to make more effective use of distance education technologies, particularly the potential of internet based education and training services which can be delivered anywhere, anytime at any pace.[55]

*Logistics, transportation, and distribution becoming more important*
In this new context of increased globalisation, rapid technical change, and shorter product life cycles, modular production and outsourcing, and the

need to get components and products to the customer quickly, logistics (transportation, distribution channels, and warehousing), which connects manufacturing and retailing, is becoming another critical factor for competitiveness.[56] Therefore, transportation infrastructure – roads, railroads, airports, seaports and transportation companies, with coordination enabled by IT – is critical for countries to participate effectively in the global market.[57]

The implication of this for many developing countries is that, even if they can produce competitively, it may still be very difficult for them to get into global value chains because of high transport costs. Typically, developing countries have very poor transportation infrastructure. In addition, they frequently do not have the volume to warrant bulk transport systems nor the frequency of service required to make the transportation costs competitive. This works against small countries far from the main markets. Most countries in Africa have very poor shipping or air links with the rest of the world, and few of these have direct links with key markets. This means that there are usually many stops and several transshipments before products get to their final destination. This increases both transportation costs as well as the inventory costs for goods in transit.

Part of the cost advantage of China is not just low wages and that it has over 200 million underemployed workers in agriculture that can be brought into industrial production, but that it has developed large scale and low cost transportation infrastructure. Combined with frequent shipping and air service to major world markets, it can place its goods virtually anywhere, for a fraction of the costs of most other developing countries.

*Efficient IT becoming new critical infrastructure*
Information technology is becoming a fundamental enabling infrastructure of the new competitive regime. "Supply chain management requires speed across global space to accomplish what a factory accomplished internally with the assembly line. Information and communications technologies (ICT) are the tools that allow flexible accumulation to function."[58] ICT is a critical part of what enables the organization and coordination of global production networks and the integration of global supply chains. It is also an essential element for monitoring what the consumers are buying and what they want, and passing that information seamlessly along to producing units which often are not even owned by brand name manufacturers. This real-time information on the changing needs of the market, indeed even direct interaction with the consumer (as in the examples of made to order computers or automobiles), as well as internal electronic exchange and management between different departments and division within firms and among firms, their suppliers and distributors, are becoming essential new ingredients of the global economy.

There are several implications for developing countries. At the national level, there needs to be modern and low cost communication systems as well as good training in the skills necessary to use these networks. For the development of e-business, there need to be appropriate legal and regulatory systems including e-signature as well as secure digital communications and safe payment systems. At the level of the firm, investments in training and hardware as well as in restructuring business processes are also necessary in order to take advantage of the reduction in transactions costs and time that can be obtained through these technologies.[59]

*The enabling environment as a still necessary factor*
The enabling environment consists of the government regulations and institutions that facilitate the operation of business and the economy. It includes the basic institutions such as government, rule of law, efficiency of capital and labour markets, ease of setting up or shutting down business. It also includes the ability of the government to create consensus and the ability to help people who fall through the cracks in the system.

## 7. The China (and India) factor(s)[60]

Figure 6 presents the current and projected size through 2015 of the world's nine largest economies in terms of purchasing power parity (PPP) comparisons.[61] Using PPP exchange rates, China is already the second largest economy in the world and India the fourth largest. Moreover, using average growth rates for the period 1991-2003 to project future size, China will become the largest economy, surpassing the US by approximately 2013, and India will surpass Japan (currently the third largest economy), by the end of next year. While past performance is not necessarily a good predictor of future performance, these projections are helpful to emphasize that China and India are already large players in economic terms and that they are going to be even larger given that they are growing almost three times faster than the world average. It is therefore useful to take stock of their strengths and challenges and to explore the potential impact of their growth on other countries.

## 7.1 China's strengths and challenges

China's strengths are numerous and varied.[62] One strength is its very large size and rapid growth. It has critical mass and economies of scale. It also has a government that has a long-term strategic vision and is able to orchestrate and implement long-term plans. Part of why it has been able to upgrade its technology so fast is because it is well integrated into the global trade system. As noted, it has the largest traded sector among the world's large countries. It gets modern technology embodied in capital goods and components and its export firms are forced to compete with the best abroad. It has also used FDI to rapidly modernize its economy.[63] Through the lure of its very large internal market and the potential to serve as an export platform as well, it attracts MNCs willing to bring the most modern technology into the country. In addition, because of its rising supply of scientists and engineers, over 700 R&D centres have been set up by MNCs in China. Moreover, it has been investing heavily in higher education. In 1997, its tertiary enrolment rate was 6.5 per cent. Since then it has been increasing new entrants by 50 per cent per year. Last year, its tertiary enrolment rate reached 21 per cent and the number of students enrolled at the tertiary level surpassed that in the US. Forty percent of them were in mathematics, science and engineering.

China also faces many challenges. One of them is increasing income inequality. Its Gini coefficient increased from 0.33 in 1990 to 0.47 in 2003. There are also very large regional income inequalities between the coastal provinces, where GDP has been growing at 15 per cent to 20 per cent per year, and the western provinces, where growth has been just 2 per cent to 5 per cent . As part of its rapid restructuring and transition to the market economy, for the past five years the state-owned enterprises have been shedding workers at the rate of 12 to 15 million workers a year. These lay-offs plus the increasing income inequality are potentially destabilizing. In addition, every year China absorbs 10 to 15 million rural migrants into the cities. Its financial sector is another weak area as there is a very large non-performing loan portfolio. Part of the problem is that the financial system still channels the bulk of the funds to the state enterprise sector. Since the social security system is still not well developed, state enterprises still act as an informal social security system and require support from the government. China also has a rapidly ageing population, and because of the one-child policy adopted some years ago, it will start to have a very high dependency ratio in 20 years.

China is also facing very severe environmental constraints. It is natural resource poor, particularly on a per capita basis. It relies on imports from the rest of the world for a large part of its raw materials. It turned from being an oil exporter until the 1990s to now being the second largest oil importer after the US. It has a water shortage. The Yellow River periodically dries up. The rate of desertification is increasing. The Gobi desert is moving toward Beijing and there are sand storms that blow red dust all the way to North America. Water and air pollution are serious problems. It is estimated that several million people die each year from air pollution. Air pollution is getting worse not only because of China's rapid industrialization, but also because it has opted for a very rapid expansion of cars as a basic means of transportation.

Finally, China also faces the challenge of how long a one party system can continue to function effectively as the country transitions rapidly to a private market economy. The number of demonstrations has been rising since the late 1990s to reach over 80,000 last year.

Thus, while China has been growing very fast, and the consensus expectation of most economists is that it can continue to grow at 7-8 per cent for another 10 to 20 years, it also has some severe structural problems.

## 7.2 India's strengths and challenges

India is a rising economic power, but one which has not yet integrated very much with the global economy and still has not achieved its potential as much as China. It has many strengths, but it will also be facing many challenges in the increasingly competitive and fast changing global economy.[64]

India's key strengths are its large domestic market, its young and growing population, a strong private sector with experience in market institutions, and a well developed legal and financial system. In addition, from the perspective of the knowledge economy, another source of strength is a large critical mass of highly trained English speaking engineers, businessmen, scientists and other professionals, who have been the dynamo behind the growth of the service sector. In fact, Blinder (2006, p. 127) sees India as a greater challenge than China to developed countries in terms of future competition because it is currently stronger in terms of the second unbundling (see Singh, 2007, in this volume, for an analysis of the strengths and limitations of India's service-led industrialization).

The reality, however, is that the supply of highly trained knowledge workers such as scientists and engineers in India is much more limited than commonly thought. There is a highly bifurcated higher education system. The premier part consists of seven Indian Institutes of Technology, six Indian Institutes of Management, the Indian Institute of Sciences, the Indian Statistical Institute, and the All Indian Institute of Medical Sciences which are world class. However, they produce only ten thousand graduates per year. The bulk of the higher education system produces graduates of very low quality. A recent McKinsey study estimates that only 10 to 20 per cent of the graduates are properly trained to work for MNCs. There are also many political economy problems to increasing the supply of the premier institutes or to improving the quality of the broader system. These constraints on the ability to expand rapidly the supply of high level human capital will constrain India's ability to exploit the second unbundling.

More generally, one of India's key challenges is its rapidly growing and young population. India's population is expected to continue to grow at a rate of 1.7 per cent per year until 2020 and to overtake China's. An important part of the challenge is that India's population has low average educational attainment. The average years of schooling of the adult population is less than 5, compared to nearly 8 in China and 12 in developed countries. In addition, illiteracy is 52 per cent among women and 27 per cent among men.

Another challenge is poor infrastructure – in terms of power supply, roads, ports and airports. This increases the cost of doing business. In addition, India is noted for an excessively bureaucratic and regulated environment which also increases the cost of doing business.

All these factors constrain the ability of the Indian economy to react to changing opportunities. Low education reduces workforce flexibility. Poor infrastructure and high costs of doing business constrain domestic and foreign investment. The high costs of getting goods in and out of India constrain the country's ability to compete internationally and to attract export oriented foreign investment except for business that can be done digitally rather than requiring physical shipments.

## 7.3 The impact of China's rise on the rest of the world

The speed, scale, and scope of China's economic growth is unprecedented in economic history. China's rapid integration into the global trading system has been spectacular and has implications for the rest of the world.[65] China's merchandise exports have surged from US$25 billion in 1984 to US$62 billion in 1990 and US$593 billion in 2004. Its share of world merchandise exports shot up from less than 0.5 per cent in 1980 to 6.5 per cent in 2004 (figure 7). Although China used to export some commodities and fuels, its exports are primarily manufactures and their share in the total has been increasing – from 72 per cent in 1990 to 91 per cent by 2004. Furthermore, as in the other Asian high performing economies, its manufactured exports started primarily as labour-intensive goods (particularly textiles and clothing), but the technology intensity of its exports has been increasing very rapidly. In 1998, the share of high technology exports in China's manufactured exports was 15 per cent. By 2004 it had doubled to 30 per cent.

Figure 8 projects the growth of merchandise exports of the eight largest economies in the world, using the average export growth rates from the past 5 years. According to these projections, China's merchandise exports surpass the US's by 2006 and those of Germany by about 2009. This is no longer based on PPP but on nominal exchange rates. Thus China already is a major force to be reckoned with and is likely to become even more important in the near future. India is still at a much earlier stage and will not be as important for some time to come, although it has the potential to increase its exports and have a more significant impact on world markets. The rest of this section will therefore focus on the impact of China's rising importance in global trade on the rest of the world.

To analyze the impact of China's trade on the global system, it is useful to distinguish direct effects from indirect effects. Direct effects include the direct impact of exports and imports on other countries. The indirect effects include the impact of exports and imports on third markets, as well as any secondary effects that China's growth may have on other international flows such as direct foreign investment and finance. These are hard to quantify but an attempt will be made to at least indicate what some of these may be for different countries.

First, it should be noted that while China is rapidly increasing its exports it is also increasing its imports. Thus, it is opening up the opportunity for many countries to export to China, or even to set up manufacturing facilities there. China's imports are primarily natural resources, and machinery and components. Therefore, developing country exporters of commodities are likely to benefit from increased exports and higher prices (indeed many are already doing so). The same goes for exporters of capital goods and components. The main exporters of capital goods are likely to be developed countries. Component exporters include many countries in East and South East Asia, as China has become the final assembler and exporter of many finished goods based on components from neighbouring countries.[66][67]

It should also be noted that an important indirect impact of China's rapid expansion of manufactured exports is that they have helped to drive the price of many manufactured products down. That has meant an increase in welfare for consumers all over the world. The problem, of course, is that the direct competition from cheaper Chinese manufactured products has diminished markets and profits for producers of those goods from other countries, and some may even be driven out of business. This is already clear in the production of textiles and garments where China has a very clear comparative advantage that was being constrained until January 2005 by the quotas of the Multi-Fibre Agreement and its successor.

An important indirect impact of China's rapid growth on the rest of the world is its pressure on global environmental resources. The impact of China's voracious appetite for natural resources has already been seen in rapidly rising prices for many natural resources and commodities, particularly oil. There are also the negative externalities of increased transboundary air pollution and global warming.

*Developed countries* probably have the most to gain from the expansion of China's trade. They are the biggest importers of Chinese manufactures, so their consumers will get the advantage of lower prices. They will feel some competition in the medium technology level and many manufacturers may have to switch to production in or sourcing from China. However, they have higher educated workers and more capability to compete through innovation, so they should be able to redeploy workers to more competitive areas. Moreover, a very large share of Chinese manufactured exports are being produced or sourced there by MNCs headquartered in developed countries. Thus, these MNCs and their stockholders are benefiting. Also, developed countries are better placed to export the capital goods and consumer durables and services in demand by China as people reach higher incomes and want more sophisticated consumer goods and services. Nevertheless, there will be considerable adjustment pains as some industries face Chinese competition. These are likely to be more pronounced in the EU than in the US as the rate of unemployment is already higher in European countries and their economies are less flexible and less innovative than the US.

*Developing countries in South East Asia* have also been benefiting from China's growing trade. The poorer natural resource rich countries are supplying China with natural resources and primary commodities. The more advanced economies, including Japan, Korea, and Taiwan, are supplying it with capital goods and components for its expanding higher technology manufacturing in special high-tech export processing zones. However, there is a risk that some suppliers will shift to producing directly in China, thus reducing exports and domestic jobs. Middle-income countries of South East Asia face perhaps the biggest competitive challenge from China in their export markets for manufactures, though they have also enjoyed increased demand for their components from Chinese assembly plants as well as increased demand for their natural resource based exports. The labour rich low-income countries (such as Vietnam, Cambodia and some South Asian countries, particularly India) may find that, as Chinese wages rise, some of the labour-intensive production that is still done in China will be transferred to them.[68]

*Latin American countries* are likely to experience two different effects. Mexico and some of the Central American textiles exporters which have had preferential arrangements with the US, such as the Dominican Republic and Nicaragua, are already feeling the pain of increased competition. On the other hand, many natural resource-rich countries in Latin American, including Brazil, are experiencing an export boom thanks to increased import demand from China. China is also sealing many long-term supply contracts. In addition, a significant inflow of Chinese FDI is emerging, mainly into natural resource sectors, but this may expand to manufacturing for domestic or regional markets. A few Latin American companies are also beginning to invest in the rapidly growing Chinese market. In the medium and long-run, Latin America is likely to find it difficult to keep up with the Chinese expansion of manufactured exports. Latin American exporters of manufactured goods are already facing increased competition from Chinese exporters not only in other Latin American markets, but also in the US and the EU, and this is likely to get more intense. As noted, even Brazil and Mexico, which are the most industrially advanced of the Latin American countries, are not investing enough in education or carrying out enough innovation efforts to become more effective competitors with China. Therefore, the Chinese competition is becoming more of a threat for their future manufacturing growth.[69]

*African countries* are likely to experience similar effects to Latin America but even more pronounced. Textiles and garments, which has been the most important manufactured export industry of Africa, is already facing very strong Chinese competition and many factories are closing down. On the other hand, many countries are benefiting from increased sales of minerals and commodities to China, and these exports are booming. In fact, they are growing so much that a problem for many African countries is going to be to manage the impact of increased export earnings in order to avoid Dutch disease effects caused by appreciation of exchange rates. In addition, there is rapidly growing Chinese foreign investment in Africa, particularly in mining and commodities and supporting infrastructure. A critical issue is whether this new Chinese investment will develop more linkages than that of preceding foreign investment from other countries.[70] Given past historical experience and the low education and institutional capability in most African countries, it is not clear that these positive linkages will develop very quickly, if at all.[71] Aid agencies will also have to consider how to adjust their policy advice given how China is pre-empting the usual one of labour-intensive export growth. Aid agencies will also have to factor in the implications of a much larger Chinese influence in Africa not just in the commercial and economic spheres, but also in terms of development assistance and policy advice.

## 8. Conclusions and implications

It is a challenge to draw together all the different strands covered in this paper, but this will be attempted here under various headings. Some are more tentative than others. Obviously much more could be done on any of these topics so they are listed here to provoke further discussion and more research.

*The international environment is becoming more competitive, demanding and fast paced.* The world has become more integrated through the expansion of trade, investment, and communications. The ICT revolution has also led to an explosion in the internationalization of all types of services that can be done digitally. Thus there is more international competitive pressure. Product life cycles have become shorter. Production, distribution, and supply chains have become more integrated globally even as production has become more fragmented across countries..

*The global system depends on efficient communications and information system, plus excellent logistics* to get goods and services in and out of countries and delivered to the customer in a matter of hours or days, rather than weeks or months. This has led to a speed-up in production and distribution systems. Suppliers have to respond immediately to customer demand.

*Most developing countries do not have the pre-requisites to compete successfully in this more demanding global system.* It is not just that they do not have the latest technologies or skills. They will have to put in place more agile procedures and ways of doing business. They also do not have the logistics and infrastructure. Even if they had the money to invest in the physical infrastructure, they do not have the economies of scale for bulk air or sea shipping via the most direct routes to key markets. This means that many developing countries are excluded from these fast paced markets.

*China and India (if it can open up more, reduce bureaucracy and red tape, and invest more in infrastructure, education, and R&D) will do well in this new competitive system.* They have the scale and critical mass of highly trained people and R&D, as well as large internal markets to play successfully in the global system. They are also large and strategic enough to be among the countries developing the rules of the global system. As such they can play an important leadership role for other developing countries.

*Developing countries have to position themselves to try to benefit as much as possible from this demanding globalised world.* This involves many things.

First, it means more investments in human capital. This is not just in basic education, but secondary, technical and higher education and a system of life-long learning. Second, it means more investment in two kinds of infrastructure. One is the traditional physical infrastructure needed to link to the global economy – roads, ports, airports. The other is the new ICT infrastructure which has already become so critical for competition in the new real-time world and for taking advantage of the second unbundling. Third, it means improvements in the economic and institutional regime – the rule of law, the efficiency of capital and labour markets. Fourth, it means improvement in governance – the ability of government to help its citizens respond successfully to the new challenges and to help people falling between the cracks.[72]

*What countries can do will depend on their level of development and their specific economic, political, and social structure.* They will need to examine carefully how to make best use of their resources and how to leverage them in this new competitive environment. They need to think and act more strategically. They can learn about creating consensus on longer term visions from some of the high performing East Asian economies. They have to learn how to make effective use of global knowledge, how to attract FDI than can contribute to their national development, and how to get positive externalities from that investment.

*Because of very strong adjustment pressures and trend towards marginalization of many countries and even within countries, there has been an increase in the difference in incomes between the richest countries and the poorest.* In 1980, the gap between the richest country and the poorest was about 170 times. Now it is 500 times.[73] Even within developed countries there is a trend toward increasing inequality. The gap in incomes between knowledge workers and those with high school education or less is increasing.

*On a global level, part of what is going on is a massive integration of labour markets and rebalancing of relative incomes.* With the entry of China, India and the former Soviet economies into the global market economy, the world's effective labour force has doubled. With reduction of transportation, communication and information processing costs there is increased trade in goods and services. Together with rapid technological change, the shifts in production locations and the redeployment of resources which globalisation is causing are resulting in large adjustment pressures.

*There is the possibility of backlash against globalisation with a risk of moving back to protectionist trade regimes.* If at all, this is likely to start in Western Europe because it is more rigid than the US, but it could spread to the US. Globalisation will also be a contentious issue for developing countries that are being left out. Note for example the movement towards the left in Latin America, seemingly largely from a feeling that the Washington Consensus reforms have failed. It will be important for the stability of the world for both developed and developing countries to resist the temptation to revert to protectionism. Developed countries in particular should focus instead on increasing the flexibility of their economies to adjust to changing comparative advantage, focusing on labour retraining, improving social safety nets, and fostering creativity and innovation. Developing countries need to work on improving their human capital and physical infrastructure as well as their capabilities to take advantages of the two unbundlings.

*Finally, there are increasing fissures in the global system.* There are large asymmetries in the global rules of the game and in the distribution of income and wealth. The least developed countries are falling further behind. The global system is not benefiting all equally. More efforts need to be made to open up possibilities for the disenfranchised.

Figure 1. The impact of technological advances on global population and GDP per capita – A two millennium perspective

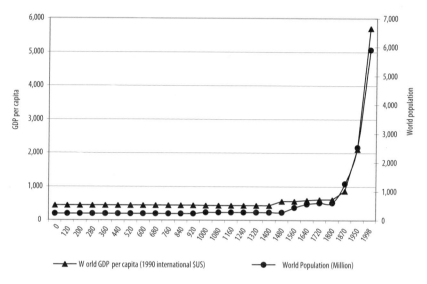

Source: Calculated from Maddison (2001).

Figure 2. The differentiation in regional and country performance since the industrial revolution, selected regions and countries

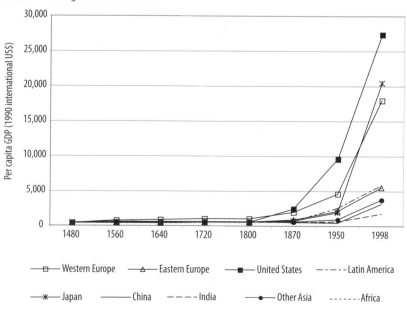

Source: Calculated from Maddison (2001).

Figure 3a. Shares of different world regions in global value added (constant 2000 US dollars),%

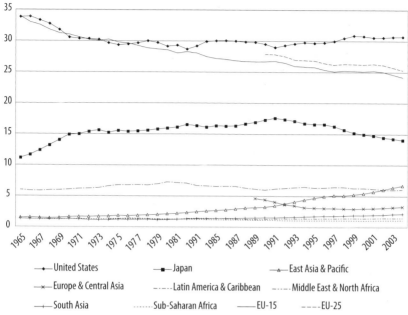

Source: Compiled from the World Development Indicators database.

Figure 3b. Shares of different world regions in global value added (PPP US$), %

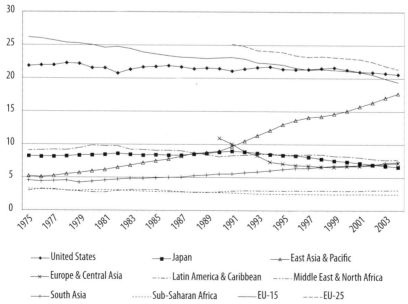

Source: Compiled from the World Development Indicators database.

Figure 4. Total gross domestic expenditure on R&D (PPP US$)

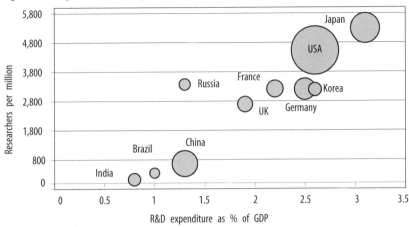

Source: Computed from data in World Bank (2006a).

Figure 5. Structure of OECD manufacturing trade by technology intensity, %

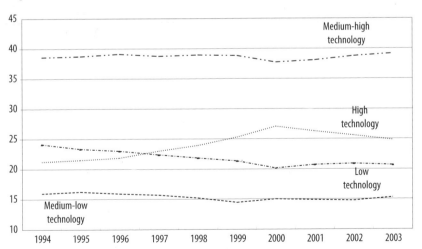

Source: OECD (2005).

Obs.: excludes Luxembourg and the Slovak Republic.
Average value of total OECD exports and imports of goods.

Figure 6. Relative economic size and projections through 2015 for largest economies, % of global GDP

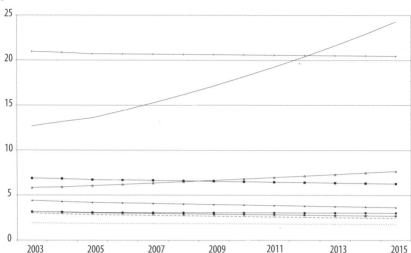

Source: Projected based on data from the World Development Indicators database.

Figure 7. Share of merchandise trade of main exporters, 1980-2004, %

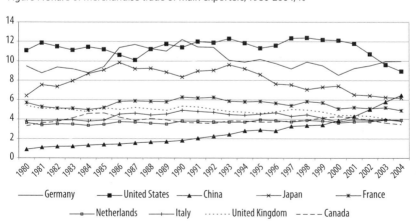

Source: Calculated based on World Bank (2006a).

Figure 8. China's share of merchandise trade surpasses US by end 2006

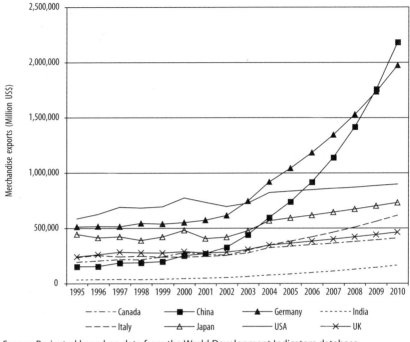

Source: Projected based on data from the World Development Indicators database.

### Table 1.
### High performing plus BRICM

| Country | 1965-1980 | 1980-2004 | 1990-2004 | 2000-2004 |
|---|---|---|---|---|
| Botswana | 13.3 | 7.8 | 5.4 | 6.0 |
| Brazil | 7.9 | 2.5 | 2.0 | 2.6 |
| China | 7.3 | 9.7 | 9.7 | 9.0 |
| Hong Kong (China) | 8.7 | 5.4 | 4.1 | 4.6 |
| India | 3.3 | 5.8 | 5.7 | 5.8 |
| Indonesia | 6.9 | 5.4 | 4.8 | 4.6 |
| Korea, Rep. | 8.2 | 6.7 | 5.9 | 5.4 |
| Malaysia | 7.4 | 6.2 | 6.5 | 5.0 |
| Mexico | 6.6 | 2.8 | 3.1 | 2.6 |
| Pakistan | 5.8 | 5.2 | 4.1 | 4.0 |
| Russian Federation | n/a | n/a | -1.1 | 6.8 |
| Singapore | 10.4 | 6.9 | 6.4 | 4.0 |
| Taiwan (China) | n/a | 6.4 | 5.3 | 3.3 |
| Thailand | 7.6 | 6.0 | 5.1 | 5.0 |

*Source: Computed from World Bank (2006a).*

Technology, Globalization, and International Competitiveness 69

**Table 2.**
**Broad characterization of strategies toward**
**trade and foreign direct investment (FDI)**

|  | Outward | Inward |
|---|---|---|
| FDI passive | Hong Kong | Brazil |
|  | Indonesia | Mexico |
|  | Malaysia | (although it turned outward with NAFTA) |
|  | Thailand |  |
|  | Vietnam |  |
| FDI strategic | China (but now increasing own R&D) |  |
|  | Singapore |  |
|  | Taiwan |  |
| Own R&D | Korea | India |
|  | [Japan] | Russia |

## Table 3.
## The four high performing East Asian economies

|  | Hong Kong | South Korea | Singapore | Taiwan |
|---|---|---|---|---|
| GDP Growth rate (1999-2004) | 4.8 | 5.4 | 4.2 | 3.3 |
| Gross Capital Formation as % of GDP (1994-2003) | 28.8 | 32.1 | 29.9 | 22.1 |
| Trade as % of GDP (2004) | 330.6 | 73.8 | n/a | 109.0 |
| Tariff & Non-Tariff Barriers* (2006) | 1.0 | 3.5 | 1.0 | 2.0 |
| Gross Foreign Investment as share of GDP (average 1994-2003) | 37.0 | 1.8 | 21.7 | n/a |
| Royalty and license fee payments (millions US$ 2004) | 491 | 4,450 | 3,334 | n/a |
| Royalty and license fee payments/ million population (2004) | 73.0 | 92.5 | 775.5 | n/a |
| Royalty and license fee Receipts (millions US$ 2004) | 196 | 1,791 | 197 | n/a |
| Royalty and license fee Receipts/ million population (2004) | 29.1 | 37.2 | 45.8 | n/a |
| Manufactured trade as % of GDP (2003) | 272.5 | 48.7 | 246.3 | 75.7 |
| High technology exports as % of manufactured exports (2003) | 12.7 | 32.2 | 58.8 | 43.0 |
| Tertiary Enrolment Rates (2004) | 26.0 | 84.7 | 43.8 | n/a |
| Science and Engineering Enrolment Ratio (% of tertiary students 1998-2002) | 30.2 | 41.1 | n/a | n/a |
| Science enrolment ratio (% of tertiary students (1998-2003) | 14.3 | 10.3 | n/a | n/a |
| Researchers in R&D (2003) | 10,639 | 151,254 | 18,120 | 87,394 |
| Researchers in R&D / million population (2002) | 1,568 | 2,979 | 4,352 | 3,937 |
| Total expenditures on R&D as % of GDP (2002) | 0.6 | 2.9 | 2.2 | 1.8 |
| Scientific and Technical Journal Articles (2001) | 1817 | 11,037 | 2,603 | 8,082 |
| Scientific and technical journal articles/ million population (2001) | 275.0 | 233.1 | 630.1 | 361.7 |
| Patent applications Grant by USPTO (2004) | 641 | 4,671 | 485 | 7,202 |
| Patent applications granted by USPTO/ million population (2004) | 93.6 | 97.0 | 111.8 | 318.5 |

Source: Compiled form WBI KAM (World Bank Institute Knowledge Assessment Methodology) 2006.
Obs.: * The lower the number, the more open the trade regime to imports and exports.

**Table 4.**
**The second wave of East Asian high performers**

| | Indonesia | Malaysia | Thailand | Vietnam |
|---|---|---|---|---|
| GDP Growth rate (1999-2004) | 4.6 | 5.1 | 5.1 | 7.1 |
| Gross Capital Formation as % of GDP(1994-2003) | 21.9 | 31.5 | 29.5 | 29.5 |
| Trade as % of GDP (2004) | 56.9 | 207.6 | 124.6 | 127.3 |
| Tariff & Non-Tariff Barriers* (2006) | 3.0 | 2.5 | 3.5 | 4.5 |
| Gross Foreign Direct Investment as share of GDP (average 1994-2003) | 3.1 | 5.4 | 2.9 | 5.9 |
| Royalty and license fee payment (millions US$ 2004) | n/a | 782 | 1,584 | n/a |
| Royalty and license fee payments/ million population (2004) | n/a | 31.5 | 25.4 | n/a |
| Royalty and license fee Receipts (millions US$ 2004) | n/a | 20 | 15 | n/a |
| Royalty and license fee Receipts/ million population (2004) | n/a | 0.8 | 0.2 | n/a |
| Manufactured trade as % of GDP (2003) | 24.1 | 139.3 | 82.7 | 64.8 |
| High technology exports as % of manufactured exports (2003) | 14.5 | 58.4 | 30.2 | 1.7 |
| Tertiary Enrolment Rates (2004) | 15.2 | 26.6 | 36.7 | 12.1 |
| Science and Engineering Enrolment Ratio (% of tertiary students, 1998-2002) | n/a | 40.1 | n/a | 19.7 |
| Science Enrolment Ratio (% of tertiary students, 1998-2003) | n/a | 16.3 | n/a | 0.00 |
| Researchers in R&D (2003) | n/a | 7,157 | 17,710 | n/a |
| Researchers in R&D / million population (2002) | n/a | 295 | 289 | n/a |
| Total expenditures on R&D as % of GDP (2002) | n/a | 0.7 | 0.2 | n/a |
| Scientific and technical journal articles (2001) | 207 | 494 | 727 | 158 |
| Scientific and technical journal articles/ million population (2001) | 1.0 | 20.8 | 11.9 | 2.0 |
| Patent applications granted by USPTO (2004) | 23 | 93 | 28 | 1 |
| Patent applications granted by USPTO/ million population (2004) | 0.1 | 3.7 | 0.5 | 0.0 |

Source: Compiled from WBI KAM 2006.
Obs.: * The lower the number, the more open the trade regime to imports and exports.

### Table 5.
### BRICM

|                                                                          | Brazil | Russia  | India   | China   | Mexico |
|--------------------------------------------------------------------------|--------|---------|---------|---------|--------|
| GDP Growth rate (1999-2004)                                              | 2.7    | 6.9     | 5.7     | 8.5     | 2.6    |
| Gross Capital Formation as % of GDP (1994-2003)                          | 20.9   | 20.9    | 23.1    | 39.5    | 22.4   |
| Trade as % of GDP (2004)                                                 | 30.0   | 52.6    | 30.5    | 66.1    | 58.5   |
| Tariff & Non-Tariff Barriers* (2006)                                     | 3.5    | 3.5     | 5.0     | 3.0     | 2.5    |
| Gross Foreign Investment as share of GDP (average 1994-2003)             | 3.4    | 1.9     | 0.7     | 5.1     | 3.0    |
| Royalty and license fee payments (millions US$ 2004)                     | 1,197  | 1,095   | 4201    | 3,548   | 805    |
| Royalty and license fee payments/ million population (2004)              | 6.7    | 7.7     | 0.4     | 2.8     | 7.8    |
| Royalty and license fee Receipts (millions US$ 2004)                     | 115    | 228     | 25      | 107     | 92     |
| Royalty and license fee Receipts/ million population (2004)              | 0.6    | 1.6     | 0.03    | 0.1     | 0.9    |
| Manufactured trade as % of GDP (2003)                                    | 15.1   | 17.8    | 13.5    | 51.3    | 46.0   |
| High technology exports as % of manufactured exports (2003)              | 12.0   | 18.9    | 4.8     | 27.1    | 21.3   |
| Tertiary Enrolment Rates (2004)                                          | 18.2   | 69.8    | 11.4    | 12.7    | 21.5   |
| Science and Engineering enrolment ratio (% of tertiary students, 1998-2002) | n/a | n/a     | 20.1    | n/a     | 31.1   |
| Science enrolment ratio (% of tertiary students, 1998-2003)              | n/a    | n/a     | 15.1    | n/a     | 12.5   |
| Researchers in R&D (2003)                                                | 59,838 | 487,477 | 117,528 | 810,525 | 27,626 |
| Researchers in R&D / million population (2002)                           | 352    | 3,415   | 120     | 633     | 274    |
| Total expenditures on R&D as % of GDP (2002)                             | 1.0    | 1.2     | 0.9     | 1.2     | 0.4    |
| Scientific and technical journal articles (2001)                         | 7,205  | 15,846  | 11,076  | 20,978  | 32     |
| Scientific and technical journal articles/ million population (2001)     | 41.8   | 109.5   | 10.7    | 16.5    | 32.3   |
| Patent applications granted by USPTO (2004)                              | 161    | 173     | 376     | 597     | 102    |
| Patent applications granted by USPTO/ million population (2004)          | 0.9    | 1.2     | 0.4     | 0.5     | 1.0    |

Source: Compiled from WBI KAM 2006.
Obs.: * The lower the number, the more open the trade regime to imports and exports.

### Table 6.
### Countries with annual growth rates of 5% or more

| Country | 1965-1980 | 1980-2004 | 1990-2005 | 2000-2004 |
|---|---|---|---|---|
| Algeria | 6.3 | 2.6 | 2.5 | 4.2 |
| Botswana | 13.3 | 7.8 | 5.4 | 6.0 |
| Bosnia Herzegovina | n/a | 7.8 | 19.5 | 5.0 |
| Brazil | 7.9 | 2.5 | 2.1 | 2.6 |
| Cambodia | n/a | 6.5 | 7.1 | 6.6 |
| Chad | -0.5 | 5.3 | 5.3 | 12.0 |
| Chile | 3.3 | 5.1 | 5.5 | 3.8 |
| China | 7.3 | 9.7 | 9.7 | 9.0 |
| Colombia | 5.4 | 3.0 | 2.8 | 2.8 |
| Congo Rep | 6.0 | 4.0 | 2.0 | 4.4 |
| Costa Rica | 6.4 | 3.8 | 4.7 | 3.4 |
| Côte d'Ivoire | 6.3 | 0.8 | 1.5 | -1.0 |
| Dominican Rep. | 6.4 | 4.1 | 4.2 | 3.6 |
| Ecuador | 5.9 | 2.4 | 2.7 | 4.2 |
| Egypt | 5.9 | 5.0 | 4.3 | 3.8 |
| Gabon | 8.0 | 2.3 | 2.4 | 1.8 |
| Greece | 5.8 | 1.9 | 2.6 | 4.2 |
| Guatemala | 5.7 | 2.5 | 3.6 | 2.6 |
| Honduras | 5.5 | 2.9 | 3.6 | 2.6 |
| Hong Kong (China) | 8.7 | 5.4 | 4.1 | 4.6 |
| Iceland | 5.3 | 2.8 | 2.6 | 3.2 |
| India | 3.3 | 5.8 | 5.7 | 5.8 |
| Indonesia | 6.9 | 5.4 | 4.8 | 4.6 |
| Iran | n/a | 3.2 | 5.0 | 5.6 |
| Ireland | 4.5 | 5.3 | 6.8 | 6.2 |
| Israel | 6.6 | 4.2 | 4.6 | 2.6 |
| Jordan | 5.0 | 4.6 | 5.1 | 5.4 |
| Kenya | 7.1 | 3.0 | 2.1 | 2.4 |
| Korea, Rep. | 8.2 | 6.7 | 5.9 | 5.4 |
| Lebanon | n/a | 3.1 | 7.9 | 3.8 |
| Lesotho | 7.6 | 3.9 | 3.3 | 2.4 |
| Libya | 8.3 | n/a | n/a | 4.6 |
| Malawi | 6.2 | 3.0 | 3.7 | 2.6 |
| Malaysia | 7.4 | 6.2 | 6.5 | 5.0 |
| Mauritius | n/a | 5.2 | 5.1 | 4.4 |
| Mexico | 6.6 | 2.8 | 3.1 | 2.6 |
| Morocco | 5.5 | 3.4 | 3.1 | 4.0 |
| Mozambique | n/a | 4.2 | 6.4 | 7.6 |

continued

| Country | 1965-1980 | 1980-2004 | 1990-2005 | 2000-2004 |
|---|---|---|---|---|
| Nigeria | 5.1 | 2.7 | 3.8 | 5.2 |
| Oman | 15.8 | 6.4 | 3.9 | 3.6 |
| Pakistan | 5.8 | 5.2 | 4.1 | 4.0 |
| Panamas | 5.7 | 3.2 | 4.7 | 3.2 |
| Paraguay | 7.1 | 2.8 | 2.1 | 1.6 |
| Philippines | 5.5 | 2.7 | 3.2 | 4.4 |
| Portugal | 5.6 | 2.7 | 2.3 | 1.0 |
| Russian Federation | n/a | n/a | -1.1 | 6.8 |
| Rwanda | 6.3 | 3.2 | 3.3 | 5.4 |
| Singapore | 10.4 | 6.9 | 6.4 | 4.0 |
| Sudan | 3.3 | 4.4 | 5.1 | 6.0 |
| Syrian Arab R. | 7.9 | 4.0 | 4.7 | 3.0 |
| Taiwan (China) | n/a | 6.4 | 5.3 | 3.3 |
| Thailand | 7.6 | 6.0 | 5.1 | 5.0 |
| Tunisia | 6.3 | 4.5 | 4.9 | 4.8 |
| Uganda | n/a | n/a | 6.5 | 5.8 |
| United Arab Emirates | n/a | n/a | 6.1 | 7.2 |
| Vietnam | n/a | 6.7 | 7.4 | 7.2 |
| Zimbabwe | 5.3 | 2.0 | -0.2 | 5.8 |

*Source: Computed based on data from World Bank (2006), data for Taiwan estimated from CIA Factbook 2006.*

### Table 7.
### Basic data on high performing East Asian countries
### plus BRICM (2004)

| | Population (millions) | GNI (billion) | GNI per Capita | GNI (PPP Terms) | PPP GNI per Capita | Merchandise Exports (billion) |
|---|---|---|---|---|---|---|
| Brazil | 184 | 552 | 3,000 | 1,460 | 7,940 | 96 |
| China | 1,296 | 1,938 | 1,500 | 7,634 | 5,890 | 593 |
| Hong Kong (China) | 7 | 184 | 26,660 | 217 | 31,500 | 266 |
| India | 1,080 | 673 | 620 | 3,369 | 3,120 | 76 |
| Indonesia | 218 | 248 | 1,140 | 757 | 3,480 | 72 |
| Korea, Rep. | 48 | 673 | 14,000 | 987 | 20,530 | 254 |
| Malaysia | 25 | 113 | 4,520 | 242 | 9,720 | 127 |
| Mexico | 104 | 705 | 6,790 | 1,001 | 9,640 | 189 |
| Russian Federation | 144 | 489 | 3,400 | 1,392 | 9,680 | 183 |
| Singapore | 4 | 105 | 24,760 | 116 | 27,370 | 180 |
| Taiwan (China) | 23 | 311 | 13,500 | 606 | 26,307 | 171 |
| Thailand | 64 | 158 | 2,490 | 505 | 7,930 | 97 |
| Sub-Total | 3,197 | 6,149 | -- | 18,286 | -- | 2,304 |
| World Total or World Average | 6,365 | 40,282 | 6,329 | 56,289 | 8,844 | 9,145 |
| These 12 Economies as % World | 50.2 | 15.3 | -- | 32.5 | -- | 25.2 |
| Total for Low- and Middle-Income Countries | 5,362 | 8,050 | 1,502 | 25,334 | 4,726 | 2,472 |
| These 12 Economies as % of Low- and Middle-Income Countries | 59.6 | 76.4 | -- | 72.2 | -- | 93.2 |

Source: Computed based on data from World Bank (2006), data for Taiwan estimated from CIA Factbook 2006.

## Notes

1 At the broadest level, average per capita income is a good summary measure of the effective application of knowledge to production of goods and services, although in comparisons across countries it is necessary to be mindful of cases where rents from sale of natural resources such as oil bias per capita income upward.

2 See Maddison (2001) for a millennial historical overview.

3 See Perez (1992).

4 As pointed out by Gershenkron (1962), the advantage for late industrializers is that they can draw on the technology and experience of the already developed countries. However it is not so easy to replicate what other countries have done, as evidenced by the very small number of countries who have made a transition from low to high incomes.

5 See Abramovitz (1986) on catching up with developed countries.

6 See World Bank (2006a) for the different country groupings.

7 In May 2005 ten Central European countries joined the EU. Figure 3 has added their shares to those of the EC-15 back to 1990 to get an estimate of the EU-25 for comparative purposes.

8 The BRICs has become a popular aggregation since the Goldman Sacks report of 2003. Here Mexico has been added to the original list of BRICs as Mexico is the second largest economy of this group. Therefore we look at the BRICKM countries (with global ranking in 2004 in terms of economic size in parenthesis): Brazil (13th), Russia (16th), India (11th), China (5th) and Mexico (10th).

9 The Philippines does not because its average annual growth rate was only 2.7 per cent for 1980-2004.

10 The World Bank's East Asia Miracle book published in 1993 covered Hong Kong, Indonesia, Japan, Malaysia, Korea, Singapore, and Taiwan (Province of China) as the high performing Asian economies. It did not give any attention to China in spite of its already impressive performance. See Stiglitz and Yusuf (2001) for an updated view of the East Asian miracle.

11 The slowdown in growth was generic in Latin American countries. In the 1965-1980 period, 10 of the 41 countries that averaged more than 5 per cent annual growth were Latin American. In the 1980-2004 period, only one of the 19 countries that grew at more than 5 per cent was Latin American. That country was Chile whose growth fizzled to an average of 3.8 per cent for 2000-2004.

12 High growth during this period was also typical for the former soviet countries. Sixteen of the 49 countries that had average growth above 5 per cent for 2000-2005 were former soviet economies. It appears that after suffering severe economic contractions and undertaking key reforms in the economic and regulatory system, many were finally beginning to grow.

13 Hong Kong, Singapore and Taiwan are actually considered developed economies by the World Bank as their per capita incomes are above the US$10,066 threshold used, but they have been included as part of the developing countries' group here because until relatively recently they were considered as such.

14 See Lall's article in Lall and Urata (2003) for an elaboration of this distinction.

15 Table 3 on the second group of Asians includes Vietnam because it has had an average annual rate of growth of 6.70 per cent for 1980-2004.

16 See Kniivilä (2007), in this volume, for a review of the industrialization of the high performing East Asian economies with a special focus on poverty reduction.

17 Westphal, Rhee, and Purcell (1981) have pointed out that Korea acquired a lot of technology from its early engagement in trade. This consisted of design and production technology that was transferred by large foreign purchasers. It also included technical assistance provided by supplies of capital goods and turnkey plants. More generally, the fact that Korean firms were forced to export, made them more aware of the technology used by the competitors and forced them to keep up with new product and process improvements.

18 Kim (2003).

19 Kim (2003).

20 Logistics contributes 5.3 per cent of Hong Kong's GDP and employs 6 per cent of its working population.

21 See Tan, Lui and Loh (1992).

22 For a good account of Singapore's foreign investment strategy see Wong (2003).

23 See Wade (1999), and Noland and Pack (2003) for more detail.

24 See Aw (2003).

25 See Dahlman and Sannanikone (1991) for an early account of Taiwan's technology strategy.

26 Strong Brazilian companies in food processing are Perdigão and Sadia, which are exporting to many countries.

27 Less than one percent of the inputs (other than labour, and infrastructure services) were sourced from Mexico. Part of the problem was that many of the firms were already committed to purchases from their US supplier networks and did not find it attractive enough to develop Mexican suppliers due to low quality and scale economies.

28 As part of this, in 1970 India enacted intellectual property legislation that did not recognize product patents for pharmaceuticals or agro-industry products, and limited the protection for process patents to just five years in these sectors; and to 14 years in other sectors. Efforts were oriented towards mission oriented national programs in defense, nuclear energy space; the large capital-intensive state enterprise sector; small scale industry; and agriculture.

29 See Rodrik and Subramanian (2004) for a good account of the business liberalization that started before the trade liberalization of the early 1990s.

30 Most notable among these was the Council for Industrial and Scientific Research (CSIR), which by 1995 came out with a new strategy and vision for 2001. It changed its orientation from state industry and import substitution, to providing industrial research and development for the new competitive needs of the industrial sector.

31 World Bank Report (forthcoming 2007), The Environment for Innovation in India, Washington, DC: World Bank.

32 For a summary of the earlier stages see Yao (2003).

33 According to Premier Weng Jiabo's speech on the 15 year technology strategy in December 2005.

34 For a more positive assessment on the prospects for developing countries see the Economist (2006), "The New Titans". This survey points out that all major 32 emerging market countries are growing and had sounder macroeconomic balances. It presents a much more positive future for these emerging market economies.

However, it does not sufficiently distinguishing short term improvement because of increases in basic commodity and natural resource prices from the longer terms trends which are primarily being taken advantage of by China and to some extent India, as will be argued below.

35 But even in more traditional industries such as cars, there in an increase in the number of variety of products. It is now common for consumers to specify the options on the particular brand and model of car they wants to purchase, and have the car made to order.

36 Average weighted tariffs ( using each country's imports from the world as weights ) in developing countries have fallen from 19.7 per cent  1980-83 to 11.0 per cent  in 2000-2001; and in developed countries from 5.8 per cent  in 1989-1992 to 3.1 per cent  in 2000 (UNCTAD, 2004).

37 See OECD (2004).

38 See Chang (2002) for a good development of this argument.

39 For a good exposition on modular production as applied to electronics see Sturgeon (2002).

40 For US MNCs, R&D undertaken by foreign affiliates increased from 11 per cent in 1994 to 13 per cent  in 2002. For Swedish MNCs it increased from 22 per cent  in 1995 to 43 per cent  in 2003.  For the world as whole, R&D expenditure by foreign affiliates is estimated to have risen from US$30 billion in 1993 to US$67 billion in 2002 – i.e., from roughly 10 per cent to 16 per cent of all global business R&D, US$403 billion (UNCTAD, 2005).

41 The use of unbundling for these trends is attributed to Baldwin (2006).

42 For a current analysis of this based on interviews with over 500 companies around the world see Berger (2006).

43 There is much debate on the number of jobs that might actually be outsourced, and Blinder's estimates tend to be on the high end, but the key point is that as ICT advances and more tasks can be digitized, many more jobs may be at risk.

44 In 2003, the top six MNCs (Ford, Pfizer, Daimler Chrysler, Siemens, Toyota, and General Motors) spent more than US$5 billion each. Only five developing countries came near to US$5 billion or more per year (Korea, China, Taiwan [Province of China], Brazil, and  Russia) – see UNCTAD (2005).

45 UNCTAD (2005, various years).

46 In 2004, the exports of MNCs were approximately US$3,690 billion out of total world merchandise and non-factor service exports of  US$11,069 billion (UNCTAD, 2000)

47 For an excellent perspective on this from no other than the CEO of IBM, see Palmisano (2006).

48 The economies, in decreasing order of FDI inflows in 2005 are: China, Hong Kong (China), United Arab Emirates, Brazil, Russia, Bermuda, Colombia, Mexico, and Taiwan—see UNCTAD (2006).

49 For a good exposition on supply chains and the difficulty of moving up see Kaplinsky (2005).

50 For example, according to a recent interview with the handicraft store chain Ten Thousand Villages, the main reason why there are so few handicraft products from Africa is that producers in African countries have trouble producing to the scale, quality, and timely delivery required.

51 Some of the most famous are companies such as Samsung, LG, and Hyundai from Korea; Acer from Taiwan; China Mobile, China Netcom, Founder, Lenovo, SAIC, Tsingtao Beer, and ZTE Corp from China; Bajaj, Bharat, Cipla, Dr. Reddy's Labs, Infosys, Ranbaxy, Reliance, Satyam, Tata, and Wipro from India; and Gerdau, Embraer, Natura, Perdigão, Sadia, and Votorantim from Brazil.

52 The World Bank developed a framework and methodology that captures indicators of all but the physical infrastructure elements ( see http://www.worldbank.org/kam).

53 Palmisano (2006, p.132) for example writes, "Real innovation is about more than the simple creation and launching of new products. It is also about how services, are delivered, how business process are integrated, how companies and institutions are managed, how knowledge is transferred, how public policies are formulated - and how enterprises, communities, and societies participate in and benefit from it all".

54 See for example De Ferranti et al. (2002).

55 For the broad architecture of the kind of systems that need to be set up in developing countries, as applied to China, see Dahlman, Zeng and Wang (forthcoming 2006).

56 For an exposition on how the traditional factory production system has been replaced by logistics and the implications that has for workers see Ciscel and Smith (2005).

57 For a good exposition of this and of how some regions in the US are organizing public private partnerships to create this enabling infrastructure see Kasarda and Rondinelli (1998).

58 Ciscel and Smith (2005, p.431).

59 Studies from many countries show that efficiency gains are much larger when investments in hardware are accompanied not only by training but also by changes in organizational processes and procedures to take advantage of the potential offered by the new technologies (see OECD, 2005).

60 For another view on the impact of these two giants on developing countries see Altenburg et al. (2006).

61 Rather than using nominal exchange rates the figure uses purchasing power exchange rates. PPP rates provide a better measure for comparing the real levels of expenditure across countries. They are derived from price surveys across countries to compare what a given basket of goods would cost and use that to impute the appropriate exchange to use.

62 See Bergsten (2006) for a good analysis of the implications of China's rise for the US. See Dahlman and Aubert (2001) for an earlier analysis of the strengths and weaknesses of China as a knowledge economy.

63 According to Palmisano (2006, p.130) just between 2000 and 2003 foreign firms built 60,000 manufacturing plans in China, some targeted at the domestic market, but many targeted at the global market.

64 For a recent analysis of India's strengths and challenges see Dahlman and Utz (2005).

65 The rate of export growth in Japan and Korea was faster than in China, but they were smaller as a share of world exports.

66 See Evans, Kaplinsky, and Robinson (2006) for an explanation of the triangular production networks which have been established in East Asia where supply chain governor economies like Hong Kong and Taiwan organize production in China using inputs for the East Asian region, for buyers in the US and EU.

67 See IDB (2005) for some data on the degree of intra regional production chains.

68 For more on the impact of China in East Asia, see Gill and Kharas (2006), and Humphrey and Smitz (2006).

69 For more on the likely impact on Latin American countries see IDB (2005) and World Bank (2006b)

70 For more on the likely impact on Africa see Goldstein et al. (2006).

71 For a more optimistic assessment of Africa's prospects in natural resource-based industries including agriculture, see Kjöllerström and Dallto (2007) in this volume.

72 See Aubert et al. (forthcoming 2007) for some of the key elements of strategy that developing countries will have to master to take advantage of the opportunities opened up by the rapid changes in technology.

73 The per capita incomes of Norway and Switzerland are around US$50,000 compared to per capita income of around US$100 for Burundi, the Democratic Republic of Congo, and Ethiopia.

# Acknowledgements

I would like to thank participants in the September 7-8, 2006 seminar in New York on the draft papers for this volume for their valuable comments. I would particularly like to thank David O'Connor for his very useful written comments on the first draft of this paper. I would also like to thank Zach Wilson and Anubha Verma for their excellent research assistance.

# Bibliography

Abramovitz, M. (1986), Catching Up, Forging Ahead, and Falling Behind, Journal of Economic History, 46 (2), 385-406.

Altenburg, T., H. Schmitz, and A. Stamm (2006),Building Knowledge-based Competitive Advantages in China and India: Lessons and Consequences for other Developing Countries, paper presented at Workshop of Asian Drivers of Global Change, St. Petersburg, Russia.

Aubert, J.-E., et al. (forthcoming 2007) Towards Knowledge Economies - Advanced Strategies for Development, World Bank Institute, Washington DC.

Aw, B.-Y. (2003), Technological Acquisition and Development in Taiwan, in Competitiveness, FDI and Technological Activity in East Asia, S. Lall and S. Urata, eds., Edgward Elgar, Northampton.

Baldwin, R. (2006), Globalization: The Great Unbundling(s), paper contributed to event on Globalization Challenges to Europe and Finland organized by the Secretariat of the Economic Council, Prime Minister's Office (June).

Berger, S., (2006), How We Compete: What Companies around the World are Doing to Make it in Today's Global Economy, Random House, New York.

Bergsten, C. et al. (2006), China The Balance Sheet: What the World Needs to Know About the Emerging Superpower, Institute for International Economics and CSIS, New York.

Blinder, A. (2006), Offshoring: The Next Industrial Revolution?, Foreign Affairs, 85 (2) (March-April).

Chang, H.-J. (2002), Kicking Away the Ladder, Anthem Press, London.

Ciscel, D. H. and B. E. Smith (2005), The Impact of Supply Chain Management on Labour Standards: The Transition to Incessant Work, Journal of Economic Issues, 39 (2), 429-437.

Dahlman, C. J., D. Zhihua Zeng, and S. Wang (forthcoming 2006), Developing a System of Life Long Learning in China to Enhance Competitiveness, World Bank, Washington, D.C..

Dahlman, C. J. and A. Utz (2005), India and the Knowledge Economy: Leveraging Strengths and Opportunities, World Bank, Washington, D.C..

Dahlman, C. J. and J.-E. Aubert (2001), China and the Knowledge Economy: Seizing the 21rst Century, World Bank, Washington, D.C..

Dahlman, C.J., and O. Sananikone (1991), Technology Strategy in the Economy of Taiwan: Exploiting Foreign Linkages and Investing in Local Capability, World Bank Industrial Strategy Policy Series Papers.

De Ferranti, D. et al. (2002), Closing the Gap in Education and Skills, World Bank, Washington DC.

Drucker, P. (1994), The Age of Social Transformation, Atlantic Monthly, Vol.274.

Economist, The (2006), The New Titans: A Survey of the World Economy, Special supplement in September 16th edition.

Evans, D., R. Kaplinsky, and S. Robinson (2006), Deep and Shallow Integration in Asia: Towards a Holistic Account, IDS Bulletin, 37 (1).

Freeman, R. (2006), Labour Market Imbalances: Shortages, or Surpluses, or Fish Stories?, paper prepared for Boston Federal Reserve Economics Conference - Global Imbalance - As Giants Evolve, June 14-16, Chatham, Massachusetts.

Gershenkron, A. (1962), Economic Backwardness in Historical Perspective: A Book of Essays, Cambridge: Belknap Press of Harvard University Press.

Gill, Indermit; and Homi Kharas (2006), An East Asian Renaissance: Ideas for Economic Growth, Washington DC: World Bank.

Goldstein, A., N. Pinaud, H. Reisen, and X. Chen (2006), The Rise of China and India: What's in it for Africa? Paris: OECD Development Centre.

Grossman, G. and E. Rossi-Hansberg (2006), The Rise of Offshoring: It's not Wine for Cloth Anymore, conference paper, Reserve Bank of Kansas, August 23.

Humphrey, J. and H. Schmitz (2006), The Implication's of China's Growth for Other Asian Countries, Institute of Development Studies, Brighton, UK.

Inter American Development Bank (2005). The Emergence of China: Opportunities and Challenges for Latin America and the Carribean, IDB Research Department, Washington DC.

Kaplinsky, R. (2005), Globalization, Poverty, and Inequality. Cambridge: Polity Press.

Kasarda, J. D. and D. A. Rondinelli (1998), "Innovative Infrastructure for Agile Manufacturers," Sloan Management Review, Vol. 39 (2), 73-82.

Kim, L. (2003). The Dynamics of Technology Development: Lessons from the Korean Experience, in Competitiveness, FDI and Technological Activity in East Asia, S. Lall and S. Urata, eds., Edgward Elgar, Northampton.

Kjöllerström, M., and K. Dallto (2007), Natural Resource-based Industries: Prospects for Africa's Agriculture, this volume.

Kniivilä, M. (2007), Industrial Development and Economic Growth: Implications for Poverty Reduction and Income Inequality, this volume.

Lall, S. (2003), Foreign Direct Investment, Technology Development and Competitiveness: Issues and Evidence, in Competitiveness, FDI and Technological Activity in East Asia, S. Lall and S. Urata, eds., Edgward Elgar, Northampton.

Maddison, A. (2001), The World Economy: A Millennial Perspective, OECD, Paris.

Noland, M. and H. Pack (2003), Industrial Policy in an Era of Globalization: Lessons from Asia, Institute of International Economics, Washington DC.

OECD (2005), Science, Technology and Industry Scoreboard 2005, OECD, Paris.

OECD (2004), Internationalization of Higher Education: Opportunities and Challenges, OECD, Paris.

Page, J., et al. (1993), The East Asian Miracle: Economic Growth and Public Policy, World Bank, Washington DC.

Palmisano, S. (2006) The Globally Integrated Enterprise, in Foreign Affairs (May- June).

Perez, C. (1992), Technological Revolutions and Financial Capital: The Dynamics of Bubbles and of Golden Ages, Edward Elgar, London.

Rodrik, D. and A. Subramanian (2004), From Hindu Rate of Growth to Productivity Surge: The Mystery of the Indian Growth Transition, National Bureau of Economic Research , Working Paper 10376 (March).

Singh, N. (2007), Services-Led Industrialization in India: Prospects and Challenges, this volume.

Stiglitz, J. and S. Yusuf (2001), Re-Thinking the East Asian Miracle, Oxford University Press and the World Bank.

Sturgeon, T. (2002), Modular Production Networks: A New American Model of Industrial Organization, Industrial and Corporate Change, 11 (3), 451-496.

Tan. W. B., C. W. E. Lui; and C. M. Loh,(1992), The Use of Information Technology by the Port of Singapore Authority, World Development, December, 1785-1795.

UNCTAD (2004), Development and Globalization Facts and Figures, Geneva.

UNCTAD (2005), World Investment Reports 2005: Transnational Corporations and the Internationalization of R&D, New York and Geneva.

UNCTAD (2006), World Investment Report 2006: FDI from Developing and Transition Economies-Implications for Development, New York and Geneva.

UNCTAD (various years), World Investment Reports. New York and Geneva.

Wade, R. (2003), Governing the Market, Princeton University Press.

Wong, P. K. (2003), From Using to Creating Technology: the Evolution of Singapore's National Innovation System and the Changing Role of Public Policy, in Competitiveness, FDI and Technological Activity in East Asia, S. Lall and S. Urata, eds., Edgward Elgar, Northampton.

Westphal, L., W. Y. Rhee, and G. Purcell (1981), Korean Industrial Competence: Where It Came From, World Bank Staff Working Paper 469, Washington DC.

World Bank (2006a), World Development Indicators 2006, Washington DC.

World Bank (2006b), Latin America and the Caribbean's Response to the Growth of China and India: Overview of Research Findings and Policy Implications, Washington, DC.

Yao, Yang (2003), In Search of Balance: Technological Development in China, in Competitiveness, FDI and Technological Activity in East Asia, S. Lall and S. Urata, eds., Edgward Elgar, Northampton.

# Developing country multinationals: South-South investment comes of age

Dilek Aykut* and Andrea Goldstein❖

## 1. Introduction

Foreign Direct Investment (FDI) has been one of the main vectors of globalization in the past and has possibly grown in importance over the past decade (Jones, 2005; OECD, 2005). The multinational corporations (MNCs) from industrialized countries, where most FDI originates, have provided a massive infusion of capital, technology, marketing connections, and managerial expertise that, under certain conditions, have played a major role in the economic transformation and growth that many less developed and newly industrialized countries from around the world have experienced over the past two decades.[1] In the process, some enterprises from emerging economies, including both transition, and developing economies, have amassed sufficient capital, knowledge and know-how to invest abroad on their own and claim the status of emerging multinationals (EMNCs). The number of Fortune 500 companies headquartered outside the Triad (the North Atlantic and Japan) and Oceania has risen from 26 in 1988 to 61 in 2005, and Samsung (Republic of Korea) has become one of the top 20 most valuable brand names in the world.[2] It seems likely that this trend will continue in the years ahead. Another indicator is the ratio of foreign assets held by the largest EMNC to those of the world's largest MNC, which has risen from 5.7 per cent in 1999 to 6.9 per cent in 2003 (UNCTAD, 2001 and 2005).[3] In April 2006, the Russian Gazprom surpassed Microsoft to become the world's third most valuable company. And China Mobile's market capitalization surpassed that of the United Kingdom telecom company Vodafone.

Developing-country MNCs first appeared as a focus of interest about 25 years ago, with the advent of some overseas expansion by companies from a few countries (Lecraw, 1977; Lall, 1983; Wells, 1983).[4] The earliest major developing-world sources of FDI in this period were a small group of economies, including Argentina, Brazil, Hong Kong (China), India, Republic of Korea, Singapore, and Taiwan (Province of China).[5] It is only since the late 1980s that an increasing number of developing countries and transition economies, including Chile, China, Egypt, Malaysia, Mexico, Russian Federation, South Africa, Thailand, and Turkey, have become significant sources of FDI. Since 2003, the growth rate of outward FDI (OFDI)

* DECPG-International Finance Team, The World Bank.
❖ OECD Development Centre.

from emerging markets has outpaced the growth from industrialized countries (UNCTAD, 2005). While OFDI from the BRIC countries – Brazil,
Russian Federation, India and China – has received more attention (Sauvant,
2005), other developing countries are also home to new important global
businesses. Cemex, a Mexican cement giant, has used acquisitions to become
the largest cement producer in the United States; Argentina's Tenaris
(although it is owned by an Italian family and is also listed in New York) is
the world's largest producer of seamless tubes thanks to its technological
edge. CP Group in Thailand is said to be the largest single investor in China.
Recent mega-deals that have received considerable attention include the purchase of Wind of Italy by Orascom of Egypt – Europe's largest ever leveraged
buyout – and of P&O (United Kingdom) by DP World of Dubai. MNCs
from new FDI source countries as "exotic" as Lebanon, Peru, or Uganda are
now emerging. Sri Lankan firms, for example, are now very important players in the export-oriented clothing industry in many countries (in particular
Bangladesh, India, and Madagascar).

Inasmuch as EMNCs have become a permanent, sizeable and growing
feature of the world economy, they can no longer be regarded as exceptions
or anomalies. This paper provides an introduction to some of the key issues
regarding EMNCs,[6] including:

- Their size, nature, motives, and patterns of internationalization;
- The challenges that they encounter in their quest abroad (e.g., difficulties in creating a sustained competitive edge over well-established
  incumbents and in managing complex operations that require both
  foreign adaptation and cross-border integration); and
- Their contribution to the global economy, not least through investment in other developing countries, as a burgeoning instance of
  south-south cooperation, in particular supporting regional integration and responding to the incentives created by regional agreements.

Section 2 examines the investment patterns and characteristics of
EMNCs in general and in selected industries; section 3 develops a simple
conceptual framework for the analysis of motivations and strategies by
EMNCs; section 4 examines how the impact of FDI by EMNCs on host
economies might differ from that of OECD-based MNCs and addresses key
policy issues arising at the national and international levels;[7] and the conclusions try to separate those questions for which there is are preliminary
answers from those where a lot of research is still necessary.

## 2. Patterns and characteristics

With increased globalization of operations and complex business networks,
it is harder than ever to assign nationalities to multinational companies, or to
define and monitor their international operations. For FDI indicators at the

aggregate level, differences in the way data are collected, defined and report-ed explain some of the oddities in global data compilations – in particular, while inward and outward FDI should in principle balance globally, the data rarely do. In 2004, global FDI outflows were reported at US$730 billion, whereas the inflows were US$648 billion. At the bilateral level, outflows reported by investing economies seldom resemble the data provided by recip-ient countries. The inconsistency in data is further exacerbated by the activ-ities of off-shore financial centres – for instance, according to official data the biggest "investing country" in India is Mauritius.

All such limitations are magnified in the case of FDI outflows from developing and transition economies, and for a number of reasons, OFDI statistics for non-OECD countries tend to be patchy and relatively unreli-able. Some of those countries that have invested abroad do not identify FDI outflows (Iran for instance), while some major emerging economies (such as Malaysia and Mexico) just started reporting FDI outflows in recent years. Moreover, for several countries, official data on FDI outflows are consider-ably smaller than the actual flows. Official statistics do not usually include financing and reinvested components of OFDI or capital that is raised abroad (Aykut and Ratha, 2004). Also, they generally only reflect large investments while excluding small and medium size transactions. In addi-tion, countries with capital controls, currency controls or high taxes on investment income provide a substantial incentive for underreporting by investors. On the other hand, liberalization of currency controls may have resulted in less attention to accounting for international financial flows. This problem is exacerbated by lax accounting standards, weak tax administration, and limited administrative capacity in agencies responsible for data collec-tion, resulting in private flows being grouped into residual categories (rather than classified as FDI, bond flows, bank lending, or portfolio equity flows).

Several country case studies based on company level data highlight the underreporting of outward FDI flows. Del Sol (2005) shows that Chilean investment abroad during the 1990s was almost twice the official data; Pradhan (2005) finds the same result for India. And some portion of the esti-mated US$245 billion capital flight from the Russian Federation during the 1992–2002 period is believed to be unrecorded FDI flows (Vahtra and Liuhto, 2004). Wong and Chan (2003) document the substantial under-reporting of FDI flows from China: the reported numbers reflect only invest-ments with official approval (which is required for initial investments only), and China's State Administration and Foreign Exchange estimates that unau-thorized capital outflows from China between 1997 and 1999 totalled US$53 billion. Similarly, the outward FDI stock of Turkey is estimated as US$15 billion in 2004, three times the official numbers (Erdilek, 2005).

## 2.1 How reliable are definitions and statistics?

Is there any prima facie reason to assume a fundamental dissimilarity in the nature of MNCs depending on the characteristics of the home country (developed vs. developing and transition countries)? The debate in economics and business studies is largely inconclusive (Goldstein, 2006c) and yet most discussions on EMNCs centre on this issue. Some see ownership as a central issue and oppose the rise in FDI from non-OECD countries, while others consider South-South investment as a blessing. We will return to this below.

At any rate, definitions count and many EMNCs are indefinable beasts. For many very large EMNCs it is not obvious how to assign nationality. Possibly the best-known example is Mittal Steel, a fortiori following its attempt to take over Franco-Luxemburgeois-Spanish Arcelor and create the world's largest steel-maker. The company is 88 per cent-controlled by an Indian citizen who lives in London. Lakshmi Mittal and his two children sit on the board of directors alongside another Indian, a Mauritian of Indian descent, and four North Americans. The team overseeing the many major acquisitions, including those in Romania, Czech Republic, Poland, and South Africa, mostly comprises Indian engineers, led by Mittal Steel's Chief Operating Officer.[8] The story of South African MNCs is also quite complex. SABMiller, for instance, is British-registered, with dual listing in London and Johannesburg; its management is overwhelmingly of South African nationality, although it is unclear where the managers reside;[9] its major shareholder (Altria) is American and the second-largest (the Santo Domingo family) is Colombian.

Other cases that are difficult to classify include:
- Subsidiaries of OECD-based MNCs in developing countries that in turn invest in other developing countries;
- Emerging-country companies that are controlled by OECD investors – for instance, the largest shareholder in Zentiva, which controls more than 50 per cent of the Czech generic drug market and also has a dominant position in Romania and Slovakia, is Warburg Pincus; and
- EMNCs which buy fixed assets from OECD-based MNCs, and which receive in turn large stakes in the latter (Lenovo/IBM, TCL/Alcatel, BenQ/Siemens).

## 2.2 What are the trends?

It is important to bear in mind these caveats, and the fact that year-on-year variance is very large, when examining the available aggregate statistics. OFDI stock from developing and transition economies has increased rapidly in recent years, from US$147 billion in 1990 to over US$1 trillion in 2004 (see figure 1). The increase in OFDI flows is equally impressive – from an average of slightly more than US$53 billion per year in 1992-98 to more than US$85 billion in 1999-2004, with a peak of US$147 billion in 2000. Global FDI flows, however, rose much faster over this period, and as a result, the share of developing and transition countries has diminished from 14.7 per cent in 1992-98 to 9.9 per cent in 1999-2004, the 2004 share being the highest since 1997. This trend does not diminish the importance of EMNCs, as much as it underlines the fact that the 1990s have seen even stronger international economic integration, led by mergers and acquisitions (M&As), among OECD economies.

Developing and transition economies together accounted for 13 per cent of the world's OFDI stock in 2005, compared with 7 per cent in 1990. OFDI flows as a percentage of gross fixed capital formation (GFCF) are considerably higher than the world average for such economies as Hong Kong (China), Taiwan (Province of China), the Russian Federation, and Singapore.

Among developing economies, those in Asia remain by far the largest FDI sources. The original East Asian Tigers accounted for almost 59 per cent of total emerging-economy OFDI in 1992-98 and 52 per cent in 1999-04. Adding China, the five largest emerging OFDI source economies, all in Asia, accounted for more than two-thirds of the total in 2004. Hong Kong (China) firms allocated 53.2 per cent of their total 2001-03 investment to foreign markets; Singapore channelled 23.3 per cent; and Taiwan (Province of China) 6.4 per cent. For the two latter economies, a large chunk of FDI outflows went to China. Again, the quality of the data on outward FDI flows as percentage of GFCF is debatable – this indicator also reaches suspiciously high levels for countries such as Albania, Gambia, and Laos.

Extreme care is important with data for China, as FDI enjoys favourable treatment compared to domestic investment, resulting in an incentive to label investments as foreign.[10] A significant part of the investments pouring in from Taiwan, Hong Kong, and Singapore is round-trip flows from China's mainland. Despite the distorting effect of round-tripping on Chinese FDI statistics, the abuse of measures intended to attract foreign investment, and the negative consequences for tax revenues, Cross et al. (2004) argue that this round-tripping has brought certain benefits – a sort of second-best practice that has promoted access to international capital markets and has catalyzed the internationalization of Chinese enterprises. As Athukorala (2006, Table 2.3) shows, another, perhaps even more important, problem with Chinese FDI data arises from "over-reporting" of inward FDI, a phenomenon that seems to affect flows from other developing Asian countries more than from OECD countries.

The Russian Federation is another major source of emerging-economy OFDI, with a heavy concentration in the natural resources and transportation sectors of other countries of the former Soviet Union. Gazprom's acquisition of Sibneft has increased the share of State-owned companies in Russian outward FDI. There are also a handful of major regional groups (Lukoil and Yukos Russia) that are emerging with ambitions of becoming regionally dominant oil and gas groups. Russian metal-makers have also become important MNCs. Flat steel producer Severstal aims to become one of the world's six biggest producers and has already completed major acquisitions in two G7 countries (Rouge in the United States, Lucchini in Italy). RusAl is the second largest aluminium company in the world, supplying 10 per cent of world aluminium with production capacities built in former Soviet Union countries as well as Guinea. In the Russian case, the Cypriot offshore sector has developed into a landing place for Russian capital, to the extent that Cyprus is currently the biggest direct investor in Russia. The investment flow from (or via) Cyprus to other Eastern European countries is also relatively big, and a significant share of these "Cypriot" investments is considered to be of Russian origin.

Companies headquartered in other transition economies in Central and Eastern Europe have only recently become outward investors, and their foreign presence is now gaining momentum in Western Europe as well as a result of the May 2004 EU enlargement, although from a very low basis. The privatization of various previously State-owned companies (INA in Croatia, Beopetrol in Serbia and Montenegro) is also opening opportunities for the emergence of regional oil companies such as Hungary's MOL.

Latin American investors such as Argentinean companies, which began cross-border production in the early part of the twentieth century and were still dominating the geography of Southern FDI in the 1970s, now account for a much smaller share (11.7 per cent in 1992-98, falling to 10.6 per cent in 1999-2004). Chile, with the smallest population among the six largest Latin American investors, has consistently ranked among the top 3 FDI sources. While FDI is still small and concentrated in financial centres, Latin American MNCs have a presence abroad in activities such as beverages, petrochemicals, petroleum, mining, steel, cement, pulp and paper, textiles and agribusiness, with little or no presence in technology- or marketing-intensive products like automobiles, electronics, telecommunication equipments and chemicals.

There are two types of *multilatinas*: those that expand regionally (what Rugman (2005) calls "regional multinationals"), and those that expand globally. Intra-regional FDI has increased significantly since the early 2000s. Reasons for this include:

- The retreat of some global MNCs from Latin America since the early 2000s, giving Latin American firms an opportunity to expand their activities in the region;
- Access to oil and gas reserves (Petrobras in Argentina, Bolivia and Venezuela); and
- State policies of regional energy integration (PDVSA in Argentina, Brazil, Cuba, etc.).

The trends in South African data reflect the decision of many of the country's traditional industrial groups and mining houses to transfer their primary listing from Johannesburg to London, as well as the reverse takeover of De Beers by Anglo-American. To further strengthen South African investment abroad, the Government adopted policies to encourage its MNCs to expand into other African countries after apartheid, and in 2004, foreign exchange restrictions were eased on South African companies' outward FDI. More than half of South Africa's FDI outflows are estimated to have gone to other countries in Africa, including other SADC members and elsewhere. South Africa is actively supporting the Maputo Development Corridor public-private partnership, with Nigeria, Mauritius, and the Democratic Republic of Congo as other significant FDI recipients. Many South African firms (ESKOM, MTN, Vodacom, SABMiller and Anglo Gold) have a strong presence both in other African countries and outside Africa, though some of them have moved their headquarters outside South Africa. Another fast-rising African MNC is the Orascom Group from Egypt (Goldstein and Perrin, 2006).

Finally, some oil exporting Gulf States (e.g. Kuwait, Qatar, Saudi Arabia, and the United Arab Emirates) are contributing to South-South OFDI flows at both the intra- and the inter-regional levels, in particular towards Africa and the Indian sub-continent. This "oil money" also provides FDI to developed countries, including the United States, targeting, for instance, hotels and automotive firms.

## 2.3 The geography of EMNCs' investments

Despite the differences in their institutional characteristics, many EMNCs share a tendency to invest regionally and in other developing countries before taking on the rest of the world (table 2). They tend to invest close to their home country and in countries where they have a certain familiarity through trade, or ethnic and cultural ties. Increasing openness to private investment and trade – in particular through privatization of state-owned firms – has provided increased opportunities for investment in developing and transition countries and played an important role in the recent surge of FDI between those countries. For example, Russian investments abroad have primarily been in the countries of the former Soviet Union; Turkey has also been actively investing regionally, particularly in West and Central Asia, and companies from India and China have been particularly active in other Asian countries. EMNCs from Chile, Brazil, and Argentina have expanded their operations mainly in other developing countries in the region, and South African investments in other developing countries are almost completely in the southern part of Africa.

Despite the advantages of intra-regional investments, there are some preliminary indications that developing-country multinationals are increasingly venturing beyond their immediate region. For example, in 2004 about half of China's outward FDI went to natural resources projects in Latin America; Malaysia has emerged as a significant new source of FDI in South Africa (Padayachee and Valodia, 1999); and Brazil has considerable investments in Angola and Nigeria (Goldstein, 2003).

## 2.4 In which industries?

The data considered so far have been largely aggregate FDI flows. Data on FDI flows by industry and source country distribution are even more problematic, as for most countries only simple tabulations based on investment approval records are available. It is well known that there are large differences between approved and realized FDI. Moreover, whether data relating to FDI projects get recorded in official approval data depends on the nature of the FDI regulatory regime. For instance in Thailand there is no requirement for foreign investors to go through any government screening process to invest in the country. As a result, official approval records grossly understate FDI in Thailand.

With these caveats, anecdotal evidence indicates that FDI flows between emerging economies are highly concentrated in the services and extractive sectors, as emerging-country firms have been successfully participating in large privatization and M&A deals in those sectors. Data on cross-border M&A deals completed in developing and transition countries in 2004 reveal that in value terms EMNCs accounted for 47 per cent of regional activity in Africa, 13 per cent in Latin America, 24 per cent in Asia and Oceania, and 25 per cent in South East Europe and the CIS (UNCTAD 2005, Annex table A.II.1). In developing and transition countries, investors from those countries accounted, in value terms, for 27 per cent of activity in energy and 18 per cent in water, versus 59 per cent in transport and 51 per cent in telecom (PPIAF 2005).

Liberalization of the services sector has been an important factor in the recent surge of FDI flows among developing and transition economies. First, privatization of state-owned assets in the infrastructure sector has provided great opportunities for emerging-country companies to acquire important assets domestically and expand regionally. Second, compared to other sectors, the services sector often requires greater proximity between producers and consumers and also favours cultural and ethnic familiarity, which may generate synergies for developing county firms.

In the case of telecommunications, companies from emerging economies have emerged as significant investors (Table 3). This has been particularly so since 2001, as local and regional operators and investors have begun to fill the gap left by the retreat of some of the traditional international operators from infrastructure projects in the developing world (PPIAF 2005). Intra-regional FDI in 1990-2003 has been as high as 49 per cent of total South-South FDI in telecommunications in sub-Saharan Africa and 48 per cent in North Africa and the Middle East (Guislain and Zhen-Wei Qiang, 2006).

Given the low fixed-line penetration and large population, Africa and the Middle East have become the world's fastest-growing telecommunications markets. In sub-Saharan Africa, Vodacom (a joint venture between Telkom (South Africa) and Vodafone (United Kindgom) and MTN (South Africa) jointly have more than 17 million subscribers outside of South Africa (March 2006). If Orascom (Egypt) is one of the Arab world's largest MNCs, in the same sector and region other operators are also raising their investment profile – UAE's Etisalat (in Saudi Arabia, West Africa, and Pakistan), Kuwait's Mobile Telecommunications Company (in the Gulf and Africa), Qatar Telecom (in Oman), and Dubai Tecom Investments (in Malta and Tunisia).

In Latin America, América Movil has been transformed in just over two years, from 2003 to 2005, from a Mexican company with some presence in Central America to the largest telecommunications company in Latin America. It took advantage of the liquidation of emerging markets' assets of United States operators such as AT&T, Bell South, and MCI to reach more than 100 million subscribers in March 2006, compared with 74 million for Telefónica Móviles, its Spanish-owned competitor. Russia's number two mobile service provider VimpelCom controls Kazakhstan's second-largest operator, KarTel, as well as the second- and fourth-largest operators in Uzbekistan, Unitel and Buztel, and Ukraine's fourth-largest operator, Ukrainian Radio Systems (URS). In addition, Altimo (formerly Alfa Group), a Russian holding company and the majority owner of VimpelCom, controls 40 per cent of the second-largest mobile service provider of Ukraine, KyivStar, and the only mobile operator in Turkmenistan, Bashar Communications Technology. In late 2005, Altimo announced its readiness to pay as much as US$3 billion for one of the largest Turkish mobile operators (Vahtra, 2006).

In the oil and gas sector, companies from emerging economies, mostly state-owned, have become active cross-border investors. With their exclusive access to domestic resources, national oil companies are leading players in the market and have expanded their operations globally, both in upstream activities (exploration and production) to diversify their portfolio, and downstream (refining and distribution) to reach consumers directly (Table 4). For example, Venezuela's PDVSA took over CITGO (United States) in 1989 and has long had investments in refineries in Germany, Belgium, United Kingdom and Sweden to process its heavy crude. More recently PDVSA has been expanding in Brazil, Argentina, Chile, and Paraguay. Using their strong technical competencies in deep-water exploration, Brazilian Petrobras and Malaysian Petronas have invested in more than twenty developing countries in exploration and production projects. High-growth economies with limited domestic petroleum resources, such as China and India, have been notably successful in acquiring oil and gas-related assets or licenses in other developing countries.

## 3. Motivations and strategies

The growth in South-North and South-South FDI flows reflects the general rise in capital flows to emerging economies, as well as the increasing size and sophistication of emerging-economy firms. As a result of the increasing globalization of economic activities, companies are faced with growing competition in sales and in access to resources and strategic assets. South-South FDI has been driven mainly by developing countries' increasing openness to capital and trade, and by their increasing participation in international production networks. Still, the question remains, do companies from emerging economies behave like OECD-based MNCs when they expand their operations abroad and hence become EMNCs?

### 3.1 From OLI to LLL?

While the conceptual and theoretical frameworks developed in the international business literature to account for outward FDI and the sustainability of MNCs are well established, the nature of the strategies that EMNCs have pursued, and their specificity compared to those developed earlier by OECD MNCs, remains a relatively neglected topic (Bonaglia et al., 2006). The OLI (ownership/location/internalization) theory is squarely based on the experiences of large, predominantly Anglo-American, successful international firms that could easily find the resources and the capabilities to expand internationally if they wished to do so.[11] On the other hand, when EMNCs decide to invest overseas, they rarely have at hand resources such as proprietary technology, financial capital, brands, and experienced management. They have to internationalize, in new conditions created by globalization, in order to capture the resources needed. Moreover, for them the option of waiting does not seem to exist anymore as protection at home is eroded by market liberalization, time-to-market is reduced, and production runs must increase continuously to control costs. The path of expansion is slow and incremental, with frequent loops of experimental learning. In sum, EMNCs internationalize in order to build advantages – a reversal of the traditional strategy.

Utilizing a perspective that focuses on firms' resources in an international setting, Bonaglia et al. (2006) consider internationalization as a strategy of increasing integration within the global economy. The nature of the competence creation process has changed. The emergence of international production networks has favoured a closer integration of the process of capability accumulation, so that the internationalization strategy becomes heavily intertwined with technological and product diversification strategies (Cantwell and Piscitello, 1999). Analyzing how EMNCs have mastered this process can therefore also offer interesting insights into the broader debate on the relationship between corporate diversification and internationalization.

One interesting facet of the internationalization of EMNCs is the way that they use and leverage various kinds of strategic and organizational innovations in order to establish a presence in industrial sectors already heavily populated with world-class competitors. In doing so, they benefit from a narrow window of opportunity available to them as latecomers. Firstly, they all internationalize very early in their corporate life – Acer (Taiwan, province of China) for instance has evolved rapidly as a worldwide cluster of independent corporate entities (Mathews, 2002). Secondly, EMNCs have been able to achieve this accelerated internationalization not through technological innovation, but through organizational innovations adapted to the emergent global economy. South African retail banks, for instance, are extending so-called mzansi accounts, aimed at domestic low-income users, to their operations in other African countries, while Illovo Sugar, also of South Africa, has enjoyed success in part due to out-grower schemes which incorporate low- and middle-income farmers and collectives (Goldstein and Pritchard, 2006). Third, EMNCs built linkages with existing MNCs in innovative ways that enabled them to exploit their latecomer and peripheral statuses to advantage – Embraer, for instance, went from being a supplier to global aircraft manufacturers to a true multinational with production facilities on four continents (Goldstein, 2002). Mathews (2006) defines this as the new LLL (linkage, leverage and learning) paradigm. A closely related question is, of course, the sustainability of this process.

If the "ownership" assets of EMNCs do not arise solely from their home country and region, but derive as well from their position in the global and regional value chain (which differs by industry), a classification of EMNC strategies must emphasize value-chain analysis and highlight differences between South-South and South-North typologies. Each cell in Table 5 provides an example. BOE Technology of China, for instance, which makes computer monitors, acquired Hynix in Korea to manufacture small-sized flat displays for use in mobile phones and other portable devices in order to improve the efficiency of its core business by exploiting economies of scale and scope. Tata Steel of India, on the other hand, took over NatSteel of Singapore to export its own billets as raw material for the acquired affiliate. Similarly, by taking over OGMA in Portugal, Embraer gained a presence in the European MRO (maintenance, repair and operation) market.

## 3.2 EMNCs' institutional characteristics

EMNCs' strategies are strongly influenced by the business environment of the countries or regions where they are based and do most of their business; by the industrial and development policies of those countries and regions; and by the position of these countries/regions in the international division of labour, including the degree and type of relationship with incumbent MNCs, all of which factors are interrelated. In particular, the fact that the corporate governance structure may differ from the public company model of widespread ownership that is increasingly prevalent in OECD countries (Morck, 2005) may have political-economy consequences, especially when an EMNC is (or is perceived to be) state-owned. A schematic synthesis of the close connections between patterns of national and regional development and the internationalization of companies is presented in Table 6. This point is not novel – the need to incorporate "the peculiar institutional characteristics of Japanese corporations, together with Japanese government policies and practices which crucially affect the foreign corporations of these corporations" was identified in early studies of Japanese MNCs (Mason and Encarnation 1995, p. xix). In fact, most charges made against EMNCs in recent months echo those common in the United States and, to a lesser extent, Europe, in the late 1980s (Goldstein, 2006b).

In the case of Latin American MNCs, the increasing competition due to liberalization in the 1990s has acted as a selection mechanism. Relatively few large companies survived, but those that did are far "leaner and meaner" and therefore able to compete on global markets. The car industry, and in particular manufacturing of parts and components, provides a fine illustration. Most Brazilian and Mexican companies that had grown under import-substitution industrialization since the 1950s have been either taken over by OECD-based competitors, or gone bankrupt. Survivors, however, have proven to be reliable suppliers to American and European assemblers, to the point of being asked to follow their customers and invest overseas. Sao Paulo's Sabó Retentores is a global supplier of oil rings, rubber hoses, and gaskets to Volkswagen and factories in Argentina, Austria, Hungary and the United States – and plans to move into China at the urging of its largest individual customer.

Another example of the relationship between trade policies and OFDI is provided by import restrictions imposed by developed countries on clothing. This was already a key factor behind EMNCs expansion in that industry in the 1980s (Wells, 1994). In recent years, Chinese firms in clothing, footwear and other light manufacturing industries have begun to invest heavily in neighbouring low-wage countries because of threats of import restrictions in the European Union and the United States.

The regional arrangements that have proliferated around the world since the mid-1990s (World Bank, 2005b) have also encouraged intra-regional trade and investments. Some of these arrangements, such as the Southern African Development Community (SADC), the Association of Southeast Asian Nations (ASEAN), MERCOSUR, and the Andean Community offer various incentives for outward investment within the region, including lower tax and tariff rates and easier profit repatriation.[12] Some members of the groups also have bilateral investment agreements and double-taxation treaties. In addition, as in many developed countries, some developing-country governments have provided fiscal and other incentives for outward investment, particularly in the context of South–South FDI flows. For example, China provides loans on preferential terms and tax rebates for investments that facilitate trade. If the investment is in an aid-receiving country, firms can receive preferential loans under Chinese aid programs or projects. Malaysia supports special deals for FDI outflows to countries such as India, the Philippines, Tanzania, and Vietnam (Mirza, 2000). The Thai government actively promotes Thai firms' involvement in infrastructure projects in Mekong countries (UNCTAD, 2005). In Brazil, the national development bank, BNDES, created a special credit line in 2002 to support outward FDI, which is granted on condition that within six years the beneficiary increase exports by an amount equal to the credit. This instrument was first used by Friboi in 2005 to buy Swift in Argentina. One of the measures of the new Brazilian *Política Industrial Tecnológica e de Comércio Exterior* launched in March 2004 is the creation of 38 multi-dimensional external trade units within the Banco do Brasil to support the internationalization of national firms. In November 2005, PIBAC (*Programa de Incentivo aos Investimentos Brasileiros na América Central e no Caribe*) was launched to stimulate Brazilian investment in Central America and benefit from CAFTA-RD, the free trade agreement between SICA (*Sistema de Integración Centro-Americano*) and the United States.

The "North" is also increasingly becoming an important destination for EMNC investments as they try to expand their markets. EMNCs usually enter these developed markets by acquiring companies with well-established market presence and brand name. For example, with very few internationally recognized brand names of their own, Chinese firms such as Lenovo and TCL have acquired well-known Western brand names such as Thompson, RCA, and IBM. Haier's attempt to buy Maytag was not only for its brand name, but also for its distribution channels. Compared to other Southern MNCs, Chinese MNCs seem to have made more attempts to acquire well-known brand names. This strategy was not followed by Japanese and Korean budding MNCs that developed their own brand names in the second half of the last century. A small but increasing number of EMNC investments, mainly from Asia, are being made in developed-country enterprises with R&D assets in order to tap into new technology in a wide range of sectors. There is also some indication that strong economic and cultural ties play a role when these companies invest in developed countries. Almost all FDI outflows from Latin America to high-income OECD countries went to the United States and Spain. Major investment destinations for East Asian investors are the Republic of Korea and Australia. The United Kingdom receives 40 per cent of African – mainly South African – investments in high-income OECD countries.

## 4. Implications for South-South cooperation

Developing countries see South-South cooperation as "an imperative to complement North-South cooperation in order to contribute to the achievement of the internationally agreed development goals, including the Millennium Development Goals" (G-77, 2004). In fact investment, and more generally private sector involvement, is increasingly seen as an area where South-South cooperation can contribute to overcome the most pressing development challenges. As has been discussed above, "in addition to growing political commitment, the new vibrancy in South-South cooperation is reflected in the trends towards increasing flows of South-South trade and investment, as well as collaboration in the monetary and energy sectors" (UN, 2005).

The emergence of Southern multinationals may have important implications for economic development. Firstly, South–South FDI represents an opportunity for low-income countries needing investment capital. Except in the extractive sector, most Northern multinationals are unlikely to invest in small markets as their location decisions are mainly driven by market size (Levy-Yeyati et al., 2002). Southern multinationals, on the other hand, tend to invest in neighbouring developing countries with a similar or lower level of development than their home country. Hence, South–South FDI flows, however small, are significant for many poor countries, particularly those that are close to major Southern investors. In many poor countries, South-South flows account for more than half of total FDI (UNCTAD, 2006). For example, India (in hotels and manufacturing) and China (in manufacturing) account for more than half of FDI in Nepal. Indian firms figure prominently among foreign firms in Sri Lankan manufacturing. Most FDI in Mongolia comes from China and the Russian Federation. In the banking sector, crossborder investment by developing-country investors is more significant in low-income countries (27 per cent of foreign bank assets and 47 per cent of the number of foreign banks) than in middle-income countries (3 per cent of foreign assets and 20 per cent of foreign banks) (World Bank, 2006). Hence, South-South FDI represents an opportunity for low-income countries, and its development impact is particularly important for poverty reduction efforts.

Secondly, in recent years, South-South FDI has played an important role in offsetting the significant decline in FDI flows to developing countries from the North. The enlargement and diversification of the pool of countries' sources of FDI may reduce fluctuations, contributing to the economic development of recipient countries. In fact, following the Argentinean default in 2001, while North-South FDI slumped, several Argentinean assets were bought by Brazilian investors. In May 2002, AmBev, a leading beer and beverage producer, unveiled plans to purchase a one-third share of Argentina's top beer-maker, Quilmes, a deal valued at US$700m. That was the first major foreign investment since the default. That same year, Petrobras, the Brazilian oil company, bought a controlling stake in Perez Companc for some US$1.1 billion.

Third, to the extent that EMNCs have greater familiarity with technology and business practices suitable for developing-country markets, they may enjoy some advantages over industrial-country firms when investing in developing countries.[13] They may for example be able to use more appropriate production processes and use locally available inputs. Moreover, to the extent that a country's absorption capacity is greater with a smaller technological gap between a foreign firm and domestic firms (Durham, 2004), the fact that this gap is smaller in the case of South-South FDI may also be an advantage.

Early work seemed to support the expectation that EMNCs have a more benign impact on host economies than OECD MNCs because they have a better appreciation of local conditions, are culturally closer, and use "intermediate", small-scale technologies" that directly substitute labour for capital. In the most rigorous such study, Lecraw (1977) controlled for industry composition and found that in Thailand foreign investors from other less developed countries (LDC) use more labour-intensive technology than either Thai firms or OECD investors (Table 7). He concluded that, "on balance, LDC firms offered significant benefits to the Thai economy without many of the costs associated with other FDI" (p. 456). In their study of Sri Lankan manufacturing, Athukorala and Jayasuriya (1988) caution against simple comparisons and argue that firm attributes other than nationality can affect capital intensity. Differences between developed countries' MNCs and Third World MNCs were found to be marked in the textiles and wearing apparel industries "where the range of technological possibilities is wide enough to enable significantly different techniques of production to be utilized" (p. 420), but not in the chemical and metal product industries.

Unfortunately, empirical research has not caught up with the policy debate and only some tentative inferences can be made. The only study on the differential impact of nationality on technology transfer and technology compares South African and OECD companies in Tanzania (Kabelwa, 2004). The results show that South-South FDI does indeed have a higher potential. Also on the positive side, the Republic of Korea's Hyundai Motors set up its largest overseas assembly factory in the Indian state of Tamil Nadu, where it also operates an aluminium foundry and a transmission line. Major suppliers from the Republic of Korea also invested in the Ulsan automobile cluster, often through joint ventures with Indian partners. Hyundai now has 85 per cent domestic content, higher than any other foreign-owned car-makers in India (Park, 2004). However, a comparison of different foreign investors in Shandong province in China finds that Korean firms developed many fewer backward linkages with local firms than subsidiaries of United States and Hong Kong (China) firms (Park and Lee, 2003). A similar study that examines whether the nationality of foreign investors affects the degree of vertical spillovers from FDI in the case of Romania found that inflows from distant source countries that are not part of the regional preferential trade agreement are more likely to be associated with positive vertical spillovers (Javorcik et al., 2004). A survey study of investments in Sub-Saharan Africa also found that developing country firms are relatively less integrated in terms of local sourcing (UNIDO, 2006). Distance, agreements and the duration of the investment, among other factors, affect the share of intermediate inputs sourced by multinationals from a host country, which is likely to increase with the distance between the host and the source economy. Given the regional tendencies in South-South FDI flows (often supported by trade agreements) and that such investments are relatively recent, South-South FDI may in some cases have less positive vertical linkages than North-South flows. Although more difficult to substantiate empirically, there is evidence that in services EMNCs have more familiarity with consumer demands and capabilities in project execution than competitors from developed countries. In Uganda, for instance, MTN (the South African telecommunications company) could tap into its in-house expertise to launch services packages more adequate than those offered by its competitor from Britain, which had the advantage of incumbency (Goldstein, 2003). América Movil was similarly successful in fine-tuning its marketing strategy across Latin America and elbowing out competitors from the United States and Europe. The South African retail banking sector has equally been an innovator in extending mzansi accounts, aimed at low-income users in South Africa, to other African countries (Goldstein and Pritchard, 2006). In a similar fashion, Illovo Sugar has enjoyed significant success in part due to its use of outgrower schemes which incorporate low- and middle-income farmers and collectives.

Managing economic and political risks is another area where EMNCs have developed a relative advantage. Egypt's Orascom is the only foreign telecom company operating in Iraq (Goldstein and Perrin, 2006). A related hypothesis is that developing-country firms may be more willing to assume the risks of post-conflict and other politically difficult situations (World Bank, 2006). For example, Chinese companies (not all of them state-owned) are the only foreigners that have invested in Sierra Leone since the end of the civil war (Hilsum, 2006).

FDI flows from other developing countries may pose risks as well as benefits. The operational and financial challenges facing developing-country multinationals, coupled sometimes with deterioration in host-country economic conditions, have contributed to several examples of unsuccessful South–South investment followed by disinvestments. In addition, increased South-South integration could also lead to increased vulnerability of developing countries to an economic crisis. The rise of cross-border flows between developing countries will likely make it easier for shocks to be transmitted between developing countries. This increases the risk of a contagious financial crisis.

South–South FDI is not always more beneficial than North–South FDI. Over the years, the transparency of Northern multinationals' foreign operations, as well as the environmental and labour standards observed in those operations, have improved thanks to corporate social responsibility (CSR) initiatives. Such initiatives are less common among Southern companies, which may have low environmental and labour standards (Save the Children

2005). That said, compliance with corporate governance standards in developing countries is increasing, although significant regional and sectoral variations remain (OECD, 2005). In addition, state ownership is much more prominent among MNCs from developing countries, indicating that considerable amounts of South-South FDI may be driven not only by economic but also by political and strategic factors, which may hinder the stability of these FDI flows in the long term.

South-South investment may also generate benefits to the investing developing economy (as it does for high-income countries). The vast literature on Northern MNCs is inconclusive on the issue and – with very few exceptions – the impact of outward FDI on the source developing countries has not yet been assessed. The impact will depend on a range of factors, including the sectors and particular operations of the EMNCs, whether outward FDI is complementary or a substitute to domestic production, and the absorptive capacity of the recipient countries for new technologies and know-how from abroad. When outward FDI is complementary, as when Southern firms increase their profits by expanding and diversifying their markets, the home economy gains from increased economic activity and employment related to FDI projects, as well as tax revenues. If in the future OFDI becomes a substitute for domestic investment, the impact would not be clear. Survey reports on Southern multinationals, on the other hand, indicate that direct presence in foreign markets has enabled many firms to increase their competitiveness and to respond better to consumer demand. For Chinese firms, foreign operations have tended to be more profitable than domestic operations (Yao and He, 2005). Geographic risk diversification and market access can be crucial for some Southern firms with volatile home markets. In a recent survey, diversification was cited most frequently as one of the benefits that developing country investors expect from outward investments (UNCTAD, 2006).

## 5. Conclusions

As trade in the world economy returns to the high levels prevailing in the early 1900s, companies intensify their cross-border investment activities in different forms and with different purposes. The number of actors that take part in this game is rapidly increasing, with more and more firms going global, or at least regional, at an earlier age. The nature of MNCs is also changing, with an increasing number of countries in developing and transition economies hosting such firms. Existing theories can address this evolution, but the inter-relationships are complex and industry- and corporate-level analyses are essential.

Is there anything inherently new in these trends? Certainly the bases on which EMNCs grow are different, as the traditional OLI advantages give way to LLL. Internationalizing firms from the periphery are pursuing strategies that enable them to catch up with established players, leveraging their latecomer advantages. These include: being able to access strategic assets, new technologies and markets; deploying low-cost engineers in innovative ways; mastering all aspects of manufacturing processes; and others. This pattern of internationalization is very different from the pattern that drove earlier MNC experience, which mostly involved export expansion and trade promotion. To the extent that developing-country firms benefit from better connections to international markets, increased productive capacities, and improved access to natural resources and strategic assets, the debate on adjustment costs, especially social costs in the case of off-shoring of labour-intensive activities, will occupy a central position in source countries. In developing policy options relating to OFDI, due consideration should be given to maximizing the benefits in relation to the costs.

Another contentious issue concerns the behaviour of EMNCs, their willingness to adopt corporate social responsibility (CSR) standards, and ultimately the developmental impact of South-South investment. Different questions are intertwined here: is foreign ownership an issue? Does nationality count? And if so, how? According to one perspective, EMNCs are "more of the same" and in due course, they will converge towards the norms of OECD MNCs. Others question this optimism and argue that insofar as EMNCs are less risk-averse, they are more likely to enter "conflict zones", and their presence may reduce the influence of bilateral and multilateral donors and jeopardize their efforts at improving governance. While it is probably far too early to reach any definitive conclusion – and research on such issues should receive a high priority in academic and policy circles – it is certainly not too early to engage in open and frank policy dialogue with all stakeholders.

The expansion of South–South FDI over the past decade has generated preliminary assessments, largely based on case studies, of the pros and cons of South–South FDI. As more data become available in the years to come, it should be possible to provide a more robust analysis of South–South flows. Greater efforts to collect data are essential to progress. Further empirical research could focus on: (i) the characteristics of Southern multinationals (How do emerging economy enterprises select foreign locations? What types of FDI diversification and product diversification strategies do they follow, and why? Can cross-border merger and acquisition strategies undertaken by developed country multinationals be generalized to emerging market multinationals? In what ways do they compete and collaborate with host country businesses?); and (ii) the extent of spillovers from South–South FDI and how these differ from spillovers from North–South FDI.

Figure 1. OFDI stock by developing and transition regions, 1980–2005 (billions of US dollars)

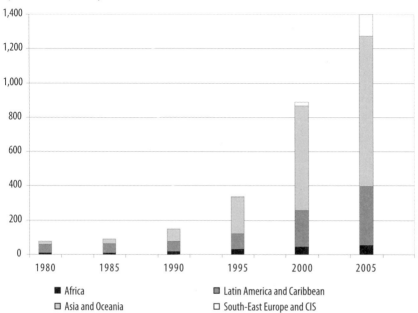

Source: UNCTAD (2006), World Investment Report.

## Table 1.
### OFDI* from emerging regions and selected economies, 1990-2004 (billions of dollars)

| Region/economy | OFDI stock 1990 | OFDI stock 2003 | OFDI stock 2004 | Change in OFDI Stock (i.e. flow in 2003-2004) | OFDI flow as % of GFCF** 2002-2004 | Selected MNCs |
|---|---|---|---|---|---|---|
| World | 1,785 | 8,731 | 9,732 | 1,001 | 8.9 | |
| Developing economies and territories | 147 | 927 | 1,036 | 109 | 2.9 | |
| Africa | 20 | 43 | 46 | 3 | 1.2 | |
| South Africa | 15 | 27 | 29 | 2 | 1.5 | TMN, AngloGold Ashanti, Illovo Sugar, Mondi, Steinhoff |
| Latin America and the Caribbean | 59 | 261 | 272 | 11 | 3.2 | |
| Argentina | 6 | 22 | 22 | 0 | 0.0 | Techint (Tenaris and Tertium) |
| Brazil | 41 | 55 | 64 | 9 | 3.7 | Odebrecht, Gerdau, Embraer |
| Cayman & Virgin Islands (UK) | 2 | 118 | 116 | -2 | 0.0 | |
| Chile | .. | 14 | 14 | 0 | 6.5 | |
| Mexico | 1 | 14 | 16 | 2 | 1.3 | Cemex, Telmex, America Movil, FEMSA, Grupo Alfa |
| Asia and Oceania | 68 | 623 | 718 | 95 | 2.9 | |
| West Asia | 8 | 15 | 15 | 0 | -0.7 | |
| Turkey | 1 | 6 | 7 | 1 | 1.2 | Koç Holdings, Sabanci Holdings, Enka |
| South, East and South-East Asia | 61 | 608 | 703 | 95 | 3.4 | |
| China | 4 | 37 | 39 | 2 | 0.2 | Sinopec, CNOOC, Haier, |
| Hong Kong (China) | 12 | 340 | 406 | 66 | 57.0 | Hutchison Whampoa, Li & Fung |
| Republic of Korea | 2 | 35 | 39 | 4 | 2.0 | Samsung Electronics, LG Electronics, Hyundai, POSCO |
| Taiwan Province of China | 30 | 84 | 91 | 7 | 10.9 | Acer, BenQ, Farmosa |
| South Asia | .. | 6 | 8 | 2 | 0.9 | |
| India | .. | 5 | 7 | 2 | 1.0 | Tata, Infosys, Bharat Forges, Ranbaxy, Mahindra & Mahindra, Cipla, ACE Laboratories |

continued

| Region/economy | OFDI stock 1990 | OFDI stock 2003 | OFDI stock 2004 | Change in OFDI Stock (i.e. flow in 2003-2004) | OFDI flow as % of GFCF** 2002-2004 | Selected MNCs |
|---|---|---|---|---|---|---|
| South-East Asia | 11 | 107 | 120 | 14 | 5.9 | |
| Malaysia | 3 | 12 | 14 | 2 | 7.7 | Petronas, Malayan Banking, Telekom Malaysia, Hong Leong |
| Singapore | 8 | 90 | 101 | 11 | 25.4 | Singapore Airlines, Neptune Orient Lines, SingTel, Keppel Corp., Capital Land, Pacific Int. Lines, Sembcorp Industries, DBS Group |
| South-East Europe and the Commonwealth of Independent States | 0.2 | 77 | 86 | 10 | 5.9 | |
| Russian Federation | .. | 72 | 82 | 10 | 9.1 | Lukoil, Novoship, Norilsk Nickel, Alfa, RusAl, Gazprom |
| Developing economies as percentage of world | 7.3 | 10.6 | 10.6 | 10.8 | .. | |

Source: UNCTAD, FDI/TNCs database.
Obs. : * Outward foreign direct investment ; ** Gross fixed capital formation.

## Table 2.
## Selected EMNCs: the geography of business (end-2005 data, % shares)

| | Own country | Region | "North" | Rest of "South" |
|---|---|---|---|---|
| **Industrial commodities** | | | | |
| Cemex [a] | 27.70 | 15.68 | 40.73 | 15.89 |
| Gerdau [b] | 65.10 | 9.00 | 25.90 | 0 |
| Sappi [b] | 45.65 | 0 | 53.71 | 0.64 |
| Severstal [b] | 75.39 | 0 | 24.61 | 0 |
| **Services** | | | | |
| Orascom [c f] | 14.18 | 25.51 | 31.74 | 28.58 |
| SingTel [c] | 2.08 | 89.82 | 8.10 | 0 |
| **Other manufacturing** | | | | |
| Embraer [b] | 85.90 | | 12.91 | 1.19 |
| Samsung [d] | 42.41 | 20.53 | 30.73 | 6.33 |
| **Natural resources** | | | | |
| CVRD [e] | 22.84 | 6.75 | 43.40 | 27.01 |

Source: Authors' calculation based on companies' reports.
Obs.: a = production ; b = employees ; c = subscribers ; d = capital ; e = sales ; f = March 2006, including Wind.

## Table 3.
## Selected telecom providers in emerging economies
## (March 2006)

| Carrier | Country | Subscribers (millions) | Foreign countries |
|---|---|---|---|
| China Telecom | China | 200 | None |
| América Movil | Mexico | 100 | Argentina, Brazil, Colombia, Ecuador, Guatemala, Nicaragua |
| SingTel | Singapore | 85 | Australia, Bangladesh, India, Indonesia, Philippines, Thailand |
| Vimpel | Russia | 48 | Kazakhstan, Tajikistan, Ukraine, Uzbekistan |
| Orascom | Egypt | 35 | Algeria, Bangladesh, Iraq, Pakistan, Tunisia, Zimbabwe |
| Vodacom | South Africa | 25 | Congo DR, Lesotho, Mozambique, Tanzania |
| MTN | South Africa | 24 | Botswana, Cameron, Congo, Ivory Coast, Rwanda, Swaziland, Uganda, Zambia |
| Hutchinson Telecom | Hong Kong | 21 | Ghana, India, Indonesia, Israel, Macau, Sri Lanka, Thailand, Vietnam |
| MTC | Kuwait | 21 | Bahrain, Burkina Faso, Chad, Congo, Congo DR, Gabon, Iraq, Kenya, Jordan, Lebanon, Madagascar, Malawi, Niger, Nigeria, Sierra Leone, Sudan, Tanzania, Uganda, Zambia |

*Source: Goldstein and Perrin (2006).*

### Table 4.
### Selected southern multinationals in the oil and gas sector

| Corporation (Home Country) | Ownership | 2004 Assets (US$ billion) | Selected countries of operation |
|---|---|---|---|
| NPC (China) | State | 110.6 | Sudan, Venezuela, Kazakhstan, Myanmar, Ecuador, Mauritania, Canada |
| PEMEX (Mexico) | State | 84.1 | Argentina |
| Petro China (China) | State | 58.8 | Sudan, Venezuela, Nigeria |
| Petronas (Malaysia) | State | 53.5 | Sudan, Turkmenistan, Chad, Iran, Myanmar, Cambodia, China, Iran, South Africa, Myanmar |
| Lukoil (Russia) | Private | 29.8 | Iraq, Romania, Ukraine, Bulgaria, Canada, Uzbekistan, Egypt, Morocco, Tunisia, Columbia |
| Petrobras (Brazil) | State (56%) | 19.4 | Argentina, Mexico, Nigeria, Tanzania, Libya, Venezuela |
| PDVSA (Venezuela) | State | 13.4 | Brazil, Argentina, Chile, Paraguay, USA, Germany, Belgium |
| Indian Oil Corp. | State | 10.9 | Ivory Coast, Iran, Libya, Sudan, Russia, Vietnam |
| Saudi Aramco (Saudi Arabia) | State | | China, US, Japan, Canada |

*Source: World Bank (2006).*

### Table 5.
### A typology of EMNCs' deals

| | South-South | | South-North | |
|---|---|---|---|---|
| | Horizontal | Vertical | Horizontal | Vertical |
| Resource-seeking | Hon Hai | | Amica Wronki – Gram | PDVSA – Citgo |
| Efficiency-seeking | BOE Technology – Hynix | Tata Steel | SingPower – SPI PowerNet | |
| Market-seeking | LAN – Argentina and Ecuador | E-valueserve | San Miguel – Berri | Embraer – OGMA |

### Table 6.
### Patterns of national and regional development
### and the internationalization of companies

| Region | Development policies since the 1980s | Characteristics of major MNCs | Competitive advantages |
|---|---|---|---|
| Latin America and the Caribbean | Washington consensus | Private firms, mostly focused on core business (Gerdau – steel; Tenaris – tubes; Embraer – aircraft) | Know-how to play the post-privatization regulatory game and have become leaner and meaner as suppliers to Western MNCs |
| East Asian Tigers | Export-oriented with strong state | Conglomerates (chaebols, Temasek) and contract manufacturers | Innovation capabilities |
| ASEAN | FDI-driven | Conglomerates (CP Group) | Management of mainland China's insertion into global value chains, Guanxi networks |
| China | FDI-driven with strong state | Public-private firms, mostly focused on core business (Lenovo – PCs; Haier – appliances; Huawei – telecom equipment) | Leverage of huge domestic market |
| South Asia | Gradual opening backed by diaspora linkages | Private conglomerates (Tata) and ICT firms (Infosys, Wipro) | Low psychic distance with the US and Commonwealth, engineering skills |
| South Africa | Post-apartheid reconciliation | Unbundled and London-listed conglomerates (Anglo-American, Rembrandt) and state-owned enterprises (Eskom, Transnet) | Regional players in services, strong in project execution capabilities that can be deployed in resource-based economies; global players in mining |
| New Europe | EU convergence | Privatized firms, Turkish conglomerates (Koç, Sabanci) | Regional players in telecoms, electricity and gas, retail |
| Russian Federation and the CIS | Big bang and crony capitalism | State-owned enterprises (Gazprom) and privatized firms still dependent on Kremlin support (Severstal) | Regional players in telecoms; global players in metals and natural resources |

**Table 7.**
**Multinational firms' nationality,**
**factor proportions and spillovers**

| Paper | Country and years | Sample | Methodology | Results |
|---|---|---|---|---|
| Lecraw (1977) | Thailand, unspecified | 88, ad hoc survey | Controlled for other firm attributes | EMNCs are more labour intensive |
| Wells and Warren (1979) | Indonesia | | Compared average factor intensity | EMNCs are more labour intensive |
| Busjeet (1980) | EPZs in Mauritius and the Philippines | 36, interviews | No matching sample | EMNCs are more labour intensive, and scaled technology provides less scope for idle capacity |
| Athukorala and Jayasuriya (1988) | Sri Lanka, 1981 | 101, from manufacturing survey | Controlled for firm size and age, export orientation, wage rate | Links between nationality and capital intensity are industry-specific |
| Kabelwa (2004) | Tanzania | 128, from IPA files | | South African companies have significant potential in terms of technology transfer and spillovers |

## Notes

1 As OECD membership widened to include emerging economies such as Mexico, Republic of Korea, the Czech Republic, Hungary and Poland, the traditional OECD versus non-OECD dichotomy, which held until the early 1990s, has now lost relevance for our purposes. Turkey has been an OECD country since 1964 even though its income level was substantially lower than the OECD average. The definition of developed countries used in this study follows the UN-DESA country classification and includes all members of the OECD Development Assistance Committee. The Republic of Korea and Singapore are not considered developed countries, even though they are now net contributors to the World Bank Group (in other words, they are not eligible for loans anymore). The term "emerging" is used in this paper to include both developing countries and economies in transition.

2 According to the annual Business Week-Interbrand survey, Samsung was ranked 42nd in 2001 and 20th in 2006.

3 Excluding Hutchinson Whampoa for which the 1999 foreign assets data is not available.

4 Note, however, the pioneering experience of Argentine investors in neighbouring countries as early as in 1910 (Kosacoff, 2001). Uruguay also appeared relatively high in the ranking of foreign investors in its two much larger neighbours, Argentina and Brazil (Jacob, 2003). There were also about 100 pre-World War II Chinese MNCs (Mira Wilkins, Professor, Economics Department, Florida International University, personal communication, 16 June 2006).

5 We draw extensively on Goldstein (2006a) and World Bank (2006).

6 Some of the main issues that are not covered in this note include, what are the preferred foreign market modes and strategies by firms from emerging markets? What are the determinants in the choice of these respective modes and strategies? How do EMNCs integrate their foreign expansion with home country operations? How do they coordinate multiple businesses in multiple countries? Can cultural fit explain for the choice of partners/targets in host countries? How does their international experience come into play in various international expansion strategies or activities? What type of hiring policy do they adopt to staff global operations? How is the top management team selected, composed, motivated and evaluated? Likewise, we don't analyze the implications for OECD countries (governments, firms, and civil society) both in the OECD countries themselves – as EMNCs become important sources of FDI, employers, and providers of goods and services (Goldstein 2006b) – and in non-OECD ones – as competitors as well as important actors in the development of the private sector in hitherto unexplored markets.

7 Mira Wilkins drew our attention to the interesting similarity with the history of Simon Patiño, a Bolivian entrepreneur who worked through companies registered in advanced countries, building a tin empire in the intra-war years.

8 As of August 2005, the only non-South African national in the executive committee (and the only woman) was the corporate affairs director, a Briton.

9 In the early years of the twentieth century, Russian interests set up and registered in London a company to make direct investments in Tsarist Russia (Gurushina, 1998). By virtue of its British nature, the Russian Tobacco Company could avoid some regulations in the Commercial Code that discouraged the creation of monopolies in the Russian Empire.

10 Xiao (2004) argues that around 40 per cent of China's FDI inflows are likely to be spurious, a much higher estimation than previous authors had suggested. Over time this share seems to have declined (see Huang, 2003).

11 Dunning (1981; 1986) examined the advantages that international firms drew from extending their operations abroad in terms of three characteristics or sources. There was the potential advantage derived from extending their proprietary assets, such as brands or proprietary technologies, bringing greater fire power to bear on their domestic competitors in foreign markets (the "ownership" advantage). There was the potential advantage of being able to integrate activities across regions of the world with very different factor costs and resource costs (the "location" advantage). Finally there were the potential advantages derived from building economies of scale and scope through internalizing activities spread across borders that would otherwise be dispersed between numerous firms (the "internalization" advantage).

12 Other regional arrangements include the South Asian Association for Regional Cooperation and the Arab South–South Preferential Trade and Investment Agreement, among others.

13 At the same time, "bureaucratic constraints on outward investment, other financial constraints, and a paucity of institutional support and business services" may hamper their competitiveness (World Bank, 2006). Moreover, the overall policy environment in the host economy may not be conducive and supportive and a vibrant entrepreneurial class may not exist.

# Acknowledgements

For detailed comments on earlier versions we thank Prema-chandra Athukorala, Federico Bonaglia, Mónica Kjöllerström, David O'Connor and participants at the conference Industrial Development for the 21st Century: Sustainable Development Perspectives, UN-DESA, New York, 8-9 September 2006. The opinions expressed and arguments employed are the authors' sole responsibility and do not necessarily reflect those of the OECD, the OECD Development Centre, the World Bank Group, or their Members.

# Bibliography

Athukorala, P. (2006), Multinational Enterprises in Asian Development. Cheltenham, UK: Edward Elgar.

---- and S. K. Jayasuriya (1988), Parentage and Factor Proportions: A Comparative Study of Third-World Multinationals in Sri Lankan Manufacturing, Oxford Bulletin of Economics and Statistics, 50 (4), 409-23.

Aykut, D. and D. Ratha, (2004), South–South FDI flows: how big are they?, Transnational Corporations, 13 (1).

Bonaglia, F., A. Goldstein, and J. Mathews (2006), Accelerated Internationalisation by Emerging Multinationals: The Case of the White Goods Sector, mimeo, OECD Development Centre.

Busjeet, V. (1980), Foreign Investors from Less-Developed Countries: A Strategic Profile, doctoral thesis, Graduate School of Business Administration, Harvard University.

Cantwell, J. and L. Piscitello (1999), The Emergence of Corporate International Networks for the Accumulation of Dispersed Technological Capabilities, Management International Review, 39, 123-147.

Cross, A, L. Xin, and H. Tan (2004), China and the 'round-tripping' phenomenon: A re-evaluation and future trends, mimeo, Leeds University Business School, Centre for Chinese Business and Development.

del Sol, P. (2005), Why Join a Chilean Firm to Invest Elsewhere in Latin America?, mimeo, Pontificia Universidad Catolica de Chile.

Dunning, J.H. (1981), Explaining the international direct investment position of countries: towards a dynamic or developmental approach, Weltwirtschaftliches Archiv, 117 (1), 30-64.

---- (1986), The investment development cycle revisited, Weltwirtschaftliches Archiv, 122 (4), 30-64.

Durham, B. J. (2004), Absorptive Capacity and the Effects of Foreign Direct Investment and Equity Foreign Portfolio Investment on Economic Growth, European Economic Review, 48 (2), 285-306.

Erdilek, A. (2005), Case study on outward FDI by Enterprises from Turkey, Background paper for the UNCTAD Conference "Enhancing the Productive Capacity of Developing Country Firms through Internationalization".

G-77 (Group of 77) (2004), Marrakech Declaration on South-South Cooperation, 16-19 December 2004.

Goldstein, A. (2002), Embraer: From National Champion to Global Player, UN-ECLAC (CEPAL) Review, 77, 97–115.

---- (2003), Regional integration, FDI, and competitiveness: the case of SADC. Paris: OECD.

---- (2006a), Emerging Multinationals in the Global Economy. Basingstoke: Palgrave MacMillan.

---- (2006b), Who's Afraid of Emerging Multinationals?, prepared for the conference "The Rise of TNCs from Emerging Markets: Threat or Opportunity?", Columbia Program on International Investment and UNDP Special Unit for South-South Cooperation, New York, 24-25 October 2006.

---- (2006c), Proprietà delle imprese e competitività dei paesi – una relazione complessa, mimeo, OECD Development Centre.

---- and S. Perrin (2006), Orascom Telecom: une multinationale arabe. M. Mezouaghi (ed.), Trajectoires d'insertion dans l'économie numérique: le cas du Maghreb, Maisonneuve & Larose.

---- and W. Pritchard (2006), South African Multinationals: South-South Co-Operation At Its Best?, in Doing Business in Africa, N. Grobelaar (ed.), Johannesburg: SAIIA.

Guislain, P. and C. Zhen-Wei Qiang (2006), Foreign Direct Investment in Telecommunications in Developing Countries, in World Bank Information and Communications for Development 2006: Global Trends and Policies, Washington, DC.

Gurushina, N. (1998), British Free-Standing Companies in Tsarist Russia, in The Free-Standing Company in the World Economy, 1830-1996, Mira Wilkins and Harm Schröter (eds.), Oxford University Press.

Hilsum, L. (2006), We Love China, Granta, 92.

Huang, Y. (2003), Selling China: Foreign Direct Investment during the Reform Era. Cambridge: Cambridge University Press.

Jacob, R. (2003), Cruzando la frontera. Editorial Arpoador.

Javorcik, B. S., K. Saggi and M. Spatareanu (2004), Does it matter where you come from? Vertical spillovers from foreign direct investment and the nationality of investors, World Bank Policy Research Working Paper, 3449.

Jones, G. (2005), Multinationals and Global Capitalism from the Nineteenth to the Twenty-first Century. Oxford University Press.

Kabelwa, G. (2004), Technology Transfer and South African Investment in Tanzania, Economic and Social Research Foundation, Globalisation and East Africa Working Paper Series, 10.

Kosacoff, Bernardo, ed. (2001), Going global from Latin America. The Arcor case. McGraw-Hill (Santiago de Chile).

Lall, S. (ed.) (1983), The New Multinationals: The Spread of Third World Enterprises. Chichester: Wiley.

Lecraw, D. (1977), Direct Investment by Firms from Less Developed Countries, Oxford Economics Papers, 29 (3), pp. 442-457.

Levy-Yeyati, E., U. Panizza, and E. Stein (2002), The cyclical nature of North-South FDI flow, IADB Research Department Working paper, 479.

Mason, M. and D. Encarnation (eds.) (1995), Does Ownership Matter? Japanese Multinationals in Europe. Oxford: Oxford University Press.

Mathews, J. (2002), Dragon Multinationals. Oxford: Oxford University Press.

------ (2006), Strategizing, Disequilibrium, and Profit, Palo Alto, CA: Stanford University Press.

Mirza, H. (2000), The Globalization of Multinational Enterprise Activity and Economic Development, chapter 9 in Business and East Asian Developing-Country Multinationals, St. Martin's Press, Inc.

Morck, R. (ed.) (2005), A History of Corporate Governance around the World, NBER and University of Chicago Press.

OECD (2005), Measuring Globalisation – OECD Handbook on Economic Globalisation Indicators, Paris.

Padayachee, V. and I. Valodia. (1999), Malaysian Investment in South Africa, Journal of Contemporary African Studies, 17.

Park, B. and K. Lee (2003), Comparative Analysis of Foreign Direct Investment in China, Journal of the Asia-Pacific Economy, 13 (1).

Park, J. (2004), Korean Perspective on FDI in India, Economic and Political Weekly, 31, July, 3551-5.

PPIAF (Public Private Infrastructure Advisory Facility) (2005), Developing Country Investors and Operators in Infrastructure, Phase 1 Report.

Pradhan, J. P. (2005), Outward Foreign Direct Investments from India: Recent Trends and Patterns, mimeo, Centre for the Study of Regional Development, Jawaharlal Nehru University, New Delhi.

Rugman, A. M. (2005), The Regional Multinationals, Cambridge: Cambridge University Press.

Sauvant, K. P. (2005), New Sources of FDI: The BRICs, The Journal of World Investment and Trade, 6 (5), 639-711.

Save the Children (2005), Beyond the Rhetoric: Measuring Revenue Transparency in the Oil and Gas Industries.

UN (2005), The state of South-South cooperation, Report of the Secretary-General. A/60/257.

UNCTAD (various years), World Investment Report, Geneva.

UNIDO (2006). Understanding the contributions of different investor categories to development: Implications for targeting strategies, in Africa Foreign Investor Survey 2005. Vienna: United Nations Industrial Development Organization.

Vahtra, P. (2006), Expansion or Exodus? Trends and Developments in Foreign Investments of Russia's Largest Industrial Enterprises, Working paper, PanEuropean Institute, Turku School of Economics <http://www.tukkk.fi/pei/pub>

Vahtra, P. and K. Liuhto (2004), Expansion or Exodus? - Foreign Operations of Russia's Largest Corporations, Electronic Publications of Pan-European Institute, 8/2004 http://www.tukkk.fi/pei.

Wells, L. T. Jr. (1983), Third World Multinationals: The Rise of Foreign Investment from Developing Countries, Cambridge, MA: The M.I.T. Press.

---- (1994), Mobile Exporters: New Foreign Investors in East Asia, in Foreign Direct Investment, K.A. Foot (ed.), Chicago, IL: University of Chicago Press: 173-91.

---- and V. Warren (1979), Developing Country Investors in Indonesia, Bulletin of Indonesian Economic Studies, 15 (1), 69-84.

Wong, J. and S. Chan (2003), China's Outward Direct Investment: Expanding Worldwide, China: An International Journal, 1 (2), 273–301.

World Bank (various years), Global Development Finance, Washington, DC.

---- (2005b), Global Economic Prospects, Washington, DC.

Yao, Y. and Y. He (2005), Chinese outward firms. A study for FIAS/IFC/MIGA, Beijing: China Center for Economic Research, Peking University, mimeo.

Xiao, G. (2004), Round-Tripping Foreign Direct Investment in the People's Republic of China: Scale, Causes and Implications, ADB Institute Discussion Paper, 7.

# Part 2

# Sector Studies

# Natural resource-based industries: Prospects for Africa's agriculture

Mónica Kjöllerström and Kledia Dallto*

## 1. Introduction

At the same time that China and other emerging markets in Asia are displacing higher cost competitors in manufactured goods and world manufactures export prices are falling, world demand for raw materials, including oil, metals, wood, some agricultural products, and precious stones has been rising since the late nineties, with the rapidly growing economies of Asia (the so-called 'Asian drivers') accounting for much of the growth (Kaplinsky, 2005).

The main premises of this paper are that the prospect of a relatively extended commodity boom can be used to the benefit of raw material rich Sub-Saharan Africa (henceforth, Africa), and that natural-resource based growth can also be sustained in that continent, as has happened elsewhere. To be sure, such a boom is bound to produce only transient benefits unless efforts to increase value-added are undertaken. It is precisely the fact that so many natural-resource rich countries have been unable to upgrade in this sense that has led researchers and policy-makers to promote industrialization in order to avoid the so-called "natural resource curse". In addition, too often primary and resource-based products have been equated to low tech, low R&D because of the limited amount of processing. In fact, many of them are nowadays intensive in knowledge and/or services, and thus can have more value-added than some processed industrial goods.

After making the case for natural resource-based growth in section 2, an overview of Africa's economic structure and quality of integration in world markets for primary and natural resource-based goods, with emphasis on agricultural products (including fisheries) is presented in section 3. Section 4 draws on the experiences of Chile, in Latin America, and Malaysia, in Asia, to show how specialization in primary or natural resource-based products led to sustained economic growth as a result of deliberate actions to create a competitive

* Policy Integration and Analysis Branch, Division for Sustainable Development, UN-DESA, United Nations, New York, and IDPM, The University of Manchester, United Kingdom (Ph.D. candidate), respectively. The views expressed in this document are those of the authors and do not necessarily coincide with those of the organizations to which they are affiliated.

advantage in these products. Section 5 discusses some of the challenges associated with pursuing such a strategy in Africa given its current capabilities, and the contributing factors to success stories, and section 6 concludes.

## 2. Making the case for natural resource-based growth

The Chilean experience shows that it is possible to sustain high export and GDP growth rates specializing in natural-resource-based high-value exports, including mining and agricultural products. In Africa, Botswana has managed to escape the natural resource curse, achieving high growth rates boosted by diamond exports. Agriculture also played an important role in the industrialization processes of Malaysia and Thailand.

While no one disputes the success stories of natural resource-based growth mentioned above, and many of the positive characteristics associated with non- traditional primary goods are acknowledged in the literature making the case for industrialization as a condition for sustained growth and competitiveness, this tends to be done to illustrate "the exception confirming the rule". The fact that rapid economic growth in East and South-East Asia has been based largely on the development of manufacturing for both domestic and export markets, and that specialization in natural resource-based sectors has produced far less satisfactory results in Latin America has been used as evidence supporting this notion (see, for instance, Lall, Albaladejo and Moreira, 2004). More broadly, it is widely held that natural resource-based sectors exhibit lower productivity growth, are less dynamic in international trade and encompass fewer linkages with the rest of the economy, thus having lower multiplier effects. In addition, expansion of the manufacturing sector is viewed to go hand in hand with the development of educational systems and modern institutions and legal structures, as well as new skills and attitudes that contribute to socio-economic development (Lall, 2005).

A growing body of literature suggests that this does not always hold. At the very least, we hope to convince the reader that specialization in manufacturing is not a necessary condition for sustained economic growth by examining critically the principal misconceptions entertained about natural resources and natural resource-based growth. At this point, we would also like to point out that the distributive consequences of such a development pattern are only addressed marginally in this chapter.

The inverse correlation between per capita GDP growth and abundance of (dependence on) natural resources has come to be known as the "resource curse" hypothesis (Sachs and Warner, 1999). The "resource curse" regularity has been used to argue that countries should focus on manufacturing for their economic development, although evidence on the underlying causes of the relationship is fairly weak. For instance, in this literature, it is implicitly assumed that resource reliance is a measure of development failure, while it could be a result of building upon a country's comparative advantage. Resource reliance does not simply reflect a country's exogenous natural endowment, but it is also a function of endogenous efforts to make natural resources economically relevant (Stijns, 2005).

More broadly, while in many countries the discovery of natural resources has led to conflicts, and/or very little of the significant rents have been used to invest in people or infrastructure, elsewhere the same discovery has been a "blessing" rather than a curse, as economies have flourished building on the income generated by natural resource exports. In Sweden and Finland, for instance, the knowledge and networks established by the thriving forestry sector were instrumental in eventually making these countries highly competitive in a range of high tech products and in helping to keep the forestry sector itself competitive in face of lower cost producers such as Chile, Brazil and some Eastern European countries (Ferranti et al., 2002). Attributing growth failures to resource endowments hence seems far-fetched and suggests that the underlying causes of growth failures lie within the realm of policy choice (Wright, 2001). Sala-i-Martin and Subramanian (2003) find that once "institutions are controlled for there is either very little effect of natural resources on growth or even a positive effect". This is in line with Acemoglu and Johnson's (2003) finding – based on a cross-section of developing countries – that institutions constraining government and elite expropriation have a large positive effect on investment rates and long-run economic growth.

"Dutch disease" effects are argued to be one of the causes of the "resource curse", but in fact there are various examples suggesting that commodity booms do not necessarily stall economic growth provided rents are managed adequately. In Norway, after the discovery of oil in the North Sea in 1969, economic growth accelerated for the following 25 years, allowing the country to catch-up and then exceed its otherwise highly similar Scandinavian neighbours, Denmark and Sweden, in terms of GDP per capita (Larsen, 2005). In Botswana, reliance on diamond exports has contributed to a notable economic performance, both in relation to the region's average GDP growth, but also in relation to other regions, including East Asia. Between 1965 and 1998, PPP adjusted GDP per capita grew at 8 per cent annually and in 1998 it was four times the average for Africa (Acemoglu, Johnson and Robinson, 2003). Key government initiatives included the establishment of a revenue stabilization and public debt service fund in 1972 (whereby windfall earnings are invested in foreign assets to avoid exchange rate pressure and the interest generated is an important part of government revenues), and implementation of National Development Plans, which determine public expenditure and are voted into force by the Parliament (ODI, 2006).

By another contention, natural-resource based sectors exhibit relatively slow (total factor) productivity growth. As productivity growth is the main determinant of economic growth in the long run, structural change away from primary production towards manufacturing is assumed to be a precondition for sustained economic growth. The dearth of comparable productivity estimates for manufacturing and non-manufacturing sectors has contributed to this being accepted as matter of fact. There is however a growing body of evidence suggesting that the opposite is true. Productivity growth has been shown to be higher in the agricultural sector than in manufacturing, in both developed and developing countries (table 1). In addition, convergence in agricultural productivity across countries appears to be relatively rapid (Martin and Mitra, 2001). One cause of concern is relatively low agricultural TFP growth in Africa, which by one estimate grew by approximately one-fifth of the growth rate in Asia (Coelli and Rao, 2003).

For a set of 14 OECD countries during the 1970-1987 period, Bernard and Jones (1996) estimate that total factor productivity growth was on average highest in agriculture, but negative in mining. Evidence for petroleum, coal and copper extraction in the United States, however, shows that while multi-factor productivity growth was indeed negative for these activities during the 1970s, it has improved significantly since then, as a result of restructuring of the industry but also significant technological developments and improvements in handling systems.[1] In fact, over the longer term, the costs of extraction of many minerals have declined substantially, despite the need to exploit lower grade and more remote and hard to process deposits (Tilton and Landsberg, 1997).

With respect to agriculture, reliance on a finite factor of production (land) means that there is a ceiling on how much can be planted (even considering that significant improvements in yields can be achieved through technological innovations and infrastructure investments). Also, the percentage of household income spent on food decreases as incomes grow. This would (and indeed generally does) translate into lower average growth rates for the agricultural sector than for the non-agricultural sector, and to the decreasing share of agriculture in GDP as a country becomes more developed. This well established empirical regularity does not, however, tell us anything with respect to the contribution of the agricultural sector[2] to economic growth in terms of spillover effects (Bravo-Ortega and Lederman, 2005b).

Research drawing on social accounting matrices (SAM) – which consider both intermediate and final demand across sectors – suggests that the declining share of agriculture in national production is in fact due to the agricultural sector's strong multiplier effects on the rest of the economy, contrary to what the early literature on linkages suggested. Even at the lowest levels of development, where linkages from intermediate demand are weak, expenditures on non-tradable goods and services from rural households following an increase in agricultural incomes – final demand linkages – are substantial (Vogel, 1994). This is in line with Bravo-Ortega and Lederman's (2005b) econometric results, which show a significant positive effect from growth in the agricultural sector to the rest of the economy in developing countries, whereas the contribution of the non-agricultural sector's growth to the agricultural sector is found to be negative or not statistically significant across regions. In their model, the impact of agriculture on other sectors depends on which dominates: (a) the resource-pull effect (for a sector to grow it needs factors of production that are in fixed supply in the short-run), or (b) positive externalities associated with productivity gains. These positive externalities can arise from the direct demand stimulus associated with technological improvements or from indirect effects (e.g. release of labour and capital from agriculture to other sectors; increased demand for non-agricultural products). The empirical analysis suggests that the second effect dominates in developing countries, whereas the opposite is true in developed countries.

By contrast, the empirical record for extractive industries suggests that linkages with the rest of the economy in developing countries are relatively poor.[3]

Yet another reason why agriculture and other natural resource-based sectors are said to lead to stalled economic growth is that they exhibit declining terms of trade. However, although increases in prices in the 2000-2004 period have been transitory for some commodities and increased supply has since brought prices down[4], overall it seems that primary and resource-based products may not be under as much relative price pressure as traditionally assumed, given the effect of mainly China's (but also India's) growing presence in world markets as net importers of many of those goods and net exporters of many manufactures (Kaplinsky and Paulino, 2004). Using Lall's (2000) classification, Kaplinsky and Paulino find that while high tech sectors have been relatively immune to price pressure, both low tech and engineering sectors have been affected by falling unit prices to a greater extent than resource-intensive sectors.

Cashin and McDermott (2002) find a downward long-run trend in real commodity prices over the period 1862-1999, but they argue that because the trend is small (one per cent annual decline) and totally dominated by the variability in prices, it is of little practical policy relevance.

While high price volatility does pose a challenge for commodity-reliant countries, and the prospects for commodity prices remain uncertain in the short to medium run, growth in demand in Asia will at the very least provide space for developing countries expanding their commodity exports in volume terms. WTO (2005) data for the volume of exports of agricultural products and fuel & mining products show an annual average growth rate of 3.6 per cent between 1990 and 2004, compared to 1.6 per cent and 0.9 per cent, respectively, between 1980 and 1990. While manufacturing exports remain the fastest growing sector in real terms (6.3 per cent between 1990 and 2004; 5.7 per cent between 1980 and 1990), the gap has been reduced.

On the other hand, it seems increasingly likely that the development of low-tech manufacturing sectors in Africa will be stymied by competition from Asia, especially from China. Hence, it may well be that, for Africa, "industrial development will be a relatively less attractive development option in the short- to medium-run" (Kaplinsky and Morris, 2006, p.33).

Below we address the related issue of innovation cum knowledge intensity in primary and natural resource-based sectors. Kaplinsky and Paulino's (2004) analysis of unit value trends across sectors of varying "innovation content" shows that there is no straightforward correlation between the two, with the exception of goods within the "high tech excluding engineering" category. However, as the authors themselves remark, using unit values as indicators of innovation intensity, and thus competitiveness, implicitly assumes that cost-reducing technical change/innovation is neutral across sectors. While primary sectors are not included in their analysis, there is a significant amount of evidence that increased productivity in primary sectors has steeply reduced production costs for many commodities even as prices were declining.

Lall, Weiss and Zhang (2006) classify products according to "sophistication", inferring product characteristics from the characteristics of the exporter rather than from the technology content of the parent industry.[5] They find that, while there is a link between sophistication and technological depth at the extremes, there is no clear relation otherwise. For instance, electronic products (classified as high-tech) have a lower sophistication score than all of the goods in medium technology categories, suggesting production relocation towards low wage countries. In addition, and more significant from our point of view, is the fact that many resource-based products do not conform at all to the assumption that high sophistication is synonymous with technological depth. While in some cases (e.g. tobacco, dairy products) a low-tech/high-sophistication combination is due to significant trade barriers, in other cases, such as essential oils, perfumes and flavours, but also chocolates and cheese, such a combination reflects product differentiation achieved through branding and specialized skills. The same is true for the (on average) low-tech fashion cluster, which includes a number of very "sophisticated" products, from special textile fabrics to lace and embroidery, which are skill and knowledge intensive.

We disagree however with these authors' view that "primary exports do not raise significant issues on technology" (p.224). Significant trade in fresh agricultural produce, for instance, is a relatively new phenomenon, intrinsically related to innovations in inputs (e.g. improved seeds and feed), post-harvest/slaughter (e.g. irradiation and temperature treatments; animal traceability; packing and labelling), logistics (transport and distribution systems) and in the use of specialized skills (e.g. in the introduction and adaptation of new varieties/species to local conditions). For many of these export products, embedded knowledge and service content are inversely related to the degree of processing (e.g. fresh fruits versus canned fruits). Among developing countries, trade in high-value agricultural products is concentrated in the richest among them (Jaffe, 1998; VEK-World Bank, 2004; UN-ECLAC, 2005).

Within dynamic global value chains (see next section), differentiated products such as organic fruits and vegetables, or free range poultry, obtain premium prices, but even in relatively stagnant commodities one increasingly observes processes of differentiation and value-addition. Premium coffees, for instance, are virtually insulated from what happens in the conventional coffee market, reaping prices up to six times higher (Kaplinsky, 2004). In Argentina, a specific classification for the corn variety Flint was introduced in 1997, effectively segmenting the market. Until then, the two main varieties of corn in Argentina (hybrid of US origin and Flint) were both classified as tipo duro, coloured. While hybrids improved productivity, average quality was reduced. The segmentation of the market has thus allowed Argentina to enter markets demanding a specific quality level (Brooks and Lucatelli, 2004). In the food industry, numerous new products and brands are brought to market every year. Packaging and branding allow for horizontal differentiation, while higher quality and service content (e.g. ready to cook meals) permit vertical differentiation (Brooks and Lucatelli, 2004).

In minerals, more sophisticated surveying techniques, improved extraction technologies and other innovations can "expand a country's resource base, effectively creating new natural resources from an economic standpoint" (Watkins, 2006, p.510).

Commodities are commonly conceived as products with low barriers to entry (Kaplinsky and Paulino, 2004). Innovating in production/extraction processes and in marketing and distribution raises such barriers; indeed, many primary products offer significant opportunities for upgrading.

In conclusion, there is substantial evidence supporting our view that specialization in primary and/or natural resource-based goods has the potential to lead to sustained economic growth. Nevertheless, while such a pattern of specialization is not necessarily a curse, it has been one in practice in many developing countries, among which African countries figure prominently.

## 3. Quality of Africa's insertion in world markets

In this section, we look at the depth and quality of Africa's insertion in world markets for primary and natural resource-based products, with emphasis on the agricultural sector (including fisheries). Recent papers have addressed at length the opportunities for Africa's mineral sector and discussed the institutional set-ups that might improve resource rent management (e.g. ODI, 2006). Whereas in a number of net fuel and mineral exporters, these products are likely to remain dominant features of the economy, a large number of African countries are dependent on agriculture for both GDP and exports. While on average the agricultural sector accounts for 20 per cent of GDP, in some LDCs this percentage reaches 50 per cent. Overall, agricultural exports (including raw materials and processed foods) represent half of total merchandise exports from African countries, exceeding 80 per cent in some.[6] Furthermore, over 30 per cent of the African population depends on agriculture for their livelihood, but this share reaches 95 per cent in some of the poorest regions (European Commission, 2005).

## 3.1 Dynamic primary products and resource-based manufactures

Goods for which demand is growing relatively fast offer opportunities for export growth. These dynamic products typically include (but do not necessarily coincide with) differentiated products which command higher prices than standardized ones. UNCTAD has authored a number of publications on this subject. In the 2002 Trade and Development Report, for instance, it finds that "primary products and resource-based manufactures have steadily lost shares over the past several decades", while "non-resource based manufactures have been driving export growth" (p.143). Aggregating products into categories conceals variations at the product level. Furthermore, increased participation of developing countries in high-tech exports has been highly concentrated in East Asia and, until recently, largely relied on the technologically simpler, more labour intensive processes.

Here we replicate the UNCTAD exercise using recent data to capture the emergence of the so-called Asian drivers and their significant impact on the demand for raw materials and natural resource-based goods. We use Lall's (2000) SITC Rev.2 commodity categories for technological content[7] but highlight the dynamics of products within the primary and resource-based categories over the 1990-2004 period. All data are from UN-COMTRADE. Import values were used to estimate world trade, which includes intra-EU trade. COMTRADE reports trade volumes only for a small number of products (basically, primary commodities). The analysis is thus exclusively based on nominal trade values.

Based on average (compounded) annual growth rates, we find that the 50 per cent fastest growing products (at the 4-digit level) in world trade (i.e. with growth rates above the median, 5.3 per cent) accounted for 84 per cent of total world imports in 2004. Medium & high tech goods accounted for roughly 60 per cent of world trade in dynamic products thus defined (34 per cent and 26 per cent, respectively), primary goods for 14 per cent, resource-based goods for 11 per cent and low tech goods for the remaining 14 per cent.

In a further refinement, we created a group of "highly dynamic" products, which in addition to exhibiting average annual growth rates above the median, also increased their share in total world trade in the period under consideration (this means in effect growing above the average for total world trade, 7.1 per cent). "Highly dynamic" products represent roughly only one-fifth of the total number of products at the 4-digit level but accounted for almost two-thirds of world trade as of 2004. While at the aggregate level only high-tech goods have gained market share over the period under consideration, we find that, in addition to mineral fuels, a few other primary products and roughly one-fifth of natural resource-based manufactures are highly dynamic. True, non-fuel highly dynamic primary commodities represent a very small share of world trade (0.5 per cent), and resource-based commodities account for only around 6 per cent (figure 1). Still, goods with very different unit values are being compared and it is noteworthy, for instance, that imports of (fresh or chilled) fish fillets[8], within primary goods, or of palm oil, within resource-based manufactures, have grown faster than many goods in the manufacturing sector, increasing their respective market shares in world trade by 75 per cent and 84 per cent, respectively, between 1990 and 2004.

Table 2 provides an illustrative list of the "dynamic"/"highly dynamic" agricultural goods under the primary and resource-based categories.

Between 1980 and 2000 Africa had a generally poor performance as far as world market share in more technologically sophisticated manufactured products is concerned, the two exceptions being South Africa and Mauritius. African resource-based manufactures and primary products increased their share of world trade. Among the former, however, only mineral-based manufactures increased their shares and, among the latter, most growth was explained by oil exports (Lall, 2005).

Although there is an improvement in world market shares for African low- and medium-tech manufactures when comparing 2004 to 1990, our estimates based on UN-COMTRADE data indicate that, as of 2004, African exports (mirrored by world imports) still accounted for a very small fraction of world trade in manufactures (0.1 per cent, 0.5 per cent and 0.6 per cent of world trade in high-tech, medium-tech and low-tech manufactures, respectively; 2.0 per cent of world trade in NR-based manufactures). The only category where Africa has an important world market share is in primary products (6.7 per cent), although without South Africa the market share drops to 5.5 per cent, largely on account of that country's significant share in the non-fuel primary mineral products category.

A more detailed analysis based on the definition of "dynamic" products adopted earlier reveals further insights into the pattern of specialization in Africa. While its share of dynamic primary products is relatively high (7.3 per cent) – actually growing by 0.1 percentage points over the 1990-2004, this is largely accounted for by high growth in demand for fuels. Its market share is relatively high in the case of fuels and other minerals (8.2 per cent and 6.5 per cent, respectively), and only 2.3 per cent in the case of dynamic agricultural goods.

Africa's share of world trade in dynamic natural resource-based manufactures, on the other hand, is small and stagnant (at 1.8 per cent), and its share in dynamic agro-based manufactures trade, which includes many goods for which demand is elastic and/or with high unit value, is growing but still incipient (0.6 per cent in 2004 vs. 0.4 per cent in 1990).[9] One important driver of this pattern of specialization is increased demand from Asia, especially from China. In 2004, China accounted for roughly 9 per cent of Africa's exports, up from 1 per cent in 1995. Minerals and forestry products account for the lion's share of Africa's exports to China (Goldstein et al., 2006).

As shown below, Africa is a major exporter of "typical" primary commodities, of which only cocoa is a dynamic one, but it has been increasing its market share, sometimes very significantly, for some dynamic, high unit value agricultural products. Unfortunately, exports of products in the latter group are still very small and concentrated in a handful of countries, and processes of value-addition and differentiation in traditional export sectors have been limited.

## 3.2 Traditional agricultural export products

Africa's agricultural exports are concentrated in a few commodities – including coffee, tea, raw cane sugar, cocoa, and cotton. Africa is the largest producer of cocoa beans (about 70 per cent of world production on average in the 2000-2004 period, representing a 25 per cent increase in volume terms over the 1980-2004 period) and has relatively significant shares in world production of green coffee (13 per cent), bananas (10 per cent), cotton (9 per cent) and sugar cane (6 per cent) (European Commission, 2005). Most exports go to countries outside the region. The European Union is Africa's most important trade partner by far in agricultural goods (table 3).

Production has increased for all of these products with the exception of coffee, which happens to be one of the most valuable export commodities where Africa has traditionally been a major player in world markets. As of 2004, Africa's green coffee production stood at 80 per cent of its 1980 level. The main determinants of this decline are increasing competition from exporters in Latin America (Brazil, Colombia) and East Asia (Vietnam) and stagnant productivity – while farm yields in the rest of the world increase (European Commission, 2005) (see box 1).

One alternative to the commodity coffee market is to focus on market niches such as organic or specialty coffee. The ability to enter these profitable markets presents significant challenges for producing countries, including the fact they are relatively small in terms of traded volumes and that they require substantial investments in developing certification bodies (Rodrigues and Torres, 2003). Foreign organic production systems are typically not recognized in developed country markets, and thus organic products must be re-certified in order to be sold as such, entailing significant costs (see Garcia and Bañados, 2004, for Chile; Gómez et al., 2005, for Mexico; Basu and Grote, 2006, for China). Still, the market for organic produce is growing fast. Expansion is likely to be enhanced as large retailers like Wal-Mart enter this market segment.[10]

Ghana and the Ivory Coast remain by far the world's largest producers of cocoa. Indonesia and Brazil are the largest producers outside of Africa.[11]

Other (significant) producing countries in Africa include Cameroon, Gabon, Nigeria and Togo. Cocoa production in Indonesia has undergone significant expansion since the early eighties, increasing by a factor of 20 between 81/82 and 96/97. The expansion programme was encouraged by a number of factors, including government grants to buy land and incorporation of planting technology and husbandry used in Malaysian plantations (ICCO, 2005 and 2003). Between 1970 and 1997, Africa's market share in cocoa is estimated to have fallen by 20 per cent in favour of Asia, which saw its share rise by roughly the same proportion (Iyoha, 2005).

---

### Box 1

In Viet Nam, as a result of reforms undertaken since 1986[12], the area cultivated with coffee grew at a phenomenal rate over the following decade and production expanded commensurably, making Vietnam the third largest world coffee producer (Minot, 1998). Most coffee grown in Vietnam is of the lower quality, lower cost Robusta variety which is mainly used in instant coffee and blends. In Africa, half of total production consists of Robusta coffee (Uganda and Ivory Coast being the main producers in the region) and the remainder the higher quality, higher price Arabica variety. The most important sources of Arabica coffee in Africa are Ethiopia and Kenya. The latter thus compete more directly with Colombia and Brazil (where Arabica coffee accounts for 100 per cent and 80 per cent of total coffee bean production respectively). While Arabica prices typically exceed Robusta prices by 50 per cent, oversupply in the coffee market has affected both, and demand for the latter has been growing faster (e.g. as a result of growing demand for espresso, which requires fewer coffee beans per serving and more robusta to increase the caffeine "kick"). New technologies have also contributed to widening the use of the Robusta variety (Scholer, 2004).

---

Global consumption of cocoa has been increasing steadily. Africa has an important market share in the world's main consuming markets, including the EU and the United States, but also in China. In 2004, cocoa bean imports from Africa accounted for 94 per cent, 59 per cent and 68 per cent, of these countries' imports, respectively. African cocoa powder exports also hold an important market share in extra-EU imports, although imports of cocoa powder are only a fraction (3 per cent) of imports of cocoa beans, as most of the grinding takes place within the EU.[13]

One interesting development in the Ivory Coast has been the increase in its share of cocoa grinding (leading to its becoming the world's third largest processing country since 1998/99, after the Netherlands and the United States). According to ICCO (2005), this "has partly resulted from government policies geared towards exporting value-added semi-finished products rather than raw cocoa beans, triggering substantial investments in cocoa processing capacity at origin by multinational companies" (p.13). At the same time, however, dismantlement of the cocoa parastatal marketing board in the early nineties, major policy errors (including withholding cocoa from the market in the late eighties in the face of growing competition from Asia), combined with more recent political turmoil have been accompanied by a steep reduction in the share of high quality cocoa beans. In Ghana, for the time being, effective operation of the cocoa state marketing board has kept production up to high quality standards (Kaplinsky, 2004). In addition to quality, low yields are a problem. A small cocoa farm in the Ivory Coast produces an average of 450 kg per hectare (ha) and in Ghana 300 kg/ha, whereas yields reach 1500 kg/ha in Indonesia. Government intervention (including the distribution of seedlings of the high yielding variety) was instrumental in the expansion of production, yields and participation of smallholders in Indonesia[14] (ICCO, 2003 and 2000).

*Sugar* is a stagnant commodity largely as a result of oversupply due to protectionism in OECD countries. Sugar's world market prices are, together with cotton, some of the most distorted. In fact, despite the fact that the cost of producing sugar from cane is approximately half the cost of producing it from beets, in 2000 27 per cent of the world's sugar came from beets, which are almost entirely produced in the EU, the United States, Japan and Eastern Europe (Mitchell, 2004). Although the EU is the second largest net exporter of sugar[15] (after Brazil, the most competitive producer in the world) as a result of import protection and export subsidies, it provides trade preferences to some ACP countries under the Sugar Protocol and an associated agreement (Mauritius being the largest beneficiary) and to LDCs under the Everything But Arms (EBA) initiative[16]. As of 2004, Africa's share of extra-EU raw sugar imports reached 53 per cent.[17] While some LDCs, such as Ethiopia and Mozambique, have been able to develop their sugar sector as a result of these preferences, overall imports from African LDCs are insignificant compared to the EU's total sugar consumption, which remains largely supplied by domestic producers (Oxfam, 2004).

The reform of the EU sugar regime (which came into force on 1 July 2006, cutting production and internal prices, but maintaining tariffs on imports) will affect different African producers differently. All countries currently benefiting from preferential treatment in the EU will be negatively affected to a certain extent, with the highest impact being felt in Mauritius (as it currently enjoys a large quota and has high production costs). Other countries, including Malawi, Mozambique, Swaziland, Zambia and Zimbabwe, are among the most competitive producers in the world and will probably withstand the ensuing fall in EU import prices. South Africa, the largest producer in Africa and seventh in the world, on the other hand, does not currently benefit from preferential treatment in the EU. If, as expected,

EU sugar exports fall as a result of the reform, new world market space would be created and South Africa, as well as other competitive producers in the continent, could potentially occupy that space, depending on their ability to compete with Brazil (Malzbender, 2003).

Production of sugar as an intermediate input to the regional biofuel industry could represent an alternative for African sugar cane growers (as happens already in Brazil) and simultaneously help reduce dependence on imported fossil fuels (most African countries are net importers of oil). Mauritius, for instance, is already looking at developing its bioethanol industry. In addition, the expansion of demand for sugar/ethanol in the EU and US markets (as a result of both regulation and market driven incentives to increase biofuels' share in total fuel consumption) could become an opportunity for upgrading in the African sugar sector as well. MFN duties applied to bioethanol are steep in both the EU and the US, but African countries (with the exception of South Africa) do not pay duties in the EU (Teixeira Coelho, 2005). Among ACP countries, Swaziland and Zimbabwe are the leading exporters. The only LDC supplying the EU with bioethanol, albeit in a highly erratic manner, has been the Democratic Republic of the Congo (European Commission, 2006).

As of 2004, EU *banana* imports were managed under a tariff-quota regime which benefited African producers to the detriment of Latin American producers. Still, the latter remain the EU's main suppliers. African exports held a 14 per cent market share as of 2004.[18] Following an agreement reached with the US and Ecuador in 2001, the EU committed to a transition to a tariff-only import system starting in January 2006. It has now put in place a dual system where an import tariff of 176 euros per metric ton on bananas is imposed on MFN suppliers, and ACP countries are allowed to export duty-free under an annual import quota of 775,000 tons.[19] A re-examination of the internal aspects of the Common Market Organisation (CMO) that regulates aid to European banana producers is now being undertaken and is due to be released this summer (European Commission, 2006). Duty phase-out under EBA for bananas took place in January 2006, which could potentially benefit African LDCs. Still, one should note that the two largest African exporters (Ivory Coast and Cameroon) are not LDCs and that yields (according to FAOSTAT) are well below those prevailing in the largest EU suppliers (Ecuador and Costa Rica).

Consumption of *cotton* has been on an expansion track since 1998 in both developed and developing countries. Among the latter, China has been a significant driver, as it is the largest world cotton producer but also a net importer. This has resulted from a combination of declining relative prices with respect to other textile fibres, population increase and rising per capita incomes, and the gradual integration of quota categories into WTO rules preceding the end of the Multi-fibre Arrangement (ICAC, 2004). As of 2004, Africa accounted for 20 per cent of China's imports of cotton (up from

18 per cent in 1990). It was furthermore an important external cotton supplier of the EU, with a market share of 26 per cent as of 2004.[20] Expansion of production in francophone (western) Africa is a result of significant improvements in yields enabled by public and semi-public support for research, input supply, production, processing, and marketing. This region is now the second largest exporter of cotton in the world (after the US) – whereas its world market share was close to zero after independence (Gabre-Madhin and Haggblade, 2004; ICAC, 2004). Nevertheless, important challenges remain (see box 2).

---

**Box 2**

The West African countries which produce low-cost high quality cotton have been unable to benefit fully from this boom, as world prices are artificially low due to oversupply of subsidized US cotton. While China, India and Pakistan are also major producers, only the United States is in addition a major exporter. Africa's cotton exports to the US accounted for less than 0.5 per cent of the total supplied to that market in 2004.[21] At the Hong Kong WTO Ministerial it was decided that developed countries would eliminate all forms of export subsidies to cotton in 2006. Since most cotton producers in Africa are smallholders, this could have a significant impact on rural incomes and rural poverty. At the same time, although there is in principle scope for developing a textile industry and producing goods with more value added, high energy and transportation costs remain a challenge. In Mali, for instance, the purchases of cotton by the nascent local textile industry have to be subsidized by the local ginning company (Goldstein et. al, 2006). Diversification towards products with more value added is particularly important as new competitors enter the market. Although Brazil has traditionally been a net importer of cotton, the introduction of the new high yielding Bt variety has turned the country into a net exporter as of 2003/04 and this change is likely to be sustained (ICAC, 2004; Oxfam, 2002). As of 2005/2006, yields were higher only in Australia[22].

---

In summary, with the exception of cotton, African producers of traditional agricultural commodities have steadily been losing market share to Asian and Latin American competitors over the last two decades. This holds even for cocoa, where the Ivory Coast remains a dominant supplier. Stagnant yields and inability to improve the price/quality ratio stand in stark contrast with trends in competing countries.

### 3.3 Fresh and simply processed high-value agricultural exports

In this section, we look at Africa's current insertion in selected world markets for fresh and simply processed high value agricultural products. This group consists of those defined as high unit value and/or high income elasticity of demand foods in Mayer, Butkevicius and Kadri (2002) – meat and meat products, dairy products, vegetables fruits and nuts (fresh, preserved and prepared), spices, and fixed vegetable oils and fats – plus dynamic inedible ornamentals (live plants and bulbs; cut flowers and foliage). Like fresh fruits and vegetables, the latter are perishable, high value-to-volume ratio products.[23] Products at the 5-digit SITC Rev.2 level are considered.

The EU is by far Africa's main market for its high value agricultural exports, accounting for almost three-fourths of the total. The second largest importers globally, Japan and the US, account for only 5 per cent each, followed closely by India. China is still a small market for African exports of this type of products, but its significance as a destination for Africa's exports has increased the most over the 1990-2004 period, and, in contrast to India, African countries have actually gained market share in China for these type of products (with potential for further growth; see section 5). The same holds for the US (where Africa's market share doubled) and the EU (where Africa's market share increased by 2.7 percentage points). Africa lost market share in Japan (table 4).

The two largest import markets globally are taken into consideration for more disaggregated analysis below: the EU (15) and the United States. Combined, these economies accounted for almost half of world imports of high value agricultural products in 2004 (table 4). Imports from Africa accounted for 12 per cent and 1 per cent, respectively, of those countries' total imports of high value agricultural products in 2004 – a proportional increase in market shares with respect to 1990 of 30 per cent and 83 per cent (table 5).

In the United States, Africa is still an incipient supplier (or not an exporter at all) in many product categories. Still, imports of high value agricultural products as a group from Africa have grown at a significantly faster rate than imports of these products from the world. Moreover, for certain products, Africa is already a large supplier. High value agricultural import categories where Africa is a relatively important supplier (at least 5 per cent market share) include: vanilla (76 per cent) and cloves (49 per cent); oranges (44 per cent); raisins (15 per cent); edible nuts nes[24] (15 per cent); mandarins (14 per cent); mixtures of fruit or vegetable juices (7 per cent); flours of leguminous vegetables, fruits, roots and tubers (7 per cent). Market shares grew in all cases, in some instances from zero in 1990. Very large market share increases (although often from a low base) have taken place in several product categories, including: frozen fish fillets, oranges, some juices and cut foliage (table 5).

In the US market, the main competition (for the products where Africa has a market share of 5 per cent or more) comes from developing countries in Latin America and from China, but also from developed countries (e.g. Australia and Spain in the case of oranges and mandarins, respectively) (table 6).

Most importantly in terms of scale, Africa has a significant (above 10 per cent) and increasing market share of the (extra) EU market in a relatively large number of product categories (see table 6). Amongst these products, the highest market shares are achieved, in descending order, by: cut flowers (53 per cent), oranges (43 per cent), grapes (41 per cent), fresh or chilled fish fillets (36 per cent) and pears (34 per cent). In one important category, fresh or chilled vegetables nes (all vegetables excluding leguminous, tomatoes and alliaceous vegetables), Africa's market share has remained stagnant at 22 per cent. Africa also has a considerable market share in the EU's imports of fresh apples (18 per cent), several tropical fruits (fresh and processed) (e.g. 38 per cent in the case of pineapples), spices (55 per cent in the case of both vanilla and cloves) and peanut oil (31 per cent), but it has lost market share in these markets.

The largest world suppliers in each selected market and Africa's suppliers for each product category are contrasted in table 6. Some stylized facts emerge. First, there is a high source-country concentration for these products (the combined market shares of the two largest competitors account for between 54 per cent and 66 per cent on average in the markets considered). Secondly, only two countries consistently appear among the two largest suppliers across product categories, Kenya (for fresh vegetables and cut flowers) and South Africa (citrus, apples, grapes, pears and quinces, stone fruit nes, prepared or preserved fruits and nuts, nes). In addition, these countries stand out in that they are suppliers of a diverse set of both fresh and slightly processed fruits and vegetables. Thirdly, only a handful of LDCs appear at all as suppliers of high value agricultural products (e.g. Uganda and Tanzania, in the case of fresh fish fillets; Mozambique and Malawi, in the case of nuts; Madagascar and Comoros in the case of vanilla and cloves; Zambia in the case of vegetables). Finally, and on a more positive note, non LDC countries such as Zimbabwe and Swaziland are emerging as growing suppliers of vegetables, fruits and flowers, while Botswana and Namibia are important suppliers of beef in the EU market and a few countries in West Africa (Ivory Coast, Ghana, Cameroon), are still among the leading suppliers of the European market for tropical fruits as well as producing for the local processing industry – although faced with increasing competition from Latin American producers.

Africa is either totally absent as a supplier or has a market share below 1 per cent for most meats (notably, the most dynamic ones in world trade, such as fresh poultry and pork), dairy products, eggs, and most vegetable oils (the exception being the least dynamic among them, peanut oil, of which the LDCs Senegal and Gambia are large exporters – see table 6).

While some of these products face steep competition from established, large supplying countries (Malaysia and Indonesia for palm/palm kernel oil; Argentina and Brazil for soybean oil), very high SPS barriers (meats, dairy), and/or high protectionism (dairy products), the same applies to a certain extent to other products where Africa has increased its market share significantly. For example, although African exports of products such as fish fillets or cut flowers benefit from preferential market access in both the EU and the US, they also face steep SPS barriers, suggesting that a process of upgrading has occurred. As discussed in section 5, this is indeed the case.

## 4. Successful agricultural-based growth: policy lessons from Asia and Latin America

This section reviews the experiences of Chile, in Latin America, and Malaysia, in Asia, in achieving sustained agricultural-based growth, with special reference to the role of the public sector in this process.

### 4.1. Lessons from Chile

While copper is the single most important source of foreign exchange and foreign investment, the agricultural sector (including fisheries and forestry) is a significant contributor to GDP, exports and employment in Chile – a contribution that substantially increases when backward and forward linkages are taken into consideration (Ferranti et al., 2005).

Chile's exports of high value agricultural products are concentrated in fish, wine and fresh fruits. Chile is the largest world exporter of fresh grapes (31 per cent world market share as of 2004) and fresh or chilled fish fillets (21 per cent). It is also the second largest exporter of avocados (19 per cent; Mexico is the first). In other fruits, it is still a relatively small player, but its market shares have consistently increased (e.g. berries). Finally, Chile is the fifth largest exporter of wine, with a 5 per cent world market share.[25]

While Chile does enjoy a comparative advantage in the production of agricultural products, as a result of relatively low fixed costs and counter-seasonal production (with respect to the northern hemisphere), its success in international markets is ultimately rooted in the ability to acquire competitiveness in new market niches and sectors, by upgrading both processes ("transforming inputs to outputs more efficiently by reorganization of the production system or introducing superior technology and process upgrading") and products ("moving into more sophisticated product lines in terms of increased unit values") (Giuliani, Pietrobelli, and Rabelotti, 2005, p. 552). We discuss key determinants using the berries and salmon sectors as illustrations.

*Berries*

Chilean fresh fruit exports are intensive in technology and services, as a result of the use of advanced technologies at different production stages, including computerized irrigation, modern selection procedures and packaging systems, controlled atmosphere storage and air-conditioned transport, to name but a few. The use of such technologies is both cost-saving and allows for better quality control, thus introducing an element of differentiation at the international level. Hence it is not uncommon that Chilean fruits appear under the country brand in OECD food retailers (Brooks and Lucatelli, 2004). The emergence of Chile as an important world producer of berries is just one example among many of how the country has excelled in diversifying its primary exports towards higher value-added products. As of 2004, Chile was the fifth largest exporter of fresh raspberries, blackberries and the like, with 8 per cent of world market share, and the second largest exporter (after Serbia and Montenegro) of frozen berries (excluding strawberries), with 21 per cent of world market share. The US and the EU are the main markets for these products.[26]

Below, we draw extensively on Guaipatín (2004) to show how early public investments in knowledge and infrastructure were instrumental in the development of this dynamic cluster already in the seventies. Increased exports of non traditional agricultural products took place much later elsewhere in the region (David, Dirven and Volgelgesang, 2000). To this day, the Chilean agricultural sector remains a recipient of important public investments in irrigation infrastructure, targeted credit and technical assistance programmes for small farmers, and sanitary and phytosanitary programmes. According to the most recent estimates available for public expenditures in the agricultural sector, Chile spends a considerable amount per person employed in the sector (almost US$500 in 2001, more than double the amount spent in 1990, compared to an average in Latin America of US$250[27]) (Kjöllerström, forthcoming).

In the late sixties, CORFO, a public development agency, instituted a programme for the development of the fruit sector ("*Plan Frutícola*") which included public investments in R&D, post-harvest infrastructure, overseas market research, soft credit lines for investments in infrastructure and working capital, and tax incentives for fruit exporters. This induced the development of specialized training programmes in the University of Chile (UC) and the National Institute for Agricultural Research (INIA). A cooperation agreement signed with the University of California allowed students of the UC to acquire state-of-the-art knowledge in fruticulture. At the same time, INIA attracted the most competent researchers offering competitive salaries and started a research programme focused on the sector (whereby, for instance, fruit varieties adapted to local conditions were developed). In summary, the *Plan Frutícola* created the necessary mass of human capital that was pivotal in the successful transfer and adaptation of foreign technology, which improved fruit production and post-harvest, and also the infrastructure required for exports of highly perishable products. Despite its elimination following the 1973 coup, the basis for private sector participation had been laid, as both risk and initial investment requirements were substantially reduced.

The take-off of fruit exports in the seventies was driven by large companies, which benefited from a duty drawback system for non traditional exports and the devaluation of the exchange rate. A large portion of the specialists that had worked under direct or indirect financing of the Plan went on to work for these companies, and the remainder were encouraged to find private financing for their research, which meant that it became very much demand driven. In 1975, Prochile, a government agency for the promotion of exports was founded, offering credit to groups of medium to large producers. INIA similarly started an agricultural extension and technology transfer programme targeting groups of large producers in the early eighties. The fact that groups of producers were targeted stimulated horizontal cooperation, ultimately leading to the creation of important private sector associations which exist to this day, such as Fepach[28] and Fedefruta. These private sector associations are today central elements of the dynamic fruit cluster. Fepach plays a prominent role in the berries niche, monitoring the adoption of good agricultural and manufacturing practices[29], negotiating better prices for international freights and production inputs, and providing market intelligence to its members.

Because of high barriers to entry (related to quality requirements and to complex logistics), the marketing of fresh raspberries is dominated by four companies and tends to be vertically integrated from the production stage, while in the case of frozen raspberries, which have lower value-added but also lower entry barriers, over 45 companies operate. Small farms are virtually excluded from the former but participate extensively in the latter, accounting today for half of the area cultivated with raspberries – from virtually zero in the beginning of the nineties. Overall, the sector makes a significant contribution to employment, as production is labour-intensive (e.g. 90 per cent of the harvest is done manually).

Both the private and public sectors contributed to increasing small producer participation in the frozen raspberry value chain. INDAP (an agency of the Ministry of Agriculture) and INIA started providing credit and agricultural extension services to small producers in the beginning of the nineties. INDAP initiated a supplier development programme for small fruit producers which included capacity building in the adoption of good agricultural practices. Large producing/exporting companies have played a significant role in this process, as the need to lower variable costs and increase flexibility in supply led them to contracting out production to small farms, becoming in the process one of the main sources of credit, inputs and technical assistance in order to keep quality under control.

*Salmon*[30]

From virtually zero exports in the early eighties, Chile is today the second largest world salmon producer after Norway. Salmon exports accounted for 9 per cent of total exports excluding the mining sector (5 per cent of overall exports) as of 2005. Productivity (measured by kilos of fish per kilo of feed) is estimated to have more than doubled over this period[31] and is now similar to Norway's. While in 1991 fish flour still accounted for 42 per cent of total exports of fish and fish products and salmon for only 14 per cent, by

2005 these shares were 16 per cent and 56 per cent, respectively. In addition, value-added salmon products (fresh and frozen fillets being the most important) have increased their share in the total cluster exports from 23 per cent in 1994 to 67 per cent in 2005. Fresh salmon fillets, like fresh berries, are transported by air (mainly to the US), and face highly stringent sanitary requirements, while frozen fillets are transported by sea, the EU and Japan being the two main markets. While salmon is a relatively homogeneous product with low value added, salmon fillets command premium prices.[32] The investment requirements of the salmon sector have led to the development of a number of supplying industries, including, among others: manufacture of fish farming cages and nets; construction of floating warehouses; manufacture of feed, vaccines and antibiotics; transportation; infrastructure maintenance services; quality monitoring services; and insurance (Association of Chilean Salmon Industries, SalmonChile, http://www.salmonchile.cl). In addition to being an important contributor to exports, GDP and employment, the development of the salmon cluster is considered to have had a significant impact in reducing poverty in Chile's main salmon producing region (Los Lagos, 1000 km south of Santiago, the capital), which dropped from 40 per cent in 1990 to 24 per cent in 2000 (Montero, 2004).

The Chilean government (through agencies like the Agriculture and Livestock Service, SAG) started to survey areas with potential for salmon farming already in the mid-sixties, with the support of international cooperation. For instance, the Japanese International Cooperation Agency (JICA) supported the introduction of the Coho species in Southern Chile. In the seventies, domestic and foreign companies gradually started to invest in the business following the establishment of the first commercial salmon operation in the country, with funding from CORFO and the leadership of *Fundación Chile*[33], which showed that this could be a profitable activity. In the nineties, joint actions led by the private sector and supported by public agencies, such as the allocation of public funds for R&D and technological upgrading, and more recently, the promotion of Chilean salmon abroad, have contributed to the strengthening of the cluster (Giuliani, Pietrobelli, and Rabelotti, 2005; Montero, 2004).

A stable macroeconomic, investment-friendly environment contributed to attract foreign direct investment. Although foreign firms played only an incipient role in the development of the cluster, they have increased their presence among large exporters and have facilitated the introduction of new technologies such as automated fishing and fish-counting systems (UNCTAD, 2006).

*Fundación Chile* continues to be an important contributor to innovation in the industry. Just recently, it has developed an automatic tool for salmon harvesting that increases harvest yields (in terms of usable meat per fish), as well as improving the processing and quality of the fillet's texture.[34] A number of public and private universities are nowadays developing new technologies and training professionals for the sector. Many of these projects are also co-funded by public funds [e.g. FONDEF – Scientific and Technological Development Fund – in the case of the development of a remote sensing system for seabed cleaning by the University of Concepción (UNCTAD, 2006)].

Throughout this process, government agencies have also had a key regulatory role: in the assignment of coastal concessions to fish farming companies, and in monitoring the sanitary conditions of inputs, output, and infrastructure. In 2000, Chilean authorities decided to introduce restrictions to salmon egg imports. This measure forced the private sector to enter the business of roe production, leading to a high degree of self-sufficiency (Chile produces 80 per cent of its needs), improved yields and reduced incidence of diseases and related antibiotic requirements, with an overall positive impact in terms of production costs (Montero, 2004).

Enforcement of regulation has increasingly been undertaken in partnership with the private sector, one example of such collaboration being the Cleaner Production Agreement signed with the Association of Chilean Salmon Industries (SalmonChile) in 2001. This is an agreement with the government and monitored by SalmonChile, whereby companies in the cluster voluntarily commit to using environmentally friendly processes, recycling and optimizing the use of materials (Iizuka, 2006).

SalmonChile also has an important role in supporting the development of quality standards, overseas marketing, and capacity-building, and in the legal defense against anti-dumping accusations in the WTO between 1997 and 2002. Concerns about increasingly stringent private sector requirements have more recently prompted SalmonChile to develop a local quality, sanitary, social and environmental standard (SiGes – Integrated Management System) that – although in line with international ones[35] – is less cumbersome and costly, allowing domestic companies with certain sustainable management practices in place to gain recognition for those efforts. Simultaneously, these standards function as guidelines towards the adoption of the stricter international standards such as ISO14000. In 2004, under the leadership of SalmonChile, the standards based on SiGes were adopted industry-wide by the Association of American Salmon (SOTA).[36] Thus the Chilean salmon industry has been able to become a standard setter in the salmon industry on the American continent. This illustrates the role of enhancing collective capabilities in the process of upgrading in natural resource-based industries (Iizuka, 2006).

## 4.2. Lessons from Malaysia

The growth of agro-industry in Malaysia was stimulated by the development of both traditional and export-oriented agriculture. Production and upgrading were encouraged by public specialized agencies, and the fiscal revenue obtained from taxes on the thriving export sector was us ed to reinvest in targeted R&D. Rapid economic growth ensued, *pre-dating* the boom in electronics. In addition to strong evidence that natural resources had a major role in Malaysian and Thai growth, and helped both countries to cope with economic recession following the Asian financial crisis, there is some evidence that rapid expansion of non-resource based exports from the mid-eighties onwards might actually have been "less favourable to the long-run development of these economies than is commonly suggested", due to relatively small learning effects, impacts on technological capabilities and backward linkages (Reinhardt, 2000, p.58).

In fact, the 2006 WTO Trade Policy Review of Malaysia states: "Malaysia's heavy dependence on exports of electronics and electrical goods means that economic growth is vulnerable to global fluctuations in the demand for these products. (...) Malaysia's economic slowdown [following the Asian crisis and up to 2003] highlighted the problems of over-reliance on an export-led growth strategy (...) and the consequent vulnerability to the industrial countries' business cycle" (WTO, 2006, p.1). The Malaysian government has now taken measures to "develop new sources of growth, focusing on agriculture, services and resource-based industries to improve the country's resilience to shocks" (WTO, 2006, p.1).

Below we focus on the determinants of expansion and upgrading of the agricultural sector in Malaysia, and particularly on the development of the palm oil industry, with a view to highlighting the role of public policy in the upgrading of the sector, just as we did for Chile.

Malaysia is currently the world's largest producer and exporter of palm oil – replacing Nigeria as the main producer as early as 1971 (Yusoff, 2006)[37] – accounting for 50 per cent of world output and 58 per cent of world exports as of 2004. Palm oil accounts for over one-third of total value added in the agricultural sector (WTO, 2006).

In the fifties, Malaysia's economy was largely dependent on tin and rubber, which combined accounted for over half of total GDP. With the emergence of synthetic rubber, Malaysian natural rubber exports went through a severe crisis. Recognizing the inadequacy of such a narrow base to sustain economic growth, the government initiated a diversification strategy in the sixties which included initiatives to develop non resource-based manufacturing (including the creation of Export Processing Zones and fiscal incentives to attract FDI) and diversification of the agricultural sector by promoting the palm oil industry. The focus on rural and agricultural development was further justified by the need to address mounting social conflict as a result of high income inequality between the Malay dominated rural areas and the ethnic Chinese dominated urban areas. Because the re-settlement of the rural landless was undertaken in connection with the development of organized smallholder oil palm schemes through government agencies such as FELDA (Federal Land Development Authority), the stage was set for palm oil to play a key role in the diversification of primary exports and ultimately in

Malaysia's rapid economic growth. Large expanses of land cultivated with rubber were converted to oil palm, which went from 55,000 hectares in 1960 to 1 million hectares in 1980, to 2 million hectares in 1990 and 3.4 million hectares as of 2000, a little over half of total agricultural land use. Over one-fourth is cultivated under FELDA schemes. The palm oil industry's share in total agricultural exports increased from a mere 7.7 per cent in 1970 to roughly 30 per cent by the mid-nineties. At the same time, palm oil development made a significant contribution to poverty reduction. As of 1997, poverty rates in agriculture were 11.8 per cent, compared to 68 per cent in 1970 (Simeh and Ahmad, 2001).

In addition to the instrumental role played in converting land to production of a new product for which there was a strong demand in international markets and which could be produced locally at a competitive price, public intervention was key in supporting market development, R&D and a conducive regulatory framework. The Palm Oil Registration and Licensing Authority (PORLA), for instance, undertook licensing and other regulatory activities so as to ensure that declared quality standards were being met. The Palm Oil Research Institute of Malaysia (PORIM), on the other hand, conducted research aimed at improving productivity, value-added and quality in the industry. PORLA and PORIM have been merged and now form the Malaysian Palm Oil Board (MPOB). Finally, the Malaysian Palm Oil Promotion Council (MPOPC) has since 1990 been promoting palm oil overseas, through diverse marketing activities, promotion of joint-ventures and provision of technical support and information to increase consumer knowledge about palm oil. Because the palm oil industry has been so successful, the agricultural sector is now deemed to have become too dependent on the commodity and hence the Malaysian Government now aims at revitalizing the agricultural sector elsewhere and has identified a number of products for purposes of diversification in its Third National Agriculture Policy (1998-2010) (Simeh and Ahmad, 2001).

With the goal of making Malaysia a "competitive global producer of high quality and safe agricultural products that meet international standards", the government is emphasizing the following three broad policy objectives: (i) adoption of modern agricultural methods, including biotechnology, through investments in R&D; (ii) development of Malaysia as a hub for processing, packaging and marketing of agricultural products; and (iii) development of the aquaculture, deep-sea fishing, ornamental fish breeding and halal produce sub-sectors (WTO, 2006).

The main incentives for selected activities in the agricultural sector are: (i) "pioneer status" (5-year partial income tax exemption); (ii) investment tax allowance (5-year allowance of 60 per cent on qualifying capital expenditure), including investments in clearing and preparation of land, planting of crops, construction of access roads including bridges, among others; (iii) incentive packages, including tax exemptions of different degree and relief of losses in some cases, for companies investing in the production of kenaf,[38] deep-sea fishing, vegetables, fruits, herbs, spices, aquaculture, and the rearing of cattle, goats and sheep; (iv) tax incentives for 'Halal' Food Production[39]; and (v) eligibility of locally-owned manufacturing companies with Malaysian equity of at least 60 per cent and reinvesting in promoted food processing activities (e.g. chocolate, processed fruits and vegetables, essential oils, aquaculture feed, etc) for another round of the Pioneer Status or Investment Tax Allowance (ITA) incentive.[40]

Like Chile in the salmon industry, Malaysia has played a leading role in the development of halal certification, in line with the government's aim of developing the country as a hub for halal products, although it is currently still a small producer. All meat and meat products, poultry, egg and egg products must receive halal certification from the Department of Islamic Development Malaysia (JAKIM). Standards have since 2004 been strengthened through the introduction of new guidelines by the Malaysian Department of Standards, which involve adopting procedures for slaughtering, processing, and other related operations as prescribed by Islamic rules. Each individual product must receive halal certification – rather than the production plant – and the certificate is issued following the joint recommendation of both JAKIM and the Malaysian Department of Veterinary Services based on on-site inspection. The Small and Medium Industries Development Plan (2001-2005) and the Third National Agricultural Policy include additional initiatives for the development of this sub-sector, such as capacity-building in inspection, monitoring and certification of halal standards, and promotion of halal industries through tax incentives such as those just described (WTO, 2006).

Common characteristics of these incentive packages include the fact they are granted for a limited amount of time, and they essentially target new investments in "new" activities (the promoted activities/products[41]). This is in line, at least to a certain extent, with Rodrik's (2004) recommendation that, in order to minimize the risks of perpetuating mistakes and to achieve spillover and demonstration effects, only "new" activities/products not previously produced locally or new technologies applied to "old" products should be given support, which should be limited in time.

At the same time as these other sub-sectors are being promoted, enhanced prospects from use of palm oil as biofuel and the enormous amount of oil palm waste available in the country have led the Malaysian government to target the development of the biofuel industry through a "four prong strategy" defined in the National Biofuel Policy released in August 2005.[42] This includes: (i) the production of a biofuel blend of 5 per cent processed palm oil and 95 per cent diesel; (ii) encouraging the use of this blend among consumers; (iii) establishing an industry standard for palm oil biodiesel quality; and (iv) promoting the establishment of biodiesel plants in Malaysia for export (e.g. through joint-ventures with the MPOB, using MPOB patented technology). Moreover, the government will be promoting the use of biofuel among government vehicles, through a voluntary scheme (Malaysian Palm Oil Board, 2005). Exports to Europe are reported to have commenced in August 2006, and biodiesel was also to have become available at local pumps in Fall 2006. Thirty-two biodiesel manufacturing licenses (out of a total of 87 applications) had received government approval as of July 2006.[43]

## 5. Creating competitive advantages in the agricultural sector in Africa

### 5.1 What products? What policies?

A central thesis stemming from Hausmann and Rodrik's (2003) work on economic development and "self-discovery" is that specialization in primary or natural resource-based products leads to sustained economic growth if this is a result of deliberate actions to build on a comparative advantage and create a competitive advantage in these products, but typically not otherwise.

The view that specialization according to comparative advantage is not a driver for economic growth is supported by empirical work showing that diversification (in terms of value added and employment, and in terms of "new" exports, i.e., products not substantially exported in the beginning of the 1990s but exported in large quantities a decade later) steadily increases with per capita income up to a relatively high threshold, and only then starts to decline (Imbs and Wacziarg, 2003; Klinger and Lederman, 2004). Furthermore, Klinger and Lederman (2004) show that "discovery" (in the sense of episodes when countries start exporting a new product) has occurred at a lower than expected frequency in Sub-Saharan Africa, given its population and income level.[44]

Specializing in traditional primary goods without innovating to increase value-added seems to be a recipe for failure. This is in line with Ferranti et al.'s (2002) paper on developing a knowledge-based economy from a natural resource base by placing emphasis on "how to produce" rather than on "what products"; and also with Bonaglia and Fukasaku (2003, p.9), who argue that low income countries "must use, rather than 'sit on' their natural wealth to build new areas of competitive advantage in non-traditional products". But how do countries (a) discover "new" products or (b) upgrade traditional ones?

Much recent research on the drivers behind the development of dynamic clusters in developing countries has focused on the governance of domestic and external networks (e.g. what firm characteristics determine the propensity to cooperate with others) and participation in global value chains, neglecting the central role played by governments in providing infrastructure, business services, technical upgrading and export assistance to the private sector (Meagher, 2005; for an exception, see Guaipatín, 2004). Finding "new" goods and services that can be supplied cost effectively has sometimes taken place without public intervention (see Jaffe and Gordon, 1998).

However, in many instances, public-private partnerships have been instrumental in starting new activities that later proved to be very profitable, and evolution towards high productivity clusters has often been backed by public interventions aimed at capturing cost-discovery externalities and at solving coordination failures (Rodrik, 2004). A survey of expert opinion concluded that public institutions were key initiators of change leading to success in African agriculture, for example (Gabre-Madhin and Haggblade, 2004). Active government intervention was found to be important in supporting crucial stages of agricultural market development in the Green Revolutions which took place in the 20th century (Dorward et al., 2004).

This is because the process of discovery and upgrading is far from trivial. First, there is uncertainty concerning the true costs of producing a new good or service under local conditions. Investments in new activities with potentially high returns which cannot, however, be fully appropriated by pioneers will be undersupplied, despite the potential to generate significant social benefits. This is particularly relevant in natural resource-based sectors, where uncertainty is particularly high and appropriability low (Giuliani, Pietrobelli, and Rabelotti, 2005). Second, in order to be profitable, many projects require complementary investments in a number of areas, often with high fixed costs which private entrepreneurs would be reluctant to bear. To address the information externalities underlying the first problem, some form of public support to investments in non-traditional activities is typically required. With coordination externalities, on the other hand, public policy can foster coordination of private investments, e.g., through measures like selective loan guarantees, and public investment can provide infrastructure with high social but low private returns (Rodrik, 2004).

The experiences of Chile and Malaysia show how horizontal and vertical diversification has led to successful natural resource-based growth and how public policy has played an important role in this process. Both countries are now large world suppliers of primary and natural resource-based agricultural products for which demand is growing and income-elastic and which are characterized by relatively high unit values. Also, in both cases, the products that eventually became success stories were not produced traditionally; rather, they are "new" products in the sense described above.

## 5.2 Special challenges and success stories in Africa

The extent to which the best practices reviewed in section 4 can be utilized in the African context to build new areas of competitive advantage within the agricultural sector is constrained by high external barriers and poor domestic capacity to overcome them. The most important of these are discussed below. Key actions in the African countries which have been able to overcome these barriers are highlighted.

While on average tariff protection remains high in developed countries for some agricultural sectors[45], Sub-Saharan Africa faces relatively low tariffs as a result of preferential treatment received under the Cotonou (ACP) and Everything But Arms (EBA) schemes (EU), the African Growth and Opportunity Act (AGOA) (US) and GSP. For instance, in the EU, African agricultural exports pay an average tariff of 7 per cent, compared to 18 per cent for developing countries of the CAIRNS group. In developed Asian countries, the tariffs applied are 12 per cent and 24 per cent, respectively. In the US the preferential margin is smaller (3 per cent compared to 3.8 per cent, respectively), but the average tariff applied is low. In addition to facing the highest tariffs, South American and Asian countries are also affected by tariff escalation in the EU to a greater extent than African countries (Bureau, Jean and Matthews, 2005).

The average tariff (including ad valorem equivalents for non ad valorem tariffs) imposed on high value agricultural goods – as defined earlier – originating from Africa was 6 per cent and 1 per cent in the EU and the US, respectively. In emerging markets, such as China and India, on the other hand, tariff protection is steep (23 per cent and 37 per cent on average). Averages for Africa, in the case of the EU, are affected by the fact that many African countries are LDCs. The more developed African countries, which are also more competitive in non commodity agricultural exports, benefit from ACP treatment, but not EBA. The average tariff applied to non LDC African countries is 11 per cent, compared to the overall average of 6 per cent[46] (in the US, China and India, the difference is insignificant).

Overall, preferences granted to developing countries seem to be well used for agricultural products. In the US and the EU, only a little over 10 per cent of eligible agricultural products are not imported under a preferential regime and those correspond to small trade flows and/or low MFN tariffs. Trade flows associated to preferential schemes for LDCs are, however, quite modest in relation to the EU and the US's total agricultural imports (0.4 per cent in the case of the EBA initiative and 0.2 per cent in the case of AGOA, for instance) (Bureau, Jean and Matthews, 2005). The inability to leverage these preferences is rooted in poor domestic capabilities to deliver goods complying with increasingly demanding standards.

By one recent estimate, the ad valorem equivalent (AVE) of TRAINS[47] Non-Tariff Barriers[48] (NTBs) is higher than the actual tariff in 57 per cent of the cases when present in a given tariff line. The incidence of NTBs on agricultural goods is particularly high, although manufactured goods are not exempt from them (AVE = 20 per cent and 8 per cent, respectively)[49]. In addition, for roughly one-third of the products subject to domestic agricultural support, the AVE of that support is higher than the tariff (9 per cent on average for products subject to support). Dairy products are the agricultural goods subject to the highest NTBs, as measured by their AVE. Within countries, tariffs tend to increase with both the AVE of NTBs and domestic agricultural support, lending support to the view that NTBs are partly used as protectionist tools (Kee, Nicita and Olarreaga, 2006).

Among the different types of NTBs, technical measures such as Sanitary and Phytosanitary (SPS) and other standards (e.g. related to labelling and packaging) have been gaining prominence over the last 10 years. In 1994, technical measures accounted for 22 per cent of all NTBs applied by developed countries, whereas in 2004 this percentage reached 50 per cent. In developing countries in Asia, which include emerging markets for Africa like China and India, the share of technical measures increased from 24 per cent to 48 per cent. Overall, by one estimate, government mandated testing and certification requirements have experienced a seven-fold increase over this period (UNCTAD, 2005).

SPS measures in developed countries often exceed multilateral norms. For instance, in the EU, maximum allowable residues of aflatoxins in nuts, dried fruits and cereals are more stringent than international standards, with an estimated significant negative impact on imports from Africa (Otsuki, Wilson and Sewadeh, 2001). The 2004 EU Directive on wood packaging material is also more restrictive than what is established in the International Plant Protection Convention (USTR, 2005).

The ITC (2003) estimated that, in 2002, 40 per cent of LDC exports were subject to NTBs, compared to 15 per cent in the case of the exports from other developing and transition economies. Respondents to a survey of low and middle income countries rated SPS standards to be the most important barrier for their agricultural exports to the EU, the most affected products being (fresh and simply processed) meat, fish, fruits and vegetables. While the EU was the market for which SPS requirements were considered to be the most significant impediment to trade, SPS requirements were also deemed problematic in Australia and the United States (Henson and Loader, 2001).

In the EU, imports of *products of animal origin* must comply with two basic requirements. First, the exporting country must be recognized as free of certain diseases (the same holds in the US); and secondly, imports into the EU must have an original health certificate from an approved establishment. Neither the EU nor the US automatically recognizes a country's (or region's) disease-free status determined by the World Organization for Animal Health. The EU also has strict requirements for the use of hormones and other substances such as antibiotics, as well as for maximum allowable residues. Exporting countries are required to have monitoring programmes in place and to submit monitoring results to the EU. Laboratories must comply with EU standards. The monitoring programmes can be limited to products for export, but traceability must be ensured. Establishments exporting meat to the EU must also comply with Directive 93/119/EC on animal welfare. Of 30 countries which responded to a survey undertaken by the European Commission on the subject, only 5 African countries (Botswana, Cape Verde, Namibia, South Africa and Swaziland) have some sort of animal welfare protection rules or industry guidelines.[50] As a result of these restrictions, and despite substantial preferences, especially for LDCs, in Africa only a handful of countries are allowed to export (some) meat products to the EU (Botswana, Namibia, South Africa, Swaziland, Zimbabwe). No African country is eligible to export fresh meat products to the US.[51]

With the exception of South Africa, these African countries are all beneficiaries of preferential quotas in the EU market under the Cotonou agreement (South Africa's beef does not benefit from preferential treatment under the bilateral trade agreement with the EU either). In Africa, Namibia and Botswana are the largest beef exporters to the EU, although with substantially smaller market shares than highly competitive countries which benefit from less generous preferences, like Brazil and Argentina (table 6). Still, maintaining a presence in the EU market is indicative of the substantial public investments that have been taking place in those African countries in order to meet the stringent requirements outlined above, including in livestock identification and trace back systems and upgraded facilities in slaughterhouses. In Botswana, the beef sector has traditionally been a recipient of considerable direct government support, namely through direct subsidies, tax incentives and provision of livestock-specific infrastructure. Government expenditures in the agricultural sector as a whole have been estimated at over 50 per cent of agricultural GDP, with the expenditures of the Department of Animal Health accounting for approximately half of that in the 2003/2004 budget (Stevens and Kennan, 2005, p.9).

According to Kaplinsky and Readman (2005): "Product upgrading (in design or quality) will be reflected by a relatively good unit price performance (in that either unit prices grow more rapidly or fall less rapidly than those of competitors) and a complementary improvement in (or stability of) market share". Namibia's market share in the EU has grown faster than Botswana's and unit values have also increased more (Stevens and Kennan, 2005). This suggests that product upgrading has occurred in Namibia to a greater extent than in Botswana. Qualitative information supports this assertion. The key determinant of Namibia's success has been the ability to persuade importers of the superior quality of its beef, which is largely a result of the Farm Assured Namibian Meat Scheme (FANMEAT), managed by the government-owned, privately financed Meat Board of Namibia. Under this scheme, both full traceability and strict veterinary and animal welfare standards conforming to EU requirements are ensured. No other comparable scheme exists in Africa today. Although currently most Namibian meat exported to the UK is used in the catering industry, supermarket chains are becoming interested in marketing this meat as well, as it is "hormone free, hygienic and reared according to higher welfare standards" (Bowles et al., 2005, p.785).

While tariffs imposed by developed countries on *fish products* from developing countries are either zero or low, sanitary standards and technical requirements (e.g. with respect to packing and labelling) are important restrictions to developing country exports. Imports to the EU and the US must have an original health certificate from approved establishments and bear the name of the country of origin. Health and quality standards are based on the stringent HACCP requirements (UNCTAD, 2005a).[52]

Despite these barriers, low-income countries like Uganda and Tanzania were able to respond to increased demand for freshwater fish in the beginning of the nineties and have become important suppliers of an essentially "new" product, fish fillets, which happens to be among the most dynamic commodities in world trade (see section 2) and has a high unit value. Production of fish fillets has stimulated the development of the animal feed sector, which uses fish waste as a main input, as well as the packing and logistics sectors. This required substantial investments in upgrading infrastructure and domestic capabilities. In Uganda, for example, following the EU's 1997 ban on imports of Nile perch[53] from East Africa due to bacterial contamination (followed by a ban in 1999 due to fish poisoning), the Fish Processors and Exporters Association (UFPEA) sought technical assistance from donors and in cooperation with the government established a reliable, EU (and US)-compliant fish safety assurance system. UFPEA members themselves undertook significant investments (Bonaglia and Fukasaku, 2003). Technical assistance from UNIDO (United Nations Industrial Development Organization) seems to have been instrumental in this regard. Essential aspects of its support included: reviewing the organizational aspects of fish inspection; updating regulations to conform with international standards; reinforcement of the capacity of the regulatory and inspection authority, the Department of Fisheries Resources; strengthening the technical support institutions (thereby creating a critical mass of national HACCP (Hazard Analysis and Critical Contro Point) and Good Hygienic Practices specialists/auditors); upgrading the capacity of public laboratories (with equipment and technical assistance); and strengthening the capacity of the private sector at the fishing, landing and processing plant levels (e.g. training of plant staff in Good Hygienic Practices and HACCP).[54] International cooperation in the start-up phase of new activities was also an important aspect of Chile's fruit and salmon sector development (see section 4) and is probably crucial to other low income countries in Africa.

Despite auspicious demand prospects, overexploitation of fisheries stocks could limit the industry's expansion. Development of commercial aquaculture is widely seen as a desirable development that would compensate for the diminishing catch of wild Nile perch, but research on its reproductive biology, spawning habits and growth potential in an artificial environment has received relatively little attention. Uganda's Fisheries Policy includes an aquaculture development plan, but funding remains a challenge (Kaelin and Cowx, 2002).

Because government standards defining quality, size and ripeness vary between markets and change frequently, they constitute a significant barrier to exports of fruits, vegetables and nuts from developing countries.[55] In addition to strict standards imposed by developed country governments, private standards such as those imposed by supermarkets and global distributors also constitute a barrier to participation in global agricultural markets. In the EU, standards were initially imposed by each supermarket chain on its suppliers of fresh agricultural produce, but this later evolved to a system of protocols defined by the supermarket industry as a whole. These constitute de facto licenses to enter the EU market, and comprise mainly food safety standards, but also environmental (e.g. restricting the use of chemicals) and labour standards in some cases [e.g. the Euro Retailer Produce Working Group (EUREP) Good Agricultural Practice (GAP) guidelines, EUREP-GAP]. In many instances, requirements exceed national norms (VEK-World Bank, 2004).

Investments in quality and food safety assurance systems are key factors underlying Kenya's success as a vegetable exporter. The establishment of a well staffed national plant inspection service (KEPHIS) in 1997 has played a key role in this regard.[56] The Kenya Horticultural Code of Practice – drafted by the Fresh Produce Exporter Association of Kenya (FPEAK) in partnership with the Horticultural Crop Development Authority – is designed to ensure European importers that Kenyan horticultural products are produced in an environmentally- and worker-friendly manner. Although there is no legal enforcement mechanism, it is expected that importers will pressure Kenyan exporters to adopt the code following European certification (Minot and Ngigi, 2003).

Substantial investments in supply control and traceability systems, upgrading of packinghouse facilities (e.g. improved water and sanitation and advanced cold treatment and storage systems), staff training and health counselling, and environmental testing have been undertaken by the leading companies in the fresh produce industry, allowing them "to service the premium-quality end of the market [of British supermarkets], including the growing demand for salads and other semi-prepared vegetable products" (World Bank, p.86). Private investments have been stimulated by a liberal investment regime, fiscal incentives for horticultural exports and political and economic stability (Zhihua Zeng, 2006; Minot and Ngigi, 2003). Overall, and despite the fact that not all exporters have been able to move to the most profitable segment of the market (they keep supplying wholesale and ethnic food markets in Europe), these proactive actions have contributed to increasing the unit value of Kenyan vegetable exports (World Bank, 2005, p.88), similarly to what Namibia achieved for its meat.

In the Ivory Coast, increased competition from Central American and Caribbean fresh pineapple exporters (the country supplied roughly 90 per cent of the European market in the mid-1980s and only two-thirds in 1990) has made the need for upgrading in the industry apparent. The *Office Centrale des Producteurs-Exportateurs d'Ananas et de Bananes* (OCAB) was formed in the nineties to represent the interests of exporters, set quality standards, facilitate communication among stakeholders and organize the chartering of reefer ships for transport of bananas and pineapples to Europe. One important action undertaken by this body has been the reduction in the number of approved exporters of fruit in order to maintain quality standards (Minot and Ngigi, 2003). Strategic investments in shipping logistics and other supporting infrastructure have also been undertaken. The development of a real time "bar code" pallet traceability system allows all agents involved in a transaction to trace individual pallets at all times of shipping, while investments financed by EU funds have been used to improve feeder roads and power lines to connect banana and pineapple producing plantations and smallholder clusters to the main road and electrical network (Voisard, 2005). Political instability since 1999 has undermined the potential impact these interventions might have had, and the Ivory Coast has lost further market share in the EU to Costa Rica and Ghana.[57] We will return to the Ghanaian experience below.

While favorable tariff quotas, fast growing demand for high value foods and historical ties have led African countries to focus on the European market, fast growing economies in the developing world, particularly in Asia, with a complementary pattern of specialization, and where less stringent quality requirements prevail, represent an opportunity for market diversification.

China is already driving Africa's pattern of specialization as a result of soaring demand for minerals, as well as cotton and cocoa.[58] Increasing per capita income and urbanization rates will lead to increased demand for feed (e.g. oilseeds), meat and other non-cereal foods (e.g. edible oils, sugar, products from aquaculture, fresh fruits and vegetables) and therefore might become an interesting market for Africa's exports of high value foods in the near future (Mayer and Fajarnes, 2005; Goldstein et al., 2006). In fact, Africa has started to supply the Chinese market with live plants, frozen fish fillets, lemons and limes, edible nuts, and grapefruit juice, and it has significantly increased its market share in dried fish and crustaceans, albeit from a very low base.[59]

Increased concentration of purchasers in global value chains only adds to the difficulties faced by potential suppliers in developing countries. A consequence of this is increased concentration in sourcing, as mentioned in section 4. Competitive global suppliers are forming alliances, joint-ventures and other networks with the goal of becoming preferred suppliers for the multinationals that dominate world food trade. Hence, in addition to investments in productivity and quality, suppliers must undertake important investments in terms of organization if they want to penetrate international markets. South African companies are among the few on the continent, which have been engaged in such alliances. Sunkist, the largest citrus cooperative in the world, has forged an alliance with a company in South Africa to supply the Asian market; and Driscolls, the largest strawberry producer in the US, is in alliance with Kentish Group in the UK, in turn allied with Vital Berry in Chile, and the latter two are together investing in Argentina and South

Africa. Elsewhere, governments have been active in promoting the formation of such organizational capital by facilitating alliances with large retailers. In Malaysia, for instance, the government promotes linkages between domestic producers and domestic/foreign supermarket chains through the Federal Agricultural Marketing Authority (FAMA), helping suppliers to integrate local supply chains and open the doors for insertion in regional and global procurement chains. In Brazil, the Brazilian Export Promotion Agency (APEX) and the Industry and Trade Ministry have facilitated an agreement with Carrefour whereby the latter will promote Brazilian fruits in its European stores and later in its stores in Asia and the Americas (Reardon and Flores, 2006). This is especially relevant for small farmers. Innovative policies in this respect include supporting the formation of farmers' associations, as well as associations between farmers and agro industry, and supporting organizations that link input supply with information dissemination.

Promoting product differentiation (e.g. through promotion of country brands) is a complement to pursuing such a strategy. In South Africa, a large supplier of fresh citrus, among other fresh fruits, Outspan International decided to market all South African citrus under the "Outspan" label after being nominated as the single desk exporter of South African citrus in 1940 (a privilege it retained until recently). This allowed the company to market a variety of cultivars sourced in distinct ecological areas as a "national product" to northern hemisphere consumers with considerable success (Mather, 1999). Most African countries, on the other hand, despite supplying unique and/or high quality fresh foods, have so far been unable to market them accordingly, one case in point being Nile Perch from Lake Victoria which is marketed in developed country markets without any reference to its origin and characteristics ("firm boneless white flesh, high level of omega 3 fatty acids, mild flavour and flexibility for use in cooking"[60]).

Some African countries could benefit from their privileged geographical position with respect to other developing regions, particularly in the case of the most perishable fruits, vegetables and flowers, which must be air-freighted. In order to utilize this advantage, however, substantial investments in distribution services and infrastructure are required (e.g. cold storage; reliable transport connections between airports and producing areas; upgrading of airports to international standards) (UNIDO, 2004). This is especially relevant in that, increasingly, buyers require consistency in volumes delivered, quality and timing, as well as "just in shape delivery", i.e., the delivery of produce which needs no additional processing/labelling before being shelved (VEK-World Bank, 2004).

Investments in logistics infrastructure for air-freighted perishable exports have been key drivers of Kenya's export diversification success, helping to both attract and increase the returns on private sector investment (Bonaglia and Fukasaku, 2004). Hence, in addition to being an important exporter of fresh vegetables, Kenya is by far the largest exporter of cut flowers in Africa (see table 6) and the 4th largest exporter in the world (after the Netherlands, Colombia and Ecuador).[61] In Ethiopia, where a flower industry is emerging, on the other hand, cargo bottlenecks created by inefficient airport infrastructure, insufficient cold facilities at the airport, and poor connection roads, are major barriers to expansion, despite generous incentives for private investors, which include: five-year tax exemptions; duty-free machinery imports, including irrigation systems and greenhouses; and easy access to bank loans.[62]

Djankov, Freund and Pham (2006) estimate that, in Africa, internal handling and transportation of goods for export takes over 1.5 months on average,[63] compared to 24 days in East Asia and the Pacific, 28 days in the Middle East and North Africa, 29 days in Latin America and the Caribbean, 33 days in South Asia and 13 days in developed countries. This is explained by poor port and road infrastructure (only one fourth of roads in Africa are paved, compared to 27 per cent in Latin America and 43 per cent in South Asia), and by excessive customs and tax procedures, clearances and cargo inspections. While each additional day a shipment is delayed reduces trade by at least 1 per cent, time-sensitive exports, such as fresh agricultural produce, are reduced by 6 times that amount.

Landlocked African countries face special challenges in dealing with inefficient customs procedures and high charges imposed for goods in transit. Whereas transport and insurance costs account for approximately 15 per cent of the value of exports originating in landlocked developing countries, this percentage reaches 32 per cent in landlocked African LDCs – against an average 8 per cent and 6 per cent in developing and OECD countries, respectively. In coastal African countries these costs reach 15 per cent. Furthermore, poor regional connections characterize the continent and contribute to explaining the relatively low share of intra-African trade (AfDB/OECD, 2006).

In light of this and the shift in the composition of Official Development Assistance (ODA) for LDCs away from the infrastructure and productive sectors towards social expenditures since the early nineties (UNCTAD, 2006a), increased FDI in basic infrastructure from China is a welcome development. While a large part of this investment will mostly benefit the mineral sector – including for the rehabilitation and construction of roads and railways connecting mineral-rich areas to ports in Angola and Mozambique – (AfDB/OECD, 2006), there is evidence of China's starting to invest in the agricultural, telecommunications and power infrastructure sectors. For instance, the China Grains & Oils Group, one of China's larger agricultural companies, has invested in a soybean processing plant in Mozambique (Bosten, 2005). China has also been providing extension services and technology transfer to small farmers and fishermen in a number of African countries in the context of the South-South Cooperation initiative of FAO's Special Programme for Food Security.

In addition to poor infrastructure and organizational capital, "underfunded knowledge creation"[64] (Laiglesia, 2006, p.52) is a major constraint to upgrading Africa's agricultural sector in general and increasing exports of non traditional agricultural products in particular. With few exceptions, the agricultural sectors' total factor productivity growth over the 1960-2000 period in low income African countries was below the rates achieved in Asia and Latin America (Bravo-Ortega and Lederman, 2005a). Yield improvements in fruits and vegetables (which worldwide have been lower than in cereals) have been especially low in Africa. For instance, between 1961 and 2004, yields in vegetables in Africa grew at an average annual rate of 0.6 per cent (versus 0.7 per cent for cereals) compared to an average 1.4 per cent for the world (Weinberger and Lumpkin, 2005).

As mentioned earlier, public R&D (e.g. identification of products with export potential, selection of suitable varieties, and adaptation of those varieties to local conditions) has a fundamental role in attracting the private sector to invest in new activities characterized by high uncertainty and low appropriability.[65] Crop breeding and research on disease control have many public good characteristics which make it fundamentally dependent on public sector intervention (Masters, 2005). Thus, it is of concern that, in Africa, the intensity of public expenditure in agricultural R&D (irrespective of whether intensity is measured in relation to agricultural GDP or economically active agricultural population) exhibits a downward trend over the 1980-2000 period, in contrast to the other regions in the developing world. In fact, approximately half of the African countries for which information is available spent less on agricultural R&D in 2000 than in 1991 in absolute terms as well (Pardey et al., 2006). While developed countries spent on average 3.5 US PPP dollars per hectare of agricultural land in 1991, and developing countries spent on average almost 2.5 US PPP dollars, Africa spent less than 1 dollar (Masters, 2005).

The trends described in the previous paragraph can be attributed to a shift of bilateral and multilateral donor support – on which African domestic R&D efforts depend for funding (exceptions are Botswana, Malawi, Mauritius and Sudan) – away from the agricultural sector in general and agricultural research in particular. For instance, USAID funding for agricultural research projects in Africa fell to 23 per cent of the levels in the mid-1980s; World Bank lending for agriculture also exhibits a downward trend in real terms since the 1980s (Pardey et al., 2006).

This is compounded by the fact that horticultural research has received relatively little attention from the international agricultural research centres until very recently. In 2002, the Consultative Group on International Agricultural Research (CGIAR) system's expenditures in horticultural research amounted to only 13 per cent of the expenditures in cereal-related research (Weinberger and Lumpkin, 2005).

Finally, especially in the cases where production is dominated by smallholders, conversion to non traditional crops – and, within these, to those cultivars and varieties for which demand is high and which can be produced at a lower cost – can be facilitated by public sector intervention (see also section 4 for examples in Chile and Malaysia). The success of the Ghanaian pineapple industry has been based on targeting the discount segment of the Northern European market and competing on price (although some companies have started to supply higher value-added products as well, such as sliced pineapple, fruit salads, and pineapple juice). One important advantage until recently was its air-freight cost advantage compared to other countries in the region. Since 1996, however, it has sustained increasing competition from a higher yielding cultivar grown in Costa Rica (the MD2) which is also sweeter and more flavourful than the main cultivar exported by Ghana (Smooth Cayenne). Because MD2 is not a proprietary cultivar and since consumer loyalty appears to be related to its intrinsic characteristics rather than to the Del Monte brand, Ghana has put in place a concerted strategy to convert production to the higher yielding cultivar. With donor support, the government is playing an important role in this process through its Agricultural Services Support and Investment Program (AgSSIP). In addition to supporting crop conversion among the smallholders which dominate pineapple production in the country, other actions in the context of this programme include developing local capacities in tissue culture multiplication techniques and investments in cold-chain facilities and other export infrastructure (Danielou and Ravry, 2005).

## 6. Conclusions

It is a broadly held view that natural resource-based sectors exhibit low productivity growth, are less dynamic in international trade, have low innovation and knowledge content and encompass fewer linkages with the rest of the economy, thus having lower multiplier effects. We have shown that this does not always hold, especially in the agricultural sector, and therefore that specialization in manufacturing is not a necessary condition for sustained economic growth.

With the exception of cotton, African producers of traditional agricultural commodities have steadily been losing market share to Asian and Latin American competitors over the last two decades. This holds even for cocoa, where the Ivory Coast remains a dominant supplier. Stagnant yields and inability to improve price/quality ratios stand in stark contrast with trends in competing countries.

While Africa is mainly an exporter of basic primary commodities, it has been increasing its market share, sometimes very significantly, for some dynamic, high unit value agricultural activities for which low labour costs are a crucial competitiveness factor. Nevertheless, exports of products in the latter group are still very small and concentrated in a handful of countries. Moreover, processes of value-addition and differentiation in traditional export sectors have been limited.

Common constraints in most countries are poorly funded R&D, poor capability to comply with SPS and other standards in developed country markets, poor "organizational capital", and poor logistics infrastructure – to be able to deliver products at the price and in the volumes, quality and timing required by international buyers. In some instances, African suppliers which had achieved important market shares at a given point in time are now losing this advantage in favour of suppliers with access to better infrastructure and/or which have been able to innovate and increase productivity in order to overcome existing infrastructure or geographical disadvantages. The development of the papaya cultivar in Brazil, which can now be sea-freighted and which has undermined Ghana's low-cost advantage in air-freighted papayas to Europe, illustrates the latter point (Danielou and Ravry, 2005).

Also, increasingly, the ability to organize in order to promote exports under a national country brand and to penetrate global supply chains has been a discriminating factor in favour of Asian and Latin American producers. High supplier concentration further suggests that scale matters. Only South Africa (fruits) and Kenya (vegetables and cut flowers) consistently emerge as one of the two largest suppliers in the US and the EU. Some countries are emerging as suppliers of meats (Botswana, Namibia), vegetables, fruits and flowers (Zimbabwe and Swaziland), fish fillets (Uganda and Tanzania) (fish fillets) and edible nuts (Malawi and Mozambique), but it remains to be seen whether the very high investments undertaken to penetrate international markets are sufficient to withstand competition from much larger suppliers elsewhere. The case of Botswana versus Namibia (see section 5) suggests that additional efforts to differentiate domestic exports may be required to exploit niche markets where competition is not (solely) based on cost advantages.

The proactive actions undertaken in Chile and Malaysia to maintain advantage in increasingly competitive international markets, by constantly innovating to increase product differentiation and finding new products that can be marketed cost effectively, suggest that concurrent public policy interventions and coordinated actions with and within the private sector are crucial in that process. Areas where public support, by direct (e.g. tax incentives and subsidized credit) or indirect (e.g. allocation of public funds through competitive bidding), means have been key include: allocation of the "commons"; promoting targeted R&D and technology transfer towards new activities; upgrading of transportation infrastructure; development of institutions for quality control and traceability; overseas marketing; and supporting the formation of producer associations and their articulation with global value chains. Once new activities achieve a certain degree of maturity, private sector associations appear as important actors in maintaining leadership in international markets and undertake activities that either complement or reinforce public intervention, including through promotion overseas, standard-setting and provision of technical assistance along value chains.

The case for concerted government interventions at many different levels is in line with recent work by Hausmann and Rodrik (2006, p.24) who argue that notions such as property rights, institutions and infrastructure involve "very many different activities that are highly [sector] specific and need to be conceived, planned and organized by a myriad of different organizations or networks of organizations".

Although there is a dearth of quantitative data regarding the overall cost of these interventions, the information available suggests they are not trivial. Focusing on fast growing but less demanding developing country markets with complementary specialization patterns could prove useful for some countries at low levels of development. The growing interest of China in Africa as an investment destination and a source for raw materials could be utilized to the benefit of Africa's agricultural sector, as evidence of increased technical assistance, investments and emerging exports seems to suggest. Support from international donors was an important aspect of Chile's fruit and salmon sectors' early development and in success stories in low income countries in Africa as well. South-South cooperation could play a similar role.

Political and macroeconomic stability have to be in place before issues such as capability to comply with developed country quality standards become relevant. Ivory Coast was on most accounts a major success story until political strife overtook the country in the end of the nineties. Some countries with great agricultural potential, such as Angola and Mozambique, have only recently emerged from decade-long conflicts, but are already attracting a lot of attention from the private sector, including foreign investment.

One caveat with respect to the distributional consequences of developing non traditional agriculture is in order. In Latin America, for instance, this process has been highly concentrated in medium to large farms (David, Dirven and Vogelgesang, 2000). There is also evidence that smallholder participation in agricultural exports has declined to a significant extent since the early 1990s in some African countries (e.g. Minot and Ngigi, 2003). The exceptions tend to go hand in hand with targeted government support. Access to subsidized credit (in the case of products requiring significant investments) and technical assistance (in the case of products with relatively complex production technologies) have proven to be critical in enabling small farmers to adopt new, higher return crops in Ecuador, Guatemala and Brazil (Damiani, 2000). In Africa, there is evidence that supermarkets will source from small horticultural producers provided there is institutional support to "upgrade" them to meet quality, safety, consistency and cost standards (Weatherspoon and Reardon, 2003, p.352). Other illustrations of the government's role in enhancing smallholder participation in new dynamic sectors are provided in section 4, and this was especially important in Malaysia. Increased smallholder participation is, however, not the only means whereby rural incomes can be enhanced. First, large operations producing fruits, flowers and other labour-intensive crops generate employment (this of course does not hold in the case of grain or soybean production, both of which are highly capital-intensive in most countries). Secondly, agricultural activities create demand for labour-intensive services such as packing, which can be better remunerated than on-farm work. In Chile, overall direct smallholder participation in the fresh fruit export sector is relatively small. Still, due to the high labour intensity of the agro-processing sector (e.g. post harvest activities such as selection and packing), and increased employment and wages in larger farms, both of which employ unskilled labour, the agricultural sector has contributed to reducing poverty (López and Anriquez, 2003a). The magnitude of the positive contribution of agricultural growth on the incomes of the poorest will thus depend on context.

From a sustainable development perspective, it is also important to consider to what extent agricultural growth entails negative environmental consequences. As mentioned before, in East Africa, fish stocks are being depleted at high rates, threatening the survival of the nascent fish processing industry. In the south of Chile, salmon farms have polluted and generated ecological imbalances in inland lakes and streams (Altieri and Rojas, 1999). The expansion of the agricultural frontier through deforestation in countries like Brazil and Malaysia is an important contributor to $CO_2$ emissions and loss of biodiversity (Wakker, 2005). However, as Bravo-Ortega and Lederman (2005b) point out, most empirical research has been focused on the negative impacts of agricultural growth, rather than on its benefits compared to other economic sectors, which are shown to be overall relatively benign. At the same time, there exists relatively little research comparing the impact of traditional agriculture and non traditional export products. In Chile, for instance, the use of agro-chemicals has increased substantially in the nineties, but it would have risen even faster if expansion in the agricultural sector had been led by traditional import-competing crops, which are more reliant on pesticide use (López and Anriquez, 2003b).

In conclusion, current domestic capabilities and endowments in the great majority of African countries suggest that it is more realistic to find opportunities for upgrading within the primary and natural resource-based sectors. The potential for generating spillovers to other sectors and sustaining growth, as well as for poverty reduction, is probably greater in agriculture than in other sectors. Thus, contrary to the commonly held view that Africa cannot industrialize and thus can not develop, we take a more optimistic stance, agreeing that much of Africa faces major challenges in the production of sophisticated manufactures in the foreseeable future, but arguing that it can probably compete in the production of some dynamic, high unit value primary agricultural products and agricultural manufactures. The current boom in commodity prices boosted by increasing demand from Asia might just provide the necessary leverage to undertake the investments this requires.

Figure 1. Distribution of world trade, by technological categories and dynamism, 2004

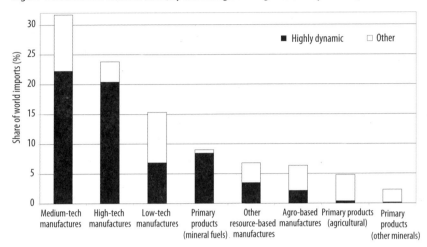

Source: the authors based on UN COMTRADE data and Lall's (2000) technological categories.

## Table 1.
### Average annual growth in multi-factor productivity across sectors (%)

| Country (region) and period | Source | Mining | Coal | Petroleum | Copper | Agriculture | Manufacturing |
|---|---|---|---|---|---|---|---|
| United States 1970-1980 | Parry (1997) | -- | -3.5 | -7.0 | -2.5 | -- | 0.8 |
| United States 1980-1992 | Parry (1997) | - | 2.6 | 1.3 | 3.9 | -- | 1.4 |
| 14 OECD countries 1970-1987 | Bernard and Jones (1996) | -0.1 | -- | -- | -- | 3.0 | 2.0 |
| 33 developing countries 1967-1992 | Martin and Mitra (2001) | -- | -- | -- | -- | 2.6 | 0.9 |
| 18 developed countries 1967-1992 | Martin and Mitra (2001) | -- | -- | -- | -- | 3.5 | 2.8 |

**Table 2.**
**Examples of dynamic primary agricultural products**
**and agro-based manufactures (1990-2004)**

|  | Dynamic (growing above the median) | Highly dynamic (growing above the median and increasing market share in total world trade) |
|---|---|---|
| Primary agricultural goods | **Pig meat** fresh, chilled or frozen; **Poultry**, fresh, chilled or frozen; **Milk and cream fresh**, not concentrated or sweetened; **Eggs**; **Fish fillets**, frozen; **Fish fillets**, fresh or chilled; **Rye**, unmilled; **Other fresh or chilled vegetables** (a); **Nuts**, edible, fresh or dried; **Fruit**, fresh or dried, nes (b); **Coffee** extracts, essences or concentrates; **Cocoa powder**, unsweetened; **Spices**, except pepper and pimento; **Margarine**, imitation lard and other prepared edible fats nes; Most **oilseeds, oilcake and oilseed flour**; **Cotton**, carded or combed; **Palm nuts and kernels** | **Milk and cream fresh**, not concentrated or sweetened; **Fish fillets**, fresh or chilled; **Cocoa powder**, unsweetened; **Margarine**, imitation lard and other prepared edible fats nes; **Soya beans**; **Cotton seeds**; **Cotton**, carded or combed |
| Agro-based manufactures | **Edible products and preparations** (e.g. soups and sauces); **Wine**; Materials and products of **rubber**; **Bakery products**; **Chocolate** and other preparations containing cocoa; **Non-alcoholic beverages** nes; **Vegetables**, prepared or preserved, nes; **Beer** made from malt; Other prepared or preserved **meat**; **Malt** extract; **Sugar confectionery** and preparations, non-chocolate; all **vegetable oils**; **Tobacco**, manufactured; **Sausages** and the like, of meat; **Jams**, jellies and marmalades; Natural **honey**; processed **animal and vegetable oils** | **Edible products and preparations** (e.g. soups and sauces); Materials and products of **rubber**; **Bakery products**; **Non-alcoholic beverages** nes; **Beer** made from malt; **Malt** extract; **Sugar confectionery** and preparations, non-chocolate; **Palm and palm kernel oil**; **Soya bean oil**; **Olive oil**; **Tobacco**, manufactured; Natural **honey**; processed **animal and vegetable oils.** |

*Obs.: (a) This group includes all fresh or chilled vegetables, except tomatoes, leguminous and alliaceous vegetables. (b) This group includes all tropical fruits, plus berries and avocados. Citrus, bananas, apples, grapes and figs are not in this group, although their growth performance was respectable, ranging between 3.5 per cent and 4.5 per cent annually.*

## Table 3.
### Main markets for Africa's traditional agricultural exports

|          | Share of world imports (a) | Share of partner in Africa's exports (b) | | Share of Africa in partner's market (a) | |
|          | 2004 | 1990 | 2004 | 1990 | 2004 |
|----------|------|------|------|------|------|
| EU15     | 31.6 | 65.0 | 55.7 | 32.4 | 36.0 |
| China    | 8.8  | 2.5  | 7.9  | 13.0 | 18.2 |
| USA      | 14.1 | 7.7  | 7.2  | 8.6  | 10.5 |
| Sum      | 54.4 | 75.2 | 70.8 | --   | --   |

Source: authors, based on UN-COMTRADE data. SITC rev.2 codes: 0573,0611,0612,0615,07111,07112,0721,0722,0723,2631,2632,2633,2634,0741.
Obs.: (a) Intra-EU trade is excluded. (b) Exports mirrored by partner's imports.

## Table 4.
### Main markets for Africa's exports of high value agricultural products, plus China

|          | Share of world imports (a) | Share of partner in Africa's exports (b) | | Share of Africa in partner's market (a) | |
|          | 2004 | 1990 | 2004 | 1990 | 2004 |
|----------|------|------|------|------|------|
| EU15     | 25.8 | 69.6 | 72.0 | 9.0  | 11.7 |
| USA      | 18.9 | 2.5  | 4.5  | 0.5  | 1.0  |
| Japan    | 16.0 | 8.4  | 5.0  | 1.6  | 1.3  |
| China    | 4.2  | 0.1  | 0.5  | 0.2  | 0.5  |
| India    | 1.8  | 1.8  | 4.3  | 10.6 | 10.0 |
| Sum      | 66.6 | 82.4 | 86.2 | --   | --   |

Source: authors, based on UN-COMTRADE data.
Obs.: (a) Intra-EU trade is excluded. (b) Exports mirrored by partner's imports.

**Table 5.**
**Africa's insertion in selected world markets for**
**high value agricultural goods**
**(sorted by value of total imports in selected market)**

| SITC Rev 2 Code & description by Country reporter | | Total imports | | Sub Saharan Africa | | |
|---|---|---|---|---|---|---|
| | | Value 2004 | Annual growth rate (%) 1990-2004 | Annual growth rate (%) 1990-2004 | Market share (%) 2004 | Growth rate (%) 1990-2004 |
| **USA** | | **37,908,240,014** | **5.6** | **10.3** | **1.0** | **83** |
| 0344 | Fish fillets, frozen | 1,587,812,433 | 2.7 | 30.5 | 1.7 | 2,731 |
| 05857 | Juice of any other fruit or vegetable | 592,707,245 | 6.1 | 42.3 | 1.6 | 5,970 |
| 05779 | Edible nuts, fresh or dry, nes | 308,057,082 | 8.0 | 21.9 | 14.7 | 445 |
| 07521 | Vanilla | 205,113,652 | 10.7 | 11.6 | 76.1 | 12 |
| 05712 | Mandarins and similar citrus, fresh or dried | 140,661,019 | 17.4 | ... | 14.0 | ... |
| 05481 | Roots and tubers, with high starch or insulin, fresh or dried | 118,782,631 | 8.9 | 21.8 | 3.0 | 379 |
| 29272 | Cut foliage, fresh, dried, bleached, etc | 114,007,879 | 5.8 | 19.5 | 1.9 | 448 |
| 05891 | Nuts, roasted (including peanut) | 112,905,995 | 11.5 | 7.0 | 1.6 | -44 |
| 05792 | Pears and quinces, fresh | 80,443,361 | 6.6 | ... | 2.3 | ... |
| 05711 | Oranges, fresh or dried | 69,916,046 | 19.4 | 79.1 | 44.1 | 29,204 |
| 07526 | Ginger (except in sugar or in syrup) | 37,004,934 | 9.8 | 7.4 | 2.4 | -27 |
| 05853 | Juice of any other citrus fruit | 30,930,477 | -1.8 | 21.1 | 4.4 | 1,788 |
| 05858 | Mixtures of fruit or vegetable juices | 24,067,694 | 4.8 | ... | 6.9 | ... |
| 05752 | Grapes dried (raisins) | 15,096,213 | 3.4 | ... | 15.1 | ... |
| 05488 | Vegetable products, primarily for human food, nes | 8,588,968 | 5.6 | ... | 1.1 | ... |
| 05643 | Flour, meal and flakes of potato | 7,214,652 | 16.9 | ... | 1.6 | ... |
| 05649 | Flours of leguminous, fruits, roots and tubers | 6,050,658 | 4.3 | 8.4 | 7.3 | 70 |
| 07523 | Cloves | 3,007,102 | -2.3 | 1.4 | 48.7 | 67 |
| **EU - 15 (excluding intra-EU trade)** | | **52,037,862,898** | **4.2** | **6.2** | **11.7** | **30** |
| 0360 | Crustaceans and molluscs, fresh, chilled, frozen, salted, etc | 4,581,225,503 | 5.3 | 6.7 | 14.6 | 21 |
| 0573 | Banana, plantain, fresh or dried | 3,507,793,803 | 3.7 | 7.6 | 13.8 | 67 |
| 0344 | Fish fillets, frozen | 2,506,160,445 | 5.5 | 12.2 | 10.8 | 136 |
| 0341 | Fish, fresh or chilled, excluding fillet | 2,274,055,069 | 3.9 | 11.6 | 9.6 | 170 |
| 0371 | Fish, prepared or preserved, nes | 1,983,860,427 | 4.1 | 8.7 | 32.3 | 84 |
| 0342 | Fish, frozen, excluding fillets | 1,466,106,754 | 0.7 | 2.3 | 21.3 | 25 |
| 01112 | Bovine meat fresh, chilled or frozen, boneless | 1,386,354,431 | 4.0 | 3.1 | 7.0 | -12 |

continued

| SITC Rev 2 Code & description by Country reporter | | Total imports | | Sub Saharan Africa | | |
|---|---|---|---|---|---|---|
| | | Value 2004 | Annual growth rate (%) 1990-2004 | Annual growth rate (%) 1990-2004 | Market share (%) 2004 | Growth rate (%) 1990-2004 |
| 05459 | Vegetables, fresh or chilled, nes | 1,302,099,713 | 9.6 | 9.4 | 21.8 | -3 |
| 0574 | Apples, fresh | 1,171,877,460 | 3.2 | 0.7 | 18.1 | -29 |
| 05798 | Other fresh fruit | 1,028,340,008 | 7.4 | 8.3 | 11.1 | 13 |
| 05751 | Grapes fresh | 990,601,424 | 9.0 | 10.8 | 41.2 | 27 |
| 05899 | Fruit and nuts, prepared, preserved, nes | 827,429,120 | 2.0 | -0.3 | 20.1 | -27 |
| 05779 | Edible nuts, fresh or dry, nes | 806,398,950 | 5.6 | 24.9 | 2.6 | 943 |
| 05659 | Vegetables prepared or preserved other than vinegar, nes | 798,433,437 | 5.7 | 8.5 | 4.9 | 46 |
| 29271 | Cut flowers and flower buds, fresh, dried, bleached, etc | 793,456,022 | 5.9 | 13.2 | 53.1 | 156 |
| 0542 | Beans, peas, other leguminous vegetables, dried, shelled | 685,181,821 | 0.9 | -1.5 | 2.6 | -29 |
| 05795 | Pineapples, fresh or dried | 672,580,290 | 12.2 | 6.8 | 37.8 | -50 |
| 0343 | Fish fillets, fresh or chilled | 644,513,293 | 21.3 | 45.8 | 35.5 | 1,207 |
| 05711 | Oranges, fresh or dried | 565,395,620 | -0.2 | 5.2 | 43.4 | 110 |
| 05797 | Avocados, mangoes, guavas, mangos-teens, fresh or dried | 460,200,688 | 5.9 | 3.5 | 27.5 | -27 |
| 05793 | Stone fruit, nes, fresh | 431,027,056 | 9.8 | 12.0 | 24.5 | 33 |
| 05461 | Vegetables, preserved by freezing | 422,625,677 | 3.1 | -3.9 | 1.6 | -63 |
| 05792 | Pears and quinces, fresh | 382,926,998 | 2.5 | 3.8 | 34.4 | 19 |
| 05752 | Grapes dried (raisins) | 374,527,873 | 1.5 | 1.3 | 6.3 | -2 |
| 29269 | Other live plants | 328,016,157 | 6.2 | 12.2 | 20.2 | 114 |
| 29272 | Cut foliage, fresh, dried, bleached, etc | 326,874,006 | 6.1 | 4.2 | 6.0 | -22 |
| 05481 | Roots and tubers, with high starch or insulin, fresh or dried | 304,092,230 | -6.9 | 2.9 | 5.5 | 301 |
| 05712 | Mandarins and similar citrus, fresh or dried | 301,737,949 | 3.7 | 15.8 | 17.0 | 370 |
| 05722 | Grapefruits, fresh or dried | 289,221,672 | -0.5 | 0.5 | 20.2 | 16 |
| 0561 | Vegetables (excluding leguminous), dried, evaporated, etc | 288,471,958 | 3.3 | -1.1 | 1.5 | -46 |
| 05799 | Other dried fruit | 287,820,256 | 4.0 | -2.7 | 1.1 | -61 |
| 05451 | Alliaceous vegetables, fresh or chilled | 275,795,982 | 3.9 | 10.6 | 3.8 | 141 |
| 05773 | Cashew nuts, fresh or dried | 269,049,071 | 11.1 | -0.5 | 1.1 | -79 |
| 01189 | Meat and edible meat offal, fresh, chilled, or frozen, nes | 268,207,154 | -0.1 | 16.0 | 9.2 | 709 |

continued

| SITC Rev 2 Code & description by Country reporter | | Total imports | | Sub Saharan Africa | | |
|---|---|---|---|---|---|---|
| | | Value 2004 | Annual growth rate (%) 1990-2004 | Annual growth rate (%) 1990-2004 | Market share (%) 2004 | Growth rate (%) 1990-2004 |
| 05721 | Lemons and limes, fresh or dried | 258,335,233 | 9.6 | 10.3 | 11.3 | 9 |
| 05651 | Vegetables and fruit, in vinegar or acetic acid | 254,339,518 | 6.9 | 21.0 | 2.7 | 471 |
| 0544 | Tomatoes, fresh or chilled | 251,627,147 | 2.9 | 14.3 | 2.7 | 336 |
| 0751 | Pepper of piper; pimento of capsicum or pimenta | 249,189,803 | 2.9 | 4.4 | 6.2 | 22 |
| 05794 | Berries, fresh | 207,478,042 | 7.9 | 1.8 | 1.0 | -56 |
| 05854 | Pineapple juice | 171,439,946 | 6.2 | 1.7 | 14.8 | -45 |
| 05796 | Dates, fresh or dried | 137,034,884 | 3.4 | 39.1 | 1.3 | 6226 |
| 4234 | Groundnut (peanut) oil | 122,612,060 | -3.4 | -8.8 | 31.2 | -56 |
| 03504 | Fish smoked | 118,433,300 | 9.6 | 13.2 | 2.2 | 59 |
| 07528 | Thyme, saffron, bay leaves; other spices | 98,698,367 | 10.0 | 9.1 | 1.9 | -10 |
| 07521 | Vanilla | 94,895,107 | 7.5 | 4.1 | 54.8 | -36 |
| 4249 | Fixed vegetable oils, nes | 91,910,602 | -0.4 | 7.7 | 12.4 | 198 |
| 05771 | Coconuts, fresh or dried (excluding copra) | 79,798,420 | 0.7 | -2.7 | 7.4 | -38 |
| 05852 | Grapefruit juice | 69,439,160 | -1.1 | 6.8 | 9.1 | 193 |
| 29261 | Bulbs, tubers, corms and others; dormant, in growth or in flower | 53,048,259 | 8.8 | 2.1 | 8.3 | -59 |
| 07526 | Ginger (except in sugar or in syrup) | 47,314,643 | 9.1 | 9.7 | 11.1 | 8 |
| 0583 | Jams, jellies, marmalades, etc, as cooked preparations | 33,516,933 | 5.9 | 3.2 | 6.9 | -31 |
| 05649 | Flours of leguminous, fruits, roots and tubers | 30,076,785 | 1.1 | 13.3 | 2.9 | 396 |
| 05858 | Mixtures of fruit or vegetable juices | 28,908,493 | 3.8 | 8.6 | 4.5 | 88 |
| 05853 | Juice of any other citrus fruit | 27,897,139 | 0.4 | -8.6 | 3.5 | -73 |
| 07522 | Cinnamon and cinnamon-tree flowers | 13,306,295 | 0.3 | -7.8 | 3.6 | -69 |
| 05864 | Peel of melons or citrus fruit, fresh, frozen, dried, etc | 7,423,435 | 4.5 | 25.5 | 18.4 | 1,195 |
| 0121 | Bacon, ham, other dried, salted or smoked meat of domestic swine | 6,731,089 | 0.4 | ... | 5.2 | ... |
| 05729 | Citrus fruit, nes, fresh or dried | 6,147,705 | 7.7 | 27.0 | 21.8 | 902 |
| 07523 | Cloves | 6,036,878 | 1.1 | -1.5 | 54.9 | -30 |
| 05645 | Tapioca, sago and substitutes obtained from starches | 2,738,705 | 2.2 | -6.8 | 1.8 | -72 |

*Source: the authors, based on UN-COMTRADE data.*
*Obs.: (a) products for which Africa has a market share below 1 per cent are not included in the table but are included in the totals. An empty cell means that no exports of that product category were registered in 1990.*

**Table 6.**
**Africa's largest exporters' and main competitors' insertion
in selected world markets for high value agricultural goods
(market shares, %, 2004)**

| Code SITC Rev.2 | Description | Largest supplier | | 2nd largest supplier | | Largest suppliers in Africa *(in addition to those found in the first two columns)* | | | |
|---|---|---|---|---|---|---|---|---|---|
| **EU-15** | | | | | | | | | |
| 01112 | Bovine meat fresh, chilled or frozen, boneless | Brazil | 51.1 | Argentina | 27.8 | Namibia | 3.7 | Botswana | 3.1 |
| 01189 | Meat and edible meat offal, fresh, chilled, or frozen, nes | New Zealand | 41.2 | Poland | 10.1 | South Africa | 7.9 | Zimbabwe | 1.1 |
| 0121 | Bacon, ham, other dried, salted or smoked meat of domestic swine | Areas, nes | 31.7 | Poland | 13.3 | Ivory Coast | 4.7 | Central African Rep. | 0.5 |
| 0341 | Fish, fresh or chilled, excluding fillet | Norway | 51.7 | Faeroe Isds | 8.0 | South Africa | 3.6 | Senegal | 2.3 |
| 0342 | Fish, frozen, excluding fillets | Russian Federation | 13.3 | USA | 11.6 | Namibia | 7.5 | South Africa | 5.0 |
| 0343 | Fish fillets, fresh or chilled | Iceland | 24.4 | Norway | 18.8 | United Rep. of Tanzania | 13.7 | Uganda | 13.0 |
| 0344 | Fish fillets, frozen | China | 16.4 | Norway | 13.3 | Namibia | 6.2 | South Africa | 2.4 |
| 03504 | Fish smoked | Poland | 68.7 | Norway | 10.8 | Ivory Coast | 1.7 | Ghana | 0.2 |
| 0360 | Crustaceans and molluscs, fresh, chilled, frozen, salted, etc | India | 8.3 | Argentina | 8.2 | Madagascar | 3.4 | Senegal | 2.3 |
| 0371 | Fish, prepared or preserved, nes | Morocco | 11.1 | Ecuador | 10.2 | Seychelles | 9.6 | Ivory Coast | 7.8 |
| 0542 | Beans, peas, other leguminous vegetables, dried, shelled | Canada | 42.2 | China | 10.6 | Ethiopia | 1.1 | United Rep. of Tanzania | 0.8 |
| 0544 | Tomatoes, fresh or chilled | Morocco | 68.5 | Israel | 12.6 | Senegal | 2.6 | South Africa | 0.1 |
| 05451 | Alliaceous vegetables, fresh or chilled | Argentina | 21.4 | New Zealand | 18.2 | South Africa | 2.8 | Kenya | 0.7 |
| 05459 | Vegetables, fresh or chilled, nes | Morocco | 16.5 | Kenya | 13.9 | Zambia | 1.3 | Zimbabwe | 1.1 |

continued

| Code SITC Rev.2 | Description | Largest supplier | | 2nd largest supplier | | Largest suppliers in Africa (in addition to those found in the first two columns) | | | |
|---|---|---|---|---|---|---|---|---|---|
| 05461 | Vegetables, preserved by freezing | Poland | 26.8 | China | 19.1 | Kenya | 0.7 | South Africa | 0.5 |
| 05481 | Roots and tubers, with high starch or insulin, fresh or dried | Thailand | 76.2 | Israel | 4.4 | Ghana | 3.3 | South Africa | 0.8 |
| 0561 | Vegetables (excluding leguminous), dried, evaporated, etc | China | 31.3 | USA | 10.3 | Zimbabwe | 0.9 | Senegal | 0.1 |
| 05645 | Tapioca, sago and substitutes obtained from starches | China | 39.5 | Thailand | 34.6 | Madagascar | 0.6 | Nigeria | 0.5 |
| 05649 | Flours of leguminous, fruits, roots and tubers | Turkey | 41.9 | USA | 21.4 | Nigeria | 1.2 | Ghana | 0.6 |
| 05651 | Vegetables and fruit, in vinegar or acetic acid | Turkey | 47.3 | Hungary | 10.9 | South Africa | 2.1 | Madagascar | 0.5 |
| 05659 | Vegetables prepared or preserved other than vinegar, nes | China | 39.5 | Peru | 13.9 | Kenya | 3.0 | Cameroon | 0.6 |
| 05711 | Oranges, fresh or dried | South Africa | 39.2 | Morocco | 17.4 | Zimbabwe | 2.5 | Swaziland | 1.7 |
| 05712 | Mandarins and similar citrus, fresh or dried | Morocco | 31.3 | South Africa | 16.5 | Zimbabwe | 0.3 | Swaziland | 0.2 |
| 05721 | Lemons and limes, fresh or dried | Argentina | 52.6 | Brazil | 16.0 | South Africa | 11.2 | Zimbabwe | 0.1 |
| 05722 | Grapefruits, fresh or dried | USA | 28.5 | South Africa | 18.0 | Swaziland | 1.4 | Zimbabwe | 0.4 |
| 05729 | Citrus fruit, nes, fresh or dried | Israel | 48.7 | South Africa | 20.4 | Zimbabwe | 1.4 | ... | ... |
| 0573 | Banana, plantain, fresh or dried | Ecuador | 22.9 | Costa Rica | 22.5 | Ivory Coast | 6.9 | Cameroon | 6.7 |
| 0574 | Apples, fresh | New Zealand | 28.8 | South Africa | 18.1 | Ivory Coast | 0.0 | Central African Rep. | 0.0 |
| 05751 | Grapes fresh | South Africa | 39.8 | Chile | 24.2 | Namibia | 1.4 | Ivory Coast | 0.0 |
| 05752 | Grapes dried (raisins) | Turkey | 59.1 | USA | 21.3 | South Africa | 6.3 | ... | ... |

continued

| Code SITC Rev.2 | Description | Largest supplier | | 2nd largest supplier | | Largest suppliers in Africa (in addition to those found in the first two columns) | | | |
|---|---|---|---|---|---|---|---|---|---|
| 05771 | Coconuts, fresh or dried (excluding copra) | Philippines | 34.9 | Indonesia | 20.1 | Ivory Coast | 7.3 | South Africa | 0.1 |
| 05773 | Cashew nuts, fresh or dried | India | 64.1 | Viet Nam | 27.7 | United Rep. of Tanzania | 0.3 | Mozambique | 0.2 |
| 05779 | Edible nuts, fresh or dry, nes | USA | 40.1 | Iran | 28.4 | South Africa | 2.0 | Malawi | 0.3 |
| 05792 | Pears and quinces, fresh | Argentina | 40.7 | South Africa | 34.4 | Fmr Ethiopia | 0.0 | Central African Rep. | 0.0 |
| 05793 | Stone fruit, nes, fresh | Turkey | 30.3 | South Africa | 24.3 | Namibia | 0.1 | Zimbabwe | 0.0 |
| 05795 | Pineapples, fresh or dried | Costa Rica | 49.2 | Ivory Coast | 23.8 | Ghana | 11.3 | South Africa | 1.2 |
| 05796 | Dates, fresh or dried | Tunisia | 50.9 | Israel | 22.0 | South Africa | 1.2 | Namibia | 0.1 |
| 05797 | Avocados, mangoes, guavas, mangos-teens, fresh or dried | Brazil | 19.1 | Israel | 15.7 | South Africa | 14.7 | Kenya | 5.4 |
| 05798 | Other fresh fruit | New Zealand | 32.7 | Brazil | 15.7 | Madagascar | 7.7 | South Africa | 1.9 |
| 05799 | Other dried fruit | Turkey | 36.8 | USA | 26.5 | South Africa | 1.0 | Madagascar | 0.0 |
| 0583 | Jams, jellies, marmalades, etc, as cooked preparations | Turkey | 38.7 | Bulgaria | 9.1 | South Africa | 5.2 | Swaziland | 0.7 |
| 05852 | Grapefruit juice | USA | 44.0 | Israel | 24.6 | South Africa | 8.3 | Swaziland | 0.8 |
| 05853 | Juice of any other citrus fruit | Argentina | 47.2 | Brazil | 19.0 | South Africa | 2.7 | Ivory Coast | 0.3 |
| 05854 | Pineapple juice | Thailand | 34.3 | Costa Rica | 11.8 | Kenya | 7.8 | South Africa | 4.5 |
| 05858 | Mixtures of fruit or vegetable juices | USA | 40.0 | Israel | 12.6 | South Africa | 4.6 | Ghana | 0.0 |
| 05864 | Peel of melons or citrus fruit, fresh, frozen, dried etc | Haiti | 19.0 | Brazil | 14.2 | Ghana | 11.5 | Senegal | 5.0 |
| 05899 | Fruit and nuts, prepared, preserved, nes | Thailand | 19.5 | South Africa | 11.5 | Kenya | 6.2 | Swaziland | 2.0 |
| 0751 | Pepper of piper"; pimento of "capsicum or pimenta"" | Brazil | 17.8 | Viet Nam | 16.7 | Zimbabwe | 2.7 | South Africa | 1.9 |
| 07521 | Vanilla | Madagascar | 47.5 | Indonesia | 18.3 | Comoros | 5.9 | Uganda | 1.3 |

continued

| Code SITC Rev.2 | Description | Largest supplier | | 2nd largest supplier | | Largest suppliers in Africa (in addition to those found in the first two columns) | | | |
|---|---|---|---|---|---|---|---|---|---|
| 07522 | Cinnamon and cinnamon-tree flowers | Indonesia | 40.8 | Sri Lanka | 27.4 | Madagascar | 2.9 | Seychelles | 0.6 |
| 07523 | Cloves | Madagascar | 30.7 | Comoros | 22.7 | Tanzania | 1.5 | Mali | 0.0 |
| 07526 | Ginger (except in sugar or in syrup) | China | 46.6 | Thailand | 15.7 | Nigeria | 8.2 | South Africa | 1.2 |
| 07528 | Thyme, saffron, bay leaves; other spices | Iran | 27.0 | India | 17.1 | South Africa | 1.3 | Mauritius | 0.3 |
| 29271 | Cut flowers and flower buds, fresh, dried, bleached, etc | Kenya | 36.1 | Israel | 14.2 | Zimbabwe | 6.2 | Uganda | 3.3 |
| 29272 | Cut foliage, fresh, dried, bleached, etc | USA | 26.8 | Costa Rica | 18.1 | South Africa | 5.4 | Kenya | 0.3 |
| 29261 | Bulbs, tubers, corms and others; dormant, in growth or in flower | USA | 14.4 | Chile | 13.6 | South Africa | 7.7 | Kenya | 0.3 |
| 29269 | Other live plants | Costa Rica | 13.0 | Israel | 12.0 | Kenya | 11.1 | Uganda | 3.3 |
| 4234 | Groundnut (peanut) oil | India | 44.5 | Senegal | 21.2 | Gambia | 7.0 | Sudan | 2.8 |
| 4249 | Fixed vegetable oils, nes | USA | 34.2 | China | 9.5 | Ghana | 4.9 | South Africa | 4.3 |
| **USA** | | | | | | | | | |
| 0343 | Fish fillets, fresh or chilled | Chile | 52.1 | Canada | 16.7 | Uganda | 0.6 | Kenya | 0.1 |
| 05481 | Roots and tubers, with high starch or insulin, fresh or dried | Costa Rica | 49.0 | Dominican Rep. | 14.9 | Ghana | 2.9 | Nigeria | 0.1 |
| 05488 | Vegetable products, primarily for human food, nes | China | 32.4 | Other Asia, nes | 20.9 | South Africa | 1.1 | ... | ... |
| 05643 | Flour, meal and flakes of potato | Canada | 56.6 | Spain | 19.6 | Ethiopia | 0.8 | Djibouti | 0.8 |
| 05649 | Flours of leguminous, fruits, roots and tubers | Canada | 30.2 | Thailand | 13.5 | Ghana | 3.6 | Nigeria | 2.1 |
| 05711 | Oranges, fresh or dried | Australia | 44.6 | South Africa | 44.1 | ... | ... | ... | ... |

continued

| Code SITC Rev.2 | Description | Largest supplier | | 2nd largest supplier | | Largest suppliers in Africa (in addition to those found in the first two columns) | | | |
|---|---|---|---|---|---|---|---|---|---|
| 05712 | Mandarins and similar citrus, fresh or dried | Spain | 76.4 | South Africa | 14.0 | ... | | ... | ... | ... |
| 05752 | Grapes dried (raisins) | Chile | 50.7 | Mexico | 22.6 | South Africa | 15.1 | ... | ... |
| 05779 | Edible nuts, fresh or dry, nes | Mexico | 45.7 | China | 17.4 | South Africa | 6.3 | Kenya | 4.0 |
| 05792 | Pears and quinces, fresh | Argentina | 37.4 | Chile | 26.3 | South Africa | 2.3 | ... | ... |
| 05853 | Juice of any other citrus fruit | Mexico | 48.4 | Argentina | 30.5 | South Africa | 4.4 | Swaziland | 0.0 |
| 05857 | Juice of any other fruit or vegetable | China | 32.5 | Argentina | 19.0 | South Africa | 1.6 | Ghana | 0.0 |
| 05858 | Mixtures of fruit or vegetable juices | Canada | 30.6 | Mexico | 29.7 | South Africa | 6.9 | Kenya | 0.0 |
| 05891 | Nuts, roasted (including peanut) | Canada | 25.7 | China | 12.7 | Kenya | 1.2 | Mozambique | 0.2 |
| 07521 | Vanilla | Madagascar | 65.6 | Indonesia | 13.5 | Comoros | 7.8 | Uganda | 2.7 |
| 07523 | Cloves | Madagascar | 32.1 | Brazil | 19.3 | Comoros | 14.0 | Tanzania | 2.6 |
| 07526 | Ginger (except in sugar or in syrup) | China | 71.6 | Brazil | 11.2 | Nigeria | 2.4 | South Africa | 0.1 |
| 29272 | Cut foliage, fresh, dried, bleached, etc | Canada | 43.3 | Italy | 8.1 | South Africa | 1.2 | Madagascar | 0.5 |

Source: the authors, based on UN-COMTRADE data.
Obs.: only products for which Africa as a whole had a market share of at least 1 per cent are included in the table. Intra-EU trade is excluded.

## Notes

1 The slowdown during the 1970s could partly be explained by exceptionally high prices inducing small, inefficient mines to enter these sectors, the introduction of a number of environmental, health and safety regulations, and the occurrence of important disruptions due to strikes. These factors would have had a negative, but transitory, effect on multi-factor productivity growth. That is, "in retrospect the 1970s look like an exceptional period, rather than marking a change in long-run productivity trends" (Parry, 1997, p.3).

2 Including agriculture, fisheries and forestry.

3 In Canada, for instance, where mineral exports still account for a significant share of the total, the mining sector has extensive backward and forward linkages, and the accumulation of geological knowledge has allowed native firms to explore mineral resources elsewhere and to export geophysical services and equipment (Ritter, 2001). In the developing world, however, even in countries where the mining sector significantly contributes to investment, production and exports, the mining sector typically exhibits relatively low linkages with the domestic economy (see Buitelaar, 2001, for Latin America; Stilwell et al., 2000 for South Africa). Even in the few which have done very well overall, and where innovation has become a productivity driver (e.g. Chile; see Nishiyama, 2005; and García, Knights and Tilton, 2001), the majority of local suppliers provide goods and services which are not essential to the competitiveness of the large mining firms. As the latter procure this type of relatively undifferentiated goods and services on a cost-minimization basis, small firms are marginalized, and domestic goods face steep competition from imported supplies. Furthermore, downstream activities, such as copper refining, are still incipient (Culverwell, 2001).

4 This is the case of cotton, of which China is an important importer but also producer. International demand is however expected to pick up again as demand for cotton in China (and India) expands following the end of the Multi-Fibre Arrangement.

5 Thus, the higher the average income of the exporter, the higher the degree of sophistication, the underlying logic being that in the absence of policy-induced trade barriers, the goods exported by richer countries will have certain specificities (e.g., related to technology content, marketing, logistics, information and familiarity, infrastructure and value-chain organization) that let high-wage producers withstand competition in world markets, i.e., where competition is not primarily based on price.

6 Data are from the World Development Indicators online database.

7 Product categories are: Primary (which we further separate into agricultural, fuel and other minerals), Resource-based (agro-based and other), Low technological content, Medium technological content and High technological content. A small group of commodities which do not fit any of the categories are excluded from the analysis. Lall classified organic chemicals in other resource-based manufactures, rather than agro-based, and thus we classified crude organic fertilizers in primary mineral products, rather than agricultural.

8 Fish is the paradigmatic example of a commodity that does not typically increase its unit value when it is processed, with the exception of the value-adding process of filleting.

9 Authors' calculations, based on UN COMTRADE data.

10 "Wal-Mart eyes organic foods", The New York Times (12/May/2006).

11 While Vietnam is currently a small producer of cocoa by world standards, its production is expected to expand significantly over the medium-term, as farmers respond to declining coffee prices by replacing or supplementing coffee with cocoa in land deemed to be highly suitable for its cultivation (USDA, 2003).

12 Including allocation of cooperative land to farm households, legalization of private ownership of productive assets, deregulation of agricultural marketing and prices, and devaluation of the exchange rate.

13 Authors' calculations based on COMTRADE data.

14 The total area planted by small farmers now accounts for more than half of the total in that country.

15 Sugar production in the EU is however expected to decline as a result of reforms of the sugar regime which came into effect in July 2006 (FAS-USDA, World Sugar Situation 2006).

16 Although full liberalization under EBA for sugar will only take place in 2009.

17 Authors' calculations based on COMTRADE data.

18 Authors' calculations based on COMTRADE data.

19 US Mission to the EU
(http://www.useu.be/Catcgories/Bananas/Index.htm).

20 Authors' calculations, based on COMTRADE data.

21 Authors' calculations, based on COMTRADE data.

22 USDA-FAS, Official estimates for May 2006 (http://fas.usda.gov/psd/complete_tables/CO-table11-177.htm).

23 This group includes bananas, which were discussed in the previous section.

24 Nes = not specified elsewhere (this category includes macadamia nuts, among other edible nuts, of which South Africa is the second largest exporter after Australia).

25 Authors' calculations, based on COMTRADE data.

26 Authors' calculations, based on COMTRADE data.

27 This average includes only expenditures through the regular budget, excluding therefore those incurred by public development banks, which are very sizeable in countries like Brazil or Costa Rica.

28 Now called ChileAlimentos.

29 Good agricultural practices comprise a set of measures implemented at farm level in order to meet certain environmental, health, worker's welfare and sanitary standards. These are formally required by large food retailers in Europe and the United States since 1997, and today Chilean exporters require their suppliers to have them in place. Good manufacturing practices are similar, but pertain to agricultural processing plants ("Nuestra Tierra" Magazine, Chilean Ministry of Agriculture, July 2003).

30 Salmon refers to salmon and trout, unless otherwise indicated.

31 Authors' calculations, based on figures in UNCTAD (2006).

32 The processing of salmon into fillets is labor intensive and Chile benefits from labor costs lower than those prevailing in its main competitors, Norway and Scotland (UNCTAD, 2006).

33 This is the largest non profit organization fostering innovation and technology transfer in the country, founded in 1976 by the Chilean government and the US-based ITT corporation.

34 The equipment utilizes a method that produces brain death in the salmon but otherwise allows it to maintain its physiological functions (http://www.fundacionchile.cl).

35 SIGes combines locally created standards with modified global standards.

36 Established in 2003 by several salmon industry associations in Canada, the US and SalmonChile in Chile.

37 The country now ranks third, after Indonesia (Malaysian Palm Oil Board, http://econ.mpob.gov.my/economy/world_8.htm).

38 Kenaf is a fiber-producing plant which is used for the manufacture of pulp and paper products. It is considered one of the most promising alternatives to wood for paper production (Taylor, 1993).

39 "To encourage new investments in 'halal' food production for the export market and to increase the use of modern and state-of-the-art machinery and equipment in producing high quality 'halal' food that comply with the international standards, companies which invest in 'halal' food productions and have already obtained 'halal' certification from JAKIM are eligible for the Investment Tax Allowance of 100 per cent of qualifying capital expenditure incurred within a period of 5 years" (Malaysian Industrial Development Authority, Investor's Guide, http://www.mida.gov.my).

40 Malaysian Industrial Development Authority, Investor's Guide (http://www.mida.gov.my).

41 For the list, see:

http://www.mida.gov.my/beta/view.php?cat=3&scat=34&pg=978.

42 "First shipment of biodiesel to Europe next week"

(http://biz.thestar.com.my/news/story.asp?file=/2006/8/11/business/15112818&sec=business).

43 "Malaysia weighs palm oil share for food, energy" (http://www.planetark.com).

44 This finding cannot be attributed to structural factors, since the observed relationship between discovery and income per capita does not significantly differ across sectors.

45 Average tariffs (including ad-valorem equivalents of specific duties) are highest in the EU and developed Asia for a broad range of products, while in the United States (and Canada) tariff protection is concentrated in a few sectors, including sugar, dairy and tobacco.

46 The WITS database was used. At the time of writing, the most recent year for which ad valorem equivalents were calculated was 2001, and thus the average tariffs presented are for 2001. Since then, South Africa has signed a free trade agreement with the EU, so these averages are probably lower. Non LDC countries in Africa are Botswana, Cameroon, Congo, Gabon, Ghana, Kenya, Mauritius, Namibia, Nigeria, Seychelles, South Africa, Swaziland and Zimbabwe.

47 UNCTAD's Trade Analysis and Information System.

48 Including price control measures, quantity restrictions, monopolistic measures and technical regulations.

49 Based on survey data, findings from several OECD reports show that the agriculture and food sectors account for the largest number of NTB complaints in relative terms, followed by mining and textiles (UNCTAD, 2005).

50 Importation of fresh meat derived from domestic and wild ungulate (hoofed) animals", European Commission

(http://europa.eu.int/comm/food/animal/animalproducts/freshmeat/index_en.htm).

51 http://www.fsis.usda.gov/regulations_&_policies/Eligible_Foreign_Establishments/index.asp.

52 HACCP=Hazard Analysis and Critical Control Point. African countries allowed to export fish and fish products to the EU are: Cape Verde, Gabon, Gambia, Ghana, Guinea, Ivory Coast, Kenya, Madagascar, Mauritania, Mauritius, Mozambique, Nigeria, Seychelles, Senegal, South Africa, Tanzania and Uganda. In the US, the responsibility to verify that that the fish and fish products comply with HACCP principles and US regulations for the "Safe and Sanitary Processing and Importing of Fish and Fishery Products" falls on the importers. One way in which importers may satisfy their verification obligation is to obtain products from a country that has an equivalence agreement with the US covering fish and fish products. As no such agreement exists with African countries, importers must take "affirmative" steps [e.g. obtaining a certificate from an appropriate foreign government inspection authority attesting that the products were produced in accordance with US requirements ("Fish and Fishery products: affirmative steps", US Food and Drug Administration,

http://cfsan.fad.gov/~frf/sfimport.html)].

53 Nile perch is the most important commercial species in Uganda. It was introduced in Lake Victoria during the colonial period and was initially sent to Kenya for processing. This ended in 1991 when the Ugandan government banned exports of unprocessed whole fish to Kenya.

54 http://www.unido.org/userfiles/timminsk/LDC3uganda.pdf.

55 New technical barriers are constantly emerging. For instance, in the US, the Public Health Security and Bioterrorism Preparedness and Response Act of 2002 increased the stringency of food (and drug) import requirements with respect to traceability (e.g. all companies supplying food products to the US must register with the Food and Drug Administration and must keep records related to processing, packaging, distribution and so forth for a 2 year period) and container security (the Container Security Programme, CSI, requires that container content be monitored prior to arrival in the US; due to the high costs of the necessary equipment, most ports in developing countries are not CSI compliant yet, and thus shipments have to be monitored in US ports, a process which takes between 2 and 6 days) (UN-ECLAC, 2004).

56 KEPHIS is seeking recognition by the European Commission as a "competent authority" (meaning that most inspection responsibilities would be delegated to KEPHIS thereby facilitating the entry of Kenyan exports into the EU).

57 Annual growth rates in market shares over the 1990-2004 period were, respectively, -64.5 per cent, 391 per cent and 11 per cent, based on UN-COMTRADE data. As a reference, Latin America held a 45 per cent market share in China's imports of agricultural products as of 2003 (up from rough-

ly 28 per cent in 1995). In India, the region's market share increased from roughly 7 per cent to 20 per cent over the same period (UN-ECLAC, 2005).

58 While India remains an incipient importer overall, for some countries and some products it is an important trading partner (e.g. cotton from Sudan and Cameroon; fruits and vegetables from Ethiopia, Ghana and Tanzania; fruits and nuts from Mozambique) (Goldstein et al., 2006).

59 Authors' calculations, based on COMTRADE data.

60 East African Business Week, May 29, 2006: "Fish exporters begin to look to value addition".

61 Authors' calculations, based on UN-COMTRADE data for 2004.

62 "Ethiopia: the next production hot spot", FloraCulture International, May/June, Vol.16 (3), by N. Laws.

63 Mauritius being an outlier, in that handling and transport take only half a month on average, just slightly above the average for developed countries. On the other extreme, export time reaches 116 days in the Central African Republic.

64 This expression is used in the OECD paper in relation to the inability to re-create the Green Revolution in Africa.

65 Even in the US, where a well-developed patent system exists, it is estimated that "seed companies retained only 30-50 per cent of the economic benefits from enhanced hybrid seed yields and only 10 per cent of benefits from non-hybrid seed during 1975-90" (Fuglie et al., 1996, quoted in Kremer and Zwane, 2005).

# Acknowledgements

The authors would like to thank David O'Connor and David Le Blanc for helpful comments and discussions.

# Bibliography

Acemoglu, D. and S. Johnson, S. (2003), Unbundling institutions, The Journal of Political Economy, October, 113 (5), 949-995.

Acemoglu, D., S. Johnson, and J.A. Robinson (2003), An African success story: Botswana", Chapter 4 in In Search of Prosperity – Analytic Narratives on Economic Growth. Ed. D. Rodrik, Princeton University Press.

AfDB/OECD (2006), African Economic Outlook.

Altieri, M.A. and A. Rojas (1999), Ecological impacts of Chile's neoliberal policies, with special emphasis on agroecosystems, Environment, Development and Sustainability, 1, 55-72.

Basu, A. and U. Grote (2006), China as a standard-setter – the examples of GM cotton and ecological and food safety standards, Paper presented at the Pre-conference Workshop (Seventh Annual Global Development Conference) on Asian and other drivers of global change, St. Petersburg, January 18-19, 2006.

Bernard, A.B. and C.I. Jones (1996), Comparing apples to oranges: productivity convergence and measurement across industries and countries, The American Economic Review, 86 (5), 1216-1238.

Bonaglia, F. and K. Fukasaku (2003), Export diversification in low-income countries: an international challenge after Doha, OECD Development Centre Technical Papers, 209, June.

Bosten, E. (2005), China's engagement in the construction industry of Southern Africa: the case of Mozambique, Paper presented at the Asian and Other Drivers of Global Change Workshop held in St Petersburg, Russia on 18-19th January 2006.

Bowles, D., R. Paskin, M. Gutiérrez and A. Kasterine (2005), Animal welfare and developing countries: opportunities for trade in high-welfare products from developing countries, Rev. sci. tech. Off. int. Epiz., 24 (2), 783-790.

Bravo-Ortega, C. and D. Lederman (2005a), Public Expenditures, RNR Productivity, and Development, Chapter 5 in Beyond the city: The Rural Contribution to Development, eds. Ferranti, D., Perry, G.E., Foster, W., Lederman, W. and Valdés, A., The World Bank, 312 pp.

Bravo-Ortega, C. and Lederman, D. (2005b), From Accounting to Economics: The Rural Natural Resource Sector's Contribution to Development, Chapter 3 Beyond the city: The Rural Contribution to Development, eds. Ferranti, D., Perry, G.E., Foster, W., Lederman, W. and Valdés, A., The World Bank, 312 pp.

Brooks, J. and S. Lucatelli (2004), International competitiveness of the A-B-C agro-food sector, Chapter 4 in Trade and competitiveness in Argentina, Brazil and Chile: not as easy as A-B-C, OECD..

Buitelaar, R. (2001), Aglomeraciones mineras y desarrollo local en America Latina, ed. Rudolf Buitelaar, Alfaomega/UN-ECLAC/IDRC, 340 pp.

Bureau, J-C., S. Jean and A. Matthews (2005), The consequences of agricultural trade liberalization for developing countries: distinguishing between genuine benefits and false hopes, CEPII, Working paper 2005-13, August.

Cashin, P. and C.J. McDermott (2002), The long-run behavior of commodity prices: small trends and big variability, IMF Staff Papers, 49 (2), 175-199.

Coelli, T.J. and D.S.P. Rao (2003), Total factor productivity growth in agriculture: a Malquist index analysis of 93 countries, 1980-2000, Plenary paper presented at the 2003 International Association of Agricultural Economics (IAAE), Durban, August 16-22.

Culverwell, M. (2001), Desarrollo de proveedores en la región de Antofagasta, Chapter IV in Aglomeraciones mineras y desarrollo local en América Latina, ed. Buitelaar, R., Alfaomega/UN-ECLAC/IDRC, 340 pp.

European Commission (2006), Towards a reform of the internal aspects of the common organisation of the market in bananas, Consultation document of the impact analysis steering group, April.

European Commission (2005), Africa's agricultural economy: its position in the world and its relations with the EU, Monitoring Agri-trade Policy, No.02-05, June, DG Agriculture & Rural Development.

Damiani, O. (2000), The State and Nontraditional Agricultural Exports in Latin America: Results and Lessons of Three case Studies, Paper presented at the Conference Rural economy and poverty reduction in Latin America and the Caribbean, New Orleans, March.

Danielou, M. and C. Ravry (2005), The rise of Ghana's pineapple industry – from successful take-off to sustainable expansion, World Bank Africa Region Working Paper series No.93, November.

David, B., M. Dirven and F. Vogelgesang (2000), The Impact of the New Economic Model on Latin America's Agriculture, World Development, 28 (9), 1673-1688.

Djankov, S., C. Freund and C.S. Pham (2006), Trading on time, World Bank Policy Research Working Paper 3909, May.

Dorward, A., J. Kydd, J. Morrisson and I. Urey (2004), A policy agenda for pro-poor agricultural growth, World Development, 32 (1), 73-89.

Ferranti, D., G.E. Perry, W. Foster, W. Lederman and A. Valdés (2005), Beyond the city: The Rural Contribution to Development, The World Bank, 312 pp.

Ferranti, D., G.E. Perry, D. Lederman and W.F. Maloney (2002), From natural resources to the knowledge economy. Trade and job quality, World Bank Latin American and Caribbean Studies, Viewpoints.

Fuglie, K., N. Ballenger, K. Day, C. Koltz, M. Ollinger, J. Reilly, U. Vasavada and J. Yee (1996), Agricultural research and development: Public and private investments under alternative markets and institutions, Agricultural Economic Report No. 735, Washington, DC: Economic Research Service, United States Department of Agriculture.

García M., M. y F. Bañados, (2004), Impact of EU organic product certification legislation on Chile organic exports, Food Policy, 29 (1).

García, P., P.F. Knights and J.E. Tilton (2001), Labor productivity and comparative advantage in mining: the copper industry in Chile, Resources Policy, 27, 97-105.

Gabre-Madhin, E.Z. and S. Haggblade (2004), Successes in African agriculture: results of an expert survey, World Development, 32 (5), 745-766.

Giuliani, E., C. Pietrobelli and R. Rabelotti (2005), Upgrading in global value chains: lessons from Latin American clusters, World Development, 33 (4), 549-573.

Goldstein, A., N. Pinaud, H. Reisen and X. Chen (2006), China and India: what's in it for Africa?, OECD Development Centre, May, 150 pp.

Gómez T., L., L. Martin, M.A. Gómez Cruz and T. Mutersbaugh (2005), Certified organic agriculture in Mexico: market connections and certification practices in large and small producers, Journal of Rural Studies, 21, 461-474.

Guaipatín, C. (2004), La aglomeración de la frambuesa en Chile: el reto común del Estado, las grandes empresas y los pequeños productores, Chapter 5 in Los recursos del desarrollo – lecciones de 6 aglomeraciones agroindustriales en América Latina, ed. C. Guaipatín, UN-ECLAC/ALFAOMEGA (pub.).

Hausmann, R. and D. Rodrik (2006), Doomed to choose: industrial policy as predicament, Paper prepared for the first Blue Sky Seminar organized by the Center for International Development at Harvard University, September 9

Hausmann, R. and D. Rodrik (2003), Economic development and self-discovery, Journal of Development Economics, 72, 603-633.

Henson, S. and R. Loader (2001), Barriers to agricultural exports from developing countries: the role of sanitary and phytosanitary requirements, World Development, 29 (1), 85-102.

ICAC (2004), Cotton: review of the world situation, International Cotton Advisory Committee, 58 (2), November-December.

ICCO (2005), 2003/2004 Annual Report of the International Cocoa Organization.

ICCO (2003), Cocoa in Indonesia, Q&A International Cocoa Organization (http://www.icco.org/questions/indonesia.htm).

ICCO (2000), How many smallholders are there worldwide producing cocoa?, Q&A International Cocoa Organization (http://www.icco.org/questions/smallholders.htm).

Iiuzuka, M. (2006), Catching up through collective capability: globalization and standards in the salmon farming industry in Chile, Paper submitted to the DRUID (Danish Research Unit for Industrial Dynamics) Summer Conference (http://www2.druid.dk/conferences/viewabstract.php?id=545&cf=8).

Imbs, J. and R. Wacziarg (2003), Stages of Diversification, American Economic Review, 93(1), 63-86.

ITC (2003), International Trade Forum, Issue 2/2003, ITC, 25-27.

Iyoha, M.A. (2005), Enhancing Africa's trade: from marginalization to an export-led approach to development, African Development Bank Economic Research Working Paper No.77, August.

Jaffe, S. with the assistance of P. Gordon (1998), Exporting high value food commodities. Success stories from developing countries, World Bank Discussion Paper 198.

Kaelin, A. and I.G. Cowx (2002), Outline of the path forward in Uganda's fisheries sector, paper prepared for the Presidential Conference on Export Competitiveness, February 12.

Kaplinsky, R. (2005), Revisiting the terms of trade: will China make a difference? Briefing Paper, March, Institute of Development Studies, University of Sussex, and Centre for Research in Innovation Management, University of Brighton.

Kaplinsky, R. (2004), Competition policy and the global coffee and cocoa value chains, Paper prepared for UNCTAD, May, Institute of Development Studies, University of Sussex, and Centre for Research in Innovation Management, University of Brighton.

Kaplinsky, R. and M. Morris (2006), The Asian drivers and SSA; MFA quota removal and the portents for African industrialization?, Paper prepared for conference on Asian and other Drivers of change, St. Petersburg, Russia, 18-19th January..

Kaplinsky, R. and A.S. Paulino (2004), Innovation and competitiveness: trends in unit prices in global trade, Second Globelics Conference Proceedings, Beijing, china, October 16-20.

Kaplinsky, R. and A.S. Readman (2005), Globalisation and upgrading: what can (and cannot) be learnt from international trade statistics in the wood furniture sector?, Industrial and Corporate Change, 14 (4), 679-703.

Kee, H.L., A. Nicita and M. Olarreaga (2006), Estimating trade restrictiveness indices, Policy Research Working Paper Series 3840, The World Bank.

Kjöllerström, M (forthcoming), Gasto público en el sector agrícola y las áreas rurales: la experiencia de América Latina en la década de noventa in Políticas públicas y desarrollo rural en América Latina y el Caribe: El papel del gasto público.

Klinger, B. and D. Lederman (2004), Discovery and development: an empirical exploration of 'new' products, World Bank Research Policy Working Paper 3450, November.

Kremer, M. and A.P. Zwane (2005), Encouraging private sector research for tropical agriculture, World Development, 33 (1), 87-105.

Laiglesia, J. de (2006), Institutional bottlenecks for agricultural development – a stocktaking exercise based on evidence from Sub-Saharan Africa, OECD Development Centre Working paper No. 248, March.

Lall, S. with the assistance of E. Kraemer-Mbula (2005), Is African industry competing?, Working Paper No. 121, QEH Working Paper Series, University of Oxford.

Lall, S. (2000), The Technological structure and performance of developing country manufactured exports, 1985-1998, Queen Elizabeth House Working Paper Series 44, University of Oxford.

Lall, S., M. Albaladejo and M.M. Moreira (2004), Latin American industrial competitiveness and the challenge of globalization, Washington D.C.: Inter-American Development Bank, Integration and Regional Programs department, INTAL-ITD Occasional Paper-SITI-05.

Lall, S., J. Weiss and J. Zhang (2006), The 'sophistication' of exports: a new trade measure, World Development, 34 (2), 222-237.

Larsen, E.R. (2005), Are rich countries immune to the resource curse? Evidence from Norway's management of its oil riches, Resources Policy, 30, 75-86.

López, R. and G. Anriquez (2003a), Agricultural Growth and Poverty in an Archetypical Middle Income Country, Photocopy, Department of Agricultural Economics, University of Maryland at College Park.

López, R., and G. Anriquez (2003b), Environmental externalities of agriculture: Chile 1980-2000, Paper prepared for the Roles of Agriculture International Conference, 20-22 October, 2003 – Rome, Italy, ESA-FAO.

Malaysian Palm Oil Board (2006), Overview of the Malaysian oil palm industry 2005.

Malzbender, D. (2003), Reforming the EU sugar regime: will Southern Africa still feature?, tralac working paper No.12/2003.

Martin, W., and D. Mitra (2001), Productivity Growth and Convergence in Agriculture and Manufacturing, Economic Development and Cultural Change, 49 (2), 403–22.

Masters, W. (2005), Paying for prosperity: how and why to invest in agricultural research and development in Africa, Journal of International Affairs, 58 (2), 35-64.

Mather, C. (1999), Agro-commodity chains, market power and territory: re-regulating South African citrus exports in the 1990s, Geoforum, 61-70.

Mayer, J. and P. Fajarnes (2005), Tripling Africa's primary exports: What? How? Where?, Discussion Paper, No.180, UNCTAD, October.

Mayer, J., A. Butkevicius and A. Kadri (2002), Dynamic products in World exports, UNCTAD Discussion Paper No.159.

Meagher, K. (2005), Social networks and economic ungovernance in African small firm clusters" Paper prepared for the Queen Elizabeth House, Oxford University, 50th Birthday Conference.

Minot, N. (1998), Competitiveness of food processing in Viet Nam: a study of the rice, coffee, seafood, and fruit and vegetable subsectors, a Report prepared by IFPRI for the Vietnamese Ministry of Planning and Investment and UNIDO.

Minot, N. and M. Ngigi (2003), Are horticultural exports a replicable success story? Evidence from Kenya and Côte d'Ivoire, paper presented at the InWEnt, IFPRI, NEPAD, CTA Conference "Successes in African agriculture", Pretoria, December 1-3.

Mitchell, D. (2004) Sugar policies: opportunity for change, World Bank Policy Research Working Paper 3222, The World Bank, February.

Montero, C. (2004), Formación y desarrollo de un cluster globalizado: el caso de la industria del salmón en Chile, Serie Desarrollo Productivo, 145, January, UN-ECLAC, Chile.

Nishiyama, T. (2005), The roles of Asia and Chile in the World copper market, Resources Policy, 30, 131-139.

ODI (2006), Meeting the challenge of the resource curse – International experiences in managing the risks and realising the opportunities of non-renewable natural resource revenue management, report prepared for UNDP by the programme on Business and Development Performance of the Overseas Development Institute, United Kingdom, January.

Pardey, P.G., N. Beintema, S. Dehmer and S. Word (2006), Agricultural research – a growing global divide?, International Food Policy Research Institute (IFPRI) report, Agricultural Science and Technology Indicators Initiative, August.

Otsuki, T., J.S. Wilson and M. Sewadeh (2001), Saving two in a billion: quantifying the trade effect of European food safety standards on African exports, Food Policy, 26, 495-514.

Oxfam (2004), Dumping on the World – How EU sugar policies hurt poor countries, Oxfam Briefing Paper, 61.

Oxfam (2002), Cultivating poverty – The impact of US cotton subsidies on Africa, Oxfam Briefing Paper, 30.

Parry, I.W.H. (1997), Productivity trends in the natural resource industries, Discussion paper 97-39, Resources for the Future.

Reardon, T. and L. Flores (2006), Global market opportunities and challenges for Central American exporters: strategies for customized competitiveness in the CAFTA era, Paper prepared for the Inter-American Development Bank and the Swedish Internacional Development Agency, and presented at the SIDA-IADB conference "Opportunities and challenges in markets, land, migration, and public investment in the context of CAFTA", February 14, 2006, Guatemala City.

Reinhardt, N. (2000), Back to basics in Malaysia and Thailand: the role of resource-based exports in their export-led growth", World Development, 28 (1), 57-77.

Ritter, A. (2001), La aglomeración en torno a la minería en Canadá: estructura, evolución y funcionamiento, Chapter II in Aglomeraciones mineras y desarrollo local en América Latina, ed. Buitelaar, R., Alfaomega/UN-ECLAC/IDRC, 340 pp.

Rodrigues, M. and M. Torres (2003), La competitividad agroalimentaria de los países de América Central y el Caribe en una perspectiva de liberalización comercial, Serie Desarrollo Productivo No. 139, 64 pp.

Rodríguez, F. and D. Rodrik (2001), Trade policy and economic growth: A skeptics guide to the cross-national literature, in NBER Macroeconomics Annual 2000, ed. Ben Bernanke and Kenneth S. Rogoff. Cambridge: MIT Press.

Rodrik, D. (2004), Industrial policy for the twenty-first century, paper prepared for UNIDO, September.

Sachs, J.D. and A.M. Warner (1999), The big push, natural resource booms and growth, Journal of Development Economics, 59 (1), Pages 43-76.

Sala-i-Martin, X. and A. Subramanian (2003), Addressing the natural resource curse: an illustration from Nigeria, NBER Working paper Series, WP 9804, June.

Scholer, M. (2004), Bitter or better future for coffee producers?, International Trade Forum magazine, 2, International Trade Centre.

Simeh, A. and T.M. Ahmad (2001), The case study of the Malaysian Palm Oil, Paper prepared for the Regional Workshop on commodity export diversification and poverty reduction in South and South-East Asia, Bangkok, 3-5 April.

Stevens, C. and J. Kennan (2005), Botswana beef exports and trade policy, Background study prepared for the World Bank-BIDPA Botswana Export Diversification Study, IDS Sussex, UK, February.

Stijns, J-P C. (2005), Natural resource abundance and economic growth revisited, Resources Policy, 30, 107-130.

Taylor, C.S. (1993), Kenaf: An emerging new crop industry in New crops, eds. J. Janick and J.E. Simon, New York: Wiley, pp. 402-407.

Teixeira Coelho, S. (2005), Biofuels: Advantages and trade barriers, UNCTAD/DITC/TED/2005/1.

Tilton, J.E. and H. H. Landsberg (1997), Innovation, Productivity Growth, and the Survival of the U.S. Copper Industry, Discussion Paper 97-41, Resources for the Future, Washington D.C..

UNCTAD (2006), A case study of the salmon industry in Chile, Transfer of technology for successful integration in the global economy Series, UNCTAD/ITE/IIT/2005/12.

UNCTAD (2006a), The Least Developed Countries Report 2006 - Developing Productive Capacities.

UNCTAD (2005), Methodologies, classifications, quantification and development impacts of non-tariff barriers, Note by the UNCTAD Secretariat, Expert Meeting on Methodologies, classifications, quantification and development impacts of non-tariff barriers, Geneva, 5-7 September 2005, TD/B/COM.1/EM.27/2.

UNCTAD (2005a), Promoting participation of developing countries in dynamic and new sectors of world trade: fishery products, Background note prepared by the UNCTAD Secretariat, Expert Meeting on dynamic and new sectors of world trade, Geneva, 24-26 October 2005, TD/B/COM.1/EM.28/3.

UNCTAD (2002), Trade and Development Report.

UNIDO (2004), Industrial Development Report.

UN-ECLAC (2005), Panorama 2005. El nuevo patrón de desarrollo de la agricultura en América Latina y el Caribe, Agricultural Development Unit, UN-ECLAC, September, 142 pp.

UN-ECLAC (2004), Access of Latin American and Caribbean Exports to the US market 2003-2004, Washington D.C., November, LC/WAS/L.71.

USDA (2003), Vietnam cocoa update, Foreign Agricultural Service GAIN Report #VM3003.

USTR (2005), National Trade Estimate Report on Foreign Trade Barriers.

VEK-World Bank (2004), Structure and dynamics of the European Market for horticultural products and opportunities for SSA exporters, Report prepared by VEK Adviesgroep for the Africa region of the World Bank.

Vogel, S.J. (1994), Structural changes in agriculture: production linkages and agricultural demand-led industrialization, Oxford Economic Papers, 46 (1), 136-156.

Voisard, J-M. (2005), Benchmarking and competitiveness analysis in horticultural supply chains, Issue notes, Strategic Development of Horticultural Supply Chains in Sub-Saharan Africa, World Bank course, Module 1.

Zhihua Zeng, D. (2006), Knowledge, technology and cluster-based growth in Africa – findings from eleven case-studies of enterprise clusters in Africa, WBI Development Study, Knowledge for Development (K4D) Program, World Bank Institute, World Bank.

Wakker, E. (2005), Greasy Palms - The social and ecological impacts of large-scale oil palm plantation development, a report prepared for Friends of the Earth, January 2005.

Watkins, G.C. (2006), Oil scarcity: what have the past three decades revealed?, Energy Policy, 34, 508-514.

Weatherspoon, D.D. and T. Reardon (2003), The rise of supermarkets in Africa: implications for agrifood systems and the rural poor, Development Policy Review, 21 (3), 333-355.

Weinberger, K. and T.A. Lumpkin (2005), Horticulture for poverty alleviation – the unfunded revolution, AVDRDC, The World Vegetable Center Working paper No.15, Taiwan.

World Bank (2005), Food safety and agricultural health standards: challenges and opportunities for developing country exports, Report No.31207, January.

Wright, G. (2001), Resource-based growth then and now, Paper prepared for the World Bank project "Patterns of integration in the global economy".

WTO (2006), WTO Trade Policy Review Malaysia.

WTO (2005), World Trade Report.

Yusoff, S. (2006), Renewable energy from palm oil – innovation on effective utilization of waste, Journal of Cleaner Production, 14, 87-93.

# The textile and clothing Industry: Adjusting to the post-quota world

Ratnakar Adhikari and Yumiko Yamamoto*

## 1. Introduction

It is just over two years since the phasing-out of the global system of quota controls which governed trade in the textile and clothing (T&C) industry. That industry generates US$479 billion in world exports and accounts for a 4.6 per cent share in global merchandise exports [World Trade Organization (WTO, 2006a)]. The quota system and policy developments since its demise illustrate the highly selective and targeted nature of production and market relations in the industry. Although 1 January 2005 was supposed to mark the end of the quota system for all countries and was expected to unleash massive adjustment challenges for a number of countries, quota elimination has shown a mixed result so far. Moreover, countries that have lost out the most had seen their exports decline earlier, which means that their dismal performance cannot merely be ascribed to the quota phase-out.

Several countries that had been projected by numerous studies to lose out in the post-quota world not only managed to hold on to their past gains, but also achieved significant growth in their export earnings. This is mainly because of the re-imposition of quotas on T&C exports from China not only by the developed countries but also by some developing countries which were making use of temporary safeguard measures as agreed to by China during the process of its accession to the WTO.

Most analysts predict that the situation will not remain the same after the phasing-out of the safeguards measures, which will expire in 2008. At the same time, the entry of Vietnam into the WTO from 11 January 2007, which enables the country to compete in the global T&C market without any quantitative restrictions on T&C exports, means that the competitive pressure is likely to become intense for the small and marginal players. Therefore, the real adjustment challenge is yet to begin.

Textiles and clothing is a unique industry in the global economy main-ly for three reasons. First, most developed countries of today and newly industrialized countries (NICs) used this industry as the springboard for their development journey and even some least developed countries (LDCs)

* Programme Specialist, UNDP Regional Centre in Colombo (RCC), Asia-Pacific Trade & Investment Initiative (APTII), and Gender and Trade Programme Advisor, UNDP RCC APTII, respectively. The opinions expressed in this document are those of the authors and do not necessarily reflect those of the United Nations Development Programme (UNDP).

were able to step onto the development ladder on the basis of their T&C industry. Millions of people, mostly women, are employed in this industry in these economies. Second, this industry has very low entry barriers; entry does not require huge capital outlay and factories can be set up with workers with relatively low skills. Therefore, this industry is characterized by high competition intensity. Third, this industry is the most protected of all manufacturing industries in the global economy, both in developed and developing countries. Protectionist interests have been extremely ingenious in creating new protectionist instruments in the past 50 years.

Taking as precedent the imposition in 1957 of voluntary export restraints (VER) on the exports of cotton textiles from Japan to appease the domestic textile industry in the United States, the regime of protection in this industry was institutionalized in 1974 with the introduction of the Multi-Fibre Arrangement (MFA). This governed international trade in textiles and clothing for almost two decades. This arrangement enabled developed countries to bilaterally negotiate quotas with supplier countries taking into account their competitiveness and the perceived threat to the domestic interests in the importing countries. During the Uruguay Round of multilateral trade negotiations (1986-93), the international community decided to integrate the MFA into the new Agreement on Textiles and Clothing (ATC), which featured a clear time table for phasing-out the quota system within a ten-year period starting on 1 January 1995 (Adhikari and Weeratunge, forthcoming).

Even during the heyday of the quota system, characterized by a distorted global market for T&C products, entrepreneurs in countries restricted by quotas found ways to exploit the system. They established factories in countries with low levels of quota utilization and in some instances even helped in the industrialization process of those countries. For example, Korean companies established factories in Bangladesh, Caribbean and Sub-Saharan Africa, Chinese companies established factories in several Asian and African locations, Indian companies in Nepal and even relatively minor players in the global market such as Sri Lankan and Mauritian businesspersons established factories in the Maldives and Madagascar, respectively, to overcome quota restrictions. While the indigenization of this industry took place in some countries (e.g., Bangladesh, Nepal) due to the entry of the local entrepreneurs, in other countries (e.g., Maldives) the industry itself got wiped off the industrial map once the foreign investors pulled out.

Against this backdrop, the objective of this paper is to discuss the current state of play in the global T&C market, identify the factors shaping and influencing the evolution of this industry including emerging trends, and provide some policy recommendations for the developing countries to help them not only to survive in the post-quota regime, but also to exploit the opportunities created by the increased competition in the industry.

The remainder of the paper is organized as follows. Section 2 summarizes the trade flows in the post-quota world and discusses the human development implications of the quota phase-out. Section 3 discusses challenges facing developing countries and LDCs in using the T&C industry as a springboard for their development efforts. Section 4 deals with emerging issues in the areas of T&C trade at the global level, which offers various opportunities as well as challenges to the T&C industry in the developing countries. Section 5 analyzes the efforts made by various developing countries to overcome the emerging challenges and critically evaluates the sufficiency of such measures in addition to proposing some measures that could help these countries minimize the human development fallout of the phasing out of quotas. Section 6 concludes.

## 2. Trade flows in the post-ATC period and their human development implications

Textiles and clothing are among the first manufactured products an industrializing economy produces. They played a critical role in the early stage of industrialization in the United Kingdom, parts of North America and Japan, and more recently in the export-oriented growth of the East Asian economies (Yang and Zhong, 1998). Hong Kong (China), the Republic of Korea, and Taiwan (Province of China) relied heavily on T&C products for their exports from the 1950s to the mid-1980s. As these economies scaled up their industrial development toward more capital-intensive and high-tech manufacturing products, Southeast Asian and South Asian developing countries and LDCs started to join the race. For example, Bangladeshi clothing exports increased ten-fold over the last 15 years and the country is now one of the leading exporters of clothing in the world (table 2). As for Cambodia, clothing exports took off in the late 1990s (Adhikari and Yamamoto, 2006, p. 46). The T&C share in total exports exceeds 70 per cent in these two economies (UNDP RCC, 2005a, p. 6). As a result, the T&C exporters' group has diversified over time, and Asia has become a hub of manufacturing production. This transition period overlaps with the time when the latecomers introduced their liberalization policies under structural adjustment programmes, acceded to the WTO and/or undertook domestic reforms.

### 2.1 Trends in the global market

Table 1 shows exports of textiles from selected economies. Global textile exports reached a historical high of US$203 billion in 2005, and this value has nearly doubled from the 1990 level of US$104 billion. In broad terms, the immediate effect of the expiry of quotas in the textile industry was a gain for developing countries and a loss for developed and semi-developed economies in Asia and European Union (EU). The growth of Chinese textile exports is remarkable – increasing by 22.8 per cent from 2004 to 2005, so that more than 20 per cent of textiles traded in 2005 originated in China. Other developing countries in Asia also experienced a significant growth during the first year   post-ATC – e.g., exports from Bangladesh, India, Indonesia, Malaysia, Pakistan and Thailand grew at between 7 and 15 per cent. On the other hand, textile exports from the top producers in East Asia – Hong Kong, Japan, Republic of Korea, Taiwan – decreased by 3-4 per cent from 2004 to 2005. The EU, the largest textile exporter in the world, also experienced a loss of exports in both intra- and extra-EU markets, recording reductions of 7.2 and 3.3 per cent respectively. Textile exports from Asia to Africa, Europe and North America increased by 14-20 per cent after the expiry of quotas (WTO, 2006a, p. 166[1]).

Products from the top 15 economies account for more than 90 per cent of global textile exports while the top 15 economies account for 77-83 per cent of global clothing exports in 2004-05 (ibid., pp. 171 and 178[2]). Table 2 displays the exports of clothing in selected economies. The clothing export market grew at a faster rate than textiles; the total value of clothing exports reached US$276 billion in 2005, 150 per cent higher than the level of US$108 billion in 1990.

In 2005, Asia was supplying nearly half of the global T&C market; China's exports alone accounted for 27 per cent of world trade in clothing. During the first year of the post-ATC regime, the value of China's clothing exports went up from US$62 billion in 2004 to US$74 billion and recorded a growth rate of 20 per cent. Among the Asian economies listed in table 2, on the one hand, NICs[3] plus Macau (China) were hit hard, with a 14-24 per cent reduction from 2004 to 2005. On the other hand, the remaining developing countries from Southeast Asia and South Asia survived the first year of quota elimination, in spite of pessimistic predictions made before the expiry of ATC. The smaller clothing producers are not listed in table 2, however. As we discuss below, Fiji, Mongolia and Nepal are struggling to survive, while the Maldives has ceased to export T&C products.

Some developing countries in other regions, including the ones which have preferential market access to the United States, also recorded a negative growth in 2005. Examples are: Morocco (which has a bilateral trade agreement with the United States); Dominican Republic, El Salvador, Guatemala, Honduras (which are part of the U.S.-Caribbean Basin Trade Partnership Act – CBTPA); and Madagascar, Mauritius, South Africa (which receive preferential market access to the US market under the African Growth and Opportunity Act – AGOA). Exports from Mauritius and South Africa started to decline in 2004 (WTO, 2006a, p. 179) and even did so in the US market in spite of the preferential arrangement under AGOA (Morris, 2006, pp. 50-51). Negative export growth rates of clothing from Mauritius and South Africa in 2005 were 20.7 per cent and 32.7 per cent respectably. Exceptions are Peru and Colombia, which benefit from preferential arrangements with the United States under the Andean Trade Promotion and Drug Eradication Act (ATPDEA) and experienced a continuous growth over time.

## 2.2 Two years after the expiry of quotas

The 2006 data will help us observe the impacts of quantitative restrictions on Chinese exports imposed by the EU and the United States in summer 2005. This section will summarize the growth of T&C exports from selected Asian and Pacific countries, based on the import data from two major markets – the EU and the United States.[4,5] For the EU, data for the first 8 months of 2006 are available; for the United States, the first 9 months of 2006 data are available at the time of writing.

The main focus is on 12 selected Asian countries (hereafter, the 'Asian 12'): Bangladesh, Cambodia, China, India, Indonesia, Lao People's Democratic Republic (PDR), Nepal, Pakistan, the Philippines, Sri Lanka, Thailand, and Viet Nam. These countries can be grouped into four categories: (1) countries with a large production capability in both textile and apparel production (China, India); (2) countries that have limited production capability in both textiles and apparel (Indonesia, Pakistan, Thailand, Viet Nam); (3) middle-income countries that mainly have apparel production capability (Philippines, Sri Lanka); and (4) LDCs (Bangladesh, Cambodia, Lao PDR, Nepal). The cases of Fiji, Maldives and Mongolia, which were severely hit by the expiry of ATC, will be also discussed.

### 2.2.1 EU market

Table 3 shows the market share and growth rates of imports from the Asian 12 and other major trading partners in EU markets from 2004 to 2006. Our analysis focuses only on imports from non-EU member countries, i.e., extra-EU trade. The share of extra-EU trade in total imports of T&C products has increased to around 50 per cent in 2006 from 46 per cent in 2004.

Asia's share of EU T&C imports continued to increase in the post-ATC period. In 2004, about 46 per cent of total EU imports were from the Asian 12; its share now accounts for more than half of EU imports of T&C products. In contrast, regions which have a trade agreement with the EU have lost their market shares in spite of their preferential market access. For example, the market shares of Morocco, Romania, Tunisia and Turkey declined, albeit slightly, in the post-ATC years.

Between 2004 and 2005, EU imports from the Asian 12 increased by 19.6 per cent; however, the gains were not distributed evenly in Asia. China was the leading contributor to this rapid growth with India a distant second. EU imports from China increased by US$6.1 billion – 42 per cent up – from US$14.7 billion to US$ 20.8 billion during the first year in the post-ATC while EU imports from India increased by US$800 million, from US$ 4.4 billion to US$5.2 billion, at the growth rate of 18.3 per cent. Other Asian 12 countries – except Viet Nam and Lao PDR – as well as the exporters in other regions – except Turkey – had a difficult start of the post-ATC regime, experiencing negative growth despite their benefits from several variants of Generalised System of Preferences (GSPs) and other preferential arrangements.

This trend changed noticeably in 2006 after the EU and China came to an agreement on restricting Chinese T&C imports to the EU in June 2005. Until 2008, the annual growth rate of 10 of the 35 categories of Chinese imports liberalized with the expiry of ATC is restricted to 8-12.5 per cent (European Commission, 2005). A comparison of the first 8 months' data in 2005 and 2006 reveals that EU imports from China slowed down to 5.5 per cent growth rate whereas the rest of the Asian 12 countries, except Nepal, revived their exports to the EU market at two-digit growth rates. Exporters in other regions ('Rest of the World' in table 3) also resumed their exports to the 2004 level by experiencing 10.8 per cent growth for the first 8 months of 2006.

## 2.2.2 US market

Table 4 shows the market share and growth rates of imports from selected Asian and Pacific countries including the Asian 12 and other major trading partners in US market from 2004-2006. The Asian 12's share of US T&C imports continued to rise. In 2004, the Asian 12's share of US T&C imports was 41.3 per cent; data for the first 9 months of 2006 show that 54.8 per cent of the total US imports are now from the Asian 12. In contrast, exporting countries from other regions, in fact, the majority of those countries which have preferential arrangements with the United States, continue to lose their market shares. For example, the share of Caribbean Basin Initiative (CBI) member nations plus Mexico declined from 21.6 per cent in 2004 to 17 per cent in 2006. The share of sub-Saharan African countries (in the category classified as AGOA) also declined from 2.1 per cent in 2004 to 1.4 per cent in 2006.

US imports from the Asian 12, like in the EU case, showed significant increase during the first year of the post-ATC regime. The growth rate of US T&C imports from the Asian 12 between 2004 and 2005 was 28.6 per cent. China is the leading contributor to this growth with a 50 per cent growth rate from 2004 to 2005. In contrast to the trend in the EU, other Asian 12 countries – except Nepal and Thailand – also showed steady growth even after the expiry of quotas. When US imports from China went down to a growth rate of 7.3 per cent for the first three quarters of 2006 as compared to the same period of 2005, the rest of the Asian 12 – except Nepal – succeeded either in exporting more or sustained their positive growth. As a result, US imports from the Asian 12 continued to grow at 11.8 per cent for the first 9 months of 2006, which is much higher than the growth rate of total US imports, 2.6 per cent.

The difference in the pattern observed between US and EU imports is that, in the US market, exports from other regions did not revive after quantitative restrictions imposed by the United States on Chinese T&C imports.[6] This was so for countries which have preferential arrangements with the United States. For example, US imports from CBI countries plus Mexico decreased by 4.9 per cent from 2004 to 2005 and 9.3 per cent from 2005 to 2006. As for Sub-Saharan African countries, the reduction rate of US imports was 16.5 per cent in 2005 and 13.2 per cent for the first 9 months of 2006.

Smaller exporters from the Asia-Pacific – e.g., Fiji, Maldives, Mongolia and Nepal – were hit hard by the elimination of quotas. As for Mongolia and Nepal, it was observed that some orders came back after the safeguards on Chinese imports. For Fiji and Maldives, US imports continued to decline in 2006.

## 2.3 Human development impact of the expiry of quotas

As discussed earlier, the ready-made garment (RMG) industry in the countries hit hard by the expiry of quotas – Fiji, Maldives, Mongolia, Nepal – was established by foreign investors whose T&C exports were bounded by the quota system. These small exporters have the disadvantage of being land-locked or small island economies as well as supply-side problems, as we discuss later. The expiry of quotas triggered the closure of factories in these countries as foreign investors shifted the production elsewhere. As a result, thousands of jobs have been lost in these countries.

### 2.3.1 Fiji

Fiji's garment industry expanded rapidly in the late 1980s and the 1990s after obtaining preferential market access to Australia and New Zealand under the 1981 South Pacific Regional Trade and Economic Co-operation Agreement (SPARTECA), with the restriction of using 50 per cent locally manufactured fabric and granting a 13-year tax holiday and other benefits to companies exporting 70 per cent or more under the 1987 Tax Free Factories (TFF) scheme. The latter attracted foreign investors to open production facilities in Fiji. Moreover, the 1991 Import Credit Scheme (ICS) allows Australian fabrics to be shipped to Fiji at competitive prices for production of garments that will be re-exported to Australia. Furthermore, Fiji enjoyed quotas from the United States under the MFA. The number of tax-free garment factories rose from 27 in 1988 to 88 by the end of 1991 (Harrington, 2000). In 2000, the industry employed nearly 20,000 people, more than 70 per cent of them women. About two-thirds of manufacturing jobs were provided by the garment industry. Exports peaked at FJ$322 million (US$163 million) in 1999, and this accounted for more than 30 per cent of total exports and 11 per cent of GDP (Storey, 2004). The coup in 2000 triggered the downfall of Fiji's garment exports, leading to the closure of a dozen factories during 2002 and retrenchment of up to 6,000 people (Global

Education Centre and Family Planning International Development, 2004). T&C exports decreased by 28 per cent from FJ$312 million (US$137 million) to FJ$223 million (US$106 million) between 2000 and 2002, but the expiry of quotas in 2005 led to a negative growth of 47 per cent with respect to 2004 (Adhikari and Yamamoto, 2006), triggered by a decrease in US RMG imports of 78 per cent (Table 4).

An immediate negative impact on employment was estimated as the retrenchment of 6,000 workers, predominantly women (ADB, 2006). The Australian government agreed to relax its rules of origin requirement to 25 per cent in January 2008, something which the Fiji's garment industry has long requested (Fiji Times, 2006). This policy change is expected to create thousands of jobs; however, the industry fears further job losses of several thousands instead, due to possible economic sanctions imposed by its trading partners as a result of the recent political instability in the country.

### 2.3.2  Maldives

Exports of RMGs took off in 1997 in Maldives and peaked in 2002. Having "guest workers" from Asia is not unique to the clothing industry in island economies given lack of trained domestic workers. In its peak time, 2,478 expatriates were employed in the industry. The number of expatriates started to decline in 2004, by January 2005 it halved to 1,228, and by the end of the year it had declined to 431. During its peak time, more than 70 per cent of expatriate garment workers were sewing machine operators, with more than 90 per cent of these women. The majority of them were Sri Lankan women who were sent home as operations slowed down (Adhikari and Yamamoto, 2006, pp. 18-19).

Given the high dependence on expatriate labour, one analysis suggests that the effects of the elimination of quotas on the economy of Maldives are expected to be negligible (United States Department of State, 2006). Although detailed data for local employment are not available, the 2000 Census data shows that 2,699 men and 5,518 women were working as "craft and related trade workers" in manufacturing (Ministry of Planning and National Development, 2004a). Female production workers in manufacturing received the lowest pay among industries (Ministry of Planning and National Development, 2004b). Since many garment factories were located in the outer atolls, where alternative jobs for low-paid garment workers are hard to find, female workers with low skills are likely to face the loss of income and the fear of long-term unemployment. Income inequality between Malé and the atolls has increased, and so has gender inequality in the labour market. Unemployment among women aged 15-24 rose from 30 to 40 per cent during 1997-2004 as compared to the male unemployment rate of the same age cohort of 10 to 23 per cent (Ministry of Planning and National Development, 2005). The loss of foreign exchange may be another factor to consider. RMGs accounted for about one-third of total merchandise exports and half of merchandise exports by the private sector in 2003 (Ministry of Planning and National Development, 2004a).

### 2.3.3 Mongolia

The T&C industry accounted for 11.3 per cent of 2004 total exports in Mongolia and employed an estimated 20,000, mostly women, as well as illegal migrants (ADB, 2006). With the elimination of quotas, US T&C imports from Mongolia recorded a 41.2 per cent decline from 2004 to 2005 (table 4). In March 2005, the number of workers reached 4,526 persons in textiles and 8,880 persons in wearing apparel, dressing and dyeing fur sectors, a 30 per cent decline from 6,401 and 12,725 persons respectively in March 2004 (National Statistical Office of Mongolia, 2005).

Products that faced severe declines in 2005 were the items in which quotas expired at the end of 2004 as well as the products that other countries are producing. Table 5 shows the top five US T&C imports from Mongolia, based on their value in 2004. Three out of the top five are knitted jerseys and pullovers of cotton, cashmere and man-made fibres, whose export value plunged by 35.1, 91.6 and 54.8 per cent respectively. Two other products, women's and girls' woven cotton trousers and knitted cotton T-shirts, are also common RMGs produced by many other countries. They recorded a negative growth of 9.7 and 56.0 per cent, respectively, during the first year of the post-ATC. Cotton is imported from China and Mongolia engages in the most labour-intensive parts of production, such as sewing.

Mongolia, which traditionally produces cashmere and wool clothing products, has not been successful in establishing vertical integration for export markets. For example, more than half of foreign exchange generated from cashmere-related trade consists of exports of raw cashmere to China. The price of raw cashmere is not stable while the price of manufactured cashmere products is; therefore, it is more profitable for Mongolia to process the raw cashmere for domestic manufactures and export the final products. However, Mongolia currently lacks a cashmere processing industry; thus, it often imports cashmere inputs back from China to produce the final products. Lecraw, Eddleston and McMahon (2005) report that if all raw cashmere produced in Mongolia were fully processed into finished knitted and woven products before export, such exports would generate about US$206 million, more than the 2005 level of the country's entire T&C exports, and employment in the processing industry would more than double. As for wool, Mongolia currently exports about US$6 million worth of uncombed sheep wool, while carpet exports generate only US$1 million. Mongolia committed to remove its export duty on raw cashmere by 2007 upon its accession to the WTO in 1997; however, Government of Mongolia has been studying the possibility of extending this period to discourage the exports of raw cashmere (GTZ, 2006).

With quantitative restrictions on Chinese T&C imports, it was hoped that foreign investors will reopen their factories and restart production in Mongolia. The first 8 months of the country's 2006 industrial production data show that the total textile output is 30.7 per cent higher compared to the previous year in real terms (ibid., p. 1). In December 2005, the EU granted Mongolia GSP-plus status for 2006-08. However, the US market accounts for more than 95 per cent of Mongolia's T&C exports; therefore, the positive impact from GSP-plus will be limited. Mongolia is currently negotiating a free trade agreement with the United States.

### 2.3.4 Nepal

The T&C industry in Nepal grew rapidly and became a major foreign currency earner after Indian exporters established an RMG industry in the early 1980s. Nepal also expanded its exports of carpets, a product in which the country traditionally has a competitive advantage. RMG exports peaked in 2000 and started to decline partly because of preferential market access granted by the United States to sub-Saharan African countries under AGOA. Uncertainties and apprehensions regarding the post-ATC scenario also seem to have contributed to the gradual decline in Nepalese garment exports between 2000 and 2004 (Dahal, 2006). Nepal's T&C exports were heavily concentrated in the US and EU markets, accounting for 98 per cent of total T&C exports. The United States alone accounted for more than 90 per cent of T&C exports in the early 1990s, but this share has been declining (Bhatt et al., 2006, p. 29).

In both the EU and US markets, Nepal's exports in 2005 and 2006 could not revive to their pre-ATC levels (tables 3 and 4). Table 6 displays the top five T&C export products to the EU and US markets, based on their value in 2004. Wool or fine animal hair carpets and other textile floor coverings (HS 570110) are the top exports of Nepal in both markets. In the EU, this commodity accounted for nearly 60 per cent of total Nepalese T&C exports in terms of value. Two other commodities that appear in both EU and US markets are woven cotton trousers for women or girls (HS 620462) and for men or boys (HS 620342). In 2004, they ranked second and fourth in the EU market and second and third in the US market. However, both the value of EU and US imports of these commodities dropped significantly in 2005 – in the EU, by 75.2 and 40.8 per cent respectively, and in the United States, by 39.4 and 33.9 per cent. The two other commodities in the top five US imports from Nepal are knitted cotton jerseys, pullovers, cardigans, waistcoats and similar articles (HS 611020) and knitted men's or boy's cotton shirts (HS 610510). The export value of these two products decreased by 57.5 and 59.7 per cent respectively in 2005. Similar to the Mongolian case described above, Nepal's loss of competitiveness in three out of the top five commodities in US market are explained by the fact that: (1) these faced more competition after the eliminations of quotas; and (2) these are also produced by other countries in the region.

During its peak time the RMG industry in Nepal employed more than 50,000 persons; when production for exports declined the number of workers also went down. A recent study by Bhatt et al. (2006) found that the industry now employs less than 5,000 persons (p. 36). Several alarming findings regarding Nepali RMG workers reported in the study can be summarized as follows: 1) Nearly a quarter of employees reported a decrease in their salaries after 2005 while about 40 per cent saw no changes in salary and 36.1 per cent received better salaries; 2) Only 14.6 per cent of the RMG employees live above the poverty line with net earnings of more than 7,500 Nepali Rupees (US$100) per month; 3) Women on average earn only 60 per cent of men's monthly salary, and gender disparity in salary is observed among similar occupations even after working hours are taken into account; 4) Two-thirds of workers who were previously employed in the RMG industry became unemployed because of factory closures and about 82 per cent of former workers did not find other forms of employment immediately after leaving the industry; and 5) The loss of garment factory jobs has resulted in declining income for almost 20 per cent of the workers while the majority feel a rise in food and housing costs.

The job losses among RMG workers indicate further negative impacts on human development. More than half of RMG workers surveyed sent remittances home; a majority of these remittances are used to buy necessities and support education of family members. With the loss of income or a reduced salary, their livelihoods are also likely to be affected.

### 2.3.5 Trade gains but not in human terms

Even in countries where export growth has been robust, increased exports do not necessarily translate into more employment, better wages or better working conditions. In general, T&C workers receive relatively low wages. In Bangladesh, where the total number of workers in RMG sector is 2 million, of which 80 per cent are women, the legal minimum earnings of 930 Takas per month (US$16), fixed in 1994, has not been revised since, in spite of a rising trend in inflation (ADB, 2006, pp. 147-148). As for Sri Lanka, a recent report on apparel industry workers estimated that the total costs to cover the basic needs of the worker, excluding saving and remittance, are 7,000 and 8,800 Sri Lankan Rupees (LKRs) (US$70-85) for outside-free trade zone (FTZ) workers and FTZ workers respectively (Prasanna and Gowthaman, 2006). The minimum wage of US$36, however, does not allow meeting workers' basic needs; in fact, 86 per cent of workers surveyed receive a basic salary of less than LKR 6,000 per month (ibid.).

In Cambodia, in spite of a rise in RMG exports, workers' earnings decreased by 8.5 per cent in 2005 compared to 2004 (CDRI, 2006 cited in Chan and Sok, 2006, p. 30). A recent study by Chan and Sok (2006) also found that 30 per cent of workers surveyed perceived that their real wage has decreased in the post-ATC years as opposed to 19 per cent who perceived that their salary is increasing. The report also found that about 60 per cent perceived that their health condition has worsened as compared to 2004 (i.e., prior to the quota expiry) and argues that longer working hours to meet an increase in orders in the post-ATC environment and less expenses on food in order to save money for other purposes such as remittances and savings might have affected workers' health conditions. Employment has become increasingly casual over time, with increasing prevalence of short-term con-tracts and piece-rate work. As we discuss later, Cambodia has adopted the industry-wide compliance monitoring system but the latest report shows that less than a quarter of the factories monitored comply with the overtime with-in the legal limit (ILO, 2006). In the case of Bangladesh, Ahmed, Rahman and Sobhan (2005) found that overtime for RMG workers has decreased in the post-ATC environment, because of buyer pressure to meet the legal limit of 60 hours a week, but this affected workers' well-being negatively because of reduced income and loss of nutritional supplements that are provided as snacks for overtime workers. The factories meet the increased orders by sub-contracting some parts of the orders (ibid.). In short, even in the countries which performed well in the post-ATC period, there are a number of factors which need to be improved from a human development perspective.

## 3. Challenges Facing Developing Countries

Getting a foothold in the T&C sector may not be a difficult task but sustain-ing and achieving growth may be a real challenge for a number of develop-ing countries. It is not advisable to lump all the countries together because a country with all necessary prerequisites to become a leading exporter of T&C products like China faces challenges that lie more on the demand side, or market access barriers, than on the supply side. However, a small land-locked LDC like Nepal faces challenges both on the demand as well as sup-ply side. Therefore, only selected and most common challenges are highlight-ed in this section, and examples from countries facing each specific challenge have been included, where available.

### 3.1    Protectionist forces

Given the existence of powerful vested interests in the T&C industry, particu-larly in developed countries, the protectionist forces are not likely to wane but rather to be further accentuated in the future. However, the form of protection may change over time. In the past, there used to be a double protection to the T&C industry – through quotas and high tariffs. In the case of China, very little would appear to have changed even after the phasing-out of quotas.

Powerful and vocal protectionist lobbies have not only found ways to protect their industries in connivance with their government, but have also managed to couch these arguments in altruistic fashion in order to remain "politically correct". Domestic job losses are the largest single argument made by these interests, followed by helping weaker countries move up the industrial ladder so as to enable them to grow out of poverty through preferential arrangements. Therefore, when it comes to the T&C industry, the normal economic rationale of the need to prevent distortion in the economy caused by trade protection becomes hollow. Moreover, the advice to follow a transparent means of protection such as tariffs, should the protection be inevitable, is also not fully heeded. This is followed by several other near-arbitrary measures such as the imposition of trade remedy measures and discriminatory measures in preferential trading agreements. The various forms of protection in the developed countries, some of which are truly ingenious, are discussed below.

### 3.1.1 Tariff barriers

On average, the tariffs imposed on T&C products are four times higher than the average industrial tariffs imposed by the developed countries. The average post-Uruguay Round tariffs on T&C products in three major industrial countries are 14.6 per cent in the United States; 9.1 per cent in the EU; and 7.6 per cent in Japan, while their average industrial tariffs are 3.5, 3.6 and 1.7 per cent respectively (Hayashi, 2005).

Disaggregated data reveal remarkably high tariffs imposed on some products. In the post-Uruguay Round era, the majority of T&C tariff lines face tariff peaks – 52 per cent of T&C imports in the United States have tariff rates of 15.7 to 35 per cent, 54 per cent of EU imports have duties of 10.1 to 15.0 per cent, and 55 per cent of Japanese imports have duties of 5.1 to 10.0 per cent (ibid.). The high tariff on T&C products has become an even more important trade policy tool in the hands of the developed countries and is not likely to come down significantly even if the stalled negotiations on non-agricultural market access (NAMA) are revived at the WTO.[7]

One of the ways to get around this barrier is to provide preferential market access – either through a GSP or a free trade agreement (FTA) – to a selected group of countries ostensibly with the objective of helping them in their developmental objectives. No doubt such preferences have helped some countries. However, the evidence shows that their impacts have been, at best, mixed as far as the export performance of the preference receiving countries is concerned. For example, Bangladesh has been able to use the duty-free-quota-free market access treatment to the EU provided under the "Everything but Arms (EBA)" initiative to the benefit of its knitted apparel exports, with the preference "take up" rate of 80 per cent. However, the country has not been able to register significant growth in the export of woven items,[8] the reason for which will be discussed below.

Similarly, Jordan, a country largely unknown regarding its prowess in textiles and clothing, has emerged as a significant player in this industry only after its 2001 free trade agreement with the United States. It has been main-taining its growth momentum for the last four years. Jordan's clothing exports to the United States have increased from a mere $43 million in 2000 to $1.1 billion in 2005 (Ahmad, 2005). During the first six months of 2006, it has posted an increase of 18.3 per cent in the US market (International Textiles and Clothing Bureau, 2006). In contrast, the value of Jordanian exports to the EU, where it does not enjoy duty free market access, was only $8.8 million in 2005 (Ahmad, 2005).

A number of other countries that enjoy preferential market access to the US or EU market did not necessarily fare well in the post-quota era. Examples include: Lesotho, Malawi, Namibia and Swaziland in Southern Africa, which are beneficiaries of AGOA; Costa Rica, Dominican Republic, Jamaica, El Salvador, Honduras which are the beneficiaries of the CBPTA; and Mexico, which is a beneficiary of the North American Free Trade Agreement (NAFTA). Similarly, a number of countries that enjoy preferen-tial market access to the EU, e.g., Morocco, Romania and Tunisia, did not achieve a significant export growth in the post-quota era as discussed above.

There are three major problems associated with countries having prefer-ential trading arrangements. First, since they have had assured market access opportunities during the MFA and ATC periods, they never felt the compet-itive pressure and did not have any incentive to improve their performance. Complacency led to their lacklustre performance in the post-quota era. Second, due to strict rules of origin (ROO) requirements, they have to rely on imported materials from relatively high cost sources like the United States and the EU, which makes them uncompetitive. The "yarn forward" require-ment included in most FTAs, which make it mandatory for the preference receiving countries to use US yarn and fabrics, as a condition for assembled textile or clothing products to enter duty-free, is a testimony to this.[9] While this scheme provides a captive market for US textile exporters, it also pre-vents the preference receiving countries from using textiles from other com-petitive sources such as China, which are seen as a threat to the survival of US textile firms.[10] The captive market hypothesis is corroborated by the export data from the United States and the EU. US exports of yarns and fab-ric to NAFTA, Central American and Caribbean Basin countries, which are the beneficiaries of duty free access to the United States, increased from less than 40 per cent in 1989 to 77 per cent in 2004. Since the EU also promotes a captive market strategy, 37 per cent of its textiles exports were destined to Eastern European, African and Mediterranean countries (Romania, Tunisia, Morocco, Bulgaria and Turkey in 2004).[11]

Third, again due to ROO requirements included in GSP preferences, most developing countries and LDCs that lack textile and other raw materi-al producing capacities are handicapped because they cannot meet the min-imum ROO threshold.[12] Among the existing ROO requirements imposed for preferential trading arrangement, the one being implemented by the EU is considered the most restrictive because it requires at least two finishing operations – a process known as "double transformation" – to occur in the exporting country to qualify for preferential market access. Therefore, despite the EBA initiative, LDCs that are not able to meet the requirement continue to have a low level of preference utilization. For example, the utilization rates for clothing preferences of the Asian LDCs under the EBA in 2004 were 33.8 per cent for Bangladesh and 65.8 per cent for Nepal (WTO, 2005). This partly explains the reason behind Bangladesh's ability to achieve impressive export growth in the knitted garments in which domestic value addition is very high and not on woven garments where domestic value addition is extremely limited due to lack of vertical integration. Low utilization of preferences means that LDCs continue to pay Most Favoured Nation (MFN) tariffs on their exports to the EU market.[13]

Preferential market access has distorted the tariff structure. The distribution can be quite regressive in nature as it penalizes the poorer countries and rewards the rich countries. For example, Asian countries that are not beneficiaries of preferential market access in the US market pay much higher tariffs on T&C products than beneficiaries (table 7). Exporters from a poor country like Bangladesh pay 82 times higher tariffs than Canada for the exports of knitted apparels and 107 times higher tariffs for the exports of woven apparels. Similarly, its knitted apparel exports contribute almost the same share as that of Canada to the US customs revenue, and its woven apparel exports contribute 2.8 times more revenue than Canada's. Another comparison between two LDCs from two different regions, Cambodia and Lesotho, is quite striking. Cambodia pays 144 times higher tariffs to access the US market for its knitted apparel than Lesotho, and it pays 233 times higher tariffs for the export of its woven apparel.

It is interesting to note that such discriminatory practices do not run foul of the multilateral rules-based and non-discriminatory systems espoused by the WTO. Efforts aimed at remedying these problems are yet to bear fruit. For example, despite the fact that there have been extensive discussions in the run up to the Hong Kong Ministerial conference to provide duty-free and quota-free market access to all LDCs, the decision now limits the duty free access to only 97 per cent of the products under the tariff lines of the importing countries. Given the strong protectionist undercurrent in the T&C industry in developed countries, many T&C products in which LDCs are competitive may not be included in the "covered list" (Adhikari, 2006a).

### 3.1.2   Non-tariff barriers

Out of the several non-tariff barriers only two – namely trade remedy measures and regulatory/standard related barriers – will be discussed in this subsection. While the first one is a traditional barrier which is still being actively used by both developed and developing countries, the second one is an emerging barrier that reduces the competitiveness of the T&C exporters of developing countries. A common element in these barriers is that they can be and have been abused for protectionist purposes.

*Trade remedy measures*

Introduced in the global trading system as measures to protect domestic industry from unfair foreign competition, trade remedies or contingent protection measures have become tools in the hands of the domestic protectionist interest in the developed and developing countries. Three types of WTO-sanctioned trade remedy measures, of which the anti-dumping measure is the most pernicious, can be imposed by the importing countries without having to wait for a verdict from a WTO dispute settlement body.

As documented by Adhikari and Weeratunge (forthcoming), such measures have had dire consequences for the industry revenue as well as employment situation in countries like India and Pakistan. T&C imports from relatively competitive countries like China, India, Pakistan and Turkey have been routinely subjected to anti-dumping investigations in the past.[14] Bed linen has been one of the most targeted products by the EU and most of the time such an action is initiated at the behest of a single industry group – in this case, Euro Cotton.

Based on a survey of anti-dumping actions initiated between 1994 and 2001, it was found that one major WTO member initiated 53 investigations into allegations of dumping, placing the T&C industry in the third position only after iron & steel and chemicals.[15] In several instances, investigations into the same products were revived back-to-back, extending over a long period (WTO, 2003). Commenting on the unfair nature of anti-dumping investigations, Oxfam International (2004) asserts, "[T]hey take a long time to resolve, impose heavy costs of arbitration, and can be prolonged by small changes to the case". Anti-dumping measures, unlike other trade remedy measures, can be applied to targeted firms in specific countries, almost with absolute impunity (Adhikari and Yamamoto, 2005).

The post-quota period has seen the burgeoning of other trade remedy measures alongside anti-dumping ones. Temporary safeguard on Chinese imports is a case in point. Although this measure is part of the WTO accession package which China signed onto, this reflects the ingenuity of the protectionist interests. Taking advantage of this provision, a number of countries/groupings, both developed and developing, have imposed various safeguards measures against China. Although the temporary safeguards will expire on December 31, 2008, two other provisions incorporated in China's Protocol of Accession pose a significant burden to China. They are: a) until 2013 it is possible for WTO members to impose "selective" safeguards against any Chinese exports that cause "market disruption"; and b) until 2016 it is possible to use the "non-market economy" criterion against China to calculate a "dumping margin" in the process of an anti-dumping investigation. This margin inflates the dumping margin, subjecting the Chinese imports to a higher anti-dumping duty.[16]

*Regulatory barriers*
Government regulations or industry standards for goods can impact trade in at least three ways: they can facilitate exchange by clearly defining product characteristics and improving compatibility and usability; they also advance domestic social goals like public health by establishing minimum standards or prescribing safety requirements; and finally, they can hide protectionist policies.[17] Tariffs cannot block market entry unless they are prohibitive. However, regulatory and standard related barriers could effectively foreclose the market for the exporters if they are stringent and complex, making compliance de facto very costly if not impossible. These are often known as "frictional" barriers in that they raise the cost to the exporters, but do not provide any revenue to the governments imposing such requirements.

Since governments are ingenious in devising various ways to inhibit imports to protect domestic producers in sensitive industries where domestic pressure for protection persists, the list of possible regulatory barriers could be infinite. The risk is that the traditional barriers such as tariffs, quotas and VERs may be replaced by a new form of regulatory barrier.[18] Baldwin (2000, p.242) succinctly describes the political economy of regulatory and technical barriers:

> Most [regulatory barriers] are highly technical, and a large fraction covers intermediate inputs – products unknown to most voters. Owing to their technical complexity and political invisibility, product norms are often written, directly or indirectly, by domestic firms to which they apply. Quite naturally, these firms write the norms in a way that favors their varieties or at least disfavors foreign varieties.

Imposition of regulatory and standards-related barriers on T&C products has been limited, but the future looks uncertain. A particularly elaborate and complex trade-restrictive barrier is posed by a new system called REACH (Registration, Evaluation and Authorisation of Chemicals) proposed by the EU. If adopted, the REACH legislation could subject textiles and clothing firms to a procedure of registration, evaluation, authorisation and restriction for a large number of chemical substances. The EU trading partners, including developed countries, are making efforts to convince the EU to modify the rules before a formal announcement in order to reduce the potentially disruptive impact of REACH on international trade and to improve its workability (the United States mission to the European Union, 2006).

The governmental barriers mentioned above would at least provide some element of predictability despite their protectionist undercurrent. Private standards, differing from firm to firm, can also pose costly barriers. Due to pressures from consumer groups, the environmental lobby and trade unions, some of the major buyers in developed countries have private "codes of conduct", which they expect all suppliers to follow. These codes mainly correspond to environmental and labour standards, which can significantly raise suppliers' costs (Adhikari and Weerantunge, forthcoming), especially where multiple codes with different monitoring and reporting requirements are involved.

It is desirable from a human development perspective to make a gradual but sustained effort aimed at reaching higher environmental and labour standards, since an abrupt switch to higher standards could erode the competitiveness of enterprises in developing countries. The necessity of ensuring compliance with multiple standards can further aggravate the problem. Due to the immense market power of the buyers, who can dictate their terms, T&C exporters are left with only two choices. Either they have to custom-tailor the working environment in the factory to fulfil different conditions imposed by their buyers, or they have to follow the most stringent buyer's standards. Both these responses can affect the competitiveness of these enterprises.

## 3.2 Supply side constraints

Even if market access barriers are removed, most developing countries still face several supply-side constraints, which impede their competitiveness. The five most common constraints, some of which cut across the entire manufacturing sector, are discussed below.

### 3.2.1 Poor human capital

The lack of skilled and/or trained human resources, which impedes productivity growth, is a major reason for most developing countries' inability to take full advantage of trade liberalization and for others to face a threat to their survival. While the wages paid to T&C workers in several Asian countries are much lower than those paid in China, they are not as competitive as Chinese workers due to poorer skills, notably of non-production workers, and other factors impacting on productivity. According to USITC (2004), the average hourly compensation for Chinese garment workers in 2002 was US$0.68, whereas the figures for Bangladesh, India, Indonesia, Pakistan, and Sri Lanka were US$0.39, 0.38, 0.27, 0.41 and 0.48, respectively. However, the report points out that the productivity levels of T&C workers in these Asian countries are significantly lower than their Chinese counterparts.

Due to the lack of technical skills, some countries are hiring expatriate staff. A survey conducted by USAID (2005, p.22) found that 40 per cent of indirect personnel positions in the factories that responded in Cambodia were staffed by expatriates. Because using expatriate staff in technical and supervisory positions raises costs, this can have a significant impact on industry competitiveness (Adhikari and Yamamoto, 2006; Chan and Sok, 2006).

The problem of skill deficit can be addressed by investments in increasing the general level of education (as was done in several East Asian countries) and by providing training opportunities. Again, China offers an example for other developing countries; even a decade ago, a Chinese firm, on average, provided about 70 hours of training per year to its workers and managers compared to only 10 hours in India (Chandra, 1998 cited in Tewari, 2006).

Investments in training can help firms achieve considerable productivity improvements. For example, after realizing the virtue of training, garment firms in Lesotho have now started to invest in the training of their staff. Some training programmes have had spectacular results (Bennet, 2006). A training programme implemented by the Lesotho National Development Corporation (LNDC)/ComMark has helped many apparel factories achieve sustainable increases in production line output, sometimes in excess of 25 per cent.[19]

### 3.2.2 Poor quality of infrastructure

The poor quality of infrastructure, whether dilapidated roads or ports, or antiquated telecommunications networks or power supply, adds to the cost of doing business. Most developing countries face these problems, but the degree may differ from country to country. Infrastructure is a major constraint in some of the Southeast Asian countries like Philippines and Indonesia, and the situation in African and South Asian countries is arguably worse.

The costs of inefficiency in two Asian countries, namely Bangladesh and India, are well documented. According to the OECD (2004), Indian companies suffer a 37 per cent cost disadvantage in shipping containers of clothing products from Mumbai/Chennai to the east coast of the United States, relative to similar container shipments originating in Shanghai. This cost disadvantage arises from delays and inefficiencies in Indian ports. Similarly, an Asian Development Bank technical assistance study in 2003 found that clothing producers in Bangladesh were likely to earn 30 per cent more if inefficiencies were removed at the Chittagong port (ADB, 2006). Out of the six major exporters from Sub-Saharan Africa, South Africa and Mauritius are the only two countries with relatively good facilities in place; others countries such as Kenya, Lesotho, Madagascar and Swaziland are known for their relative weaknesses in infrastructure provisioning.

### 3.2.3 Limited trade facilitation measures

Trade facilitation is defined as the simplification and harmonization of international trade procedures. These procedures encompass the activities, practices and formalities involved in collecting, presenting, communicating and processing data required for the movement of goods in international trade.

Procedural hurdles can be corrected with adjustments in customs rules and formalities and investment in computerization to speed up the process. However, efforts in this direction have been extremely limited, particularly in South Asia and Sub-Saharan Africa where total time taken for import reaches 46.5 and 60.5 days, respectively, against the best performing country's (Denmark) average of five days (table 8).

South Asian countries are marginally better than Sub-Saharan African countries in terms of trading across borders, although there are inter-country variations within regions. Hummels (2001) estimates that each day saved in shipping time is worth 0.8 per cent ad valorem duty for manufactured goods. While the time taken for export or import is influenced by several factors including the quality of transportation and other infrastructure as discussed above, the lead time can be reduced by doing away with the number of documents and signatures required for import and export, e.g. via automated customs and certification processing. This will have a significant pay-off not only for the T&C industry but for the trading sector as a whole.

In the post-quota era, improved trade facilitation is even more critical for the survival of the T&C industry in these two regions, not least because this is one industry that involves both imports of inputs as well as exports of finished products. Given the move towards vertical specialization and the slicing up of the value chain, each day saved could provide enormous benefits in terms of enhancing the industry's competitiveness. This is important as some RMG products are time-sensitive products and delayed consignments could lead to the cancellation of orders (Adhikari and Weeratunge, forthcoming).

### 3.2.4 High costs of inputs

Except for countries with vertically integrated production structures, most developing countries have to rely on imported fabrics and accessories in the process of production. The absence of a vertically integrated production structure may not be a major disadvantage provided the inputs can be obtained in a short time period at international prices. However, due to the problems mentioned in the section on infrastructure and trade facilitation, it is not possible for most South Asian and Sub-Saharan African countries to access inputs on short order.

The high cost of inputs can be reduced by lowering tariffs on inputs across the board. However, this may not be a desirable option given the reliance of developing countries on customs for raising government revenue (Adhikari and Yamamoto, 2006). Therefore, many countries allow the import of inputs to be used for export processing at reduced or even zero duty rates. In order to ensure that the inputs are actually used for manufacturing exportable items, several governments have made use of a bonded warehouse facility.

This system can, however, be burdened with bureaucratic problems, as the example of Nepal shows. The exporters who have not exported for a year have faced administrative hassles to benefit from this facility. Even for regular exporters, refunds are not delivered in time and take more than 30 days to process from the date of the claim. Moreover, it has become extremely difficult to get the bank guarantee released, particularly after the introduction of value added tax (VAT)-related regulation.[20]

### 3.2.5 Limited access to finance

Access to credit, especially for small and medium-sized enterprises, including T&C ventures, is a major problem in many Asian and African countries that hinders the prospect of unleashing entrepreneurial potential. Due to the time and hassle involved in recovering loans in the event of default, and generally the high level of non-performing assets, financial institutions exercise extra caution while lending. Accordingly, they do not consider small enterprises and/or those enterprises with limited ability to provide collateral security as creditworthy. Consequently, these enterprises have to finance the majority of their operations through internal resources or rely on informal sources of funding, which tend to be extremely costly (ibid.).

For example, as stated in a study conducted by International Business and Technical Consultants, Inc. (2003) for the Ministry of Commerce, Bangladesh, a large number of knitwear garment exporters with a capital of Taka 10 to 20 million (US$0.17-0.34 million), and a workforce of 150-300, were forced to borrow from local moneylenders at a monthly interest rate close to 11 per cent. Exporters are compelled to take such loans when they fail to obtain timely bank financing (Adhikari and Yamamoto, 2006).

In the case of Nepal, the story is slightly different. While small entrepreneurs' access to credit as well as other banking facilities is severely restricted by discriminatory interest rates and the need for collateral, exporters are facing new problems after the phase-out of quotas. Nepalese commercial banks are increasingly becoming reluctant to make new investments in this sector and are initiating stricter actions against debtors (Shakya, 2005).

### 4. Emerging issues

Apart from the conventional issues discussed above, trade in T&C products is going to be influenced by several others emerging issues, some of which are discussed below.

### 4.1 Changing buyers' behaviour

Textiles and clothing, particularly clothing, is a classic example of a buyer-driven commodity chain, which is characterized by decentralized, globally dispersed production networks, coordinated by lead firms who control design, marketing, and branding at the retail level. Many of the most powerful branded retailers such as Gap, Nike, Wal-Mart and Liz Claiborne own no factories and do not necessarily "make" in order to sell. Yet, by controlling design, input sourcing, branding and distribution these powerful retailers capture the largest share of value added in apparel and textiles production (Gereffi, 1999). The economic power of large retailers, predominantly in developed countries, has increased substantially over the last few years (WTO, 2005). In the United States, for example, the 29 biggest retailers account for 98 per cent of sales (UNDP RCC, 2005a). The trend now is toward greater product specialization and brand-name and market segmentation. These large retailers collect market information about the latest trends in styles and tastes, and their integration of this information combined with the volume of their business gives them considerable leverage in dealing with suppliers (Kelegama and Weeraratne, 2005).

Because of the sheer market power, it is the buyers' preference that is going to shape market response in the exporting countries. Although price and quality used to be the two dominant variables, buyer preferences these days represent an interplay of various factors, of which five are critically important.[21]

*Price and cost factors*: The price of final delivery of goods into the warehouse is still a factor that influences the sourcing decision of the majority of buyers.[22] While several Asian countries including Bangladesh, Pakistan, Indonesia and Vietnam seem to have followed a low-cost strategy, the sustainability of this approach has been challenged on the ground that the focus on low costs makes them always vulnerable to competition from the next lower cost supplier (Tewari, 2006).

*Critical mass:* Buyers will be reluctant to place orders with producers with a small share in the world market. According to this view, countries with large production capacities and the ability to deliver huge quantities are likely to be preferred by buyers as this keeps down input costs of those suppliers, the transaction costs of dealing with multiple suppliers, and the trading costs of shipping from those countries. This view is supported by the US Department of Commerce, which estimates the number of countries from which major items would be sourced by the US buyers would drop to 25 per cent of current levels by 2010 (UNDP RCC, 2005a).

*Risk spreading:* A possible scenario opposing the critical mass sentiment is the risk-spreading argument. Buyers, desirous to maintain uninterrupted supply, would like to diversify the sources from which they import T&C products. For example, according to the US International Trade Commission: "To reduce the risk of sourcing from only one country, the US importers also plan to expand trade relationships with other low-cost countries alternative to China (USITC, 2004)". For example, stores such as Wal-Mart and Dillards make spatial distinctions among the location of the suppliers from whom they source certain categories of apparel (Tewari, 2006). Indeed, because they were anticipating the re-imposition of quotas on China, several buyers continued to source products from countries like

Bangladesh and Cambodia during the first few months of phasing out of quotas, and this contributed to the continued success of these countries.

*Total solution providers:* Buyers' preferences are likely to be tilted in favour of suppliers which can cover all stages of the value chain in production, ranging from product design to input sourcing, manufacturing, packaging and shipping of the final product (Adhikari and Yamamoto, 2005). Several East Asian manufacturers have now moved up from assembly of cut fabric into more complex operations entailing coordination, supply of machinery and finance, and management of subcontractors. They are now full-package suppliers for international buyers and are operating as transnational intermediaries receiving orders from large retailers and subcontracting to their network of producers, which are located in Asia, Latin America and Africa (Hayashi, 2005). This issue is further discussed below under the heading "value chain management".

*Ethical concerns:* As discussed above, pressures from consumer groups in industrialized countries, including boycotting of products manufactured in sweatshops or in environmentally-unfriendly manner, have brought ethical concerns into the decision-making matrix of the buyers. Most buyers have themselves developed a "code of conduct" with which they want all their suppliers to comply. This includes issues such as working conditions, workers' health and safety, minimum wages, maximum working hours and overtime.

## 4.2 Graduation and loss of competitiveness

The history of the T&C industry suggests that, as economies developed and workers' incomes increased, countries gradually moved up the technology ladder and started producing either value added T&C products or moved to other manufactures like electronics and consumer durables. Even within the T&C sector, textiles being more capital and often knowledge intensive compared to clothing, countries continue producing textiles even after reaching a certain threshold in the development ladder. Mayer (2005) argues that the shift of labour-intensive activities in textiles and clothing away from the first-tier NICs towards other Asian countries has clearly reflected industrial upgrading associated with wage increases and a move in production and export patterns towards more technology-intensive goods.

Of late, China's changing comparative advantage has been a topic of general discussion as well as empirical studies. Based on a Heckscher-Ohlin-type trade model that concentrates on relative endowments of labour, land, and human capital, Mayer and Wood (2001) show that China's comparative advantage is not in low-skill-labour-intensive production, such as clothing, but in manufacturing sectors with higher skill content. Compared to other countries including China, important clothing exporters from South Asia such as Bangladesh, India and Pakistan have an unusual combination of low levels of both skill per worker and land per worker that gives these countries a strong comparative advantage in labour-intensive manufactures, which use little of either skill or land per unit of labour (Mayer, 2005).

Similarly, according to the ILO (2005a), China is in the process of outgrowing its comparative advantage for the most labour-intensive manufacturing industries. It is evolving towards higher value-added industries. During this process, China is developing not only as a manufacturing hub, but also as an important consumer market which is likely to absorb a larger share of its own production as well as total world imports. Rising income in China is likely to be associated with rising wages for low-skilled workers so that the share of skill-intensive items in China's manufactured exports is likely to rise. It is interesting to note, in this context, that wages in China's export industries are indeed rising and that this may jeopardize the international competitiveness of Chinese exporters of labour-intensive manufactures, especially if productivity fails to keep pace (Harney, 2004 cited in Mayer, 2005).

## 4.3 Lean retailing

As yet another reflection of their market power, buyers are unwilling to maintain high levels of stock in their warehouses or stores. Moreover, taking advantage of the latest technology, they would like to respond promptly to consumer demand in line with rapidly changing fashions. With this trend toward "lean retailing," producers that can provide quick turnaround time enjoy an important competitive advantage. Most studies argue that proximity to large markets, e.g., Mexico, Central America and the Caribbean countries to the United States and Turkey, and Central and Eastern European Countries to the EU, is a key factor to ensure quick turnaround (WTO, 2005). The importance of "timeliness" and speedy delivery in lean retailing practices has significantly affected supplier location over and above consideration of price (Nordas, 2004; Berger, 2006 cited in Tewari, 2006). Emphasizing the promptness in delivery as a key factor to remain competitive in the post-quota era, Abernathy and Weil (2004) argue that the proximity advantage will become even greater as retailers raise the bar higher on the responsiveness and flexibility required of their suppliers.

However, it is necessary to see if this is the case even at a disaggregated level. For example, in high-fashion products such as women's clothing, which does not require replenishment after one season, the issue of proximity may not matter. On the other hand, for replenishment products such as men's jeans, it would seem that producers closely located to the world's major markets are at an advantage (Abernathy, Volpe and Weil, 2004). For example, replenishable products make up a greater share of US apparel imports from Mexico than they do from Asian locations despite the cost advantage associated with the sourcing from the latter. In 2003, US buyers sourced over US$4 billion worth of replenishable products from Mexico and Caribbean Basin (amounting to 22 per cent of all apparel sourced from these countries) as compared to US$1.3 billion of those products from China and other Asian countries (ibid.).

However, declining shares of Mexico, Caribbean and other South American countries in US imports and declining shares of Eastern European, Mediterranean and North African countries in EU imports of T&C products show that, on the whole, proximity has a limited role in shaping and influencing buyers' decisions. It might continue to be important in a limited range of products, but its overall significance is gradually declining due to decreasing communications costs and shipping transit time and improved efficiency of trade-related services.

## 4.4 Value chain networks

Large retail chains such as Wal-Mart and "branded marketers" such as Nike and Reebok have been outsourcing their production to low-wage countries but have retained control, as noted above, over the major portion of the value chain. By keeping control over the design and marketing functions, they also maintain close control over the global T&C value chain through standard-setting, often sourcing raw materials themselves, distributing them globally and then importing the made-up garments.[23] However, it is difficult for these large-scale buyers to coordinate all these activities by themselves. As Abernathy, Volpe and Weil (2004) argue:

> Making sourcing decisions in the global apparel market is a daunting task. Due to factors including language and custom barriers, communications hurdles, and the sheer number of producers scattered across the world, U.S. retailers have had to change the way they approach the world market. Some large retailers have established their own buying offices overseas to administer the outsourcing of their private label products. Others work with large and sophisticated independent sourcing agents to handle this intricate task.

Buyers' inclination toward the second option mentioned has led to the emergence of intermediaries, which are essentially "sub-contracted" by large buyers to perform critical tasks in the value chain. Drawing on tacit knowledge gained from years of immersion in the garment industry, their ability to master the process of fulfilling large orders to the exact specification of their buyers and to exacting delivery schedules, as well as their specific knowledge about production management, many companies from East Asia (mainly Hong Kong, Korea and Taiwan) have been acting as intermediaries for global buyers since the 1980s and 1990s (Tewari, 2006, p. 29). Their capacity to mobilize and coordinate full-package manufacturing in global T&C value chains led to what Gereffi (1999) terms "triangular production networks". This implies production is done in one country (usually less developed), organized and coordinated by firms in another country (usually middle-income), and sold to a buyer in yet another country (usually developed).[24]

---

**Box 1: Organizational skills in the changing landscape of T&C trade**

A Hong Kong based company, Li & Fung Ltd[25] – founded in China in 1906 – has evolved from an exporting agent of porcelain and silk from China to a professional manager of the entire supply chain – from product design and development, through raw material and factory sourcing, production planning and management, quality assurance and export documentation, to shipping consolidation. The company gained expertise in buying and selling quotas from Asian markets for shipment into the United States in the 1970s and 1980s as an important element of its garment exporting business. As a buying agent and broker in quotas, it established backward links with more than 2,000 Asian suppliers and forward links to manufacturers and retailers. In the late 1980s and 1990s, the company took advantage of its network of Asian suppliers and its growing familiarity with logistics management to offer US retailers an efficient means of sourcing products in Asian nations. Currently, the Group has more than 70 offices in over 40 countries and employs 8,000 staff globally to cover a global network of over 10,000 suppliers. It has achieved a turnover of US$7 billion and aims to maintain the growth rate of 18 per cent achieved in 2005 to be able to achieve a turnover of US$10 billion by 2010.

Perhaps indicative of the next step of evolution, the company entered into a licensing agreement with Levi Strauss & Co. in which it will design, manufacture and market men's tops for the US market under various Levi's® labels, including Levi Strauss Signature™ branded jeans sold to US mass marketers (Abernathy, Volpe and Weil, 2004).

---

Companies such as Li & Fung Ltd. are emerging as successful intermediaries of such triangular networks (Box 1).

## 5. Adjusting to the post-quota world

The temporary safeguards imposed on China have changed the entire dynamics of the T&C trade, with several countries either holding on to their past gains or achieving remarkable export growth. However, many analysts believe that this situation is short-lived (Razzaque and Raihan, 2006; Bhatt et al., 2006; Sisouphanthong et al., 2006; Chan and Sok, 2006). On this view, the real competition in the world T&C market will begin only after 2008 with the phasing-out of these temporary quotas.

Safeguard measures on Chinese imports can be seen as yet another breathing space for a number of countries who are expected to lose out in the post-2008 period. Efforts have already been made in several countries, even before the phasing-out of ATC either as a "preparedness strategy" or as a "survival strategy". While some support measures have been taken only by the government, others were undertaken through public-private partnership or with the private sector reacting to incentives provided by the government.

## 5.1 Efforts made so far

### 5.1.1 Government support to the T&C industry

Governments all over the world are known for providing targeted support to priority sectors, including protection from outside competition to grow, prosper and face global competition. A recent study by Adhikari (2006b) on the magnitude and type of government support provided in seven Asian countries (Bangladesh, China, India, Indonesia, Pakistan, Sri Lanka, Vietnam) suggests the emergence of the following pattern.

First, support is a function of the ability as well as the willingness of governments to provide assistance. Therefore, better resourced countries like China seem to have provided more assistance compared to, say, Indonesia. The Chinese government supported heavily the modernization of its factories[26] and provided tax forgiveness to the state owned enterprise (SOEs),[27] apart from creating textile cities and providing export credit insurance to the T&C enterprises. Governments that pursue active industrial policies tend to provide higher levels of support, which can also be seen from the examples of China and India vis-à-vis Indonesia or Sri Lanka.

Second, maintaining and improving competitiveness being the key to survive in the post-quota world, investment in technological upgrading or modernization of the T&C sector has been the most widely utilized form of support for all the countries reviewed. While some countries reduced tariffs on imports of machinery and equipment, others provided preferential credit or cash support to help their firms modernize themselves. Examples include, besides China as mentioned above, countries like Bangladesh, India, Indonesia, Pakistan and Vietnam.

Third, a reduction in the prices of infrastructure, such as rebate/reduction in utility charges was found to be the least used (or least reported) form of government support. Even in the case of Bangladesh, where this facility is provided to export-oriented enterprises, the scheme seems to have been only recently introduced into its industrial policy of 2005.

Fourth, income tax exemption for the exporting sectors, an extensively used form of government support in the past, is not the norm anymore with some governments not providing such a facility and some recently discontinuing the same. For example, income tax exemption is not provided by Indonesia, and India has recently discontinued it. Others charge income tax at reduced rates for export oriented enterprises.

Fifth, the operation of special economic zones (SEZs) or export processing zones (EPZs), which is not only targeted at the T&C industry, is common in all the seven countries reviewed. A separate discussion on this special measure has been included below. Moreover, the refund of and reduction in excise duty, sales tax and VAT for the inputs – goods and/or services – used in export processing, which is provided in all the countries reviewed, is another general support measure not confined to the T&C sector. Similarly, duty reduction on the imports of inputs also figures as one of the prominent means to support export-oriented industries in a majority of countries reviewed.

Sixth, although all the countries studied have achieved export growth in the post-quota period, no systematic study has been conducted to establish any casual link between the magnitude of government support and its contribution to export growth. Moreover, much of the support seems to have resulted from a "demonstration effect", with countries trying to replicate a successful model without conducting proper cost-benefit analysis. Government support to the industry has important fiscal implications and its sustainability can be questioned.

Seventh, most governments seem to have provided such support in a WTO-compliant manner. This has been made easier by the fact that the LDCs and developing countries with less than US$1,000 per capita Gross National Product (GNP) are exempted from rules on subsidies under the Agreement on Subsidies and Countervailing Measures (ASCM). Moreover, general subsidies, i.e., the subsidies given for production across the board to the entire industrial sector, based on some generally applied criteria can be provided, as can subsidies for research and development (R&D) and/or environmental conservation (Das, 2006). The fact that these subsidies have not been challenged so far is also a testimony to the fact that they do not run afoul of WTO provisions.

## 5.1.2  Export processing zones

One of the major supply-side constraints faced by most least developed and low-income countries is the lack of ability to enhance competitiveness, resulting, among others, from poor infrastructure, inability to obtain inputs at international prices with the shortest possible lead time, inability to meet the deadline for orders because of frequent interruptions in operation from labour unrest or political disturbances, and other regulatory barriers. Because these barriers severely constrain the ability of the private sector to earn an attractive return on investment, the private sector in turn is reluctant to invest in sectors like light manufacturing such as T&C and electronics, despite their export potential. Foreign investors are even more hesitant (Adhikari and Yamamoto, 2006). Therefore, in order to attract investments[28] in these sectors, many governments in developing countries have established various EPZs and SEZs. Within these Zones, governments provide incentives to enterprises that mimic – and go beyond – the free trade scenario. For example, enterprises within the EPZ can obtain inputs such as equipment and raw materials duty-free; a certain level of regulatory relief is assured;[29] foreign exchange controls are not applied; profit repatriation is guaranteed; strikes and other labour actions are prohibited; and, in some cases, freedom of trade unions is also restricted. Moreover, trade services and infrastructure facilities available within an EPZ are higher than national average standards. However, certain conditions are also imposed on EPZ enterprises; they are, for example, either not allowed or severely restricted from making domestic sales.

The primary goals of EPZs are to create conducive business environments and to enhance earnings by promoting non-traditional exports, direct investment, technology transfer and knowledge spillover. EPZs' greatest contribution seems to be job creation and income generation. They also can contribute to building human capital, through their demonstration and catalyst effects on the country entrepreneur pool (Madani, 1999).

Although EPZs have attracted considerable attention in the empirical literature, studies focusing on efficiency of the T&C sector within an EPZ are rare. According to one analysis, which focused exclusively on LDCs, conducted by the WTO (2005), EPZs in some cases not only offered beneficial business to domestic and foreign firms, but also boosted economic development by helping countries enhance their competitiveness. However, that report cautions: "In the majority of cases, success of EPZ was limited and contributed only to a minor extent to an improvement of LDC competitiveness in the T&C sector" (ibid.).

One reason for this could be the very limited backward or forward linkages between the EPZ and the local economy. Because of the incentive structure, along with the quality and reliability of inputs demanded by EPZ-based exporting firms, most prefer not to purchase inputs from local industries. This acts as a barrier for creating a reliable backward linkage. Moreover, because firms located in the EPZ are prevented from making domestic sales, their forward linkage with the local economy is severely constrained (Adhikari and Yamamoto, 2006).

Another important consideration is whether the incremental net value of the expected benefits justifies the huge investment to be made, at least initially, by the public sector,[30] as well as the costs to be incurred in the form of foregone revenue. Jayanthakumaran's (2003) research on the performance of EPZs, using a benefit-cost analytical framework, finds that zones in China, Indonesia, Malaysia, Republic of Korea, and Sri Lanka are economically efficient and generate returns well above estimated opportunity costs. On the other hand, the heavy infrastructure costs involved in setting up such zones in the Philippines resulted in a negative net present value.

In some countries, EPZs can become controversial mainly because of the tug of war between the Ministry of Finance, which is concerned over revenue foregone, and the Ministry of Industry, which wants to create industries as well as employment opportunities. For example, currently two ministries are at loggerheads in India over the proposed plan to upscale the creation of SEZs. According to an estimate prepared by the Finance Ministry, the country will have to forego about US$22 billion, on account of the SEZ-granted tax rebates, by the year 2009-10. According to the estimate by the Commerce and Industry Ministry, one million new direct jobs will be created on account of SEZs in the next five years, with corresponding impacts on incomes and potential tax revenue as well as spillovers on the economy, including creation of indirect employment.[31]

### 5.1.3 Case studies

This sub-section, building on an earlier study (Adhikari and Yamamoto, 2005), discusses three case studies from Asian countries which have achieved success in maintaining or even increasing their exports in the face of phasing-out of quotas. These case studies were initially prepared when the impact of safeguards imposed on China was yet to be felt. However, even after the imposition of safeguards on China, the contributions of these strategies have not diminished.

*Improved labour standards: The case of Cambodia*

Cambodia's access to the US market from 1999 to 2004 was contingent on its record of compliance with labour standards, with quota rates increased every year based on successful compliance. In order to satisfy this requirement, Cambodia adopted a corporate social responsibility programme in collaboration with the International Labour Organization (ILO), known as Better Factories Cambodia (formerly known as the ILO Garment Sector Project).

Begun in 2001 to help Cambodia's garment sector achieve and maintain improvements in working conditions, the project monitors and reports on working conditions in Cambodian garment factories against national and international standards, helps factories to improve their productivity, and works with the Government and international buyers to ensure a rigorous and transparent cycle of improvement. The main objective of the programme is to help Cambodian garment factories constantly improve the conditions of labour by strictly adhering to national labour legislation as well as international conventions that Cambodia has signed as a member of the ILO. The programme aims at setting minimum standards as agreed by the decision of a tripartite body (Government, private sector and trade union), monitoring compliance, and providing advisory support and capacity building training to stakeholders to support compliance (ILO, 2005a; ILO, 2005b).

As per a buyers' survey conducted by the Foreign Investment Advisory Services (2004) of the World Bank Group, more than 60 per cent of buyers interviewed said compliance with labour standards was of equal or more importance compared to considerations of price, quality and lead times. The survey also found that Cambodia's labour standards were seen as higher than other Asian countries (Bangladesh, China, Thailand and Viet Nam). It also revealed that 60 per cent of the buyers planned to increase their garment purchases from Cambodia, while none said they would cut back.

Cambodia's ability to achieve an overall export of US$2.2 billion in 2005, an increase of 11.7 per cent over the 2004 figure,[32] lends credence to the findings of the study. Based on the import figures of the EU and the United States for the first eight and nine months of 2006, respectively, Cambodia has done extremely well in both markets. While improved labour standards could have partly contributed to this, safeguards against China's exports may have had a greater role to play in this regard. Although Cambodia's bilateral agreement with the United States has expired and securing increased quotas is no more an incentive for Cambodia, the programme of labour standards is to be continued by the government of Cambodia in all likelihood (Chan and Sok, 2006).

However, there are four clear problems associated with this programme. First, as expressed by the Garment Manufacturers Association of Cambodia (GMAC), compliance with labour standards has led to increased costs for exporting enterprises, thereby eroding their competitiveness. Second, greater freedom of association has led to an increase in strikes and disruptive activities, which is detrimental to the interest of the industry (Chan and Sok, 2006). Third, despite the success of this model in the garment industry, it has not been replicated in other industries in the country and certainly not in other LDCs having similar socio-economic conditions and export profiles. Fourth, this scheme covers only the formal sector, but not the informal sector (Adhikari and Yamamoto, 2005).

*Focus on a niche product: The case of Sri Lanka*

The growth of the Sri Lankan garment industry, like that of many other developing countries, can be mainly ascribed to the existence of the quota system. Several studies predicted that Sri Lanka would be one of the losers in the post-quota regime. This became almost true in 2005, when Sri Lanka's export to EU market declined by 1.3 per cent in value terms. Fortunately, due to the 5.9 per cent growth in the US market, Sri Lanka still managed to post a positive growth of 3 per cent in dollar terms at the end of 2005 (ibid.). Since the Sri Lankan T&C sector is not considered highly competitive due to several factors – higher wages, low productivity of workers, high cost of utilities and lack of backward linkages – private entrepreneurs realized that they should focus on niche products in order to create an opportunity for themselves.

Taking advantage of the relatively high level of education of its workers,[33] coupled with fast learning aptitude, Sri Lanka started focusing on a distinct segment of apparel, i.e., women's undergarments. Another distinct advantage of Sri Lanka is that some of the manufacturers in the country were already concentrating on this segment for a relatively long period and have established reputation in the export market. Table 9 provides growth rates for this sector since 2004. According to the figures, the category in which fastest export growth was attained in the US market between 2004 and 2006 was cotton briefs and panties: growth reached 910 per cent in the first nine months of 2005 compared to the corresponding period in 2004, and 58.7 per cent in same period of 2006. In the case of the EU market, brassieres showed consistently strong import growth, at 18.6 per cent in first eight months of 2005 and 52.2 in same period of 2006.

The figures suggest that there is tremendous potential for expansion in the US market. With combined exports of US$240 million to the US and EU markets, these items represented 11 per cent of the total Sri Lankan export of T&C products in 2005. In 2006, these exports, which have increased to US$321 million, represent 15 per cent of all T&C exports of the island to these two major markets.

For a country that has recognized its limitations in terms of competing with other low-cost economies and that has a pool of skilled and educated human resources, focus on a niche product may be an option for survival. This sector is not likely to face increased competitive pressure in the immediate future because other developing countries with limited skills may not be able to replicate this model easily, mainly because of the lack of educated and skilled human resources.

The Sri Lankan private sector's continuous search for niche products was also demonstrated by the recent success of a single firm in carving a global niche by penetrating an even more lucrative market – body armour, flak jackets and bullet proof vests for troops in Saudi Arabia as well as for the United Nations (Daily Mirror, 2006). Therefore, it is not surprising that Sri Lanka has the second lowest export (product) concentration among T&C products in South Asia, second only to India (Adhikari, 2006c).

*Focus on regional trade: The case of Thailand*

While Thailand was able to increase its exports of garment products to the United States, its exports to the EU market declined in 2005. This may in part be due to competition from more efficient players like China and India after the quotas were eliminated. However, Thailand, as a member of the ASEAN Free Trade Agreement, was able to export to its immediate neighbours to make up for the losses it incurred in other large markets. It has become a major supplier of fabrics to all other ASEAN countries, as seen by the profile of its fabric exports. Except for Singapore and Brunei, which do not have strong T&C sectors, all other member countries of ASEAN have increased their imports from Thailand.

The EU's policy of allowing for ASEAN cumulation to achieve ROO requirements under the EBA seems also to have indirectly helped Thailand. Since its immediate LDC neighbours such as Cambodia and Lao PDR do not have well-developed textile and other accessories manufacturing, the EU's requirement to use fabrics from ASEAN to qualify for ROO requirements provides a captive market for Thai textiles. Likewise, export diversification in the case of garments is quite impressive, and there are lessons to be learned for other Asian developing countries.[34]

It might be possible for other ASEAN developing countries like Indonesia and Viet Nam to follow the same trajectory, and LDCs like

Cambodia and Lao PDR probably will have to wait for several years to make this happen. Due to a relatively liberal and hassle-free preferential trade regime within ASEAN, increasing intra-regional trade to make up for losses in multilateral trade seems feasible. However, it might not be possible in the South Asia region not only because the intra-regional trade in the region is very low but also because most member-countries have included a majority of T&C products under the "sensitive list" negotiated under the Agreement on South Asian Free Trade Area (SAFTA).[35]

## 5.2 Efforts required

Developing countries have designed and implemented a variety of survival strategies to keep themselves afloat in the post-quota era. While some of them have paid off as well as provided a sustained advantage to the T&C industry, others may not be sustainable. For example, Sri Lanka's continuous search for identifying niche products and product diversification and the Thai model of South-South trade look more sustainable than the Cambodian strategy, which can be replicated by other countries. Since the competition in this industry is bound to be intense post-2008, there is no substitute for enhanced competitiveness. However, achieving cost competitiveness alone is not enough. It might be possible to replicate one of the above models by fine tuning them to suit the national conditions. Developing countries should consider a broader range of policy responses to be able to survive in a fiercely competitive post-2008 market.

### 5.2.1 Market access

Improved market access is necessary to overcome trade barriers. It is in the interest of most developed countries to promote a rules-based, multilateral trading system rather than promoting a "spaghetti bowl" of frequently overlapping rules of origin. However, in the context of Asian LDCs, who have been deprived of market access opportunities in the US market, a campaign for unconditional duty free market access with flexible ROO, taking account of the stage of industrialization of such LDCs, should continue. Other non-tariff barriers should also be addressed as a part of the Doha Round of negotiations.

### 5.2.2 Human capital

Increased productivity is a major tool to improve competitiveness at the enterprise level. However, in order to enhance the productivity of the country as a whole, investments in health and nutrition are as important as investments in education and skills development. A combination of public-private partnerships and mobilization of donor support could be an effective way to create better human capital critical for survival in the post-quota world.

### 5.2.3 Value chain management

Given the increased importance of full-package service delivery, timeliness and consistency in delivery, quality assurance and adaptability, developing country suppliers should try to learn these techniques. Constant improvement and upgrading in trade facilitation measures is a must for achieving these objectives. Such efforts not only will help improve competitiveness of the T&C sector, but will also provide economy-wide benefits.

### 5.2.4 Sustainability of government support

In order to reduce the burden on budgetary resources, both due to support provided and revenue foregone, governments could usefully explore several approaches to sector support. First, the potential of public-private partnerships between the government and consortia of exporters should be utilized to the extent possible to develop this sector. Cost sharing should be encouraged in every support programme. Second, it may be possible to charge nominal user fees for various services provided by government to industry and gradually increase the same over time. Third, governments should try to obtain technical assistance from various multilateral and bilateral donors to support some of these initiatives. Subject to the outcomes of cost-benefit analysis, this type of support can be a perfect candidate for utilizing the benefits of "Aid for Trade" – a proposal currently being discussed at the WTO.

### 5.2.5 Access to credit

Reforms aimed at infusing more competition, including encouraging FDI and joint ventures, can help unlock the potential of the financial sector. This can be achieved through enactment/implementation of competition laws in developing countries. Another option is to empower the regulatory institutions to play a more active role in promoting competition in the financial sector. Moreover, legal reform to improve the loan recovery system could go a long way towards building the confidence of the banking system and providing it incentives to treat small- and medium enterprises more or less at par with other borrowers. If both the instruments mentioned above are not possible to implement, government may have to resort to directed lending. However, this should be conditional on performance requirements and should have a credible "sunset" clause to prevent the same from being captured by vested interests.

### 5.2.6   South-South cooperation

While the starting point for South-South cooperation is trade, it should go much beyond that. Areas of South-South cooperation for the development of the T&C sector may include the flow of investment not only in the rather "footloose" RMG sector, but also in helping create vertically integrated facilities by making investments in textiles or accessories industries and the south-south transfer of technology. Countries like China and India could take the lead in these initiatives. Another possible area of cooperation could be to encourage training institutions in relatively better-off developing countries to partner with such institutions in countries with limited capacities.

## 6. Conclusion

The paper finds that the post-quota world has not brought about a dramatic transformation in the T&C market as well as in sourcing patterns. Among the losers of the post-quota era, not all are on the same footing. While some have graduated into the production of higher value products, others have lost out because of their lack of competitiveness and their inability to adapt. The current status quo is the result of the re-imposition of quotas on China as a part of the temporary safeguard measures agreed by the country at the time of its accession to the WTO. Countries that did not manage to withstand competition in the first six month period after the phasing out of quotas need to be extremely cautious and make every possible effort to enhance their competitiveness before the expiry of this temporary measure in 2008.

Given the history of protection in this industry and rather strong political economy factors, market access remains the largest single problem for the developing countries. However, this can be resolved mainly through international and regional cooperation. There are several supply side issues which are impeding the growth prospects of several developing countries. These problems need to be addressed first at the domestic level. International support in the form of "aid for trade" can, however, be instrumental in supplementing the domestic reforms initiatives.

Despite protectionist barriers, the T&C industry has not remained static over the past five decades or so. It keeps evolving due to changing demand of the buyers, sourcing patterns, availability of and access to technology, shifting levels of economic growth and increased consciousness as well as sensitivity towards corporate social responsibility and ethical procurement. While some of these emerging issues offer opportunities for developing countries, others pose challenges. In order to survive in the present T&C market characterized by rapidly changing consumer demand and retailer market power, organizational skills and flexibility become more important than merely achieving cost competitiveness.

Some of the efforts made by the government as well as the private sector to help the T&C exporters survive the the phasing out of quotas have produced encouraging results. However, some other endeavours have either not been successful or could yet prove unsustainable. Therefore, concerted efforts should be made by various stakeholders aimed at addressing the market access anomalies and supply side constraints keeping in view the emerging challenges and the future evolution of the T&C industry and trade.

## Table 1.
### Textile exports of selected economies, 1990, 2004-05

| Region/ economies (ranked by value in 2004) | Value (million dollars) | | | Change (%) | Share in world exports (%) |
|---|---|---|---|---|---|
| | 1990 | 2004 | 2005 | 2004-05 | 2005 |
| **World** | **104,354** | **195,378** | **202,966** | **3.9** | |
| **Asia** | | | | | |
| China [a] | 7,219 | 33,428 | 41,050 | 22.8 | 20.2 |
| Hong Kong, SAR, China | 8,213 | 14,296 | 13,830 | -3.3 | 6.8 |
| Korea, Republic of | 6,076 | 10,839 | 10,391 | -4.1 | 5.1 |
| Taiwan, Province of China | 6,128 | 10,038 | 9,706 | -3.3 | 4.8 |
| Japan | 5,871 | 7,138 | 6,905 | -3.3 | 3.4 |
| India [b] | 2,180 | 7,009 | 7,850 | 12.0 | 3.9 |
| Pakistan | 2,663 | 6,125 | 7,087 | 15.7 | 3.5 |
| Indonesia | 1,241 | 3,152 | 3,447 | 9.4 | 1.7 |
| Thailand | 928 | 2,563 | 2,764 | 7.8 | 1.4 |
| Malaysia [a] | 343 | 1,227 | 1,356 | 10.4 | 0.7 |
| Singapore | 903 | 977 | 916 | -6.3 | 0.5 |
| Iran, Islamic Rep. of [b] | 510 | 817 | 848 | 3.8 | 0.4 |
| Macao, SAR, China | 136 | 313 | 275 | -12.2 | 0.1 |
| Philippines [a] | 132 | 257 | 265 | 3.1 | 0.1 |
| Bangladesh | 343 | 204 | 221 | 8.4 | 0.1 |
| Sri Lanka [b] | 25 | 149 | 136 | -8.8 | 0.1 |
| **EU and North America** | | | | | |
| European Union (25) | -- | 72,196 | 67,977 | -5.8 | 33.5 |
| intra-EU (25) exports | -- | 47,889 | 44,464 | -7.2 | 21.9 |
| extra-EU (25) exports | -- | 24,307 | 23,513 | -3.3 | 11.6 |
| United States | 5,039 | 11,989 | 12,379 | 3.3 | 6.1 |
| Canada | 687 | 2,431 | 2,464 | 1.4 | 1.2 |
| Mexico [a] | 713 | 2,071 | 2,133 | 3.0 | 1.1 |
| **Other Regions** | | | | | |
| Turkey | 1,440 | 6,428 | 7,068 | 9.9 | 3.5 |
| Brazil | -- | 1,244 | 1,326 | 6.5 | 0.7 |

Source: WTO (2006a).
Obs.: [a] Includes significant exports from processing zones ; [b] Includes Secretariat estimates.

## Table 2.
## Clothing exports of selected economies, 1990, 2004-05

| Region/ economies (ranked by value in 2004) | Value (million dollars) | | | Change (%) 2004-05 | Share in world exports (%) 2005 |
|---|---|---|---|---|---|
| | 1990 | 2004 | 2005 | | |
| World | 108,129 | 259,147 | 275,639 | 6.4 | -- |
| Asia | | | | | |
| China [a] | 9,669 | 61,856 | 74,163 | 19.9 | 26.9 |
| Hong Kong, SAR, China | 15,406 | 25,097 | 27,292 | 8.7 | 9.9 |
| India [b] | 2,530 | 6,632 | 8,290 | 25.0 | 3.0 |
| Bangladesh | 643 | 5,686 | 6,418 | 12.9 | 2.3 |
| Indonesia | 1,646 | 4,454 | 5,106 | 14.6 | 1.9 |
| Viet Nam [b] | -- | 4,441 | 4,805 | 8.2 | 1.7 |
| Thailand | 2,817 | 3,985 | 4,085 | 2.5 | 1.5 |
| Korea, Republic of | 7,879 | 3,391 | 2,581 | -23.9 | 0.9 |
| Pakistan | 1,014 | 3,026 | 3,604 | 19.1 | 1.3 |
| Sri Lanka [b] | 638 | 2,776 | 2,877 | 3.6 | 1.0 |
| Malaysia [a] | 1,315 | 2,326 | 2,479 | 6.6 | 0.9 |
| Philippines [a] | 1,733 | 2,157 | 2,276 | 5.5 | 0.8 |
| Cambodia [b] | -- | 1,981 | 2,199 | 11.0 | 0.8 |
| Singapore | 1,588 | 1,972 | 1,696 | -14.0 | 0.6 |
| Macao, SAR, China | 1,111 | 1,952 | 1,654 | -15.3 | 0.6 |
| Taiwan, Province of China | 3,987 | 1,951 | 1,561 | -20.0 | 0.6 |
| Myanmar | 12 | 568 | 331 | -41.7 | 0.1 |
| Iran, Islamic Rep. of [b] | -- | 222 | 273 | 22.6 | 0.1 |
| EU and North America | | | | | |
| European Union (25) | -- | 76,887 | 80,354 | 4.5 | 29.2 |
| intra-EU (25) exports | -- | 57,759 | 57,737 | 0.0 | 20.9 |
| extra-EU (25) exports | -- | 19,128 | 22,617 | 18.2 | 8.2 |
| Mexico [a] | 587 | 7,490 | 7,271 | -2.9 | 2.6 |
| United States | 2,565 | 5,059 | 4,998 | -1.2 | 1.8 |
| Other Regions | | | | | |
| Turkey | 3,331 | 11,193 | 11,818 | 5.6 | 4.3 |
| Romania | 363 | 4,717 | 4,627 | -1.9 | 1.7 |
| Tunisia [b] | 1,126 | 3,289 | 3,332 | 1.3 | 1.2 |
| Morocco [a] | 722 | 3,023 | 2,783 | -7.9 | 1.0 |
| Honduras [b] | 64 | 2,680 | 2,626 | -2.0 | 1.0 |
| Dominican Republic [a, b] | 782 | 2,121 | 1,908 | -10.0 | 1.0 |
| El Salvador [a, b] | 184 | 1,815 | 1,702 | -6.3 | 1.0 |

continued

| Region/ economies (ranked by value in 2004) | Value (million dollars) | | | Change (%) | Share in world exports (%) |
|---|---|---|---|---|---|
| | 1990 | 2004 | 2005 | 2004-05 | 2005 |
| Guatemala | 24 | 1,651 | 1,506 | -8.8 | 0.5 |
| Mauritius [a, b] | 607 | 939 | 745 | -20.7 | 0.3 |
| Peru | 120 | 883 | 1,057 | 19.7 | 0.4 |
| Colombia | 460 | 853 | 904 | 6.0 | 0.4 |
| Madagascar [b] | 7 | 552 | 530 | -4.0 | 0.2 |
| South Africa | 85 | 258 | 173 | -32.7 | 0.1 |

Source: WTO (2006a).
Obs.: [a] Includes significant exports from processing zones ; [b] Includes Secretariat estimates.

### Table 3.
### Share in the value of EU imports of textiles and
### clothing products, 2004-06 (percentage)

| EU (25) Imports Country/region | Market Share (%) | | | Growth Rate (%) | |
|---|---|---|---|---|---|
| | 2004 | 2005 | Jan-Aug 2006 | 2004-05 | Jan-Aug 2005-06 |
| Extra-EU Trade (ranked by 2004 value of imports) | 100 | 100 | 100 | 6.4 | 12.4 |
| Asian 12 | 45.9 | 51.5 | 52.8 | 19.6 | 13.9 |
| 1    China | 21.8 | 29 | 28 | 41.9 | 5.5 |
| 3    India | 6.6 | 7.3 | 8.1 | 18.3 | 18.4 |
| 5    Bangladesh | 5.8 | 5.2 | 6.1 | -5 | 34.8 |
| 8    Pakistan | 3.4 | 2.8 | 2.9 | -13.2 | 14.9 |
| 10   Indonesia | 2.6 | 2.2 | 2.3 | -9.6 | 30.8 |
| 15   Thailand | 1.7 | 1.5 | 1.5 | -8 | 16.9 |
| 16   Sri Lanka | 1.2 | 1.2 | 1.2 | -1.3 | 26 |
| 18   Vietnam | 1.1 | 1.1 | 1.4 | 6.2 | 56.9 |
| 22   Cambodia | 0.8 | 0.7 | 0.6 | -8.3 | 22.7 |
| 29   Philippines | 0.5 | 0.3 | 0.4 | -33.1 | 36.2 |
| 46   Lao PDR | 0.2 | 0.2 | 0.2 | 0.7 | 10.8 |
| 53   Nepal | 0.1 | 0.1 | 0.1 | -6.1 | -6.2 |
| Rest of the World | 54.1 | 48.5 | 47.2 | -4.7 | 10.8 |
| 2    Turkey | 15.5 | 15.2 | 14.5 | 4.1 | 5.1 |
| 4    Romania | 6.3 | 5.6 | 5 | -5.1 | -0.6 |
| 6    Tunisia | 4.2 | 3.7 | 3.5 | -5.5 | -1.5 |
| 7    Morocco | 3.8 | 3.3 | 3.2 | -6.9 | 2.6 |
| 9    Hong Kong, SAR | 3 | 2.5 | 3.7 | -13.4 | 221.8 |

Source: Eurostat external trade database (COMTEXT).

## Table 4.
### Share in the value of US imports of textiles and clothing products, 2004-06 (percentage)

| US Imports Country/ region | Market Share (%) | | | Growth Rate (%) | |
|---|---|---|---|---|---|
| | 2004 | 2005 | Jan-Sept 2006 | 2004-05 | Jan-Sept 2005-06 |
| World | 100 | 100 | 100 | 6.8 | 2.6 |
| Asian 12 (ranked by 2004 value of imports) | 41.3 | 49.8 | 54.8 | 28.6 | 11.8 |
| China | 17.2 | 24.2 | 26.4 | 50.2 | 7.3 |
| India | 4.6 | 5.4 | 5.8 | 26 | 11.7 |
| Indonesia | 3 | 3.3 | 4.1 | 18.9 | 27.2 |
| Vietnam | 3 | 2.9 | 3.5 | 5.9 | 24.1 |
| Pakistan | 2.9 | 3.1 | 3.4 | 13.2 | 16.2 |
| Thailand | 2.5 | 2.4 | 2.3 | -1.3 | 1.5 |
| Bangladesh | 2.3 | 2.6 | 3.1 | 19.8 | 24.4 |
| Philippines | 2.1 | 2 | 2.2 | 1 | 11.8 |
| Sri Lanka | 1.8 | 1.8 | 1.8 | 5.9 | 1.2 |
| Cambodia | 1.7 | 1.9 | 2.2 | 19.9 | 26.8 |
| Nepal | 0.2 | 0.1 | 0.1 | -25.8 | -9.2 |
| Lao PDR | 0 | 0 | 0 | 34.3 | 303.2 |
| CBI+Mexico | 21.6 | 19.2 | 17 | -4.9 | -9.3 |
| AGOA1 | 2.1 | 1.6 | 1.4 | -16.5 | -13.2 |
| Rest of the World | 35 | 29.4 | 26.9 | -10.3 | -4.6 |
| Fiji | 0.1 | 0 | 0 | -77.7 | -81.5 |
| Maldives | 0.1 | 0 | 0 | -94.2 | -100 |
| Mongolia | 0.3 | 0.1 | 0.1 | -41.2 | -15 |

*Source: USITC Interactive Tariff and Trade Data Web.*

### Table 5.
### Top 5 T&C products of US imports from Mongolia, 2004-05

| Top 5 Commodity (HS code) | 2004 | 2005 | % change 2004-05 |
|---|---|---|---|
| Knitted cotton jerseys, pullovers, cardigans waistcoats and similar articles (611020) | 53,072,983 | 34,443,733 | -35.1 |
| Women's or girl's woven cotton trousers (620462) | 38,832,389 | 35,084,568 | -9.7 |
| Knitted cashmere jerseys, pullovers, cardigans waistcoats and similar articles (611012) | 34,369,618 | 2,887,544 | -91.6 |
| Knitted man-made fibres jerseys, pullovers, cardigans waistcoats and similar articles (611030) | 21,323,058 | 9,637,070 | -54.8 |
| Knitted cotton T-shirts, singlets and other vests (610910) | 5,860,528 | 2,580,009 | -56 |

*Source: USITC, Interactive Tariff and Trade Data Web.*

### Table 6.
### Nepalese top five export products to the EU and US markets, 2004-2005

| | EU ( in 1,000 euro) | | | | US (in US dollars) | | | |
|---|---|---|---|---|---|---|---|---|
| | HS | 2005 | Change (%) | | HS | 2004 | 2005 | Change (%) |
| 1 | 570110 | 41,890,749 | -9 | 1 | 570110 | 28,489,601 | 32,257,750 | 13.2 |
| 2 | 620462 | 1,386,703 | -75.2 | 2 | 620342 | 21,200,101 | 12,844,170 | -39.4 |
| 3 | 621420 | 5,597,784 | 10.7 | 3 | 620462 | 18,489,193 | 12,214,687 | -33.9 |
| 4 | 620342 | 1,194,459 | -40.8 | 4 | 611020 | 14,159,360 | 6,022,073 | -57.5 |
| 5 | 621410 | 1,457,607 | -18.9 | 5 | 610510 | 4,663,232 | 1,879,954 | -59.7 |

*Source: Eurostat and USITC.*

### Table 7.
### Discriminatory tariffs charged by the United States
### on imports of apparels (based on Jan-May 2006 figures)

| Countries/Groups/ product categories | Calculated duties as a percentage of customs value | | Customs value share in percentage | |
|---|---|---|---|---|
| | Knit (HS chapter 61) | Woven (HS chapter 62) | Knit (HS chapter 61) | Woven (HS chapter 62) |
| **Non-beneficiaries Asian exporters** | | | | |
| Bangladesh | 17.96 | 17.12 | 2.04 | 5.38 |
| Cambodia | 17.29 | 16.36 | 3.47 | 2.43 |
| China | 13.2 | 11.58 | 14.5 | 27.04 |
| India | 16.62 | 13.38 | 4.22 | 7.34 |
| Indonesia | 19.33 | 17.4 | 3.9 | 6.32 |
| Sri Lanka | 15.86 | 16.54 | 2.12 | 2.9 |
| Vietnam | 18.4 | 16.92 | 4.47 | 4.56 |
| **NAFTA beneficiaries** | | | | |
| Canada | 0.22 | 0.16 | 2.09 | 1.94 |
| Mexico | 0.34 | 0.24 | 7.78 | 8.62 |
| **CBTPA beneficiary** | | | | |
| Honduras | 3.13 | 1.9 | 6.06 | 1.58 |
| **AGOA beneficiaries** | | | | |
| Kenya | n/a | 0.68 | n/a | 0.52 |
| Lesotho | 0.12 | 0.07 | 0.68 | 0.38 |
| Madagascar | n/a | 0.38 | n/a | 0.33 |
| **Bilateral FTA beneficiary** | | | | |
| Jordan | 0.19 | 0.41 | 2.5 | 1.27 |

*Source: EmergingTextiles.com (2006).*

### Table 8.
### Trading across borders

| Region /Economy | Documents for export (number) | Signatures for export (number) | Time for export (days) | Documents for import (number) | Signatures for import (number) | Time for import (days) |
|---|---|---|---|---|---|---|
| East Asia & Pacific | 7.1 | 7.2 | 25.8 | 10.3 | 9 | 28.6 |
| Europe & Central Asia | 7.7 | 10.9 | 31.6 | 11.7 | 15 | 43 |
| Latin America & Caribbean | 7.5 | 8 | 30.3 | 10.6 | 11 | 37 |
| Middle East & North Africa | 7.3 | 14.5 | 33.6 | 10.6 | 21.3 | 41.9 |
| OECD | 5.3 | 3.2 | 12.6 | 6.9 | 3.3 | 14 |
| South Asia | 8.1 | 12.1 | 33.7 | 12.8 | 24 | 46.5 |
| Bangladesh | 7 | 15 | 35 | 16 | 38 | 57 |
| India | 10 | 22 | 36 | 15 | 27 | 43 |
| Pakistan | 8 | 10 | 33 | 12 | 15 | 39 |
| Sub-Saharan Africa | 8.5 | 18.9 | 48.6 | 12.8 | 29.9 | 60.5 |
| Kenya | 8 | 15 | 45 | 13 | 20 | 62 |
| Madagascar | 7 | 15 | 50 | 9 | 18 | 59 |
| Malawi | 9 | 12 | 41 | 6 | 20 | 61 |
| Zambia | 16 | 25 | 60 | 19 | 28 | 62 |
| Denmark | 3 | 2 | 5 | 3 | 1 | 5 |

*Source: World Bank and IFC (2006).*

## Table 9:
## Sri Lankan exports of women's undergarments

| HS | Product description | Jan-Sep 2004 | Jan-Sep 2005 | Jan-Sep 2005 | Change (%) 2004-05 | Change (%) 2005-06 |
|---|---|---|---|---|---|---|
| Imports into US market (in million US$) | | | | | | |
| 610821 | Women's or girls' briefs and panties of cotton, knitted or crocheted | 5 | 53 | 84 | 909.9 | 58.7 |
| 610822 | Women's or girls' briefs and panties of man-made fibres, knitted or crocheted | 18 | 22 | 35 | 22.1 | 60.7 |
| 621210 | Brassieres of all types of textile materials | 64 | 89 | 79 | 38.9 | -11.5 |
| Imports into EU market (in million euro) | | | | | | |
| 610821 | Women's or girls' briefs and panties of cotton, knitted or crocheted | 17 | 13 | 20 | -22.4 | 53.4 |
| 610822 | Women's or girls' briefs and panties of man-made fibres, knitted or crocheted | 11 | 9 | 22 | -19.5 | 143.3 |
| 621210 | Brassieres of all types of textile materials | 28 | 33 | 51 | 18.6 | 52.2 |

Source: Authors' calculation based on data from USITC Interactive Tariff and Trade DataWeb and Eurostat (COMTEXT).

## Notes

1 Table IV. 70

2 Table IV. 74 and Table IV. 82.

3 The composition of 8.7 per cent growth of Hong Kong (China) is domestic exports (11.1 per cent reduction from 2004 to 2005) and re-exports (18.3 per cent growth).

4 Analysis based on the countries' export data is ideal; however, the disaggregated export data of many countries in the region are not available in a timely manner and the period of coverage based on the calendar/fiscal year and timing of releasing data differ country by country.

5 Data are complied by the Harmonised Commodity Description and Coding System (HS) at six-digit and 10-digit levels. Agricultural raw materials such as silk, cotton, wool and vegetable fibres are excluded from HS 50-53. EU data from HS 54 to 63 include trade data broken down at chapter level only, corrections due to erroneous codes, and confidential trade at chapter level.

6 For an example of quantitative restrictions by the United States, see USTR (2005).

7 Although the major demanders of the NAMA negotiations are the developed countries, developing countries' major interest lies in the possibility of being able to reduce tariff peaks on products of their export interests to the developed countries such as textiles, apparel and footwear. However, due to a call made by several powerful textiles lobby to have a "sectoral" negotiation on T&C tariffs with the average tariff capped to 15 per cent (which in itself is a very high figure), the chances of a substantial reduction in tariffs on these products are very slim. Moreover, On 13 June 2006, 44 members of Congress sent USTR Ambassador Susan Schwab a letter demanding that textiles be negotiated in separate sectoral negotiations in the Doha Round of trade talks. See National Council of Textiles Organizations (NCTO) (2006).

8 See Razzaque and Raihan (2006).

9 See UNDP RCC (2005b).

10 See NCTO and AMTAC (2005).

11 See Ahmad (2005).

12 For a detailed discussion on Rules of Origin, see Adhikari and Yamamoto (2005) and Adhikari (2005).

13 Inama (2002) asserts that at least one-third of all LDC exports pay MFN tariffs due to restrictive ROO.

14 See Adhikari and Weeratunge (forthcoming) for a detailed discussion.

15 See WTO (2003).

16 This is particularly striking because on the average the anti-dumping duties on dumped imports from non-market economy tend to be more than 12 times higher than normal anti-dumping duties. Messerlin, P.A. (2004) reveals that in the anti-dumping investigations initiated by the US (between 1995 and 1998), which resulted in a positive determination the average dumping margin with price comparison as the basis for estimated normal value of exports was only was 3.2 per cent, whereas following the non-market economies principle as the basis for arriving at estimated normal value of exports resulted in an average dumping margin of 40 per cent.

17 See Sanitary and Phytosanitary Measures and Technical Barriers to Trade (Summary), Center for International Development at Harvard University, http://www.cid.harvard.edu/cidtrade/issues/spstbt.html

18 See Maskus and Wilson (2000).

19 See ComMark Trust (2006).

20 See Dahal (2006) for further details.

21 See also Kelegama and Weeraratne (2005)

22 For example, Wal-Mart is well known for its "notorious practice of squeezing its supplies' margin." See Tewari (2006, p. 16).

23 See Morris (2006).

24 See Morris (2006).

25 Figures in Box 1 are updated based on the company's website, http://www.lifung.com/eng/global/home.php, accessed on 14 December 2006.

26 During 1997 and 2000, over US$30 billion of state-of-the-art textiles machinery was imported in China. See Ministry of Commerce (2005) cited in WTO (2006b).

27 Grants or tax forgiveness totaled Yuan 3.1 billion in 1997 and 1998. See WTO 2001.

28 In several countries, foreign investors are the main beneficiary of the positive environment created by EPZ, whereas Governments could provide incentives to local investors to benefit equally from the favorable setting. See WTO (2005).

29 For example, in Sri Lanka the Board of Investment (BOI) encourages investors to locate their factories in BOI-managed industrial processing zones to avoid land allocation problems. See USTR (2004).

30 The assumption is that the private sector will also be made participate in the EPZ investment both by contributing financial as well as managerial inputs.

31 See Mehta (2006) for further details.

32 See Chan and Sok (2006).

33 The literacy as well as education level of Sri Lanka is considered "one of the best" in South Asia. In 2004, the literacy rate (ages 15 and above) was 90.7 per cent, compared to 61 per cent in India, 48.6 per cent in Nepal and 49.9 per cent in Pakistan. The only South Asian country to have a higher literacy rate than Sri Lanka is Maldives (96.3 per cent). See UNDP (2006).

34 See Adhikari and Yamamoto (2005) for a detailed account of Thailand's success story.

35 See Adhikari and Weeratunge (forthcoming) for a detailed account of regional cooperation on T&C trade in South Asia.

# Acknowledgements

The authors would like to thank Manuel F. Montes (UN-DESA) for helpful comments.

# Bibliography

Abernathy, F. H., A. Volpe, and D. Weil (2004), The apparel and textile industries after 2005: Prospects and choices, Harvard Center for Textile and Apparel Research. Draft. December.

Abernathy, F. and D.Weil (2004) Apparel apocalypse? The America's textile industries won't die when quotas do, The Washington Post, 18 November 2004.

Adhikari, R. (2005), Sense and nonsense of rules of origin. Trade Insight, Vol.1, No. 2. Kathmandu: South Asia Watch on Trade, Economics & Environment (SAWTEE).

Adhikari, R. (2006a), LDCs should stay the course. The Kathmandu Post, 20 and 21 January.

Adhikari, R. (2000b), Governments' support to T&C sector in select Asian countries, Mimeo, UNDP RCC APTII, Colombo.

Adhikari, R. (2006c), One year after phasing-out of T&C quotas: where does South Asia Stand? Trade Insight, Vol. 2, No. 1, Kathmandu: SAWTEE.

Adhikari, R., and C. Weeratunge (forthcoming), "Textiles & clothing sector in South Asia: coping with post-quota challenges" in B.S. Chimni, B. L. Das, S. Kelegama and M. Rahman (eds.) Multilateralism at Cross-roads: Reaffirming Development Priorities', South Asian Yearbook of Trade and Development 2006. Delhi: Centre for Trade and Development and Wiley India.

Adhikari, R. and Y. Yamamoto (2005), Flying colours, broken threads: one year of evidence from Asia after the phase-out of textiles and clothing quotas, Tracking Report, UNDP RCC APTII, December.

Adhikari, R., and Y. Yamamoto (2006), Sewing thoughts: how to realise human development gains in the post-quota world, Tracking Report, UNDP RCC APTII, April.

Ahmad, M. (2005), Developments in textiles and clothing trade, post-ATC: modellers off mark — EU/US trade policy remains the predominant influence, Paper Presented at a Panel Discussion on Textiles and Clothing: One Year of Evidence after the Phasing out of Quotas in Hong Kong, 16 December 2005.

Ahmed, I., A. Rahman and F. Sobhan (2005), Impact of trade changes on labour standards – lessons to be learned from the response to the MFA phase out in Bangladesh, A study prepared for Department for International Development (DfID), November.

Asian Development Bank (ADB) (2006), Asian Development Outlook 2006: Routes for Asia's Trade, Manila: ADB.

Baldwin, R. E. (2000), Regulatory Protectionism, Developing Nations and a Two-Tier World Trade System, Brookings Trade Forum.

Bennet, M. (2006), Lesotho's export textiles & garment industry in H. Jauch and R. Traub-Merz (eds.) The Future of the Textile and Clothing Industry in Sub-Saharan Africa. Bonn: Friedrich-Ebert-Stiftung.

Berger, S. (2006), How We Compete. New York: Currency/Doubleday.

Bhatt, S. R., B. Shakya, M. Udas, S. Thapa, G. Sharma, M. Pradhananga and A. Shrestha (2006), Human Development Impact Assessment in the Post ATC period: The case of Nepal, a revised draft report submitted to UNDP RCC APTII, September, Kathmandu: SAWTEE and Action Aid Nepal.

Cambodia Development Resource Institute (CDRI). (2006), Cambodia Development Review, 10 (1), January-March 2006.

Center for International Development at Harvard University (2004), Sanitary and phytosanitary measures and technical barriers to trade summary, http://www.cid.harvard.edu/cidtrade/issues/spstbt.html, accessed 14 December 2006.

Chan, V. and H. Sok (2006), Cambodia's Garment Industry Post-ATC: Human Development Impact Assessment, Report prepared for UNDP RCC APTII, Phnom Phen: EIC.

Chandra, P. (1998), Competing through capabilities: strategies for global competitiveness of Indian textile industry. Economic and Political Weekly 34 (9): M 17-M-24, February 27.

ComMark Trust (2006), Annual Report 2006, Johannesburg: ComMark Trust.

Dahal, N. (2006), Review of Nepalese garments industry in the quota free regime, Report prepared for UNDP RCC.

Daily Mirror (2006), Bullet-proof Jackets New Weapon in Sri Lankan Export Armoury 2 September 2006.

Das, B. L. (2006), World Trade Organization: Notes on the Content and Process, Colombo, UNDP RCC APTII.

EmergingTextiles.com (2006), US tariff impact for knitted and woven apparel imports: Asia pays a high price for accessing the US apparel market, 1 August,
http://www.emergingtextiles.com/?q=art&s=060801Amark&r=search&n=1 accessed on 7 September 2006.

European Commission (2005), EU-China textile agreement, memo, 12 June 2005,
http://ec.europa.eu/trade/issues/sectoral/industry/textile/memo100605_en.htm , accessed 13 December 2006.

Fiji Times (online) (2006), Australia to Relax Fiji Garment Import Fees, 8 September, www.fijitimes.com

Foreign Investment Advisory Services (2004) Cambodian Garment Sector: Buyers' Survey Results, December 2004, Washington, D.C: World Bank.

Gereffi, G. (1999), International trade and industrial upgrading in the apparel commodity chain. Journal of International Economics, 48 (1), 37-70.

German Technical Cooperation (GTZ) (2006), Economic Monitor of Mongolia (January-August 2006), Ulaanbaatar: GTZ.

Global Education Centre (GEC) and Family Planning International Development (FPAID) (2004), Just Next Door: Development Themes for Fiji and Samoa. Wellington: GEC and FPAID.

Harney, A. (2004), Going home: Chinese migrant workers shun long factory hours and low pay, Financial Times, 3 November.

Harrington, C. (2000), Fiji's women garment workers: negotiating constraints in employment and beyond. Labour and Management in Development Journal, 1 (5), 3-22.

Hayashi, M. (2005), Weaving a new world: realizing development gains in a post-ATC trading system. United Nations Conference on Trade and Development (UNCTAD) Series on Assuring Development Gains from the International Trading System and Trade Negotiations, New York and Geneva: United Nations.

Hummels, D. (2001), Time as a Trade Barrier. West Lafayette, Indianapolis: Purdue University Economics Department.

International Labour Organization (ILO) (2005a), Promoting Fair Globalisation in Textiles and Clothing in a Post-MFA Environment, Report for discussion at the Tripartite Meeting on Promoting Fair Globalisation in Textiles and Clothing in a Post-MFA Environment, Geneva.

ILO (2005b), Fifteenth Synthesis Report on Working Conditions in Cambodia's Garment Sector. October 2005, Geneva.

ILO (2006), Seventeenth Synthesis Report on Working Conditions in Cambodia's Garment Sector, October 2006, Phnom Penh: ILO and Better Factories Cambodia.

Inama, S. (2002), Market access for LDCs: issues to be addressed, Journal of World Trade, 36 (1), 85-116.

International Business and Technical Consultants, Inc. (2003), A Study on the efficiency and effectiveness of banking and financial services for exporters. A Report Submitted to Ministry of Commerce, Dhaka, Bangladesh.

International Textiles and Clothing Bureau (2006), Few, yet important changes in US textiles and clothing imports in first half of 2006, Mimeo, http://www.itcb.org/Documents/ITCB-TD6-06.pdf, accessed on 12 December 2006.

Jayanthakumaran, K. (2003), Benefit-cost appraisals of export processing zones: a survey of the literature, Development Policy Review, 21 (1), January.

Kelegama, S. and B. Weeraratne (2005), Trade in textiles and apparel in South Asia. South Asian Yearbook of Trade and Development 2005 – Mainstreaming Development in Trade Negotiations: Run up to Hong Kong. New Delhi: Centre for Trade & Development.

Lecraw. D. J., P. Eddleston and A. McMahon (2005), A Value Chain Analysis of the Mongolian Cashmere Industry, A report for Mongolia Economic Policy Reform and Competitiveness Project (EPRC), Ulaanbaatar: USAID and EPRC, May 2005.

Madani, D. (1999), A Review of the role and impact of export processing zones, Policy Research Working Paper, 2238, Washington, D.C: World Bank.

Maskus, K. E. and J. S. Wilson (2000), Quantifying the impact of technical barriers to trade: a review of past attempts and the new policy context', Paper prepared for the World Bank Workshop on Quantifying the Trade Effect of Standards and Technical Barriers: Is it Possible?, 27 April 2000.

Mayer, J. and A. Wood (2001), South Asia's export structure in a comparative perspective, Oxford Development Studies, 29, 5 – 29.

Mayer, J. (2005), Not totally naked: textiles and clothing trade in a quota-free environment. Journal of World Trade, 39 (3), 393 – 426.

Mehta, P. S. (2006), Broad benefits of special economic zones. Financial Express, 14 December 2006.

Messerlin, P. A. (2004), China in the WTO: antidumping and safeguards, in D. Bhattasali, S. Li, and W. J. Martin (eds.) China and the WTO: Accession, Policy Reform, and Poverty Reduction Strategies, Washington, D.C: World Bank

Ministry of Commerce, China (2005), Intellectual Property Protection in China, March, Beijing.

Ministry of Planning and National Development, Republic of Maldives (2004a) Statistical Yearbook of Maldives 2004. www.planning.gov.mv

Ministry of Planning and National Development, Republic of Maldives (2004b) Household Income and Expenditure Survey 2002-2003. www.planning.gov.mv

Ministry of Planning and National Development, Republic of Maldives. (2005) Millennium Development Goals: Maldives Country Report. Ministry of September 2005. www.planning.gov.mv

Morris, M. (2006), Globalisation, China, and clothing industrialisation strategies in Sub-Saharan Africa in H. Jauch and R. Traub-Merz (eds.) The Future of the Textile and Clothing Industry in Sub-Saharan Africa. Friedrich-Ebert-Stiftung.

National Council of Textiles Organizations (NCTO) (2006), U.S. House of Representatives calls for USTR to adhere to textile negotiating objectives in WTO talks: appropriations Committee Mandates Report on Progress of Textile Negotiations, Press Release, 29 June, http://www.ncto.org/newsroom/pr200610.asp, accessed on 12 December 2006.

NCTO and American Manufacturing Trade Action Coalition (AMTAC) (2005), Members of Congress call for United States to oppose the E.U.-led LDC duty-free, quota-free initiative on textiles and to endorse separate textile talks in upcoming WTO negotiations, Press Statement, 8 December 2005, http://www.ncto.org/newsroom/pr200542.asp, accessed on 13 December 2006.

National Statistical Office of Mongolia (2005), Monthly Bulletin of Statistics, March. www.nso.mn (accessed November 2006).

Nordas, H. K. (2004), The Global Textile and Clothing Industry and Clothing, Discussion Paper No. 5, Geneva: WTO.

Organisation for Economic Co-operation and Development (OECD) (2004), Structural Adjustment in Textiles and Clothing in the Post-ATC Trading Environment. TD/TC/WP 2004/4/FINAL, Paris.

Oxfam International (2004), Oxfam International, Stitched Up: How rich-country protectionism in textiles and clothing trade prevents poverty alleviation, Briefing Paper 60, April 2004, Oxford.

Prasanna, R.P.I.R., and B. Gowthaman (2006), Sector specific living wage for Sri Lankan apparel industry workers, Survey Findings and Preliminary Report for Wider Discussion prepared for Apparel-industry Labour Rights Movement (AlaRM), Colombo, Sri Lanka.

Razzaque, M. A. and S. Raihan (2006), Two years after MFA phase out: concerns for Bangladesh" in multilateral and regional trade negotiations — implications for the Bangladesh economy, Report submitted to UNDP RCC APTII. Dhaka: Unnayan Shamannay.

Shakya, B. (2005), Sustaining Nepalese Garment Industry after Quota Abolition, A Report Prepared for Ministry of Finance and Asian Development Bank, Kathmandu.

Sisouphanthong, B., K. Phimmahasay, V. Ngonvorarath, V. Phonepraseuth and V. Syvilay (2006), Human Development Impact Assessment in Post ATC period, Report prepared for UNDP RCC APTII, November, Vientiane: National Statistics Centre.

Storey, D. (2004), The Fiji Garment Industry. New Zealand: Oxfam.

Tewari, M. (2006), Is price and cost competitiveness enough for apparel firms to gain market share in the world after quotas? A review. Global Economy Journal, 6 (4): Art. 5.

The United States Mission to the European Union (2006), "REACH Requires Further Improvements, According to EU Trading Partners", Brussels, 8 June 2006.

United Nations Development Programme Regional Centre in Colombo (UNDP RCC) (2005a), International Trade in Textiles and Clothing and Development Policy Options: After the Full Implementation of the WTO Agreement on Textiles and Clothing (ATC) on 1 January 2005, Policy Paper, UNDP RCC.

UNDP RCC (2005b), The grate maze: regional and bilateral free trade agreements in Asia – trends, characteristics, and implications for human development, Policy, Paper, UNDP RCC.

UNDP (2006), Human Development Report 2006, New York: Palgrave Macmillan.

United States Department of State (2006). Investment Climate Statement: Maldives. http://www.state.gov/e/eb/ifd/2006/63586.htm, accessed 31 March 2006.

United States Trade Representative (USTR) (2004), National Trade Estimate Report on Foreign Trade Barriers (online).

http://www.ustr.gov/assets/Document_Library/Reports_Publications/2004/ 2004_National_Trade_Estimate/2004_NTE_Report/asset_upload_file10_4 797.pdf

USTR (2005), Memorandum of understanding between the governments of the United States of America and the People's Republic China concerning trade in textile and apparel products, August.

http://www.ustr.gov/assets/World_Regions/North_Asia/China/asset_upload_file 91_8344.pdf, accessed 13 December 2006.

USAID (2005) Measuring Competitiveness and Labour Productivity in Cambodia's Garment Industry, Phnom Penh: USAID.

US International Trade Commission (USITC) (2004), Textiles and apparel: assessment of the competitiveness of certain foreign suppliers to the U.S. market, USITC publication, No. 3671, Washington D.C.: USITC. http://hotdocs.usitc.gov/pub3671/pub3671.pdf, accessed 31 March 2006.

World Bank and International Finance Corporation (IFC) (2006), Doing Business in 2006: Creating Jobs, Washington D.C.: The International Bank for Reconstruction and Development/ The World Bank.

World Trade Organization (WTO) (2001) Accession of the People's Republic of China - Decision of 10 November, WT/L/432, Annex 5B, 23 November 2001, Geneva.

WTO (2003), Anti-dumping actions in the areas of textiles and clothing, proposal for a specific short-term dispensation in favour of developing members following full integration of the sector into GATT 1994 from January 2005. WT/GC/W/502, 14 July 2003, Geneva:WTO.

WTO (2005), Options for least-developed countries to improve their competitiveness in the textiles and clothing business, WT/COMTD/LDC/W/37, 28 June, Geneva: WTO.

WTO (2006a), International Trade Statistics 2006,
    http://www.wto.org/english/res_e/statis_e/its2006_e/its06_toc_e.htm, accessed 13 December 2006.

WTO (2006b) China: Trade Policy Review, WT/TPR/S/161, Geneva.

Yang, Y. and C. Zhong (1998), China's textile and clothing exports in a changing world economy. The Developing Economies, 36 (1), 3–23.

*Electronic Sources*

Eurostat. External Trade Database (COMEXT), http://europa.eu.int/

Li & Fung limited. (corporate website)
    http://www.lifung.com/eng/global/home.php, accessed 14 December 2006.

United States International Trade Commission (USITC) Interactive Tariff and Trade DataWeb, http://dataweb.usitc.gov/

# Services-led industrialization in India: Assessment and lessons

Nirvikar Singh*

## 1. Introduction

India has become one of the fastest growing economies in the world over the last two decades, arguably aided in this performance by economic reforms. One of the striking aspects of India's recent growth has been the dynamism of the service sector, particularly information technology (IT) and IT enabled services (ITES), while, in contrast, manufacturing has been less robust. The contribution of the service sector was particularly striking in the 1990s, which not only saw rapid growth (averaging over 6 per cent since 1992), but also a high contribution – over 60 per cent (Hansda, 2001) – from services. This growth trajectory, which has been termed "services-led" industrialization, or even a "services revolution" (Gordon and Gupta, 2004), seems to stand out from the previous experience of economic development, which followed the traditional path from agriculture to manufacturing, with services becoming important at a later stage. In India, in contrast, there was a sharp increase in the share of services in GDP, from 37 per cent in 1980 to 49 per cent in 2002,[1] while the share of manufacturing remained about the same, at 16 per cent (Kochhar et al., 2006). Thus questions arise about India's development pattern, including its nature, sustainability and replicability. This paper reviews the recent growth experience of India, identifies the major contributing factors to its pattern of development, and examines the prospects for further "services-led" industrialization in India. The analysis will draw on theoretical models as well as case studies of the Indian experience.

The structure of the paper is as follows. The next section provides a conceptual framework for the examination of the Indian experience. In particular, we discuss the nature of services, their distinction from products, and their categorization. We argue that the precise nature of the services being considered is important for any analysis of growth impacts, and that one therefore has to go beyond broad national income accounts categories to understand the role of services in industrialization. Section 3 provides a brief overview of India's overall growth experience, followed by a more detailed examination of the contribution of the service sector to growth, and the relative performance of manufacturing and agriculture in Section 4. Section 5

* Department of Economics and Santa Cruz Centre for International Economics, University of California, Santa Cruz.

examines the potential for spillovers from IT, ITES and other service sectors such as financial services, to the rest of the economy. We draw on econometric work on productivity growth, as well as input-output analysis of linkages to understand these possible spillovers. It is possible, based on this evidence, to hypothesize that India's manufacturing sector development may have been constrained, at least in part, by weaknesses in key service sectors such as transportation and electricity. In fact, other evidence suggests that telecommunications reforms were also critical for the rapid growth in IT and ITES.[2]

In Section 6, we consider the particular role of international trade in services. This deserves special treatment because of its growing importance, and because balance of payments constraints have often been major barriers to stable growth for developing countries. In Section 7 we discuss the consequences for employment of different growth paths, and the challenges of education and manpower training to support and sustain India's development path. Section 8 briefly considers the social and environmental issues associated with "services-led" or alternative development paths. The focus in this section is on regional inequality issues, as well as impacts that do not necessarily manifest themselves in the national income accounts and growth statistics. Section 9 relates the Indian experience as analyzed in this paper to some of the recent discussions of industrial policy, and development policy more generally. Section 10 offers a summary conclusion of the paper's findings.

## 2. Conceptual framework

Much of the literature on service-led growth begins with broad national income accounting categories. However, it is important both to disaggregate services to identify important differences within that category, and stepping back from the accounting, to understand the key ways in which services differ from products, which themselves are classified as outputs of the manufacturing sector. A good starting point for analysis is a consideration of the precise nature of services vis-à-vis other kinds of productive activities. The differences will be seen to depend on the nature of market transactions as well as intrinsic characteristics of services vs. products, and both are subject to change as economies and technologies evolve.

The classical writers, such as Adam Smith and, earlier, the Physiocrats discussed services from the perspective of a distinction between productive and unproductive labour. Smith's idea of "unproductive labour" included the servants of wealthy individuals and government employees, as well as the military, the clergy, lawyers, doctors, writers and musicians, all of whom are now included in the service sector.[3] Of course, modern economics, based on utility and demand theory, has jettisoned this view, and services, however defined, are counted as productive activities. Various modern conceptual discussions of the distinct nature of services make similar observations. Hill (1977), for example, emphasizes the non-storability of services, which requires that services must be consumed as they are produced. Griliches (1992) defines services as anything that is the result of labour that does not produce a tangible commodity. Lack of tangibility is fundamentally what leads to non-storability, and to non-transferability (Economic Council of Canada, 1991). However, intangibility must, in the digital age, be carefully interpreted. Thus, software programs and various forms of digital electronic content have only limited tangibility, but are storable and transferable. The creation of these digital products may often be classified as a service, as also their delivery.

The marketing literature pays considerable attention to the nature of services, and in this literature, the dimensions that distinguish services from products are summarized as follows: (1) intangibility, (2) heterogeneity, (3) simultaneity of production and consumption, and (4) perishability (e.g., Parasuraman, Zeithani and Berry, 1985; Rust and Chung, 2005).[4] Several more fundamental economic implications are drawn from these distinguishing characteristics. For example, in this schema, intangibility, perishability and simultaneity all work against maintaining inventories. Heterogeneity and simultaneity (where the consumer is involved in creating the service) makes it more difficult to achieve scale economies. All of these features make display and consumer assessment of characteristics harder to achieve.

Of course, the use of the above four characteristics to distinguish services from products is subject to several caveats. First, the differences are mostly of degree, especially in comparing services to certain kinds of products.[5] Second, and more fundamentally, the distinction between products and services is often based on the contractual nature of the market transaction. At the most fundamental level, every product either provides services directly, or is combined with other products to generate services. Thus, an automobile is purchased as a product, but its value is based on the stream of services that it will provide over time. All such durable goods may be leased or rented, in which case the service is more explicitly contracted for than in the case of a product transaction. The more expensive the product (e.g., an airplane vs. an automobile), the less possible or economically desirable it is for an individual to access the services through a purchase. In fact, contracting for services from specialist providers is often a way to achieve economies of scale in providing services (or in making the underlying products) that would not be possible otherwise. The general point is that the boundary between products and services is often a function of market and economic conditions, rather than the intrinsic characteristics of what is being exchanged.

Previous analysts of this issue do recognize that the practical application of these conceptual distinctions in classifying services incorporates the contractual nature of the transaction. For example, in the case of utilities, Melvin (1995) points out that they are typically classified as services in the national income accounts, although gas, electricity and water are tangible goods. In these cases, the distribution systems are a critical aspect of enabling consumption of these goods, and the contractual relationship is primarily for delivery services using the distribution systems.

One exception to this blurring of the boundary between products and services is the case of personal services. To take a simple example, a practitioner of traditional Indian medicine (*Ayurveda*) may make a diagnosis based only on an examination of the patient, consisting of visual inspection and pulse reading, without any tools whatsoever. No product is involved in this service provision. Such pure personal services, without the use of any capital or tools, are increasingly rare: a modern doctor's services typically incorporate the use of large quantities of expensive equipment. Other personal services, such as those of lawyers and accountants, also involve the use of physical capital in their delivery, just as in the case of the utility services discussed in the previous paragraph. One idea that we develop in this section is the increasingly "industrial" or "manufacturing-like" character of such personal services. It is also worth noting that knowledge services, which have traditionally been personal services, are becoming more "industrialized" through the use of information technology: we also develop this point further in this section. By these characterizations, we mean the development of standardization, routinization, scalability and replicability for these services.

Besides the marketing literature, one area where the conceptual distinction between products and services has been explored in detail is that of international trade, where the categorizations are important for shaping international trade policies and agreements. Locational characteristics are central to discussions of services in international trade. For example, Bhagwati (1984) argues that services can be divided into two classes: those that require physical proximity of the user and provider; and those that do not. Services that require physical proximity can be further divided into three groups:

a) Mobile provider and immobile user, e.g., transporting labour to a construction site;

b) Mobile user and immobile provider, e.g., a patient going to a hospital;

c) Mobile user and mobile provider, e.g., students and professors meeting in a university for lectures.

A variation on the above classification is the basis for the World Trade Organization's (WTO's) categorization of services trade, which categorizes different "modes of supply" (Sampson and Snape, 1985; and Sapir and Winter, 1994 – see section 6 of this chapter for details).

Digital technology has also reduced the need for contact or physical proximity in many cases – these changes are at the heart of the new tradability of various knowledge-based services. Bhagwati (1985) was an early observer of the trend toward removal of proximity requirements through technological change, i.e., the increased richness and lower cost of long-distance communications. Melvin (1989, 1990) also explores this trend, characterizing services either as activities that require the double coincidence of time and location, or as activities that overcome constraints of time (e.g., storage services) and location (e.g., transportation services). He describes knowledge or information services as also overcoming a constraint – that of ignorance. Digital communications technology is, of course, behind the new wave of international trade in information or knowledge services.

In the international trade context, the skill content of services can be an important distinguishing feature (Delaunay and Gadrey, 1991; Economic Council of Canada, 1991; Melvin, 1990). Some kinds of low-skill services are susceptible to routinization and automation, whereas others are not (Dossani and Kenney, 2004). The former are easier to trade. In some cases, service activities can be unbundled or "splintered" (Bhagwati, 1984) to allow the offshore outsourcing of the lower skill components (e.g., software testing in the overall process of software development).[6] One trend that also seems to be emerging, however, is trade in services with higher skill content, such as financial analysis or patent preparation.

After one has clarified some of the conceptual characteristics of services, and their distinction from products, it is important to consider how measurement and classification are done in practice: "rather than discussing definitions, it may be more useful to take an operational approach and to examine what are actually called services in the national accounts and related statistical sources" (Griliches, 1992, p. 6). The Central Statistical Office in India provides a standard breakdown of services into 15 sub-sectors for that country (Gordon and Gupta, 2004), as shown in Table 1.[7] Note that this Indian classification does not include utilities, which are often classified as services elsewhere. The salient point is the heterogeneity of the activities that are classified as services, in terms of capital intensity, skill content, need for physical contact, and importance of tangible products as part of the service.

## 3. India's growth experience: overview

Since our interest is in the role of services in India's recent growth, it is useful to have some perspective on the nature and extent of that growth. As we noted in the introduction, in the 1980s India's growth sped up from a moderate or slow rate prior to that decade and has since ranked among the highest in the world. There are numerous detailed reviews of India's growth experience in the last couple of decades, and we shall be selective and relatively brief. These reviews often discuss causal factors, albeit typically without formal econometric modelling, with the importance of economic reforms in the growth acceleration being the subject of some controversy. In other cases, econometric techniques have been used to identify structural breaks in the growth process, but without any causal modelling (e.g., Wallack, 2003). In this section, in addition to discussing aggregate growth performance, we also examine studies that focus on the performance of the service sector.

Panagariya (2005) provides a very careful appraisal of India's growth experience in the 1980s and 1990s, and of the 'revisionist' view, articulated by DeLong (2003), Rodrik (2003) and Rodrik and Subramanian (2004a), that economic policy reforms in the 1990s were not key to India's growth performance in that decade. Those authors further argue that India's growth surge is properly understood as beginning in the 1980s, before the 1991 and subsequent economic reforms. Based on a careful examination of the data, Panagariya reaches three conclusions about India's growth experience in the last 25 years:

1.   Growth during the 1980s was inconsistent, with the last three years of that decade contributing 7.6 per cent annual growth, without which growth in the 1980s was only marginally better than that of the previous three decades.

2.   The high growth in the last three years of the 1980s was preceded or accompanied by significant economic reform, including trade and industrial policy liberalization.

3.   Growth in the 1980s was fuelled by expansionary policies that entailed accumulation of a large external debt and contributed to an economic crisis.

Panagariya's final conclusion from his review of policy changes and growth performance is that it was "the 1991 market reforms and subsequent liberalizing policy changes that helped sustain growth".

Ultimately, the positive impact of economic policy reforms seems to have been accepted, even in the revisionist view. For example, while Rodrik and Subramanian (2004b) – based on their earlier analysis (2004a) – use a growth accounting methodology to evaluate and project India's growth performance which de-emphasizes economic liberalization policies, they do not dismiss such policies. They focus on "meta-institutions" such as democracy and the rule of law, as well as conventional economic inputs such as human and physical capital, and productivity growth. In emphasizing these fundamentals,[8] they highlight the infrastructure and human capital built up under the pre-liberalization policy regime. At another level, however, their assumptions about the impacts of policy are not that different from those of Panagariya, since they state that "policy liberalisation will progressively erode the licence-quota-permit raj as a source of corruption and patronage that has had such a corrosive effect on public institutions." In addition to this indirect effect, they also attribute productivity growth directly to reforms that removed the "shackles on the private sector." The case of IT illustrates the positive impact of the 1990s reforms, with telecommunications reform and liberalization leading the way for that sector. One of the best-known, most successful participants in this industry has documented the positive impact of liberalization, including general steps to ease the conduct of business (Murthy, 2004).

While Panagariya shows that average growth rates are very sensitive to how one divides the period under consideration, one might argue that the data itself should be allowed to reveal when a growth acceleration occurred for India, rather than being determined subjectively. Time series methods to test for structural breaks are designed to achieve this. Wallack's (2003) study is the most comprehensive along these lines, and examines time series data for 1951-2001.[9] The tests are applied to aggregate GDP data as well as to sectoral data. The latter, in particular, is of interest for understanding the recent pattern of economic development in India. Since these are pure time series estimations, there are no structural explanatory variables, but one can plausibly compare the identified break dates with what we know independently about policy changes or other macroeconomic events.

The results are summarized in Table 2 and provide some plausible connections between growth and economic environment changes (such as low interest rates, an investment surge, or the IT boom). As Wallack herself emphasizes, the results are not as robust as one would like, since other years often have F-statistics close to the maximum values.[10] However, there are two important conclusions. First, there is evidence for a break in the aggregate GDP growth rate in 1980 (and in 1987 for GNP). Second, there is little evidence that this was caused by a break in the growth of any sector – instead, as T.N. Srinivasan has emphasized, much of the growth rate change probably came from a shift in activity from slower-growing to faster-growing sectors (Srinivasan, 2003).[11] The results of the statistical tests suggest some exceptions to this observation (Table 2). One is the breaks in financial, real estate and business services in 1974 and 1980. Wallack suggests these were the result of low interest rates in 1974, and an investment boom beginning in 1980.[12] There is also a break in trade, transport, storage and communication services in 1992: Wallack relates this to telecommunications reform and the growth of IT, but those factors may have come into play somewhat later. Clearly, this empirical approach needs to be explored further to understand the behaviour of the Indian economy.

In addition to the time series evidence for structural breaks in some service sectors, there are more general empirical observations on service sector growth in India. For example, the share of services in gross capital formation declined from 57.7 per cent in 1950-51 to 48.8 per cent a decade later, and further to 43.7 per cent in 1970-71. Thereafter, however, the share has not changed that much, hovering around 40 per cent. One can make conjectures about changes in capital and labour productivity in the service sector (Hansda, 2002), but since the composition of the sector has changed substantially over time, and these sub-sectors have different capital intensities, it is difficult to reach any definite conclusion from the data as presented (Hansda, 2002, Tables 7 through 9). Hansda also suggests that the terms of trade moved against the service sector in the latter part of the 1990s, with finance, insurance, real estate and business services and trade, transport, storage, and communication together contributing to that decline. Liberalization, competition and technological progress may all have contributed to this development.[13]

A disaggregated view of service sector growth in India, using the CSO classification as described in Table 1 (Gordon and Gupta, 2004), gives a stronger indication of growth acceleration than the formal time series analysis. Gordon and Gupta note that 12 of 15 service sub-sectors in India grew faster than GDP over the 50 year period beginning in 1951, but the growth acceleration in the 1990s, which was responsible for India becoming an outlier in the service sector share (as compared to typical developing countries at that income level), was the strongest in business services, communication, and banking services, followed by hotels and restaurants and community services (Gordon and Gupta, Table 5). These five sub-sectors together accounted for the entire acceleration in services growth in the 1990s. They assert that growth in other sub-sectors in the 1990s was broadly similar to, or lower than, that in the previous decades.[14] This pattern of growth is considered further in Sections 4 and 5 of this chapter, in the context of service sector contributions and linkages in the economy.

Two other aspects of the performance of India's service sector are noteworthy. First, following an international trend, FDI inflows into India have moved increasingly away from manufacturing, and towards services sector, even as they have increased overall. These flows have been heavily concentrated in telecommunications and financial services (Banga, 2005, Figure 7). Second, the structure of indirect taxation in India, with historically light or zero taxation of services due to the nature of constitutional tax provision, has meant that the recent growth of the service sector has been associated with an overall tax-GDP ratio below the norm for countries at similar income levels.[15] While services crossed 50 per cent as a share of GDP in the 1990s, they contributed only about 10 per cent of total tax revenue (Hansda, 2002, Table 11). This situation is changing, with moves to change constitutional tax assignments and bring services broadly into the indirect tax base.

In addition to analyses of aggregate and sectoral growth, summarized above, a recent review of India's pattern of development (Kochhar et al., 2006) focuses on skill intensity, and suggests that the nature of the economic policies followed by India from independence onward created a pattern of specialization that was already somewhat distinct from the typical developing country at comparable income levels. This, in turn, shaped the country's development pattern in the post-1980 reform period. In particular, India's manufacturing sector was more diversified, more skill-intensive, and less (unskilled) labour-intensive than average. In fact, it is suggested that the data indicates that India's service sector was smaller than normal up to the early 1980s.[16] Thus, while the last two decades have seen a continuation of unusually skill-intensive growth, the rapid growth since the 1980s in services (still chiefly skill-intensive, however) represents a departure from the past.

Kochhar et al. examine the performance of the Indian economy in the 1980s and 1990s, starting from these apparently unusual 1980 preconditions. GDP per worker and total factor productivity (TFP) both grew more rapidly in these two decades, as compared to the 1970s. Cross-country level regressions for the year 2000 suggest that India's services share of GDP was significantly higher than the norm in that year (by 3.8 percentage points), but only when a country size variable was included. On the other hand, services employment was always significantly lower than the norm, and by a large magnitude, of 17 percentage points. This result is consistent, then, with the kind of skill-biased development observed in India pre-1980. Regressions using the change in the share of services also indicated that India was a positive outlier during the period 1981-2000 (Kochhar et al., Table 5). According to this analysis, the 1980s and 1990s also saw an accentuation of the skill bias in India's manufacturing, including whatever is measured of the informal sector. A conjecture is that incomplete labour market reforms and continued skewed education sector spending might be underlying factors behind the observed pattern of growth, in which case it might be altered by policy changes. On the other hand, hysteresis in development paths might accentuate the observed biases in the future. State-level sectoral growth data seems to support the latter possibility: states such as Tamil Nadu and Maharashtra, according to this analysis, appear to be behaving more like advanced skill-intensive countries in their growth pattern.

The concerns raised by Kochhar et al. about India's somewhat skewed pattern of development, and its implications for income and regional inequality, will be taken up in more detail in later sections, particularly in the context of employment, education and training (Section 7), social issues (Section 8), and broader lessons for development policy (Section 9). Here, we offer one word of caution on their analysis. Historical patterns of development and cross-country comparisons are an important component of empirical analysis.[17] Nevertheless, these comparisons may miss certain kinds of innovations that are not captured in the data. In particular, the development of modern business process outsourcing represents a rather new form of organizing economic activity, and an opportunity at many skill levels, that may not have been possible in the past. This goes back to our conceptual discussion in the previous section. To offer an imperfect analogy, Japan in 1950 was not viewed as a likely candidate for building a world class automobile industry. The industry was both capital-intensive and technologically advanced. Nevertheless, Japan not only succeeded, but there were arguably positive spillovers from this effort to other engineering-intensive manufacturing. The imperfections in this analogy include substantial differences in initial conditions and social heterogeneity, but the caveat on extrapolating from the past should be kept in mind.

## 4. Understanding service sector growth and its impacts

The discussion in the last section has suggested that India's more rapid growth in the 1980s and, especially, the 1990s has been the result of policy changes as well as initial conditions. The pattern of growth has been skewed toward the service sector, as well as toward skill-intensive activities. As noted in the introduction, India's service sector was responsible for over 60 per cent

of its GDP growth in the 1990s, well above the sector's contribution in previous decades. A small number of service sub-sectors seems to have led the
overall contribution of services to GDP growth. In fact, the five fast-growing
sub-sectors in the 1990s accounted for effectively all of the more rapid services growth.

In this section, we begin with the empirical question of what factors can
explain observed service sector and sub-sector growth in India. One possible
answer is increased specialization, or splintering (Kravis et al., 1983; Bhagwati, 1984), which, if it occurs across sectors, would alter the aggregate
accounting. More precisely, if services components of manufacturing activity
such as accounting, research and development, or logistics are splintered off
and outsourced to other firms, they will be accounted for as service sector
contributions to GDP, rather than being subsumed in manufacturing value
added. Using input-output coefficients constructed by Sastry et al. (2003),
Gordon and Gupta (2004) provide one estimate of this effect, based on
changes in those coefficients. The input coefficients of services in agriculture
and manufacturing increased enough in the 1980s to add 0.5 percentage
points to service sector growth in that decade.[18] Using input-output coefficients constructed from 1998-99 data, we are able to repeat this calculation
for the 1990s, obtaining essentially no contribution of splintering in the
1990s, if measured in this manner.[19] However, this data and methodology
does not permit an analysis of the extent to which cross-country splintering,
which became more important in the 1990s, e.g., through offshore outsourcing of business services, would explain the observed patterns of service sector
growth. In the latter case, there is a real shift in economic activity to India,
whereas domestic splintering is more of an accounting change. Even in the
latter case, however, when specialization is associated with efficiency improvements, purely domestic splintering may reflect a positive economic change.

Along with increased specialization, another basic reason for an increasing share of services in GDP as an economy grows is a higher than average
income elasticity of demand.[20] Thus, the share of services in private final
consumption expenditure grew faster in the two decades beginning 1980
than did services as a share of GDP (Hansda, 2002, Table 5). Aside from a
big jump in the share of the sub-category "operation of personal transport
equipment" in the 1980s, the shares of different kinds of final consumption
services were relatively stable in this period (Hansda, 2002, Table 6). Gordon
and Gupta (2004, Table 8) estimate that final consumption of services grew
at a similar rate to overall services in the 1990s, but slower in the 1980s,
which would be consistent with our calculation (and their argument) that
splintering through specialization was a less significant contributing factor to
services growth in the latter decade. Finally, the accelerated growth in services in the 1990s, along with a decline in their relative prices,[21] is not consistent with a purely demand driven explanation of services growth.

A third possible factor in explaining service sector performance in India is the role of policy liberalization. Based on an industry case study (Murthy, 2004), we have noted the importance of liberalization in general, and telecommunications reform in particular, as a factor in the growth of IT and ITES. Gordon and Gupta (2004) make essentially the same point using patterns in the data. In the absence of any good measure of liberalization, they note that the communications sub-sector grew rapidly in the 1990s coincident with deregulation, that the private sector share in the service sector grew in this period, and that FDI was positively correlated with services growth. This period also saw a rapid increase in service sector exports, which may have been aided by domestic liberalization: the international aspects of India's service sector growth are taken up in Section 6.

Some further quantification of the contribution of the various factors affecting services growth (splintering, high income elasticity, exports and policy reforms) in the 1990s is provided by Gordon and Gupta through a basic growth accounting exercise. They first estimate a pre-1990 trend growth rate of about 1.5 per cent for service sub-sectors that accelerated in the 1990s. This is assigned to splintering and high income elasticity, as relatively constant factors. The residual is about 1.75 percentage points of service sector growth. Growth due to exports is estimated at about 0.5 percentage point.[22] The remaining residual, of 1.25 percentage points, is assigned to policy liberalization and technological progress. These estimates are somewhat rough and ready, but can provide a basis for examining more detailed econometric work on the contributions of and to service sector growth. A set of sub-sector specific and pooled time series regressions to estimate the factors determining services growth are consistent with the conclusion of a positive impact of reform on services growth (Gordon and Gupta, 2004, Tables 9 and 10). There also appears to be a positive impact of industrial growth on services growth, as one might expect.[23]

A complementary question to that of the impacts of industrial growth on services growth concerns the impact of services on manufacturing production and productivity (Banga and Goldar, 2004). These authors perform a sources-of-growth analysis, in which services are included as an input to manufacturing.[24] They first use panel data for 148 three-digit level industries covering 18 years, 1980-81 to 1997-98, to estimate a production function, and based on this econometric estimation, the sources of growth analysis is carried out. It is estimated that, although service inputs contributed little to the production of the registered manufacturing sector during the 1980s (only 1 per cent of output growth), the contribution of services increased substantially in the 1990s (to about 25 per cent of output growth). This, in turn, implies that excluding services inputs overstates the extent of manufacturing TFP growth in the 1990s. In fact, when the authors regress their TFP index on a set of explanatory variables that includes the ratio of services input to employment, a statistically significant positive relationship is found between services input and industrial productivity, though the estimated elasticity is not large. These results suggest that the increasing use of services in manufacturing in the 1990s favourably affected TFP.[25] The results of this analysis also suggest that trade reforms played an important role in increasing the use of services in the manufacturing sector. It is not clear, however, to what extent this increased use reflects splintering, or other changes in the organization of manufacturing.[26]

Finally, Bosworth, Collins and Virmani (2007) examine the role of services as part of a detailed, up-to-date growth accounting for India. A major result is that TFP growth in the service sector has been very high (almost 3 per cent per year) in recent decades, while the contribution of capital is relatively low. Since half this sector's growth has come in 'traditional' sub-sectors such as trade, transportation, and community and personal services, where great productivity improvements might not be expected, they argue that price increases in services may be underestimated, leading to an overestimate of real growth in this sector. If correct, this view has serious implications for overall Indian growth measures. However, an alternative explanation, discussed later in this section, may lie in reductions in transaction costs associated with policy reforms.

Combined, the empirical results summarized above suggest that services have not only played a positive, direct role in India's economic growth in the last decades, but may have also helped spur manufacturing growth. While the latter impact was not visible in aggregate data for the 1990s (barring a two-year boom in 1994-96), more recent data suggests stronger manufacturing growth (Ministry of Finance, 2006). Furthermore, since the growth of the services sector has been more robust than that of manufacturing, a relatively clear picture emerges of services driving the Indian growth process. There are serious concerns about skill intensity and employment, which we consider in Section 7, but the central conceptual question from a growth perspective is whether the empirical experience can be related to an underlying theoretical understanding. The traditional development paradigm of "agriculture to manufacturing to services" (e.g., Kuznets, 1959; Kaldor, 1966; Pack and Westphal, 1986) not only makes manufacturing central to the transition to modernity, but also necessary for sustained productivity growth, since an increasingly important service sector is viewed as a symptom of a mature economy and slower growth (Baumol, 1967).

Therefore, in addition to the above empirical studies, we also consider the conceptual role of services, and information technology in particular, in reducing transaction costs and improving productivity in manufacturing. In fact, a recent major empirical study of the United States (Triplett and Bosworth, 2004) concludes that services sector productivity increases were responsible for the strong growth in the US in the latter half of the 1990s, with information and communication technologies (ICTs) playing a significant role in this productivity effect. One aspect of this impact is the possibility that technological change, including the use of ICTs in particular, has made some services more routinized, and therefore more like manufacturing. For example, a large-scale call centre is run more like a factory, reaping economies of scale, rather than a traditional services organization, which would have traditionally provided customized or differentiated services at a relatively small scale. While there is some scepticism about the long-run impacts of ICTs (e.g., Joshi, 2004), there seems to be a well understood case for focusing on ICTs, providing both services and products, in the growth process. For example, Dasgupta and Singh (2005a, footnote 8) state that, "IT [information technology], however, produces both new products and processes. Nevertheless, from the Kaldorian perspective, what is important is whether IT, be it product, service or process, and manufacturing are subject to increasing or decreasing returns to scale, to dynamic economies of scale and to spill over effects for the rest of economy." While the macroeconomic data may not answer this question, microeconomic studies of developed countries directly establish the positive impacts of IT use on productivity (e.g., Bresnahan, Brynjolfsson and Hitt, 2002; OECD, 2004).

Another key aspect of ICTs' development impacts comes through reductions in transaction costs. This term can be interpreted broadly, to include various kinds of costs of communication, transportation, and other aspects of exchange, such as costs of searching for options, negotiating contracts and enforcing agreements.[27] Singh (2004a) constructs an illustrative model to show precisely how transaction cost reductions can increase short run efficiency, as well as boost the long run steady state of the economy. The simplest and most basic aspect of transaction costs is that they result in resources' being used up in exchange, and drive a wedge between the supply price and the demand price in a competitive market. If transaction costs are high enough, the relevant market will not exist, in the sense that the quantity exchanged is zero. If the transaction cost consists purely of resources used up in the process of exchange, then the welfare loss from its existence consists of the usual Harberger deadweight loss triangle, plus the transaction cost rectangle, which can be substantially larger. If the transaction cost is actually a payment to an intermediary, or a tax imposed by the government, then the welfare loss is just the Harberger triangle. Romer (1994), in an influential paper, argues that even if the rectangles represent redistribution, and not a resource cost, there is a welfare cost that goes well beyond the usual Harberger triangles. The basic idea is that if there is a fixed cost of producing a good, transaction costs can reduce operating profits to the extent that some goods are no longer produced, leading to a larger loss of welfare than would otherwise be the case.

From a development perspective, the main implication of domestic transaction costs, i.e., their effect on the equilibrium number of intermediate goods, and hence on output and welfare, must be sought in a dynamic model. Romer hints at this, but the first formal model is that of Singh (2004a), building on the analysis of Ciccone and Matsuyama (1996). This uses a dynamic monopolistic competition model, in which an economy that inherits a small range of differentiated intermediate inputs can be trapped into a lower stage of development. In particular, the model may have multiple steady state equilibria, and the starting point of the economy can determine which steady state is approached. Singh (2004a) shows that if transaction costs determine the initial number of varieties of the intermediate good, then reducing transaction costs can jump start the economy, moving it to a path that leads to a higher steady state. In addition, transaction costs will affect the long-run equilibrium number of varieties, and hence the level of the steady state. Transaction costs can reduce the long-run steady state level of the economy, and even arrest the process of development.[28] The use of ICTs, by reducing transaction costs, can mitigate both these effects.[29] Note that, although Singh (2004a) emphasizes ICTs, improved transportation and distribution can also bring down transaction costs. The connection to the empirical work on the growth of the Indian service sector reviewed earlier in this section should be clear: the fast growing services have included some sub-sectors that are critical determinants of major aspects of transaction costs for the Indian economy. From this perspective, one might also view infrastructure constraints in transportation as one manifestation of high transaction costs.[30]

In addition to affecting transaction costs, certain kinds of services may impact the rate of innovation, so that their growth is critical in determining development. The obvious perspective to take in this case is that of the endogenous growth literature, which emphasizes the role of innovation (e.g., Grossman and Helpman, 1991; Romer, 1990). In this context, the critical aspect of services growth is their knowledge intensity. The comprehensive study of Dahlman and Utz (2005) analyzes the development of a "knowledge economy" in India. These authors emphasize R&D quite broadly, and range over issues of governance institutions and education, as well as the national system of innovation. Implicitly their treatment of education partially deals with the concerns about skill intensity expressed by Kochhar et al. (2006), by highlighting the importance of skilled labour in development: we postpone details until Section 7. Their perspective converges with the transaction cost approach in emphasizing the need to improve the ICT infrastructure, which will in turn speed and enhance the acquisition, creation, dissemination, and use of knowledge.

Singh (2003) provides a formal analysis of how improving ICTs can enhance growth. His growth model, designed to capture the special role of ICTs in economic growth as an enabler of efficient communication and storage of information, is an extension of the recombinant growth model of Weitzman (1998). The central idea of this approach is that new ideas are formed through combinations of old ideas. A key property of this formulation is that the increase in the number of ideas is faster than geometric growth (Weitzman, 1998, Lemma, p. 338). The rate at which potential ideas are converted into new ones depends on a "success rate", which is a function of the current level of resources spent per potential new idea, i.e., the level of R&D. In Weitzman's model, all ideas are the same, and the actual number of new ideas is given by the number of potential new ideas multiplied by the success rate. Singh (2003) modifies Weitzman's model to allow the stock of ICT knowledge to independently affect this success rate, so that ICT gives the growth process an extra 'kick,' beyond that which comes from recombinant growth in general.

## 5. Linkages and spillovers

The analysis of the previous section can be extended and complemented by explicitly considering linkages in an input-output framework. The goal is to quantify the extent to which services, manufacturing and agriculture have spillover effects on each other. A single year's input-output data provides this information in a static context, whereas examining changes in coefficients over time can provide some insight into structural changes in the economy. For example, Sastry et al. (2003)[31] construct input coefficient matrices for four years: 1968-69, 1979-80, 1989-90 and 1993-94 (see Table 3). The basic observation is that, over this period, agricultural production became more industry- and services-intensive, whereas industrial production became less agriculture-intensive and more services-intensive. For the production of services, the main change was greater service intensity. Some of these changes took place more uniformly through this time period, but the greatest changes in the Indian economy's production structure, by this measure, came in the 1980s and 1990s. These observations are, of course, consistent with the analyses presented earlier.[32]

The input-output approach is applied at a much more disaggregated level by Hansda (2001). His goal is to address the larger question of the sustainability of services-led growth for the Indian economy. He uses input-output transactions tables for 1993-94, disaggregated at the level of 115 activities (22 in agriculture, 80 in industry, and 13 in services), as well as at the level of 10 broad sectors. At these disaggregated levels, Hansda's analysis suggests that the Indian economy is quite services-intensive with industry being the most services-intensive sector. Table 4 (adapted from Hansda, 2001, Table 5, and partially updated to 1998-99), summarizes the pattern of above average intensity for sectors falling into the three overall categories of agriculture, industry and services. The main conclusion, on the services intensity of industrial activities, is validated by the bold numbers in Table 4, indicating a large fraction of industrial activities with above-average services intensity. This conclusion is in line with the Sastry et al. aggregated data for 1993-94, and our calculations for 1998-99 (Table 3).

One can also examine the data at an intermediate level of aggregation, as in Table 5 (adapted from Hansda, 2001, Table 6 and partially updated). The numbers here are the direct (for 1993-94 and 1998-99) and indirect (for 1993-94) sectoral intensities, corresponding to the numbers reported by Sastry et al., but at a level of disaggregation that allows a greater understanding of the pattern of linkages of the different services sub-sectors. Note that the columns are further aggregated at the level of the three sectors – agriculture, industry and services. The different aggregation gives intensities somewhat at variance with the Sastry et al. calculations, but the conclusion of the importance of services still emerges clearly. Manufacturing, construction and "electricity, gas and water supply" are all services intensive. On the other hand, among services activities, "transport, storage and communication" are together quite industry intensive, while "personal, social and other services," and "trade, hotels and restaurants" are also somewhat industry intensive. As one might expect, the level of linkages to and from agriculture, as indicated by these intensities, is quite low. Surprisingly, the same is true for "financing, insurance and real estate."

The results for 1998-99, for direct intensities only, indicate relatively little change in magnitudes of agriculture and manufacturing intensities, as well as for their rankings, which capture relative intensities. Services intensities seem to have changed somewhat more from 1993-94 to 1998-99. In particular, "transport, storage and communications," "financing, insurance and real estate," and "personal and social services" all became more services intensive in absolute and relative magnitude. The level of linkages to financial and real estate services remained relatively low, however. Given the expansion of this sub-sector in the 1990s, and policy statements about creating an international financial hub in Mumbai, it would be important to investigate how these linkages have changed since 1998-99.[33]

One can also calculate backward and forward linkages more formally, using a procedure due to Rasmussen (1956). Backward linkages refer to stimulus from a sector to its input-providing sectors, while forward linkages capture stimuli in the opposite direction, i.e., downstream in production. Linkage measures are constructed as indices. An index value greater than one indicates a greater than average linkage.[34] Applying this method to 1998-99 data,[35] we find that 43 out of the total of 115 activities – 6 of 22 agricultural activities, 28 of 80 industrial activities and 9 of 13 services activities – had relative backward index values above one. In fact, 8 of the 9 service activities exceeded the threshold by substantial margins. Therefore, we may conclude that services activities had proportionately the largest inducing effect on the rest in terms of backward linkage. The results for the forward linkage indices are qualitatively similar, in terms of the relative importance of services: 19 of 115 activities – 5 of 22 agricultural activities, 5 of 80 industrial activities and 9 of 13 services activities – had high forward linkage indices. Hansda's aggregated results for 1993-94 (his Table 7) are quite similar to these disaggregated indicators, finding strong backward linkages for "personal, social & other services" and "transport, storage & communication" in particular. Forward linkages from services are weaker at this level of aggregation, emphasizing the need to consider as disaggregated a view of the economy as possible.

Two additional pieces of analysis are possible. Hansda (2001) calculates the coefficients of variation for the linkage indices. These coefficients measure the evenness across sub-sectors of a particular sector's purchases (backward linkages) or sales (forward linkages). The low proportion of services activities with low backward coefficients of variation suggests that the backward linkages from services tend to be concentrated, i.e., their purchases are from a relatively small segment of the economy. Hansda also finds that the forward linkages from services are more evenly spread. Second, given conceptual criticisms of the Rasmussen indices of linkages (e.g., Claus, 2002), he constructs an alternative index of vertical integration, based on the work of Heimler (1991). The results are that 14 out of the 115 activities have index values higher than the average, with 7 of those activities in the services sector, 6 in industry and 1 in agriculture. This supports the view that the services sector has the largest multiplier effect on the rest of the economy.

One way to interpret the results from the disaggregated input-output analysis is in keeping with the idea that India is a high transaction cost economy (Singh, 2004a). Transportation, trade and communications in India, all sectors which have high impacts on transaction costs, have all been markedly inefficient, held back by inefficiencies in government and by barriers to private participation. The 1980s and 1990s saw this situation begin to change, and a plausible interpretation of Hansda's results is that, through linkages, this change has stimulated the entire economy to some extent. One must bear in mind that this kind of input-output analysis is static, and there is no growth mechanism postulated. Nevertheless, one can argue that, to the extent that growth is driven by innovation, innovations in the services sector are likely to have positive implications for the growth of the rest of the economy. We can explore this hypothesis more explicitly by selectively perturbing input-output coefficients and tracing out the implications.

The theoretical basis for the following exercise is developed in an important paper by Majumdar and Ossella (1999). They show that in an input-output economy, under some further conditions,[36] the long-run optimal growth factor (i.e., the growth rate plus one) is given by $g = (\delta\lambda)^{1/\alpha}$, where $\delta$ is the discount factor for the representative consumer, $\alpha$ is the parameter of the constant elasticity one-period utility function (equivalent to the coefficient of relative risk aversion), and $\lambda$ is the inverse of the largest eigenvalue of the input-output matrix. Efficiency gains in sector $j$, such as would result from any kind of innovation, are modelled as proportional reductions in all the input requirements of that sector, i.e., the elements of column $j$ of the input-output matrix. The maximal eigenvalue decreases in this case, implying an increase in the optimal growth rate of the economy. Since the other two parameters are unchanged, the ranking of growth rates is equivalent to the ranking of the $\lambda$'s across all the individual sector perturbations. Hence, the sectors for which exogenous efficiency improvements would have the greatest growth impacts can be clearly identified. These sectors are termed "leading sectors" for the economy.[37]

Majumdar and Ossella, using data from 1989, consider both 2 and 5 per cent reductions in input requirements, and identify the five leading sectors of the Indian economy for that year in each case as, in order of growth rate impacts, (1) electricity, gas and water supply, (2) iron and steel, (3) paper and paper products, (4) other chemicals, and (5) other manufacturing. Using $\alpha = 0.9$,[38] the growth factor for a 5 per cent reduction in input requirements in the electricity, gas and water supply sector, relative to the original growth factor, is 1.0081. To translate this into a growth rate impact, assume that the initial optimal growth rate was 6 per cent – the efficiency gain would change the optimal growth rate to 6.9 per cent.

We carry out the analysis along the lines of Majumdar and Ossella, using input-output data for 1998-99. We have 115 sectors instead of the 60 sectors used in 1989. Nevertheless, major sectoral classifications are quite similar. We only calculate the impacts of 5 per cent efficiency improvements, but consider the 10 leading sectors of the economy. The results are presented in Table 6. Electricity, gas and water supply remains the most important leading sector, and its growth impact is estimated to be even higher than for the earlier data. Several heavy industry sectors feature in the top 10, paralleling the earlier results. The new feature of our results, however, is the prominence of services. Four services sub-sectors are in the list, and their nature and presence strongly bears out the transaction cost interpretation provided previously in this section.

As an alternative to using disaggregated input-output data, it is also possible to undertake a dynamic analysis of sectoral growth and linkages within the Indian economy through reduced-form time series modelling. Sastry et al. (2002) add a (non-oil) export sector to agriculture, industry and services, and estimate this four equation specification for annual data from 1981-82 to 1999-2000. Linkages from agriculture and industry to services, and agriculture and services to industry are incorporated by including those sectors' outputs as causal variables. On the other hand, agricultural growth is assumed to be determined independently. Their empirical results for the industrial sector come from a straightforward levels regression, and indicate that a 1 per cent rise in services (agriculture) would stimulate industrial output by 0.40 (0.25) percentage point.

The services sector presents several additional challenges in terms of assumptions required for empirical analysis. Sastry et al. focus only on construction, "trade, hotel and restaurants" and "transport, storage and communication" as endogenous services, subject to linkages, leaving finance, and "community, social and personal services" as exogenous to the system.[39] The results for the entire sample period, with the equation estimated in growth rate terms, suggest that a percentage point increase in the growth rate of services would lead to a 0.32 percentage point increase in the growth rate of industry. Given the substantial changes in the input-output coefficients over this period, and tests that reject parameter stability, they re-estimate the equation for the 1990s only. The impact of services growth now increases to 0.49 percentage points, and they argue that this is consistent with the 1993-94 input-output tables. In fact, the match is less good than the authors suggest, since the coefficient for agriculture is much higher in the time series specification than in the input-output table. Nevertheless, there is broad consistency from this approach concerning the importance of services.

The input-output linkage analysis is limited by its focus on what are essentially pecuniary externalities. As noted by Dasgupta and Singh (2005a), the Kaldorian hypothesis of the mechanisms of growth through structural change emphasizes technological externalities or spillovers, rather than pecuniary externalities. In this view, technological externalities are what made manufacturing special in the past, and now explain why ICTs (whether acting through products or services or both) are a special driver of growth.[40] This perspective is also consistent with the analysis of Singh (2003) with respect to the special role of ICTs in the innovation process, as discussed in Section 4. In this context, Singh (2005) also surveys fieldwork and case studies which suggest that there are spillovers from ICTs in rural areas of India. In particular, the introduction of a range of rural ICT-based services not only reduces transaction costs, but also provides spillovers through knowledge acquisition and information access. It has also been argued (e.g., Singh, 2003) that there were substantial spillovers from the IT services industry in India to IT enabled services (ITES), as well as to knowledge intensive sectors in general. These included specific organizational expertise, customer knowledge, and general reputational effects.[41] In turn, there are linkages and spillovers from ITES to sub-sectors such as construction and transportation, not only through demand stimulus but also by creating a different set of requirements and expectations.[42]

## 6. International trade in services

Theoretical considerations and empirical evidence both suggest a positive role for trade liberalization in India's growth since the 1980s. Theories of comparative advantage and inter-industry trade (based on product differentiation and economies of scale) do not necessarily distinguish between agriculture, manufacturing and services as likely export sectors for a developing country, though developing nations are almost invariably those with a relative abundance of unskilled labour. Since much of India's export growth has come in skill-intensive services,[43] the international aspects of India's "services-led" growth bear examination from empirical and theoretical perspectives. Panagariya (2005) summarizes India's experience with external liberalization, starting in the late 1970s. He documents the acceleration in India's growth rate in the 1980s, and ties this improvement to the external liberalization that took place. Several studies (e.g., Joshi and Little, 1994; Chand and Sen, 2002) formally establish a positive linkage between opening the economy and productivity improvements in manufacturing: this supports the conventional view connecting trade liberalization and development through improvements in manufacturing.

Many developing countries have had to struggle with maintaining balance of payments equilibrium. In India's case, balance of payments crises in the 1970s and before tended to shape a policy of keeping the Indian economy substantially closed to international trade and investment. In this respect, one of the most important aspects of services sector (particularly IT and ITES) growth in India has been its favourable international trade and balance of payments consequences. Hansda (2002) provides some basic documentation of the change in the role of services in India's international trade. For example, India's share in world export of commercial services doubled from 0.6 per cent in 1990 to 1.2 per cent in 2000, while its share in global merchandise exports went up only marginally, from 0.5 per cent to 0.7 per cent, in the same period.[44] Data going back to the 1950s (Hansda, 2002, Table 10) show that, while India has run a persistent deficit in merchandise trade, there has been a consistent surplus in trade in services. This surplus, only 10 per cent of the merchandise trade deficit in 1990-91, grew to one-third of that deficit by 2001-02. In aggregate, the ratio of services exports to merchandise exports increased from 25 per cent to 45 per cent in that period. Much of this increase came in the category of miscellaneous services, which include IT services and ITES such as business process outsourcing (BPO) and call centres.[45] Hansda also notes the higher positive balance in travel services, and suggests this may be related to a more favourable exchange rate, which was also a consequence of liberalization. Travel connected to IT services and ITES may also have contributed to this increase.

Numerous authors (e.g., Bhagwati, 1985; Gordon and Gupta, 2004; Dasgupta and Singh, 2005a) note the increased ability to deliver services over long distances at a reasonable cost as a result of technological progress in ICTs, which has led to increased worldwide trade in services. Gordon and Gupta estimate that, in India, exports of services (in U.S. dollars) grew by an average of 15 per cent a year in the 1990s, compared with 9 per cent annually in the 1980s. Using the Sastry et al. input-output matrix, and making some assumptions about input usage for services exports relative to services overall, they estimate the contribution of exports to annual average services growth to be about 0.2 percentage points in the 1980s, and 0.6 percentage points in the 1990s. In their regression analysis, they find that exports of services were highly significant for explaining overall growth of business services, which includes IT services and ITES – seemingly an unsurprising result. On the other hand, the growth of other kinds of services did not show much sensitivity to exports.

We have suggested that, in many respects, the recent services growth in India comes from outsourcing by developed country firms that has characteristics of manufacturing, namely scale and routinization. Even in general, trade in services can be analytically treated as similar to trade in goods. This includes trade based on comparative advantage as well as that driven by economies of scale and product differentiation. Bhagwati, Panagariya and Srinivasan (2004) provide some analytical foundations for understanding outsourcing to countries like India in the context of general trade in services. This offshore outsourcing is properly defined, they note, as "offshore trade in arm's length services," distinct from offshore purchases of manufactured components and FDI.[46] The authors go on to model three kinds of international outsourcing. The result of their analysis in each case is that the welfare impacts of this kind of trade in services are akin to the conventional benefits of trade in goods.[47] These models and some extensions focus on the impacts on the developed country from which the outsourcing comes. In each case, though, the receiving country should benefit from the new trade, since there is an increased demand for its labour. This kind of theoretical analysis supports the view that new trade in services, such as India is experiencing, provides positive welfare gains. At the same time, these models do not incorporate labour with different skill levels, nor can they quantify the benefits of trade.

Putting aside concerns about the magnitude and nature of the growth and employment effects of services trade, one can examine barriers to realizing whatever benefits there are. In addition to IT services and ITES, sub-sectors such as health, education and travel may all have growth and development impacts that are affected by international trade. One possible focus is on the external and demand constraints on India's international trade in services (Banga, 2005). External trade barriers can arise from limits on foreign equity participation, licensing provisions, immigration and labour market regulations and discriminatory treatment with respect to taxes, subsidies, and other policies. Domestic constraints can result from infrastructure inadequacies, poor quality and standards, lack of clear-cut responsibilities between centre and state governments and other policy-related disincentives.

To examine the extent of the constraints to trade in India's services sector, Banga classifies services in terms of their external trade barriers, i.e., the extent of liberalization, as well as growth rates and the share in exports of services (Table 7, adapted from Banga, 2005, Table 5). The extent of liberalization of services is captured by the FDI cap and restrictions on trade in Mode 4, as classified by the WTO under the General Agreement on Trade in Services (GATS).[48] The period considered for the extent of liberalization is from 1997, since many services were liberalized after that, so the average share in exports is estimated for the period 1997-2003. Banga uses this classification to suggest that services that face high trade barriers (the right hand column) have mostly grown slowly, while others, which have seen moderate liberalization, such as health and education, have had their growth held back by domestic constraints.

Several sector-specific studies provide more detail on the services sub-sectors in Table 7 (see Banga, 2005 for a review and references). The various external and domestic constraints for these sub-sectors include explicit constraints on FDI and other restrictions, but often just a lack of a coherent set of policies and modern regulatory institutions. Banga offers several policy prescriptions. In particular, health and education are identified as service areas with high growth rates and low export shares, suggesting potential for more trade in these services. Currently, India's trade in health services occurs mainly from mode 4 (movement of health personnel) and mode 2 (inflows of foreign patients for treatment in India from developed and developing countries). The latter is limited by technological and infrastructure constraints (Srinivasan, 2005). Continued telecommunication reforms, such as reduced connectivity costs and lower tariffs will expand the scope for cross-border supply of these services. Even with medical tourism to India, where doctors do not go abroad, there can be issues of diverting care from the poor. Thus, liberalization and investment in this area would ideally be accompanied by a strengthening of the public health care system.[49] Regarding trade in education services, Banga emphasizes the need to develop a more robust system of regulation and accreditation of educational institutions. Srinivasan (2005) similarly notes the possibilities and constraints for mode 2 services trade in education.

Conventional tourism, which can complement health services in particular, as in medical tourism, is particularly constrained by infrastructural shortcomings. Srinivasan (2005) notes that tourism grew by 24 per cent in 2004, making India one of the leading tourist destinations in the world. At the same time, the inadequacy of affordable quality hotel rooms, transport and communications still constrains India's ability to attract and absorb tourists. Even in the case of fast-growing IT and ITES, Srinivasan notes the infrastructure constraints can still hurt growth: "Reliable electric power, efficient and inexpensive telecommunications and access to venture capital are essential infrastructures for the IT sector. Although telecommunications infrastructure has vastly improved, as noted earlier, there are still some unresolved issues relating to the authority of the regulatory agency (Telecommunications Authority of India (TRAI)) vis-à-vis the Department of Telecommunications and the state-owned providers. The situation regarding electric power continues to be abysmal" (Srinivasan, 2005, Section 4).

One other important potential growth area is financial services (Banga, 2005). Banking and insurance have seen high growth with moderate liberalization of the sector (Table 7). Some of the developments in the financial sector have come from the adoption of information technology, and others from improvements in regulation and legal and institutional frameworks, though much remains to be accomplished in the latter arena. The problem of financially weak and inefficient public sector banks and insurance companies contrasts with modern equity markets that enjoy high trading volumes and some aggressive and competitive private sector banks such as ICICI Bank.

The input-output analyses of Section 5 do not show much evidence of strong linkages to and from the financial sector, but to the extent that the efficiency of capital allocation is increased through financial development, one can make a case for encouraging the financial services sector, as recent government policy pronouncements have suggested. Since conventional input-output analysis ignores the financial sector, and is static, its enabling role for investment and growth is neglected in that approach. However, several empirical studies for India do support the conclusion that financial sector development would stimulate economic growth (e.g., Bell and Rousseau, 2001; Athukorala and Sen, 2002).

## 7. Employment, education and training

Studies of the development of the services sector in India typically highlight the lack of job growth that has taken place, even as the sector has, to some extent, driven overall GDP growth. The problem is a bigger one, however, since overall job growth has also been anaemic. For example, organized sector employment in 1991 was 26.73 million (19.06 public and 7.67 private). By 1997, this had grown a bit, to 28.25 million (19.56 public and 8.69 private). However, in 2003, the numbers had shrunk: 18.58 million public sector employees, 8.42 million private, and 27 million total. Clearly, there are some well-known institutional and legal constraints in the labour market that inhibit job growth. Aside from these overall constraints, understanding the consequences of India's particular pattern of service sector growth for employment is important. In fact, while some fast-growing segments of IT services have not been subject to restrictive labour laws, they have not altered the overall services employment picture.

There are several accounts of the slow growth of employment in services. Hansda (2002) points out that, while the share of services in employment increased from 20 per cent in 1970-71 to 23.5 per cent in 1999-2000, this was much less than the growth of the services sector's share of GDP, which was from 32.1 per cent in 1970-71 to 48.5 per cent in 2000-01. Gordon and Gupta (2004) note that, while services rose from 42 per cent to 48 per cent of GDP during the 1990s, the employment share of services actually declined by about one percentage point during the decade. Of course, the flip side of these observations is that labour productivity in services has grown much faster than in the rest of the economy. Hence, one might re-pose the question of low employment growth in services as one of relatively low productivity growth in the rest of the economy. We will return to this issue later in this section. The productivity issue may also be examined to some extent through the input-output coefficients of the Indian economy. Lower coefficients imply not only lower linkages, but also simply lower input intensity. Thus the low linkages of financial services (Table 5) may be partly an indicator of high productivity. The caveat in reaching this as a definite conclusion, of course, is that one does not have a technology benchmark for each sector. Furthermore, splintering complicates any attempt to interpret changes in the coefficients over time.

More disaggregated data on employment in services is presented in Tables 8 and 9. The difference in the pattern of employment generation as well as overall employment growth in the two periods (Table 8) is striking.[50] Joshi (2004) points out that the slowdown in tertiary (services) sector employment growth in the latter period is chiefly due to the sharp decline in the growth of employment in community, social and personal services. Other, more disaggregated data (Hansda, 2002, Table 4) does suggest that a squeeze on public employment in the 1990s may have been behind the slowdown in employment in community, social and personal services, and hence of services employment. If that was a proper result of controlling wasteful government expenditure, the question that follows is why private sector employment did not compensate more. Possible answers may lie in the quality of the labour force, and the skills it possesses, as well as labour laws.[51] There may also have been cyclical effects at work, since employment growth picked up subsequently (see below).

Total employment impacts for the economy were determined more by changes in agricultural employment growth than by any slowdown in services employment growth. In the decade 1983-93, half of employment growth came from the primary sector, chiefly agriculture (see Table 9). However, in the subsequent six years, primary sector employment actually shrank, while neither industry nor services could pick up the entire slack. Part of this phenomenon can be explained, as suggested by Joshi (2004), by the possibility that the employment absorption capacity of agriculture has reached a saturation point (see, in particular the discussion in Planning Commission, 2001), while employment growth in the high productivity industrial sector was sluggish in this latter period because of a combination of an industrial sector recession and continued use of relatively capital-intensive-technology.

Joshi goes on to emphasize the services sector as a key area for employment generation – however, the figures in Table 9, and the organized sector employment numbers quoted earlier in this section, do not give a clear indication that this is happening in any automatic way.[52] On the other hand, the figures for organized sector employment miss over 90 per cent of employment in India. In fact, the most recent National Sample Survey Organisation data, released in 2004, estimate that the employment growth rate from 1999-2000 to December 2002 averaged about 2 per cent: the same as that in the 1983-94 period, and double the growth rate in the 1994-2000 period. This translated into about 8 million jobs added per year, with growth coming chiefly in urban areas and particularly in the small-scale sector. Thus, unorganized sector employment growth outweighed job losses in the corporate sector.[53]

Sectoral employment data going back to 1951 (Banga, 2005, Table 3) emphasize the strikingly poor record of manufacturing employment growth over five decades, though the GDP growth rate was, of course, lower before the 1980s. This would support the view that the real problems in employment generation lie with long-run structural and policy constraints that inhibit employers from hiring, rather than more recent policy changes. Employment elasticities for the 1980s and 1990s (Table 10) may be interpreted similarly. While there is some decrease in employment elasticities in the 1990s, they are low in the 1980s as well, supporting the long-run view of the employment problem.[54] One is also tempted to conclude from the data that the employment problem is somewhat independent of the fact that employment has lagged GDP growth – the latter, as noted, is an indicator of rising productivity. The cause for concern is that this rising productivity of labour has not translated into a stronger and wider demand for that factor. The answer to that may have something to do with India's pattern of skill-intensive development, itself determined by educational patterns.

Clearly, the pattern vis-à-vis agricultural employment (Tables 8 and 9) is consistent with a Kaldorian or similar story of development (Dasgupta and Singh, 2005a), with manufacturing somewhat replaced, and definitely supplemented, by services that are organized more on industrial lines. However, as discussed in detail by Kochhar et al. (2006), both services and manufacturing in India are apparently more skill-intensive than is commensurate with India's level of income and development. This has implications for the pattern of development, in two ways. First, since the scarcity of the requisite skills (e.g., fluency in non-accented English, or a good quality undergraduate engineering degree) acts as an entry barrier to these sectors, rather than development drawing in new job seekers and increasing employment, the earnings of the skilled are being pushed up, often toward developed country levels.[55] There may be trickle down demand effects, but the consequences for income distribution and social implications may be of concern.

The second implication for development is on the demand side, with the pattern of goods and services being skewed toward the demand pattern of the upper end of the income distribution. In this case, there may not be the kinds of spillovers that would occur in manufacturing, where expertise developed for mass produced goods for the middle classes in rich countries can be transferred to an array of goods that also satisfy wants of the masses in the developing country. The same degree of spillovers may not be available for call centres and BPO operations, which do not necessarily lead to efficiency benefits for the kinds of manufacturing that will employ lower-skilled workers. Of course there are some positive examples: in southern India, in particular, world-class manufacturing firms do seem to be emerging, partly driven by the business environment and culture created by IT and ITES firms.

Some of the above ideas can be incorporated in formal models, which typically assume full employment – the employment issues are then really about the quality of the jobs, and employment in high productivity sectors. New growth theories go beyond considering homogeneous investment as a driver of growth (where diminishing returns will always set in) to emphasize the importance of technical progress, embodied in new varieties of capital and consumption goods, in driving long run or sustained economic growth (e.g., Romer, 1990; Grossman and Helpman, 1991). Those models typically assume homogeneity of consumers, but Sarkar (1998), for example, allows heterogeneity of demands, and shows how demand thresholds can matter for growth,[56] and how a sufficiently large middle class can be crucial in enabling growth. In Sarkar's model, there are three classes of income earners: rich, middle class and poor. Having a large enough middle class is crucial for generating sufficient demand and profits to drive innovation, which in turn creates economic growth. In his formulation, the only feasible way to increase the growth rate is to promote the poor to the middle class by permanently increasing their productivity – through education, for example.

Thus, both theoretical and empirical analyses of the employment aspects of India's growth experience suggest that constraints on employment can be traced to the labour supply side, in the educational system, as well as to the more obvious labour demand side disincentives that are heavily built into the labour laws (e.g., Besley and Burgess, 2004). The distortion of Indian public spending toward higher education and away from primary education is well known. A significant aspect of the 1990s and the years since has been that a relatively small proportion of Indian higher education graduates, either with professional or technical degrees, or with English communication skills, were able to take advantage of the rapid development of globally-oriented IT services and ITES in this period. Financial and professional services have also started to come under this umbrella, as Indians provide a pool of managerial talent that is small relative to the population, but large in absolute numbers. The constraints on higher education in India create rents for this educated group, as they are now able to participate in an effectively global labour market.

Among the many authors who have analyzed the current state of India's higher education system, Kapur and Mehta (2004) and Kapur and Khilnani (2006) analyze the structural and institutional shortcomings of the organization of the sector. Interestingly, the educational services sector itself does not figure explicitly in all the empirical analyses reviewed here, with the exception of Banga (2005), but it provides the underpinnings for all modern sectors of the economy through its outputs. Kapur and Mehta argue that the dismal overall state of higher education in India is a result of a withering away of public education funding support, because of the unsustainable subsidies required by the existing model. At the same time, political interference and capture by vested interests have increased. The result has been a haphazard and uneven privatization, coupled with exit by those who can afford to send their children abroad. Kapur and Khilnani echo these points, and stress the need for removing subsidies to and controls on so-called elite institutions, allowing them to expand efficiently, and transferring resources to areas such as vocational education. They point out that the vocational Industrial Training Institutes (ITIs) receive just 3 per cent of the higher education budget, and are in even worse shape than the rest of the higher education system.

The policy measures that would correct the present quality and quantity constraints on the supply of higher education in India are well understood by economists,[57] but political battles have instead been focused on dividing up the existing rents in the system, through controls on FDI in higher education and quotas for various societal groups. Instead, free entry into higher education, coupled with a new and more effective system of regulation through certification, disclosure requirements, and media rankings would lead to transparent competition and an expansion of supply precisely where it is needed. Kapur and Mehta fault Indian industry for not being more proactive, since they would benefit, but one can see that in narrow areas such as IT services, firms have been quick to develop training programs and push for their employees to acquire needed qualifications and skills. The problem is with more general skills, which give larger opportunities for benefits to be captured by non-training firms. Even here, in areas such as ITES, firms have tried to develop collective action solutions through industry associations. Wider adoption of such approaches, as well as the alternative of private philanthropy to fund education, will require the government to overhaul its archaic regulatory system and legal frameworks for the provision of education services. Of course, many of these problems are endemic to primary education as well, and similar solutions (though with a stronger public sector involvement because of the greater public good elements of primary education) are desirable. In the end, what will matter for the sustainability of India's development will be its educational system, and not particular emphasis on manufacturing, services or any sub-sector among them, with the caveat that sub-sectors with greater labour intensities will obviously have more beneficial employment effects.[58]

## 8. Social and environmental issues

We have already touched on the concerns about income distribution that arise from India's skill-intensive pattern of growth. Particular kinds of inequality in income may feed into consumption demand in a manner that negatively impacts innovation and growth. To some extent, the skill-intensity observed in India may be exacerbated by the rapid increase in services exports, in sub-sectors where skills that are only available to a relatively small minority (quality engineering and science education, and/or English fluency) are necessary. Increased political battles over entrance to elite educational institutions are an indicator of competition for acquiring a skills set that is increasingly valuable but in very short supply.

The regional dimensions of India's recent growth are also important, politically as well as for shaping subnational economic policies. Kochhar et al.

(2006) suggest that the shortage of skilled managerial and supervisory workers, which has already led to their wages rising rapidly, may also give an advantage to those Indian states that are already ahead in the growth race, by magnifying the economic advantages of scale: those states with access to managerial talent can scale up enterprises more easily. The constraints on availability of management may also inhibit the growth of labour-intensive manufacture. If the more advanced states attract skilled migrants, who are more mobile than unskilled labour (except, perhaps, at the very bottom rungs such as itinerant construction workers), the poorer states will be further constrained over time. Differences in fertility rates (with economically laggard states like Bihar and Uttar Pradesh seeing greater population increases) will be yet another inequalizing factor. The policy prescriptions offered by Kochhar et al., in addition to reforming and liberalizing higher education, include broader reforms to promote labour-intensive activities in agriculture and manufacturing.

The regional picture of growth and structural change is somewhat complicated. Kochhar et al., analyzing the period 1980-2000, find no correlation between growth and the share of manufacturing or of labour-intensive industries, but do find a small positive relationship between growth and the share of services. Using data for the period 1993-94 to 2003-04 (RBI, 2006), we measure structural change for a set of states[59] in two ways, as percentage changes in sectoral shares, and as percentage point changes in those shares. An index of structural change is constructed by simply adding the absolute values of these sectoral changes (Table 11). While some states like Tamil Nadu, Haryana and Karnataka are expected examples of states ranking high in structural change, Bihar is surprising in this respect. On the other hand, Gujarat ranks very low in terms of structural change. We also calculate ten-year per capita NSDP growth rates for the states (Table 12) and correlations between growth, initial conditions and structural change. In keeping with the well-documented evidence on income divergence across Indian states, the correlation between growth rates and initial-year per capita levels was positive and quite large (0.47). On the other hand, the correlation between the structural change index and initial year levels was negligible (0.01), and that between growth and structural change was negative (-0.30).[60] In addition, we found that the correlation between the change in the share of the service sector and the growth rate was also negative (-0.29), in contrast to Kochhar et al.'s finding for the longer, earlier time period. In the absence of obvious or expected links between structural change and growth at the level of the state, our conclusion is that further investigation of this issue is required, disaggregating the three sectors further.

Aside from income distribution issues, there have also been concerns about cultural loss associated with the training required by, and lifestyles associated with, outsourced services such as call centres. While surveys suggest that such fears about identity or cultural loss may be somewhat exaggerated,[61] these factors are real, though non-quantifiable. These fears are also part of broader concerns with growth and modernization (which go back to the industrial revolution), although identity issues such as changing one's name and accent for work, or having to deal with racism from call centre customers in developed countries, cut deeper than simply changing patterns of consumption and saving as a consequence of economic growth. In the latter case, one has the extreme perspective embodied in a quote from an Indian middle-class consumer, "I can't resist buying newer models of electronic goodies" (Basu, 2003), but the changes are more far-reaching than just an impulsive desire to consume more, and sooner rather than later. They include a greater awareness of, and aspiration for, developed country lifestyles and consumption; greater attention to personal convenience and individuality; greater willingness to experiment and question traditional modes of behaviour; and greater optimism about the future. It is not at all clear that these changes are all negative, and recently it has been suggested (in the context of the United States) that innovative attitudes among consumers can actually spur domestic innovation (Bhidé, 2006) in production.

Another aspect of services-led development that goes beyond standard economic growth accounting is that of environmental impacts. In many respects, service sector growth can be more environmentally friendly, to the extent that it avoids heavy industry and its polluting impacts. However, transportation is a service sector that must grow rapidly as well, and which has substantial negative environmental impacts. To some extent, the benefits of services-led industrialization may be that the environmental impacts occur less dramatically in the short run, allowing time for income effects (favouring a clean environment) to work their way through to environmental regulation: in other words, the environmental Kuznets curve may be flatter in this case, though not completely flat.[62] Services-led industrialization may also avoid problems that come from natural resource export paths of development. In India's case, its forest cover is already heavily depleted, and the problems lie more in domestic consumption of resources than with exports. Any kind of development will increase the domestic demand for resources. This is a function of rapid growth, and the issue of appropriate institutional and regulatory regimes transcends any implications that follow from a specific pattern of development.

## 9. Lessons for development policy

In reviewing India's experience with respect to service-sector-led development, we have noted policy implications for international trade, education, and employment generation. In many respects, these are traditional concerns of development policy, and a large theoretical and empirical literature exists on each of these aspects of economic development. While there is some degree of consensus on the importance of education, economic openness, and encouragement of labour-intensive activities, debate continues with respect to the degree and specificity of government targeting of particular sectors of a developing economy. The variety of views is considerable, even for a single country like India.

Dasgupta and Singh (2005a, b) offer several policy prescriptions based on their examination of the Indian case. These include government support for the informal sector through financial and technical services, a Keynesian attention to maintaining aggregate demand, and a traditional industrial policy approach of identifying dynamic industries that have positive technological and pecuniary externalities for the rest of the economy. ICT-related activities are emphasized in their discussion (see footnote 41), but they also reiterate the importance of encouraging knowledge-intensive industries more generally. Dahlman and Utz (2005) develop the latter point in great detail for India, and Dahlman (2006) provides a more general context and framework for this view. Rodrik (2006) makes a more general case for government intervention, based on the view that economic development is fundamentally driven by structural change in the economy, and that this change is "fraught with externalities and spillovers of all kinds." In doing so, he draws on China and India as examples of fast-growing countries with export profiles skewed toward high productivity goods.

Ocampo (2004-5) summarizes several areas where the Washington consensus has been insufficient. What concerns us here is "the role of productive development strategies." In this category, Ocampo emphasizes the need to build institutional capacity, the importance of Schumpeterian innovation (e.g., Amsden, 2001) and structural change, and the standard externality arguments with respect to markets such as those for long-term capital and technology. The Latin American case, in particular, is often used to illustrate the inadequacy of mere liberalization and policy neutrality (e.g., Hausmann, Rodrik and Velasco, 2005; Velasco, 2005; Rodrik, 2006). One might add, however, that all these studies beg the question of political will and feasibility. In particular, the interplay of different interest groups may be the fundamental determinant of which policies are implemented (e.g., Rajan and Zingales, 2006), and of the quality of implementation.

Returning to the Indian case, one can argue that policy reforms that have enabled greater openness, more competition, and better government regulation have spurred growth but have not gone far enough. Impediments to internal trade, labour market rigidities, and barriers to doing business all seem to be factors in keeping economic growth below potential.

The Indian IT sector, as a major success story, has typically been highlighted as one where government policy made a difference. The key claim here is that the cluster of human and institutional capital in Bangalore, more general government investments in technology education, and government policies that promoted import-substituting industrialization all created the initial conditions that allowed the IT sector to flourish (e.g., Balakrishnan, 2006). On the other hand, there is a case to be made for the "benign neglect" interpretation of the IT sector's success (Kapur, 2002; Murthy, 2004;

Singh, 2004c). Government policy certainly did not pick a winner in this case, since there was little or no understanding of, or foresight with respect to, the market for software services. Many of those who were drawn into the sector came with general technical training, rather than skills specifically geared toward the markets that were being served from the 1990s onward.

Nor is it the case that government investment in telecommunications infrastructure in India was based on any analysis or deep understanding of its potential role in facilitating or spurring development and growth. Certainly, government made policy moves from the 1980s onward to improve telecommunications infrastructure and access, but in every case, the impetus came from outside the government (non-resident Indians, in particular), and the slow pace of reform is evidenced in how much India lags behind China in telecommunications access. Thus, the Indian case in the past hardly fits even the weak notion of industrial policy outlined in Rodrik (2006):

> "The critics of industrial policy are correct when they argue that governments do not have adequate knowledge to pick "winners." [I]ndustrial policy is more appropriately conceived as a process whereby the state and the private sector jointly arrive at diagnoses about the sources of blockage in new economic activities and propose solutions to them. … It simply requires [the government] to build the public-private institutional arrangements whereby information on profitable activities and useful instruments of intervention can be elicited".

Having cautioned against an overly rosy view of past "state-led" development in the Indian case, one can note that this does not preclude such a process from operating beneficially in the future, in the limited manner described by Rodrik. Numerous central and state government actions encouraged and supported IT and ITES once the success of these sectors became evident. A similar dynamic is potentially under way with respect to financial services.[63] However, the political realities of interest groups are evident in Indian policies that effectively ration access to education at all levels, and various other policies that impose unnecessary costs on the private sector, reduce efficiency and inhibit innovation. We have suggested that broadening economic and institutional reforms, and extending them to government itself, may be more significant in terms of positive impacts than selective interventions in particular sub-sectors, provided that this process tackles emerging inequalities (thus avoiding "Latin Americanization"). In some respects, competition among state governments that has resulted from India's economic reforms (e.g., Singh and Srinivasan, 2005, 2006) may also shape India's political economy in a more favourable direction, ameliorating some of the conflicts highlighted in the abstract by Rajan and Zingales (2006).

## 10. Conclusions

India's pattern of development, with relatively slow growth of manufacturing, and a more rapid increase in the size of the service sector than would be typical, has received considerable attention. The contribution of this paper has been to provide an integrated appraisal of India's experience and future potential along this growth path. It is straightforward to argue, as several authors have done, that manufacturing, services and agriculture are all important, and broad policy steps to improve growth and employment across the economy are desirable. Specific policy suggestions with respect to improving the tradability and productivity of particular services also emerge from various analyses. Analyses of linkages suggest that certain service sub-sectors of the economy, such as trade, transportation and communications, may be particularly important, but this is also an intuitive conclusion.[64]

Several less obvious implications do emerge from this research. First, some of the dichotomy between services and manufacturing may be over-drawn, as certain kinds of services can be organized in ways that are closer to modern manufacturing. Nevertheless, there are some differences in educa-tion requirements, and employment and social impacts, particularly in the skill intensity required by some of the services that have seen the highest growth in India in the last decade or two. Indeed, the constraints on appro-priate skill acquisition that face the majority of the population in India rep-resent the greatest barrier to any kind of sustained growth, and a major pol-icy challenge in the politically charged arena of education. Tackling the edu-cation bottleneck, and adding some labour market reform, may go a long way to allowing Indian industry and its services sector to draw on the large numbers of underemployed, poorly productive people in India's rural heart-land.

A few years, ago, the debate on the role of services in India's growth was couched in somewhat simplified terms, as services substituting for manufac-turing. Recognizing the blurring conceptual distinction between the modern components of the two sectors helps to refocus the issues on productivity, linkages and distributional concerns, rather than any simple dichotomous choice. China's recent major revision of its GDP figures upwards by one-sixth, with most of that increase coming from a revaluation of services sector activity, is also significant in this context. At a stroke, the estimated contri-bution of services to China's GDP went up by nine percentage points, cross-ing 40 per cent. This is a much more plausible figure than previous estimates, even though it is still short of the average for countries with similar per capi-ta income levels. The difference between India and China in terms of servic-es' contribution to the economy has therefore become much less stark. Just as China has focused on manufacturing exports, but seen a stimulation of services activity, in India's case, there may be positive spillovers from services growth to manufacturing, through income and demand, or through organi-zational learning (as occurred from IT services to ITES). Ultimately, the bland but appropriate conclusion may be that making the conditions right for enterprise and innovation throughout the economy is more important than any targeted intervention toward particular sectors of the economy.

### Table 1.
### Services sub-sectors for India

| Sector | Activities included |
|---|---|
| **Trade, hotels and restaurant** | |
| Trade (distribution services) | Wholesale and retail trade in commodities both produced at home (including exports) and imported, purchase and selling agents, brokers and auctioneers |
| Hotels & Restaurants | Services rendered by hotels and other lodging places, restaurants, cafes and other eating and drinking places |
| **Transport, storage and communication** | |
| Railways | |
| Transport by other means | Road, water, air transport, services incidental to transport |
| Storage | |
| Communication | Postal, money orders, telegrams, telephones, overseas communication services, miscellaneous |
| **Financing, insurance, real estate and business services** | |
| Banking | Banks, banking department of RBI, post office saving bank, non-bank financial institution, cooperative credit societies, employees provident fund |
| Insurance | Life, postal life, non-life |
| Dwellings, real estate | |
| Business services | |
| Legal services | |
| **Community, social and personal services** | |
| Public administration, defense | |
| Personal services | Domestic, laundry, barber, beauty shops, tailoring, others |
| Community services | Education, research, scientific, medical, health, religious and other community |
| Other services | Recreation, entertainment, radio, TV broadcast, sanitary services |

*Source: Banga (2005).*

## Table 2.
### Structural breaks in India's growth rates

| Series | Break year 1 | Break year 2 |
|---|---|---|
| GDP | 1980** | |
| GNP | 1987** | |
| Trade, transport, storage, and communication | 1992** | |
| Finance, insurance, real estate, and business services | 1974** | 1980*** |
| Agriculture, forestry and logging, fishing, mining and quarrying | 1979 | |
| Manufacturing, construction, electricity, gas and water supply | 1964 | |
| Registered manufacturing | 1964 | |
| Public administration, defense and other services | 1993 | |

Source: Wallack (2003).
Obs.: ** indicates sup-F statistic significant at 5% level, *** at 1% level.

## Table 3.
### Sectoral production linkages

| | Agriculture | Industry | Services |
|---|---|---|---|
| **1968-69** | | | |
| Agriculture | 0.182 | 0.127 | 0.017 |
| Industry | 0.043 | 0.333 | 0.132 |
| Services | 0.016 | 0.135 | 0.096 |
| **1979-80** | | | |
| Agriculture | 0.160 | 0.130 | 0.039 |
| Industry | 0.068 | 0.345 | 0.105 |
| Services | 0.020 | 0.149 | 0.096 |
| **1989-90** | | | |
| Agriculture | 0.166 | 0.042 | 0.035 |
| Industry | 0.144 | 0.373 | 0.172 |
| Services | 0.047 | 0.188 | 0.185 |
| **1993-94** | | | |
| Agriculture | 0.145 | 0.035 | 0.034 |
| Industry | 0.140 | 0.365 | 0.150 |
| Services | 0.048 | 0.213 | 0.195 |
| **1998-99** | | | |
| Agriculture | 0.117 | 0.081 | 0.019 |
| Industry | 0.075 | 0.397 | 0.145 |
| Services | 0.050 | 0.173 | 0.144 |

Source: pre-1998-99 figures, Sastry et al. (2002); 1998-99 figures, author's calculations.

**Table 4.**
**Distribution of activities with above average sectoral intensity**

| Activity Categories (number) | Agriculture intensive | | | Industry intensive | | | Services intensive | | |
|---|---|---|---|---|---|---|---|---|---|
| | Direct intensity | | Direct & indirect intensity 1993-94 | Direct intensity | | Direct & indirect intensity 1993-94 | Direct intensity | | Direct & indirect intensity 1993-94 |
| | 1993-94 | 1998-99 | | 1993-94 | 1998-99 | | 1993-94 | 1998-99 | |
| Agricultural activities (22) | 15 | 14 | 15 | 0 | 0 | 0 | 1 | 1 | 1 |
| Industrial activities (80) | 18 | 19 | 22 | 57 | 61 | 55 | 56 | 57 | 59 |
| Service activities (13) | 1 | 1 | 1 | 3 | 3 | 3 | 6 | 7 | 2 |
| Total activities (115) | 34 | 34 | 38 | 60 | 64 | 58 | 63 | 65 | 62 |
| Average intensity | 7 | 6 | 12 | 29 | 24 | 59 | 15 | 14 | 30 |

Source: 1993-94 figures, Hansda (2001, Table 5); 1998-99 figures, from author's calculations.

## Table 5.
## Sectoral intensity — aggregate categories

| Sector | Agriculture | | | Industry | | | Services | | |
|---|---|---|---|---|---|---|---|---|---|
| | G (Rank) | | G* (Rank) | G (Rank) | | G* (Rank) | G (Rank) | | G* (Rank) |
| | 93-94 | 98-99 | 93-94 | 93-94 | 98-99 | 93-94 | 93-94 | 98-99 | 93-94 |
| Agriculture | 0.131 (2) | 0.093 (3) | 0.172 (3) | 0.092 (7) | 0.091 (7) | 0.211 (8) | 0.057 (10) | 0.051 (9) | 0.122 (8) |
| Allied activities | 0.179 (1) | 0.173 (1) | 0.220 (1) | 0.039 (10) | 0.038 (10) | 0.127 (9) | 0.068 (8) | 0.049 (10) | 0.121 (9) |
| Mining & quarrying | 0.000 (9) | 0.000 (9) | 0.028 (9) | 0.190 (5) | 0.143 (6) | 0.358 (5) | 0.070 (7) | 0.059 (8) | 0.152 (7) |
| Manufacturing | 0.091 (3) | 0.110 (2) | 0.179 (2) | 0.420 (2) | 0.417 (2) | 0.811 (1) | 0.185 (2) | 0.179 (2) | 0.385 (1) |
| Construction | 0.024 (5) | 0.021 (5) | 0.095 (4) | 0.362 (3) | 0.340 (3) | 0.706 (3) | 0.202 (1) | 0.171 (4) | 0.381 (2) |
| Electricity, gas & water supply | 0.004 (8) | 0.003 (8) | 0.038 (8) | 0.453 (1) | 0.440 (1) | 0.800 (2) | 0.166 (4) | 0.176 (3) | 0.330 (3) |
| Transport, storage & communication | 0.023 (6) | 0.005 (7) | 0.074 (5) | 0.282 (4) | 0.276 (4) | 0.560 (4) | 0.175 (3) | 0.191 (1) | 0.317 (4) |
| Trade, hotels & restaurants | 0.034 (4) | 0.048 (4) | 0.060 (6) | 0.091 (8) | 0.083 (8) | 0.214 (7) | 0.160 (5) | 0.131 (6) | 0.227 (5) |
| Financing, insurance & real estate | 0.000 (10) | 0.000 (10) | 0.006 (10) | 0.044 (9) | 0.056 (9) | 0.089 (10) | 0.061 (9) | 0.105 (7) | 0.087 (10) |
| Personal, social & other services | 0.016 (7) | 0.013 (6) | 0.048 (7) | 0.152 (6) | 0.157 (5) | 0.301 (6) | 0.090 (6) | 0.144 (5) | 0.167 (6) |
| Average Intensity | 0.050 | 0.064 | 0.092 | 0.212 | 0.241 | 0.418 | 0.123 | 0.139 | 0.229 |

Source: 1993-94 figures, Hansda (2001), Table 6; 1998-99 figures, from author's calculations.
Definitions: G: Direct sectoral intensity; G*: Direct and indirect sectoral intensity.

## Table 6.
## Leading sectors, 1998-99

|  | Relative growth factor | Growth rate (base 6 percent) |
|---|---|---|
| Electricity, gas & water supply | 1.0108 | 7.14 |
| Iron, steel and ferro-alloys | 1.0049 | 6.52 |
| Non-ferrous basic metals | 1.0037 | 6.40 |
| Other services | 1.0031 | 6.32 |
| Other transport services | 1.0028 | 6.29 |
| Railway transport services | 1.0020 | 6.21 |
| Coal and lignite | 1.0018 | 6.19 |
| Trade | 1.0016 | 6.17 |
| Miscellaneous manufacturing | 1.0016 | 6.17 |
| Inorganic heavy chemicals | 1.0013 | 6.14 |

*Source: author's calculations.*


## Table 7.
## Categorization of services by extent of
## trade liberalization and growth

|  | Substantially liberalized | Moderately liberalized | Less than moderately liberalized / Restricted |
|---|---|---|---|
| High growth (10% and above) | Software Services H Telecommunication M | Banking M Insurance M Travel H Health L Education L | |
| Moderate growth (5-9%) | | | Legal L |
| Low growth (0-5%) | Road Transport L | Construction L Air Transport M | Professional Services, e.g., Postal, Accountancy L Rail Transport L |

*Source: Banga (2005), Table 5.*
*Obs.: H: High share in exports of services (10% and above) ; M: Moderate share in exports of services (5-9%) ; L: Low share in exports of services (less than 5%).*

### Table 8.
### Growth of employment by sectors

| Industry | Employed workers, millions (%) | | | Annual growth rates, % | |
|---|---|---|---|---|---|
| | 1983 | 1993-94 | 1999-2000 | 1983-94 | 1994-2000 |
| **Primary** | **208.99 (69.0)** | **245.16 (65.5)** | **239.83 (60.4)** | **1.60** | **-0.34** |
| 1. Agriculture | | | | 1.51 | -0.34 |
| 2. Mining and quarrying | | | | 4.16 | -2.85 |
| **Secondary** | **41.66 (13.8)** | **55.53 (14.8)** | **66.91 (16.8)** | **2.91** | **3.14** |
| 3. Manufacturing | | | | 2.14 | 2.05 |
| 4. Electricity, gas and water supply | | | | 4.50 | -0.88 |
| 5. Construction | | | | 5.32 | 7.09 |
| **Tertiary** | **52.11 (17.2)** | **73.76 (19.7)** | **90.26 (22.7)** | **3.53** | **2.42** |
| 6. Trade | | | | 3.57 | 5.04 |
| 7. Transport, storage and communication | | | | 3.24 | 6.04 |
| 8. Financial services | | | | 7.18 | 6.20 |
| 9. Community, social and personal services | | | | 2.90 | 0.55 |
| **Total employment** | **302.76 (100)** | **374.45 (100)** | **397.00 (100)** | **2.04** | **0.98** |

Source: adapted from Joshi (2004).

### Table 9.
### Shares of different sectors in increase of employment (million)

| Sectors | 1983 | 1993-94 | Increase during 1983-93 | Share in increase, % | 1999-2000 | Increase during 1994-2000 | Share in increase, % |
|---|---|---|---|---|---|---|---|
| Primary | 208.99 | 245.16 | 36.17 | 50.5 | 239.83 | -5.33 | -23.6 |
| Secondary | 41.66 | 55.53 | 13.87 | 19.3 | 66.91 | 11.38 | 50.4 |
| Tertiary | 52.11 | 73.76 | 21.65 | 30.2 | 90.26 | 16.50 | 73.2 |
| Total | 302.76 | 374.45 | 71.69 | 100.00 | 397.00 | 22.55 | 100.00 |

Source: adapted from Joshi (2004).

## Table 10.
### Sectoral employment elasticities

| Sectors | 1983 to 1987-88 | 1983 to 1993-94 | 1993-94 to 1999-2000 |
|---|---|---|---|
| Agriculture | 0.87 | 0.70 | 0.01 |
| Mining and quarrying | 1.25 | 0.59 | -0.41 |
| Manufacturing | 0.59 | 0.38 | 0.33 |
| Electricity, gas and water supply | 0.30 | 0.63 | -0.52 |
| Construction | 2.81 | 0.86 | 0.82 |
| Trade, hotels and restaurants | 0.87 | 0.68 | 0.62 |
| Transport, storage and communication | 0.47 | 0.55 | 0.63 |
| Financing, insurance, real estate and business services | 0.49 | 0.45 | 0.64 |
| Community, social and personal services | 0.52 | 0.68 | -0.25 |
| **All** | **0.68** | **0.52** | **0.16** |

*Source: Planning Commission (2002).*

## Table 11.
### Structural change in selected Indian states

| | | Agriculture | Industry | Services | Sum of absolute values | Structural change rank |
|---|---|---|---|---|---|---|
| Andhra Pradesh | 1993-94 share | 35.9 | 15.5 | 48.5 | 100.0 | |
| | 2003-04 share | 28.3 | 15.3 | 56.4 | 100.0 | |
| | Per cent change | -21.3 | -1.6 | 16.3 | 39.2 | 14 |
| | Percentage point change | -7.7 | -0.3 | 7.9 | 15.8 | 13 |
| Bihar | 1993-94 share | 51.4 | 5.2 | 43.5 | 100.0 | |
| | 2003-04 share | 38.0 | 2.8 | 59.1 | 100.0 | |
| | Per cent change | -26.0 | -45.3 | 36.1 | 107.4 | 2 |
| | Percentage point change | -13.4 | -2.3 | 15.7 | 31.4 | 4 |
| Chhattisgarh | 1993-94 share | 34.3 | 30.0 | 35.7 | 100.0 | |
| | 2003-04 share | 23.8 | 30.1 | 46.1 | 100.0 | |
| | Per cent change | -30.5 | 0.3 | 29.1 | 59.8 | 10 |
| | Percentage point change | -10.5 | 0.1 | 10.4 | 20.9 | 9 |
| Goa | 1993-94 share | 15.9 | 32.4 | 51.7 | 100.0 | |
| | 2003-04 share | 7.8 | 32.5 | 59.7 | 100.0 | |
| | Per cent change | -51.1 | 0.5 | 15.4 | 66.9 | 9 |
| | Percentage point change | -8.1 | 0.1 | 8.0 | 16.2 | 12 |
| Gujarat | 1993-94 share | 24.3 | 30.9 | 44.9 | 100.0 | |
| | 2003-04 share | 21.3 | 30.5 | 48.2 | 100.0 | |
| | Per cent change | -12.1 | -1.4 | 7.5 | 21.0 | 18 |
| | Percentage point change | -2.9 | -0.4 | 3.4 | 6.7 | 18 |
| Haryana | 1993-94 share | 42.6 | 18.0 | 39.4 | 100.0 | |
| | 2003-04 share | 25.8 | 24.0 | 50.3 | 100.0 | |
| | Per cent change | -39.6 | 33.4 | 27.6 | 100.5 | 3 |
| | Percentage point change | -16.9 | 6.0 | 10.9 | 33.7 | 3 |
| Jharkhand | 1993-94 share | 26.4 | 38.8 | 34.9 | 100.0 | |
| | 2003-04 share | 24.2 | 35.9 | 39.9 | 100.0 | |
| | Per cent change | -8.2 | -7.5 | 14.5 | 30.1 | 17 |
| | Percentage point change | -2.2 | -2.9 | 5.1 | 10.1 | 17 |

continued

| | | Agriculture | Industry | Services | Sum of absolute values | Structural change rank |
|---|---|---|---|---|---|---|
| Karnataka | 1993-94 share | 37.5 | 19.2 | 43.3 | 100.0 | |
| | 2003-04 share | 19.3 | 18.9 | 61.8 | 100.0 | |
| | Per cent change | -48.5 | -1.7 | 42.8 | 93.0 | 5 |
| | Percentage point change | -18.2 | -0.3 | 18.5 | 37.0 | 2 |
| Kerala | 1993-94 share | 32.0 | 12.3 | 55.7 | 100.0 | |
| | 2003-04 share | 18.6 | 10.9 | 70.4 | 100.0 | |
| | Per cent change | -41.8 | -10.7 | 26.4 | 78.9 | 7 |
| | Percentage point change | -13.4 | -1.3 | 14.7 | 29.4 | 6 |
| Madhya Pradesh | 1993-94 share | 42.9 | 16.0 | 41.1 | 100.0 | |
| | 2003-04 share | 33.7 | 16.4 | 49.9 | 100.0 | |
| | Per cent change | -21.5 | 2.5 | 21.5 | 45.6 | 12 |
| | Percentage point change | -9.2 | 0.4 | 8.8 | 18.5 | 11 |
| Maharashtra | 1993-94 share | 20.7 | 26.4 | 52.9 | 100.0 | |
| | 2003-04 share | 12.7 | 19.8 | 67.4 | 100.0 | |
| | Per cent change | -38.5 | -25.0 | 27.6 | 91.1 | 6 |
| | Percentage point change | -8.0 | -6.6 | 14.6 | 29.2 | 7 |
| Orissa | 1993-94 share | 44.3 | 13.8 | 41.9 | 100.0 | |
| | 2003-04 share | 36.5 | 13.9 | 49.6 | 100.0 | |
| | Per cent change | -17.5 | 0.8 | 18.2 | 36.5 | 15 |
| | Percentage point change | -7.8 | 0.1 | 7.6 | 15.5 | 14 |
| Punjab | 1993-94 share | 48.2 | 15.3 | 36.4 | 100.0 | |
| | 2003-04 share | 38.3 | 15.6 | 46.1 | 100.0 | |
| | Per cent change | -20.7 | 1.9 | 26.6 | 49.1 | 11 |
| | Percentage point change | -10.0 | 0.3 | 9.7 | 19.9 | 10 |
| Rajasthan | 1993-94 share | 35.2 | 15.5 | 49.3 | 100.0 | |
| | 2003-04 share | 29.1 | 16.3 | 54.5 | 100.0 | |
| | Per cent change | -17.2 | 5.5 | 10.5 | 33.2 | 16 |
| | Percentage point change | -6.0 | 0.8 | 5.2 | 12.1 | 16 |

continued

| | | Agriculture | Industry | Services | Sum of absolute values | Structural change rank |
|---|---|---|---|---|---|---|
| Tamil Nadu | 1993-94 share | 25.6 | 27.2 | 47.1 | 100.0 | |
| | 2003-04 share | 12.1 | 18.2 | 69.7 | 100.0 | |
| | Per cent change | -52.8 | -33.2 | 47.9 | 133.9 | 1 |
| | Percentage point change | -13.5 | -9.0 | 22.6 | 45.2 | 1 |
| Uttar Pradesh | 1993-94 share | 41.1 | 15.3 | 43.6 | 100.0 | |
| | 2003-04 share | 36.3 | 13.1 | 50.6 | 100.0 | |
| | Per cent change | -11.7 | -14.0 | 16.0 | 41.7 | 13 |
| | Percentage point change | -4.8 | -2.1 | 7.0 | 13.9 | 15 |
| Uttaranchal | 1993-94 share | 39.8 | 17.0 | 43.2 | 100.0 | |
| | 2003-04 share | 31.1 | 10.3 | 58.5 | 100.0 | |
| | Per cent change | -21.7 | -39.2 | 35.4 | 96.3 | 4 |
| | Percentage point change | -8.6 | -6.7 | 15.3 | 30.6 | 5 |
| West Bengal | 1993-94 share | 34.7 | 17.9 | 47.4 | 100.0 | |
| | 2003-04 share | 27.1 | 13.3 | 59.6 | 100.0 | |
| | Per cent change | -21.8 | -25.8 | 25.7 | 73.4 | 8 |
| | Percentage point change | -7.6 | -4.6 | 12.2 | 24.4 | 8 |

*Source: author's calculations from RBI (2006).*

### Table 12.
### Per capita net state domestic product (NSDP)
### changes in selected Indian states

| State | 1993-94 | 2003-04 | Growth (percent) | Growth rank | Structural change index |
|---|---|---|---|---|---|
| Andhra Pradesh | 7,416 | 11,756 | 58.52 | 5 | 15.8 |
| Bihar | 3,037 | 3,557 | 17.12 | 18 | 31.4 |
| Jharkhand | 5,897 | 7,732 | 31.12 | 13 | 20.9 |
| Goa | 16,558 | 30,506 | 84.24 | 1 | 16.2 |
| Gujarat | 9,796 | 16,780 | 71.29 | 3 | 6.7 |
| Haryana | 11,079 | 15,752 | 42.18 | 9 | 33.7 |
| Karnataka | 7,838 | 13,141 | 67.66 | 4 | 10.1 |
| Kerala | 7,983 | 12,328 | 54.43 | 7 | 37 |
| Madhya Pradesh | 6,584 | 8,284 | 25.82 | 16 | 29.4 |
| Chhattisgarh | 6,539 | 8,383 | 28.20 | 14 | 18.5 |
| Maharashtra | 12,183 | 16,479 | 35.26 | 11 | 29.2 |
| Orissa | 4,896 | 6,487 | 32.50 | 12 | 15.5 |
| Punjab | 12,710 | 16,119 | 26.82 | 15 | 19.9 |
| Rajasthan | 6,182 | 9,685 | 56.66 | 6 | 12.1 |
| Tamil Nadu | 8,955 | 12,976 | 44.90 | 8 | 45.2 |
| Uttar Pradesh | 5,066 | 5,975 | 17.94 | 17 | 13.9 |
| Uttaranchal | 6,896 | 9,471 | 37.34 | 10 | 30.6 |
| West Bengal | 6,756 | 11,612 | 71.88 | 2 | 24.4 |

Source: author's calculations from RBI (2006).

# Acknowledgements

I am grateful to David O'Connor and Mónica Kjöllerström for very perceptive and detailed comments. I also greatly benefited from comments on an earlier draft from T.N. Srinivasan, and from comments on my presentation by Dilek Aykut and participants in a project workshop at UNDESA. I am grateful to Shubhashis Gangopadhyay for providing me with more recent input-output data, Sanjay Hansda for his advice on the data, and Mukul Majumdar and Ilaria Osella for guidance on calculating leading sectors. Todd Feldman provided outstanding research assistance. Remaining errors are my responsibility.

## Notes

1 As observed by authors such as Hansda (2002) and Gordon and Gupta (2004), most of this increase in the service sector's share of GDP came in the 1990s, not the 1980s. In keeping with this, the service sector's contribution to GDP growth was highest for the decade of the 1990s.

2 I am grateful to David O'Connor for emphasizing these points to me.

3 Ricardo, Malthus, James Mill, and others shared this perspective, as did Marx, whose views influenced the national accounting systems of communist countries, where services were not counted in national output and as a result service industries were neglected. See Delaunay and Gadrey (1991) for a detailed historical account. Hansda (2001) also provides a survey of some of the literature on the role of services in an economy.

4 These two references are merely illustrative of a significant literature in the field of marketing, which focuses on how firms' strategies must be tailored to deal with services as opposed to product marketing, including in particular the issue of managing service quality and customer relationships. Rust and Chung (2005) survey this literature, the concerns of which are quite distinct from the focus in this chapter.

5 In the marketing literature, Lovelock and Gummeson (2004) and Vargo and Lusch (2004) have recently challenged this framework, but from a particular, pragmatic perspective, arguing that these differences of degree have shrunk over time, for many kinds of services. This point can be made more generally, and we shall develop it further in this chapter.

6 Splintering means separating service activities into components that can then be performed by different organizations, i.e., outsourced. Other examples, in addition to the software testing component of software development, are medical transcription and basic reading of x-rays as components of healthcare, checking for routine arithmetic or other errors as part of tax preparation services, and basic financial calculations as part of investment advice services. Outsourcing may allow economies of scale and specialization to be reaped, and may also permit the use of lower cost locations, as in offshoring.

7 This categorization is slightly different from that used in the United Nations International Standard Industrial Classification (ISIC): see Banga (2005).

8 Based on this analysis, these authors suggest that sustained growth of 7 per cent or more is feasible for India. Mukherji (2006), in a recent paper, suggests that 8 per cent is feasible, but not 10 per cent, though there is no exact connection between his qualitative discussion and these quantitative projections. Kelkar (2004) and Shome (2006) both provide arguments that 10 per cent growth is feasible with the right policies in place. In April 2006, the Prime Minister, Manmohan Singh, articulated this figure as a feasible target in a speech to an industry group. Evaluating the feasibility of such growth targets requires an understanding of the determinants of India's growth, and this chapter may have a contribution in that direction.

9 The methodology consists of taking all possible structural break dates, calculating each possible F-statistic, and using the maximum of these statistics to choose an initial break date. This is termed the sup-F statistic. The process is repeated for sub samples on either side of the initially identified break to isolate additional break dates. See Wallack (2003) for details and references on the statistical methodology.

10 This can be seen in the broad confidence intervals for the break years reported in Wallack (2003) – for example, that for GDP is 1973 to 1987, while for the trade, transport, storage and communication sector, it is 1988 to 1996.

11 This point is recognized by Wallack, and also emerges from the analysis of Bosworth, Collins and Virmani (2007).

12 She also finds weaker evidence for a break in 1993 for finance and related services. Gordon and Gupta (2004) suggest that there was a structural break in overall services sector growth in 1980 (their Figure 4), but the statistical methodology for this conclusion is not explained.

13 Hansda compares a services deflator with the GDP deflator. These observations on relative price trends are repeated and updated by Gordon and Gupta (2004, Figure 8). They analyze this as follows. If the growth in services output was largely a demand side phenomenon, there would not be this decline in the relative price of the fast-growing services. On the other hand, prices in sub-sectors that grew at trend rates rose faster than the GDP deflator, suggesting that a different mix of supply and demand factors were at work there. T.N. Srinivasan (personal communication) has suggested to me that the deflators used for these calculations are unreliable in their construction. That point is also raised in Bosworth, Collins and Virmani (2007).

14 In some cases, they appear to confuse statements about growth levels with growth differences. For example, banking services grew at 11.9 per cent in the 1980s and 12.7 per cent in the 1990s, which is not much of an acceleration, but well above the total for the service sector (Gordon and Gupta, Table 1). On the other hand, personal services grew at 2.4 per cent in the 1980s and 5 per cent in the 1990s, a greater acceleration, but below the overall service sector growth in each case.

15 There have been conflicting analyses of India's tax-GDP ratio, but Rao (2005) seems to provide definite support for the assertion made here.

16 This conclusion is reached from a cross-country regression which controls for per capita GDP as well as land area. See Kochhar et al. (2006), Table 2. The rationale for the size variable is not apparent.

17 Gordon and Gupta (2004, Section 2) also provide a brief survey of some of this kind of evidence. Dasgupta and Singh (2005a, b) provide further cross-country regressions.

18 The calculation is as follows. The input-output coefficients for services input in agriculture and industry increased by 0.03 and 0.04, respectively, during the 1980s. These coefficient changes would have increased demand for services (as a first round

effect) by $\Delta Y_s = 0.03Y_A + 0.04Y_I$, where $Y_i$ is the output in sector i. Dividing through by total output Y and evaluating at the average sectoral shares during the 1980s (0.35, 0.25 and 0.40 for agriculture, industry and services, respectively), yields $\Delta Y_s/Y_s = ((0.03*0.35) + (0.04*0.25)) /0.4 = 0.051$.

19 The calculation is available from the author: see Table 3 for the data. Gordon and Gupta argue that since some of the fastest growing service sub-sectors in the 1990s were geared toward final consumption (e.g., community services, communication services, and hotels and restaurants), this would fit with splintering having been less important in boosting growth in the 1990s versus the 1980s. On the other hand, business and financial services growth was also important in the 1990s, consistent with splintering of these services out of manufacturing.

20 This factor can apply to certain goods as well, especially consumer durables. The Japanese decision to pursue automobile production in the 1950s was apparently based on the high income elasticity of demand for automobiles.

21 Recall Hansda's discussion of changes in the sectoral terms of trade, summarized in the previous section. Again, the data on sectoral price deflators must be applied with caution.

22 The immediate justification for this number is not provided, but appears to be based on the Sastry et al. input-output matrix, with some assumptions about input usage for services exports relative to services overall.

23 The time series estimates use annual data from 1952 to 2000. In sub-sector specific regressions, the dependent variable is the annual growth rate for that services sub-sector. The right hand side variables include the growth rates of the commodity producing sectors, the volume of the external trade of goods, and the value of exports in services, and dummies for the 1980s and 1990s. To smooth out noise in the annual data, the authors use three-year moving average growth rates. Alternative regressions with separate dummies for the two halves of the 1990s also fit with the observation that policy reform in services such as communications only took hold in the latter part of the decade. The pooled regressions are estimated for the period 1970-2000, with similar averaging and explanatory variables. The main difference in these regressions is that sub-sector specific dummies are used, measuring whether reforms were implemented in each sub-sector. These dummy variables turn out to be most significant.

24 In the absence of direct data on services inputs at the disaggregate level used by the authors, they calculate services as a residual, i.e., the difference between total input costs and the cost of materials and energy.

25 A set of regressions by Dasgupta and Singh (2005b) using aggregate data is relevant in this context. Using cross-section data for 42 developing countries, they find that manufacturing and services have similar, strongly positive effects on TFP growth.

26 I am grateful to David O'Connor for raising this issue. The impact of splintering on manufacturing productivity would depend on the relative productivity of ancillary service activities versus core manufacturing activities. If the service activities are both low productivity and more efficient when outsourced, there would be two sources of measured productivity gains in manufacturing.

27 While Coase (1937) does not use the term, his 'marketing costs' are the essence of the modern concept. Williamson, for example (1975, 1981), extends the analysis of transaction costs to relationships within organizations, which allows us to interpret the work of Bresnahan et al. (2002) and the studies in OECD (2004) in a transaction cost context.

28 The economic intuition is that, as intermediate goods producers must increase their prices to compensate for transaction costs, the substitutability of undifferentiated

labour for their inputs reduces their share of final value, and forces marginal intermediate goods out of production.

29 Singh (2004b, 2005) consider how these impacts can be realized in practice in rural areas, using case studies and examples from fieldwork in rural India.

30 See also Gulyani (2001) for an empirical analysis of transportation costs and their impacts on the Indian automobile industry. I am grateful to David O'Connor for the point made in the text, and this reference.

31 As noted earlier, their calculations are used by Gordon and Gupta (2004) in the latter's informal growth accounting exercise. The Sastry et al. approach to linkages draws on earlier work of Ahluwalia and Rangarajan (1986).

32 An alternative to the production linkages in Table 3 uses the Leontief inverse to calculate what can be termed demand linkages (Sastry et al., 2002, Table 4). While statements about production intensity are based on the direct input-output coefficients, summarized in a "Leontief" matrix A, the matrix $(I - A)-1$ (the Leontief inverse), represents the direct and indirect requirements of gross output in all activities needed to support one unit of final demand in each activity: these requirements are the basis for considering demand linkages. As one would expect, agriculture became more connected to industry and services, in terms of demand for the outputs of those sectors. Sastry et al. calculate that during 1968-69, a rise in agricultural output by one unit would have raised demand for industrial goods by 0.087 units, and demand for services by 0.035 units. In 1993-94, on the other hand, one unit of increase in the agricultural output would have raised the demand for industrial goods by 0.297 units, with this sharp increase having occurred largely in the 1980s. Conversely, and as expected, demand linkages of industry weakened with respect to agriculture (again, largely in the 1980s). However, they increased by 50 per cent in the 1980s with respect to services, with a further increase by 1993-94. Demand linkages of the services sector remained almost constant in the case of agriculture over the whole time period, whereas there was an increase in the demand linkages with industry, again mostly in the 1980s. The overall story of the changes in demand linkages is thus consistent with that of production linkages.

33 The issue of linkages is one important aspect of the national economic benefits of pursuing the creation of an international financial services hub. For example, de Jonquieres (2006), in drawing an analogy with national airlines, criticizes the desirability of such a move if it merely serves as a national status symbol. One can conjecture that the linkages from a vibrant, diverse financial sector would be much greater than those from simply operating a national airline, but this needs to be established empirically. Interestingly, Singapore Airlines is a success story partly because it is a national carrier for a regional travel and trade hub – this has an obvious linkage interpretation.

34 The procedure is as follows. The elements of the Leontief inverse matrix (footnote 33) are adjusted by weighting by the final demand vector. Row sums yield the total forward linkage for each sector or sub-sector, and the individual row sums relative to their average yield an index or normalized measure of the forward linkage in each sector. The same procedure with column sums yields an index of backward linkages. In each case, indirect as well as direct linkages are accounted for, since the Leontief inverse is used.

35 Detailed calculations are available from the author. These results are similar to Hansda's figures for 1993-94 data. He finds that 46 of 115 activities – 7 of 22 agricultural activities, 31 of 80 industrial activities and 8 of 13 services activities – had relative backward index values above one. For the forward linkage indices, 15 out of the total of 115 activities – 5 out of 22 agricultural activities, 3 out of 80 industrial activities and 7 out of 13 services activities – had indices greater than one.

36 In particular, the theory is developed for a closed economy. Mukul Majumdar (personal communication) has pointed out to me that this assumption may have been a tenable approximation for the 1989 data used in their paper, but is less appropriate for the current Indian economy. Nevertheless, we follow the previous methodology, leaving extensions to an open economy to future research.

37 Majumdar and Ossella also consider efficiency improvements in combinations of sectors. We leave that to future research as well. Note that the approach is similar in spirit to, and considerably predates, the more recent attempt by Hausmann, Rodrik and Velasco (2005) to formalize the relative importance of policy or sectoral constraints. One difference is the focus here on technical efficiency, rather than policy, but the two are naturally connected.

38 Since one is looking at a ratio of growth, the discount factor cancels out and does not affect the calculations.

39 Sastry et al. have construction in the services sector, while Hansda includes it in industry. Neither author discusses this choice, and the implications of this different classification are unclear.

40 An important conceptualization in this context is that ICTs are 'general purpose technologies' (GPTs), distinguished by pervasiveness, technological dynamism and innovational complementarities. See Bresnahan and Trajtenberg (1995), where the term was introduced, and Singh (2003) for a discussion of its applicability to ICTs in India.

41 Thus, the argument here is that learning is much more general than specialized or context-specific learning: cf. Ethiraj et al. (2005). The importance of reputation in the Indian software industry has been established in Banerjee and Duflo (2000).

42 The involvement of multinationals and the need to serve foreign clients in ITES led to an emphasis on quality of workspaces, and of reliable transportation for employees, affecting both construction and transportation: see, e.g., Khan (2003).

43 Rodrik (2006) calculates that India's exports of goods are also more skill-intensive than would be predicted by overall factor endowments. Interestingly, China's exports show the same pattern: Rodrik argues that this indicates the role of policy. This issue is taken up in Section 9.

44 See also Banga (2005) for additional data on services and overall trade for India.

45 For a discussion of India's comparative advantage in the IT services sector, see Singh (2004c) and the references therein.

46 These distinctions may seem obvious to the economist, but have been blurred in US policy debates, as is discussed in more detail by Bhagwati et al. (2004).

47 The models considered are: 1. A single good, produced with two inputs, labour and capital. Electronically hiring labour from abroad increases welfare, but labour loses while capital benefits. 2. A two-good, three-factor model, with trade in goods. Outsourcing increases national income for a small country, but terms-of-trade effects may cause welfare losses. 3. A three-good two-factor model where a nontraded service becomes tradable. Here owners of both factors of production become better off.

48 This classification is based on the constraints on the physical location of producer and consumer in realizing the transaction, The four "modes of supply" are:

Mode 1: cross-border supply of service (i.e., not requiring the physical movement of supplier or customer);

Mode 2: provision implying movement of the consumer to the location of the supplier;

Mode 3: services sold in the territory of a Member by (legal) entities that have established a presence there but originate in the territory of another Member;

Mode 4: provision of services requiring the temporary movement of natural persons.

49 An important domestic constraint identified by Banga in the health sector is that it is on the concurrent list of constitutional assignments, so there is a complex set of state and local regulations. Thus, even without a cap on FDI in health services, the share of health services in total trade and FDI is low (only 0.4 per cent of total FDI approvals are in health).

50 Joshi (2004) characterizes the 1980s as a pre-reform period, but recent work, as summarized in Section 2 above, suggests that this sharp distinction may not be completely justified. Data for 2000-02 also suggests caution in associating reform with slow employment growth.

51 India's labour laws introduce rigidities, and although there is considerable de facto labour market flexibility (Sharma, 2006), it comes about through costly methods of bypassing labour laws and regulations – these costs would discourage employment.

52 In particular, some service sub-sectors appear to be especially capital intensive. Panagariya (2006) calculates that finance, insurance, real estate and business services, which accounted for 13 per cent of the GDP in 1999-00, employed only 1.2 per cent of the labour force.

53 Dasgupta and Singh (2005b), based on calculations from NSSO data, report that, comparing the two periods 1987-88 to 1993-94 and 1993-94 to 1999-2000, manufacturing employment growth increased from 1.23 per cent to 2.58. However, the organized manufacturing sector had almost no growth in employment during the latter period (0.87 per cent), while informal manufacturing sector employment (over 80 per cent of the total) grew at 2.95 per cent. A similar point is made in more detail in Sundaram (2004). He also distinguishes carefully between private and public sector employment, discusses some problems in the statistics, and notes that some of the overall employment slowdown is explained by reductions in female workforce participation associated with poverty reduction.

54 This discussion is in terms of overall employment elasticities. Note that the sub-sectoral elasticities in Table 9 indicate that the recent decline in employment elasticities has been concentrated in a few sectors, which include large proportions of employment.

55 For example, see the evidence presented in Bosworth, Collins and Virmani (2007).

56 A similar point is made by Murphy, Shleifer and Vishny (1989a) in the context of a static model. This idea is also related in broad terms to the 'big push' view of development advanced in the 1940s by Rosenstein-Rodan – see Murphy, Shleifer and Vishny (1989b) for detailed references and a formal model.

57 In fact, economists seem to be in total agreement here – see also Kochhar et al. (2006), and the comments by Banerjee (2006).

58 Of course, one still needs sensible economic policies that make sure that the demand for labour is not stifled. For decades, India was producing more well-trained graduates than it could productively employ in the private sector.

59 The states were selected by excluding all special category states except Uttaranchal, which was included as it was formerly part of Uttar Pradesh. The results reported are not sensitive to excluding Uttaranchal, or the small general category state of Goa.

60 This last result was qualitatively insensitive to omitting Goa and Gujarat: the sign did not change. It should be noted that the initial year NSDP figure for Gujarat appears to be surprisingly low.

61 For example, Kamath (2005) uses a 2003 survey made of Indian youth by Taylor Nelson Sofres (TNS), an Indian market research agency, and argues that consumption patterns have changed more than have deeper attitudes towards parents, marriage and religion.

62 Pandit (2002) does try to incorporate the growth costs of environmental protection into a simple aggregate macroeconometric model for India. Since these costs are borne independently of the pattern of development, there is no implication for the environment of changes in the sectoral distribution of growth. However, one could conceivably calibrate an extended version of Pandit's model to explore differential growth implications of environmental protection, and even allow for feedback effects from such protection. Pandit suggests the latter, but does not implement it in his simulations.

63 It is useful to relate these concerns to the discussion of linkages and leading sectors in Section 5. Neither IT nor financial services showed up as leading sectors in that analysis, which identified more traditional services sectors such as trade and transportation, as well as heavy industry sectors as having greater linkages and potential growth impacts. This may reflect the limitations of the closed-economy input-output model, and suggests that further analysis is required to reliably identify where government can make a difference beyond its basic role in providing public goods and infrastructure.

64 Here it is worth repeating the observation that financial services may matter beyond their role as measured in the input-output data. Interestingly, if one goes back in time before the industrial revolution, there was a merchant and finance (i.e., services) revolution that got the whole process going, as Sir John Hicks (1969) argued.

# Bibliography

Ahluwalia, Isher J. and C. Rangarajan (1986), Agriculture and Industry: A Study of Linkages the Indian Experience, processed, World Congress of International Economic Association, December.

Amsden, Alice (2001), The Rise of "The Rest": Challenges to the West from Late Industrializing Countries, New York, Oxford University Press, September.

Athukorala, Prema-Chandra, and Kunal Sen, (2002), Saving, Investment, and Growth in India (New Delhi: Oxford University Press).

Balakrishnan, Pulapre (2006), Benign Neglect or Strategic Intent? Contested Lineage of Indian Software Industry, Economic and Political Weekly, September 9, pp. 3865-3872.

Banga, Rashmi and B.N Goldar (2004), Contribution of Services to Output Growth Productivity in Indian Manufacturing: Pre and Post Reform, ICRIER Working Paper No. 139, August.

Banga, Rashmi (2005), Critical Issues In India's Service-Led Growth, ICRIER Working Paper No. 171, October.

Banerjee, Abhijit V. (2006), The Paradox of Indian Growth: A Comment on Kochhar et al., processed.

Banerjee, Abhijit V. and Esther Duflo (2000), Reputation Effects and the Limits of Contracting: A Study of the Indian Software Industry, Quarterly Journal of Economics 115(3), 989-1017.

Basu, I. (2003), India's Growing Urge to Splurge, Asia Times Online, http://www.atimes.com/atimes/South_Asia/EH22Df01.html, accessed January 4, 2005.

Baumol, W. J. (1967), Macroeconomics of Unbalanced Growth: The Anatomy of Urban Crises, American Economic Review 57(3), June, 415-26.

Bell, Clive and Peter L. Rousseau, (2001), Post-Independence India: A Case of Finance- Led Industrialization?" Journal of Development Economics, 65(1), pp. 153-75.

Besley, Tim, and Robin Burgess, (2004), Can Labour Regulation Hinder Economic Performance? Evidence from India, The Quarterly Journal of Economics, 119(1), 91-134.

Bhagwati, Jagdish, Arvind Panagariya and T. N. Srinivasan (2004), The Muddles over Outsourcing, Journal of Economic Perspectives, Fall.

Bhagwati, Jagdish, N. (1984), Splintering and Disembodiment of Services and Developing Nations, World Economy, 7(2), June, 133-43.

Bhagwati, Jagdish, N. (1985), Why are Services Cheaper in the Poor Countries?, Wealth and Poverty, edited by Gene Grossman Essays in Development Economics Series, vol. 1, Cambridge, MIT Press, England, Blackwell, 82-91.

Bhidé, Amar (2006), Venturesome Consumption, Innovation and Globalization, Paper for a Joint Conference of CESifo and the Centre on Capitalism and Society "Perspectives on the Performance of the Continent's Economies," Venice, 21-22 July.

Bosworth, Barry, Susan Collins and Arvind Virmani (2007), Sources of Growth in the Indian Economy, India Policy Forum, forthcoming.

Bresnahan, Timothy, Erik Brynjolfsson, and Loren Hitt (2002), Information Technology, Workplace Organization and the Demand for Skilled Labour: Firm-Level Evidence, Quarterly Journal of Economics, 117(1), 291-303.

Bresnahan, Timothy and Manuel Trajtenberg (1995), General Purpose Technologies: "Engines of Growth", Journal of Econometrics, 65, 83-108.

Chand, Satish and Kunal Sen (2002), Trade Liberalization and Productivity Growth: Evidence from Indian Manufacturing, Review of Development Economics, 6(1), 120-32.

Ciaschini, M. (1988), (ed.), Input-Output Analysis, London: Chapman and Hall Ltd.

Ciccone, Antonio and Kiminori Matsuyama (1996), Start-up Costs and Pecuniary Externalities as Barriers to Economic Development, Journal of Development Economics, 49(1), 33-59.

Claus, Iris (2002), Inter Industry Linkages in New Zealand, Working Paper 02/09, June, New Zealand Treasury.

Coase, Ronald (1937), The Nature of the Firm, Economica, 4, 386–405.

Dahlman, Carl (2006), Technology, Globalization, and International Competitiveness: Challenges for Developing Countries, UNDESA project paper draft.

Dahlman, Carl and Anuja Utz (2005) India and the Knowledge Economy: Leveraging Strengths and Opportunities, Report No. 31267-IN, World Bank, Washington DC, April.

Dasgupta, Sukti, and Ajit Singh (2005a), Will Services be the New Engine of Economic Growth in India? Centre for Business Research, University of Cambridge Working Paper No. 310, September.

Dasgupta, Sukti, and Ajit Singh (2005b), Manufacturing, services and premature de-industrialisation in developing countries: a Kaldorian empirical analysis, paper presented at WIDER Jubilee Conference in Helsinki.

De Jonquieres, Guy (2006), Asia seeks fortune in a field of dreams, Financial Times, April 17, www.ft.com (accessed through LexisNexis).

Delaunay, Jean-Claude, and Jean Gadrey, Services in Economic Thought: Three Centuries of Debate, Kluwer Academic Publishers, Boston, 1991

DeLong, J. Bradford (2003), India Since Independence: An Analytic Growth Narrative, in In Search of Prosperity: Analytic Narratives on Economic Growth, ed. Dani Rodrik, Princeton, New Jersey: Princeton University Press.

Dossani, Rafiq and Martin Kenney (2004), The Next Wave of Globalization? Exploring the Relocation of Service Provision to India, Working Paper 156, September, The Berkeley Roundtable on the International Economy

Economic Council of Canada (1991), Employment in the Service Sector, Minister of Supply and Services, Canada, Ottawa.

Ethiraj, Sendil K., Prashant Kale, M. S. Krishnan and Jitendra V. Singh (2005), Where Do Capabilities Come From and How Do They Matter? A Study in the Software Services Industry, Strategic Management Journal, 26: 25–45

Gordon, James, and Poonam Gupta (2004), Understanding India's Services Revolution, IMF Working Paper WP/04/171, September.

Griliches, Zvi (1992), (ed.), Output Measurement in the Service Sectors, NBER Studies in Income and Wealth, Vol. 56, University of Chicago Press, Chicago.

Grossman, Gene M. and Elhanan Helpman (1991), Innovation and Growth in the Global Economy, Cambridge, MA: MIT Press.

Gulyani, Sumila (2001), Effects of poor transportation on lean production and industrial clustering: Evidence from the Indian auto industry, World Development, 29(7), July, 1157-1177.

Hansda, Sanjay K. (2001), Sustainability of Services-led Growth: An Input-Output Analysis of Indian Economy, RBI Occasional Working Paper, Vol 22, No. 1,2 and 3.

Hansda, Sanjay K. (2002), Services Sector in the Indian Growth Process: Myths & Realities, The Journal of Income and Wealth, Vol. 24, No. 1 & 2, January-December 2002.

Hausmann, Ricardo, Dani Rodrik and  Andrés Velasco (2005), Growth Diagnostics, working paper, Kennedy School of Government, Harvard University.

Heimler, A. (1991), Linkages and Vertical Integration in the Chinese Economy, The Review of Economics and Statistics, 73, May, 261-267.

Hicks, John R. (1969), A Theory of Economic History, New York, Oxford University Press.

Hill, T. P. (1977), On Goods and Services, Review of Income and Wealth, 23(4), December, 315-338..

Joshi, Seema (2004), Tertiary Sector-Driven Growth in India- Impact on Employment and Poverty, Economic and Political Weekly, Special Article, September 11, 2004.

Joshi, Vijay and Ian M. D. Little (1994), India: Macroeconomics and Political Economy: 1961–91, Washington, DC: World Bank.

Kaldor, N. (1966), Causes of the Slow Rate of Economic Growth of the United Kingdom (Cambridge: Cambridge University Press).

Kamath, M.V. (2005), A Changing, Moving, Resurgent India, http://samachar.com/features/130105-features.html, accessed January 21, 2005.

Kapur, Devesh (2002), The Causes and Consequences of India's IT Boom, India Review, 1, 1, 91-110.

Kapur, Devesh and Sunil Khilnani (2006), Primary Concerns, Hindustan Times, New Delhi, April 24th and 25th.

Kapur, Devesh and Pratap Bhanu Mehta (2004), Indian Higher Education Reform: From Half-Baked Socialism to Half-Baked capitalism, CID working paper No. 108, Harvard University, September.

Kelkar, Vijay (2004), India: On the Growth Turnpike, K.R. Narayanan Oration, Australian National University.

Khan Sabith Ullah (2003), Backward & Forward Linkages in the ITES/BPO Industry, Centre for Civil Society, New Delhi.

Kochhar, Kalpana, Utsav Kumar, Raghuram Rajan, Arvind Subramanian, Ioannis Tokatlidis (2006), India's Pattern of Development: What Happened, What Follows?, IMF Working Paper WP/06/22.

Kravis, Irving B., Alan Heston, and Robert Summers (1983), The Share of Service in Economic Growth, in Global Econometrics: Essays in Honor of

Lawrence R. Klein, (ed.) F. Gerard Adams and Bert G. Hickman, Cambridge MA, 188-219.

Kuznets, S. (1959), Six Lectures on Economic Growth, The Free Press of Glencoe, New York.

Lovelock, Christopher, and Evert Gummesson (2004), Whither Services Marketing? In Search of a New Paradigm and Fresh Perspective, Journal of Service Research, 7(1), 20-41.

Majumdar, Mukul and Ilaria Ossella (1999), Identifying Leading Sectors that Accelerate the Optimal Growth Rate: A Computational Approach, in Trade, Growth and Development: Essays in Honor of Professor T.N. Srinivasan, Amsterdam: Elsevier Science, 273-290.

Melvin, James R., (1989), Trade in Services: A Theoretical Analysis, Institute for Research on Public Policy, Halifax.

Melvin, James R.. (1990), Time and Space in Economic Analysis, Canadian Journal of Economics, 23, November, 725-747..

Melvin, James R., (1995), History and Measurement in the Service Sector: A Review, Review of Income and Wealth, 41(4), December, 481-494.

Ministry of Finance (2006), Economic Survey of India, 2005-06, http://india-budget.nic.in/es2005-06/esmain.htm.

Mukherji, Joydeep (2006), Economic Growth and India's Future, Occasional Paper 26, Centre for Advanced Study of India, University of Pennsylvania.

Murphy, K.M., A. Shleifer, and R.W. Vishny, (1989a), Income Distribution, Market Size and Industrialization, Quarterly Journal of Economics, 104: 537-564.

Murphy, K.M., A. Shleifer, and R.W. Vishny, (1989b), Industrialization and the Big Push, Journal of Political Economy, 97(5) October, 1003-1026.

Murthy, N. R. Narayana (2004), The Impact of Economic Reforms on Industry in India: A Case Study of the Software Industry, in in India's Emerging Economy: Performance and Prospects in the 1990's and Beyond, ed. K. Basu, Cambridge, MA: MIT Press, 217-222.

Naastepad, C.W.M., 1999, The Budget Deficit and Macroeconomic Performance: A Real-Financial Computable General Equilibrium Model for India (New Delhi: Oxford University Press).

Ocampo, Jose Antonio (2004-5), Beyond the Washington Consensus: What Do We Mean? Journal of Post Keynesian Economics, 27(2), Winter, 293-314.

OECD (2004), The Economic Impact of ICT: Measurement, Evidence and Implications, Paris, France: OECD.

Pack, Howard and Larry Westphal (1986), Industrial Strategy and Technological Change: Theory versus Reality, Journal of Development Economics, 22, 87-128.

Panagariya, Arvind (2005), The Triumph of India's Market Reforms: The Record of the 1980s and 1990s, Policy Analysis, November 7, No. 554.

Panagariya, Arvind (2006), Transforming India, paper presented at the conference "India: An Emerging Giant," October 13-15, 2006, Columbia University.

Pandit, V. N., 2002, Sustainable Economic Growth for India: An Exercise in Macroeconomic Scenario Building, CDEDSE Working Paper 100.

Parasuraman, A., Valarie A. Zeithaml, and Leonard L. Berry (1985), 'A Conceptual Model of Service Quality and Its Implications for Future Research,' Journal of Marketing, 49 (Fall), 41-50.

Planning Commission (2001), Report of the Task Force on Employment Opportunities, chaired by Montek S. Ahluwalia, New Delhi, Government of India.

Planning Commission (2002), Report of the Special Group on Targeting Ten Million Employment Opportunities per year over the Tenth Plan Period, chaired by S.P. Gupta, New Delhi, Government of India.

Rajan, Raghuram, and Luigi Zingales (2006), The Persistence of Underdevelopment:

Institutions, Human Capital, or Constituencies? Working Paper 12093, National Bureau of Economic Research.

Rao, M. Govinda (2005), Should Indians pay more in taxes?, Business Standard, February 12, available at http://www.business-standard.com/search/story-page_new.php?leftnm=lmnu5&leftindx=5&lselect=1&autono=180612, accessed April 27, 2005

Rasmussen, P. N. (1956), Studies in Intersectoral Relations, Amsterdam: North Holland.

Reserve Bank of India (RBI) (2006), Handbook of Statistics for the Indian Economy, www.rbi.org.in.

Rodrik, Dani (2003), Introduction: What Do We Learn from Country Narratives? in Dani Rodrik, ed., In Search of Prosperity Analytic Narratives on Economic Growth, Princeton, New Jersey: Princeton University Press.

Rodrik, Dani (2006), Industrial Development: Stylized Facts and Policies, UNDESA project paper draft.

Rodrik, Dani and Arvind Subramanian (2004a),From Hindu Growth to Productivity Surge: The Mystery of the Indian Growth Transition, National Bureau of Economic Research Paper, No 10376.

Rodrik, Dani and Arvind Subramanian (2004b), Why India Can Grow at 7 Per Cent a Year or More: Projections and Reflections, Economic and Political Weekly, April 17.

Romer, Paul (1990), Endogenous Technological Change, Journal of Political Economy, October, 98(5), S71-102.

Romer, Paul (1994), New Goods, Old Theory, and the Welfare Costs of Trade Restrictions, Journal of Development Economics, 43 (1), 5-38.

Rust, Roland T., and Tuck Siong Chung (2005), Marketing Models of Service and Relationships, working paper, Robert H. Smith School of Business, University of Maryland, College Park.

Sampson, Gary P., and Richard H. Snape (1985), Identifying the Issues in Trade in Services', World Economy, 8(2), June, 171-82.

Sapir, A. & C. Winter (1994), Services Trade, in D. Greenaway and L. Winters (eds.), Surveys in International Trade, Blackwell Economic Theory and the Role of Government in East Asian Industrialization, Princeton University Press, Princeton.

Sarkar, Abhirup (1998), Endogenous Growth and the Size of the Market, Keio Economic Studies, 35 (1), 29-44.

Sastry, D.V.S., Balwant Singh, Kaushik Bhattacharya, and N. K. Unnikrishnan (2003), Sectoral Linkages and Growth Prospects: Reflections on the Indian Economy, Economic and Political Weekly, June 14, 2392-2397.

Sharma, Alakh N. (2006), Flexibility, Employment and Labour Market Reforms in India, Economic and Political Weekly, May 27, 2078-85.

Shome, Parthasarathi (2006), At the Threshold of 10 Per Cent Economic Growth?, Economic and Political Weekly, March 18.

Singh, Nirvikar (2002), Information Technology as an Engine of Broad-Based Growth in India, in The Knowledge Economy in India, ed. Parthasarathi Banerjee and Frank-Jürgen Richter, London: Palgrave/Macmillan, 34-57.

Singh, Nirvikar (2003), India's Information Technology Sector: What Contribution to Broader Economic Development? , OECD Development Centre Technical Papers, No. 207, March.

Singh, Nirvikar (2004a), Transaction Costs, Information Technology and Development, UCSC Economics Department Working Paper, October.

Singh, Nirvikar (2004b), Information Technology and Rural Development in India, in Integrating the Rural Poor into Markets, Bibek Debroy and Amir Ullah Khan, eds., New Delhi: Academic Foundation, 221-246.

Singh, Nirvikar (2004c), Information Technology and India's Economic Development, in India's Emerging Economy: Performance and Prospects in the 1990's and Beyond, ed. K. Basu, MIT Press, 223-261.

Singh, Nirvikar (2005), ICTs and Rural Development in India, University of California, Santa Cruz, USA, Draft, in progress, December.

Singh, Nirvikar and T.N. Srinivasan (2005), Indian Federalism, Economic Reform and Globalization, in Jessica Wallack and T.N. Srinivasan, eds., Federalism and Economic Reform: International Perspectives: Cambridge University Press, 301-363.

Singh, Nirvikar and T.N. Srinivasan (2006), Federalism and Economic Development in India: An Assessment, October, UCSC Economics Department Working Paper No. 625.

Srinivasan, T.N. (2003), Indian Economy: Current Problems and Future Prospects, Working Paper No. 173, Stanford Centre for International Development, July.

Srinivasan, T. N. (2005), Information Technology Enabled Services and India's Growth Prospects, Forthcoming in Lael Brainard and Susan M. Collins (editors): Offshoring White-Collar Work – The Issues and Implications, The Brookings Trade Forum.

Sundaram, K. (2004), Growth of Work Opportunities In India: 1983 – 1999-2000, Centre for Development Economics, Delhi School of Economics, India.

Triplett Jack E., and Barry P. Bosworth, Productivity in the U.S. Services Sector: New Sources of Economic Growth, Brookings Institution Press, 2004.

Vargo, Stephen L., and Robert F. Lusch (2004), Evolving to a New Dominant Logic for Marketing, Journal of Marketing, 68 (January), 1-17.

Velasco, Andres (2005), Why Doesn't Latin America Grow More, and What Can We Do About It?, working paper, Kennedy School of Government, Harvard University, October.

Wallack, Jessica (2003), Structural Breaks in Indian Macroeconomic Data, Economic and Political Weekly, October 11th, 4312-4315.

Weitzman, Martin (1998), Recombinant Growth, Quarterly Journal of Economics, 113(2), 331-360.

Williamson, Oliver E. (1975), Markets and Hierarchies: Analysis and Antitrust Implications, New York: The Free Press.

Williamson, Oliver E. (1981), The Economics of Organization: The Transaction Cost Approach, American Journal of Sociology, 87(3), 548-577.

# Part 3

# Social and Environmental Dimensions
# of Industrial Development

# Industrial development and economic growth: Implications for poverty reduction and income inequality

Matleena Kniivilä*

## 1. Introduction

The share of poor people in the global population has declined during recent decades. According to Chen and Ravallion (2004), one-third of the population of the world lived in poverty in 1981, whereas the share was 18 per cent in 2001. The decline is largely due to rapid economic growth in population-rich countries like China and India. There are, however, remarkable differences between countries and between regions in the developing world. Some regions and countries, notably in East Asia, are rapidly catching up to industrialized countries. Others, especially in Sub-Saharan Africa, are lagging far behind and the share of poor people in the population has even increased in some countries.

Industrial development has had an important role in the economic growth of countries like China, the Republic of Korea (Korea), Taiwan Province of China (Taiwan), and Indonesia. Along with accelerated growth, poverty rates have declined in many countries. Some countries have managed to achieve growth with equity, whereas in others inequality has remained high. In this chapter, the growth stories of seven countries – China, India, Korea, Taiwan, Indonesia, Mexico and Brazil – are described and discussed. The main emphasis is on describing their growth processes and strategies, the role of industrial development, the contribution of a range of policies to growth performance, and the impact of growth on poverty and income inequality. The study begins with a short theoretical discussion of the impact of industrial development on growth and the impact of growth on poverty and income inequality and then proceeds to the country examples. The final section discusses the lessons learnt.

## 2. The role of structural change in economic growth

The current understanding of economic growth is largely based on the neo-classical growth model developed by Robert Solow (1956). In the Solow model, capital accumulation is a major factor contributing to economic growth. Productivity growth – measured as an increase in output per worker – results from increases in the amount of capital per worker, or capital accumulation (e.g. Fagerberg 1994). Capital deepening will continue until the

* Pellervo Economic Research Institute, Helsinki, Finland.

economy reaches its steady state – a point at which net investments grow at the same rate as the labour force and the capital-labour ratio remains constant. The further the economy is below its steady state, the faster it should grow (see e.g. Jones 1998). In the steady state, all per capita income growth is due to exogenous technological change. The rate of technological process is assumed to be constant and not impacted by economic incentives. Several authors have found that capital and labour actually explain only a fraction of output growth and that allowing for the quality of the labour force (human capital) only partially reduces the unexplained growth – or Solow residual.

Endogenous growth theory, initiated by Romer (1986, 1990) and Lucas (1988), focuses on explaining the Solow residual. Technological change becomes endogenous to the model and is a result of the allocative choices of economic agents (see Aghion and Howitt 1998, Veloso and Soto 2001). Technological progress is driven by R&D activities which in turn are fuelled by private firms' aim to profit from inventions. Unlike other production inputs, ideas and knowledge are nonrivalrous (see Romer 1990). Moreover, new knowledge can augment the productivity of existing knowledge, yielding increasing returns to scale. Because of this, the marginal productivity of capital does not decline with increasing GDP per capita, and incomes need not converge across countries.

Technological change and innovations are essential sources of structural change. In Schumpeter's view, innovations lead to "creative destruction", a process whereby sectors and firms associated with old technologies decline and new sectors and firms emerge and grow (see Verspagen, 2000). More productive and profitable sectors and firms displace less productive and less profitable ones and aggregate productivity in the economy increases. Technological change is thus at the very centre of modern economic growth. Based on the observation that, beginning with the Industrial Revolution, technological change took place mainly in the manufacturing sector, authors like Kaldor (1970) and Cornwall (1977) have asserted that the expansion of this sector is a driving force for economic growth (see Verspagen, 2000). Moreover, Cornwall (1976, 1977) saw technological change in certain manufacturing sectors as a driving force for productivity growth in several other sectors.[1] Syrquin (1986) observes that, when overall growth accelerates, manufacturing typically leads the way and grows faster than other sectors. At low income levels, the share of manufacturing in GDP is, however, low and its immediate contribution to aggregate growth minor. When manufacturing increases its output share – often as a response to changes in domestic demand and in comparative advantage – faster sectoral growth noticeably raises the aggregate growth rates of output and labour productivity.

In developed countries, research and development (R&D) activities are the main driver of technological change. This is not, however, the only mechanism of technological change. Firms and individual employees learn by doing, increasing output and productivity even if technology or inputs remain unchanged (see e.g. Arrow 1962). As R&D activities in developing countries are relatively limited and countries are far from the technological frontier, international technology diffusion is essential for productivity growth. International economic relations, especially international trade but also foreign direct investment, are important channels of technology transfer and increased productivity growth. However, technology diffusion can only be efficient if the level of human resources is high enough, incentives for technological improvement are strong, and institutions are relatively well-functioning.

One of the driving forces for structural change is the change in domestic and international demand. At relatively low income levels, individuals spend a significant part of their income on food. As income rises, this share tends to decline, whereas demand for manufactures rises. Similarly, as income rises further, demand for manufactures increases at diminishing rates, whereas demand for services rises rapidly. Changes in demand will also change sectoral employment and output shares and impact the economy's labour productivity. Furthermore, trade has an impact on countries' specialization patterns and on the rate of industrialization or structural change within industries. Under an open trade regime, countries tend to specialize in the production of commodities for which they have a comparative advantage and import commodities which are relatively expensive to produce domestically. Trade openness is also likely to bring foreign investment into the country. This is often vital, and especially so at early stages of development. It is also likely to increase productivity as domestic companies are facing external competition.

However, the composition of foreign trade matters as well as the openness of trade (e.g. Amable, 2000; also, Rodrik in this volume). Moreover, specialization in itself does not necessarily lead to higher growth rates. This is most evident in the case of developing countries dependent on exports of primary products. As real international prices of non-oil commodities have trended downward over time and are subject to sizeable short-term fluctuations, specialization in primary production seldom promotes sustained economic growth.

## 3. Economic growth and the poor

Rapid economic growth is often essential for achieving a reduction in absolute poverty. As growth may be associated with increased income inequality, it does not automatically address the whole poverty problem. The traditional economic development literature considered highly unequal income and wealth distribution as a necessary condition for continued and rapid economic growth. The basic economic argument to justify large income inequalities was that high incomes (personal and corporate) were a necessary condition for higher savings, which in turn were needed for investment and economic growth (Todaro, 1994).

The new political economy literature, on the other hand, links greater inequality to lower future growth paths, and considers it an impediment to poverty-reducing growth, as the elasticity of poverty with respect to growth is found to decline when inequality increases (e.g. Nissanke and Thorbecke, 2004). The research in this area has not, however, been able to identify the mechanisms through which this happens (Helpman, 2004). One possible explanation is credit market failure, whereby the poor are unable to use growth-promoting investment opportunities (in physical and human capital). The higher the proportion of credit-constrained people, the lower the level of investment and the rate of growth are. High inequality, manifested in a large proportion of population having poor health, nutrition, and education, is also likely to impact on overall labour productivity and to cause slower economic growth (Todaro, 1994). Raising income levels of the poor, on the other hand, stimulates demand for domestic products and increases employment and production. More equitable distribution of income may also act as a material and psychological incentive to widespread public participation in the development process (Todaro, 1994), whereas inequality may cause political and economic instability.

Even if there is no consensus on the proportion of the world's population living in absolute poverty, it is highly likely that the share of the poor in the global population has declined during the last two decades (see e.g. Wade, 2004).[2] This is largely due to rapid economic growth in countries like China and India. Differences between regions are, however, remarkable in the developing world. Especially in Sub-Saharan Africa, the number of poor people [living on less than $1.08 a day (PPP)] significantly increased between 1981 and 2001 (Chen and Ravallion, 2004). Inequality between countries seems to have increased (e.g. Wade, 2004) . Evidence on that is, however, somewhat controversial (as examples see e.g., Sala-i-Martin, 2002, and Milanovic, 2002) and depends e.g. on the methods used, countries included, timeframe and so on.

During the 1950s and 1960s there was a widespread move towards greater egalitarianism in many developing countries. Despite a decline, however, inequality remained high in many places because of the persistence of the traditional causes of inequality like high land concentration, unequal access to education and other public services, and the dominance of the mining and plantation sectors (Cornia, 2005). During the past twenty five years, inequality has been increasing again in many developing and developed countries. In Latin America, income inequality increased in many countries in the 1980s and also in the 1990s. Trend reversal also occurred in highly successful East Asian countries – where inequality decreased between the late 1950s (or early 1960s) and the late 1970s and early 1980s – and in India and China. Over the past 50 years, income inequality in China has followed a U-shaped pattern with the turn-around point located around the mid-1980s. Due to rapid economic growth there has, however, been a dramatic reduction in overall poverty in the 1981-2001 period. In India, the Gini coefficient of household consumption expenditure fell in the 1950s as a result of the partial land reform and affirmative action in favour of low caste groups, and stayed more or less at the same level until it rose in the 1990s during the years of gradual liberalization and globalization (Cornia and Kiiski, 2001). However, due to rapid growth India has also experienced a significant decline in poverty since the 1980s.

As the growth experiences of Taiwan and South Korea show, rapid economic growth does not inevitably lead to increased inequality at the early stages of development. Taiwan and South Korea have been able to combine economic growth and industrialization with decreased inequality, even if inequality has somewhat increased during recent years. However, some other countries have been less successful. In Thailand, for instance, rapid growth was accompanied by increased income inequality (e.g. Sarntisart, 2000). In general, the impacts of inequality on growth and of growth on inequality depend very much on national characteristics and initial levels of poverty and inequality, but especially on the nature of the development process – how growth is achieved, who participates, which sectors are given priority. The choice is not so much between growth and equality, but about the type of economic growth to be pursued (Todaro, 1994) and the policies to achieve it.

## 4. Impact of industrialization and trade on the poor

Industrialization is often essential for economic growth, and for long-run poverty reduction. The pattern of industrialization, however, impacts remarkably on how the poor benefit from growth. Pro-poor economic and industrial policies focus on increasing the economic returns to the productive factors that the poor possess, e.g. raising returns to unskilled labour, whereas policies promoting higher returns to capital and land tend to increase inequality, unless they also include changes in existing patterns of concentration of physical and human capital and of land ownership. Use of capital-intensive methods instead of labour-intensive ones tends to increase income disparities, as does the employment of skill-biased technologies, especially where the level of education is low and human capital concentrated. Also, the location of industrial facilities has an impact on overall poverty reduction and inequality. As enterprises are often concentrated in urban areas – because of ready access to skilled labour force, better infrastructure, larger markets and technological spillovers (e.g. Lanjouw and Lanjouw, 2001), industrialization may increase inequality between urban and rural areas. Promoting development of rural non-agricultural activities, like production in small and medium-sized enterprises (SMEs), may decrease this disparity.

The degree of economic openness of a country can have an important influence on its pattern of specialization and industrialization. If countries are open to trade they should, according to Heckscher-Ohlin theory, specialize in the production of commodities in which they have a comparative advantage. In labour-abundant countries, trade liberalization would tend to shift production from capital-intensive import substitutes towards labour-intensive exportables. Due to this change, domestic inequality in those countries is expected to decline because of the increased demand for labour, whereas inequality would increase in countries with an abundant endowment of capital. Liberalization of foreign direct investment can also decrease inequality in capital-importing countries, but that depends in part on the degree of skill-bias of technologies employed by foreign invested firms.

In several countries, trade and investment liberalization has, indeed, decreased absolute poverty and sometimes also inequality. Bourguignon and Morrison (1990), for example, analyze the determinants of inequality in 35 developing countries and conclude that the phased removal of trade protection in manufacturing reduces the income of the richest 20 per cent of the population and increases the income of the poorest 60 per cent. Dollar and Kraay (2004), who examined impacts of increased trade on growth and inequality, found changes in growth rates to be highly correlated with changes in trade volumes. No systematic relationship between changes in trade volumes and changes in household income inequality was found, and they conclude that on average greater globalization is a force for poverty reduction. Still, the impact of trade liberalization is likely to vary between countries, depending for instance on factor endowments, and liberalization creates both winners and losers. Similarly to international trade, the impact of foreign direct investments on income inequality is likely to vary between countries. Any foreign direct investment (FDI)-inequality relation depends e.g. on the sectoral composition of FDI, its impact on demand for unskilled workers, the skill bias of technical change induced through FDI, and the regional distribution of FDI (see e.g. Cornia, 2005).

## 5. Industrialization, economic growth, poverty and inequality: Country examples

### 5.1 China

After World War II, China adopted a development strategy that included deliberate insulation from the world economy, industrialization and economic dominance of the state. As the country was falling far behind Western countries, however, it began reforming its closed and centrally planned economy in 1978. Since reforms, growth has accelerated and in the 1980s and 1990s GDP growth rates were the highest in the world, 9.9 per cent and 10.3 per cent respectively, up from 6 per cent in the 1970s (World Bank, 2004a). Growth has been especially high in industry, the compound annual growth rates being 11.3 per cent between 1980 and 2002, with services also growing fast (10.4 per cent). The share of industry in GDP has increased from 35 per cent in 1965 to 46 per cent in 2004 (World Bank 2006), whereas the share of agriculture has declined from 38 per cent to 13 per cent (Figure 1). At the same time, the ratio of exports of goods and services to GDP has increased from 3 per cent in 1970 to 34 per cent in 2004 (World Bank, 2006). Despite remarkable decline in the share of agricultural value added in GDP, the decline in agriculture's employment share has been much more modest. In 2002, 44 per cent of the labour force still worked in agriculture (World Bank, 2006). Compared with employment profiles of mature industrialized countries, China is still very much dependent on its agricultural sector (Dutta, 2005).

Between 1980 and 2001, the share of machinery and transport equipment in manufacturing value added has somewhat increased, from 22 per cent to 32 per cent (World Bank, 2006). The share of textiles and clothing has been declining, and while the sector produced 18 per cent of manufacturing value added in 1980, it produced 12 per cent in 2001. While exports of light industry manufactures like textiles are large and growing (Figure 2), their relative importance has declined somewhat and that of more skill-demanding manufactures has increased. In general, the volume of Chinese exports significantly expanded during the 1990s, and the share of manufactures in total merchandise exports also increased, exceeding 90 per cent in 2004 (World Bank, 2006).

In its reforms, China has followed a model similar to that of other successful East Asian countries. Growth has been based on rapid industrialization, increased trade openness and exports, and gradual liberalization of financial markets. Growth has been import-export led: technology and know-how have been imported from abroad and adapted to the domestic resources, in particular to the abundant labour force (Dutta, 2005). This has made the extensive production of export goods possible. The high domestic savings rate coupled with large foreign direct investment inflows have made massive investments in infrastructure possible. In addition, labour markets have been increasingly deregulated, facilitating labour mobility.

China's reforms started in the late 1970s and early 1980s with agricultural reform, which de-collectivized agricultural land and privatized land-use rights. Investments in rural infrastructure were increased, mandatory delivery of output to the state by farmers was reduced, and farmers were enabled to have a more market-oriented output mix (Ahya and Xie, 2004). Due to reforms, agricultural growth averaged almost 10 per cent per year during 1980-1984 and 6.2 per cent per year in the 1980s as a whole (Ahya and Xie, 2004), decreasing poverty in rural areas. Successful reform in the agricultural sector contributed substantially to reform and expansion of the manufacturing sector. Due to increased productivity in agriculture, surplus labour became available to migrate to the manufacturing sector. Furthermore, due to increased income, farmers were able to increase their expenditure on goods and services produced by the domestic manufacturing sector (Dutta, 2005). Industrial reforms started after agricultural reform with the opening up to foreign investment and the establishment of township and village enterprises.

In the late 1980s and early 1990s, reforms focused on creating a pricing system and market institutions, and also on reducing the state's role in resource allocation. Since then, the focus has been on banking sector reform and state enterprise reform, which has included closing many unprofitable state-owned factories.

Due to high economic growth, the share of people living in absolute poverty has declined steeply during recent decades in China. The role of agricultural growth has been very important in poverty reduction, far more important during the 1980s and 1990s than growth in the secondary or tertiary sectors (Ravallion and Chen, 2004). According to Ravallion and Chen (2004), in the 20-year period after 1981, the proportion of population living under the poverty line fell from 53 per cent to 8 per cent. World Bank estimates, using one dollar a-day consumption as a measure of poverty, suggest that between 1990 and 2000 the poverty rate fell from 33 per cent to 16 per cent. Poverty reduction has not, however, been smooth and half of the decline took place in the early 1980s (Ravallion and Chen, 2004). Poverty reduction has also been more difficult in provinces that started the reform period with high inequality (Ravallion and Chen, 2004). Furthermore, despite poverty reduction at the national level, income inequality between regions and between rural and urban areas is still high.

After agricultural reform in the early 1980s, incomes tended to become more equal across the country. In the mid-1980s, however, economic reform favoured coastal cities with the development of special economic zones, which increased inequality between regions. While eastern China has attracted a remarkable amount of foreign direct investment and generated large export flows (see e.g. Wan et al. 2004), the inland and western regions, disadvantaged by scarce skills, low agglomeration economies and expensive transport, have fallen behind. Also, rural industrialization has been concentrated in eastern regions, which has increased inequality between rural areas. Rural industrialization has also widened income disparities within rural areas as labourers have become wealthier relative to those who have relied only on the land. According to Ravallion and Chen (2004), inequality in general has been increasing within rural and urban areas, and absolute inequality between urban and rural areas has increased appreciably.

China's fast growth has been based on rapid industrialization, high savings, massive investment in infrastructure and productive capacity, an increasingly deregulated labour market and an internationally open and competitive economy. The huge labour supply has made labour-intensive production possible, which in turn has increased average income and reduced poverty. While the investment rate has been remarkable in China, the efficiency with which capital is used is still low (Wolf, 2005).

## 5.2 India

The economic development strategy that India chose after the Second World War was very similar to China's – near autarky, industrialization and the dominance of the state in the economy. Development was considered synonymous with industrialization and industry was concentrating mainly on basic goods like steel and machinery. Private capital was not seen as an efficient motor for development, and it was considered to have a tendency towards monopolization. Because of that, state control was considered to be essential. The chosen development strategy was one of import substitution. Development policies included licensing of industrial activity, the reservation of key areas for state activity, controls over foreign direct investment, and interventions in the labour market (Kaplinsky, 1997).

As the chosen strategy turned out to be ineffective, bureaucratic and conducive to rent-seeking behaviour, policy reforms were started in the 1980s, and some provisional moves to encourage capital-goods imports, rationalize the tax system and relax industrial regulations were made. In the 1980s, however, reforms were less consistent than in China, and they only became systematic and broader at the beginning of 1990s, following a severe macroeconomic crisis. Acceleration of economic growth, however, started already in the 1980s, and Rodrik and Subramanian (2004) and DeLong (2001) consider the reforms and attitudinal changes of the 1980s as important reasons for India's current success. In the 1980s, the allocative role of the state in India's industrialization remained important, and only after the 1991 reforms did the driving force of resource allocation shift in favour of the market. The reforms undertaken in 1991 and thereafter included relaxation of the licensing system controlling internal production, currency devaluation, relaxation of restrictions on the inflow of foreign capital and technology transfer, abolition of quantitative restrictions on imports of raw materials, intermediates and capital goods, reduced tariff levels, relaxation of rules restricting large companies to expand existing units and construct new ones, and simplification of exchange controls (Kaplinsky, 1997). Furthermore, reforms included breaking public sector monopolies, reducing foreign currency debt dependence and tax reforms. However, most of the restrictive labour legislation was left intact and, in addition, the agricultural sector was left largely untouched. In general, the approach to liberalization in India has differed from the standard, Washington consensus, approach. Liberalization has been gradual and controlled, slow liberalization of trade and very gradual privatization have been emphasized, and capital account liberalization has been avoided thus far (Jha, 2002).

During the past 40 years, the Indian economy has undergone remarkable structural change. The share of agricultural value added in GDP has more than halved between 1965 and 2005, from 45 per cent to 19 pre cent (Figure 3). Despite structural changes, agriculture still accounts for a very high share of employment. At the same time, the expansion of services has been sizable, with its share of GDP increasing from 35 per cent in 1965 to 54 per cent in 2005. In contrast to many rapidly growing developing countries (especially in East Asia), there have not been sizable changes in the share of manufacturing (16 per cent in 2005 vs. 14 per cent in 1965). The share of textiles and clothing in manufacturing value added decreased between 1965 and 2000 (from 25 per cent to 13 per cent) (World Bank, 2006). The share of machinery and transport equipment was 19 per cent of manufacturing value added in 2000 (roughly the same as in 1965) and the share of chemicals was about the same (up from 10 per cent in 1965), with much of the increase in the 1990s.

In the 1980s and 1990s, GDP growth was moderately strong in India, the compound annual growth rate being 5.8 per cent in the 1980s and 5.4 per cent in 1990-2002. Growth has been occurring mainly in manufacturing and services. Between 1980 and 2002, the growth rate of manufacturing value-added averaged 6.6 per cent and that of services 7.1 per cent, while agriculture grew at only 2.8 per cent per year. In the 1990s, growth was remarkable in services.

High growth has been accompanied by increasing trade flows. For example, during the period 1991/92-2001/02, India's gross trade flows almost tripled, and the trade-GDP ratio increased from 21.3 per cent to 33.1 per cent. Growth has been especially rapid in services exports, which grew by 275 per cent, whereas merchandise exports grew by 145 per cent (Kelkar, 2004). The share of manufactures in merchandise exports has been increasing gradually but significantly. In 1962, manufactures made up 43 per cent of merchandise exports, while in 2003 the share was already three-quarters. Food exports comprised 11 per cent of merchandise exports in 2003 (World Bank, 2006). Within manufactures exports, light industries have significance, especially textiles and clothing. Gems (part of sub-category 66 in Figure 4) are also important exports. Recently, India has developed significant exports of chemicals, mostly drugs and dyes, and automotive components (Economist Intelligence Unit, 2005a).

In addition to rapid GDP growth, a sharp reduction in growth volatility has been important for the Indian economy. In the 24 years after 1980, the standard deviation of GDP growth has fallen to 1.9 per cent (Kelkar, 2004), one reason being the shift in the sectoral composition of output and the decrease in the importance of agriculture.

According to government estimates (presented e.g. in Srinivasan, 2004), the proportion of poor people in the total population (using national poverty lines) declined from 45.7 per cent in 1983 to 27.1 per cent in 1999–2000 in rural areas, and from 40.8 per cent to 23.6 per cent in urban areas. For the country as a whole, poverty declined from 44.5 per cent to 26.1 per cent. The widening of regional disparities has, however, been significant. After reforms, per capita expenditure differences between states have increased, with already better-off states growing more rapidly than poorer states (Deaton and Drèze, 2002). Southern and western states have been doing relatively better, as they have been able to utilize the opportunities of globalization and the market economy, whereas in some other states weaknesses in human capital and governance have generated reduced growth rates in the post-1990 period (Kelkar, 2004). Furthermore, rural-urban disparities of per capita expenditure have risen (Deaton and Drèze, 2002), even if inequality has increased faster within urban areas than in rural areas (see e.g. Deaton and Drèze, 2002; Jha, 2002). Due to slow liberalization, however, changes in inequality following reforms have been relatively modest in India compared e.g. to transition economies (Jha, 2002).

The impact of the reforms of the early 1990s on manufacturing firms depended, inter alia, on their location and technological level. According to Aghion et al. (2003), liberalization fostered innovation, profits and growth in industries that were close to the technological frontier, while it reduced them in industries that were far from the frontier. Also, pro-worker labour regulations at state level discouraged innovation and growth in all industries and this effect increased with liberalization (Aghion et al. 2003, 2006). Lall and Chakravorty (2004) conclude that structural reforms have had different impact on different states. In seeking efficient locations, private sector investments favoured existing industrial clusters and coastal districts, whereas state-owned industry has been less oriented towards such locations (Lall and Chakravorty, 2004). Due to reforms, the role of the state as industrial owner and industrial location regulator has been substantially curtailed and the dominance of private sector industrialization has increased, which is likely to lead to higher inequality between regions. According to Mishra and Kumar (2005), however, trade liberalization has decreased wage inequality in industry. In sectors with large tariff reductions, wages increased relative to the economy-wide average. Since the tariff reductions were relatively larger in sectors with a higher proportion of unskilled workers and these sectors experienced an increase in relative wages, these unskilled workers experienced an increase in income relative to skilled workers (Mishra and Kumar, 2005).

The sectoral composition of growth is likely to matter to the aggregate rate of poverty reduction and changes in income inequality. Jha (2002) argues that the rise of inequality during the years of rapid growth has been due to a shift in earnings from labour to capital income, rapid growth of the services sector, a decrease in the rate of labour absorption during the reform period, and rapid growth of banking, financial institutions, insurance and real estate. Real wages for agricultural labourers have grown at around 2.5 per cent per year in the 1990s, whereas public sector salaries have grown at 5 per cent per year (Deaton and Drèze, 2002), which is one of the reasons for increased inequality between rural and urban areas. According to Ravallion and Datt (1996), changes in poverty (during the period 1951-1991) have responded more to rural than to urban economic growth. They also argue that primary and (informal) tertiary sector growth has had greater impact on poverty than secondary sector growth. Over the long term, the secondary sector has not been a significant source of poverty reduction (Ravallion, 2004). One reason for that is likely to be high inequality in human resource endowments, preventing the poor from participating in the non-farm formal sector (see e.g. Ravallion, 2004), especially in the more skill demanding activities. As absolute poverty in India is principally a rural problem, the greatest poverty reduction can be attained by emphasizing rural development, in particular, agricultural development. In some regions, however, poverty reduction is not possible through investments in agriculture, and employment in manufacturing or services is the only possible way to reduce poverty.

The reform process has had clearly beneficial effects on the Indian economy. Growth rates have been high and growth more stable than earlier. The service sector has expanded particularly rapidly, in terms of both output and exports. Along with economic growth, poverty has significantly declined. India's economy, however, still confronts many obstacles hindering its growth. Limiting factors for development have included: an inefficient legal system and extensive regulations like those of the labour market; a low savings rate which has limited capital formation; a minor role for FDI, especially when compared to China; lack of access to finance, especially for small businesses; high tariff levels which restrict competition in domestic markets and hinder the development of potential exporters.

## 5.3 South Korea

Economic growth in South Korea has been rapid during the last 40-45 years. During its rapid industrialization, the country was able to achieve remarkable growth with steep reductions in poverty and inequality. In 1960-2002, the compound annual GDP growth rate (CAGR) was 7.5 per cent. Growth has been high especially in manufacturing. Between 1960 and 1969, the CAGR of manufacturing value added was 16.5 per cent and between 1970 and 1979 it was 17.6 per cent. Growth in agriculture's value-added has been continuously declining, falling from 5.1 per cent in the 1960s to only 1.7 per cent during 1990-2002. Rapid growth has been associated with significant structural changes (Figure 5). In 1965, the share of manufacturing in GDP was 14 per cent and that of agriculture 39 per cent. In 1977, the shares for both sectors were around 24 per cent, and in 2004 they were 29 per cent and 4 per cent, respectively (World Bank, 2006). Employment in agriculture has also declined. In 1980, 34 per cent of all employees (18 per cent in 1990) still worked in agriculture; in 2003 the share was only 9 per cent (World Bank, 2006). The industrial employment share has had an inverted U-shape form during the last 25 years: in 2003 industry employed 28 per cent of employees, compared with 37 per cent in 1991 and 29 per cent in 1980. The share of employment in services has been continuously increasing during the last decade, reaching 64 per cent in 2003.

In the late 1950s, the Korean government still pursued a relatively pro- tectionist import substitution strategy. Imports were restricted by high tariffs and import licensing systems. Most of the products exported were primary products, and exports remained negligible (Lee 1997). In the early 1960s, however, government policy shifted from import substitution towards export orientation. Policies included trade reforms and export promotion, direct export subsidies, tax exemption and low-interest export loans. Government intervention was strong, and export targets were formulated in a detailed way by product, market and exporting firm. Exporters also enjoyed duty-free access to imports (Noland and Pack, 2003). Infant industries were protect- ed. In general, however, successful export performance was likely to bring on more favourable treatment by government. Export promoting policies were highly successful, since during the 1962-73 period the share of exports in GNP increased from 6 per cent to 30 per cent (Lee, 1997). At the same time, the export structure changed dramatically, with the share of manufactures exports in total merchandise exports increasing from 20 per cent to 84 per cent. Within industrial products, the export of light manufactures, in which Korea had a comparative advantage, was especially important in the 1960s. In the 1970s, economic policy changed and massive investment programs were introduced to promote heavy industries, like shipbuilding, steel and chemicals. The aim was to change the export composition, reduce depend- ence on low-wage sectors and sustain growth. Also, efforts at selective indus- trial policies were intensified and, in contrast to the rule-based policies of the 1960s, greater policy discretion was introduced. This included an increase of direct government control in the banking sector in order to channel funds to preferred sectors, projects or firms (Noland and Pack, 2003). Priority indus- tries also received tax incentives as well as trade protection. Basic metals and chemical industry received a remarkable share of investments, whereas textile and light industry benefited little from the policy shift (see e.g. Noland and Pack, 2003). The impacts of this selective industrial policy can be seen in the current export structure of Korea (Figure 6). During the recent years, exports of labour-intensive goods like clothing have been in decline or stagnant. At the same time, the sophistication of engineering exports has grown, and the car industry has been evolving rapidly (Economist Intelligence Unit, 2005b).

With rapid economic growth, absolute poverty has decreased sharply in Korea. Even as late as the 1960s, poverty was widespread, but in the late 1990s the share of population living on less than $1 a day (PPP) was only 2 per cent (World Bank, 2004a). Export-oriented industrialization, which gen- erated rapid economic growth, has had a major role in the reduction. It cre- ated high demand for labour and rapid expansion of employment, increasing incomes and reducing poverty (World Bank, 2004b). At the outset, econom- ic growth was heavily based on export of labour-intensive manufactures. Subsequently, an increase of human capital has made possible the specializa- tion on more sophisticated export items. It has also enabled productivity to rise, and increased innovative ability and adaptation of technology developed elsewhere (see e.g. World Bank, 2004b), all of which have contributed to continued high growth. Compared to many other developing countries, investment in human resources has been extensive in Korea. Education has provided avenues of upward social mobility[3].

In addition to growth based on industrialization, the land reform of the late 1940s also contributed to the reduction of poverty, especially in rural areas (see e.g. Henderson et al., 2002). Land reform facilitated a vast transfer of arable land ownership to the peasantry. There were major improvements in productivity (Henderson et al. 2002). An increase of agricultural product prices in the late 1960s and the green revolution of the 1970s, as well as government investments in rural development, all increased income in rural areas and reduced rural poverty (World Bank, 2004b). The government growth strategy, however, has laid emphasis on industrialization and urbanization, which have led to more rapid growth of income in urban areas and increasing income disparity between rural and urban areas.

Poverty decline has been extremely rapid in Korea. After the rapid improvements between 1960s and 1980s, the rate of decline has slowed down (Henderson et al., 2002), but as of the beginning of the 1990s growth was generally still highly pro-poor (see e.g. Kakwani and Pernia, 2000). However, the change in income inequality has not been as impressive as the decrease in poverty. According to Choo (1993), there was no significant change in the size distribution of income between 1965 and 1990 (see also Lee, 1997). On the other hand, Fields and Yoo (2000) argue that labour income inequality, as measured by the Gini coefficient, fell remarkably between the late 1970s and early 1990s. Since the economic crisis of the late 1990s, inequality has been increasing. Compared to many Southeast Asian countries, however, income distribution in Korea has been and still is distinctly more equitable. Government social welfare programs, which have provided the poor with subsistence assistance and medical services, have been one of the reasons for relatively low inequality.

## 5.4 Taiwan Province of China

Like Korea, Taiwan has experienced rapid economic growth over the past half century. The average annual growth rate during that period has been 8.4 per cent, reaching almost 10 per cent in the 1960s and 1970s (Liang and Mei, 2005). Economic growth has been heavily based on the growth of manufacturing, and from the 1960s onwards on export-orientation. At the outset, the country specialized in labour-intensive production and later shifted towards capital-intensive and high-tech production.

As in Korea, government intervention in Taiwan has also been remarkable. In the 1950s, the development strategy was one of import substitution, but in the 1960s, policy started to change towards export-orientation. Over the years, and especially before the 1990s, government policies included extensive use of tariffs and non-tariff barriers on imports (especially in agriculture), selective credit policies favouring preferred sectors, a government-led push for exports of manufactures, sectoral industrial policies to support specific industries, and the promotion of state-owned firms (see e.g. Noland and Pack, 2003). The government also set up special industrial parks, in which several privileges, like duty free imports of materials, were provided for occupant firms. Policies have also included the establishment of institutions designed to identify, transfer, diffuse and absorb foreign industrial technologies and undertake innovation (Noland and Pack, 2003), in order to ease Taiwan's transfer to high-tech production.

Taiwan's post-war growth pattern has to a large extent been one of growth with equity. Already in the 1950s, when rapid growth and industrialization were at the beginning, Taiwan had a much more equal income distribution than many other developing countries. Major land reforms introduced after the war which reduced inequality and rural poverty are one of the reasons. From the mid-1960s onwards, income inequality further declined due to low inequality of wage income as a result of rapid growth of employment in export-driven, labour-intensive manufacturing industries. Demand for all types of labour was at that time expanding, but demand for low-skill workers was expanding at the fastest rate. Average wage rates rose and, as the wages of low-educated workers were rising faster than higher educated ones, wage differentials narrowed. In addition, due to improvements in education, the supply of higher educated workers was relatively high, which decreased marginal returns to education (Chu 1995, Kanbur 2000). However, in the 1980s the development of skill-intensive sectors pushed up wage inequality, while the share of capital and property in total income increased. This was linked to the increasing importance of larger private enterprises and escalation of land values (Kanbur, 2000; Cornia and Kiiski, 2001). In general, economic growth in Taiwan has been associated with even less income inequality than in Korea. In Korea, capital-intensive industries and large conglomerates were favoured over light industries, whereas in Taiwan SMEs have had greater importance.

## 5.5 Indonesia

From the late 1960s until the Asian economic crisis of 1997, economic growth in Indonesia was very rapid, averaging 7 per cent per year (Hofman et al., 2004). During that 30-year period, the country moved from a predominantly agricultural production base to a more industrialized base – the share of agriculture in GDP declined from 56 per cent in 1965 to 16 per cent in 1997, and the share of industry increased from 13 per cent to 44 per cent (Figure 7). In the 1970s and 1980s, oil production had a high importance – e.g., in 1980 the share of mining and quarrying (including crude oil) in GDP was 25.7 per cent (Ishida, 2003). From the mid-1980s onwards, manufacturing has been the driving force behind economic growth. Agriculture remains, however, a very important sector in terms of employment: in 2004 it accounted for 43 per cent of total employment, whereas industry's share was 13 per cent (World Bank, 2006). Rapid growth of the economy has benefited a large share of the population, as poverty fell from more than 70 per cent in the mid-1960s to 11 per cent in 1996 (Hofman et al., 2004). The Asian economic crisis in 1997, however, caused an increase in poverty rates.

In the mid-1960s, Indonesia was still one of the least industrialized of the large developing countries (Feridhanusetyawan, 2000), poverty was widespread and society in economic and political chaos. In 1966, after a regime change, thorough reforms were started. The first phase of economic liberalization involved a shift away from a closed economy and heavily interventionist policies to a more market oriented economy (Feridhanusetyawan, 2000). Liberalization entailed the restoration of external stability, fiscal constraints, restoration of the banking system, liberalization of the investment regime, and agricultural support programs aiming especially at self-sufficiency in rice production. Liberalization of the investment regime included incentives and assurances to new foreign investors, and the return of previously nationalized foreign-owned industrial and trading properties. Preferential treatment for state enterprises was reduced. New investment laws provided the same incentives to domestic and foreign investors. Export and import procedures were simplified. Indonesia also moved to a unified, fully convertible fixed exchange rate, which gave a boost to exports and foreign direct investment. Most of the price controls were eliminated, and a balanced budget policy was adopted. Restoration of the banking system included creation of a national central bank, improved access to credit, authorized establishment of foreign bank branches and of private domestic banks (Hofman et al. 2004). Chosen policies fostered broad-based industrial growth in the country (Hofman et al. 2004), but the liberal policy period did not last long. During the 1970s, Indonesia experienced a rapid growth of income due to an increase of oil production. Oil revenues made it possible for the government to finance capital-intensive investments and engage directly in production, and there was less need to rely on external sources of capital (Feridhanusetyawan, 2000). Furthermore, the open door policy at the end of 1960s and beginning of the 1970s had already brought vital foreign investments to the country. As a result, Indonesia reverted to a public sector-dominated economic strategy emphasizing import substitution and public financing (Hofman et al., 2004). State-owned banks provided subsidized credits to favoured clients, the state was the owner of strategic capital-intensive industries, and barriers to imports were erected (Feridhanusetyawan, 2000). State-owned factories operated especially in such areas as oil refining, fertilizers, cement and basic metals. Exports were mainly of oil and gas, mining and quarrying sector products – e.g. in 1980, 70 per cent of Indonesian exports were products of this sector (Ishida, 2003). However, once the oil boom ended at the beginning of the 1980s, the import-substituting pattern of industrialization, financed by oil revenues, could not be sustained, and the government shifted towards an export-promoting strategy. Indonesia moved from government-led growth to greater private sector participation. A series of deregulation measures were introduced to improve the investment climate. Trade reforms were introduced, including exemption of export-oriented firms from all import duties and regulations on imported inputs. Investment controls, including investment licensing, were relaxed. Also, financial sector reforms were started in the early 1980s and major reforms were carried out at the end of the 1980s (Hofman et al., 2004). Reforms eased restrictions on the opening of new private banks, allowing e.g. foreign banks to open offices. Freedom for banks to mobilize deposits in support of new lending was increased.

As a result of the improvement in the investment climate, foreign and domestic direct investments started rising rapidly in the late 1980s (Hofman et al., 2004), and exports of manufactures started to increase at a remarkable rate (Figure 8). In 1980, the share of manufacturing exports in merchandise exports was only 2.3 per cent, but by 1996 the share had expanded to 51.4 per cent. Oil-based exports remained important, however, with the share of fuels in merchandise exports at the beginning of 2000s still amounting to approximately one-fourth. Food exports are also of importance. Within the category of manufacturing exports, the importance of resource-based manufactures diminished in the 1980s and, by the early 1990s, they had been overtaken by low- and medium-technology manufactures (Aswicahyono and Feridhanusetyawan, 2004). Since the mid-1990s, the share of low-tech product exports has declined and that of medium and high-tech products increased (see Aswicahyono and Feridhanusetyawan, 2004). This trend can also be seen in the structure of manufacturing production, as the share of machinery and transport equipment production in manufacturing value-added increased from 13 per cent in 1980 to 22 per cent in 2002 (World Bank, 2006). Over the same period, the share of the food sector (food, beverages and tobacco) decreased from 32 per cent to 23 per cent (65 per cent in 1970), while the share of textiles and clothing, which is also a low-tech industry, has been relatively steady – between 15 per cent and 21 per cent during the 1990s.

Rapid and persistent economic growth, which continued until the late 1990s, had a significant impact on poverty. In the late 1960s a large part of the population was still living in poverty, but in 1996 the share was only 11 per cent (Hofman et al. 2004; according to World Bank figures, the share was 15.7 per cent). From 1967 to 2002, the income of the bottom 20 per cent of income earners grew at the same pace as the overall average per capita income (Timmer, 2004), and growth was thus on average pro-poor during that period, even if there was considerable variance between sub-periods. Changes in inequality were relatively minor during the 1964-1996 period, and the Gini coefficient fluctuated between 0.32 and 0.38 (see Feridhanusetyawan, 2000).[4] Investment of the oil rents in the financing of the green revolution caused a decline of inequality, especially in rural areas, as employment and production opportunities increased in the rural sector (Cornia and Kiiski, 2001). Oil revenues allowed large investments in infrastructure, education and health, all of which also benefited the poor. The period from the mid-1970s to the late-1980s can in particular be considered a successful example of fast and equitable growth accompanied by rapid poverty reduction. However, from the late 1980s until the economic crisis of the late 1990s, during the period of rapid globalization, the development of the urban-based manufacturing, financial and other sectors was emphasized, and there was a slowdown in agricultural growth, which caused a widening of the rural-urban gap and an increase of overall inequality (Cornia and Kiiski, 2001). Rural development programs were also retrenched during that period. As the overall growth was rapid, however, the poverty rate declined during that period as well.

Rapid economic growth has significantly decreased poverty in Indonesia. Growth has been built on strong macroeconomic policies, support for agriculture, investment in physical and human capital, and increasingly liberal policies in the financial sector, trade, and foreign investment (Hofman et al., 2004). Rapid growth has tended to be based on labour-intensive production; thus, growth has in general been pro-poor. As in China, Taiwan or South Korea, development of and increased productivity in the agricultural sector have contributed significantly to the reduction in poverty. The oil boom of the 1970s caused a significant increase in export income and made possible investments in infrastructure and public goods that also benefited the poor. Following the oil boom, an increase of manufacturing exports has been the driving force of growth. Private sector manufacturing has been highly labour-intensive and sectors like textiles and clothing, wood processing, and the food industry have created employment opportunities for the poor.

## 5.6 Mexico

Compared to South Korea, Taiwan or China, Mexico's economic development has been far less noteworthy. Especially during the 1980s and 1990s, the country experienced several economic crises. From the 1940s until the mid-1980s, Mexico's economic policy was based on import-substituting industrialization (e.g. Esquivel and Rodríguez-López, 2003). The strategy included high protective tariffs and other import barriers, especially to consumer goods. Industrial expansion was promoted through public investment in energy and transportation infrastructure. During those years, the Mexican economy industrialized and the economy performed well. In the 1960s, for example, GDP grew by 6.8 per cent per annum and industry also grew rapidly (7.9 per cent per year, 1965-1969). By 1970, Mexico had diversified its export base – the share of manufactures in merchandise exports was already 32 per cent, while eight years earlier it had been less than half of that – and it was also self-sufficient in many consumer goods. Rapid economic growth continued in the 1970s, but growth was undermined by fiscal mismanagement and deterioration of the investment climate. Foreign borrowing increased, and the public sector deficit rose rapidly. Also, inflation started to rise. The poor investment climate led to massive capital flight. In general, the macroeconomic policies of the 1970s left the economy vulnerable to external shocks and, at the beginning of the 1980s, rising inflation, increasing debt, falling oil prices and higher world interest rates caused an economic crisis. The crisis forced the country to start economic reforms, and in the mid-1980s economic policy was re-oriented toward trade liberalization, export promotion and privatization. Trade barriers were reduced, Mexico joined the General Agreement on Tariffs and Trade (GATT), and Mexico's US debt was re-scheduled. The economy stagnated, however, throughout the 1980s and the growth of GDP was negative as late as 1986. By the end of the 1980s, the inflation rate fell significantly and growth resumed. Trade liberalization further progressed as Mexico joined the North American Free Trade Agreement (NAFTA) in 1994. A new economic crisis occurred, however, in 1994-1995, and in 1995 GDP growth was significantly negative. With international support, growth recovered by the end of the 1990s before declining again at the beginning of the next decade, when industry in particular stagnated. During the past few years, the country's economic health has improved and, compared to the period of the mid-1990s economic crisis, it is more resilient to external shocks. Tighter monetary and fiscal policies have dampened inflation: in 2002 consumer price inflation was 5 per cent, compared to 69 per cent in the 1980s.

The services sector is the largest contributor to Mexican GDP, accounting for 70 per cent in 2005 (Figure 9). The importance of the sector has somewhat increased during recent decades, but it accounted for 59 per cent of GDP already in the mid-1960s (World Bank, 2006). The contribution of agriculture to GDP has been minor. In 1965, its share was 14 per cent and the share has declined further since then – in 2005 it was only 4 per cent. The agricultural sector is, however, still an important employer, absorbing 16 per cent of total employment in 2003, and in some regions significantly more than that. The share of manufacturing has been relatively constant over the years, accounting for 18 per cent of GDP in 2005. The importance of manufacturing exports has, however, significantly increased. In the late 1970s and early 1980s, Mexico relied heavily on oil for foreign-exchange earnings (in 1982 the share of fuels in merchandise exports was 77.2 per cent), but since the mid-1980s, when trade liberalization started, the share of manufacturing exports began to increase, and in 2004 they accounted for approximately 80 per cent of total merchandise exports.

The most important manufacturing sub-sectors in terms of output are currently metal products, machinery and related equipment; food, beverages and tobacco; and chemicals, petroleum products, rubber and plastics (see e.g.

Economist Intelligence Unit, 2004). The first of these is also the most important manufacturing export sector. During the last 15 years, the importance of some skill-intensive exports (including road vehicles, telecommunication equipment, and electrical machinery) has been increasing, as has the share of some light industries (Figure 10). Among individual light industries, the clothing and accessories sector is the most important, accounting for more than one-fourth of total light industry export income in 2003. The share of food and agricultural raw material exports in total merchandise exports has been steadily declining, from more than 40 per cent of total merchandise exports in the 1960s to 12 per cent in 1980 and 5 per cent in 2004 (World Bank, 2006). A remarkable part of Mexico's production of manufactures for export is currently occurring in *maquiladoras* (in-bond assembly for re-export plants), which generally have a large content of imported inputs.

Poverty and inequality are still significant problems in Mexico. In 2002, one-fifth of the population was living in poverty (measured using a food-based poverty line, close to the international $2 per day poverty line) (World Bank, 2004c). Over the past decade, the pattern of overall poverty has closely followed the macroeconomic cycle and the changes in the labour market (World Bank, 2004c). During the 1994-1995 crisis, poverty increased significantly, and it later declined with economic growth. The period 2000-2002 was exceptional, however, and poverty fell despite economic stagnation.

Inequality is high in Mexico – the Gini index for the year 2000 was 54.6, while for India it was 32.5 (World Bank, 2004a). Wage inequality increased between the mid-1980s and the mid-1990s (see e.g. Cortez, 2001). In manufacturing, according to Esquivel and Rodríguez-López (2003), wage income inequality between skilled and unskilled workers increased substantially between 1988 and 1996, after which it did not change much until 2000. Between 2000 and 2002, overall income inequality declined (World Bank, 2004c). In addition to inequality between the skilled and unskilled labour force, there are large differences across regions, and poverty is highest in the southern parts of the country (e.g. World Bank, 2004c).

There are several possible reasons that can explain why inequality increased even if, according to standard factor-proportions trade theory, trade liberalization could have been expected to reduce inequality in Mexico. According to Esquivel and Rodríguez-López (2003), technological change was responsible for the increase in manufacturing wage inequality in the late 1980s and 1990s. In the absence of technological change, trade liberalization would have led to a reduction in the wage gap, particularly in the pre-NAFTA period. Moreover, the structure of effective protection before liberalization may have favoured unskilled labour-intensive industries (e.g. Ros and Bouillon, 2002). Furthermore, even if Mexico has an abundance of unskilled labour compared to the United States (Mexico's main trading partner), it does not necessarily have it vis-à-vis the rest of the world (see e.g. Ros and Bouillon, 2002).

Slow economic growth and high inequality have inhibited progress in poverty reduction (World Bank, 2004c). Manufacturing, which could be an engine of growth, has been growing slowly in recent years. Exports have been expanding, but a significant share of exports is produced in relatively skill-demanding industries, which has decreased the possibilities of poor people to participate. Nevertheless, during recent years, Mexico has made major progress in some poverty dimensions, e.g. in health and education (World Bank, 2004c). The progress in raising the monetary incomes of the poor has, however, been slow, even if Mexico has slightly lower poverty rates than the Latin American average.

## 5.7 Brazil

Similarly to many other Latin American countries, economic performance in Brazil has been volatile. The contribution of the industrial sector (including manufacturing, construction, mining and utilities) has, however, remained relatively constant over the past three decades (Figure 11). In 2004, industry comprised 34 per cent, agriculture 9 per cent and services 57 per cent of GDP.

Manufacturing, the single most important sub-sector of industry, accounts for nearly two-thirds of industrial GDP. Within manufacturing, the most important sub-sectors are food processing, basic metallurgy, machinery and equipment, and chemical products. The production of motor vehicles, aircraft, certain electronic products and machinery and equipment are world class. Some of these industries are recipients of generous public incentives (World Trade Organization, 2004).

The contribution of the agricultural sector to GDP has been less than 10 per cent since the early seventies, but has increased by approximately 2 per-centage points between 2001 and 2003, which reflects increased production for some crops but also higher productivity (World Trade Organization, 2004). Despite a relatively small contribution to GDP, agriculture is still an extremely important sector for Brazil, as it is a major source of export revenues and an important employer (Economist Intelligence Unit, 2005c).

The share of services increased between the mid-1980s and late 1990s, but declined somewhat after that. However, the sector still accounts for about 60 per cent of GDP, and it is the most important employer, absorbing approximately two-thirds of the labour force. The Brazilian government has increasingly liberalized the services sector, particularly in telecommunications, financial services, and port and airport services. Public banks are still important, but private participation, as well as foreign investment, has increased over the years. Public administration is the most important sub-sector, followed by real estate, finance, commerce and communications. (World Trade Organization, 2004).

Exports have been a key factor in stimulating production in Brazil (UN ECLAC, 2005a). The share of high-tech manufactures in total commodity exports has increased (e.g. aircraft, from 1.8 per cent in 1990 to 3.5 per cent in 2004), as has the share of manufactures of intermediate technology (e.g. passenger vehicles, from 5.0 per cent in 1990 to 8.3 per cent in 2004). The share of low-technology manufactures, on the other hand, has decreased as a result of increased exposure to competition from lower cost producers in Asia (e.g. textiles, clothing and footwear, which in total accounted for 7.0 per cent of total exports in 1990 and only 3.7 per cent in 2004). The share of primary products, including agricultural and mining, plus processed goods of agricultural origin, beverages and tobacco, and chemicals and fuels, remains high, oscillating around 50 per cent of total exports (Figure 12). Increased demand, especially from China, and strong prices in world markets have positively affected both mining and agricultural exports in recent years.

Brazil is a net exporter of agricultural products (primary and processed) and mining products (including ores), whereas it is a net importer of other industrial products and services (World Trade Organization, 2004). Interestingly, whereas transnational companies account for approximately half of Brazil's merchandise exports, only a small portion is either medium or high-tech – mostly automobiles and telecommunications equipment (UN ECLAC, 2005b).

As a whole, industry accounts for approximately 50 per cent of total commodity exports, machinery and transport equipment being the most important sub-group. Within the latter, the automotive industry has been especially dynamic. This has been partly a result of an aggressive export development strategy, which included targeted support programs to the automotive, shipbuilding and aircraft industries (World Trade Organization, 2004).

The trade liberalization measures[5] implemented by the Brazilian government between 1988 and 1994 led to a substantial reduction of the average rate of protection (Ferreira and Facchini, 2005). Whereas Brazil has become increasingly more open to trade, as measured by the weight of external trade flows in GDP, it is still – together with Argentina – below the regional average, as it was in the beginning of the 1980s[6] (UN ECLAC, 2004a). In addition, contrary to most countries in the region, Brazil continues to impose high effective tariffs on several manufactured goods, with those imposed on motor vehicles, some food products (poultry, dairy, and vegetable oils), beverages, apparel, and textiles being above average. Imports of primary agricultural and mining products, of which Brazil is a very efficient producer, face low effective tariffs (World Trade Organization, 2004).

The manufacturing sectors that are relatively shielded from international competition, such as the motor vehicle industry, are also highly concentrated and represented by strong lobbies. Less concentrated sectors have not been able to benefit from tariff protection, nor tax breaks or subsidies, to the same extent. In the auto-parts sector, for instance, as tariffs rapidly decreased, most Brazilian firms were closed or sold to foreign companies. In the context of the MERCOSUR preferential trade arrangements, the motor vehicle industry and other well established, politically organized industries (e.g. refrigerators, bicycles, audio and video equipment) were successful in maintaining tariffs well above average (Ferreira and Facchini, 2005).

The industrial specialization pattern followed by Brazil and other Southern Cone countries, based on capital-intensive industries, contributed to exacerbate the negative effects of sluggish and volatile GDP growth on employment and informality. While natural resource-based industries generate little new employment, labour-intensive sectors such as footwear, clothing and furniture have been displaced by foreign competition. For instance, in Brazil, labour-intensive traditional industries' share in total manufacturing output fell from 36 per cent in 1970 to 26 per cent in 1996 (Cimoli and Katz, 2002).[7] This has led to increases in unemployment rates and informal employment. Unemployment rose on average from 4.3 per cent in 1990 to 12.3 per cent in 2003. Informal employment is estimated to have risen from 40.6 per cent in 1990 to 46 per cent in 2003. Average wages of formal employees in the industrial sector fell by 1 per cent annually between 1990 and 1999 and by 4.3 per cent between 2000 and 2003. Overall, increases in unemployment and the expansion of the informal sector have worsened income distribution, as wages are a significant source of household income (almost two-thirds of household income on average in Brazil), and income levels in the informal sector are substantially below those prevailing in the formal one[8] (UN ECLAC, 2004a).

Finally, poverty rates in Latin America in general remain above 1980 levels despite improvements since 1990, and even with those improvements the absolute number of people living in poverty has increased. In Brazil, poverty reduction was significant especially in the 1990/1999 period, with poverty rates, measured using national poverty lines, falling by 10 percentage points. Since then, however, the poverty rate remained largely unchanged, at least through the early 2000s (more recent data being unavailable) (UN ECLAC, 2004b).

## 6. Discussion

For the countries analyzed here, industrial development has been an important basis for economic growth. Output expansion has been associated with export promotion, increased trade opening, economic liberalization and an improved business climate in most of the countries. However, import protection and selective government intervention have been employed as well.

As poverty in many developing countries is a predominantly rural problem, increased agricultural productivity is often a key to poverty reduction at the outset of economic development. This has been the case e.g. in China and Indonesia. Countries that have started their economic reforms – as China did – with agricultural reform or otherwise emphasized rural development have – at the beginning – typically experienced declining inequality due to a decrease of rural poverty. In Korea and Taiwan, due to land reforms of earlier decades, income distribution was relatively even when rapid industrialization began. In Indonesia, oil rents were used in financing rural development.

After the early stages of economic development, growth in the industrial sector is, however, essential for sustained long-run growth and poverty reduction. In the countries studied, the growth of the manufacturing sector has created employment opportunities outside agriculture and, as manufacturing in many of these countries has been – at least at the beginning – intensive in unskilled labour, the poor have benefited. In some countries, like Korea, growth during certain periods has clearly been pro-poor, with the poor benefiting proportionally more than the non-poor. There are, however, significant differences between countries as far as the impact of industrialization on the poor is concerned. In Mexico, for example, the growth of the manufacturing sector in the late 1980s and early 1990s benefited skilled workers to a greater extent than unskilled ones. Often, economic growth has been accompanied by increasing inequality over some periods, even if poverty in absolute terms has declined – as shown by the recent experience in China.

The extent to which industrial development effectively decreases poverty and inequality depends on the pattern of industrialization. Industries which employ a high proportion of unskilled workers and/or use domestic inputs and raw materials produced with labour-intensive technologies can have positive effects on incomes of the poor. In Taiwan, for example, during the early phases of industrial development, the demand for unskilled workers increased relative to that for skilled workers, which reduced inequality and poverty. At later stages, demand for skilled workers significantly increased, along with a change in Taiwan's export and manufacturing structure. By that time, Taiwan had made major investments in human capital, so the effect on income distribution of changing skill demands was relatively muted. The Republic of Korea has followed a similar path. In Brazil and India, on the other hand, manufacturing has tended to be relatively capital intensive, creating relatively modest employment opportunities for the poor. Also in India, the service sector has been a major contributor to recent growth, but the dynamic service industries like software and back-office processing have provided few jobs for the unskilled directly. Still, with strong growth performance for the past 15-20 years, the poverty rate in India has significantly declined.

The geographical location of industry can also affect the extent to which industrialization is pro-poor. In China, industrialization has significantly increased per capita income, but as industrial development has been concentrated in the eastern coastal regions of the country, inequality between regions has increased and industrial development has contributed relatively little to poverty reduction in much of the interior. Still, inter-regional labour mobility is high and the remittances sent home by migrant workers can help mitigate effects of geographic concentration of industry on regional inequality. Geographical reasons – or economic distances – also partly explain why some parts of Brazil, India, Indonesia or Mexico are much less developed than other parts of those countries.

Initial conditions significantly impact on whether major industrial development occurs, and whether industrialization accelerates economic growth and reduces poverty. Fundamental conditions for sustainable economic growth and industrial development include political, social and macroeconomic stability, well-functioning institutions and rule of law. The role of government is essential in creating these. If these framework conditions are lacking, investments – whether foreign or domestic – are likely to be few and growth limited and fluctuating. Economic instability is likely to impact especially the poor, as has happened e.g. in Mexico in the mid-1990s and in Indonesia in the late 1990s. In Korea and Taiwan, on the other hand, economic development has been much more stable.

Government has an important role in infrastructure and human resources development as well as in encouraging and supporting innovation and technological upgrading. For poor people, education is often an avenue to better employment and income opportunities. The existence of universal education, as in China or Korea, gives the poor better possibilities to participate in the development process.

At the outset of their development, countries may rely on primary resources or a cheap labour force, and all the countries analyzed here have begun their development process by relying on one or both of these factors. In the long run, however, investment in human capital and technological upgrading are essential if a country wishes to remain internationally competitive and sustain economic prosperity. Korea and Taiwan are good examples of countries where human resources development has had a significant impact on industrial development and broad economic growth. Due to rapid technical change and globalization, competition is becoming more and more intense, and the capacity to employ state-of-the-art technologies is increasingly crucial to succeed. That capacity is above all a function of the educational attainment and skills level of the workforce.

Countries may choose to build their industrial capabilities through domestic research and development as Taiwan and Korea did to a considerable extent. A more common approach has been to plug into global value chains and become a supplier of labour-intensive products (UNIDO, 2002), gradually upgrading technological capabilities through foreign investments. This is the strategy used e.g. by Mexico and to a somewhat lesser extent by Brazil. The two approaches are not mutually exclusive, and many countries rely on a mix of technology imports and development of domestic technologies and technological capabilities, with the balance tending to shift towards the latter as economic development proceeds. Governments have a significant role in capability-building as well as in attracting FDI.

All countries analyzed here have, at some point in time, carried out selective industrial policies, by which they have aimed to change the sectoral structure of production towards sectors believed to offer greater prospects for faster productivity growth. Taiwan and especially Korea are examples of export-manufacturing-oriented countries which have successfully used government intervention and import protection in the early phases of development of their manufacturing sectors.

Today, the degree of policy freedom left to developing countries is narrower than it was some decades ago, even if some well-planned government intervention may seem justified based on the success stories of the earlier decades. However, governments still have a primary role in promoting sustainable economic growth and especially poverty-reducing growth. In addition to ensuring stability, well-functioning institutions and appropriate legislation (e.g. labour laws), other essential government actions are related to skills formation, technology support, innovation financing, infrastructure development, and provision of a variety of public goods. All these have an impact on the growth and trade performance of a country. Rapid economic growth as such tends to decrease poverty. Rapid growth may increase income inequality, but this is not inevitable. Whether or not it does, depends not only on the skill bias of technical change in an economy but on human capital formation measures and on the nature of taxation and expenditure policies. In addition to promotion of job creating industries and SMEs and supporting the creation of domestic linkages, inequality can be decreased e.g. by subsidized access to education, subsidized housing, progressive taxation or economic asset redistribution like land reforms.

Figure 1. Sectoral shares of GDP in China, 1965-2004

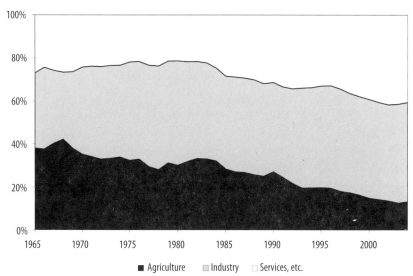

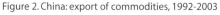

■ Agriculture    ▨ Industry    ☐ Services, etc.

Source: World Bank (2006).

Figure 2. China: export of commodities, 1992-2003

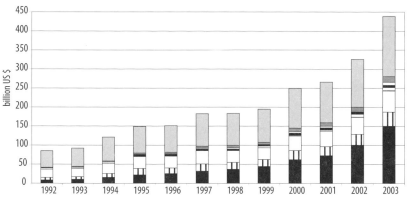

☐ Textiles & clothing, leather goods & other light industry manufactures (SITC rev . 3: 61, 63, 65, 8)

▨ Road vehicles & other t ransport equipment (SITC rev.3: 78, 79).

≡ Power generating machinery, industrial machinery etc. (SITC rev.3: 71, 72, 73, 74)

☐ Other commodity exports (primary commodities, food and beverages, chemicals, fuels etc., (SITC rev. 3: 0, 1, 2, 3, 4, 5, 9)

Ⅱ Iron & steel, non-metallic mineral manufactures & other heavy industry manufactures exc. machinery & transport equip. (SITC rev.3: 62, 64, 66, 67, 68, 69)

■ Electrical machinery, telecommunications equip., office machines etc. (SITC rev.3: 75, 76, 77).

Source: UN Comtrade database. Obs.: re-exports included.

Figure 3. Sectoral shares of GDP in India, 1965-2005

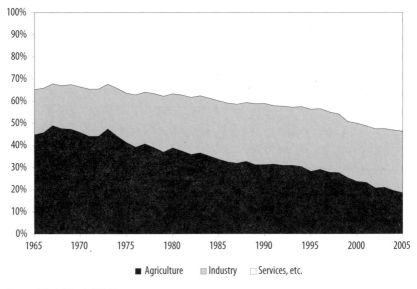

Source: World Bank (2006).


Figure 4. India: Export of commodities, 1988-2003

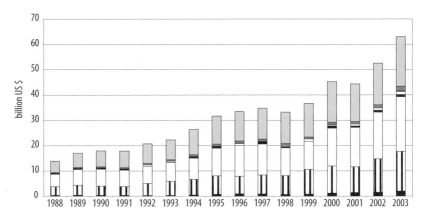

☐ Textiles & clothing, leather goods & other light industry manufactures (SITC rev . 3: 61, 63, 65, 8)

■ Road vehicles & other transport equipment (SITC rev.3: 78, 79).

➡ Power generating machinery, industrial machinery etc. (SITC rev.3: 71, 72, 73, 74)

☐ Other commodity exports (primary commodities, food and beverages, chemicals, fuels etc., (SITC rev. 3: 0, 1, 2, 3, 4, 5, 9)

⊓ Iron & steel, non-metallic mineral manufactures & other heavy industry manufactures exc. machinery & transport equip. (SITC rev.3: 62, 64, 66, 67, 68, 69)

■ Electrical machinery, telecommunications equip., office machines etc. (SITC rev.3: 75, 76, 77).

Source: UN Comtrade database. Obs.: re-exports included.

Figure 5. Sectoral shares of GDP in South Korea, 1965-2004

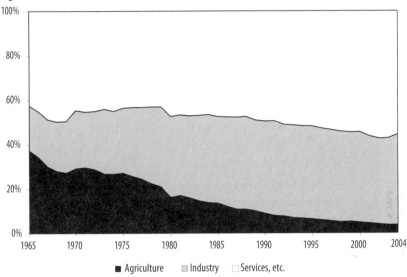

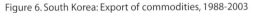

■ Agriculture   ▨ Industry   □ Services, etc.

Source: World Bank (2006).

Figure 6. South Korea: Export of commodities, 1988-2003

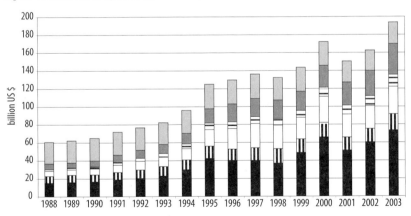

▨ Textiles & clothing, leather goods & other light industry manufactures (SITC rev . 3: 61, 63, 65, 8)

■ Road vehicles & other t ransport equipment (SITC rev.3: 78, 79).

▬ Power generating machinery, industrial machinery etc. (SITC rev.3: 71, 72, 73, 74)

□ Other commodity exports (primary commodities, food and beverages, chemicals, fuels etc., (SITC rev. 3: 0, 1, 2, 3, 4, 5, 9)

‖ Iron & steel, non-metallic mineral manufactures & other heavy industry manufactures exc. machinery & transport equip. (SITC rev.3: 62, 64, 66, 67, 68, 69)

■ Electrical machinery, telecommunications equip., office machines etc. (SITC rev.3: 75, 76, 77).

Source: UN Comtrade database). Obs.: re-exports included.

Figure 7. Sectoral shares of GDP in Indonesia, 1965-2005

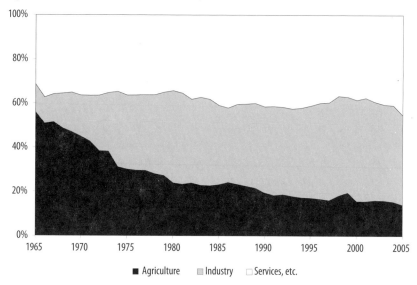

Source: World Bank (2006).

Figure 8. Indonesia: export of commodities, 1989-2004

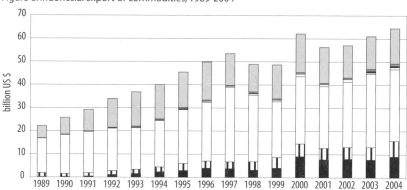

  ▦ Textiles & clothing, leather goods & other light industry manufactures (SITC rev . 3: 61, 63, 65, 8)

  ▦ Road vehicles & other t ransport equipment (SITC rev.3: 78, 79).

  = Power generating machinery, industrial machinery etc. (SITC rev.3: 71, 72, 73, 74)

  ☐ Other commodity exports (primary commodities, food and beverages, chemicals, fuels etc., (SITC rev. 3: 0, 1, 2, 3, 4, 5, 9)

  ⌐ı Iron & steel, non-metallic mineral manufactures & other heavy industry manufactures exc. machinery & transport equip.
     (SITC rev.3: 62, 64, 66, 67, 68, 69)

  ■ Electrical machinery, telecommunications equip., office machines etc. (SITC rev.3: 75, 76, 77).

Source: UN Comtrade database. Obs.: re-exports included.

Figure 9. Sectoral shares of GDP in Mexico, 1965-2005

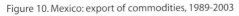

Source: World Bank (2006).

Figure 10. Mexico: export of commodities, 1989-2003

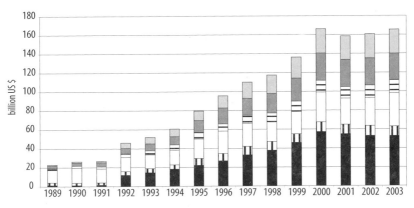

▨ Textiles & clothing, leather goods & other light industry manufactures (SITC rev . 3: 61, 63, 65, 8)

■ Road vehicles & other transport equipment (SITC rev.3: 78, 79).

▬ Power generating machinery, industrial machinery etc. (SITC rev.3: 71, 72, 73, 74)

▢ Other commodity exports (primary commodities, food and beverages, chemicals, fuels etc., (SITC rev. 3: 0, 1, 2, 3, 4, 5, 9)

▯ Iron & steel, non-metallic mineral manufactures & other heavy industry manufactures exc. machinery & transport equip.
    (SITC rev.3: 62, 64, 66, 67, 68, 69)

■ Electrical machinery, telecommunications equip., office machines etc. (SITC rev.3: 75, 76, 77).

Source: UN Comtrade database. Obs.: re-exports included

Figure 11. Sectoral shares of GDP in Brazil, 1970-2003

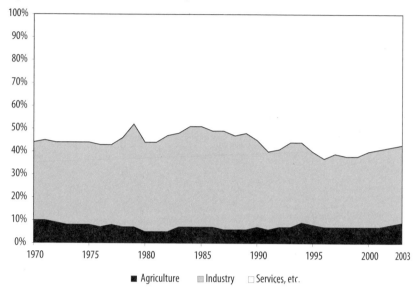

Source: UN National accounts database.


Figure 12. Brazil: export of commodities, 1989-2004

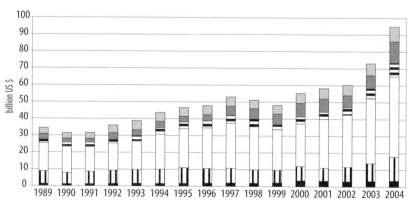

☐ Textiles & clothing, leather goods & other light industry manufactures (SITC rev . 3: 61, 63, 65, 8)

■ Road vehicles & other t ransport equipment (SITC rev.3: 78, 79).

▬ Power generating machinery, industrial machinery etc. (SITC rev.3: 71, 72, 73, 74)

☐ Other commodity exports (primary commodities, food and beverages, chemicals, fuels etc., (SITC rev. 3: 0, 1, 2, 3, 4, 5, 9)

Ⅱ Iron & steel, non-metallic mineral manufactures & other heavy industry manufactures exc. machinery & transport equip. (SITC rev.3: 62, 64, 66, 67, 68, 69)

■ Electrical machinery, telecommunications equip., office machines etc. (SITC rev.3: 75, 76, 77).

Source: UN Comtrade database. Obs.: re-exports included.

# Acknowledgements

I wish to thank David O'Connor (UNDESA/Policy Integration and Analysis Branch) for his comments throughout the writing process. Mónica Kjöllerström (UNDESA/Policy Integration and Analysis Branch) has written the section on Brazil. This is gratefully acknowledged. Mr. Jukka Jalava and Mr. Kalle Laaksonen of Pellervo Economic Research Institute have provided feedback on selected sections.

## Notes

1 It is important to notice, however, that technological change is not only relevant to manufacturing, but similarly has significant impacts in other sectors of the economy. A good example of this is increased productivity in agriculture, which has been essential for accelerated economic growth in many developing countries.

2 According to some analysts, the distribution of income among all people in the world has become more equal over the last two decades.

3 It has also had negative impacts on income distribution. During the 1970s, for instance, demand for skilled workers in heavy and chemical industries pushed up domestic wages and increased wage differentials between skilled and unskilled workers.

4 The validity of official inequality measures has been questioned, however.

5 These included reduction in tariff levels, tariff dispersion and elimination of major non-tariff restrictions.

6 Mexico is on the other extreme, having increased its openness to trade five times between the early eighties and the first years of the current decade.

7 Job creation has shifted towards the private services sector, in both highly remunerated activities (financial services, telecommunications, etc.) and activities with low barriers to entry, such as informal commerce and personal services (UN ECLAC, 2004a).

8 In 2000, income levels in the informal sector were 72 per cent lower than those prevailing in the formal sector on average in the region, up from a 59 per cent differential in 1990.

# Bibliography

Aghion, P. Burgess, R., Redding, S., and Zilibotti, F. (2006), The unequal effects of liberalization: Evidence from Dismantling the License Raj in India. Discussion Paper No. 5492, Centre for Economic Policy Research (CEPR), February 2006, 31 p.

Aghion, P. Burgess, R., Redding, S., and Zilibotti, F. (2003), The unequal effects of liberalization: theory and evidence from India. October 2003.

Aghion, P. and Howitt, P. (1998), Endogenous growth theory. MIT Press, Cambridge.

Ahya, C. and Xie, A. (2004), New tigers of Asia. India and China: a special economic analysis. Morgan Stanley, July 26, 2004, 59 p.

Amable, B. (2000), International specialization and growth. Structural Change and Economic Dynamics, Vol. 11, pp. 413-431.

Arrow, K. (1962), The economic implications of learning by doing. The Review of Economic Studies, Vol. 29, No. 3, pp. 155-173.

Aswicahyono, H. and Feridhanusetyawan, T. (2004), The evolution and upgrading of Indonesia's industry. CSIS Working paper series, WPE 073, Centre for Strategic and International Studies, 27 p.

Bhalla, S.S. (2003), Not as poor, nor as unequal, as you think – Poverty, inequality and growth in India, 1950-2000. Final report of a research project undertaken for the Planning Commission, Government of India, December 2004.

Bourguignon, F. and Morisson, C. (1990), Income distribution, development and foreign trade. European Economic Review, Vol. 34, No. 6, pp. 1113-1132.

Chen, S. and Ravallion, M. (2004), How have the world's poorest fared since the early 1980s?, World Bank, processed.

Choo, H. (1993), Income distribution and distributive equity in Korea. In Krause, L.B. and Park, F.-K. (eds.): Social issues in Korea: Korean and American perspectives. KDI Seoul, Korea.

Chu, Y.-P. (1995), Taiwan's inequality in the postwar era. Working Paper No. 96-1, Sun Yat Sen Institute, Taiwan.

Cimoli, M. and Katz, J. (2002), Structural reforms, technological gaps and economic development. A Latin American Perspective. Desarrollo Productivo Series No. 129, ECLAC, United Nations, Santiago, Chile, August 2002.

Cornia, G.A. (2005), Policy reform and income distribution. Paper presented in the DESA development forum: Integrating economic and social policies to achieve the UN development agenda. New York, 14-15 March 2005.

Cornia, G.A. and Kiiski, S. (2001), Trends in income distribution in the post-World War II period. Evidence and interpretation. Discussion paper no. 2001/89, United Nations University, World Institute for Development Economics Research.

Cornwall, J. (1977), Modern capitalism. Its growth and transformation. London, Martin Robertson.

Cornwall, J. (1976), Diffusion, convergence and Kaldor's laws. Economic Journal, Vol. 86, pp. 307-314.

Cortez, W.W. (2001), What is behind increasing wage inequality in Mexico? World Development, Vol. 29, No. 11, pp. 1905-1922.

Deaton, A. and Drèze, J. (2002), Poverty and inequality in India: a reexamination. Working Paper No. 107, Centre for Development Economics, August 2002, 64 p.

DeLong, J.B. (2001), India since independence: an analytic growth narrative. July 2001.

Dollar, D. and Kraay, A. (2004), Trade, growth, and poverty. The Economic Journal, 114: F22-F49.

Dutta, M. (2005), China's industrial revolution: challenges for a macroeconomic agenda. Journal of Asian Economics, Vol. 15, pp. 1169-1202.

Economist Intelligence Unit (2005a), India. Country profile 2005. 59 p.

Economist Intelligence Unit (2005b), South Korea. Country profile 2005. 59 p.

Economist Intelligence Unit (2005c), Brazil. Country profile 2005. 52 p.

Economist Intelligence Unit (2004), Mexico. Country profile 2004. 60 p.

Esquivel, G. and Rodríguez-López, J.A. (2003), Technology, trade, and wage inequality in Mexico before and after NAFTA. Journal of Development Economics, Vol. 72, pp. 543-565.

Fagerberg, J. (1994), Technology and international differences in growth rates. Journal of Economic Literature, Vol. 32, No.3, pp. 1147-1175.

Feridhanusetyawan, T. (2000), Globalization, poverty and equity in Indonesia. Country background paper for the OECD conference: Poverty and income inequality in developing countries – a policy dialogue on the effects of globalization. Paris, November 30- December 1, 2000, 29 p.

Ferreira, P.C. and Facchini, G. (2005), Trade liberalization and industrial concentration: evidence from Brazil. The Quarterly Review of Economics and Finance, Vol. 45, pp. 432-446.

Fields, G. and Yoo, G. (2000), Falling labor income inequality in Korea's economic growth: Patterns and underlying causes. Review of Income and Wealth, Series 46, No. 2, June 2000, pp. 139-159.

Helpman, E. (2004), The mystery of economic growth. The Belknap Press of Harvard University Press, 223 p.

Henderson, J., Hulme, D., Phillips, R., and Kim, E.M. (2002), Economic governance and poverty reduction in South Korea. August 2002, 44 p.

Hofman, B., Rodrick-Jones, E. and Thee, K.W. (2004), Indonesia: Rapid growth, weak institutions. A case study from: Scaling up poverty reduction. A global learning process and conference, Shanghai, May 25-27, 2004. The International Bank for Reconstruction and Development/The World Bank.

Ishida, M. (2003), Industrialization in Indonesia since the 1970s. IDE Research Paper no. 5, Institute of Developing Economies (IDE-JETRO).

Jha, R. (2002), Reducing poverty and inequality in India: has liberalization helped? Departmental Working Papers 2002-04, Australian National University, Economics RSPAS, 65 p.

Jones, C.I. (1998), Introduction to economic growth. W.W. Norton & Company Ltd.

Kakwani, N. and Pernia, E.M. (2000), What is pro-poor growth? Asian Development Review, Vol. 18, No. 1, pp. 1-16.

Kaldor, N. (1970), The case for regional policies. Scottish Journal of Political Economy XVII, pp. 337-348.

Kanbur, R. (2000), Income distribution and development. In: Atkinson, A.B. and Bourguignon, F. (eds.): Handbook of income distribution, vol. 1. North Holland.

Kaplinsky, R. (1997), India's industrial development: an interpretative survey. World Development, Vol. 25, No. 5, pp. 681-694.

Kelkar, V. (2004), India: On the growth turnpike. 2004 K. R. Narayanan oration, Australian National University, Canberra, April 27.

Lall, S.V. and Chakravorty, S. (2004), Industrial location and spatial inequality: theory and evidence from India. Research paper No. 2004/49, United Nations University, World Institute for Development Economics Research.

Lanjouw, J.O. and Lanjouw, P. (2001), The rural non-farm sector: issues and evidence from developing countries. Agricultural Economics, Vol. 26, pp. 1-23.

Lee, J.-W. (1997), Economic growth and human development in the Republic of Korea, 1945-1992. UNDP, Human Development Office, Occasional Paper 24.

Liang, C.Y. and Mei, J.Y. (2005), Underpinnings of Taiwan's economic growth: 1978-1999 productivity study. Economic Modelling, Vol. 22, pp. 347-387.

Lucas, R.E. Jr. (1988), On the mechanics of economic development. Journal of Monetary Economics, Vol. 22, pp. 3-42.

Milanovic, B. (2002), True world income distribution, 1988 and 1993: first calculations based on household surveys alone. Economic Journal, Vol. 112(476), pp. 51-92.

Mishra, P. and Kumar, U. (2005), Trade liberalization and wage inequality: evidence from India. IMF Working Paper WP/05/20, International Monetary Fund.

Nissanke, M. and Thorbecke, E. (2004), The impact of globalization on the world's poor – channels and policy debate. WIDER Angle No. 2/2004, World Institute for Development Economics Research, pp. 10-13.

Noland, M. and Pack, H. (2003), Industrial policy in an era of globalization: Lessons from Asia. Institute for International Economics, Washington D.C.

Ravallion, M. (2004), Less poverty and more inequality in China, India. Financial Express, December 11, 2004 (Summary of a lecture at the Council of Applied Economic Research, Delhi).

Ravallion, M. and Chen, S. (2004), China's (uneven) progress against poverty. World Bank Policy Research Working paper 3408, September 2004.

Ravallion, M. and Datt, G. (1996), How important to India's poor is the sectoral composition of economic growth? World Bank Economic Review, Vol. 10, No. 1, pp. 1-25.

Rodrik, D. and Subramanian, A. (2004), From "Hindu growth" to productivity surge: the mystery of the Indian growth transition. BREAD Working Paper no. 055, Bureau for Research in Economic Analysis of Development, March 2004.

Romer, P.M. (1990), Endogenous technological change. Journal of Political Economy, Vol. 98, S71-S102.

Romer, P.M. (1986), Increasing returns and long-run growth. Journal of Political Economy, Vol. 94, pp. 1002-37.

Ros, J. and Bouillon, C. (2002), Mexico: Trade liberalization, growth, inequality and poverty. In: Vos, R., Taylor, L. and Paes de Barros, R. (eds). Economic Liberalization, Distribution and Poverty. UNDP, Edward Elgar, pp. 347-389.

Sala-i-Martin, X. (2002), The distributing "rise" of global income inequality. NBER Working Paper w8904.

Sarntisart, I. (2000), Growth, structural change and inequality: the experience of Thailand. WIDER Working Papers no. 207, WIDER Institute.

Solow, R. (1956), A contribution to the theory of economic growth. Quart. J. Econ., vol. 70, No. 1, pp. 65-94.

Srinivasan, T.N. (2004), China and India: economic performance, competition and cooperation: an update. Journal of Asian Economics, Vol. 15, pp. 613-636.

Syrquin, M. (1986), Productivity growth and factor reallocation. In: Chenery, H., Robinson, S. and Syrquin, M. Industrialization and growth – a comparative study. A World Bank Research Publication. The International Bank for Reconstruction and Development/ The World Bank, Oxford University Press, pp. 229-262.

Timmer, C.P. (2004), The road to pro-poor growth: The Indonesian experience in regional perspective. Working Paper 38, Center for Global Development, April 2004.

Todaro, M. P. (1994), Economic development. Longman Singapore Publishers.

UN ECLAC (2005a), Economic Survey of Latin America and the Caribbean, 2004-2005. LC/G.2279-P/I, August 2005.

UN ECLAC (2005b), Foreign investment in Latin America and the Caribbean – 2004.

UN ECLAC (2004a), Desarrollo productivo en economías abiertas. ECLAC, Executive Secretary, June 2004.

UN ECLAC (2004b), Panorama social de América Latina 2004. LC/L.2220-P/E.

UNIDO (2002), Industrial development report 2002/2003. Competing through innovation and learning. United Nations Industrial Development Organization.

Veloso, F. and Soto, J.M. (2001), Incentives, infrastructure and institutions: Perspectives on industrialization and technical change in late-developing nations. Technological Forecasting and Social Change, Vol. 66, pp. 87-109.

Verspagen, B. (2000), Growth and structural change: Trends, patterns and policy options. Paper prepared for the conference on "Wachstums- und Innovationspolitik in Deutschland und Europa. Probleme, Reformoptionen und Strategien zu Beginn des 21. Jahrhunderts", Potsdam, 14 April 2000. First draft, April 2000.

Wade, R.H. (2004), Is globalization reducing poverty and inequality? World Development, Vol. 32, pp. 567-589.

Wan, G., Lu, M. and Chen, Z. (2004), Globalization and regional income inequality: evidence from within China. Discussion Paper No. 2004/10, United Nations University, World Institute for Development Economics Research.

Wolf, M. (2005), On the move: Asia's giants take different routes in pursuit of economic greatness. Financial Times, February 23, 2005.

World Bank (2006), World Development Indicators. Online database.

World Bank (2004a), World Development Indicators 2004. CD-ROM.

World Bank (2004b), Republic of Korea: Four decades of equitable growth. A case study from: Scaling up poverty reduction: A global learning process and conference, Shanghai, May 25-27, 2004.

World Bank (2004c), Poverty in Mexico: An assessment of conditions, trends, and government strategy.

World Trade Organization (2004), Trade policy review: Brazil. WT/TPR/S/140.

# Industrial energy and material efficiency: What role for policies?

Mohan Peck and Ralph Chipman*

This chapter is divided into two parts which explore the role for policies in promoting industrial energy and material efficiency. Economic and environmental pressures for energy and material efficiency have been increasing in the past few decades, resulting in noticeable advances in process and product design and in making waste more recyclable and reusable.

According to the World Energy Council, energy efficiency has a broader meaning than mere technological efficiency of equipment; it encompasses all changes that result in decreasing the amount of energy used to produce one unit of economic output (e.g. the energy used per unit of GDP) or to achieve a given level of comfort. Energy efficiency is associated with economic efficiency and includes technological, organizational and behavioural changes.[1] The importance of energy intensity of national economies as an indicator of sustainable development was agreed in Agenda 21, which states that "reducing the amount of energy and materials used per unit in the production of goods and services can contribute both to the alleviation of environmental stress and to greater economic and industrial productivity and competitiveness."

Material efficiency in industrial production, on the other hand, can be defined as the amount of a particular material needed to produce a particular product. Material efficiency can be improved either by reducing the amount of the material contained in the final product ("lightweighting"), or by reducing the amount of material that enters the production process but ends up in the waste stream. In a slightly broader sense, taking into account the industrial production-consumption cycle, material efficiency can refer to the amount of virgin natural resources required for producing a given amount of product, with recycling of post-consumption waste material back into production contributing to material efficiency. Three components of material efficiency can therefore be identified: lightweighting in the production process; waste reduction in the production process; and recycling of material in the production-consumption cycle.

Public policies have generally focused on the third of these, recycling, with improvements in material efficiency within industrial production,

* Policy Integration and Analysis Branch, Division for Sustainable Development, UN-DESA, United Nations, New York. The views expressed in this document are those of the authors and do not necessarily coincide with those of the organization to which they are affiliated.

either through lightweighting or waste reduction, generally left to industry. The discussion here will therefore focus on policies promoting recycling.

## A. Energy efficiency in industry

Energy efficiency is rising toward the top of many national agendas for a number of compelling reasons that are economic, environmental and inter-governmental in nature. As many industries are energy-intensive, this is resulting in new impetus to industrial energy efficiency policies. The economic reasons are quite clear. Most important has been the rise in energy prices from 2005-2006 and their likely continuation at a high level. Increasing concerns over energy security (reliability of supply) are a second factor. Energy supply in many countries increasingly depends on imported oil and gas, and supply is being constrained by geopolitical events while global economic growth is resulting in greater energy demand. Additionally, in many developing countries energy efficiency is also a way to alleviate the investment costs for expanding energy supply infrastructure in the face of tight fiscal constraints.

Environmental pressures are also exerting influence. There is now the need to reduce greenhouse gas emissions to meet commitments under global environment agreements, particularly for Annex 1 signatories to the Kyoto Protocol. In the European Union and in other countries, cap and trade carbon dioxide ($CO_2$) emission trading schemes are now in place, compelling them to reduce greenhouse gas (GHG) emissions, and the focus is often on energy-intensive industries. Moreover, environmental directives in major markets are influencing global industrial supply chains. For example, the European Union's Directive for Energy-using Products (EuP) encompasses the entire life cycle of a product: design, manufacturing, use and disposal, and sets legal requirements for energy use of manufactured products.

Finally, energy efficiency has recently been high on the intergovernmental agenda, where it was a main topic of discussion in the G8 meetings at both Gleneagles and St. Petersburg. Energy efficiency and industrial development are also currently on the agenda of the 14th and 15th sessions of the United Nations Commission on Sustainable Development, which will result in recommendations for international action. Industrial energy efficiency also figures prominently in the "Marrakech Process" on sustainable consumption and production.

Industry is the largest energy end-use sector in the world today and consumed 30 per cent of delivered energy in OECD countries in 2003.[2] Moreover, energy use in the industrial sector is forecast to grow an average of 2.4 per cent per year through 2030 – 3.2 per cent in developing countries and 1.2 per cent in developed countries.[3]

A wide variety of energy efficiency policies, programmes, products, services and delivery mechanisms have been implemented by countries in efforts to improve energy efficiency in industry. Results in developed countries due to such efforts have been significant. For example, while the manufacturing output of the OECD countries has doubled since the 1970s, the amount of energy used in manufacturing has not changed (World Energy Council, 2004). While it is true that most of those gains were achieved between 1973 and 1986 as a response to high oil prices, many opportunities for significant energy savings continue to exist.

Energy efficiency efforts have been shown to be more likely to succeed if a supportive framework of policies and regulatory environment exists. This framework may include: overall energy policy; power sector reform; energy efficiency policies, laws and targets; the establishment of energy efficiency agencies within governments; utility demand-side management programs; negotiated agreements with industry; support and promotion of energy audits; and energy efficiency standards, codes, testing, certification and labelling.

## 1. Trends in industrial energy intensity

Energy efficiency is a main determining factor of industrial energy intensity, but another important factor is structural change in the economy (such as growth of the service sector). At the world level, there has been a continuous decline in primary energy intensity. Global energy intensity is expected to decline at a rate of between 1.5 - 1.9 per cent per annum between 2003 and 2030, depending on economic growth.[4] As shown in Figure 1, there is considerable regional variation in industrial energy intensity. The clear trend has been a continuous decline in industrial energy intensity with significant strides made in China and North America. The exceptions are the Middle East and Africa where energy intensities are still climbing.

Figure 2 highlights energy use and trends in energy-intensive industries in the EU-15. Primary metals, non-metallic minerals and chemicals, as the largest energy-consuming sectors, have over the past decade been the focus of negotiated agreements to achieve energy efficiency and, as a result, significant progress has been made in reducing their energy intensities. Other sectors such as paper, food and textiles show minor increases in the amount of energy required for a unit of output.

## 2. Market-based measures for energy efficiency

During the past decade, liberalization of energy markets, as a process, was initiated in the Australia, Canada, United Kingdom and United States. The EU established rules to liberalize its electricity market, which became operational in 1999, and liberalization of the natural gas market is now being phased-in over time. Liberalization of the energy markets in developing countries and economies in transition has taken place in a number of countries under World Bank structural adjustment programmes, one of the main objectives being to attract private capital to expand and improve the sector.[5]

The change from vertically integrated, monopolistic sectors to competitive markets has also changed the way governments intervene in the energy sector. Instead of regulating monopolies, governments are now in the process of introducing a range of market-based measures. A number of these measures promote energy efficiency either directly or indirectly (for example through reduction of greenhouse gases).

Tax and fiscal policies encourage investment in energy efficient equipment by increasing the cost of energy or reducing the cost of investments. Main targets for these policies are energy-intensive industries, energy service companies and equipment vendors. Such incentive programmes typically have short-term objectives of increasing energy efficiency by 10 per cent and long-term objectives as high as 25 per cent as compared to a baseline year. For example, fiscal incentives in Japan encourage the acquisition of energy efficient equipment. The Energy Conservation Law enacted in 1993 introduced several special tax measures related to energy efficient equipment. These included: a corporate tax rebate equivalent to 7 per cent of the purchase price; and accelerated tax depreciation for new equipment yielding at least a 5 per cent energy savings. As a result of the incentives, investment in energy efficient products increased by US$4 billion per year for several years during the 1990s (Price et al., 2005).

---

### Case Study on Economic Incentives: China

Price reform in China has increased economic incentives for conservation. In 1994, except for coal used for power generation, all price subsidies for coal were withdrawn. In 1998, for the first time, domestic crude oil prices were allowed to float with international oil prices. Controls on the prices of oil products were removed in 2000. Prices rose substantially once these subsidies were lifted and, as economists would expect, energy-intensive industries reduced consumption of these resources. As an example, energy prices in the iron and steel industry increased by a factor of three between 1986 and 1995. Forced to pay the full cost of their energy inputs, firms responded by finding ways to conserve energy and reduce energy expenditures. Over this ten-year period, the iron and steel industry realized energy savings of 15 Mtoe and avoided an estimated 3.87 billion Yuan in energy expenditures (World Energy Council, 2004).

---

## 2.1 Taxes and charges

*Energy or energy-related $CO_2$ taxes* have the advantages that they reduce demand for the taxed product, they increase public revenues and they reduce pollution and its related impacts. These taxes have the disadvantage that they may negatively affect the competitiveness of an industry. Such taxes were first introduced in the 1990s in Europe and are now in practice throughout the EU.

---

## UK Climate Change Levy

Established in 2001 with an environmental goal of reducing $CO_2$ emissions by 2 Mt per year, this is a levy on the sales of electricity, coal, natural gas, and liquefied petroleum gas to the business and public sectors. The levy adds 15 per cent to typical energy bills for the business and public sectors, but companies that meet negotiated energy efficiency improvement targets receive an 80 per cent levy discount. The revenues collected contribute in part to government support for energy efficiency measures and energy-saving technologies. The levy is not set in relation to carbon content of various fuels (Oikonomou and Patel, 2004).

---

*Pollution levies* are imposed by a wide number of countries for violations of pollution emission standards that are often associated with energy use. Such levies are usually imposed on energy-intensive industries and levels of penalties for offences have been rising over time. Efforts are often made to balance the social and economic benefits of the services violators produce with the environmental harm. Countries have developed systems with both civil and criminal penalties. Civil penalties have the advantage that it is only necessary to show that a violation of regulations has occurred, and no lengthy judicial hearings are required; consequently, the majority of penalties imposed come as a result of civil actions. Penalties for pollution levies can range from warning notices or small fines issued in field actions, to substantial administrative penalties, to legal settlements requiring payments of large sums and requirements to install pollution mitigation equipment (see table 1). For example, several manufacturers of diesel engines were jointly penalized over US$1 billion for installing special computer chips that allowed their engines to pass laboratory inspections when in conditions of actual operation they exceeded the emissions standards.[6]

Restructuring of public electric utilities in the 1990s introduced competition but also reduced incentives for demand-side management programmes. To regain the benefits of DSM programmes, *public benefits charges* were introduced whereby a fee is imposed on electricity distributed to all users. Most experience has been in the United States where 25 states currently have energy efficiency programmes funded by public benefits charges. But other countries, such as the UK, Australia, Norway, and Sweden, found the same underinvestment in energy efficiency after deregulation and developed similar programs funded through general revenues or through charges on energy consumption. In the US, as of 2005 these funds have financed over US$900 million of spending on energy efficiency programmes leading to average annual reductions in power demand of 0.4 per cent and a total reduction in demand of over 1,000 MegaWatts (MW) (Price et al., 2005)

---

**Public Benefits Charge in New York**

New York's Energy and Research Development Authority (NYSERDA) provides a number of energy efficiency related services to the industrial sector using funding from a public benefits charge. Services include 50 per cent cost-shared on-site engineering studies, an ESCO-administered industrial performance programme, and a loan fund that provides interest rate reductions on energy efficiency investment projects.

---

## 2.2 Financial incentives

A range of incentive measures may aim at reducing costs associated with increasing energy efficiency, including subsidies or grants for energy efficiency investments, tax relief for purchase of energy efficient equipment or for participation in negotiated agreements, subsidies for energy audits, and loans or guarantee funds for energy efficiency projects.

*Subsidies or grants* for the purchase of energy efficient equipment are the most widespread fiscal incentive in use today. Subsidies and grants are particularly useful to encourage energy efficiency investments in developing country environments where perceived risks may be higher and where competition with infrastructure projects may put energy efficiency projects at a disadvantage. They also effectively stimulate energy efficiency measures in countries where energy prices do not reflect the real costs of energy and are too low to allow financial benefits to accrue to energy projects through energy savings. To make a subsidy programme more effective, care should be given to avoid free riders (those companies that would have upgraded their equipment even without a subsidy) and to reduce transaction costs.

One market-based approach to energy efficiency is the development of an *energy service company* (ESCO) industry. An ESCO is a company that is engaged in developing, implementing and financing performance-based projects that seek to improve energy efficiency or reduce electricity loads of facilities owned or operated by customers. ESCOs are promoting energy efficiency around the world but particularly in countries experiencing increased competition and privatization in the electric utility business, as well as in other sectors undergoing liberalization, e.g., heat production in Central and Eastern Europe. Since ESCO remuneration is often tied to the level of energy savings, it makes good business sense for them to target energy intensive industries.

*Energy audits* of industrial enterprises are key to assessing the potential for energy savings and for identifying energy efficiency measures that could be employed. Energy audits of industrial enterprises are often subsidized or provided free of charge to encourage participation and to facilitate the adoption of modern energy efficient technologies. For example, in France ADEME provides a subsidy of 50 per cent for audits conducted on Industrial sites. About 75 per cent of the companies that received the subsidy stated that they made investments immediately after the audit. The subsidy programme cost the public about € 76 per toe saved and yielded investments with an average cost of € 570 per toe savings per annum, which yields a savings of approximately € 1500 for every toe saved at 2006 oil prices. In some countries, regular audits are mandatory for large energy consumers. In Portugal, Thailand and Tunisia, audits are mandatory for buildings and large factories using over 1000 toe per year. According to the World Energy Council, subsidies generally cover 40-100 per cent of the cost of an energy audit. The Korea Energy Management Corporation performs approximately 2000 energy audits every five years and roughly 80 per cent of the audits are performed for free. A sample of eight audits in the industrial sector required an investment of US$48.65 million and yielded energy savings of 198,604 toe annually. This amounted to annual cost savings of US$37.33 million with an average pay back period of 1.3 years (World Energy Council, 2004).

In many countries, financing of energy efficiency investments is made possible via a combination of soft *public loans and innovative private financing*, aimed at increasing the involvement of private capital. Such innovative financing instruments include ESCO funding, guarantee funds, revolving funds and venture capital. ESCOs sometimes use a shared savings approach in which the ESCO guarantees the energy savings of the project and secures the needed upfront financing. Guarantee funds provide a repayment guarantee to banks granting loans for energy efficiency projects and thus cover the associated credit risk. This is particularly useful in developing countries where financial institutions have little experience in making loans to often asset-free energy efficiency projects.

France, Hungary, Brazil and China have established *loan guarantee* funds for energy efficiency projects. The guarantee fund set up in France is directed to energy efficiency projects of small and medium-size companies (SMEs) which typically have trouble financing energy efficiency due to the small size of their projects. The national guarantee fund covers 40 per cent of the risk, the French Agency for Environment and Energy Management (ADEME) covers an additional 30 per cent of the risk, and a national bank supporting SME growth provides soft lending terms. This fund guarantees up to € 242 million for loans to the private sector. Its goal is to provide SMEs with the option to obtain loans for energy efficiency and renewable energy investments.[7]

Taxes and fiscal incentives promoting industrial energy efficiency in selected countries are summarized in table 2.

One of the most significant co-benefits of energy efficiency is its contribution to GHG emission mitigation. *Carbon dioxide emission trading schemes* are now in place both within the EU and among signatories of the Kyoto Protocol. While designed with environmental goals, these market mechanisms also provide incentives for energy efficiency. The EU Emission Trading Scheme (EU ETS) will cover about one-half of the EU-25's total $CO_2$ emissions by 2010, including all the energy intensive industries. While significant energy efficiency gains are expected as a result of the EU ETS, greater gains could be realized if there was tighter and more consistent target setting. International commitment to post-2012 Kyoto targets is also needed. The Clean Development Mechanism within the Kyoto Protocol supports, among other things, energy efficiency projects that can certify emission reductions with an approved methodology. The first such projects are now being piloted.

White certificate programmes for energy efficiency are being implemented in Italy, the UK, France, Belgium and New South Wales, Australia. In these programmes electricity and gas utilities are required to promote energy efficiency among end-users and to show that they have saved an amount of energy that is a percentage of the energy they distribute. That amount of energy saved is certified through "white certificates". These certificates can then be traded, with those parties that do not meet their energy saving targets having to purchase certificates in the market (Farinelli et al., 2005). The white certificate program in Italy was launched in January 2005. Figure 3 shows the energy savings targets and projected evolution of energy savings over the first 5-year compliance period in Italy with respect to the electricity sector due to white certificates. During this phase of the programme, 3 million tons of oil equivalent (Mtoe) of cumulative primary energy savings are projected to be realised, of which 1.6 Mtoe by electricity distributors and 1.3 Mtoe by natural gas distributors (Bertoldi and Rezessy, 2006).

## 3. Policies for industrial energy efficiency

Figure 4 depicts the various energy efficiency policies employed by over sixty countries[8] and identifies the percentage of countries that use a particular policy. The survey was conducted in 2004 by the World Energy Council and the French Agency for Environment and Energy Management. The chart does not indicate the effectiveness of those policies, their impact, or whether the targets or stipulations of those policies were ambitious or lax.

*Negotiated agreements* between government and industry to improve energy efficiency are playing a significant role in both developed and developing countries (see table 3). While most programmes are voluntary, they generally provide either incentives and/or penalties to encourage participation by companies. Typically, companies or industry associations set targets for reducing energy use or greenhouse gas emissions in exchange for government support, such as financial incentives, publicity, or relief from other environmental or tax obligations. Negotiated agreements may be categorized in three ways: 1) those that are entirely voluntary; 2) those that have implied threats of regulation or taxation; and 3) those with a mix of incentives and penalties for non-compliance. As voluntary programmes have few incentives and lack penalties, they tend to have less participation by industry and results are usually small improvements on business-as-usual. Programmes with implied future threats of regulation or taxation promise easy environmental permitting, relief from regulations, and avoidance of energy or GHG emissions taxes in return for participation. As a result these negotiated agreements have been more successful; for example, the Netherlands achieved an industrial energy efficiency improvement of 22.3 per cent between 1989 and 2000. Programmes with a mix of incentives along with penalties for non-compliance achieved both wide participation and strong results. Participation by industrial enterprises in these agreements is generally high, representing about 90 per cent of industrial GHG emissions in Canada, Denmark, New Zealand, Switzerland and UK.[9]

## Negotiated Agreements in The Netherlands

Under a new Long Term Agreement entitled "The Covenant on Benchmarking Energy Efficiency", industrial enterprises commit to achieving "best of class" energy efficiency amongst comparable companies by 2012. This level is determined as being 90 per cent as efficient as the best performing enterprise. Implementation begins in 2006 and if a company is not in the best of class by 2008 it has the option to make additional energy efficiency improvements or make trade-offs using the Kyoto mechanisms (Rezessy, Bertoldi and Persson, 2005).

Higher levels of end-use energy efficiency can allow deferral of a part of the investment needed to meet growing energy demand. While electric utilities in developed countries have been implementing *demand-side management (DSM) programmes* aggressively during the past 25 years, the electricity sectors in developing countries have had little exposure to the DSM process. Until the early 1990s, subsidized energy prices, non-competitive end-use markets, lack of sufficient DSM knowledge and expertise, and the absence of adequate regulatory and institutional support were the primary factors limiting DSM activities in developing countries. However, as increasing numbers of these countries adopt pricing schemes that reflect actual costs in their electricity sectors, the incentives are likely to increase for realizing energy and capacity savings through DSM.

## Case Study on Demand Side Management: Thailand

In Thailand, the national utility's DSM program, supported by a GEF project, has exceeded targets, with a 566-MW peak load reduction and 3,140 GWh annual energy savings. The utility created a dedicated DSM office that now has a staff of 375 people. The DSM office is implementing 13 different energy efficiency programs for refrigerators, air conditioners, green buildings, industrial cost reduction, industrial ESCO development, motors, compact fluorescent lamps, street lighting, thermal storage, stand-by generation, interruptible loads, time-of-use tariffs, and public awareness campaigns. The private sector has been engaged, through workshops with distributors and retailers to encourage sale of high-efficiency refrigerators and air conditioners, and through negotiations with manufacturers to produce high-efficiency equipment (Singh and Mulholland, 2000).

*Energy performance standards and labels:* Electricity consumption is rising worldwide every year as people gain access to electricity and become increasingly dependent on electrical equipment. In industry, electricity motors power pumps, compressors, fans and a wide variety of machinery. One of the most cost-effective and proven methods for increasing energy efficiency at industrial enterprises is to establish energy efficiency standards for industrial motors. Currently, minimum energy performance standards for motors have been adopted in 30 countries. According to a study by the European Copper Institute, European industry could save over 200 billion kilowatt hours (kWh) of electricity per year by using more energy-efficient electrical motor systems. Research by the EU's motor challenge programme found that industry across the EU-25 could save € 10 billion per year on its electricity bills plus a similar amount from reduced maintenance. Carbon dioxide emissions would be reduced by 100 million tonnes per year, equivalent to one quarter of the EU-15's Kyoto commitment.[10] Labelling of efficient motors has been shown to boost their sales. At present 26 countries use a labelling scheme to help industrial purchasers identify energy efficient motors. Examples of labels for energy efficient motors from four countries are shown in figure 5.

Benchmarking provides a means to compare the energy use within one company or plant to that of other similar facilities producing similar products. Benchmarking can be used to compare plants, processes or systems. For example, systems such as compressed air systems can be benchmarked to evaluate energy efficiency, such as Germany's REN Strom programme. Benchmarks are typically employed as part of negotiated agreements and are supplied to all participating companies. Those companies participating in the negotiated agreement then agree to achieve the efficiency level of the top 10 per cent of plants.

## Benchmarking Tool

The Lawrence Berkeley National Laboratory in the US has produced a Benchmarking and Energy-Saving Tool (BEST) that compares each process used at a plant with world best practice. The software allows industrial users to select from a broad array of energy-efficiency technologies and measures that could be implemented. The software tool is process-related and includes motor systems, boilers, steam distribution and cogeneration, among other things. Apart from characterizing the energy savings, the software also captures non-energy benefits such as reduced emissions, reduced water use, increased productivity, etc.[11]

*Monitoring and targeting* (M&T) is a tool that often provides useful information when implementing other energy efficiency measures, thus making them more effective. It also ensures accountability by providing feedback on performance improvement measures that have been implemented, assessing energy savings achieved. It can also be an effective tool to change corporate thinking about energy saving at all levels from corporate management to operational staff and, as such, can lock in efficiency gains through a strategy that influences corporate culture and promotes behaviour modification. M&T has a long history in the UK, which launched a national programme in 1980. Over 50 industry sector studies have demonstrated the benefits of monitoring and targeting. These benefits include:

- Energy savings of 5 to 15 per cent with similar reductions in emissions of $CO_2$ and other pollutants;
- Coordination of energy management policy through targeting of initiatives that achieve the maximum benefit;
- Assisting with financing for energy efficiency projects, through determination of baseline energy use levels for energy efficiency project proposals, and verification of savings (critical for performance contracting by ESCOs);
- Improved product and service costing, through better understanding of the energy content of products and services;
- Improved budgeting, by providing improved data for the accurate projection of future energy use.

Apart from the UK, the World Bank and others have supported activities that apply the M&T approach in improving energy efficiency in the industrial sector in Brazil, Peru, Colombia, and Slovakia. A recent European Commission Green Paper on energy has set a target of reducing EU energy consumption by 20 per cent compared to projections for 2020.

## M&T Case Study: Unilever Canada

In the late 1990s, Unilever Canada analyzed several alternatives in a bid to reduce the utility bills at one of its facilities. A study concluded that an in-house monitoring and targeting (M&T) program could bring a potential saving of US$700,000 per annum - US$260,000 from technical projects and US$440,000 from operational efficiency improvements. The M&T program was implemented in 2001 and the actual results exceeded initial projections with a year-end total energy savings of US$1million.[12]

*Websites* for industrial energy efficiency are proliferating rapidly and contain tools, guidebooks, information and links on energy efficiency programmes, policies, technologies, financing and technical assistance. The EU's CORDIS website provides access to information on available support programmes, databases and reports, while its ManagEnergy website has similar tools and includes links to over 400 energy agencies, events and partner searching capabilities. Sweden's STEM website includes a calendar of energy efficiency events online (Galitsky, Price and Worrell, 2004).

An overview of industrial sector energy efficiency program products and services of industrialized countries is presented in table 4.

*Market transformation policies and programmes* for energy efficiency have been widely employed by industrialized countries and in recent years are being increasingly adopted by developing countries and economies in transition. Market transformation programmes for energy efficiency a) intervene strategically in the market, b) create long-lasting changes in the structure or functioning of the market, and c) lead to widespread adoption of energy efficient products, services and practices. Market transformation efforts that have been employed to "push" technology innovation include a range of measures such as promoting technology transfer for domestic manufacturing, adopting minimum energy performance standards for energy consuming equipment, developing voluntary agreements with manufacturers, developing new lines of distribution through electric utilities or retailers, and arranging soft financing terms for manufacturers. Other efforts have been designed to "pull" the market; these have included helping consumers to make informed purchase decisions through media campaigns or point-of-purchase aids such as energy efficiency labelling, lowering prices via subsidy or rebate, encouraging bulk purchase/procurement, establishing buy-back or recycling programmes, and providing financing of purchases through banks or utility bills. To date, a host of market transformation initiatives have been implemented in a number of countries that targeted residential appliances (e.g., lighting, refrigerators, and air conditioners), commercial buildings, industrial sectors, and government facilities.

---

### Market Transformation of China's Refrigerator Industry

A project funded by UNDP/GEF and implemented by China's Environmental Protection Administration in cooperation with UN/DESA has succeeded in transforming the Chinese refrigerator market. China has the world's largest refrigerator industry but, prior to the project, the average refrigerator consumed up to 2.5 kWh a day (compared to 1.5 kWh a day in Europe).

Project partners worked with 16 refrigerator manufacturers to help build capacity for research and design of energy efficient refrigerators. New government regulations were also researched and implemented that changed the rules of the market and forced manufacturers to make technology upgrades. In addition, innovative incentive programs were introduced for manufacturers and retailers in order to spur competition.

The project obtained commitments from each participating refrigerator manufacturer to design one new top-rated equivalent refrigerator (that consumes less than 55 per cent of the average current energy use); improve the efficiency of the average refrigerator by at least 10 per cent; and invest at least 10 per cent of their advertising budgets to promote energy efficient refrigerators.

A US$3 million national consumer education campaign raised awareness of the benefits of energy efficient refrigerators in terms of lower operating costs and mitigation of environmental impacts. The advertising campaign directed to television, radio and print media was highly successful and won two national awards for excellence in advertising.

As a result of the above measures which all came together in 2005, the overall project goal of 20 million refrigerators sold yielding lifetime product emission reductions of 100 million tons of $CO_2$ and energy savings of 66 billion kWh was not only met but doubled (UN-DESA, forthcoming).

---

## 4. Policies for supply-side efficiency in energy industries

Both developed and developing countries have pursued regulatory reform and liberalization of the electric power industry. They have done so in the expectation that such reform and restructuring could yield important benefits, namely improving economic efficiency, lowering costs and consumer prices and stimulating economic growth and competitiveness. These expectations have to some extent been realized. For example, in some formerly public-owned companies, labour productivity has improved by up to 60 per cent and generating costs in some cases have declined by 40 per cent. In other countries, availability of generating plants has improved significantly (from 60 per cent to 87 per cent), customer outages have been reduced, distribution company productivity has improved, and prices have been reduced by 13-20 per cent in electricity markets (OECD, 2000). Wider economic benefits are also possible, given that electricity is an input to almost all productive activities. However, the impact of market liberalization on long-term investments in generating capacity is not yet fully clear, particularly in developing countries.

The improvement in efficiency after privatization of four South American distribution companies is summarized in Table 5. These improvements were measured in terms of the change in performance between the date of privatization and a point in time approximately five years later (ten years in the case of Chile). The four companies showed substantial improvements in performance according to all the indicators. These improvements show the benefit of having private management focus on commercial performance, which has been a major weakness of state-owned utilities.

---

### Case Study on Electricity Market Reform: Colombia

Colombia undertook a "middle of the road" approach to electricity sector reform beginning in 1994 which continues today. In 1994, 100 per cent of the electricity sector was publicly owned but it suffered from inadequate capitalization and inability to attract investment. In 2005, 55 per cent of the generation capacity and 50 per cent of the distribution capacity is in private hands. The sector is efficient and transparent, system availability and reliability have markedly improved, and electricity losses have been reduced. There still remains a challenge of rural electrification (30 per cent of the population still has no access). The regulatory authority has significantly changed the "rules of the game" but it has only limited independence. Privatization has resulted in the participation of 37 private companies valued at US$2 billion. Tariffs are competitively priced but competition is affected by cross-subsidies. Since 2003, operations have yielded a financial surplus (Herz, 2005).

---

Another area of significant potential energy savings in the electricity sector lies in the reduction of transmission and distribution losses, which in many developing countries are high due to technical and non-technical losses. For example, at the end of 2005, India had 122,275 MW of installed capacity but only 66 per cent of that capacity was available due to inefficient transmission and distribution.[13] The result was frequent power shortages and load shedding. Although the generating capacity is set to increase, the transmission and distribution sector remains congested and inadequate with losses amounting to approximately 25 per cent, compared to less than 15 per cent which is an acceptable rate in most developing countries[14] and approximately 5 per cent in developed countries. Countries facing a similar challenge to that posed in India might consider a number of possible solutions, including:

- Attracting further investment for transmission infrastructure through easing licensing requirements for entering the transmission and distribution business.[15]
- Strengthening metering, billing and enforcement efforts as a means of reducing the high level of electricity theft.
- Introducing availability based tariffs to improve grid discipline and reduce transmission losses.
- Promoting distributed generation to both industrial parks and remote locations to avoid transmission losses.
- Raising consumer awareness regarding practical energy conservation measures and the benefits of choosing energy efficient appliances.
- Increasing the percentage of renewable sources in the energy mix to provide more options for decentralized generation and to reduce emissions.[16]

*Combined heat and power, or cogeneration,* represents another clean energy path for industry. Worldwide, 65 per cent of fuel energy consumed in electricity generation is lost as waste heat. Building or adapting power plants for cogeneration of electricity and heat can reduce those losses to 20-30 per cent. After generating electricity, the waste heat can be recovered and then used for, among other things, process steam, space heating, air conditioning, water cooling and product drying. Alternatively, clustering of industrial enterprises in industrial parks facilitates opportunities for cogeneration of electricity using waste heat from industrial processes. Auto-production of electricity by industry has the co-benefit of reducing peak load on the electricity network. Installed cogeneration capacity in 2004 amounted to 6,926 GW and has been growing at between 2.5 to 3.0 per cent annually.[17] The share of cogeneration in global electricity generation is just over 7 per cent, despite its enormous potential. Furthermore, most industrial cogeneration is on-site and thus avoids transmission losses, reduces energy costs and security vulnerabilities, and improves reliability and power quality. By significantly reducing the environmental footprint of industry, cogeneration plays a central role in enhancing corporate environmental responsibility. While significant potential for expansion of cogeneration capacity exists, it is typically constrained by outdated framework policies for the electricity sector and by electric utilities that perceive cogeneration as a threat to their sales of electricity and, therefore, their revenue. The extent of cogeneration in selected countries is shown in Figure 6.

---

### Power plants and water use

Conventional electric power plants require large amounts of water for cooling. Half the water used is evaporated in the cooling process and the other half is discharged into waterways, often at higher temperatures or in a degraded state. For example, in the United States 39 per cent of available freshwater is used in power supply, 39 per cent for irrigation in agriculture, while only 14 per cent is consumed by public water supply and 6 per cent by industry. Since cogeneration systems do not require water for cooling, they save water and avoid environmental impacts to natural bodies of water.[18]

---

*The petroleum refining industry* provides fuel to practically every economic sector with the largest shares going to the transport sector and chemical industry. Refineries themselves are large consumers of energy with approximately 50 per cent of operating costs attributable to energy needs. The United States accounts for about one quarter of all refinery capacity in the world and this industry is the largest industrial energy user in the country. Competitive benchmarking data indicates that most petroleum refineries can economically improve energy efficiency by 10-20 per cent. A number of refining companies have adopted energy management programmes that are yielding significant results. BP has implemented a GHG emission reduction programme that reduced its global emissions to 10 per cent below 1990 levels after just five years. ExxonMobil identified over 200 best practices for processes and equipment that are reducing energy use by 15 per cent. All the refineries operating in the Netherlands participated in Long Term Voluntary Agreements that concluded in 2000 and achieved a total energy efficiency improvement of 17 per cent.

### 5. Conclusions: Policies for promoting energy efficiency

It seems clear that the new drivers for industrial energy efficiency – in particular, higher energy prices and concerns about climate change – are going to remain with us for some time. The eco-design of more energy efficient industrial products that is being mandated by environmental directives in major markets will only become more stringent over time.

While there is broad experience and history of innovation in industrial energy efficiency policies in developed countries, there remains much potential for further improvement. Moreover, while some developing countries have shown notable improvements in energy efficiency, there is an urgent need for wider diffusion of industrial energy efficiency policies and application of technologies in developing countries.

## B. Material efficiency in industry

In the broadest sense, the material intensity of an economy can be defined as the total quantity of all raw materials consumed relative to total production, e.g. tons of raw materials consumed per unit of GDP. This broad concept was developed as a parallel to the concept of overall energy intensity of an economy. The quantity of material consumed is measured as "resource flows" or "total material requirement", a concept pioneered by the World Resources Institute (WRI).[19] This work will be briefly reviewed below.

Reducing the environmental impact of industrial production and moving toward sustainability can also be achieved by changing the materials used, replacing toxic materials or non-renewable resources for example. However, material substitution would need to be analyzed in different and more complex terms, particularly regarding the specific environmental impacts of different materials, so this issue will not be addressed here.

The analysis here will not cover material efficiency in agriculture or fisheries, as they are generally considered outside the industrial sector. Similarly, forestry will not be covered generally, although paper will be covered as it is an important industry and central to recycling programmes. Water efficiency will only be covered briefly as it relates to industrial consumption.

## 1. Benefits of increasing material efficiency

There are a number of benefits of increasing material efficiency. First, natural resources are conserved, ensuring both that they will be available for future generations and that use of the most accessible and lowest-cost resources will be extended, reducing the cost of production and improving the standard of living. While scarcity of natural resources, other than water and energy, does not appear to impose a substantial restraint on development, conserving those resources does provide benefits.

Second, reducing the demand for raw materials will reduce the impacts of raw material extraction, including both environmental and social impacts. The environmental impacts of mining and primary processing, in particular, can be severe, including water pollution, air pollution and land degradation. Environmental regulation of mining and primary processing has often been less effective than regulation of large-scale industry and the energy sector, in part because mining enterprises tend to be small, in some cases consisting of one mine, so that enterprises can disappear or declare bankruptcy after deposits are depleted, leaving the damage to be cleaned up by others.[20] In the United States, for example, many of the largest Superfund toxic waste sites are metal mines, and mining operations produce a large share of industrial toxic releases. The costs of these environmental impacts are not reflected in market prices of raw materials. Analyses have generally found that the environmental impacts of recycling materials are substantially less than the impacts of extracting the same raw materials. The impacts of raw material extraction will not be examined here, other than to note that increasing material efficiency will reduce such impacts.

Third, energy will be conserved and greenhouse gas emissions reduced. As indicated in the consideration of energy efficiency above, the metals sector in particular is very energy intensive. Recycling of materials can save most of the energy required for refining and processing. Typical energy savings from recycling relative to raw material extraction are estimated at: aluminium 95 per cent, iron and steel 74 per cent, plastic 80 per cent, paper 64 per cent and glass about 10 per cent.[21]

Fourth, increasing material efficiency will reduce the amount of waste material going to landfills or incineration, reducing land use, water and air pollution and other negative impacts from waste handling. Industrial production and consumption are involved in almost all solid waste disposal in developed countries, whether through wastes from extraction of industrial raw materials, wastes from industry, or household or office waste of industrial products. In the United Kingdom, industrial production and consumption account directly for almost one-third of solid waste, with mining and quarrying, and construction and demolition accounting about equally for most of the remaining two-thirds. Within the 33 per cent due directly to industrial production and consumption, 14 per cent is directly from industry, 10 per cent is from commercial sources, and 9 per cent is household waste. Only the 5 per cent of solid waste due to dredging, and a few per cent due to household yard waste (leaves and grass) and food waste would be independent of industrial production. Agricultural residues are generally not included in solid waste statistics, nor are livestock wastes, which are considered liquid waste.[22]

Fifth, and finally, improved collection and recycling of waste, particularly drink containers and plastic bags, could reduce the amount of litter cluttering land and water and in some cases clogging drainage systems. In fact, the desire to reduce litter for aesthetic reasons has been a major driving force behind municipal recycling schemes in many areas.

## 2. Resource scarcity

Scarcity of natural resources other than water and energy, as noted above, does not appear to be a critical problem for development. Deposits of most mineral resources are fairly abundant relative to demand. As the richest and most accessible deposits have been gradually depleted, improvements in extraction and processing technology have reduced extraction costs, and prices of raw materials have generally trended downwards in recent decades, with short-term fluctuations due to cycles of supply and demand. As a result, there has been little economic pressure for increasing material efficiency.

Since 2004, however, prices of metals have increased substantially, with the IMF metals index increasing to almost three times the 2002 level. This increase in prices has been primarily due to high growth in demand, largely from China. Prices are expected to decline over the next few years as new extraction and refining capacity comes on line in response to high prices. Energy prices are considered more likely to remain high, and since material extraction and refining tends to be energy intensive, particularly for metals, raw material prices are likely to remain somewhat above the prices of recent decades (IMF, 2006). As a result, there is likely to be strong short-term pressure for increased material efficiency and recycling, and more modest long-term pressure.

## 3. Total material consumption

From an economy-wide perspective, material intensity is measured and monitored through material flow accounting (MFA), a concept developed by the World Resources Institute and elaborated in detail by Eurostat, including the development of a statistical database (Eurostat, 2001).

According to the Eurostat database, overall material consumption, including fossil fuels but excluding water, in the EU-15 amounted to 15.7 tonnes per capita in 2002. In broad categories, this includes, per capita, 7.0 tonnes of construction minerals (sand, gravel, crushed stone), 4.0 tonnes of biomass (food, fodder and wood), 3.7 tonnes of fossil fuels, and 1.0 tonnes of industrial ores and metals. Over the period 1970-2000, this broad measure of material consumption grew closely with economic growth in the lower-income countries of the EU-15 (Spain, Portugal, Greece, Ireland, Italy), keeping material intensity fairly constant relative to GDP, while in the richer countries (Sweden, UK, Netherlands, Belgium, Germany), economic growth has been largely "de-coupled" from total material consumption, leading to a steady reduction in material intensity per unit of GDP. In the UK, Sweden, and particularly Germany, total material consumption has declined over the period. This de-coupling of material consumption from economic growth appears to occur between a GDP per capita of about US$20,000 and US$30,000 (Weisz et al., 2005, pp.19-22).

Analyses to date of total material flows have aggregated mass flows without taking into account the specific environmental impacts of particular flows, due in part to lack of data and techniques for such analysis. A more detailed system of MFA accounts for policy development might take into account both large flows – usually with low specific environmental impacts – and small flows with large impacts, such as heavy metals and hazardous chemicals. Such an analysis has been proposed but would need to include hundreds of different materials and would be a complex undertaking (Eisenmenger, Fischer-Kowalski and Weisz, 2006).

There have been few if any policy efforts focusing on reducing aggregate material flows as such, in part because no single policy could address this broad aggregate, and in part because the different material flows have very different impacts on sustainability and the environment, and policies generally focus on more specific problems.

The main direct driver of overall industrial material efficiency is raw material prices, but general policy measures such as taxes on raw materials to increase prices (other than on fossil fuels) have not generally been used to reduce consumption or increase material efficiency. One exception to this is taxes on construction aggregate in a few countries intended to promote recycling of those materials and reduce landfill. Increased charges for logging on public land, or restrictions on such logging, could increase prices of wood and promote efficiency in wood and paper use, but there has been little use of such instruments for these purposes.

## 4. Lightweighting

The simplest and most direct form of improving material efficiency in industry is reducing the amount of material that goes into a product, or "lightweighting". The average weight of aluminium cans in the United States has decreased from 20.6g in 1972 to 15.6g today, a reduction of 24 per cent. Glass bottles are now about 25 per cent lighter than they were in 1984. Plastic soft drink bottles made of polyethylene terephthalate (PET) had an average weight of 67g in 1984 and 48g in 2000. Plastic milk jugs made of high density polyethylene (HDPE) weighed 120g in the mid-1960s and 65g in 2000. The thickness of the most common plastic grocery bag has been reduced from 30 microns to 18 microns (Rathje and Murphy, 2001, p.101). This industrial lightweighting has contributed substantially to improving material efficiency in the last few decades and to stabilizing, but not reducing, total material requirements.

However, there is probably limited scope for much more lightweighting (distinct from material substitution) in most products, perhaps with the exception of electronics, a modest but growing component of waste (considered below). With respect to material efficiency, increased recycling generally appears to offer the greatest potential for further progress, with material substitution contributing to eco-efficiency. In addition, industrial lightweighting is driven, at least directly, by internal production economics, production technologies, and raw material prices, with limited influence from public policies. Lightweighting will therefore not be analyzed in detail here.

## 5. Recycling

Recycling of waste materials back into industrial production, as noted above, not only reduces requirements for the extraction and processing of virgin natural resources, but also saves much of the energy consumed by extraction and processing, and reduces the amount of waste going to landfills or incineration. It is therefore an important contributor to material efficiency, in terms of natural resource requirements, and the component that has been the main focus of public policy.

Recycling is generally more cost-effective for waste from industry and business than for household waste, as industrial and commercial activities generally produce large volumes of relatively uniform waste. Collection and recycling of household waste is less cost-effective because of the high costs of collecting and sorting mixed wastes in relatively low volumes, particularly considering that most households, to a greater or lesser extent, contaminate recyclables with non-recyclable material and throw out recyclables with the general garbage. In the United Kingdom, while recycling of household waste amounted to 6.3 million tonnes in 2003 (22 per cent of household waste), industrial and commercial recycling amounted to 30.7 million tonnes (45 per cent of total industrial and commercial waste).[23]

Economic analyses of municipal recycling of household waste indicate that recycling is often more expensive than landfill disposal (usually excluding externalities), particularly where inexpensive land is available, as in most parts of the United States. Recycling is most cost-effective for aluminium, other metals and paper, and is least cost-effective for plastics and glass. Assessing the costs and benefits of household waste recycling, including all externalities, is rather complex, and different analyses come to different conclusions. Nonetheless, it seems fairly clear that recycling of household waste does reduce consumption of virgin raw materials and thus contributes to material efficiency.

Demand, and therefore prices, for many recycled materials have been low, particularly for the mixed recyclables derived from household waste. This is in part because industries are reluctant to invest in production systems using recycled material, which often differ significantly from systems using virgin raw materials because of uncertainties about availability and price of recycled material and variability in the characteristics of the material. Recycling paper, for example, requires processes for removing ink, staples and other artificial contaminants, but not for removing lignin and other natural contaminants of pulpwood.

It should be noted that household waste recycling is a traditional as well as a recent phenomenon, with a historical gap between the two. In the industrialized countries, until the early to mid-twentieth century, small-scale and informal commercial collection of municipal waste for reuse and recycling (e.g. "rag and bone men" in the United States), was common, sometimes as barter exchange. There were specialized collectors and recyclers for rags, used clothing, paper, scrap metal, and food waste – particularly bones and fat – as well as used but still usable household goods. Industry, both large and small, commonly used recycled materials as inputs. Then, in the early twentieth century, rising wages and standards of living, health and safety concerns, declining prices of virgin raw materials, and new technologies of mass production gradually reduced demand for most recycled materials, and collection of household waste for recycling largely disappeared (Strasser, 1999). Informal waste scavenging and recycling are still common in developing countries, where formal municipal waste collection and disposal systems are very limited. However, modern systems are gradually being introduced, reducing traditional recycling, for better or worse.

While traditional informal scavenging has declined and environmental recycling of household waste has increased over the 20th century, commercial scrap recycling has continued, sometimes in competition with municipal recycling. In the United States, member enterprises of the Institute of Scrap Recycling Industries (ISRI), operating on a purely commercial basis, recycle over 130 million tons of material per year, compared to 79 million tons of household waste recycling.[24]

Reducing solid waste and littering were the main political drivers of the introduction of modern municipal recycling programmes in the 1970s. In the United States, it was estimated that by 1990, there were more than 140 laws related to recycling in 38 states (Rathje and Murphy, 2001, p.200). By 2006, some 9000 communities had introduced collection of separated household waste for recycling, alongside general waste collection, up from one in the 1970s. Some states have now achieved municipal waste recovery rates of about 50 per cent.[25] Figure 7 shows the components of municipal solid waste in the United States, amounting to a total of 245 million tons in 2005. Figure 8 shows the recycling rates for various components – using different categories than figure 7.[26]

In the United Kingdom, where modern household recycling began a little later, recycling, including composting, increased from 11 kg per capita per year in 1991 to 113 kg in 2004 (figure 9). Over the same period, total annual household waste per capita, including recycled waste, increased from 428 kg to 517 kg. Recycling thus accounted for 22 per cent of total municipal waste by 2004. As a result, unrecycled waste declined from a peak of 456 kg per capita in 2001 to 404 kg in 2004.[27]

In OECD countries, all of which now have a variety of recycling programmes, municipal waste recycling rates are increasing and now average over 80 per cent for metals, 40-55 per cent for paper and cardboard, and 35-40 per cent for glass (de Tilly, 2004). Recycling of municipal solid waste, including composting of organic waste, in the EU-15 varies from 4 per cent in Portugal to 64 per cent in the Netherlands. The remainder of the waste goes to either landfill or incineration, with incineration, generally with energy generation, dominating in the Netherlands, Denmark, Sweden, Belgium and Germany, as well as Japan, and landfill in most of the other European countries, as well as in the United States and Canada.[28]

Also affecting industrial material efficiency are product and packaging take-back requirements, also known as "extended producer responsibility", which make industry responsible for their associated waste products, including end-of-life products. These requirements, recently introduced in Europe and Japan (see below), in addition to providing recycled material to the originating industry at no charge beyond that of meeting the take-back requirements, also provide an incentive to design the products to reduce the amount of waste and facilitate recycling. These policies appear to be fairly effective in increasing recycling and, in the case of packaging at least, in reducing waste generation rates. It is still too early to assess their effectiveness in reducing waste generation and recycling through product design.

Charges and restrictions on waste disposal can also promote industrial recycling by increasing the cost of disposal and thus making recycling more economically attractive. In many places in the United States, for example, it is illegal to dispose of automobile lead-acid batteries in landfills. Such batteries must be returned to dealers, making it economical to recover the lead for use in new batteries.

To reduce waste generation and promote recycling generally, particularly from industry and business which pay directly and volumetrically for waste disposal, Denmark in 1987 introduced a landfill tax, which has gradually increased to € 50 per tonne, roughly doubling the cost of landfill disposal. Lower taxes are charged on incineration, particularly for incineration with energy recovery, as that is the preferred option for final disposal in Denmark. As a result of this and other measures, reuse and recycling of waste in Denmark increased from 21 per cent in 1985 to 60 per cent in 2000. The Netherlands also has a high landfill tax, which was increased in 2000 to € 70 per tonne (OECD, 2003).

In the Republic of Korea, following the introduction of a Volume-based Waste Fee System and a Waste Deposit-Refund System, an Extended Producer Responsibility system was introduced in 2003, covering TVs, refrigerators, air conditioners, tires, lubricating oil, metal cans, glass bottles, paper packaging and plastic packaging material. Responsibility was subsequently expanded to cover fluorescent light bulbs and packaging film, and responsibility for electronic products is planned. Under the system, the Ministry of the Environment sets annual recycling obligations for each product and each producer or importer. The producers and importers than submit annual recycling plans and progress reports, and fines are imposed if the obligations are not met.[29]

The growth of recycling programmes in recent decades has, in some cases, created a glut of recycled materials that exceed industrial demand, even if they are free. Indeed, for most materials, recycling of material back to industry is limited by demand more than supply. In 1987, when the state of New Jersey in the United States introduced requirements for municipal recycling, the collection rate for newspapers increased from 50 per cent to 62 per cent, and the price of used newsprint fell from US$45 per ton to minus US$25 per ton, i.e. the collectors had to pay to get rid of it (Rathje and Murphy, 2001, p.206). To increase demand, and therefore prices, for recycled material, and to encourage the introduction of technologies using recycled material as input, some communities have passed laws requiring government offices, and in some cases private businesses, to buy products such as paper with a certain proportion of recycled material. These measures, however, have been difficult to administer and enforce. The fact that waste collection and recycling is commonly the responsibility of municipal authorities rather than national governments can make it difficult to develop national policies or build national markets.

## 5.1 Metals

Recycling of metals, unlike many other types of recycling, has a long and continuous history as a commercial business, to which modern municipal recycling of household waste makes a modest contribution. And metal recycling makes a major contribution to material efficiency in industry, as well as to energy efficiency. In the United Kingdom, the contribution of recycled metal to total production is: lead 74 per cent, steel 42 per cent, aluminium 39 per cent, copper 32 per cent and zinc 20 per cent. Energy savings from the use of recycled metals were about: aluminium 95 per cent, copper 85 per cent, steel 68 per cent, lead and zinc 60 per cent.[30]

In the United States, the volume of metal scrap recycling, like metal production, is dominated by iron and steel, with about 78 million tons recycled, compared with 2.5 million tons of aluminium, 1.5 million tons of copper, and 1.3 million tons of lead.[31]

In the United States in 2005, the 78 million tons of scrap iron and steel recovered for recycling, represent 76 per cent of domestic production (103 million tons). Most of the recycled scrap was used domestically, but an increasing share, about 17 per cent, was exported, with China as the largest importer. The recycling rate of 76 per cent was up from about 65 per cent in the late 1990s. The major components of scrap steel are vehicles (almost 100 per cent recycled), construction beams (97 per cent recycled), appliances (90 per cent recycled), construction rebars (65 per cent recycled), as well as rail components, machinery and other large items. Municipal solid waste recycling contributed 14 million tons to recycled steel in 2005. A modest but significant growth component of this was steel cans, with the recycling rate increasing from 15 per cent in 1998 to 65 per cent in 2005.[33] The international price of high-grade scrap steel has increased in the last few years to US$300-US$400 per ton in 2006, up from US$100-US$200 a few years ago. The price of basic finished steel products, such as wire rods and rebars, is now about US$400 to US$500 per ton, indicating that a major share of the cost of steel is in mining and refining. The recent price increases have substantially increased the profitability of scrap steel recycling. The increased recycling over the last decade has reduced United States demand for iron ore, as the trends in production and consumption have been generally flat.

Scrap steel is the input for steel-making in the electric arc furnace (55 per cent of steel production in the United States), while iron ore, along with some scrap, is used in the blast furnace and basic oxygen furnace (45 per cent of steel production). Steel production from scrap in the electric arc furnace requires about one-third of the energy required for steel production from iron ore in a blast furnace, reduces air pollution by 85 per cent and water use by 40 per cent.

Aluminium production, including both primary production from bauxite and secondary production from recycled scrap, increased from 16 million metric tons globally in 1976 to 43 million tons in 2005. Aluminium production from recycled material increased from 2.8 million tons to 13 million tons over the same period, increasing from less than 18 per cent of total aluminium production to about 30 per cent. This represented a reduction in the increase in bauxite mining and refining by about 40 per cent. Recycling of aluminium generally provides greater economic benefits than other materials, as primary production from bauxite is highly energy intensive, while aluminium production from scrap can be accomplished with as little as 5 per cent of the energy input. The capital cost of an aluminium recycling plant is about one tenth the cost of a bauxite smelter complex.[34]

In the United States, which accounts for almost half of recycled aluminium, 59 per cent of recycled aluminium was manufacturing scrap recycled within the industry, with 41 per cent coming from post-consumer recycling. About half of the post-consumer recycling consisted of used beverage cans, about 60 per cent of which were recycled, mostly for making new cans. The average aluminium can now contains more than 50 per cent recycled aluminium.

In the United Kingdom, recycling of aluminium cans increased greatly in the 1990s as a result of recycling programmes, from 1,200 tonnes (2 per cent of aluminium can production) in 1990 to 34,400 tonnes (40 per cent) in 2001. Over the same period, the weight of the average aluminium can was reduced from 18.5g to 15.5g (a 16 per cent reduction), making an additional smaller contribution to overall material efficiency. Total consumption of virgin aluminium for beverage cans was reduced slightly, as total production almost doubled, and would have more than doubled had plastic bottles not increased their share of the beverage container market. The recycling rate for other aluminium packaging, mostly aluminium foil, is lower, resulting in an overall aluminium recycling rate of 24 per cent. In addition to recycling into beverage cans, recycled aluminium is used for making lightweight vehicle components. Aluminium recycling in the United Kingdom is lower than in other industrialized countries, largely due to lower rates of household waste recycling.[35]

From 1970 to 2003, the price of aluminium in real terms fluctuated, with an overall downward trend to less than US$1,500 per tonne. As noted above, the increase in recycling during that period, while profitable, was driven more by the desire to reduce waste and litter through deposit-return schemes and household recycling programmes than by shortage of bauxite or high prices for aluminium. Since 2004, the price of aluminium has increased to about US$2,600 per tonne, providing increased incentives for recycling.[36]

Global copper consumption has been increasing steadily, from about 15 million tonnes in 1993 to 20 million tonnes in 2005. The share of recycled scrap, about 30 per cent in 2005, has fluctuated between 30 per cent and 40 per cent since 1970. In absolute terms, recycling of copper scrap increased steadily until 1995 to 6.5 million tonnes, and has since fluctuated in the range of 6 to 6.5 million tonnes. In the United States, about half of the copper consumed is used in buildings, particularly for wiring, with the other half used in electrical and electronic equipment, transportation equipment, and machinery. There is little copper in ordinary household waste. Copper products such as building wiring can have a lifetime of decades in use, limiting the availability of scrap.[37] The overall trend of copper prices from 1970 to 2000 was downward, with the price falling by about half in real terms between 1970 and the late 1990s. Fluctuations in copper prices have tended to be reflected in fluctuations in recycling rates, with recycling rates declining when copper prices fall (Chipman, and Dzioubinski, 1999). However, since 2002, the price of copper has more than quadrupled, from about US$1,500 per tonne to almost US$7,000 per tonne. The scrap price has also increased, substantially increasing the incentive for copper recovery and recycling.

Total world production and consumption of lead has been increasing steadily in recent years, with recycling increasing and primary production declining, in both absolute and relative terms. Recycled lead increased from under 30 per cent of the total in 1976 to almost 60 per cent in 2003. Recycled lead is mostly post-consumer recycled from lead-acid vehicle batteries, which account for about 60 per cent of global lead consumption. Lead-acid batteries account for almost 90 per cent of the lead used and recycled in the United States, where many other uses of lead, such as paint and leaded gasoline, have been banned. Most states legally require recycling of lead-acid batteries and prohibit disposal in landfill. Over 90 per cent of lead-acid batteries from motor vehicles are recycled in the United States, Canada, the United Kingdom and other OECD countries. The energy required for processing recycled lead is about one quarter that for primary lead.[38]

Mining subsidies, often implicit, reduce the cost of mining and the economic incentives for metal recycling. In the United States, for example, an 1872 law still in effect allows hard rock mining enterprises (but not coal, oil or gas enterprises) to buy public land for US$5 per acre and not pay any production royalties to the government. Relative to actual land values, this amounts to an implicit subsidy of about US$500 million per year.[39] In addition, the lack of guarantees for clean-up costs often leaves those costs to the public. The cost of cleaning up some 550,000 abandoned hard rock mining sites in the United States is estimated to be in the range of US$32 billion to US$72 billion.[40] Ensuring that the prices of metal reflect the full costs of mining, including externalities, would increase incentives for recycling.

## 5.2 Paper and packaging

The United States in 2005 consumed 100 million tons of paper (including cardboard), with 51 million tons (51 per cent) recovered for recycling, up from 92 million tons consumed and 35 million tons (39 per cent) recovered in 1993. The volume of waste paper going to landfill declined from 47 million tons in 1987 to 38 million tons in 2003. Unlike metals, most recycled paper derives from municipal solid waste. Two-thirds of the paper recovered goes back to paper mills, providing 37 per cent of the paper industry's fibre requirements. It is estimated that each ton of paper recycled conserves roughly 17 trees.[41]

Two-thirds of that recycled paper is used for making cardboard (including both smooth paperboard and corrugated packaging), with most of the rest going into tissue, sanitary paper and newsprint. Cardboard generally has a high recycled content, newsprint and tissue have variable amounts, and most high quality printing and writing paper has relatively low recycled content. As a result of this "downgrading" of recycled paper, due to damage to the pulp fibres in the recycling process as well as to contamination of the collected paper, it is estimated that the maximum overall recycled content of paper and cardboard would be 70-80 per cent. Most of the recovered paper not used by paper mills in the United States was exported, with little going to incineration or landfill. As a result of the increased recycling, paper industry requirements for virgin fibre, and the amount of waste paper and cardboard sent to landfills, have been fairly constant, despite steadily increasing total production.[42]

Germany, in 1991, began a programme to reduce and recycle packaging waste, including product and transport packaging, through a Packaging Ordinance that requires manufacturers to pay the cost of recycling the packaging from their products and to achieve a recycling rate of 60-75 per cent, depending on the material. While some companies developed schemes to comply with the Ordinance on their own, many manufacturers joined forces with retail firms and waste collection companies in the German Dual System or Green Dot system in order to reduce costs through economies of scale. Participating manufacturers place a green dot on their packaging and pay the waste collection companies for the green dot packaging they collect for recycling. Packaging recycling in Germany is thus a national programme, rather than a municipal programme as elsewhere. As a result, packaging in Germany declined from about 96 kg per person per year in 1991 to 77 kg in 2002, a reduction of about 20 per cent. Of over 6 million tonnes of packaging waste collected, some 5.3 million tonnes went back to industry for reuse, an 84 per cent recycling rate.[43] At the same time, the printing industry in Germany, in order to avoid regulation, adopted a voluntary quota for the recycling of printing paper, with the quota increasing from 53 per cent in 1994 to 60 per cent in 2000.

The Green Dot programme has been expanded to the European level in response to the 1994 European Packaging Directive and is now operational in 25 European countries with some 130,000 participating enterprises. Participating waste collection programmes are organized in the Packaging Recovery Organization Europe (PRO-Europe). For goods imported from outside Europe, the European importer is responsible for meeting the requirements. As a result, the paper recycling rate in Europe has increased to 55 per cent in 2005, up from 38 million tonnes in 1998 to 46 million tonnes, accounting for over half of the paper produced.[44]

In Japan, efforts to increase corporate responsibility for waste recovery since the mid-1990s have increased paper recovery and reuse rates from about 50 per cent in 1993 to about 67 per cent in 2003 (Bowyer, et al., 2005).

Recycling requirements for paper increase the amount of material available for reuse and reduce its cost, making it more attractive to paper producers. However, increasing recycling requirements in Germany, as in other places, resulted in an initial rapid increase in volumes of recovered paper, which reduced the market price of recovered paper to below zero, i.e. recyclers had to pay producers to accept recovered paper in order to dispose of all of the available supply. Subsequently, the high availability and low price of recovered paper induced producers to invest in production facilities designed for recycled material, which raised prices again (Baumgärtner and Winkler, 2003). In order to increase the market for recycled paper as well as reduce the impact of government paper consumption, the United States Government requires that the paper it procures have at least 30 per cent recycled content. California requires that at least 50 per cent of the newsprint used by each printer and publisher must contain at least 40 per cent post-consumer recycled fibre. In Wisconsin, newspapers are required to use newsprint with a least 35 per cent recycled content. Procurement policies of many private companies also specify recycled content for paper and packaging. These policies have encouraged companies to invested in systems for recycling paper, increasing the demand and price for recovered paper, and making recycling more economical.

The economic incentive for paper recycling is undermined by subsidization of timber extraction. The United States Forest Service spends about US$34 million per year on building, maintaining and subsidizing roads in national forests, which are used without charge by logging companies. Charging industry for these services would increase the price of virgin timber and paper made from it, increasing the demand for recovered paper.[45]

The cost of paper and other wood products also depends on the price wood harvesters pay for the right to harvest the wood, sometimes called "stumpage fees". In the United States, most harvested timber comes from private land, with prices set by supply and demand, but a significant share of wood comes from public land. In recent years, environmental concerns have reduced or stopped timber sales from public lands, reducing supply and increasing prices, particularly for construction lumber.

It should also be noted that waste paper products contribute to energy recovery from incineration of municipal solid waste, replacing fossil-fuel energy generation. As renewable biomass energy, it also reduces net emissions of greenhouse gases. In some circumstances, using waste paper as an energy source may be more sustainable than recycling. Logging residues are also burned for process heat in paper production, and increasingly for district heating and power generation through combined heat and power (CHP) systems, reducing fossil fuel consumption. In Finland, wood fuels, mostly from logging residues, provide 21 per cent of total primary energy. This can also be considered as an increase in material efficiency in forest industries, including pulp and paper (UNEP, 2006).

More general questions of sustainable forest management and forest productivity, deforestation, timber trade, "industrial" tree farming, biodiversity, carbon sequestration and other such questions, all of which affect timber prices, will not be addressed here, as they are more part of discussions on forest management than industrial efficiency.

## 5.3 Beverage containers

In the United States, a deposit-return system was introduced in the state of Oregon in 1972, with a 5 cent deposit required on all bottles and cans of beer and carbonated soft drinks. As a result, over 90 per cent of the beverage containers covered were returned, although the rate gradually declined to 82 per cent in 2002, in part due to increasing consumption in public places where recycling was less convenient. In states without such "bottle bills", about 30 per cent of beverage containers are recycled. In addition, the share of roadside litter consisting of beverage containers in Oregon declined from 40 per cent to 10 per cent, which was a primary purpose of the law.[46] Ten other states have since introduced bottle bills. Other countries with deposit-return systems for various kinds of beverage containers include Canada (1970), Netherlands (1974), Finland (mid-1970s), Sweden (1984), Denmark (1989), Switzerland (1990), Austria (1990) and Kiribati (2004).[47]

Some countries have other charges or restrictions, in some cases in addition to deposits, on various types of beverage containers. In Finland a system of taxes, together with deposits, ensures that 81 per cent of beer and soft drinks are sold in refillable glass or PET bottles, with most of the rest recycled in other ways. Norway has a tax on all packaging, including non-refillable beverage containers, with partial exemption depending on recycling rates. In Denmark, domestic beer and soft drinks must be sold in refillable glass or plastic bottles, with standardized beer bottles allowing reuse without sorting by brand. The German Ordinance on Packaging Waste (1993) requires that at least 72 per cent of most beverages be sold in refillable bottles. Sweden required (1984/1994) that aluminium cans and PET bottles must achieve 90 per cent recycling or face a ban, leading to the adoption by bottlers of standard bottles to facilitate reuse.[48]

## 5.4 Plastics

Some plastics, notably PET (polyethylene terephthalate) and HDPE (high density polyethylene), both of which are used for bottles and other containers, can be reused by the plastics industry and are included in many municipal recycling schemes. Recycling plastic, compared to virgin plastic production from natural gas or petroleum feedstock, reduces energy and water consumption by 70-80 per cent, including conservation of the chemical feedstock in their production, and substantially reduces air pollution.[49] Globally about 4 per cent of oil and gas is used as feedstock for plastics production, and another 4 per cent (equivalent) is used for energy for plastics processing.

In the United Kingdom, a total of 4.7 million tonnes of plastics are consumed annually, 35 per cent of which consists of bottles, containers and other packaging, with building and construction accounting for another 23 per cent. About 3 million tons is disposed of as waste, of which about 7 per cent is recycled. Some 24,000 tons of plastic bottles are recycled, amounting to 5.5 per cent of the bottles sold.[50]

In the United States in 2004, some 500,000 tons of PET bottles were collected, representing about 20 per cent of PET bottle production. The volume collected has increased slightly in recent years, but the recycling share has declined from 40 per cent in 1995 to 20 per cent in 2002, apparently because people are consuming more drinks in small containers away from home (Royte, 2005, p.177). In Europe, 665,000 tons of PET bottles were collected in 2004, representing a 30 per cent collection rate.

Used PET can be recycled into new plastic bottles – Coke and Pepsi have committed to using 10 per cent recycled material in their PET bottles – as well as for fibrefill for winter coats and sleeping bags, polyester carpeting, fleece jackets, or plastic strapping. One-third of the used PET collected in the United States is exported to China, with the amount doubling between 1995 and 2004. Clean recycled PET flakes now (November 2006) fetch US$600-US$700 per tonne on the international market, providing a strong incentive for recycling. In the German Green Dot packaging recycling programme, reuse of recovered plastic by industry has increased from 51 per cent of the recovered plastic in 2001 to 63 per cent in 2005 (Schedler, 2006).

In the United States in 2002, about 2 million tons of HDPE bottles and containers were used, with 370,000 tons recycled, for a recycling rate of about 20 per cent. This was a dramatic increase from 40,000 tons recycled (a 5 per cent rate) in 1990. Recycled HDPE is used in the production of bottles (28 per cent), plastic film (17 per cent), pipes (15 per cent), shipping pallets (14 per cent), and plastic lumber (11 per cent), with the remaining 15 per cent going to other uses or exported, mostly to Asia. Recycled HDPE thus replaces both petroleum and wood in production. The increase in recycling since 1990 has been accompanied by longer-term light-weighting of HDPE bottles, with the weight of a one gallon milk container, for example, declining from 95g in the 1970s to 60g in 2000.[51]

Recycling of HDPE from municipal solid waste, like most plastics, is not generally profitable, as the cost of collecting household HDPE is about US$1000-US$1400 per ton, with processing costs of about US$120 to US$250 per ton, while used HDPE currently (November 2006) fetches about US$200-US$400 per ton on the international market, depending on quality.[52]

While the tonnage of PET and HDPE recycled has increased rapidly, it has been from a low base and is not keeping up with the rapid increase in total PET and HDPE production and consumption. Plastic recycling is therefore not reducing in absolute terms the amount of petroleum and energy consumed in its production. On the other hand, the increase in PET and HDPE production and consumption has, in part, replaced the use of glass, paper cartons and other plastics, so a full examination of the evolving impact of PET and HDPE would need to take into account the impact of substitution as well as the impact of recycling. It should also be noted that waste plastics contribute to energy recovery from waste incineration.

Some countries have also adopted policies to reduce the use of plastic bags. In response to such bags littering the landscape and clogging drains, South Africa has banned bags under 80 microns thick (standard supermarket bags are 18 microns), Bangladesh and Taiwan (province of China) have banned free distribution of bags by stores, and Ireland has imposed a 15 cent charge for each bag (Royte, 2005, p.193).

The recycling rate for plastics remains very low relative to other materials, providing a large potential for substantial increases in material efficiency, with benefits for reducing energy consumption, waste, air pollution and greenhouse gas emissions.

## 5.5 Glass

Recycled glass, which is collected in some municipal recycling programmes in the United States and not in others, is used to make new bottles, for fibreglass, and for road construction aggregate. The inclusion of some recycled glass reduces the energy required for glass-making. In general, however, the benefits of improving material efficiency in glass production are less than those for other materials. Waste is reduced, but the energy saved is small, and the raw material, sand, is abundant and cheap everywhere (Royte, 2005, p.266).

## 5.6 Electronic waste

Computers and other electronic equipment, which contain lead, mercury, chromium, cadmium, barium, beryllium, PVCs, brominated flame retardants and other toxic elements as well as plastic, copper, glass and other materials, are of growing concern with respect to waste. In the United States, the volume of e-waste entering the waste stream is uncertain, with estimates ranging from 1-4 per cent of municipal solid waste. It is estimated that about 70 per cent of the heavy metals in landfills come from electronic waste, and Silicon Valley in California has become seriously contaminated with toxic waste from electronics production. Observations indicate that the amount of electronic equipment, particularly computers, that is discarded is much less than the numbers being replaced by consumers, suggesting that most households are storing old computers and other electronic devices, and that the quantity entering the waste stream will soon increase rapidly. A large quantity of discarded computers and other electronic products from the United States, Japan and the Republic of Korea is exported to China and other developing countries in Asia for recycling, often under unsafe conditions.[53]

To reduce electronic waste going to landfills and incinerators, the European Union in 2003 adopted a Waste Electrical and Electronic Equipment (WEEE) Directive requiring industry, starting in August 2005, to take responsibility for recovering and recycling electronic waste without charge to consumers. On products sold before 2005, the costs of collection and recycling are to be shared by all producers, while for later products, producers will be responsible for collecting and recycling their own products. This is intended not only to promote recycling, but also as an incentive to producers to design products to reduce waste and facilitate recycling.[54] In the Netherlands, Norway, Sweden and Switzerland, the purchase price of some electronic items includes an advance disposal fee to fund recycling.

Japan, as part of its Basic Plan for a Recycling Society, has been developing legal requirements for recycling. The 1998 Home Appliance Recycling Law came into effect in 2001. By 2003, collection of used air conditioners, TV sets, refrigerators and washing machines had increased by about 20 per cent, metals were recovered for recycling, and CFCs (ozone depleting substances and greenhouse gases) were recovered for disposal.

In the United States, the Environmental Protection Agency (EPA) estimates that electronic waste amounts to 2.5 million tons per year, of which about 10 per cent is recycled. National law regulates disposal of electronic equipment by businesses and government agencies, but only six states require recycling of electronic equipment by households. A growing number of municipalities are taking action to ban the disposal of electronic equipment in landfills, but without adequate infrastructure for recycling.[55]

Recycling of electronic products can include recovery of gold, platinum, silver, copper and steel, as well as plastic and glass, although little such recovery is now done. Usable electronic components can be recovered by disassembly, plastic and steel can be recovered by mechanical shredding, and other metals can be recovered by incineration and/or chemical extraction. In China, copper wire is recovered by burning the plastic covering, while acid baths are used to recover precious metals, but under very unsafe conditions. Electronic products can be considered as ores in that circuit boards contain much higher concentrations of gold, copper and other metals than natural ores, and fewer polluting contaminants. However, recovering these materials is not currently economical. Recycling of these materials could be encouraged by simple design changes to facilitate component extraction and material recovery.[56]

## 5.7 Automotive waste

The EU has adopted a Directive on End-of-Life Vehicles to reduce waste going to landfills and promote recycling. By 2007, 85 per cent by weight of every new vehicle must be made from recyclable components, up from the 75 per cent metal that is now recyclable.[57]

In 1995, the Danish government entered into an agreement with a number of organizations on a take-back scheme for used tires, with a goal of recycling 80 per cent of scrap tires. Previously most scrap tires ended up in landfills. A consumer charge of about US$1 per tire on purchase is used to subsidize enterprises that collect tires and convert them into rubber granulate. In 1999, the take-back rate reached 87 per cent.[58]

## 5.8 Construction and demolition waste

The building sector accounts for a large amount of waste (mostly concrete and bricks from demolition), accounting for an estimated 10 per cent to 44 per cent of total solid waste in various OECD countries. As it is difficult to reduce the amount of material in buildings without reducing performance, the potential for waste reduction is mainly from recycling materials. Currently the estimated recycling rate ranges from 5 per cent to 90 per cent in various OECD countries, with much of the waste going to engineering fill or road foundation, where the quality of the material is less important than in the case of building materials. The annual volume of waste generated by demolition also depends on the lifetimes of buildings before replacement, with average lifetimes of commercial buildings in OECD countries ranging from 31 years in the United States to 62 years in the United Kingdom.

To reduce the volume of demolition waste going to landfill or incineration, some OECD countries have imposed mandatory separation of demolition waste and restrictions on the disposal of recyclable construction material to landfills. In some cases, demolition contractors must get disposal plans approved before demolition can begin, which also helps to protect against illegal dumping. These measures are often in addition to general landfill taxes and virgin material taxes (e.g. aggregate taxes), which increase the economic incentive for recycling. In Denmark and the Netherlands, both of which have had, since 1997, strict limitations on the disposal of recyclable demolition waste in landfills, landfill taxes, permission requirements for demolition, and other incentives for recycling, 90 per cent of demolition waste is recycled. In Japan, the Construction Recycling Act came into effect in 2002, requiring the sorting of debris from demolition to facilitate recycling of stone debris for road and building construction, and reuse of lumber for particle board, paper or energy generation.[59]

Builders, however, are often hesitant to use recycled materials due to concerns over quality. Furthermore, due to low levels of recycling, recycled materials are often less conveniently available than virgin material available through construction supply houses, and transport costs are relatively high for low-cost construction materials. As part of efforts to address this problem, the United Kingdom, in 1998, established an internet-based Material Information Waste Exchange to allow contractors with unwanted materials or wastes to find others who could use them.

## 5.9 Water

In considering industrial water efficiency, it is important to distinguish between water withdrawals and water consumption, although the terms are often used interchangeably. Commonly used figures indicate that in developed countries, industry, including power-generating plants, accounts for 59 per cent of water withdrawals. Most of this water, however, is used by power plants, which use it for cooling purposes and then return it to watercourses slightly warmer, but available for other use downstream. Actual consumption of water, with evaporation ultimately making it unavailable for further use, is much lower.

In the United States, power plants account for 39 per cent of total water withdrawals (131 billion gallons per day), but only 3 per cent of that (3.5 billion gallons per day) is actually consumed, amounting to 4 per cent of total water consumption. Industry and mining, excluding power plants, account for 8 per cent of withdrawals (28 billion gpd) and 5 per cent of water consumption (4.5 billion gpd). Domestic and commercial uses account for 10 per cent of withdrawals (34 million gpd) and 7 per cent of consumption. Agriculture (as well as livestock and landscape watering) actually consume most of the water withdrawn for those purposes.[60] The major problem with industrial water use in relation to sustainable development is not water consumption in this sense, but pollution of the water that is used and returned to watercourses. In other words, water quality is more important than water efficiency.

In the United States, since the 1970s, there have been large increases in water efficiency in terms of production per unit of water withdrawn, particularly in the industrial sector. Total water withdrawals by non-agricultural businesses, including the mining, industrial and commercial sectors, but excluding power plants, declined by 38 per cent from 1970 to 1995, from about 45 billion gallons per day to about 31 billion, while output increased by 69 per cent. From 1980 to 1995, reductions of about 10 per cent were achieved in the much larger water withdrawals for thermal-electric power plant cooling and for agricultural irrigation. These reductions in absolute volume are substantially larger when calculated on a per capita basis or per unit of GDP (Hawken, Lovins, and Lovins, 2000, pp.216-217, 225).

Improving water efficiency in industry through reducing withdrawals is generally achieved by recycling water within the facility, with pollution treatment as necessary to make the water reusable. While reducing water withdrawals and reducing pollution, it also reduces the water returned to watercourses by about the same amount, and thus does not make any more water available to other users downstream. In the case of cooling water, the only effect is to reduce the warming of the watercourse from which the water is withdrawn and to which it is returned.

The recycling of water and reduction in water withdrawals by industry in recent years has generally been in response to public policy measures limiting the discharge of polluted water. Rather than treating water to public standards and discharging it, industry has found it more economical to recycle the used water, treating it sufficiently to meet internal water quality requirements. Where industry pays for water from municipal water systems, a reduction in water withdrawals also saves money for the enterprise, so increasing water prices will also promote water efficiency in this sense.

Pulp and paper mills have been heavy users and polluters of water. As an example of more efficient water use, a German manufacturer of paper products for packaging was able to reduce water withdrawals by over 90 per cent by treating and recycling wastewater, withdrawing only enough new water to compensate for evaporation and the water content of the paper products. The resulting water withdrawals were 15 to 20 times less than the recent German norm (Hawken, Lovins, and Lovins, 2000, p. 225).

Reducing water withdrawals can be particularly important in urban areas in dry regions where competition for clean freshwater is particularly intense. In India, water withdrawals for the Bhilai Steel Plant in Madhya Pradesh State, which suffers severe water scarcity, were reduced from 17,000 $m^3$/hr to 3000 $m^3$/hr, or from 52 $m^3$ per ton of steel to 10 $m^3$ per ton, through a water conservation project undertaken in response to drought conditions in 1988. This was achieved through rainwater harvesting, treatment and recycling of wastewater, reduction in water leakage, improved operation and maintenance of the pumping system, and reducing water use in landscaping. The water conservation measures required improved water quality monitoring and treatment to meet water quality requirements for process water and waste water discharge (UNEP, 1998a).

In some cases, reducing water withdrawals and pollution discharges can be combined with measures to recover useful material from process water, thus increasing material efficiency. In Concepción, Chile, for example, fish processing companies that produced fishmeal were a major source of organic water pollution going into the sea. Faced with impending effluent regulations, the Fisheries Association of 16 companies found that the fish wastes in the effluent could profitably be recovered, increasing fishmeal production while reducing water withdrawals and pollution. Improved pumps reduced losses in pumping fish from ship to shore, while substantially reducing water use and damage to the fish. Screens captured fish particles from the effluent and returned them into the fish processing system, further reducing fish losses and pollution. The new system reduced organic pollution (chemical oxygen demand) by 85 per cent while increasing productivity and reducing water withdrawals, such that the investment paid for itself within two years. In urban coastal situations such as this, where water is withdrawn from municipal water supplies and discharged to the sea, reducing water withdrawals can increase the amount of freshwater available for other uses (United Nations, 1999, p.34).

Use of wastewater for industrial purposes that do not require water of drinking quality can increase the availability of clean water for uses which require the highest quality. In Chennai (formerly Madras), India, which suffers from severe and increasing water scarcity, Madras Fertilizers Ltd. has switched from using potable groundwater that can be used for other municipal purposes to partially treated municipal wastewater, which the company treats further. The company uses about 20 million litres/day, about two-thirds for cooling and one-third for process water and general uses. The company installed advanced wastewater treatment technologies to remove biological oxygen demand (BOD), hardness and ammonia, together with reverse osmosis to remove dissolved solids to ensure adequate water quality. This has freed about 14 million litres/day of drinking water for use in Chennai (UNEP, 1998b).

In general, as noted above, the primary issue concerning industrial water use is water quality rather than water efficiency. As the issue of freshwater management and water quality protection is a very broad issue beyond the scope of this chapter, it will not be considered further here.

## 6. Conclusions: Policies for promoting material efficiency

As indicated above, a variety of public policies have been used effectively in many countries, most often in developed countries, to promote material efficiency. These policies include legal and regulatory requirements, taxes and charges, other economic incentives, and supportive public services.

The broadest and best known set of policies for promoting material efficiency in the production-consumption cycle is to promote recycling of used or waste material back into the industrial production system. While recycling of industrial metal, and to a lesser extent paper and plastic, has long been a profitable commercial activity without policy support, this commercial recycling has, since the 1970s, been supplemented by policy-driven municipal waste recycling, which has made a modest contribution to metal recycling, and a much larger contribution to paper recycling.

Since the 1970s, many communities have set up recycling programmes as part of household waste collection services. Households are required to separate recyclable material, most often cans, bottles, paper and yard waste, from other household waste. The municipality collects the material for recycling, usually does further sorting, and sells the saleable material to commercial recyclers who sell it to industry. Household separation is often legally mandatory and households can be fined for putting recyclables in the regular waste, but enforcement is difficult and voluntary participation is generally good although imperfect.

Some communities, in the United States, Republic of Korea and other countries, have introduced financial incentives for waste reduction and recycling through volume-based waste collection charges ("pay-as-you-throw") that exclude recycled material. Households may pay for collection of a certain volume of waste on a regular basis, or may buy pre-paid bags or tags for their waste. A few programmes are weight-based but these are more complicated to manage. Recyclable material is placed in separate containers for which there is no charge. They appear to be effective in increasing recycling, but their effect on waste reduction is unclear. As they are mostly volume-based, they tend to increase household waste compaction more than reduction.

Deposit-return systems for beverage containers were among the earliest policy-driven recycling efforts. Those systems have been very effective, greatly increasing the recycling of containers, often up to rates of around 90 per cent. In various countries, such schemes have applied to various types of containers (cans, glass bottles, plastic bottles), and various types of beverages (soft drinks, beer, water, milk, wine). The deposits have ranged from about US$.05 to US$.50. They require arrangements for collection and return of deposits and handling of returned containers, a burden imposed on retailers, wholesalers and bottlers, leading to opposition to such systems. In addition to promoting recycling, such schemes can provide some income for informal scavengers, who can make a substantial contribution to the effectiveness of the system.

In some cases, such as in Denmark, deposit-return schemes have been complemented and supported by requirements for the use of refillable glass or plastic bottles. Such containers may be heavier and stronger than non-refillable containers to survive the rigours of recycling, and hence will conserve raw materials only if they are effectively recycled. Again, such requirements have sometimes aroused the opposition of bottle manufacturers, bottlers, distributors and retailers who have to fund and manage the system.

In most cases, the deposit-return scheme, including specification of the containers covered, deposit amounts and other arrangements, is mandated by public policy. In some cases, however, as in extended producer responsibility systems, public policy establishes general requirements for recovery and allows industry to set up the mechanisms, which may include deposit-return mechanisms.

While most deposit-return schemes have applied to beverage containers, they have also been used for lead-acid batteries in Germany and in some states of the United States, for old cars in Norway and Sweden, for appliances and tires in the Republic of Korea, and for pesticide containers in the United States (state of Maine).

Landfill taxes have been used in some countries to increase the price of waste disposal and provide an economic incentive for recycling. These are effective more for businesses and industries that pay directly for waste disposal than for households. They may be particularly effective for demolition debris, which involves a large volume of waste. Landfill taxes have been used in Denmark, Netherlands and the United Kingdom to substantially increase the cost of disposal to landfill. Denmark and the Netherlands, as well as Japan, also have regulatory restrictions on the disposal of demolition debris to landfill in order to promote recycling of construction material for roads and buildings. The United Kingdom has an "aggregate tax" to reduce quarrying of construction aggregate and promote recycling.

Bans on disposal to landfills are used as policies to compel recycling. In the United States, many communities ban disposal of lead-acid batteries to landfills and require their recycling. In many cases, almost 100 per cent of lead-acid batteries are recycled.

Extended producer responsibility (EPR) requirements have been used in a number of countries, in particular in the EU and Japan, as an effective means to promote recycling of a variety of materials and products, including packaging, old vehicles, electronics, appliances and batteries. In contrast to municipal recycling programmes, extended producer responsibility puts the cost and management responsibility for collection and recycling on industry, although some programmes also provide for government involvement and support. EPR also provides an incentive for industry to design products to be more recyclable, although its effectiveness for this purpose is unclear.

Increasing recycling means not only increasing the supply of recovered material, but also increasing the demand from industry. In the United States, ten state governments have established mandatory recycled-content requirements for products produced in or imported into the state, including newsprint, trash bags, glass and plastic containers and fibreglass. In Belgium, disposable beverage containers are subject to a tax unless they have 50 per cent or more recycled content.

Public procurement also provides a public mechanism for promoting recycling by increasing demand for recycled material. The United States Federal Government and many local authorities require procurement of recycled-content paper for themselves and contractors, as well as more general recycled-content requirements for other procurement. To assist government procurement agents, the US Environmental Protection Agency has developed standards for recycled content for a range of products and lists of products meeting those standards. Such requirements for government procurement not only increase demand directly, but also provide a model and incentive for procurement requirements by industry, other institutions and households. Making government standards and databases publicly available also helps other institutional consumers in buying recycled products. This increases demand for recycled material, which raises prices, which encourages commercial recycling and helps pay for municipal recycling.

Governments can also intervene in some cases to increase the prices of raw materials, thus increasing the economic incentive for industrial material efficiency and recycling. In many countries, for example, wood comes in part from national forests, and policies controlling access to those public resources can increase the price of wood products, including paper. Restricting logging on public land, reducing government support for logging operations, or increasing "stumpage fees" will tend to increase the cost of virgin paper and other wood products.

Stronger environmental laws on mining, including requirements for remediation of the land after mining is exhausted, with financial guarantees to cover the costs of environmental damage and clean-up, would internalize the environmental costs of mining, raise the price of minerals, and promote material efficiency and recycling.

Finally, governments can facilitate industrial recycling by promoting waste exchanges and industrial ecology that link industries producing a certain type of waste product with other industries that can use those waste products as inputs.

Figure 1. Regional variation in industrial energy intensity
[Kg oil equivalent/industrial output (1995 US $ ppp)]

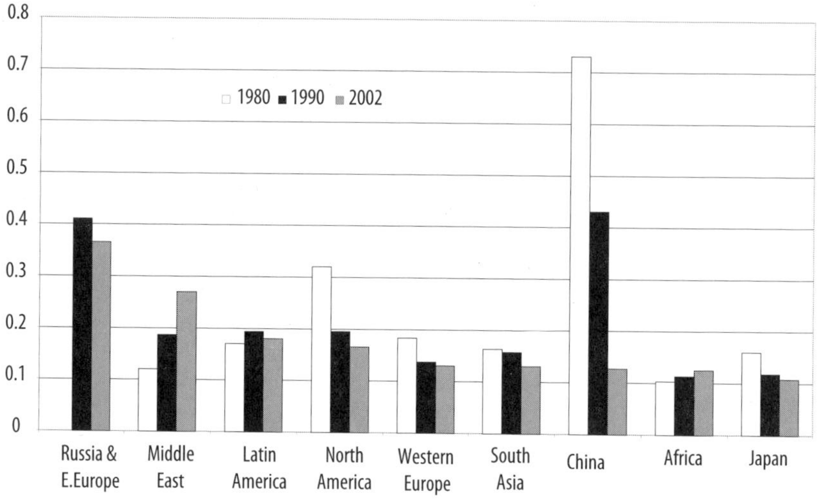

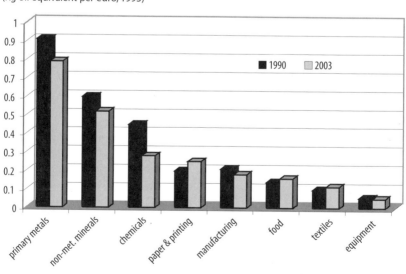

Source: World Energy Council using data from Enerdata.

Figure 2. Energy intensities by sub-sector in the EU-15
(Kg oil equivalent per euro, 1995)

Source: Odyssee and Enerdata.

Figure 3. White certificate electricity savings target and evolution of savings in Italy (million tons of oil equivalent)

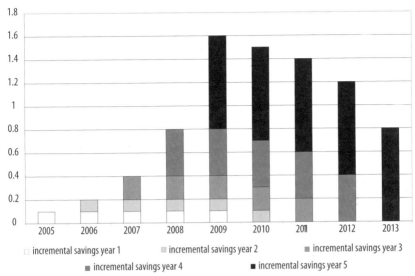

Source: Odyssee and Enerdata. Source: Pavan, M., White Certificates can foster ESCO development. In: ESCOs in Europe conference, 6-8 October 2005. Vienna.
Note: The data for this chart were compiled by WEC-ADEME from a survey of 63 countries. Energy savings projects are expected to contribute to the achievement of targets for up to five years, therefore the chart begins in 2005 and ends in 2013.

Figure 4. Energy efficiency policies – most frequent measures (% of countries where policy is used)

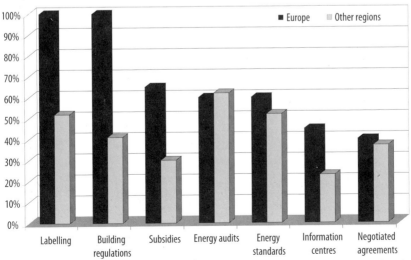

Source: François Moisan, Energy efficiency: a worldwide review -- Indicators, policies and evaluation, World Energy Council – French Agency for Environment and Energy Management, 2006.

Figure 5. Energy efficiency labels for motors from China, Colombia, Singapore and Thailand, respectively.

Figure 6. Extent of cogeneration in selected countries in 2004

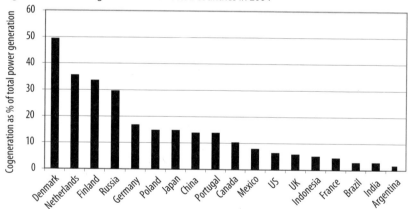

Source: World Survey of Decentralized Energy 2005, World Alliance for Decentralized Energy, 2005.

Figure 7. Municipal solid waste (United States, 2005)

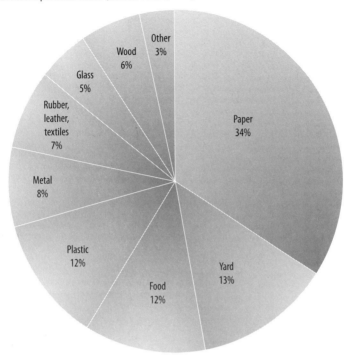

Source: US EPA, Municipal Solid Waste (*www.epa.gov/msw/facts.htm*).

Figure 8. Recycling rates - selected materials (United States, 2005)

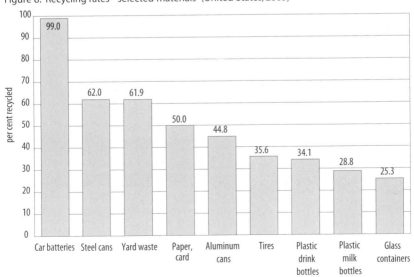

Source: US Environmental Protection Agency (November 2006), Municipal Solid Waste: Basic Facts (*www.epa.gov/msw/facts.htm*).

Figure 9. Household waste recycling, UK

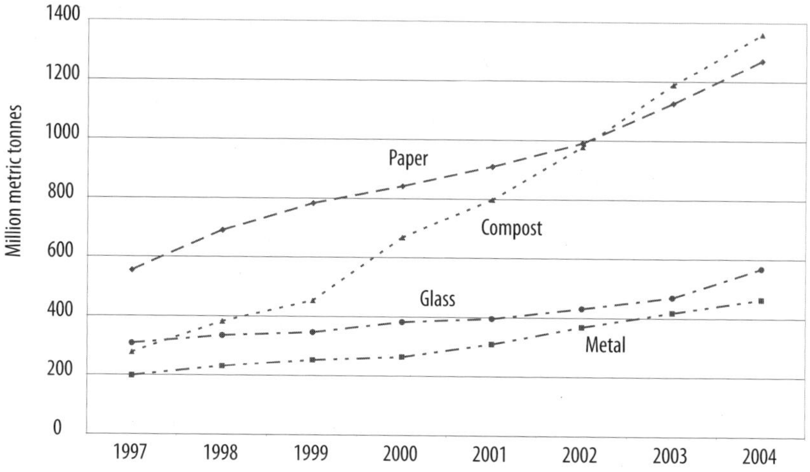

Source: Defra (www.defra.gov.uk/environment/statistics/waste/download/xls/wrfg15.xls).

## Table 1.
### Pollution levies in selected countries

| Country | Administrative/ civil penalties | Criminal penalties | Remarks |
|---|---|---|---|
| Australia | X | | Currently under review |
| Austria | X | X | Fines depend on income of violator |
| Czech Rep. | | X | In addition to fines and imprisonment, other sanctions may be imposed |
| Denmark | X | X | Civil penalties are under consideration |
| Finland | | X | Fines set according to discretion of court |
| France | | X | Fines doubled for repeat offenses |
| Germany | X | X | In corporate cases, managers may be imprisoned |
| Greece | X | X | |
| Hungary | | X | Imprisonment is typically applied |
| Ireland | X | X | Fines unlimited under some statutes |
| Portugal | X | X | |
| Slovakia | X | X | Fines doubled for repeat offences |
| Spain | | X | |
| Netherlands | X | X | Civil penalties are under consideration |
| UK | X | X | Civil penalties are under consideration |
| USA | X | X | Fines vary depending on statute; doubled for repeat offences |

Source: adapted from Price et al. (2005).

## Table 2.
### Taxes and fiscal incentives promoting industrial energy efficiency in selected countries

| Country | Taxes or Fees | | | Fiscal Incentives | | | | |
|---|---|---|---|---|---|---|---|---|
| | Energy or CO2 tax | Pollution levy | Public benefits charge | Subsidies or grants | Subsidized audits | Soft public loans | Innovative private funds | Technology tax relief |
| **OECD** | | | | | | | | |
| Australia | | A/C | X | X | X | | E | EX |
| Austria | X | A/C, CR | | X | X | | E | |
| Canada | | | | | X | | E, RF | AD |
| Denmark | X | CR | | X | X | | | |
| Finland | X | CR | | X | X | | E | |
| Fraance | X | CR | | X | X | | GF, IF | |
| Germany | X | AC, CR | | X | X | X | E, IF | EX, R |
| Hungary | | CR | | X | X | X | E, GF | |
| Italy | X | | | X | X | | E | R |
| Japan | | X | | X | X | | E | AD, R |
| Korea | | | | X | X | X | E | R |
| Mexico | | | | X | X | X | E, IF | |
| Netherlands | X | CR | | X | X | | | AD, R |
| UK | X | CR | | X | X | X | E, VC | R |
| USA | | A/C, CR | X | X | X | X | E | EX |
| **Non-OECD** | | | | | | | | |
| Brazil | | | | | X | | GF, RF | R |
| Egypt | | | | X | X | | E | R |
| Indonesia | | | | | X | | | |
| Jordan | | | | X | X | X | E | R |
| Philippines | | | | X | X | | E | R |
| Thailand | | | | X | X | X | E, RF | |
| Tunisia | | | | X | X | | E | |

*Sources: World Energy Council 2004, Energy Efficiency: A Worldwide Review — Indicators, Policies, Evaluation, London; Galitsky, Price and Worrell (2004).*
*Obs.: X = program exists; A/C = administrative/civil penalties; CR = criminal penalties; E = ESCOs; GF = guarantee fund; RF = revolving fund; VC = venture capital; AD = accelerated depreciation; R = reduction; EX = exemption.*

## Table 3.
## Selected voluntary/negotiated agreements with industry

| Country | Agreement | Program years | Government and public recognition | Information | Assistance and training | Energy audits | Financial assistance & incentives | Emissions trading | Relief or exemption from regs & taxes | Reduced/ avoided energy/ GHG taxes | More stringent env. permitting | Increased reg's | Penalty/ fee | Energy or CO₂ tax |
|---|---|---|---|---|---|---|---|---|---|---|---|---|---|---|
| | | | Incentives | | | | | | | | Penalties | | | |
| **Completely voluntary** | | | | | | | | | | | | | | |
| Australia | Greenhouse Challenge | 1996-present | X | X | X | | | | | | | | | |
| China (Taipei) | Energy Auditing Programme | 2002-2020 | X | X | X | X | | | | | | | | |
| Finland | Promotion of Energy Conservation in Industry | 1997-present | X | X | X | X | X | | | | | | | |
| Korea, Rep. | Energy Conservation & Reduction of GHG Emissions | 1998-present | X | X | X | | X | | | | | | | |
| USA | Climate Vision | 2003-present | X | X | X | X | | | | | | | | |
| **With threat of regulations or taxes** | | | | | | | | | | | | | | |
| France | AERES Negotiated Agreements | 2002-present | X | | X | | X | | | | | | X | |
| Germany | Agreement on Climate Protection | 2000-2012 | | | | | | | X | X | | | | |
| Japan | Keidanren Voluntary Action Plan on the Environment | 1997-present | X | | | | | | | | | | | |
| Netherlands | Benchmarking Covenants | 2001-2012 | X | X | | | X | | X | | X | | | |
| **Energy/GHG taxes or regulations** | | | | | | | | | | | | | | |
| Canada | Large Final Emitters Programme | 2003-2012 | | X | X | X | | X | X | | | X | X | |
| Denmark | Industrial Energy Efficiency | 1993-present | | X | X | X | X | | | X | | | | X |
| New Zealand | Negotiated Greenhouse Agreements | 2003-2012 | | | | | | X | | X | | | | X |
| Switzerland | CO₂ Law Voluntary Measures | 2000-2012 | | | | | | X | | X | | | | X |
| UK | Climate Change Agreements | 2001-2013 | X | X | X | X | X | X | | X | | | | X |

*Source: Price (2005).*

## Table 4.
### Overview of industrial sector energy efficiency program products and services of industrialized countries

| | Australia | Canada | Denmark | EU | France | Germany | Japan | Netherlands | Norway | Sweden | Switzerland | UK | USA |
|---|---|---|---|---|---|---|---|---|---|---|---|---|---|
| Audits/assessments | | | | | | X | | X | | X | | X | X |
| Benchmarking | | X | | | | X | | X | X | | | X | |
| Case studies | X | X | | X | | X | | X | X | X | | X | X |
| Demonstration: commercialized technologies | | X | | | X | X | X | X | | | | X | X |
| Demonstration: emerging technologies | | X | | X | X | | | X | | X | | | X |
| Energy awareness promotion materials | X | X | X | | X | X | | X | X | X | X | | |
| Fact sheets | X | | | X | | | | | | X | X | X | X |
| Industry profiles | | X | | X | | | | X | X | | | | X |
| Reports/guidebooks | X | X | | X | X | X | X | X | X | X | X | X | X |
| Tools and software | X | X | X | X | | X | | X | X | | | X | X |
| Verification | X | X | | X | X | X | | X | X | | | | X |
| Visions/roadmaps | X | X | | | | | | X | X | | X | | X |

Source: Galitsky, Price and Worrell (2004).

## Table 5.
### Improvement in performance of four South American electricity distribution companies

| Performance criteria | Peru Luz Del Sur | Argentina Edesur | Argentina Edenor | Chile Chilectra |
|---|---|---|---|---|
| Year privatized | 1994 | 1992 | 1992 | 1987 |
| Energy sales (GWh/y) | +19% | +79% | +82% | +26% |
| Reduction in energy losses | -50% | -68% | -63% | -70% |
| No. of employees | -43% | -60% | -63% | -9% |
| Customers/employee | +135% | +180% | +215% | +37% |
| Net receivables (days) | -27% | -38% | n/a | -68% |
| Provisions for bad debts, % of sales | -65% | -35% | n/a | -88% |

Source: Bacon and Besant-Jones (2001).

## Notes

1 International Energy Agency, http://www.sourceoecd.com.

2 International Energy Outlook 2006, U.S. Energy Information Administration, 2006.

3 World Energy Council, http://www.worldenergy.org/wec-geis/publications/reports/ weepi/introduction/definition.asp.

4 International Energy Outlook 2006, U.S. Energy Information Administration, 2006.

5 Climate Change 2001, Intergovernmental Panel on Climate Change, 2001.

6 Johnson, J., 1998, "EPA Fines Engine Makers", http://www.ttpnews.com/members/ printEdition/0000164.html.

7 International Energy Agency,

http://www.iea.org/textbase/pamsdb/detail.aspx?mode=gr&id=24.

8 Countries that responded to the survey include: the EU-25 countries, Russia, Turkey, Canada, USA, Mexico, Costa Rica, Brazil, Chile, Colombia, Peru, China, Rep. of Korea, Japan, Thailand, Myanmar, Malaysia, Singapore, Indonesia, Philippines, Australia, New Zealand, Iran, Jordan, Algeria, Egypt, Tunisia, Morocco, Mali, Mauritania, Guinea, Cote d'Ivoire, Ghana, South Africa, Botswana, Kenya, Tanzania.

9 Collaborative Labeling and Appliance Standards Program,

http://www.clasponline.org/disdoc.php?no=171.

10 "Energy Efficient Motor Driven Systems", European Copper Institute, http://www. eurocopper.org/eci/jsp/index.jsp?idx=48.

11 Lawrence Berkeley National Laboratory, hrtp://china.lbl.gov/china_industry-iee-best.html.

12 Canadian Energy Efficiency Agency: best practices,

http://www.energyefficiency.org/.

13 Press article, "Cautious optimism? The Indian Power Sector", Sachin Kerur, Dec. 2005 http://www.pinsentmasons.com/media/1096940727.htm.

14 "Power" EquityMaster, Quantum Information Services Private LTD. http://www. equitymaster.com/research-it/sector-info/power/.

15 Prem K. Kalra, " Transmission and distribution loss minimization", Indian Institute of Technology, Kanpur,

http://www.electricityindia.org/dca_stanford/presentations/Prem_Kalra.pdf.

16 "Power" EquityMaster, Quantum Information Services Private LTD. http://www. equitymaster.com/research-it/sector-info/power/

17 World Survey of Decentralized Energy 2005, World Alliance for Decentralized Energy, 2005.

18 Combined Heat and Power White Paper, American Council for an Energy Efficient Economy, 2006.

19 World Resources Institute (1997), Resource Flows: The Material Basis of Industrial Economies. http://materials.wri.org/resourceflows-pub-2742.html.

20 US Government AccountabilityOffice (GAO) (17 August 2005), Environmental Liabilities: EPA Should Do More to Ensure That Liable Parties Meet Their Cleanup Obligations. Report GAO-05-658, www.gao.gov/htext/d05658.html.

21 Worldwatch Institute (November 2006), Beverages: The Price of Quenching our Thirst. www.worldwatch.org/node/1479.

22 UK Department for Environment, Food and Rural Affairs (DEFRA) (November 2006), e-Digest Statistics About: Waste and Recycling. www.defra.gov.uk/environment/statistics/index.htm.

23 UK Department for Environment, Food and Rural Affairs (DEFRA) (November 2006), Key Facts About Waste and Recycling. www.defra.gov.uk/environment/statistics/waste/kf/wrkf03.htm

24 Institute of Scrap Recycling Industries, Statement of ISRI Chair Joel Denbo to Congress, Sept. 2005. www.isri.org

25 USEnvironmental Protection Agency (November 2006), Municipal Solid Waste: Recycling. www.epa.gov/msw/recycle.htm. See also Royte, Elizabeth (2005), Garbage Land: On the Secret Trail of Trash. Little Brown & Co., New York, p.264.

26 US Environmental Protection Agency (November 2006), Municipal Solid Waste: Basic Facts. www.epa.gov/msw/facts.htm.

27 UK Department for Environment, Food and Rural Affairs (DEFRA) (November 2006), Key Facts About Waste and Recycling. www.defra.gov.uk/environment/statistics/waste/kf/wrkf04.htm.

28 UK Department for Environment, Food and Rural Affairs (DEFRA) (November 2006, e-Digest Statistics About: Waste and Recycling, www.defra.gov.uk/environment/statistics/index.htm

29 Ministry of Environment, Republic of Korea (November 2006), Waste and Recycling. eng.me.go.kr/docs/index.html

30 British Metals Recycling Association (November 2006), What is Metals Recycling. www.recyclemetals.org/whatis.php

31 Harmony Enterprises (November 2006), Non-Ferrous Recycling. www.harmony1.com/recycling/nonferrous.cfm

32 Steel Recycling Institute (November 2006), Steel Recycling Rates at a Glance: 2005. www.recycle-steel.org. See also Royte (2005).

33 MEPS International Ltd (November 2006), World Steel Prices. www.meps.co.uk.

34 Alupro (November 2006), Facts and Figures. www.alupro.org.uk/facts%20and%20figures.htm

35 UK Department for Environment, Food and Rural Affairs (DEFRA) (November 2006), e-Digest Statistics About Waste and Recycling: Aluminium. www.defra.gov.uk/environment/statistics/waste/wraluminium.htm. See also Aluminum Packaging Recycling Organization (Alupro) (November 2006), Facts and Figures. www.alupro.org.uk/facts%20and%20figures.htm

36 Aluminum Packaging Recycling Organization (Alupro) (Sept 2006), www.alupro.org.uk/facts%20and%20figures.htm. See also Chipman and Dzioubinski (1999).

37 Copper Development Association (November 2006), The US Copper-base Scrap Industry and its By-products. www.copper.org/resources/pub_list/pdf/scrap_report.pdf.

38 Lead Development Association International (November 2006), Lead Information. www.ldaint.org/information.htm. See also Chipman and Dzioubinski (1999). (1999)ww.un.org/esa/desa/papers/1999/esa99dp5.pdf.

39 Grassroots Recycling Network (November 2006), Welfare for Waste. www.grrn.org/reports/w4w/ExecSum.pdf

40 Green Scissors (November 2006), Cutting Wasteful and Environmentally Harmful Spending. www.greenscissors.org/publiclands/1872.htm.

41 US Environmental Protection Agency (November 2006), Municipal Solid Waste: Basic Facts. www.epa.gov/msw/facts.htm.

42 Paper Industry Association Council (November 2006), 2005 Recovered Paper Annual Statistics. www.paperrecycles.org.

43 The Green Dot (2005), www.gruener-punkt.de.

44 Confederation of European Paper Industries (July 2006), Europe Global Champion in Paper Recycling. www.paperchain2000.org.uk/news/06/pr0307erpcfigs.pdf

45 Green Scissors 2004 Report: Cutting Wasteful and Environmentally Harmful Spending. Friends of the Earth, Taxpayers for Common Sense, and US Public Interest Research Group. www.greenscissors.org/publications/gs2004.pdf.

46 Oregon Department of Environmental Quality (November 2006), The Oregon Bottle Bill: Fact Sheet.

www.oregondeq.com/wmc/pubs/factsheets/sw/OregonBottleBill.pdf.

47 Container Recycling Institute (November 2006), Bottle Bill Resource Guide. www.bottlebill.org/index.htm

48 Container Recycling Institute (November 2006), Bottle Bill Resource Guide. www.bottlebill.org/index.htm

49 Waste Online (November 2006), Plastics Recycling Information Sheet. www.wasteonline.org.uk/resources/InformationSheets/Plastics.htm

50 Waste Online (November 2006), Plastics Recycling Information Sheet. www.wasteonline.org.uk/resources/InformationSheets/Plastics.htm

51 Miller, Chaz (2001), Profiles in Garbage: High-Density Polyethylene. Waste Age, July. images.wasteage.com/files/121/ArtPackSample.pdf. See also Toto, Deanne (2004), Consumers of Recycled PET and HDPE are Hungry for More Material. Recycling Today, July.

52 Miller, Chaz (2001), Profiles in Garbage: High-Density Polyethylene. Waste Age, July. images.wasteage.com/files/121/ArtPackSample.pdf. See also Toto, Deanne (2004), Consumers of Recycled PET and HDPE are Hungry for More Material. Recycling Today, July.

findarticles.com/p/articles/mi_m0KWH/is_7_42/ai_n6124430.

53 WorldWatch Institute (2004), State of the World 2004, pp. 44-45. See also US Environmental Protection Agency (November 2006), eCycling. www.epa.gov/epaoswer/hazwaste/recycle/ecycling.

54 Europa (November 2006), Waste Electrical and Electronic Equipment. europa.eu.int/scadplus/leg/en/lvb/l21210.htm

55 Vitello, Paul (2006), Clearing a Path from Desktop to Recycler. New York Times, 11 Nov. 2006.

56 US Government Accountability Office (GAO) (November 2005), Electronic Waste. www.gao.gov/new.items/d0647.pdf.

57 Europa (November 2006), Waste Management.

europa.eu.int/scadplus/leg/en/s15002.htm.

58 Danish Ministry of Environment and Energy (1995), Environmental Administration in Denmark, Chapter 8, Environmental Requirements for Consumers. www.mst.dk/udgiv/Publications/1995/87-7944-324-9/html/8.htm.

59 Japan Ministry of the Environment (November 2006), www.env.go.jp/en/.
60 US Environmental Protection Agency (November 2006), National Trends in Water Use. www.epa.gov/OW/you/chap1.html.

# Bibliography

Bacon, R. W. and J. Besant-Jones (2001), Global Electric Power Reform, Privatization and Liberalization of the Electric Power Industry in Developing Countries, World Bank.

Baumgärtner, S., and R. Winkler (2003), Markets, Technology and Environmental Regulation: Price Ambivalence of Waste Paper in Germany. Ecological Economics, Vol. 47, p.183-195.

Bertoldi, P. and S. Rezessy (2006), Tradable Certificates For Energy Savings (White Certificates), Theory and Practice, European Commission, Directorate-General, Joint Research Centre, Institute for Environment and Sustainability.

Bowyer, J., J.Howe, P. Guillery and K. Fernholz (2005), Paper Recycling in the United States: How Are We Doing Compared to Other Nations. Dovetail Partners Inc.

Chipman, R., and O. Dzioubinski (1999), Trends in Consumption and Production: Selected Minerals. DESA Discussion Paper No.5, United Nations.

Eurostat (2001), Economy-wide Material Flow Accounts and Derived Indicators: A Methodological Guide.

Farinelli, U. et al. (2005), "White and Green": Comparison of market-based instruments to promote energy efficiency, Journal of Cleaner Production 13.

Galitsky, C., L. Price and E. Worrell (2004), "Energy Efficiency Programs and Policies in the Industrial Sector in Industrialized Countries", LBNL-54068, Lawrence Berkeley National Laboratory, USA.

de Tilly, S. (2004), Waste Generation and Related Policies: Broad Trends Over the Last Ten Years: The Economics of Waste, OECD.

Eisenmenger, N. M. Fischer-Kowalski and H. Weisz (2006), Indicators of Natural Resource Use and Consumption, in Moldan, B., T. Hak and P. Bourdeau (eds.), Assessment of Sustainability Indicators, Washington, D.C., SCOPE, Island Press.

Herz, R. (2005), "Sector Eléctrico Colombiano: Hacia la Profundización de un Esquema de Competencia Efectiva y Participación Privada", ENERCOL.

Hawken, P., A. B. Lovins, and L. H. Lovins (2000), Natural Capitalism: Creating the Next Industrial Revolution, Chapter 11, Aqueous Solution. Back Bay Books.

IMF (2006), World Economic Outlook, Chapter 5, "The Boom in Non-Fuel Commodity Prices: Can It Last?", www.imf.org/Pubs/FT/weo/2006/02/index.htm.

OECD (2003), Environmentally Sustainable Buildings: Challenges and Policies. OECD, Paris.

OECD (2000), Electricity Market Reform.

Oikonomou, V. and Patel, M., 2004. An Inventory of Innovative Policies and Measures for Energy Efficiency. Phase 1 of the EU SAVE "White and Green" Project. Utrecht, The Netherlands: Universiteit Utrecht.

Price, L. (2005), "Voluntary Agreements for Energy Efficiency or GHG Emissions Reduction in Industry: An Assessment of Programs Around the World", 2005 ACEEE Summer Study on Energy Efficiency in Industry.

Price, L., C. Galitsky, J. Sinton, E.Worrell, and W. Graus (2005), Tax and Fiscal Policies for Promotion of Industrial Energy Efficiency:   A Survey of International Experience, LBNL-58128.

Rathje, W. and C. Murphy (2001), Rubbish: The Archeology of Garbage. University of Arizona Press, Tucson, p.101.

Rezessy, S., P. Bertoldi and A. Persson (2005), "Are Voluntary Agreements an Effective Energy Policy Instrument? Insights and Experiences from Europe", 2005 ACEEE Summer Study on Energy Efficiency in Industry.

Royte, F. (2005), Garbage Land: On the Secret Trail of Trash. Little Brown & Co., New York.

Schedler, M. (2006), PET Bottle Recycling Status Report. Resource Recycling, February.

Singh, J. and C. Mulholland (2000), "DSM in Thailand: A Case Study", World Bank/ESMAP Program.

Strasser, S. (1999), Waste and Want: A Social History of Trash.  Metropolitan Books, New York.

UN-DESA (forthcoming), Case Studies of Market Transformation.

UNEP (2006), Bioenergy in Finland. www.unep.org/GC/GCSS-IX/Documents/FINLAND-bioenergy.pdf.

UNEP (1998a), Integrated Water Conservation: Bhilai Steel Plant, India. Sourcebook of Alternative Technologies for Freshwater Augmentation in Some Asian Countries, UNEP/DTIE/IETC.

UNEP (1998b), Reclaimed City Sewage as Industrial Water: Madras Fertilizers Ltd., Madras, India, UNEP/DTIE/IETC.

United Nations (1999), Business and the UN: Partners on Sustainable Development. United Nations, New York, p. 34.

World Energy Council (2001), Energy Efficiency:A Worldwide Review.

Worrell, E. and C. Galitsky (2005), "Energy Efficiency Improvement in the Petroleum Refining Industry", 2005 ACEEE Summer Study on Energy Efficiency in Industry.

Weisz, H., F. Krausmann, C. Amann, N. Eisenmenger, K.-H. Erb, K. Hubacek, and M. Fischer-Kowalski (2005), The Physical Economy of the European Union: Cross-Country Comparison and Determinants of Material Consumption, Social Ecology Working Paper 76, Institute for Social Ecology, Klagenfurt University, Austria.

# From supply chains to value chains: A spotlight on CSR

Malika Bhandarkar and Tarcisio Alvarez-Rivero*

## 1. Introduction

Corporate social responsibility (CSR)[1] has become a hot topic in boardrooms across the world. Changes in corporate value systems are being driven by pressures from different actors, including governments, consumers, non-governmental organizations (NGOs) and institutional investors (diagram 1). Multinational corporations (MNCs) have operations spread across the globe, relying on both foreign affiliates and arm's-length suppliers arrayed along global supply chains, many of which encompass developing countries. What then does the growing CSR movement mean for developing country producers? The chapter addresses this question.

### Diagram 1

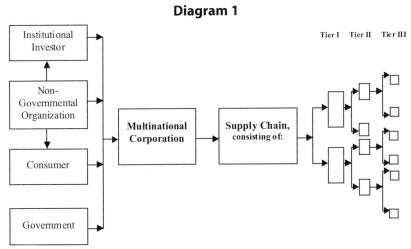

CSR has relevance to many facets of a corporation's operations. Strong CSR policies can help to recruit the right people for the job, keep attrition rates low by promoting a "feel good" quotient, improve corporate image, prepare for future regulation, empower "soft" laws (Vogel, 2005, p.162), appease green customers, and convince institutional investors that the corporation is following sustainable practices that positively impact the bottom line.

---

* Policy Integration and Analysis Branch, Division for Sustainable Development, UN-DESA, United Nations, New York. The views expressed in this document are those of the authors and do not necessarily coincide with those of the organization to which they are affiliated.

Managers are being asked to raise profits but in more socially and environmentally responsible ways. The bottom line continues to be the baseline for measuring corporate success. CSR activities must be seen as providing a measure of shareholder value (e.g., reputation, goodwill) which enhances a company's ability to produce income now and in the future. Multinational firms have created a new global economic space, sourcing products from far-flung global production networks and supply chains (Palmisano, 2006), and CSR advocates argue that MNCs ought therefore to be accountable not only to their shareholders but also to the communities that are affected by their decisions and transactions with suppliers wherever they may operate. Simultaneously, companies are finding business value in increasingly engaging in community programs across the world, as larger shares of their revenues and profits are earned from international operations.

## 2. CSR in international supply chains

With globalization of production networks, corporations have to extend the reach of their CSR policies not only to their overseas subsidiaries but also to suppliers over which they have varying degrees of operational control. The magnitude of the challenge involved in promoting CSR within MNCs and along their supply chains is illustrated by the fact that there are over 63,000 MNCs with over 800,000 subsidiaries multiplied by millions of suppliers and distributors (UNCTAD, 2001).

For developing country firms, the challenge is how to use CSR to competitive advantage, avoiding the risk that weak CSR practices exclude them from global supply chains. CSR is a considerable investment for small and medium-sized enterprises (SMEs) but at the same time the investment has the potential to contribute to long term competitiveness.[2]

### 2.1 Supply chains & SMEs in developing countries

Developing country firms can at times face contradictory pressures: on the one hand, buyers want to be able to certify that their suppliers comply with one or another CSR code of conduct; on the other, they require low prices and tight delivery schedules. While some suppliers in developing countries will be able to meet the challenge, others may face difficulty, none more so than SMEs. For, they are likely to have greater difficulty than large firms in bearing the fixed costs of CSR compliance.

Of the 2,909[3] business participants in developed and developing countries that have signed up with the UN Global Compact, slightly less than half are SMEs and more than a quarter are SMEs from developing countries.

### 2.2 The European experience of CSR & SMEs

One key difficulty in assessing the adoption of CSR by SMEs in supply chains is the dearth of available information on SMEs in developing countries. Insights gained from discussions and surveys of SMEs in developed countries provide a broad understanding of the issue and possible lessons for developing countries.

An October 2005 survey of more than 1,000 Danish SMEs revealed that ethical and moral considerations were the main reason for implementing CSR, although many SMEs are also motivated by aspects of the business case (improved company reputation, attracting and retaining employees, improving financial performance). Thirty six per cent of enterprises believe that CSR activities in general have a positive financial impact, while only 4 per cent are of the opinion that CSR activities in general have a negative financial impact. The relative importance of the impact on financial performance as a reason for engaging in CSR increased with the size of the company, which suggests that there may be important economies of scale in undertaking CSR investments (Kramer, Pfitzer and Lee, 2005).

## 3. The evolution of value systems

As illustrated in diagram 1, the business system is ruled by multiple relationships, some of which are explicitly contractual in nature, but most of which are not.

Sections 3.1 to 3.4 discuss the various relationships between the firm and those stakeholders which have a direct or indirect influence on the commercial success of the firm. An enabling environment for CSR is created if business is pushed to act by the presence of pressure actors like the government, institutional investors, NGOs and consumers. Depending on the nature and extent of those pressures, businesses will in turn demand compliance with more or less stringent CSR codes on the part of their suppliers, whether in developed or developing countries.

### 3.1 Pressure actor: Government as regulator & consumer

The government is the first non-business actor to pressure corporations to change behaviour. The pressures arise mostly from regulatory efforts that affect a business even before the first product is produced or sold. These efforts are considered to be the "least common denominator" for behavioural change and their effectiveness depends greatly on the ability of the government to ensure and enforce compliance. Governments typically exert pressure on business behaviour in areas related to employment conditions and pollution. In some cases these pressures evolve into investor and consumer protection programs.

Governments have a significant role to play in shaping the public policy environment in which businesses operate. Apart from playing the role of regulator, governments can actively engage in promoting CSR as consumers.

### 3.1.1 Government as regulator, facilitator & enabler

Compliance with an increasing number of CSR codes of conduct[4] can be technically difficult and expensive to achieve, in particular for SMEs in developing countries. While some CSR requirements mean complying with the law (e.g. international labour standards), others go beyond legal requirements. The local industry may find it impossible to cope in the short term, due to high costs, obsolete technology, lack of capacity and knowledge, and imperfect information. Governments in developing countries will need to work actively to enable companies to adapt to these requirements and avoid loss of export markets. Key reasons why governments should get involved in corporate social responsibility are discussed below.

• *Creating access to markets & international leverage*

Trade and investment promotion is an important reason why governments should promote CSR. Domestic companies attempting to gain access to global supply chains and markets may need to present evidence of environmental and labour conditions that are consistent with international CSR codes of conduct. To maintain and build the export capacity of national industry, government needs to ensure that local companies have the ability, capacity and the support infrastructure to respond to these new market requirements.

• *Improving regulatory compliance & enforcement*

Most CSR practices are in concert with international labour, humanitarian and environmental agreements and standards. In many developing countries, however, the ability of governments to effectively enforce the law is relatively weak. The adoption of CSR practices by large firms and their supply chains exerts an upward pull on the regulatory performance of suppliers in developing countries , which might contribute to promote legal compliance and reduce the cost of monitoring and enforcement for developing country governments.

• *Achieving social & environmental goals*

Some CSR activities focus on the provision of welfare or environmental services that would in principle be provided by the government but are not because of budget or institutional limitations. These have included basic services such as access to electricity, clean water and sanitation, education and healthcare, as well as restoration of polluted sites and improved management of natural resources.

• *Establishing consistent best practices*

CSR practices required by MNCs could be in conflict with national regulations and cultural or social practices in a given country. The government is in a position to ensure that CSR as practiced within its borders by MNCs does not run against regulatory mandates or conflict with accepted cultural norms.

## 3.1.2 Government as a consumer/buyer

Another clear area of influence for governments is through procurement processes. In most countries, government is the single largest individual consumer. If directed towards products manufactured with explicit concern for environmental and social aspects, this purchasing power can provide a critical mass for supplier companies to embrace CSR and can offer standards and information that support other consumers in implementing sustainable procurement practices. A recent study of European countries shows a sizable potential environmental benefit from "green purchases" of selected product groups. For example, if all public administrations in the European Union (EU) switched to green electricity, they would be able to reduce $CO_2$ emissions by 60 million tonnes, equivalent to 18 per cent of the EU's obligation under the Kyoto Protocol (OECD, 2003).

A number of governments, including Canada, Switzerland, USA and the United Kingdom, have initiated "green" procurement programs, focusing on a variety of goods and services. Also, a number of governments have used public procurement to advance targeted social goals, such as decent employment, anti-discrimination, and human rights.

It is thus clear that governments have significant interest in supporting and monitoring CSR activities domestically, and can also be a driving force for change in global supply chains.

## 3.2 Pressure actor: Non-Governmental Organizations

The not-for-profit sector, excluding religious organizations, has become a US$1 trillion-plus industry (Salamon et al., 1999, p.8). More than 30,000 NGOs operate international programs, and roughly 1,000 have memberships drawn from three or more countries (Sikkink and Smith, 2002).

Getting some large corporations to change their policies is often easier than changing public policy (Vogel, 2005). NGOs have succeeded in installing elements of public accountability into the transnational activities of corporations where national or international regulatory pressures for accountability are weak or non-existent.

### 3.2.1 Knowledge navigators: NGOs vs. MNCs

To many in the NGO community, CSR is viewed as a means to ensure that the profit-driven behaviour of international companies is governed by consideration of broader impacts on society and environment (Ruggie, 2004). The ability of the NGO community to exert pressure on MNCs to change their behaviour depends crucially on the ability to move public opinion through the media. Thus, media and image management have become increasingly important.

NGOs have successfully utilized internet-enabled social networks, tapping into what Waterman (1998) terms "communication internationalism" for near instantaneous dissemination of information about corporate activities to global audiences (O'Sullivan, 2000).

A number of large corporations have responded to the adverse publicity propagated by NGOs by using the media to disseminate their own message. While NGOs use systems that require little or no investment and are decentralized, corporations have tended to rely on cash-intensive media strategies that flood the print media and TV air time with messages of their social and environmental responsibility. Nothing is to prevent them, however, from communicating through the same web-enabled social networks and they could be expected to do so in targeting certain audiences, especially youth.

## 3.2.2 Shifting gears: The changing NGO interface

Some of the larger NGOs have begun to cooperate with, rather than merely confront, the private for-profit sector, working as CSR advisors or partners to corporate actors.. One such example is that of the Environmental Defense Fund (EDF) and its cooperation with McDonalds. As Fred Krupp, the EDF President, recently explained, EDF's informal motto used to be to sue MNCs, whereas now the official tagline is, "Finding the ways that work." So after years of campaigns to pressure McDonalds into improving its operations, the EDF is not only working closely with the fast food giant to change its internal practices, but it has also enlisted McDonalds to pressure chicken suppliers to reduce antibiotic use. The EDF is also working closely with Federal Express in converting a part of the FEDEX truck fleet to hybrid vehicles.[5]

NGO-corporate relationships appear thus to evolve through three broad stages:
*Stage 1: The NGO shame game*
In this first stage, NGOs develop corporate "shame" lists. Companies engage in defensive public relations (PR) actions, which tend to go hand in hand with the adoption of superficial CSR practices.

With so many companies active in the CSR area and openly cooperating with NGOs, the activist community has now shifted criticism towards industry laggards. An example of this is the relationship between the Dogwood Alliance and Forest Ethics and some of the largest office supplies retailers. The two groups applauded Staples and Office Depot for their efforts to stop the sales of paper produced from endangered forests. It also staged, however, a series of demonstrations against OfficeMax and publicly denounced the company's lack of effort on the issue (Deutsch, 2006).

Because some NGO campaigns have led companies to sever ties with noncompliant suppliers, resulting in unintended negative consequences for workers and communities, the focus of such campaigns has tended to shift towards helping MNCs to support their suppliers in the implementation of CSR practices.

*Stage 2: Partnering*

In this stage, NGOs move away from applying pressure to companies responsible for social and environmental problems to identifying corporate partners to help solve problems. "Nonprofits often have a deeper understanding of the social problem, which enables them to help companies devise more comprehensive strategies and set more ambitious and attainable goals" (Kramer and Kania, 2006, p. 28). Company resources can be harnessed to complement NGO goals, but as NGOs fear tarnished reputations by aligning with MNCs, and MNCs fear public distrust, the partnership is a balancing act, which needs to come across as a credible and output-oriented process for it to be judged a success.

*Case study #1: Greenpeace's inside-out approach[6]*

> After the record-breaking heat waves in 2006, from Athens to Mumbai, the fall out from climate change has become an issue of great concern for governments and the public alike. To combat global warming and other environmental problems, Greenpeace's strategy is both to protest against environmental offenders and to help companies craft comprehensive and achievable CSR strategies. Using this inside-out approach, Greenpeace catapulted Greenfreeze, an obscure ozone- and climate-safe refrigerant, into widespread use (Hartman and Stafford, 2006).

*Stage 3: MNCs as CSR thought leaders*

In this stage, corporations are increasingly active in the field of CSR (e.g. Nike and Danisco) and no longer need to be prodded by NGOs to undertake such activities. Many have developed their own business cases for staying active in CSR and see it now as part and parcel of just being successful at business, with CSR activities being mostly driven by internal management systems.

## 3.3 Pressure actor: Consumers

In developing countries, MNCs interact with local consumers by engaging in CSR activities that enhance the standard of living in the community, through better access to education, healthcare, etc. These programs help MNCs to build a relationship with the consumer, bringing credibility to the product sold and building brand loyalty. Nevertheless, producing and selling what consumers want – including poor consumers – can be as important as engaging in broader community welfare activities.

*Case study #2: Building a relationship with rural India*

> Part of Unilever India's business model is a long-term commitment to contribute to economic development locally by serving the "bottom of the pyramid" consumer (those with income of less than US$2 a day). Its commercial success is highlighted by the extensive distribution network which reaches deep into the villages of India. Unilever India has helped its bottom line by tapping into the purchasing power of the once ignored rural consumer while at the same time helping to improve rural livelihoods. For example, acknowledging the water shortages that affected its rural consumers, Unilever introduced water-saving technology in its detergents, and bacteria-fighting soaps to reduce the incidence of diarrhoea fatalities due to poor hygiene (HLL, *www.hll.com*; Unilever, *www.unilever.com/ourvalues/environmentandsociety/default.asp*).

The needs and values of consumers have changed and will continue to change. A growing segment of consumers, particularly in developed countries, are wealthy enough to be concerned with more than basic product characteristics, i.e. with quality, timeliness and the environmental and social dimensions of production processes. In response to these changes, the business sector has been developing new non-functional features for brand differentiation such as environmental or social qualities of the manufacturing, transportation and marketing process.

## 3.3.1 Consumers' choice: Value over values

How far are consumers willing to pay for various environmental and social attributes of a product, extending to the way in which it was produced? Consumer surveys and other market research provide a complex picture of how far consumers' stated preferences translate into spending decisions.

Social and environmental certification systems provide opportunities for producers to gain market recognition for strong CSR performance. They also provide consumers with the ability to distinguish between products, based on the social and environmental qualities of the production process and impacts throughout the lifecycle of the product.

• *Boycotts vs. convenience*

Vogel (2005) notes that few consumers will change their purchasing habits in response to corporate practices that do not affect them directly. Consumers appear more willing to avoid a product produced in ways they regard as irresponsible, than to purchase a responsibly produced product. Yet "ethical boycotts" affect less than 2 per cent of market transactions and tend to be short-lived (Porter and Kramer, 2002, p. 67).

• *The gap between green consciousness & green consumerism*

There is evidence suggesting a major gap between what consumers say they would do and their actual behaviour (see for instance, Makower et al.,

1991). In fact, this key insight has been a recurrent one in consumer polls and studies, which emphasize the primacy of a "value for money" calculation in consumers' purchasing decisions. A 2004 European Survey found that only 3 per cent of consumers actually modified their purchasing decisions because of social or environmental criteria, even though 75 per cent indicated that they would do so (Willard, 2002; Carrigan and Attalla, 2001; Boulstridge and Carrigan, 2000).

There is evidence, however, of growing consumer preference for certain classes of products thought to have health benefits in consumption – e.g., organic foods – also an increased willingness to base spending decisions on consideration of global environmental impacts (as for example with voluntary carbon offsets in travel and the purchase of hybrid or other less polluting motor vehicles).

### 3.4 Pressure actor: Institutional investors

A growing number of institutional investors are becoming increasingly sensitive to perceived corporate risk exposure related to CSR issues, including environmental management, child labour standards, women's employment criteria, corruption, etc. Companies have begun to recognize that there can be market rewards to "socially responsible" companies which manage to achieve or maintain robust bottom lines with sustainable practices. Some would argue that a strong CSR policy and practice reflects broader management strengths which can enhance corporate financial performance. Still, it remains unclear whether socially responsible investments can be expected consistently to outperform the market average.

### 3.4.1 Social investment: A growing trend

According to the Social Investment Forum (2005), by 2005 more than US$2.3 trillion or 9.4 per cent of all professionally managed assets in the US were managed with "social screens". During the period 1995-2005, professionally managed assets using one or more "social screens" grew by 258 per cent, approximately 10 percentage points above the total for all professionally managed assets.

More than half of institutional investors use two or more social screens. Tobacco, human rights, environment, equity in employment, community and labour relations are among the top 10 social screens used among institutional investors. Most of the growth in socially screened funds is accounted for by institutional investors such as government pension funds, unions and university endowments, which often have non-financial agendas.

### 3.4.2 Institutional investors: Taking charge

Institutional investors are more influential in the allocation of resources than individual shareholders. Many of these investors have begun to take a more aggressive position towards the activities of corporate management. The California Public Employees Retirement System (CalPERS), for instance, has since 1987 flagged relatively poor performers on corporate governance, termed "Focus Companies". The companies are targeted by CalPERS activists in the form of partial take-overs to influence the board as a major shareholder or a significant threat of de-listing, in order to focus the management on change. This strategy, which has been called the "CalPERS effect", while criticized by conventional fund holders as distracting the fund's attention from returns, has proven to have positive financial results on the target companies and on CalPERs itself. A Wilshire Associates study of the "CalPERS Effect" examined the performance of 95 companies targeted by CalPERS between 1987 and 1999. The results indicate that the same stocks outperformed the Standard and Poor's index by 14 per cent in the 5 years following CalPERS intervention, adding approximately US$150 million annually in additional returns to CalPERS (Nesbitt, 2001). In the UK, the Pensions Committee of the Environmental Agency of England and Wales (2004, p. 35-36) decided to become an active shareholder and compel managers to analyze environmental performance across the entire portfolio for fiduciary reasons.

If the number of funds requiring CSR related conditions continues to grow and gather significant market power, this segment of the financial market could eventually become the single most powerful relationship driving corporations towards increased CSR.

Evidence of this growth is found in platforms such as the UN Global Compact, which recently received commitments to its "Principles of Responsible Investment" from 50 institutional investors managing funds totalling over US$4 trillion.

## 4. Multinational corporations & their supply chains

Global supply chains encompass contractors and subcontractors in a multi-tier system of intermediaries. CSR compliance along supply chains is usually monitored up to first tier suppliers, but stakeholders are increasingly demanding assurances that CSR codes are being respected further down the supply chain. In its 2005 triennial International Survey of Corporate Responsibility Reporting in over 1600 companies across 16 countries, KPMG found that supplier issues are mentioned in 80 per cent of reports, although generally without specifics. Developing countries' importance as suppliers in global supply chains has increased significantly, often making regulation and monitoring a challenge.

In what follows, we review different aspects of CSR adoption in global supply chains, including the rationale for MNCs and challenges to monitoring compliance, with a focus on implications for SMEs in developing countries.

## 4.1 Expanding market access

By engaging in community-support programs, MNCs are able to connect with their target consumer and establish relationships with key business partners in the local market. These CSR programs help guide business decision-making processes by acquainting companies with cultural norms in the host community and enabling better assessment of public expectations. The insight gained helps ensure that the company is recognized as a good corporate citizen within the community. Many companies also find that community involvement reduces local regulatory obstacles, provides access to the local political process, generates positive media coverage, and increases access to markets for their products and services.

*Case Study #3: Bristol-Myers Squibb in Africa*

In June 2005, Bristol-Myers Squibb and Baylor College of Medicine announced the creation of a Pediatric AIDS Corps whose mission was to send 250 doctors to Africa to treat approximately 80,000 children over five years and to train local healthcare professionals. Additional children's clinical centres of excellence are to be built in Burkina Faso, in Uganda and in China, in a US$40 million program. This is in addition to the US$150 million "Secure the Future" program launched in 2000 as a partnership between the company and governments, physicians, and NGOs to help alleviate the HIV/AIDS crisis in this region (Bristol-Myers Squibb Foundation And Corporate Philanthropy, *www.bms.com/sr/philanthropy/data/globhiv.html*; *www.bms.com/sr/data/index.html*).

The benefit of CSR compliance is not straightforward, however. Body Shop is an exception in that it leverages compliance with strict CSR policies as part of its branding; but for most companies, compliance is an "invisible" attribute in the final product.

## 4.2 Relationship between intermediate producers & final product brands

Intermediate producers are becoming more sensitive to and aware of CSR. If they choose not to adopt and implement basic CSR policies, they may lose markets. By embracing CSR, on the other hand, supply chain contractors can differentiate themselves and possibly attract new clients.

Suppliers can reduce obsolete inventory, cut delivery time and streamline management systems, but adjusting supply chains to implement CSR policies is trickier. The concept of supply-chain innovation can be extended to include CSR. Supply chains are constantly being reviewed/updated to optimize costs and performance. Implementation of CSR policies should be given consideration at the stage of supply chain planning.

Most studies only address implementation of CSR practices at the level of first-tier suppliers in global supply chains (see, for instance, Jørgensen et al. 2003). The challenge is to enable more suppliers to implement CSR standards more easily and to monitor compliance beyond the first level of intermediaries. For example, Mattel Inc. has extended its audits of code compliance from plants where it controls 100 per cent of the output to second-tier plants where it buys between 40 per cent and 70 per cent of the output. Companies like IKEA conduct audits among second and third tier suppliers – e.g. in India and Pakistan, in order to address the use of child labour in the textile and carpet making industries (Andersen, 2005; The IKEA Group, 2005 and 2002).

## 4.3 MNCs driving change: If retailers pave the way…CSR is here to stay

What do Wal-Mart and Tesco have in common? Apart from being among the top 5 retailers worldwide[7], these expanding corporate mammoths have been on the cover of business magazines (Fortune and Newsweek International respectively) extolling their greening campaigns. While potentially very positive for the environment, social impacts may be less so. If Wal-Mart plans to focus on organic cotton and other organic fresh produce, the question is whether poor farmers are able to get the necessary certification, or whether a lucrative new market will be dominated by large farmers able to bear the certification costs.

In Zambia, a number of enterprises in the high value horticulture sector have established outgrowers schemes, some of which cover over 1,000 local smallholder farmers, where output is sold through the world's top companies such as Tesco, Wal-Mart, Sainsbury, and McCormick Spices. Such outgrower schemes have been effective in vertically integrating rural smallholder farmers into a global supply chain, while at the same time creating better access to markets, networks and new skills (World Bank, 2004a). Compliance of such small growers with corporate CSR codes may open up opportunities for NGOs to work with major corporate buyers to build capacities, especially among poor producers in the developing world.

*Case Study #4: Kraft Foods Raises Consumer Awareness*

In 2005, Kraft Foods bought 13 million pounds of Rainforest Alliance certified coffee beans grown by sustainable sources in coffee-growing communities around the world. Coffee from Rainforest Alliance Certified farms commands a higher price in the market which allows farmers a better standard of living. The move benefited more than 100,000 farmers, families and workers on 3,574 farms of all sizes in coffee-growing areas. It preserved more than 50,000 acres of forest in Central and South America and increased availability and awareness of certified sustainable coffees to mainstream consumers. In 2005 Kraft Foods began working with 1,000 cocoa suppliers in Ecuador as part of a pilot project to expand sustainable cocoa production (Kraft Foods, *www.kraft.com/responsibility/overview_building_trust.aspx*; Business in the Community, *www.bitc.org.uk/*).

If these giant retailers are serious about their new found "calling", then CSR will finally be given the boost it needs to become mainstream and be widely adopted. By making CSR products competitively priced and available at their local outlets, Wal-Mart and other large retailers are addressing some of the constraints that have made consumers reluctant to shift on a larger scale to "green" products, while at the same time capturing attention and consumer loyalty.

*Case Study #5: Wal-Mart Tapping New Market Potential*

Can Wal-Mart's green PR campaign lead a supply-chain revolution? Will Wal-Mart be able to set an example for companies that believe the environment and the economy are in conflict?

According to a Wal-Mart poll, 8 per cent of shoppers stopped visiting their outlets due to their stand on social issues (Mallaby, 2006). This may partially explain why the world's largest retailer has recently decided to launch a US$500 million environmental makeover with a number of clothing lines with environmental and social screens. The move not only aims to appease critics but is a new way to attract customers and build consumer loyalty. The interesting part of this move is the type of consumer that Wal-Mart serves. Wal-Mart apparently believes that the desire for more environmentally and socially sound products is not confined to the well-to-do shopper and that it can introduce successfully these lines to its core customer at Wal-Mart level prices.

This move holds immense promise for the development and strengthening of markets in socially and environmentally sound products given the company's huge purchasing power and its influence over the world's suppliers of consumer products. Should Wal-Mart's competitors follow suit, then consumer markets may change faster than predicted.

## 4.4 Are supply chains implementing comprehensive CSR policies?

Many suppliers operate on thin margins and short-term business horizons. Compounded by low barriers to entry in labour-intensive industries leading to overcapacity in the supply chain, and the high costs involved in adopting different codes of conduct for different clients, they are often wary of CSR. While some supply chain partners are beginning to appreciate the opportunities for greater market access provided by CSR, most are sellers of intermediate or generic final goods (where CSR compliance is not a visible attribute associated with their own brand) and hence are less likely to feel threatened by challenges to their reputation for non-compliance with codes (Vogel, 2005).

One way to address the potentially high costs to small producers of participation in CSR initiatives is for industry associations to assume some of those costs on behalf of their members. Progressive industry participants have an interest in such schemes to the extent that they can limit the risk of negative publicity spillovers from less responsible industry participants. The chocolate industry, for example, has developed an industry-wide program aimed to prevent child labour.

*Case Study #6: Monitoring the supply chain*

> In 2000, Carrefour, the second largest retailer in the world worked with FIDH (Fédération Internationale des Droits de l'Homme), a group of 116 human rights organizations from around the world, to establish INFAS, a monitoring agency to help Carrefour establish a code of conduct for its suppliers. The purpose of the code was to commit the company's suppliers to recognize and respect international standards regarding working conditions set out in various ILO Conventions with regard to the abolition of child labour and forced labour, freedom of association and collective bargaining, non discrimination, etc. The basic goal was to contribute to the gradual and total elimination of child labour while respecting cultural diversity (Carrefour, *www.carrefour.com*; CSR Europe, *www.csreurope.org*).

*Case Study #7: Cambodia in a post-quota regime*

The US-Cambodia Bilateral Textile Agreement of 1999 offered Cambodia a quota in lucrative segments of the market based on adherence to core labour standards. The 2002 ILO synthesis report confirmed compliance with internationally recognized core labour standards and provided the US confidence that Cambodia was largely adhering to its international labour commitments. Even after the expiration of the aforementioned agreement, the Government of Cambodia hopes to maintain CSR as a source of competitive advantage. While some buyers will prefer Cambodia for this reason, this strategy would be more viable in combination with other efforts to raise skills to pursue higher value product niches.

Though Cambodia is trying to differentiate itself through CSR, domestic micro-enterprises and SMEs are only weakly linked as suppliers to large companies and MNCs. Thus, the ripple effect of CSR through the tiers of the supply chain, even for a country like Cambodia that is invested in the process, may be limited (International Labour Organization, 2002; and World Bank, 2004b).

## 4.6 Monitoring supply chain CSR

The outsourcing trend has stretched supply chains around the globe (Pande, Raman, and Srivatsan, 2006). The different players in the supply chain are at different tiers in the process, and each has different capabilities and incentives to implement a given MNC's CSR program, making management of the supply chain increasingly intricate. Management aside, the issue becomes complex due to the pressure from multiple stakeholders requiring the corporation to be more responsible through the lifecycle of the product. The pressure from some quarters is to ensure a sustainable product lifecycle, from environmental and social impacts arising from material extraction and manufacturing, to product use and disposal. This is a challenging task that requires additional company investment. Monitoring suppliers from around the world requires significant financial and human resources. Partly as a response to CSR pressures, but partly also for competitiveness reasons, the overall trend is to collapse the supply chain and develop longer-term relations with a smaller number of suppliers.

Large companies often prefer to rely on in-house programs to evaluate and strengthen CSR along supply chains. Hewlett-Packard (HP), for example, monitors its supply chain by using a self-assessment questionnaire. HP then works collaboratively with suppliers to achieve the required standard in areas identified as falling below requirements.

Where cost control of CSR initiatives is a priority, on-site monitoring by external independent monitoring firms can reduce costs by streamlining the travel and maintenance of large internal departments of company auditors. Industry initiatives – as illustrated by the following three examples – can help share costs and risks:

- ICT industry: the EICC[8] Implementation Group is made up of Cisco, Dell, IBM, Intel, HP, Microsoft, Sony and five contract manufacturers. The group coordinates with the supply-chain working group of the Global eSustainability Initiative (GeSI) to create common tools and applications for the ICT supply chain.

- Garment industry: Criticisms related to working conditions in the garment industry have prompted the formation of the Fair Labour Association (FLA), which represents a multi-stakeholder coalition of companies, universities and NGOs. More than a dozen apparel industry leaders like Adidas-Salomon, Liz Claiborne, Nike, Patagonia, Reebok, Eddie Bauer, Phillips-Van Heusen, and Polo Ralph Lauren are members. The strong involvement of human rights and child advocacy NGOs gives consumers greater confidence about working conditions in the garment factories of suppliers to member companies.

- Consumer goods industry: the SA 8000 (Social Accountability 8000) program combines an "auditable" code of conduct that can be applied across consumer products industries with a system for its verification. This certification program for factories and workplaces includes signatory members like Avon, Dole Food, Eileen Fisher, Otto Versand and Toys "R" Us.

## 4.7 Ownership and incomplete implementation of CSR in supply chains

Implementation of good social and environmental practices will not survive in the long term if owners, managers, and supervisors along the supply chain are not convinced of the benefits of CSR.

Indeed, the lack of ownership among factory managers in the apparel industry has resulted in half-hearted implementation of externally imposed codes of conduct. Oxfam (2004) discovered that, while managers made sure of zero child and forced labour, they gave priority to fulfilling an order according to the requirements of time, cost and quality and had little patience for CSR policies regarding excessive working hours, forced overtime, and harassment of workers who attempt to form unions. The same is true of other industries where cost and time pressures are intense.

## 5. Barriers

In this section, we describe the different barriers affecting the adoption and dissemination of CSR practices from the point of view of the different stakeholders involved. We first outline the generic challenges to mainstreaming CSR as a tool for sustainable business practices.

First of all, CSR is very much a moving target. The scope and focus of CSR definitions is different among multilateral institutions, NGOs and the private sector. This makes it difficult to establish universal codes of conduct, resulting in mixed expectations of outcomes from the different stakeholders.

Furthermore, there is a lack of comprehensive global indices to measure environmental practices, labour conditions and other CSR practices within and between industries. Today, most companies measure progress in CSR by assessing progress towards meeting internal CSR targets year on year. These targets are unique to each company. The lack of coordination on code definition can result in excessive costs to all involved. To some extent this is being addressed through industry-wide initiatives or broader initiatives like the Global Compact. The more generic the CSR code, however, the less guidance it is likely to provide to a specific company's operations.

Operationalizing such codes remains a company-specific challenge. There seems to be much scope for improvement in this regard, as CSR policies often remain at the level of principle and are rarely contractually specified. For instance, a recent survey in Denmark has shown that the share of SMEs receiving buyer requirements that are contractual or subject to verification is a fraction of those receiving requirements in principle, and that the same discrepancy exists in the case of requirements applied by SMEs to their own suppliers (figure 2).

Efforts at greater standardization of CSR reporting have been gaining momentum. At least five European countries have already issued national guidelines for quality assurance of Sustainability or CSR reports and the accountancy profession has endorsed the need for an international standard. Greater rigor and consistency in CSR reports would allow the financial markets and other stakeholders to rely more meaningfully on the information provided by companies in these reports.

More specifically, key challenges for MNCs and their suppliers include:

- *Lack of compliance due to insufficient understanding of business benefits*

Many suppliers remain sceptical about the tangible benefits of CSR to their bottom line. A number of suppliers do not fully accept code compliance as part of the contractual agreement and see it more as an encroachment of a Western value system. Staff too, need to be convinced of the necessity of codes of conduct and are unlikely to take compliance seriously unless they face the consequences of non-compliance. A number of companies now publish information about the number of investigations and disciplinary events.

- *Second-hand corporate commitments*

Some companies look at CSR more as a fashionable trend rather than a "coherent practical program," resulting in low commitment and investment in code compliance. The adoption of environmental and social requirements by SMEs in the supply chain depends on their perception of buyer requirements, as very few of them are contractual and subject to verification. Most CSR initiatives are understaffed – i.e. CSR is usually a line or a project added to a job profile of existing employees. Some companies do appoint staff to monitor CSR progress, but most are not empowered or assigned adequate resources.

*   *Inefficiencies & confusion due to conflicting buyer requirements*

It is estimated that 1,000 buyer codes existed as of 2003 (Jørgensen et al., 2003). The overlapping codes, generate inefficiencies and confusion as suppliers becomes preoccupied with meeting the different requirements (codes of conduct) of each of their buyers and get caught in "compliance limbo," unable to offer time and resources to address real implementation.

*   *Free-riders & first mover disadvantage*

Firms that are serious about CSR invest in setting up an enabling infrastructure, bridge gaps in compliance and commit both financial and human resources into realizing social goals. Because a large number of firms have not as yet embraced CSR, this sends mixed signals to suppliers and undermines the efforts of CSR-progressive buyers. Free-riders compound the problem and act as a disincentive for further investment by buyers. An interesting example highlighted in the IFC paper on "Establishing CSR Drivers in Agribusiness" (Tallontire and Greenhalgh, 2005) is that of brand name firms producing chocolate. The suppliers of these firms are widely dispersed smallholder producers, making it practically impossible to trace a batch of cocoa beans to a particular grower. The business case for a single firm to take responsibility for social conditions along the supply chain is not strong, as other firms are also likely to benefit from such action as free riders. One lesson is that traceability and strong market linkages are important if single firms are to be motivated by a business case to take responsibility for social issues along the supply chain.

*   *Mixed messages to suppliers*

Suppliers often find it difficult to determine a firm's true priorities. Firms demand adherence to CSR policies, but at the same time demand delivery on lower prices and shorter lead times. While subscribing to both is possible, suppliers are willing to take up the challenge only if the firm's commitment is concrete and relayed through clear signals and incentives.

Challenges for institutional investors are twofold:

*   *Weak evidence of CSR's impact on consumer behaviour*

It is difficult to forecast the impact of CSR on the bottom line because of the lack of relevant market information. Consumer polls show major gaps between what consumers say they would do and their actual behaviour. A 2004 European Survey, for instance, found that while 75 per cent of consumers indicated that they are ready to modify their purchasing decisions because of social or environmental criteria, only 3 per cent actually did so (Capron and Quairel-Lanoizelee, 2004, p.57).

• *Inadequate CSR reporting*

Although more and more companies are producing separate reports on corporate responsibility and achievement of social and environmental goals, most of the information being provided is not specific enough to be of value to financial analysts and institutional investors, thus limiting its usefulness to those with the most power to influence corporate behaviour.

Finally, key challenges to governments include the following:

• *Tension between developing & developed country perspectives of CSR*

While most developing-country governments and suppliers believe that national laws and regulations take precedence in guiding corporate behaviour, the concept of CSR often implicitly takes a developed-country perspective on complex societal and cultural issues.

• *Government capacity building*

CSR initiatives in developing countries range from regulating code compliance through a supply chain to building schools and making healthcare service available to communities, a function traditionally performed by governments. Such services are often provided in a public-private partnership with governments and this is generally to be preferred to simply replacing government, since corporate presence in the community may be time-bound and the services must not be. Thus, it is important that such partnership involve strengthening of government capacities to sustain such programs over the long run.

## 6. Conclusions

CSR could be seen as a model of extended corporate governance whereby those who run a company (managers, directors, entrepreneurs) have responsibilities that range from fulfilment of fiduciary duties towards owners to fulfilment of broader environmental and social objectives as responsible corporate citizens.

CSR issues are likely to become more important as companies in developing countries expand abroad. Identifying the barriers to CSR is half the battle. By engaging in dialogue, suppliers, buyers, NGOs and government can aim to define the scope of CSR, align financial incentives with CSR goals and create a critical mass of CSR-committed enterprises that permits the realization of scale economies, e.g., in compliance monitoring.

Large multinational buyers have an important role to play in helping their smaller suppliers address resource constraints through capacity-building initiatives. The capacity-building process involves a needs assessment of each supplier, training and workshop activities. By improving the social and environmental situation of suppliers, large buyer firms expect a return on their investment in the form of long term relationships, quality improvements (Observatoire sur le Responsabilité Sociétale des Entreprises, 2003) and fewer risks of supplier failure, while benefits for suppliers include development of business through social and environmental improvements, access to specialist advice from MNC professionals and stronger ties with multinational buyers.

Finally, adoption of CSR by supply chain firms in developing countries can result in positive spillovers and redefine industry standards. By linking to communities of CSR practice, developing country firms may be able to compensate for weak enabling environments – e.g., absence of the rule of law and weak local standards of corporate governance.

Figure 1. Number of global compact companies and SMEs in developed and developing
countries

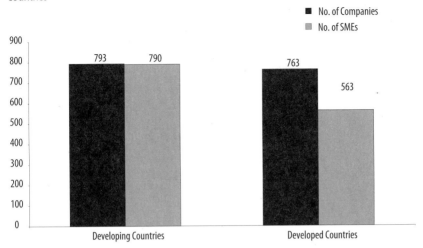

Source: The authors based on UN Global Compact's participation database (as of November
8, 2006).
Obs.: The country groupings follow the WDI definitions, where all low-income, low-middle
income and upper middle income economies are considered developing countries and all
high-income economies are considered developed countries. SMEs are defined by the UN
Global Compact as 'business participants with less than 250 and more than 10 full-time
employees.'

Figure 2. CSR requirements and SMEs in global supply chains

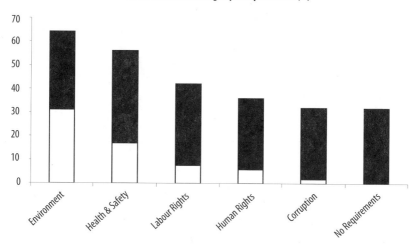

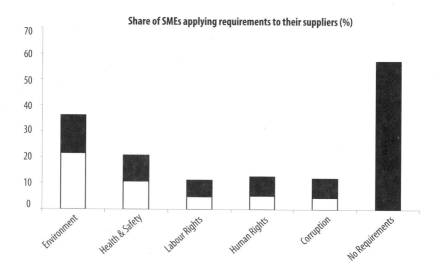

## Notes

1 The Johannesburg Plan of Implementation that emerged from the World Summit on Sustainable Development in 2002 refers to 'corporate social and environmental responsibility and accountability'. CSR, the more familiar term, is defined by the World Business Council for Sustainable Development as "the continuing commitment by business to behave ethically and contribute to economic development while improving the quality of life of the workforce and their families as well as of the local community and society at large" (WBCSD, Corporate Social Responsibility: Meeting Changing Expectations, 1999).

2 Expert Group Resources on CSR, SMEs and Regional Competitiveness (January 2006), Enterprise and Industry, European Commission http://ec.europa.eu/enterprise/csr/ms_sme_topic1.htm.

3 As per figures of the UN Global Compact's participation database (www.unglobalcompact.org), November 8, 2006.

4 Codes of Conduct are defined as the mechanism by which MNCs establish social and environmental guidelines for their suppliers.

5 Environmental Defense Fund WorldWide (www.environmentaldefense.org).

6 Case studies in the text are "leadership" practices in CSR. They have been chosen as illustrative examples to represent innovation, higher than average commitment, or a comprehensive approach to the issue.

7 Wal-Mart, Carrefour, Home Depot, Metro and Tesco are the top 5 retailers worldwide – according to the Deloitte 2006 Global Retailing Powers study.

8 EICC is the Electronic Industry Code of Conduct.

# Bibliography

Andersen, M. (2005), Corporate Social Responsibility in Global Supply Chains: Understanding the uniqueness of firm behaviour, Copenhagen Business School PhD Series 15, Copenhagen.

Boulstridge, E. and M. Carrigan (2000), Do consumers really care about corporate responsibility? Highlighting the attitude-behaviour gap, Journal of Communication Management, 4 (6), 421-433.

Capron, M. and F.Quairel-Lanoizelee, (2004), Mythes et réalités de l'entreprise responsable, Ed. La Découverte.

Carrigan, M. and A. Attalla (2001), The Myth of the ethical consumer – do ethics matter in consumer behaviour?, Journal of Consumer Marketing, 18, 560-576.

The Environmental Agency of England and Wales (2004), An Alternative Business Plan, Engaged Investor, November/December.

Deutsch, C. H. (2006), Companies and Critics Try Collaboration, New York Times, 17 May.

The Economist (20 January 2005), A Survey of Corporate Social Responsibility.

Hartman, C. L., and E. R. Stafford (2006), Chilling with Greenpeace from the Inside Out, Stanford Social Innovation Review, Summer.

The IKEA Group (2005), IKEA Facts and Figures 2003-2004.

The IKEA Group (2002), IWAY – The IKEA Way on Purchasing Home Furnishing Products.

International Labor Organization (2002), Second Synthesis Report on the Working Conditions Situation in Cambodia's Garment Sector.

Jorgensen, A. L., and J. Steen Knudsen (2006), Sustainable competitiveness in global value chains- How do Small Danish Firms Behave?, The Copenhagen Centre for Corporate Responsibility.

Jørgensen, H. Bank, P. M. Pruzan-Jørgensen (PricewaterhouseCoopers, Denmark), M. Jungk (Danish Institute for Human Rights), and A. Cramer, (Business for Social Responsibility) (2003), Strengthening Implementation of Corporate Social Responsibility in Global Supply Chains, Corporate Social Responsibility Practice, World Bank Group.

KPMG (2005), International Survey of Corporate Responsibility Reporting.

Kramer, M. and J. Kania (2006), A New Role for Non-Profits, Stanford Social Innovation Review, Spring.

Kramer, M., M. Pfitzer, and P. Lee (2005), Competitive Social Responsibility Uncovering the Economic Rationale for Corporate Social Responsibility among Danish Small- and Medium-Sized Enterprises, Foundation Strategy Group and Center for Business and Government, John F. Kennedy School of Government, Harvard University.

Makower, J., J. Elkington and J. Hailes (1991), The Green Consumer Guide, Penguin Publisher (USA).

Mallaby, S. (2006), A New Brand of Power, The Washington Post (7 August).

Nesbitt, S. L. (2001), The "CalPERS Effect" on Targeted Company Share Prices, Wilshire Associates, January.

O'Sullivan, M.(2000), Corporate Governance and Globalization, Annals, AAPSS, 570.

Observatoire sur le Responsabilité Sociétale des Entreprises (ORSE) (September 2003), Very Large Enterprises and their support for SMEs in the context of sustainable development, Exploiting CSR best practice within the framework of relations between customers and suppliers.

OECD (2003), The Environmental Performance of Public Procurement: Issues of Policy Coherence.

Oxfam GB (2004), Clean Clothes Campaign, and Global Unions, Play Fair at the Olympics, March.

Palmisano, S. J. (2006), The Globally Integrated Enterprise, Foreign Affairs, 85 (3), May/June.

Pande, A., R. Raman and V. Srivatsan (2006), Recapturing your Supply Chain Data, McKinsey Quarterly, March.

Porter, M. E. and M. R. Kramer (2002), The competitive advantage of corporate philanthropy, Harvard Business Review, December.

Ruggie, J. G. (2004), Reconstituting the Global Public Domain: Issues, actors and practices, Corporate Social Responsibility Initiative, Harvard University.

Salamon, L. M., H. K. Anheier, R. List, S. Toepler, S. W. Sokolowski, and associates (1999), Global Civil Society, Dimensions of the Nonprofit Sector, The Johns Hopkins Comparative Nonprofit Sector Project, The Johns Hopkins Center for Civil Society Studies.

Sikkink, K. and J. Smith (2002), Infrastructure for Change: Transnational Organizations, 1953-93, University of Minnesota Press.

Social Investment Forum (2005), Report on Socially Responsible Investing Trends in the United States; http://www.socialinvest.org

Tallontire, A. and P. Greenhalgh (2005), Establishing CSR Drivers in Agribusiness, International Finance Corporation, August.

UNCTAD (2001), Promoting linkages, World Investment Report 2001.

Vogel, D. (2005), The Market for Virtue: The Potential and Limits, Brookings Institution Press.

Waterman, P. (1998), Globalization, social movements, and the new internationalism, London: Mansell.

Willard, B. (2002), The Sustainability Advantage: Seven Business Case Benefits of a Triple Bottom Line, New Society Publishers.

World Bank (2004a), Public Sector Support for the Implementation of Corporate Social Responsibility in Global Supply Chains: Conclusions from Practical Experience, study prepared for the Foreign Investment Advisory Service Investment Climate Department, World Bank, by Business for Social Responsibility and PricewaterhouseCoopers (Denmark), December.

World Bank Group (2004b), Public-Private Infrastructure Advisory Facility, Seizing the Global Opportunity: Investment Climate Assessment and Reform Strategy for Cambodia, June.

# The Way Forward

# Policy lessons for 21st century industrializers

David O'Connor*

Industrial development is not the only possible route to a developed country standard of living, but it is a well-proven one. It is for this reason that industrial development remains a high policy priority of governments in the developing world. While less vital to maintaining high incomes in developed countries, industry remains an important source of well-paying jobs, especially for those workers with less than a college education.

The past several decades have witnessed a major restructuring of the global economy, one in which more and more industrial output and employment is now located in emerging developing countries, while the developed countries have become ever more service-oriented economies. Globalization through increased trade and investment flows is driving this restructuring, along with technological and associated organizational change.

Industrialization is proving a potent force for economic growth in countries of Asia, most recently China and India. In the former at least, it has also been an important contributor to poverty reduction. In China, vast numbers of people have left agriculture to work in factories, as – in the past – did rural populations in the now industrialized world. Given its very different demographic profile, with many more new labour force entrants expected over coming decades, India faces an even bigger challenge than China to create enough productive jobs, and strong industrial development will have to be an important part of the job-creation process.

Between them, China and India will occupy a huge industrial space in coming years, and those on their periphery will most likely reap some benefits of proximity which may offset in part the effects of heightened competition. On the other hand, developing countries farther afield and with less abundant labour reserves may struggle to find a competitive niche in global markets, especially for labour-intensive manufactures.

At the same time, there are new opportunities which some such countries can hope to seize. One set of opportunities is created precisely by the rapid economic growth of China, India and other so-called emerging economies, with the associated demand for imports of raw materials and semi-processed goods to feed their factories and to satisfy changing consumption patterns associated with rising incomes. Africa, Latin America and the Middle East have already enjoyed benefits from this new commodities

* Policy Integration and Analysis Branch, Division for Sustainable Development, UN-DESA, United Nations, New York. The views expressed in this chapter are those of the author and do not necessarily coincide with those of the organization to which he is affiliated.

boom. Another set of opportunities is being created by changing consumption and production patterns in developed countries, for example as they struggle to lower their emissions of greenhouse gases to meet international commitments. Biofuels are one example of a sector with significant potential from this cause, and Brazil is well positioned to gain in the first instance, while other major sugar, soybean and palm oil producers could also benefit. Also, consumer willingness to pay in developed countries for "fair trade", "organic", certified timber and "sustainable" products has created new and fast-growing markets. Coffee growers, for example, in Africa, Latin America and Asia are sharing in the gains. Finally, there are opportunities which have been opened up by new technologies and reduced costs of transport. For instance, the production of fresh fruits and flowers in tropical climates and in southern hemisphere temperate climates to supply markets in Northern hemisphere developed countries is an example where reduced transport costs have been decisive. Also crucial has been the capacity developed by some countries in the tropics and the southern hemisphere to provide the supporting infrastructure and services, from irradiation treatment to uninterrupted cold chains to controlled temperature containers.

In the case of services, lower communication costs are revolutionizing the way that different types of service industries function, with many functions not dependent on face-to-face interaction being sourced remotely where costs are competitive. India has thus far been the principal beneficiary of the growing 'trade in tasks', but other countries have also shared in the gains – notably the Philippines. Lower travel costs have created mass tourism on an unprecedented scale, which opens up significant opportunities for well-endowed countries – including for ecotourism – while at the same time placing enormous stresses on local environments and cultures in some popular tourism destinations. African countries as well as others have the potential to reap significant rewards from nature-based tourism, but the capacity to maintain destinations in their natural states while providing the sort of infrastructure and services which wealthy tourists expect is a non-trivial skills set which needs to be built over time.

As suggested by the range of activities and sectors just enumerated (and this is only a partial list), this volume seeks to broaden the terms of the discussion on industrial development. The traditional 'metal-basher' perspective is no less antiquated than one which fixates on so-called 'high-tech' sectors like electronics as the engine of industrial transformation.

Technology and its mastery are undoubtedly crucial to successful economic development, but it is clear from the cases discussed in this volume that technology is not the monopoly of industry. Nor is technology development the alpha and the omega of successful innovation. Indeed, especially at an early stage of development, there may be other forms of innovation which are more important – e.g., simply being able to identify and seize profitable new product or geographic market opportunities, to deliver goods to market more efficiently, or to serve a new class of customers through improved marketing.

The biggest challenge facing national governments in low-income developing countries is to discover how and where their countries' economies can best compete in this global marketplace. The next biggest challenge is how to do so in a sustainable manner, ensuring that breakneck growth does not contain the seeds of its own undoing.

A major theme of this volume has been the importance of policies, including macroeconomic and exchange rate policies as well as industrial and technology policies, trade and foreign investment policies, and policies to promote workforce education and training, to successful industrial development.

Several lessons which emerge from the preceding chapters deserve emphasis.

First, there are many possible patterns of specialization open to any given country, and a process of "self-discovery" (Hausmann and Rodrik) is important to finding which one yields the biggest dynamic gains. Thus, policies which promote experimentation and exploration of new markets are vital – which fits within a broad, Schumpeterian view of innovation as creating new value-generating activities. Competition and labour market policies are part of the story, as firms need to be able to reorganize easily in the event of failure and entrepreneurs need to be able to risk multiple failures in pursuit of a winning formula. Financing to support such risk taking is another critical ingredient, and where private venture capital markets are underdeveloped there may be a role for government as venture capitalist or backer of venture capitalists.

Second, for many low-income developing countries, just getting and staying on the first rung of the ladder of industrial development is a daunting task. For countries like Bangladesh, Cambodia, and Sri Lanka, textiles and clothing remain the core of their industrial sectors. Technological innovation per se and the ability to exploit it would seem the least of their worries. They are struggling to survive in an increasingly competitive global market with countries having strong competitive advantages which have been unbound from quota restrictions (or will be in a matter of a few years). For those countries, innovation is mostly about finding a viable strategy for facing such competition. Product niche marketing is one (Sri Lanka); branding as a 'socially responsible' production location is another (Cambodia); achieving economies through backward integration could be a third. For others countries, however, it may already be too late to save this industry, and innovation will mean embarking on a new search for potential areas of comparative advantage. International cooperation is needed to assist those countries with the difficult adjustments they face and to shoulder a share of the adjustment costs. A question of great importance to policy makers in such countries is how to organize and conduct that search in a way which maximizes the likelihood of success or, put differently, yields a winner with the lowest costs in time and resources.

For many developing countries, external orientation and openness to foreign direct investment can be crucial to fostering rapid search and cost discovery in new products and sectors. If foreign investors are willing to risk their capital in a sector which is not ring fenced by protectionist measures, this can provide useful information about which sector(s) hold promise of becoming internationally competitive. The policy challenge for governments is then one of balancing the need to attract foreign investment with the need to ensure meaningful linkages and spillovers to the local economy and local enterprises. Large countries with diversified domestic economies and vast domestic market potential are better positioned than small, specialized economies to encourage FDI with strong domestic linkages. Thus, a country like China is apt to be more effective in negotiating favourable technology transfer agreements as part of FDI projects than many smaller countries. Mineral extraction and processing economies are often characterized by FDI investment enclaves. While domestic linkages may in such cases remain weak, the use of government revenues from the minerals sector to invest in human capital and infrastructure with a view to long-term economic diversification can provide insurance against eventual stagnation once resources are depleted.

Third, knowledge and technology intensity is rising across most economic activities, and not only in industry (manufacturing plus mineral and materials processing). Modern agriculture is also knowledge-intensive, as the Chilean experience in developing high value fresh fruit and fish exports suggests. Moreover, new service activities (e.g., business process outsourcing) have been spawned by the development of information and communications technologies and existing ones have been revolutionized (witness telecommunications and finance). For this reason, policies that strengthen the knowledge base of an economy take on ever greater importance. This includes above all investments in education and training institutions and programmes, but it extends to other institutions which support knowledge creation, acquisition and application, like R&D laboratories, standards, testing and certification bodies, and (again) venture capital and other entrepreneurial financing. In recent years, some developing countries have become increasingly attractive as locations for R&D facilities of multinational corporations. While an existing human capital and technological base is apt to be a precondition for attracting such investment, the presence of foreign R&D facilities may generate a number of positive spillover effects for domestic technological capabilities – e.g., providing stronger incentives for pursuing advanced education in science and engineering, attracting foreign-educated scientists and engineers back to their home countries, and training both research scientists and research managers who may be able to set up and/or upgrade the quality and productivity of domestic R&D laboratories.

Fourth, small- and medium-sized enterprises can be important sources of innovation, especially radical innovation. An industrial environment which encourages and supports start-up companies is more likely to breed dynamism and experimentation.

In many developing countries, small- and medium-sized enterprises dominate the industrial structure. Historically, many successful enterprises have started as SMEs, even the Microsofts and Intels of the world. In some countries, however, the regulatory regime and investment climate is strongly biased against SMEs and inhospitable to their growth. Weak capital markets and cautious banks may starve SMEs of investment capital needed to expand beyond a rate sustainable from retained earnings and informal borrowing. Large firms may be subjected to costly regulations and controls on their operations which discourage expansion. While policies should support a dynamic SME sector from which eventual winners will emerge, they should not discourage graduation from the SME league.

While high costs of R&D can pose a formidable barrier to entry to new firms in economies operating on the technological frontier, in developing countries operating well behind the frontier the barriers to innovation are likely to be less steep. For, in this context innovation does not depend crucially on state-of-the-art R&D. What can be highly problematic in such countries are the coordination failures which make it hard for a pioneer in one area to succeed where key supporting activities, industries and infrastructures are not in place.

What sorts of government policies or other measures can be effective in remedying such coordination failures? One lesson which emerges from this volume is the importance of a formalized consultative mechanism whereby government agencies and departments can interact with business people and better understand their needs and problems. While business surveys generally yield predictable general complaints about high taxes, bureaucratic red tape, corruption, bad roads and port delays, more intensive consultations between government and industry can provide guidance on concrete, industry-specific obstacles and constraints. If, for example, it happens that the unavailability of a low-cost local supply of a particular component is a binding constraint on developing an otherwise promising component-using sector, this may signal to government the need to consider offering targeted incentives to the first investor(s) in that component manufacture. To work effectively, such government-business consultations must be accompanied by policy flexibility, i.e., a willingness to learn by doing and to adjust policies accordingly.

Another way by which governments – e.g., in the Asian newly industrialized countries, or NICs – have dealt with coordination externalities is by resorting on public investment, including through state-owned enterprises, to fill certain production gaps deemed critical to supporting priority downstream sectors but too risky and/or capital-intensive to attract private investors (e.g., steel, oil and gas, petrochemicals in some countries in the early days of industrial development).

Another possible barrier to innovation and entrepreneurial risk taking in developing countries is the limited private appropriability of the rewards to pioneering a profitable new industry or activity. Since innovation in this case involves discovering an area where local producers can be internationally competitive, not developing patentable technology, intellectual property rights protection offers little incentive. Where domestic market protection combined with strong export incentives might once have helped resolve this problem, changes to international trade rules have made this approach more difficult to pursue. In the current competitive environment, an industry pioneer can expect to reap rewards from innovation only by continuing to innovate, staying ahead of the competition, either by improving product quality or other characteristics, or by moving on to new and more profitable sectors once a particular sector becomes overcrowded. Thus, government policy needs more than ever to encourage firms to build technological and organizational capabilities for continuous adaptation.

While the most successful recent examples of the effective employment of industrial policies are the Asian NICs, the international rules of the game have changed since they industrialized. Thus, there is limited scope for late industrializers today to seek to emulate their policies, even assuming they had the capacity to do so. Today, the main forms of selectivity available to government industrial policy makers pertain to skill formation, technology support, innovation financing, FDI promotion and targeting, infrastructure development (including for IT) and all types of general subsidies which do not affect trade performance (Lall, 2003). How far today's late industrializers are constrained by these new rules of the game remains a point of contention, with Lall suggesting the constraints may be binding and Rodrik taking a contrary view (Rodrik, 2006). Lall's list contains a number of areas of intervention critical in a globalized knowledge economy. Lall himself suggests that the constraints on policy space may encourage more focused and effective policy. That will not simply happen on its own, however, so Lall stresses the need for the international community – and developed countries in particular – to provide support to developing country governments in building capacity to design and manage effective industrial promotion policies.

Until now, the focus has been on policies to promote industrial development, to ensure that such development is sustainable in an economic sense. The other big challenge noted above is how governments can ensure that industrial development is environmentally and socially sustainable. The history of industrialization in the West, in the former Soviet Union, in Japan and in the NICs tells a cautionary tale about the adverse environmental effects of rapid and weakly regulated industrialization. China today faces many of those same challenges of coping with heavy industry-induced environmental pressures, and India and other 21st century industrializers can be expected to do likewise. It is certainly true that environmental problems in these late industrializers could be far worse if their industrialization were based on 1950s or 1960s technologies rather than, say, 1990s or new millennium technologies. Still, the sheer scale of industrial production concentrated in a given geographic area can be so great as to offset in large measure the environmental benefits of cleaner, more efficient technologies.

There is no area in which the case for vigorous government policy intervention is less incontrovertible than in that of environmental regulation. Still, in many countries there remains a hesitancy about too strict regulation of industrial pollution out of concern for raising costs and reducing competitiveness. Thus, much of the discussion of feasible policies and measures has focused on those which would yield potential financial rewards to enterprises and thus generate the least resistance. Policies and measures to encourage energy efficiency and reduce materials wastage fall into this category. One of the findings to emerge from the chapter on energy and material efficiency is that the financial and economic rewards to improvements in the latter are largely attributable to improvements in the former. That is to say, increased use of recycled materials often yields significant energy savings by averting the need for energy-intensive primary materials processing. Thus, policies aimed at encouraging recycling are, in a sense, energy-efficiency policies.

The social dimension of industrial development is multi-faceted. The improvements which rapid, labour-intensive industrial development have made possible in the living standards of low-skilled workers, and in the social and economic status of women through new employment opportunities, are major contributions to social development. On the other hand, rapid structural transformation in an economy, from agricultural to industrial, from largely rural to increasingly urban, brings major social dislocations which can have both individual and social costs. Newly arrived rural migrants, possibly uninformed about workers' rights, may be especially susceptible to mistreatment, and even well-informed ones may lack attractive alternatives. Labour law protections exist in most countries, but their enforcement – as with environmental regulations – is often discretionary and partial. It is in this context that multinational corporations have felt compelled to extend their codes of corporate social responsibility, developed in response to pressures from domestic stakeholders, to their overseas subsidiaries and supply chains. Developing country governments have an interest in ensuring that their domestic enterprises – including their SMEs – are not disadvantaged in global markets by new CSR codes. Thus, where this is not already done, they may well choose to encourage if not require foreign investors and buyers producing and/or sourcing in their countries to provide technical assistance to domestic enterprises in complying with these codes.

# Bibliography

Lall, S. (2003), Reinventing industrial strategy: The role of government policy in building industrial competitiveness, for The Intergovernmental Group on Monetary Affairs and Development (G-24), September, second draft.

Rodrik, D. (2006), Powerpoint presentation to FONDAD/UN-DESA Roundtable on Policy Space, New York, 7-8 December.